The Introduction To Health Care Administration

Completely Revised for the New Century

Winborn Davis

PROFESSIONAL
PRINTING &
PUBLISHING, INC.

P.O. Box 5758 • Bossier City, LA 71171-5758
318-746-6880 • 1-800-551-8783 • FAX 318-746-6995
Web Site: http://www.ppandp.com
E-mail: order@ppandp.com

Completely Revised for the New Century

ISBN 0-929442-41-5

Professional Printing & Publishing, Inc.
P.O. Box 5758
Bossier City, LA 71171-5758
318/746-6880
WATS 1-800/551-8783 - FAX 318/746-6995
Web Site: http://www.ppandp.com
E-mail: order@ppandp.com

ABOUT THE AUTHOR

Winborn E. Davis, Author, Lecturer, Educator – During the past five decades of service in the health-care profession and in state and federal government, Winborn Davis has achieved the respect and admiration of professionals throughout the United States. He received his BA from Louisiana State University and his MSW from Tulane University. Mr. Davis is a licensed nursing facility administrator and a licensed social worker.

Mr. Davis served as the first State Director of Mental Health and the first State Director of Training and Research, Louisiana State Department of Hospitals. He also served as Administrator of the LSU Baton Rouge Hospital, associate professor of management, and associate professor of health-facilities administrator. From 1977 to 1982 he worked as administrator of the Skilled and Intermediate Care Facility at the Baton Rouge General Medical Center and then director of staff development for the Center.

Prior to writing this publication he coauthored one book and published nineteen articles on management, consultation, training, and related health subjects and received numerous awards and citations. Mr. Davis' newest publication, "Supervision in Health Care Facilities," is a companion book to the "Introduction To Health Care Administration." As an active member of the National Association of Boards of Examiners of Long Term Care Administrators and the Past Executive Director of the Louisiana State Board of Examiners for NHA, he has been instrumental in achieving progress and quality care in the long-term care profession. Mr. Davis was honored as the first distinguished member of NAB.

ACKNOWLEDGEMENTS

This publication is the result of the efforts of many people involved in long term care. I am indebted to all of them but especially to Joseph Townsend, NHA, Charles Purcell, RN, Gary McGarity, RPh, NHA, C. Kemp Wright, NHA, and Louis Champagne, personnel management specialist. Each provided expert information in his area of specialization. Government officials in the offices of FDA, OSHA, Wage and Hour Division, National Labor Relations Board, EEOC, Civil Rights, Medicare, Medicaid, Drug Enforcement Administration, and IRS were generous with time and information. They helped to pinpoint government regulations affecting nursing facilities.

I am especially grateful to my wife Claire and son Michael for their patience during long periods of isolating myself to produce this book.

Appreciation is due my publisher and editor, Dr. Robert W. Haacker, who continuously urged and encouraged me to devote the necessary time and effort to produce a useful publication for individuals entering the field of long-term care and a publication/textbook for use by colleges and universities in preparing the long-term care professional.

Winborn E. Davis

PREFACE

In order to be a nursing home administrator one must master a sizeable body of knowledge about organizational, personnel, financial, resident care, and environmental management, about marketing and public relations and about government regulations. Federal, state, and local governments carefully regulate the long-term care industry to ensure that residents receive the care they need. Every nursing facility is built according to rigid building and fire and safety codes to assure the provision of a comfortable, secure, healthy environment conducive to proper care. These standards are updated frequently, incorporating new and significant changes.

Even the administrator is regulated by government standards. Currently, an administrator must be licensed and is required to practice according to prescribed standards. The administrator's performance and the nursing facility are regularly monitored by state and sometimes federal surveyors to determine whether resident care and the facility meet required standards. A nursing home administrator must be far more knowledgeable about standards and the operations of each department in the facility than is required of hospital administrators. Hospital administrators generally have highly trained department heads – an accountant or CPA for business, nurses with bachelor and master degrees, one or more qualified dietitians, a maintenance engineer, a full time licensed pharmacists, an executive housekeeper, and others. Most likely the only one of these a nursing home administrator can employ full-time will be the director of nursing (DON). This means you must provide more frequent monitoring of every unit of your facility and be able to evaluate performance in each.

An administrator must be qualified beyond management knowledge and skills through licensing. Availability, understanding, compassion, and patience are mandatory, both with residents and staff. Administration is not a "nine to five" job. Administrators must be available, at least by telephone, at all times. Also a desire to continue learning about resident care and management is absolutely necessary to success.

This publication is designed to orient you to the long-term care industry. It introduces you to the areas of knowledge that you must master to prepare for the national examination and to become a licensed administrator. No topic is discussed in depth. You are referred to other publications and other sources from which you may obtain the additional information needed to increase your professional knowledge.

Some states administer a second licensing examination on state minimum standards. This publication does not specifically prepare you for a state examination, although a state administering its own examination may include some of this material. Each state has some standards that differ from federal guidelines, and these may be included in your state examination. It is recommended that you obtain a copy of your state minimum standards for licensing nursing homes and of state Medicaid standards for payment to help prepare you for your state examination.

Each chapter of this publication deals with a segment of long-term-care practice. The material presented is based on federal guidelines and on accepted principles and practices in the areas of management listed above. When material presented is directly defined by federal guidelines, the source (law or Code of Federal regulations) follows in parentheses. Principles and practices discussed are followed by the author's name in parentheses. At the end of each chapter is a reference list of the sources of information used in this publication, and from which you may obtain additional information. Rather than overwhelm the reader with an exhausting number of sources, several are presented that will be particularly helpful to persons entering nursing home administration. There are many other publications of equal value.

Also a glossary of frequently used terms follows each chapter except Chapter 10. Terms are those an administrator needs to know. The glossaries are not all-inclusive as new terms continue to develop and old terms sometimes take on new meaning. The terms as used herein may have particular meaning in the field of nursing home administration.

Since there is no pronoun in the English language that includes male and female, the pronoun "he" is used to include both he and she. When the word mankind is used it includes man and woman. Certainly no hierarchy of importance or values, nor slight or offense are intended. It is used simply for the sake of brevity and readability.

TABLE OF CONTENTS

CHAPTER 5 **MARKETING AND PUBLIC RELATIONS**

CHAPTER 6 **PERSONNEL MANAGEMENT**

CHAPTER 7 **FINANCIAL MANAGEMENT**

CHAPTER 10

LEGAL MANAGEMENT

CHAPTER 11

REGULATORY MANAGEMENT

CHAPTER 12

RESIDENT CARE MANAGEMENT

INDEX

CHAPTER 1

INTRODUCTION

INTRODUCTION

EARLY BACKGROUND

Health care practices can be traced back to the very earliest history of mankind. In the 13th century B.C., the terms physician, nurse, medicine, and patient were used by the Vedas, a native group in India. The Vedas developed considerable health care knowledge which they passed from generation to generation by word of mouth. (Sigerist) Later health care moved from medicinal watering holes, sacred groves, and caves to religious temples in both Egypt and Greece. (Rogers)

Various types of facilities for the aged and the sick were established in Asia, Southern Europe, and North Africa. However the health care institutions of today apparently had their beginnings in 325 A.D. in the Roman Empire. Constantine I, whose mother Helena had been converted to Christianity, wanted the sick, the poor, the lame, and the aged removed from the streets. Believing that Christians were the only people who kept their word and who could be trusted to do what they promised, Constantine authorized the Council of Nicaea to direct the Christian bishops to build and operate health care facilities. Subsequently the bishops required that some type of **hospitalis** be attached to each bishopry, cathedral, and monastery.

Even then there were three types of health care institutions: (1) nosocomia—for care of the sick, (2) ptochia—for care of the helpless poor, and (3) gerontochia—for care of the aged. Later government and the public lost sight of these classifications as poverty and disease became blended. The hospitalises were filled to capacity with the diseased poor and the aged. To this day poverty and disease are linked together and much public concern focuses on this segment of the population.

The hospitalises were **financed** by voluntary almsgiving. The practice of almsgiving was extremely popular since it was considered a guaranteed "ticket to heaven" for the donor. Alms were given for the benefit of the donor, not primarily to help the poor and the sick. The government gave no financial support to the early hospitalis, although Constantine did restore confiscated property to Christians so they could build facilities.

The hospitalises were not hospitals as they are known today. Physicians did not practice in these institutions. The clergy and religious orders operated the hospitalises and took care of the sick. They were untrained in health care, although they became proficient in dressing wounds and sores and in giving comfort to their patients.

Physicians first attended patients in health care institutions about 1850. With the many advances in science after 1875, these institutions truly became treatment facilities for the first time. Physicians used the hospital's laboratory and other diagnostic facilities, operating rooms, and treatment facilities. The poor, chronically ill, disabled, and the aged who needed long-term care were relegated to such care-giving institutions as almshouses and the workhouses first established in England. Once again they were in facilities that only offered food and shelter and whatever human comforts the institution could afford. The able-bodied poor, or paupers, were required to work to provide relief for the disabled who had no relatives to provide for them.

The concept of almshouses and workhouses spread from England to America. Municipalities and communities farmed out to the lowest bidder the care of the poor and elderly who had no family to provide such care. Since America was largely rural, these facilities became known as **poor farms**. Even though many were chronically ill, they were required to perform chores and assist with their upkeep. Certain other groups needing long-term care were isolated into tuberculosis, mental, and convalescent sanatoriums.

SOCIAL SECURITY ACT OF 1935

The Social Security Act is indirectly responsible for the nursing home industry as it exists today. Social Security's original and sole **purpose** was to provide a **supplemental** retirement for working people and their dependents. It also provided Old Age Assistance (OAA) to needy people aged 65 and older who lived in the community.

Many of the aged needed a place to live where their basic needs could be met. Boarding homes sprang up to care for the OAA beneficiaries. Large numbers of aged who were ill or blind left state and county institutions to claim OAA and to reside in boarding homes.

President Franklin D. Roosevelt's four freedoms should have included **freedom from pain**. People's attitude had begun to change from a high tolerance of pain to a desire to be free of suffering. In the 1940's discovery of sulfa drugs and penicillin meant illnesses such as pneumonia that plagued the aged could be cured. People lived longer and no longer wanted to tolerate pain. They wanted care and treatment appropriate to their needs.

In 1950 amendments to the Social Security Act extended OAA to residents of public medical institutions (except tuberculosis and mental hospitals). This accelerated the exodus of older people. Many took up residence in boarding homes now that they could afford to pay for their support.

Boarding homes became nursing homes largely because there was no place to put the aged, sickly resident. Nursing homes became a natural haven for the aged who now had longer life expectancy and could pay for basic nursing care with OAA income.

The origin of the term **nursing home** is not clear. In 1936, the Chicago area had an association of nursing homes. The Detroit area used the title **nursing home** in 1939. It appeared in the Illinois Legislature for the first time in 1945. The convalescent home was defined as a facility **commonly called a nursing home** by the Ohio Legislature in 1946. (Rogers)

The nursing home as it is known today was given impetus by the 1950 amendments to the Social Security Act mentioned earlier. These amendments required states to establish a standard setting or licensing agency for nursing homes. This gave official status to nursing homes as facilities to provide long-term care.

Although the Federal Government never intended Social Security to be involved in health care, these same amendments, for the first time in history, made grants-in-aid to states for direct payment of medical care for public welfare cases. The Kerr-Mills Act of 1960 established medical aid to the aged to be administered by the states. It required a **means test** to ensure that funds went only to health care for the needy. The Kerr-Mills Act was the predecessor of **Medicaid** which began July 1, 1965. Medicaid was established by Title XIX, an amendment to the Social Security Act.

Medicare (Title XVIII) also was born in 1965. Designed as health insurance for the aged, it was and is administered by the Federal Government with some assistance by the states. These two programs, especially Medicaid, were a real boon to nursing homes.

The Omnibus Budget Reconciliation ACT of 1987, referred to as OBRA-87 and as the Nursing Home Reform Act, changed the name nursing home to **nursing facility**. (42CFR 483.5) Now all states have a nursing facility program substantially supported by Medicaid. Each state has an agency that licenses and regulates nursing facilities. These agencies also participate in federal certification of the facilities for Medicare. States use federal guidelines published in the Code of Federal Regulations. (CFR)

Many states impose additional guidelines on nursing facilities to ensure adequate care is provided. If federal and state guidelines are in conflict, nursing facilities are required to follow the more stringent regulation. Examples are (1) some states have stricter building, fire, and safety codes than prescribed by federal regulations, and (2) some require that medical records be kept for a greater duration.

All beginning administrators should contact their state's nursing facility licensing and certification agency for detailed information regarding its operation and how it regulates nursing homes.

THE NURSING HOME ADMINISTRATOR (NHA)

Wesley Rogers contends that the practice of nursing home administration probably had its beginnings in the story of the good Samaritan. (Luke 10:30-36) Certainly, basic elements of nursing home administration are identified: compassion first, a sick person, need for care, a caretaker, a facility, treatment, funding, and long-term care.

Through the ages there were administrators for hospitals, almshouses, leper colonies, and workhouses. As the nursing home evolved, the title of the person in charge also evolved from **operator** to **nursing home administrator**. Since the term nursing home has changed to nursing facility a few states changed nursing *home* administrator to nursing *facility* administrator. However, the term nursing facility has not caught on. Predominantly they are called nursing *homes*, so the title nursing *home* administrator (NHA) is likely to remain in vogue.

Section 1902 of the Social Security Act as amended in 1965 required nursing home administrators to be **licensed** by the states. In order to participate in Medicaid and Medicare, states were required to license administrators provisionally by July 1, 1970, and by examination after July 1, 1972. No nursing facility providing Medicare or Medicaid services may operate except under supervision of a duly licensed administrator. Most states require that nursing facilities serving private-pay patients only also operate under direction of a licensed administrator.

Each state must license through its healing arts provisions or appoint a Board of Examiners that is required to (1) develop, impose, and enforce standards of licensing, (2) monitor their performance, (3) issue, revoke, or suspend licenses, and (4) conduct studies and investigations that will help to improve standards. (42 CFR 431.700 - 431.708) All states except Connecticut licenses through a Board of Examiners.

In all states it is a crime, usually a misdemeanor, to represent oneself as a nursing home administrator without being duly licensed. Such practice may be punishable by a fine and/or imprisonment.

Licensing requirements vary from state to state since licensing of professionals is a state prerogative. Educational requirements range from an evaluation of education and experience to a master's degree in health care administration. After meeting specific eligibility requirements of a given state, applicants for licensing must pass a national examination in all 50 states and in the District of Columbia. In addition, most states require the applicant to pass a state examination, either written or oral. In many states the applicant must undergo an administrator-in-training (AIT) program either before or after passing examinations. Duration of the AIT program may vary from 300 hours to one year. This period is spent as an intern in a nursing home(s) under the direction of a qualified preceptor, who in some states is certified by the State Board. (See Table 1.1)

Reciprocity has been established by some states. These states endorse an administrator's license held in another state without requiring the administrator to go through the entire licensing procedure again. Reciprocity is important as an administrator may practice only in the state(s) in which he holds a valid license. Administrators working with homes that operate homes in several states are often transferred from state to state.

Imminent change - An amendment to the Social Security Act now provides that the Secretary of the U.S. Department of Health and Human Services will establish minimum standards for nursing home administrators. This is to replace the practice of each state setting its own standards. Some members of Congress felt the Secretary's new duty was a duplication of the Social Security Act requirement for licensing. In October 1990, Congress repealed those sections of the Social Security Act that mandated licensing administrators. Repeal is to be effective at the time the Secretary promulgates minimum standards for administrators. At the time of this publication, the amendment has not been implemented.

Table 1.1:

Licensure Requirements Summary

LICENSING REQUIREMENTS			AIT TRAINING		EXAM		CE Hrs Required
State	Education	Renewal	Period	*Cert.	Nat'l	State	
Alabama	BA and AIT	Annually	1000 - 2000 hrs	Yes	Yes	Yes	24/yr
Alaska	BA and 1 yr exp	Biennially	None	–	Yes	No	None
Arizona	BA, courses, AIT	Biennially	1000 hrs	No	Yes	Yes	50/2 yrs
Arkansas	AA, or HS + exp	Annually	12-24-mos	No	Yes	Yes	20/yr
California	MA and exp/or BA plus AIT	Biennially	1000 hrs	Yes	Yes	Yes	40/2 yrs
Colorado	AA and AIT/BA/AA and exp	Annually	6-12 mos	Yes	Yes	Yes	None
Connecticut	BA, courses, AIT/MA	Annually	500-900 hrs	No	Yes	Yes	None
D.C.	BA degree/15 hr course/exp	Biennially	1 year	No	Yes	Yes	20/yr
Delaware	BA and AIT	Biennially	3-12 mos	Yes	Yes	No	48/2 yrs
Florida	BA and intern or AIT	Biennially	1000-2000 hrs	Yes	Yes	Yes	40/2 yrs
Georgia	MA and AIT or exp/BA, AIT	Biennially	6 mos	Yes	Yes	Yes	40/2 yrs
Hawaii	BA and courses and AIT	Biennially	2080 hrs	Yes	Yes	No	None
Idaho	BA and AIT/HS and exp	Annually	12 mos	Yes	Yes	Yes	20/yr
Illinois	BA/AA and exp/NHA course	Biennially	None	–	Yes	Yes	36/2 yrs
Indiana	BA and AIT/AA LTC and AIT	Biennially	6 mos	Yes	Yes	Yes	40/2 yrs
Iowa	AA in LTC/HS and AIT	Biennially	720 hrs	No	Yes	Yes	36/2 yrs
Kansas	BA and 480 hr practicum	Biennially	480 hrs	Yes	Yes	Yes	60/2 yrs
Kentucky	BA and 6 mos exp	Biennially	None	–	Yes	No	30/2 yrs
Louisiana	AA or 60 hrs and AIT	Biennially	6 mos	Yes	Yes	Yes	30/2 yrs
Maine	BA, courses/BA in LTC	Annually	6 mos	Yes	Yes	Yes	24/yr
Maryland	BA or MA and AIT/BA courses	Biennially	12 mos	Yes	Yes	Yes	40/2 yrs
Massachusetts	MA in HCA/BA and AIT	Annually	6 mos	Yes	Yes	No	30/2 yrs
Michigan	BA or MI RN lic./app courses	Biennially	None	–	Yes	Yes	36/2 yrs
Minnesota	BA with 12 courses in NHA	Annually	400-500 hrs	No	Yes	Yes	30/yr
Mississippi	Educ and exp	Annually	300 hrs	Yes	Yes	Yes	20/yr
Missouri	AA or exp in LTC	Biennially	6 mos	Yes	Yes	Yes	40/2 yrs
Montana	3,600 points of ed, exp	Annually	None	–	Yes	Yes	25/yr
Nebraska	AA and courses, and AIT	Biennially	None	–	Yes	Yes	50/2 yrs
Nevada	Educ and exp	Biennially	None	–	Yes	No	40/2 yrs
New Hampshire	BA and AIT	Biennially	12 mos	No	Yes	Yes	25/yr
New Jersey	BA and exp/Educ and AIT	Biennially	450 - 1750 hrs	Yes	Yes	No	40/2 yrs
New Mexico	BA and intern or AIT	Annually	None	–	Yes	No	24/yr
New York	BA or Educ and exp	Biennially	24 mos	Yes	Yes	No	72/2 yrs
North Carolina	2 yr col/courses/AIT	Biennially	12 to 50 wks	Yes	Yes	Yes	30/2 yrs
North Dakota	BA in LTC/BA courses	Annually	Developing AIT Program		Yes	Yes	25/yr
Ohio	BA, AIT or MA, BA in NHA	Annually	3 to 9 mos	No	Yes	Yes	20/yr
Oklahoma	HS, NHA course; BA, MA	Annually	560 hrs	Yes	Yes	Yes	20/yr
Oregon	BA	Annually	960 hrs	Yes	Yes	Yes	30/yr
Pennsylvania	120 hr study/exp/training	Biennially	None	–	Yes	Yes	48/2 yrs
Rhode Island	BA w/NHA and exp	Biennially	None	–	Yes	No	40/2 yrs
South Carolina	AA or 60 hrs and AIT	Annually	6 mos	Yes	Yes	Yes	20/yr
South Dakota	BA in NHA & exp/BA & exp	Annually	None	–	Yes	Yes	20/yr
Tennessee	BA in LTC/BA and AIT	Biennially	6-12 mos	Yes	Yes	Yes	18/yr
Texas	BA, practicum, NHA course	Biennially	520 hrs	Yes	Yes	Yes	24/2 yrs
Utah	BA w/health adm courses	Biennially	1000 hrs	Yes	Yes	No	40/2 yrs
Vermont	AA, and/or exp	Biennially	None	–	Yes	Yes	TBD
Virginia	BA in NHA and AIT	Annually	2080 hrs	Yes	Yes	Yes	20/yr
Washington	BA and AIT	Annually	500-1500 hrs	Yes	Yes	Yes	54/3 yrs
West Virginia	BA in HA and AIT	Annually	12 mos	Yes	Yes	Yes	20/yr
Wisconsin	AA NHA/course	Biennially	None	–	Yes	Yes	24/2 yrs
Wyoming	BA and AIT	Annually	6 mos	No	Yes	Yes	25/yr

* Are AIT Preceptors certified by the Board?

Source: National Association of Boards of Examiners of Long-Term Care Administrators, 1997

Repeal of the licensing requirement is very unpopular with administrators, state surveyors, advocacy groups and others who believe the requirement is helpful in upgrading standards and in promoting quality care. Unless the Secretary includes licensing as a minimum standard it is possible some states may sunset their nursing home administrator licensing programs. This is seen as a backward step. It could result in an entirely new system of selecting administrators, one that might not utilize the experience and the gains of licensing programs. The struggle for professionalism could be undermined.

Need for administrators - Table 1.2 shows a total of 16,332 nursing homes and 45,322 licensed administrators. At first glance it appears the industry does not need additional administrators; it has an oversupply already. Since 1970 when licensing began, there has been a ratio of almost three licensed administrators per nursing home. This is due to several factors: (1) some owners are licensed but do not practice; (2) many surveyors are licensed but do not plan to serve as administrators; (3) most nursing home chain organizations have numerous regional or district supervisors who are licensed but are not in charge of an individual nursing home; (4) larger nursing homes often have one or more licensed administrators serving as assistant administrators, and (5) an increasing number of administrators are retired from practice but maintain their licensed status. The three to one ratio of administrators per nursing home does not mean the field is overcrowded. There is a continuing need for a new supply of administrators, and most competent administrators are able to obtain employment with little difficulty.

THE NATIONAL ASSOCIATION OF BOARDS (NAB)

In 1971, representatives of several state boards of examiners organized the National Association of Boards of Examiners of Nursing Home Administrators. During the 1990's some states began licensing administrators of other residential long-term care facilities, as assisted living, group homes and continuing care retirement centers. NAB expanded its membership to include licensing boards for administrators of these facilities. In 1996 NAB changed its name to National Association of Boards of Examiners of Long-Term Care Administrators. The Associations purposes are:

1. To conduct research and make recommendations on questions of common interest to the long-term care administrators' examinations and licensing boards and to licensing authorities of the States, Commonwealths, District, and Territories of the United States of America.

2. To study and recommend professional and educational standards for long-term care administrators in order to promote and protect public health and welfare.

3. To cooperate in obtaining uniformity of the laws, rules, regulations, and procedures concerning state boards examiners and/or licensing authorities in order to create efficiency for those receiving licenses as long-term care administrators.

4. To consider, establish, and maintain a uniform code of ethics and standards of professional conduct and practice for boards of examiners and/or licensing authorities of long-term care administrators.

5. To work toward reciprocal endorsement and/or recognition of long-term care administrator licenses by the licensing boards and authorities of the States, Commonwealths, District, and Territories of the United States of America.

Each state and the District of Columbia are eligible to appoint one representative to the NAB Board of Governors upon payment of state membership dues. Other state board members and staff, organizations and individuals concerned with LTC are eligible for membership in the Association. A majority of the states actively participate and contribute to operations of NAB.

NAB has developed the national licensing examination which is used by all 50 states and the District of Columbia. Common testing dates - the second Thursday of the first month of each quarter - have been set so that a state can offer the examination as many as four times per year.

During 1998 NAB developed its first national examination for residential care/assisted living administrators. This is an examination separate from the NHA's examination.

NURSING FACILITIES TODAY

Congress amended the Social Security Act in 1972 to include Section 1122. It allowed the federal government to withhold Medicare and Medicaid funds from a hospital, nursing home, or other health care facility if prior approval was not obtained from the official state health planning agency for capital expenditures of $100,000 or more.

The Planning and Resource Development Act of 1975 (P.L. 93-641) sought to bring together into one package all of the Federal Government's interests in health care matters. The Act required each state to set up a State Health Planning and Development Agency (SHPDA). The SHPDA developed a "State Health Plan" that was used as a guideline in reviewing need for additional facilities. It included population and health care facility statistics upon which decisions to approve building applications were based. The plan also gave information on how to apply for needs review. A copy of the state plan could be secured from the SHPDA.

The primary purpose of Section 1122 and the State Health Plan was to prevent overbuilding health care facilities and the duplication of highly specialized, expensive equipment. Such actions accelerated health care costs. A measure of control was to ensure that unapproved facilities could not participate in Medicare and Medicaid. Under this program a state could declare a *moratorium* on building or adding facilities eligible for such funding.

In October 1987 the Federal Government **terminated** its Section 1122 agreements with the states. Also, it abolished the requirement for a State Health Plan. Now, each state may establish its own facility **needs review program**, setting its own standards on new construction eligible for Medicare and Medicaid.

TYPES OF FACILITIES

The Federal Government recognizes several types of nursing facility care.

1. **Skilled Nursing Facility (SNF)** is a nursing home that provides 24-hour per day skilled nursing services which cannot be provided in a facility other than a hospital. Formerly, there were two types of SNF's.

   a. **Medicare SNF** offers, under direction of a physician, skilled nursing services for residents who have Medicare insurance. To be eligible the resident must be undergoing treatment from which the SNF staff may reasonably expect a certain degree of improvement within a given period of time. When the Medicare beneficiary reaches maximum treatment benefits and is no longer expected to improve, he is not eligible for further SNF treatment under Medicare. This can be confusing to a responsible party since the patient may still need skilled nursing care just to maintain some degree of health. But, remember Medicare is an insurance program with specific limitations. Private-pay individuals may stay in the SNF as long as the physician agrees. OBRA-87 leaves this type SNF intact.

   b. **Medicaid SNF** offers, under direction of a physician, skilled nursing services to individuals aged 21 or older who require skilled nursing care on a 24-hour daily, inpatient basis. Often, these residents are said to be at a maintenance level and are not expected to show significant improvement. Residents eligible for Medicaid and individuals able to pay their own expenses are cared for in an SNF certified for Medicaid.

2. **An Intermediate Care Facility (ICF)** was the term applied to a nursing facility which met state licensing standards to provide, on a regular basis, health-related care and services to individuals who do not require hospital or SNF care, but whose mental or physical condition requires services (a) above the level

Table 1.2:

Nursing Home and Nursing Home Administrator Statistics

STATE	Number of Nursing Homes	Number Licensed Admin.	BOARD COMPOSITION			
			Admin	Public	Other	Total
Alabama	214	560	3	1	4	7
Alaska	14	47	No	Board		
Arizona	142	435	4	2	3	9
Arkansas	260	871	2	1	7	10
California	1340	3964	4	5	0	9
Colorado	207	568	3	4	0	7
Connecticut	255	907	No	Board		
D.C.	44	166	3	6	0	9
Delaware	18	51	2	1	2	3
Florida	612	1514	3	2	2	7
Georgia	355	893	6	3	4	13
Hawaii	42	175	3	1	3	7
Idaho	72	126	2	1	2	3
Illinois	819	2240	6	3	0	9
Indiana	588	1435	5	1	5	11
Iowa	468	763	4	2	3	9
Kansas	425	784	3	4	0	7
Kentucky	271	762	6	1	2	9
Louisiana	334	865	7	1	5	13
Maine	147	230	4	2	1	7
Maryland	228	580	5	4	2	11
Massachusetts	537	1300	5	1	5	11
Michigan	440	1310	6	3	1	10
Minnesota	459	925	4	3	4	11
Missouri	510	1778	4	2	5	11
Mississippi	169	401	3	0	4	7
Montana	102	245	2	3	0	5
Nebraska	232	439	4	2	6	12
Nevada	39	80	2	2	3	7
New Hampshire	78	199	4	5	0	9
New Jersey	315	1190	7	6	2	15
New Mexico	73	198	2	3	2	7
New York	630	4220	6	3	4	13
North Carolina	359	715	3	4	0	7
North Dakota	84	164	4	0	5	9
Ohio	981	2010	4	5	0	9
Oklahoma	422	975	6	2	7	15
Oregon	166	480	3	3	3	9
Pennsylvania	710	1971	6	3	6	15
Rhode Island	99	347	3	2	2	7
South Carolina	114	305	5	2	4	11
South Dakota	159	312	3	3	4	10
Tennessee	308	710	4	1	4	9
Texas	1193	2579	6	3	0	9
Utah	90	313	4	1	1	5
Vermont	50	107	4	1	4	9
Virginia	282	660	5	2	0	7
Washington	284	628	4	1	4	9
West Virginia	134	250	6	4	1	11
Wisconsin	421	2504	5	2	3	10
Wyoming	37	71	2	1	2	5
TOTALS	16,332	45,332	202	120	131	451

Source: National Association of Boards of Examiners of Long-Term Care Administrators, 1997.

of room and board, and (b) that can be provided only by an institution. State standards set more detailed requirements, as care under the direction of a physician and under supervision of a registered or a practical nurse over a continuous 24-hour period.

State standards often provided for establishing two or more levels of ICF's. Some states have ICF-I, ICF-II and ICF-III, each providing a slightly different level of care. In one state the ICF-I may provide service for the most debilitated patient, and the ICF-III for those requiring the least amount of care and supervision. In another state, it may be reversed, with the ICF-III caring for the most debilitated.

In addition to Medicaid residents, the Medicaid certified ICF accepted private-pay individuals. Some states allowed homes to charge a higher rate for services for private-pay than for Medicaid residents.

3. **Nursing facility** Effective October 1, 1990, OBRA discontinued the terms *nursing home* and *Intermediate Care Facility*, substituting nursing facility. In spite of the name change facilities continue to be referred to as nursing homes. The two are used interchangeably in this publication. All levels of care reimbursed by Medicaid may be provided in a single facility, except those specialized services provided in ICF-MR's which were left intact. (42CFR 440.40) The Health Care Finance Administration (HCFA) is considering reimbursement on the basis of type of illness or disability and the cost of providing service to each type. This plan is discussed in more detail in Chapter 7.

4. **Intermediate Care Facility—Mentally Retarded (ICF-MR)** is a facility whose primary purpose is to provide health and rehabilitative services for mentally retarded individuals or persons with related conditions, using a plan of care that includes professionally developed and supervised activities, experiences, or therapies. The objective of the services offered is to maintain the optimal physical, intellectual, social, and/or vocational level at which the individual is presently or potentially capable of functioning. (42 CFR 483.400)

5. **Non-participating nursing facility** is one not certified for, nor participating in Medicare or Medicaid. It is licensed by the state but is not subject to Medicare and Medicaid standards. The state Medicaid agency does not survey the facility nor monitor its performance unless such action is provided for by state law. Non-participating facilities accept only private pay or insurance cases. They are more numerous in areas in which retirees have substantial retirement income or personal resources.

Number of nursing homes The American Health Care Association (AHCA) in its publication *Facts and Trends* provides a wealth of statistical information on nursing homes, number of beds, occupancy rates, and others. It is a valuable sourcebook by which administrators can obtain an overview of averages and determine where their facilities rank compared to national and state averages. Its primary information source is the Health Care Finance Administration (HCFA), the agency within the U.S. Department of Health and Human Services that states deal with regarding Medicare and Medicaid. HCFA has established an On-line Survey, Certification, and Reporting (OSCAR) system that receives information from each state on nursing homes certified for Medicare, Medicaid, or both. (Refer to Chapter 11 for details on certification.)

AHCA's table showing number and types of nursing homes is reproduced as Table 1.3 of this chapter. It shows that predominantly nursing facilities are certified for both Medicare and Medicaid – 77 percent – whereas, 14 percent are certified for Medicaid only, and 9 percent Medicare only. These figures do not include non-participating facilities which are private-pay only. However, these nursing homes make up only a small portion of total facilities.

Number of beds AHCA's table showing number of nursing home beds nationally and by state is also reproduced in this publication. (See Table 1.4) Although only 14 percent of nursing homes are certified for Medicaid only, their beds make up 63 percent of total nursing home beds. On the other hand, 77 percent of facilities are certified for both Medicare and Medicaid, but their beds comprise only 34.3 percent of total beds.

Table 1.3:

Nursing Facilities by Certification by State - 1997

STATE	TOTAL FACILITIES	MEDICARE ONLY	MEDICAID ONLY	MEDICARE and MEDICAID
		Percentage of Facilities		
United States	**16,608**	**1,061**	**4,357**	**11,190**
Alabama	219	12	5	202
Alaska	15	0	4	11
Arizona	149	28	2	119
Arkansas	266	20	153	93
California	1,370	122	136	1,112
Colorado	213	25	38	150
Connecticut	267	8	20	239
D.C.	20	1	4	15
Delaware	44	4	6	34
Florida	634	53	18	563
Georgia	356	10	95	251
Hawaii	42	3	10	29
Idaho	77	4	0	73
Illinois	835	75	339	421
Indiana	590	25	193	372
Iowa	468	5	341	122
Kansas	433	32	248	153
Kentucky	289	23	0	266
Louisiana	342	52	252	38
Maine	143	5	3	135
Maryland	226	14	31	181
Massachusetts	545	5	99	441
Michigan	441	9	86	346
Minnesota	461	6	26	429
Mississippi	171	6	91	74
Missouri	528	48	138	342
Montana	100	1	4	95
Nebraska	335	2	141	92
Nevada	39	2	3	34
New Hampshire	78	2	55	21
New Jersey	314	13	75	226
New Mexico	78	5	15	58
New York	638	0	3	635
North Carolina	380	7	4	369
North Dakota	85	1	0	84
Ohio	997	80	312	605
Oklahoma	438	27	342	69
Oregon	163	5	41	117
Pennsylvania	722	70	49	603
Rhode Island	96	0	0	96
South Carolina	162	15	2	145
South Dakota	115	1	62	52
Tennessee	312	21	104	187
Texas	1,224	174	471	579
Utah	93	10	19	64
Vermont	48	0	14	34
Virginia	275	8	85	182
Washington	283	7	12	264
West Virginia	132	9	52	71
Wisconsin	419	4	149	266
Wyoming	38	2	5	31

Source: HCFA - OSCAR Form 671: F9, current surveys as of 3/1/98. American Health Care Association

Table 1.4:

Nursing Facility Beds by Certification Type - 1997

STATE	TOTAL BEDS	AVERAGE BEDS PER FACILITY	MEDICARE ONLY	MEDICAID ONLY	MEDICARE AND MEDICAID	NOT CERTIFIED
United States	**1,836,657**	**107**	**56,183**	**1,034,882**	**618,556**	**127,036**
Alabama	24,726	111	334	15,073	8,996	323
Alaska	812	54	16	241	460	95
Arizona	17,738	108	712	12,298	3,543	1,185
Arkansas	31,765	119	868	21,790	2,453	6,654
California	140,576	99	4,798	71,363	50,894	13,521
Colorado	20,105	90	880	13,488	4,539	1,198
Connecticut	32,775	126	270	10,967	20,468	1,070
Delaware	5,012	114	548	2,466	1,481	517
Florida	77,779	111	5,673	47,183	19,575	5,348
Georgia	39,179	110	461	25,197	12,869	652
Hawaii	3,920	89	96	1,018	2,774	32
Idaho	6,362	75	279	2,197	2,661	1,225
Illinois	108,730	125	3,892	82,169	12,997	9,672
Indiana	62,232	108	2,379	44,245	8,241	7,367
Iowa	45,699	97	344	21,233	13,182	10,940
Kansas	29,138	70	571	20,080	6,460	2,027
Kentucky	25,387	80	1,188	11,347	11,606	1,246
Louisiana	39,053	113	1,476	31,505	4,198	1,874
Maine	9,253	69	965	5,731	2,520	37
Maryland	31,562	125	851	16,785	12,242	1,684
Massachusetts	58,039	103	415	32,462	24,169	993
Michigan	51,362	115	1,689	28,966	18,489	2,218
Minnesota	45,143	101	393	9,402	34,798	550
Mississippi	17,431	84	848	13,712	2,560	311
Missouri	55,987	97	2,012	41,914	6,692	5,369
Montana	7,546	773	128	3,410	3,948	60
Nebraska	18,186	77	230	11,709	5,408	839
Nevada	4,215	90	854	281	3,045	35
New Hampshire	8,241	99	123	5,059	2,812	247
New Jersey	49,119	148	1,298	28,658	18,318	845
New Mexico	6,928	84	143	5,162	1,353	270
New York	113,380	179	0	194	112,747	439
North Carolina	39,554	98	7779	24,104	14,378	293
North Dakota	7,040	81	121	141	6,778	-
Ohio	121,184	120	2,519	58,746	32,384	27,535
Oklahoma	34,398	83	832	29,909	2,690	967
Oregon	13,980	86	221	10,074	3,388	297
Pennsylvania	96,517	121	4,421	53,191	37,906	999
Rhode Island	10,120	102	10	5,709	4,196	205
South Carolina	17,531	100	1,186	7,455	7,789	1,101
South Dakota	8,079	71	45	3,225	4,793	16
Tennessee	39,089	112	1,270	28,395	8,750	674
Texas	126,230	97	6,789	90,420	17,344	11,677
Utah	7,553	80	1,533	5,553	341	126
Vermont	3,611	84	0	1,810	1,796	5
Virginia	29,405	110	589	22,805	5,019	992
Washington	27,575	97	228	18,373	7,933	1,042
Washington DC	3,116	142	58	1,611	1,440	7
West Virginia	13,221	96	430	7,409	3,372	2,010
Wisconsin	47,929	113	385	26,773	20,536	235
Wyoming	3,144	81	33	1,874	1,225	12

Source: HCFA - OSCAR Form 1538: L13, L37-L39, current sureys as of 3/1/98. American Health Care Association

These percentages change from year to year as nursing homes frequently change certification between Medicare and Medicaid. Also, homes may drop beds or add beds dependent on market demands and state regulatory limitations.

TRENDS IN THE LONG-TERM CARE (LTC) INDUSTRY

Population A study by the American Health Planning Association (AHPA) revealed concern about the *graying of America*. In 1980 there were 25 million people age 65 and over (11 percent of the population). This is expected to increase to 36 million (13 percent of the population) by the year 2000. By the year 2030, 64 million people in the U.S. will be age 65 or over (20 percent of the population).

The American Health Care Association (AHCA) reports that in 1996 there were 30,099,000 people in the 65-84 age group (11.3 percent of the population), and 3,762,000 (1.4 percent of the population) in the 85 and over age group. In some states rates vary significantly from the national average. As an example, Florida's age 65-84 population is 11.5 percent of its total, whereas Utah has only 2.9 percent in this age group.

Population trends The Census Bureau estimates that the elderly population will continue to increase through the year 2025 and more than double between 2025 and 2050. Table 1.5 reflects latest estimates of the Census Bureau statisticians.

Table 1.5:
Estimated Growth in Population over Age 85

Year	No. Over 85
1991	3,400,000
2000	4,600,000
2025	7,000,000
2050	15,300,000

The significance of this information lies in the percent of elderly occupying nursing homes. Latest figures available in 1990 show some 1.4 percent of the 65 to 74 age group resided in nursing facilities, 6 percent of the 75 to 84 age group, and 25 percent of the 85 and older group. Of the 1.6 million people in nursing homes 53 percent were in the oldest age group. If these rates and trends continue, the LTC industry will need 3,825,000 beds for the 85 and over group by the year 2050 — more than double the total nursing home beds now in use.

Thus far, the focus has been on the **aged** in nursing facilities. There are other types of residents, but they are in the minority. These include the mentally retarded, individuals of all ages suffering from strokes, individuals with congenital deformities, accident victims (particularly the brain damaged), and others of any age who need long-term care.

Costs Nursing facility expenditures were $20 billion in 1980, $53.1 billion in 1990, $59.5 billion in 1991, and $78.5 billion in 1996. It is estimated that at the current rate of increase total costs will be $147 billion by the year 2000 — an increase of more than 176 percent. **Medicaid** expenditures are the primary concern of the government since they make up to 48 percent of the total. This means Medicaid outlay was approximately $37.2 billion in 1996. Medicaid is projected to be 49 percent of the total in the year 2000 which means $72 billion – an increase of 152.5 percent. It is obvious the government cannot continue to fund a program that increases at such phenomenal rate. Resources are simply not available.

Service Trends A number of services involving nursing homes have developed in recent years. Some of these may be provided by the nursing home while others may be a resource for the facility.

1. **Luxury Wing** Certified facilities are permitted to develop a wing of the nursing home to be used by private pay residents. This may provide a wider variety of services including catered meals, plush rooms, and others. The facility may set the rates at whatever level the traffic will bear.

2. **Sub-acute care** Largely because of the Diagnosis Related Groups (DRG's) program by which hospitals are reimbursed, patients tend

to be discharged earlier while still showing sub-acute symptoms. Many of these are discharged to nursing homes resulting in a larger population of sicker residents. Some states are establishing a sub-acute care level to accommodate these changes. Timmreck points out that this trend presents long term care facilities with legal issues previously limited to hospitals. He contends that providing service to sub-acute cases as hip factures, terminally ill, massive strokes, unhealed surgical wounds with drain, urinary catheters, and so on are heavier risks for malpractice.

States determine if they wish to add this category of services as separate from SNF and NF. Some states do not use this distinction, and this category of resident is classified as skilled.

3. **Geriatric Evaluation Centers** In larger metropolitan areas centers have been developed to offer evaluation, referral, counseling, and other related services to the elderly and their families. These centers are usually staffed by a social worker who has detailed knowledge of all diagnostic, treatment, long term care, financial, and other services available to the elderly. Some centers will do a diagnostic workup on the patient as a part of the evaluation and provide counseling services. Their greatest value is in helping families to secure the proper services for the elderly.

Alternative Care The Federal Government supports and encourages development of home care and community services that serve as alternatives to nursing facility placement. The range of housing options for elderly is growing rapidly. Some see the nursing home as a last resort with a wide middle ground between home and the nursing home. Virginia Morris identifies many alternatives.

1. **Retirement housing,** sometimes called **senior apartments,** is promoted by private enterprise. Units are constructed with needs of the elderly in mind--wheelchair accessible, sturdy and stable furniture, good lighting, tight security, and others. They may be single story or high rise. Generally, residents may prepare their own meals or purchase them at a central cafeteria. Laundry and housekeeping services are usually available. Some are condominium type where individuals purchase a condo or make a substantial deposit, some or all of which may be refundable.

2. **Assisted living units** provide additional services to those offered in retirement housing. These may include meals, recreation, some nursing service, and others. Often these units are attached to a nursing facility or are a part of retirement housing. During the past five years this form of alternative care has mushroomed into a sizeable industry. During 1995 the industry generated $16.8 billion, and this is expected to increase to $33.1 billion by the year 2000. Hospitals are especially interested, primarily because they want to remain the center of community health care. Expansion is typified by five companies going public and being listed on the stock market. (Fisher)

   Assisted living concepts appeal to the elderly since most prefer a setting that provides as much independence as they can accommodate for as long as they are physically and mentally capable.

3. **Life Care Centers** provide it all--retirement, assisted living, and nursing home. They are also called **continuing care retirement centers.** Most accept only people who are ambulating and can live independently. The center offers a variety of activities--golf, swimming, bowling, lectures and others. The assisted living complex offers more services as residents become less able to care for themselves. A nursing home unit provides full care for those who are so frail or chronically ill they need 24-hour supervision. The life care center provides a mix of residents so the atmosphere is improved over a nursing home that has only debilitated residents.

4. **Accessory Apartments,** sometimes called mother-daughter or grown-up apartments, are accessory dwellings within or attached to a home. They usually have bedroom, bath, kitchen, and living area with a separate entrance. This type housing often works well for

a parent residing in a unit attached to a son or daughter's home.

5. **ECHO housing**, (Elders Cottage Housing Opportunity) are temporary, modular homes that can be placed on single-family property, perhaps in the back yard of a family member. They are designed especially for older people because they are single level, wheelchair-accessible, energy-efficient, and well lighted. Usually they are about 500 square feet and sell in the $25,000 range. They usually can be moved when no longer needed.

6. **Shared Housing** involves someone or several people with an elderly person sharing his home and various household chores. It is less expensive, provides companionship, and allows residents to maintain autonomy.

7. **Congregate Housing** is called **group homes** in many states where they are licensed as a facility. Usually this involves a large house where residents have their own bedrooms. Some may have separate small apartments, but these are generally not referred to as group homes. Meals are usually provided as are housekeeping services.

8. **Foster homes** provide meals, laundry, transportation, and other services to an elderly person on a fee basis. Most people in foster care have some limitations and need help with daily activities. This can be a good option if the foster family embraces and nurtures their resident.

Assisted living services is a term many states apply to programs that provide home care and other services that serve as an alternative to nursing facility care. Most of these programs are now licensed by states, or provided by state and local government agencies.

1. **Day care** facilities are increasing in popularity. They provide care usually between the hours of 8:00 a.m. and 5:00 p.m. Some provide transportation and others require family to provide it.

2. **Non-emergency medical transportation** has developed into an expansive program that provides transportation to and from medical, dental, and other healthcare providers. It is extensively used by the needy who reside at home. However, it is also used by nursing facility and other residential facility residents. Medicare and Medicaid reimburse providers for eligible users of this service.

3. **Home health** is an assisted living service provided to the homebound. It provides a wide variety of health care services including nursing care, personal care, and rehabilitation services. It is financed by both Medicare and Medicaid. Home health was the major alternative service to entering a nursing facility until 1997 when the program was cut back extensively by the government largely due to excessive cost.

4. **Meals on wheels** delivers nutritious meals to many homebound. This program is usually operated by a local Council on Aging which may also offer transportation, counseling, and a variety of other services to the elderly.

5. **Sitters service** is another popular trend. Whereas, earlier it was largely practiced in hospitals and nursing facilities, many sitter services now extend to the home.

6. **Hospice care** has gained wide acceptance during the last few years. Hospice is the philosophy and practice of caring for the dying. It is based on the concept that death is a natural and inevitable part of life and at some point the focus should be on enhancing whatever life remains rather than battling illness and warding off death. The more than 2,100 hospice organizations in the United States provide home care, respite care and rehabilitation. (Morris)

   Most hospices require physician verification that a person has less than six months to live before they accept the patient. However, most hospices begin to counsel with families as soon as it is decided the patient has a terminal illness and that treatment should be palliative. This is the point at which Medicare,

Medicaid, and other health care coverage begins to cover costs of hospice care.

Administrators should be aware of hospice organizations in their area and how to use their services. This service should be an integral part of the social worker's resources file. Some nursing homes, however, offer hospice services within the facility.

Managed care The most significant trend affecting long-term care is the managed care concept used by Health Maintenance Organizations (HMOs). The number of people purchasing health care through HMOs is growing rapidly as shown in Table 1.6.

Table 1.6:
Number of Americans in HMOs

Year	Number	Average Increase/Year
1983	33,000,000	
1993	45,000,000	600,000
1995	51,000,000	3,000,000
1997	75,500,000	12,250,000

The trend is easily identified as the average yearly increase from 1983 to 1993 was only 600,000; whereas, in the two-year period between 1993 and 1995 the average yearly increase was five times as great. Between 1995 and 1997 the increase jumped to 12,250,000 per year, which is four times the 1993-95 rate. John Durso points out that although HMOs were known for going after young, healthy subscribers, they are now signing up nursing home residents under Medicare contracts. This puts LTC providers in the position of having to negotiate for the same patients they formerly admitted on a private pay or voucher basis – a rather frightening prospect.

Durso recommends that the LTC provider respond to this trend by cutting costs either at the facility level or by forming provider alliances or networks. While the HMOs say they are looking for quality care, they are really after low costs. The HMO's purchase decisions are based on price. Durso believes that in the Medicaid program of the not-too-distant future, selection of the nursing home will be taken out of the patient's hands and turned over to a managed care bureaucrat. Most likely their choice of a facility will be negotiated on the basis of facilities undercutting one another.

Survival tips advanced by Durso include:

1. Form a provider alliance or network that is a continuum of care. It could allow facilities to keep costs at a reasonable level. Such alliances, or networks, give LTC bargaining power with a purchaser that holds most of the cards.

2. Have a clear understanding of the facility's costs per patient, rather than on a per facility or cost center basis. Cost per patient will be used in negotiating with HMOs.

3. Learn to better manage care of the individual by providing a continuum of care that has a step-down, such as assisted living and home care. The LTC provider would then offer assisted living and home care as alternatives to help push down the risk. This is no different than hospitals stepping down their patients to subacute or skilled Medicare.

4. Hire a good lawyer who knows how to put all of this into contracts. It should be one who can identify the risks and that portion of the risk to be shared with the provider and how. One such risk is the 30-day notice of discharge which prevents the facility from discharging a resident at a certain time. The facility will be at risk, and it must make sure its rates include this risk factor.

Administrators may want to look at Oregon's situation where there has been an influx of managed care residents from California. In addition to the Medicare-Medicaid trends listed above, Oregon passed a law requiring private pay residents to discuss their long-term care options with a government agency before they are admitted. The result of Oregon's total program was a nursing home census drop from 95 percent to 85 percent.

Nursing facility owners and operators must be alert to and prepare for these changes.

In spite of the proliferation of alternative care services and facilities, all indicators point to continued growth of the need for residential nursing facilities. The continued increase in elderly population means continued growth of numbers of elderly whose needs can only be met by 24-hour nursing facility care. Furthermore, current findings, not yet fully validated, indicate that the anticipated reduced costs of alternatives to nursing homes may not be realized. It is the writer's opinion that when further financial data is compiled the nursing home will be identified as the best bargain in health care. Although expensive, the care nursing homes provide on a 24-hour basis exceeds in efficiency and economy anything offered by hospitals and alternative care.

GLOSSARY

ACHA American Health Care Association A national organization of nursing facilities that monitors legislation, conducts studies, and provides other services to its members and to the public.

Administrator A person who is duly licensed by a state to practice as a nursing home administrator, one who in the future will meet Federally imposed minimum standards.

Aged People who by definition in their culture have reached an advanced age during which they may become less productive. In the U.S. they are often referred to as senior citizens, especially after reaching age 65.

AIT Administrator-in-training, a person undertaking on-the-job training, or an internship approved by a given state in preparation for licensing as a nursing home administrator.

Alternative care Any type of service that helps a person meet his long term care needs outside a nursing home or hospital.

Assisted living service Programs that provide health and other services in the home or in the community, such as day care, home health, meals on wheels, and transportation.

Assisted living units A type of residential care providing room, board, and some 24-hour supervision, such as group homes, apartments attached or proximal to a retirement housing unit or a nursing facility. May be referred to as residential care facility.

Boarding home A facility that offers room and board and sometimes supervision of daily activities. It does not offer health care.

CFR Code of Federal Regulations Guidelines issued by Federal Government interpreting how a given law is to be administered.

ECHO Elders Cottage Housing Opportunity is temporary, modular housing units for the elderly that may be moved onto property of a family member.

Facility A nursing facility unless otherwise designated.

HCFA The Health Care Finance Administration Within the U.S. Department of Health and Human Services. States deal with this agency in financing the licensing and certification programs and Medicaid services in nursing facilities.

HMO Health Maintenance Organization is a type of health insurance program that covers all approved health care costs which the HMO negotiates with provider.

Home health Services provided in the home through Medicare, Medicaid, and private pay, including nursing, social service, rehabilitation and other.

ICF An **intermediate care facility**, the term previously used for nursing facility (NF) which offers nursing care on a 24-hour per day basis.

ICF-MR An **intermediate care facility** offering care and services to **mentally retarded**.

License A duly-issued certificate that permits a person to practice or a nursing facility to operate in a given state.

Lifecare center A facility that provides a continuum of services including retirement housing, assisted living units, and nursing home care.

LTC Long-term care refers to the extended care of people with chronic and/or degenerative disabilities. It especially applies to nursing facilities.

Managed care A concept used by HMOs in which the patient has a primary physician; and all specialty services, hospitalization, and nursing home care must have prior approval of the HMO's Medical Director, with emphasis on prevention.

Means test Identifying a person's income and financial status to determine whether they are eligible for Medicaid.

Moratorium A suspension of activity.

NAB National Association of Boards of Examiners of Long Term Care Administrators, Inc. A private organization.

Non-participating nursing facility A long-term care facility not certified for Medicare or Medicaid.

Nursing facility (NF) A health care facility duly licensed by the state and which offers room, board, nursing care and certain other therapies.

Nursing home The name previously applied to what is now nursing facility, but in practice is still used.

OAA Old Age Assistance A program of federal/state financial assistance to the needy, aged 65 and older.

OBRA-87 The Omnibus Budget Reconciliation Act of 1987 Also referred to as the Nursing Home Reform Act, that effected major changes in the operations of nursing facilities.

OSCAR The On-line, Survey, Certification, and Reporting system developed by HCFA from information gathered by surveyors during the standard certification survey for participation in Medicare and Medicaid.

Reciprocity The endorsement by one state of a person's license held or issued in another state.

Resident A person who resides in a nursing facility. They were previously called patients, especially in SNF's. OBRA specifies that all be referred to as residents.

Responsible party A family member, or other person , who agrees to look after the affairs of a nursing home resident and who is responsible for the resident's financial needs.

SNF Skilled Nursing Facility offers 24-hour nursing care and other services, primarily for the elderly.

Standards Guidelines that spell out policies, procedures and other regulations for practice and/or operation of facilities.

State Board of Examiners of Long Term Care Administrators An agency duly authorized by a state to license nursing home administrators and sometimes LTC administrators and monitor their performance.

Sub-acute care Care provided by nursing facilities to patients discharged from hospitals still needing specialized care for such problems as fractured hips, massive strokes, and unhealed surgical wounds.

Title XIX Provides for Medicaid which is medical assistance available to needy people through federal funds granted to states. Federal funds are matched by state funds according to a prescribed formula and funds are administered by the state.

Title XVIII Provides for Medicare which is medical assistance in the form of insurance for people 65 and over and certain disabled persons.

Treatment facility An institution to which patients are admitted by physician's orders and which offers medical, nursing and other forms of treatment for health problems.

REFERENCES

Anderson, Arthur, *The Guide to the Nursing Home Industry,* Baltimore: H.I.C.A., Inc. and Arthur Anderson, LLP, 1995.

A Guide for Planning Long Term Care Health Services for the Elderly, Washington: American Health Planning Association.

Barnett, Alicia A., "Hospitals Lured by Assisted Living", *Provider,* Vol. 22, No. 7, Washington: AHCA, 1996.

Bylaws, Policies and Procedures, Washington: National Association of Boards of Examiners for Nursing Home Administrators, Inc., June 1996.

Directory of U.S. Colleges and Universities Offering a Curriculum in Long Term Care Administration and State Board Licensure Requirements of Long Term Care Administrators, Washington: National Association of Boards of Examiners of Long Term Care Administrators and University of North Carolina at Chapel Hill Long Term Care Administration Teaching Resources Project, 1994.

Durso, John J., "Confronting Managed Care", *Nursing Homes,* Vol. 45, No. 6, Cleveland:MEDQUEST Communications, Inc. 1996.

Facts and Trends: The Nursing Facility Source Book, Washington: American Health Care Association, 1997.

Fisher, Christy, "Assisted Living Takes a Walk Down Wall Street", Provider, Vol. 22, No. 3, Washington: AHCA, 1996.

Health Care Financing Review, HCFA, Pittsburgh: Superintendent of Documents, Fall 1992.

Managed Care Digest Series, Long Term Care Edition, Kansas City, MO: Hoechst, Marion Roussel, 1997.

Morris, Virginia, *How to Care For Aging Parents,* New York: Workman Publishing, Company, Inc., 1996.

Rogers, Wesley W., *General Administration in the Nursing Home,* Boston: Cahners Books, International, 1980.

Sigerist, Henry E., *A History of Medicine,* New York City: Oxford University Press, 1961.

State Operations Manual, Provider Certification, Revisions one and two, Springfield, VA: National Technical Information Service, 1998.

Statistical Abstract of the United States, U.S. Bureau of the Census, Washington: U.S. Government Printing Office, 1993.

The Holy Bible, New King James Version, Nashville: Thomas Nelson Publishers, 1994.

Timmerich, Thomas C., "Legal and Administrative Aspects of Sub-acute Care", *Journal of Long Term Care Administration,* Vol. 16, No. 3, Alexandria, VA: American College of Health Care Administrators, 1988.

Title 42 Code of Federal Regulations, Public Health, Part 400 to 429, Washington: U.S. Government Printing Office, 1995.

Title 42 Code of Federal Regulations, Public Health, Part 430 to end, Washington: U.S. Government Printing Office, 1996.

CHAPTER 2

CONCEPTS OF AGING

CONCEPTS OF AGING

SOCIAL ATTITUDES TOWARD AGING

Attitudes toward the aging vary widely from culture to culture. While some cultures still practice a degree of ancestor worship, there are others in which the young can hardly wait for the aged to die and get out of the way. In the United States certain groups of the young see the aged as fair game to be bilked of their possessions, and sometimes their lives, through con games, high-pressure sales, theft, and even assault.

In earlier times both Chinese and Hebrews taught and practiced the concept of children taking responsibility for the care of their aged parents. The Hebrew nation formalized the teaching and wrote it into law, made it religious tradition, and structured their society around it. Honoring the aged and the care given to them in later years by their children gave unity to the family and provided comfort and care as family members became debilitated.

Christian teachings incorporated this concept. Christ elevated the practice to one of love and compassion when he rebuked neglect and commended those who honored parents. (Rogers) Christianity teaches: "Honor thy father and mother; which is the first commandment with promise; that it may be well with thee, and thou mayest live long on the earth." (Ephesians 6:23) This practice prevailed to some degree for hundreds of years, especially in the seventeenth, eighteenth, and nineteenth centuries.

During the second quarter of the twentieth century Americans gave more and more of the duties of family and church to government and private enterprise. First, Americans gave up education from kindergarten through college, then care of the needy, recreation, and health care. With the rapid rise in costs and levels of living, husband and wife had to seek employment to survive. Child care and protection, as well as care of infirm aged parents, shifted to government and private enterprise. Young parents with children feel they cannot provide for the aged. Parents whose children are grown and on their own reach for freedoms they were denied during parenthood. They are sometimes resentful, hesitant, or unable to care for aged, infirm parents. Then, of course, there is the reality that many aged people need 24-hour care which few families can afford or provide within their own homes.

Fortunately, the aged themselves have joined together and developed a strong force in government. Now, they exert their rights, and demand more for their later years than languishing in a facility where they simply await death.

Frequently, the general public looks on the aged as fragile, unable to think and do for themselves, senile, and helpless. They believe the aged normally decrease in intellectual functioning and cannot care for themselves. The truth is that most of the aged continue to function fairly well in spite of their infirmities. More and more the person retiring from work has substantial retirement income through business or government retirement programs, social security, independent retirement accounts, investments, and personal income or other sources.

Nursing facility staff can no longer **stereotype** the aged by declaring "You know how old folks are." Their meaning, of course, is they are all alike: senile, crotchety, forgetful, and in their second childhood. Health-care givers sometimes see the more debilitated elderly as "out of it," so why have regard for their dignity, they don't know what's going on anyway.

THE AGING PROCESS

It is extremely important that staff understand the aging process and know what is normal and what is abnormal. Failure to understand can result in staff **infantilizing** the elderly, treating them as if they are in a second childhood. Generally, this results in further dependency and regression.

The aging process is both psychological and physiological. A division of these two is for discussion purposes only as they are intermingled and cannot actually be separated. This is especially true of the oldest-old who frequently respond to physical illness or psychological distress with cognitive confusion. (Rock and Sorensen)

1. **Psychological aging** People generally expect behavior and attitude changes as individuals age. A person who does not show expected changes as they age is considered exceptional. One hears people say to this type person, "You look great for your age." "You really don't talk or act like a person your age." On the other hand, an older person with these characteristics is heard complaining about forgetfulness or other behaviors that are normal to aging.

Normal psychological changes include **slowed memory retrieval** which may occur at any adult age. Like a computer, as mountains of information are stored in the brain a person often experiences an information overload. It is difficult to recall a certain detail. They often say, "It's on the tip of my tongue, but I just can't say it". When an older person complains their memory is getting bad they need reassurance that this can be very normal, everyone is forgetful at times.

Increased **difficulty in handling change** may be quite normal. Generally, the elderly's resilience and ability to relate to new stimuli are reduced. They simply do not like change which may involve much energy and giving up comfortable ways of doing things. This may result in normal **depression**, especially upon admission to a nursing home which involves giving up old stimuli — home, family, privacy, lights, sounds, odors, and so on — and trying to accommodate different stimuli, including a strange environment and people they do not know.

Resistance to change can be quite normal in the elderly. Many tend to "get set in their ways" and do not want change even though it benefits them. Some mental confusion in the elderly may be normal, especially when it involves major change in life style. They may not understand or remember all that is expected of them. However, staff must take care to distinguish this as a situational matter, not confusion due to organic changes.

Abnormal psychological changes include marked memory loss in which the resident cannot remember important things in their life. This may lead to confusion and a loss of judgment. However, confusion is often a result of illness or medication so that it does not always fall within the pathological category. Dementia, delusions, and hallucinations represent pathological thought processes. A delusional person may believe people are trying to poison him and refuse to eat or take medicine.

2. **Physiological aging** In developing care plans staff must consider the usual physical effects of aging, such as loss of vision and hearing, loss of physical reserves, declining sense of smell and taste, problems with balance, loss of muscle and thinner skin that bruises easily. These degenerative processes reduce the elderly's ability to compensate and causes more stress in the elderly than is seen in younger people.

Pathological physical aging includes Parkinson's disease, the dementia's like Alzheimer's, depression, strokes, glaucoma and cataracts, incontinence, arthritis, osteoporosis, prostate disease, heart disorders, and many others. (Rock and Sorensen) Most are chronic disorders brought on or hastened by deterioration of tissues or organs, resulting in diminished vitality of body processes.

Mild strokes may be particularly confusing to staff. Individuals often have mild strokes that are hardly noticeable when they occur. The resident may not make any complaint or only call attention to a mild headache. Frequently, this type of stroke is only identified by a sudden change in behavior, usually in the area of social judgment. The stroke victim begins to make remarks that they previously considered inappropriate, such as swearing, telling shady stories, and referring to sex. He may begin to ignore rules of behavior that he previously followed.

Staff must always consider both psychological and physiological changes in their plans to deal with sudden changes of behavior. As Virginia Morris points out, residents usually are not suffering because they are old, they suffer because they are sick. Something can be done about almost all of their symptoms, some are preventable, most are treatable, and a few are curable. Virtually any disability can be made more manageable. (Morris) Recognizing and working with both psychological and physiological changes are discussed in more detail in Chapter 12.

There is no support for the concept of **stereotyping** the aged. Physically they may have many similarities, but psychologically they are perhaps as individual as other age groups. Their psychological and social needs do not seem to change with age. It is cultural attitude, characterized by social withdrawal from the aged, that changes.

CHARACTERISTICS

Many older people are far from this stereotyped description. They are active, interested in life around them, and able to take care of many of their needs. Some simply cannot do so adequately while living alone and unsupervised.

They are, and want to be seen as individuals with rights, dignity, and very human needs that can only be met with the help of their fellow man. Those who must live alone, or with minimal social contact, often are lonely and malnourished. Loneliness can lead quickly to crotchetiness, resentment, and anger. It's not that they have always been this way, or that they want to be. They can, and usually do, respond when their environment meets both their social and personal needs.

A characteristic often overlooked is **reduced resilience** and the **ability to relate** to new stimuli. When an aged person enters a nursing home, he is uprooted from old, familiar surroundings and stimuli. He is asked to give up privacy and control of his daily schedule. He is asked to relate to new stimuli, a diverse resident population, and a staff unknown to him. He may be afraid, anxious, and angry at the move. Staff must recognize he cannot relate or adapt as easily as in his younger years.

Nathan Pepper describes common forms of maladaptive responses that characterize old age. He lists eight major losses most often affecting the aged and to which they must adapt. These are loss of:

1. Spouse
2. Friends
3. Work
4. Work peers
5. Social roles
6. Income
7. Health
8. Mobility

These losses may be accompanied by sorrow, disappointment, depression, anger, feelings of futility or worthlessness, fear, and others. To combat these feelings and attitudes Pepper suggests individuals must make adaptations by trying to replace the losses through developing:

1. New social relationships
2. A new social role
3. Activities to regain lost capacities
4. New conditions to help them function

Too often the role of **depression** in the aged is either overlooked, misunderstood, or mishandled. A major symptom of depression is withdrawal from social contact whether in the aged or others. Examples are not inviting friends over anymore, not visiting others, not going out to eat with friends, discontinuing family reunions, no longer getting together with friends on Saturday night, and other small traditions. The aged who do not wish to take part are often depressed and need assistance to reestablish healthy social contacts.

In the nursing facility depression may be mistaken for dementia since the resident is slowed, complains of poor memory, and is withdrawn. It may be overlooked because the person presents physical complaints instead of dysphoria. Also, a resident may be restless, pacing, and agitated, whereas depression is usually associated with a general slowing. Cognitive impairment is sometimes mistaken for depression. The important thing is geriatric depression can be treated. (Rock and Sorensen)

It is true that the aged often have **chronic and degenerative** disorders that may prevent their return to independent community living. However, they still have the capacity to respond to warm, understanding care, and many times to improve physically and mentally, or at least to maintain some level of happiness and satisfaction until the end of their days.

NEEDS

One of the greatest needs in the American culture is a "raison d'etre"—a reason for being. When a person awakens in the morning and there is really no reason to get up—no one depends on, needs, or is waiting for him—the reason for being is lost. The aged frequently experience this loss, yet they still need to feel someone cares, someone loves them, and they are of value.

The need for **closeness** to other human beings is never lost by most of the aging. Companionship, affection, and gentle touch continue to be needed, although there are some **no-touch** people who reject this kind of closeness.

Independence is strong in some of the aged. They want to do for themselves, to tidy up their rooms, and sometimes do for others. They need to be allowed and encouraged to do as much for themselves as possible, to have the freedom to manage their own affairs insofar as they are able.

The American culture has long considered that **sexuality** retires with age. Studies show this is far from the truth. **Sexual urges** continue throughout life although not always at the same intensity. Many of the aged experience sexual needs and can be active sexually into their 80's and 90's. The aged cannot be treated as sexless creatures who have no rights in this area of need. In fact, nursing facilities must provide privacy to married couples who reside in the facility.

Participation in their own treatment and care is important to many aged. They have the right to refuse treatment if they desire. Some older people want the opportunity to participate in planning their daily activities, recreation, and special events and to have input concerning the menus and meals they are served. This, too, is a right that should not be denied. Many of those who say they do not want to participate or to be bothered, or are too tired, are simply depressed. They may need more encouragement to participate than others. Motivating the depressed is difficult, but it is an important staff function in nursing facilities.

Relationships are an important need throughout life. Many residents lose some family contacts upon entering a home. They need to develop personal relationships with certain residents and with staff. They need people who accept and like them as they are. It is a means of combating loneliness and depression.

Privacy continues to be an important need. Every resident needs some place to retreat to for meditation, consultation, intimate discussion, personal activities, and rest. The resident's room is the logical place but most rooms are occupied by two or more people. This need frequently goes unrecognized and unmet in nursing facilities. (Pepper)

FAMILIES OF THE AGING

Frequently families experience much difficulty with the aging parent, grandparent, or relative for whom they are responsible. As the individual ages, sometimes deteriorating before their very eyes, family members may have difficulty accepting this change in a loved one's life. It may be the first time the family member is confronted with his own mortality. It is painful to uproot a loved one from the home they have always occupied and take them to a nursing facility.

Much has been written about the **guilt** family members feel and the anger which results. These and other family feelings must be dealt with or they may interfere with nursing facility services. A family member with this problem frequently finds fault with the facility and is discontent with the care provided. When there seems to be no way to satisfy family members, their dissatisfaction may be due to never resolving their feelings about placement.

Our culture seems not to have learned that a nursing facility is often the place of choice. It is the only place that can adequately meet the needs of some aged people, more especially those who require care on a 24-hour per day basis.

Families frequently need **counseling** which must be an integral part of a good nursing facility program. Administrators and staff must seek the help and support of family and other responsible parties. Without it they will experience great difficulty in meeting standards of care and satisfying both the residents and the responsible parties. The family is still the resident's **primary source of emotional support,** especially during the weeks following admission.

GLOSSARY

Attitudes A feeling or posture that one assumes and often acts on without thinking.

Chronic Of extended duration, long-term, or tending to recur repeatedly.

Counseling The act of listening to another person's problem, providing expert information, advice or recommendations, and assisting in decision making.

Culture A society's typical ways of behaving; its customs, mores, and beliefs.

Debilitated Weak and infirm, unable to care for many personal needs.

Degenerative Disorders in which tissue or an organ deteriorates and vitality is diminished.

Depression An abnormal state of mind in which a person usually becomes inactive and disinterested in his environment and lacks motivation.

Stereotyping A simplified and standardized conception or attitude that assumes any one group of people have common characteristics and are lacking in originality and individuality.

REFERENCES

Brody, Stanley J. & George E. Ruff, *Aging and Rehabilitation*, New York: Springer Publishing Co., 1986.

Morris, Virginia, *How to Care for Aging Parents*, New York: Workman Publishing Company, Inc., 1996.

Pepper, Nathan H., *Fundamentals of Aging, Disabled, and Handicapped in the Nursing Home*, Springfield Illinois: Charles C. Thomas, 1982.

Rock, Barbara, K., & Carolyn Sorensen, *"Resident Care Management" in NAB Study Guide*, Washington, DC: National Association of Boards of Examiners of Long-Term Care Administrators, Inc., 1997.

Rogers, Wesley E., *General Administration in the Nursing Home*, Boston: Cahners Books, International, 1980.

The Holy Bible, New King James Version, Reference Edition Nashville: Thomas Nelson, Inc. 1994.

CHAPTER 3

ORGANIZATIONAL MANAGEMENT

ORGANIZATIONAL MANAGEMENT

ORGANIZATION

What is an **organization**? Actually, there are several meanings. Some management theorists define it as an enterprise, which it is if we refer to **the** organization. Some believe it includes all the behaviors of all participants, while others contend it is the internal, formalized, intentional structure of roles or positions within an enterprise. (Weihrich and Koontz) In this book it is used as **the** organization, meaning an enterprise in which people are working together to accomplish the goals of the enterprise.

The enterprise is organized, for there is an internal structure of roles that specifies the grouping of activities and people. The group consciously coordinates its efforts toward given goals. This type of **organizing** is a management function discussed later in this chapter.

MANAGEMENT

Every organization (enterprise) must be **managed** in order to operate efficiently and economically. Without management individuals and groups resort to meeting their own rather than organizational goals. A basic management principle is to put one person in charge when three (or more) employees work together. The reason is that at some point one employee will side with another against the third, internal conflict begins, and work is not completed. In any group some one person must be responsible for ensuring that work is performed properly.

So, what is **management**? The simplest definition is getting work done with and through other people. Weihrich and Koontz say it is designing and maintaining an environment within an enterprise in which individuals, working together in groups, can accomplish selected missions and objectives. Managers are responsible for taking actions that enable their employees to make their best contributions to group objectives.

Arthur Bedelian defines it somewhat differently. He says management is a process of achieving desired results through utilization of human and material resources. He notes that the pattern in earlier years of one individual working alone is now almost totally replaced by groups of people working together. Working together requires managers who know how to utilize human and material resources to accomplish desired goals. Managing is essential in the nursing facility and at all levels of the organization. It is the duty of the administrator, the assistant administrator, the department heads, and the line supervisors. All individuals responsible for the work of others are managers and must understand and use management principles. They may be called president, director, administrator, department head, supervisor, or chief, but overall, they are managing.

THE MANAGEMENT HIERARCHY

Organizational management begins with a **governing body** which represents the ownership of the nursing facility. OBRA regulations require that a facility have a **governing body**, or designated persons functioning as a governing body. (42 CFR 483.75) This is discussed in more detail in Chapter 4.

Within the organization, functioning under the governing body, there are **three levels of management.**

1. **Top management** of the hierarchy is comprised of the administrator or the president. It may also include assistant administrators or vice-presidents and may be referred to as the "executive staff." The hierarchy is sometimes called the management pyramid since there are few at the top, more at the middle, and still more at the line level.

2. **Middle management** is comprised of supervisors who have managers over them and who direct subordinate supervisors. They are

usually division or department heads. There is little middle management in nursing homes. The director of nursing (DON) with at least two shift supervisors (charge nurses) is middle management. The dietary manager often has an early supervisor (morning) and a late supervisor (afternoon) which places her in middle management.

3. **Line management** is comprised of supervisors who have managers over them but only employees or line workers under their direction. Line supervisors are at the bottom of the administrative hierarchy. Charge nurses and supervisors under direction of the dietary manager are examples.

These levels are sometimes referred to as "echelons." Upper echelon is top management. Lower echelons are line supervisors and line workers. The latter are at the end of the line of command.

Types of management Organizations look for the best management **type** to use in practice. There are many types, and they come and go in popularity. Actually, there is no management type that works in all enterprises. A type that is effective in one may not be as effective in another field of endeavor. Three types have been recommended and often tried in nursing facilities.

1. **Management by Objectives (MBO)** means to identify goals, determine procedures, set time limits and continuously measure progress. Everyone knows what is expected and how long it should take. Problems are anticipated and preventive measures planned. Supervisors and employees know each day what progress they have made toward achieving their goals. MBO requires more frequent supervisor/employee contact than some other types of management. It emphasizes self-control and self-direction. (Drucker)

   Many management consultants to nursing facilities are abandoning this management concept. They feel it is too complex and is not as employee centered as some other methods.

2. **Total Quality Management (TQM)** is the current popular participative management type. When used properly it results in **continuous quality improvement** (CQI). It is a management approach that builds employee interrelationships through work teams. It utilizes employee knowledge as well as their time, effort, and skill. TQM is based on open communication, trust, and mutual respect among employees and management.

   Through group problem solving by work teams staff becomes more involved, more committed to their work and much more productive. Teams focus on improving their skills and the quality of their output. They become more concerned about productivity, safety, cost, and customer satisfaction. This in turn results in greater job satisfaction and motivation.

   Administrators do not give up their role as leaders nor do they switch to a permissive style. They involve their supervisors and staff in joint efforts to determine the best way to perform tasks, to improve quality, and to continuously promote employee growth.

   This is a form of participative management developed by W. Edward Deming who originated and taught quality control methods that focus on employee involvement in problem solving and decision making in regard to improving quality and quantity of work. This management style facilitates free flow of information needed to make group decisions. (Weihrich and Koontz)

3. **Management by Walking Around** (MBWA) or as Hewlett-Packard executives say Management by *Wandering Around* is an increasingly popular management style. The administrator is interested in operations at all levels. The administrator should enter by a different door at a different time as often as possible and visit each area of the facility. He should note **what** is being done, the **quality** of staff performance, and the **environment** in which work is performed. It is the most effective means of monitoring services the facility provides. This sends a strong message to staff,

residents, and families: "I am here, I'm interested in what goes on, I am appreciative of quality performance, I know you, I'm available."

While making rounds each day the administrator should call everyone by name. If he knows anything complimentary about an employee or a family member, he should mention it to the employee. Examples are the son who kicked the winning point in last night's football game, a new baby in the family, a wedding, a write-up in the paper, and any accomplishment the administrator is aware of. It is an opportunity to commend employees as they do good work. This is the most effective time to recognize quality performance.

This management style meets the recognition need that all employees have. How much more recognition can one give than to call employees by name, know something about pleasant occurrences in the family, give a pat on the back for work well done?

TQM and MBWA styles are **employee centered** which means managers are not just interested in employee efforts, skill and work completion. They are interested in the employee's needs and interests. They want employees to enjoy their work and experience job satisfaction. This style of management promotes a positive work atmosphere and improves work performance.

To be efficient in practicing any style of management the administrator and his management staff must undertake specialized training. It is readily available on a seminar basis through universities, state health care associations, and private management training organizations.

MISUSED MANAGEMENT TERMS

Before discussing functions of managers, the three most misused terms in management should be identified.

1. **Authority** is the right or power to act, to decide, to command others. It is not a privilege. It must be used when it is entrusted to any manager at any level. Authority promotes unity in the organization. The person who has authority can use it in three ways: (a) he can initiate action, get things started; (b) he can modify action when a task is not being performed correctly; and (c) he can terminate action if an employee is doing something that should be stopped.

Authority is **delegated** by a higher authority. When a manager delegates authority to a subordinate he gives up some of his control over work performance and results. However, he retains final responsibility for the work and its completion. Since authority is given by a higher authority, it can also be taken away.

Some managers cannot effectively delegate authority because they fear losing control over work performance and the final product. They delegate in such exact terms, directing subordinates in every detail of how tasks are to be carried out, that there really is no delegation. Other managers delegate in such general terms a supervisor may not know what authority he has.

There are three types of authority: (a) line, (b) staff, and (c) functional.

Line authority is a relationship in which a supervisor exercises direct supervision over a subordinate employee. He can give instructions, approve or disapprove, veto action, give or withhold rewards, and usually hire and fire. It is directive and operational, and results in action. An administrator has line authority all the way down the organization to the line worker.

Staff authority is a relationship that is advisory. A staff person's duties are to investigate, research, give advice, problem solve, and report to line managers. He cannot give instructions or veto action. He has no authority to enforce instructions or decisions. He may teach or make recommendations but not direct.

Consultants' use of authority is more often classified as staff since they are an outside source of expertise. They provide information, recommend, problem solve, and teach, usually within one department. Since they cannot enforce their decisions, when an employee they consult with does not carry out agreed upon action, the consultant can only report the error to the administrator who has line authority.

Functional authority is the power an individual or department has over specified practices, policies, or other matters relating to activities undertaken by personnel in other departments. This does not help unity of command, but it is frequently practiced. A small slice of the line supervisor's authority is held by someone else. Examples are the personnel officer, purchasing agent, and quality control officer. This functional authority is usually limited to *how* and sometimes *when*. It seldom involves *who*, *what*, or *where*. (Weihrich and Koontz)

2. **Duties** are the tasks or activities to be carried out. They are **assigned** by a person with authority. Each employee is assigned a group of related duties he is required to perform.

3. **Responsibility** is the most misused term of these three. It is the response to assigned duties and the authority delegated to accomplish them. A person is responsible if delegated authority is used and duties are carried out. Responsibility can neither be assigned nor delegated. It is exacted from employees. They are required to respond and to be accountable for results after duties are assigned and authority delegated. Never confuse an employee by referring to his duties as his responsibilities. Make sure job descriptions list **duties**, not **responsibilities**.

FUNCTIONS OF MANAGERS

There must be some framework around which management knowledge can be organized. Most theorists agree that **functions** of managers provide that framework. Everything that a manager does falls into one of five functions: (1) planning, (2) organizing, (3) staffing, (4) directing (or leading), and (5) controlling. All new research findings, ideas, and techniques can be readily placed in these classifications. (Weihrich and Koontz)

PLANNING

Before beginning any task, an administrator must decide in advance (1) what is to be done, (2) how and when it will be done, (3) who will do it, and more. Planning is decision making. Weihrich and Koontz identify eight types of plans that are used by most enterprises. Failure of administrators to recognize this variety of plans has often caused problems in making planning effective.

1. **Purpose or mission** is the basic task assigned to an enterprise by society. The purpose of the nursing home industry is to develop and provide care and treatment of a long-term nature for the aged, disabled, and chronically ill. Administrators and their staff must understand this mission if they wish to establish and attain certain goals. Whether this mission is attained is of great social importance. Society looks for and deserves the accomplishment of the nursing home industry's mission. Managers know they must live up to these expectations, and this motivates them to produce.

2. **Goals or objectives** are the end results toward which all activities and efforts are directed. They are statements of **what** is to be accomplished. A goal should be expressed in measurable terms, such as to reduce absenteeism by fifty percent by January 1st. Figures realized at a specific future period of time should be measurable against the figures experienced when the goal is set. Certainly the facility will set goals for occupancy, profit margin, quality of care, and others.

Short-range and **long-range** goals are needed. The short range is as it sounds, goals to be attained in a few days, weeks, or a year or two. Long-range goals are those one wishes to attain in three, five, ten or more years, and may want to maintain in the future. An example of a short-range goal could be an occupancy rate of 80 percent by January 1st. A long-range goal could be to attain and maintain an occupancy rate of at least 92 percent.

Goal-orientation focuses on a distinct future accomplishment. A goal-oriented individual knows what the end result should be. Goals, or objectives, are designed to stimulate action, and managers use them for this purpose. For further discussion of the types of goals in an organization, refer to Chapter 6 on personnel management.

3. **Strategies** are a general plan of action that focuses largely on long-range goals of the nursing facility. What does management plan for the nursing facility to be in the future? The same size? Will it add more beds? Will management plan to keep abreast of community needs and change objectives and programs accordingly? What will management do if the need for the facility's services diminishes due to loss of population, change in funding, or some other factor?

Purpose of strategies is to determine and communicate what kind of enterprise is envisioned for the future. They do not outline details of how the enterprise will accomplish these objectives. This is the task of the many supporting programs within the facility. It is a valuable framework for thinking and action. It is a guide to planning. (Weihrich and Koontz)

4. **Policies** are plans in the form of general statements which guide or channel **thinking** and action in **decision making**. They begin to tell how goals will be accomplished. Policies are guidelines to keep in mind as specific tasks are performed. An example is "We provide the best nursing care possible using modern health care practices and resources." This does not tell how any task will be carried out, but it tells what is to be kept in mind while tasks are performed.

Policies allow considerable **flexibility** in decision making. Supervisors may have a task performed several different ways and still be within the policy of providing the best care possible. Policy encourages use of discretion and initiative, but within prescribed limits. Strategies and policies give direction to all other plans by furnishing a framework for them. The more care exercised in developing clearly understood strategies and policies, the more effective the framework of plans.

Policies should be developed by the administrator and his supervisors. They should be approved by the **governing body** since it is legally responsible. In a corporation this is the board of directors, whereas, in partnerships and sole proprietorships it is the owner(s).

5. **Procedures** are the step by step guides by which a task is to be performed in order to attain a goal. They are guides to **action** rather than thinking. They allow some flexibility in decision making, but less than policies. Procedures for the same activity, as paying an expense account varies from level to level in management. Procedures are found throughout an organization, but they tend to be more numerous and exacting at lower levels. In fact, there must be a procedure covering every activity carried out in a facility, otherwise employees do not know how tasks are to be performed.

A **standard operating procedure** (SOP) is a written guide that everyone follows in a given situation. An example: If a resident falls, do not try to pick him up. Call the nurse and remain with the resident. SOP's are more often found in resident care management.

Procedures should be prepared by supervisors and their employees and submitted to the administrator. They, too, should be approved by the governing body. This method of preparing standards gives all staff input on how tasks should be performed, an important factor in the TQM style of management.

6. **Rules** are specific and authoritative guides to specific action that make no allowance for decision making. They direct that certain action be taken or not be taken. Rules have no time sequence regardless of when or to whom they apply. An example: **No smoking** is a rule only when it applies at all times in a given area. If it is **no smoking** only when residents are present, there is a variable factor. It becomes a procedure as judgment is now allowed.

Rules restrict thinking, so they should be developed and used when an employee is not to use discretion. Examples of nursing facility rules are: (a) Never strike a resident, (b) sign in at the exact time you report to work, (c) count and document all Schedule II drugs at the end of each shift, and (d) do not remove any resident, staff, or nursing facility property without permission, since this could often be referred to as stealing or theft. Many administrators feel there should be as few rules as possible since they do restrict thinking and allow employees no discretion in carrying out tasks.

Every rule should be associated with some form of discipline, ranging from oral reprimand to termination, depending on severity. This helps employees understand the importance of rules and why they should follow them.

Rules should be developed by employees, supervisors, and the administrator. It is **unwise** to develop a set of rules and **command** employees to follow them. Giving everyone input to establish rules will more likely help in their enforcement. Rules should be approved by the governing body.

7. **Programs** are a summation of goals, policies, procedures, rules, work and space assignment, schedules, plans of action, resources to be used, and other items necessary to carry out a given course of action. Programs include the entire what, how, who, when, and where of undertaking a group of interrelated activities. A **major** program has impact on, or involves the entire facility or several departments. An example: The facility sets up a program to do away completely with overtime. A **minor** program involves some aspect of work within a given department or unit. An example: Nursing service develops a program to conserve use of underpads.

8. **Budgets** are plans expressed in numerical terms that outline expected results. Budgets say there is a certain amount of money for each category of expenditure (equipment, supplies, salaries, utilities, etc.) for a given period of time, usually one year. Ideally, major programs are always supported by a budget. Budgets are discussed more fully in Chapter 7.

Planning then is the process of developing all of these guidelines for the operation of the nursing facility. It continues throughout the existence of the facility and it pervades every activity. Planning is the central function of management. The **purpose** of planning is fourfold: (1) to focus all work on attaining organizational goals — perhaps the most important, (2) to offset uncertainty and change, (3) to develop an economical operation, and (4) to facilitate control.

Program Evaluation and Review Technique (PERT) is a relatively new approach to planning and control. PERT is a time-event network analysis. It involves development of a flow chart which shows an **event**, and a plan with a completion that can be measured at a given **time**. PERT has proven highly successful in manufacturing, and is used increasingly in other industries and businesses. PERT has certain definite **advantages** to an administrator as it:

1. Forces managers to plan.
2. Forces planning all down the line since each supervisor must plan the event for which he is responsible.
3. Concentrates attention on critical activities that need correction.
4. Makes possible a kind of feedback control.
5. Makes possible the aiming of reports and pressure for action at the right spot and level in the organization structure at the right time.

PERT also has **limitations** since it is (1) not useful when no responsible estimate of schedule can be made, (2) not practical for routine planning of recurring events, as mass production, (3) focuses on and emphasizes time only.

PERT is sufficiently complex so that administrators need specific training in a PERT seminar focused on nursing facility management. (Weihrich and Koontz)

Differentiating plans Employees are primarily concerned with three plans: policies, procedures, and rules. (PPR's) Every facility must have a set of these which serve as a **guideline** to behavior and performance of employees. Unfortunately, policies, procedures, and rules usually are not sufficiently differentiated. Employees who must follow them often do not know one from the other. In fact, most facilities do not even list **rules**; they have a policy and procedure manual which lists no rules. Many of these manuals do not adequately separate their policies and procedures so that supervisors and workers are aware of the difference. They do not know how much flexibility is allowed by a specific guideline.

Administrators should issue PPR's so that employees know immediately what judgement and leeway is allowed. Some administrators do this by color coding. **Policies** are issued on **white** paper, procedures on **green**, and rules on **yellow** or **red**. With this method staff knows that a guideline on yellow or red means **caution** or **stop**; there is no judgement or leeway allowed; it will be done or not be done as indicated.

Value of PPR's A primary value of PPR's is that predeciding all possible issues in advance allows the administrator to be in control whether he is present or not. Another value is they provide criteria to measure performance by. It makes controlling possible. Employees know what and how they are supposed to perform and they understand the consequence of inadequate performance. Without proper PPR's, evaluation of employee performance is not possible. Planning and controlling are said to be the Siamese twins of management– they are inseparable.

Evaluating PPR's How does the administrator know whether the facility's PPR's are adequate? What measuring device is available? The following **guidelines for writing PPR's** is one helpful device. The management staff should determine if these guidelines are met.

1. They should **reflect goals** and **plans** and help to attain them. When asked why a task is performed a certain way there should never be a response such as "no particular reason" or "we just do it that way."

2. They must be **consistently** tied in with actual practice. It is not unusual to detect a procedure that specifies certain action, and then observe that the action is not carried out according to the procedure. If a task is performed in a certain manner, the procedure or rule should be in conformity.

3. PPR's must be **flexible** in terms of change. When goals or other plans change then policies and procedures must change. They are not engraved in stone, so if they do not help attain goals, change them.

4. Policies, procedures, and rules should be **distinguished** from each other as discussed earlier.

5. They must be in **writing**. Some feel this will make PPR's too rigid or reduce creativity. If they cannot be written, the facility should not have them. Even when written they may not be clear enough, but writing will help eliminate fogginess and promote understanding.

6. PPR's should be **taught**, explained, and interpreted on a regular basis. Employees cannot use or trust what they do not understand. Feedback reveals whether staff understands and utilizes them. Gaining feedback is easy. Ask any employee why he is performing a particular task in a certain way. "I don't know, they just told me to" indicates lack of understanding. The answer should be along these lines "Because that's the best way to do a good job and take care of our residents."

7. They should be **controlled**. Someone or a committee should carefully review and update PPR's on a regular basis. Do they fulfill their purpose? Are they obsolete? Are new treatment modalities covered? Are they written, distributed, and taught?

ORGANIZING

Organizing is the second function of managers. It is the grouping of people and activities, the assigning of roles, and delegating authority for their supervision in a way that prevents friction and other unsought consequences. Its **purpose** is to carry out plans, accomplish goals, make possible effective working relationships and efficient operations, and make it possible for the organization to expand. Organizing, properly carried out, ensures proper work distribution among departments.

Departmentalization, or departmentation as it is often called, makes it possible for organizations to **expand**. Without it an enterprise is limited in size. It is limited to the number of people that one top manager can effectively supervise. Primary departmentalization is done according to the three basic functions of all organizations: (1) production, (2) sales, and (3) finance. Nursing facilities have a large **production** force since nearly everyone is involved in producing resident care. **Finance** may not be a separate department as it may involve only one person. Few nursing facilities have a **sales** program or department, although they have become more conscious of marketing and public relations in recent years.

Departmentalization within the nursing facility follows tradition and is not necessarily carried out on any conscious basis. Administrators may not know why they have nursing, dietary, housekeeping, business, and maintenance departments. They simply do what other institutions have done. It seems practical to assign all activities, or functions, of a like nature to the same department. In practice there are exceptions. For example, making beds is normally a housekeeping activity. Then why assign making resident beds to nursing service? That activity is assigned to nursing on the basis of **intimate association**. Making resident beds and resident care cannot be separated. The activity is too much a part of resident care to be assigned to housekeepers untrained in resident care. Federal guidelines say no housekeeping duties may be assigned to nursing but there is this exception.

Also, housekeeping duties in the dietary department are assigned to dietary employees. Housekeeping personnel from resident care areas where there may be infections are not allowed to do housekeeping where food is prepared and served.

Departmentalization in nursing facilities is not accomplished solely on the basis of function. It is done on a mixed basis: intimate association, territory, product, and others.

In organizing, administrators must develop a **chart of organization** that shows the organizational structure. The **scalar chain** is most frequently used, as outlined by Figure 1, to show relationships and line authority. This chain demonstrates a **line organization** in which the structure is characterized by a vertical flow of authority. It clearly shows who has authority over whom, to whom each position is responsible, and the lines to follow in communicating upward, laterally, and downward. This type of organization structure has been used since the days of Moses in the wilderness. (Exodus 18:13-26) Other systems, such as the satellite have been tried, but most return to the scalar chain as most useful. Of course, the intricacies of an enterprise can never be fully shown on paper, but the scalar chain continues to be the most widely used.

Span of management is an important factor in departmentalization. Some refer to it as the span of control, but it is more than control. It involves all aspects of directing and controlling employees. Span of management means the number of employees a manager is required to direct and control. A top manager may effectively manage only three to five subordinates reporting directly to him. This is because he usually deals with a board and has duties regarding government, the community, and his profession.

The number of employees one can **effectively** manage depends on several factors: (1) how difficult the task, (2) how clear the policies and procedures, (3) how well-trained employees are, (4) how well the supervisor communicates, (5) whether close control is required, etc. If a task is as simple as digging a ditch with a shovel, the supervisor can manage as many people as he can see. (Weihrich and Koontz) In a nursing facility a line supervisor can effectively supervise no more than 8 to 12 people. Duties are usually quite diverse and resident care duties often require a greater frequency and intensity of contact between supervisor and employee. However, one must remember that the number of people a person can supervise varies considerably.

Unity of command is very important in organizing. It means that insofar as possible each employee is responsible to one supervisor only. Employees who report to more than one supervisor often experience conflicting orders and divided loyalties. Naturally, they will act first on instructions given by the supervisor they like best, unless they are acting in fear. Sometimes the instructions not acted on should have priority and should be carried out first. Unity of command promotes job satisfaction and increases efficiency. Clear lines of authority and communication promote unity of command, which in turn enhances staff rapport or job satisfaction, and teamwork.

Decentralization of authority is the tendency to disperse decision-making authority in an organization structure. When organizing the nursing facility into departments there is no question about whether to decentralize authority. It is a matter of **how much**. When authority is not delegated, it and decision making are centralized. The organization operates as a one man executive show.

Decentralization is more than **delegation** of authority. It reflects the philosophy of organizing and managing a facility. One decides which decisions to push downward on the organization structure and which to retain at the top. Control is maintained by developing written policies to guide decision making and by carefully selecting and training people to whom management delegates. This reflects management concepts which serve as a basis for decision making.

Figure 3.1: **Chart of Organization**

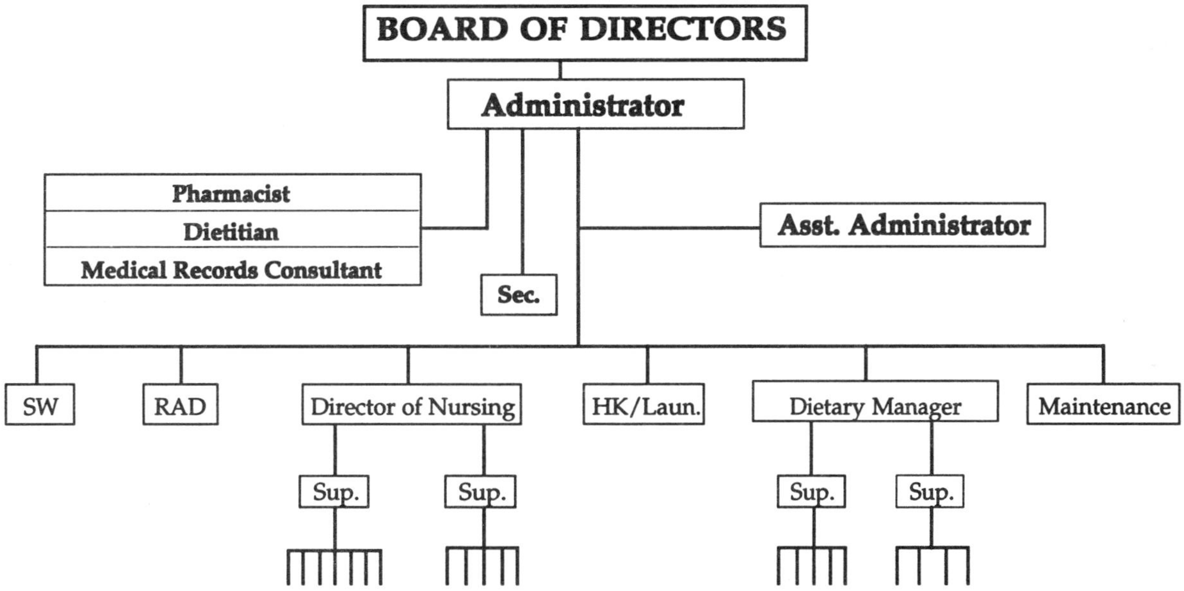

How to read a chart.

1. The depth of the box shows the degree of authority delegated to that position. The Board has greatest authority, the administrator next and on down the line.
2. Positions on the same level have equal authority in their department or unit.
3. A downward line means line authority over everyone the line reaches.
4. A lateral line as for the assistant administrator means he has limited authority over all below his position. Department heads may go directly to him or directly to the administrator. If his position were placed directly under the administrator, the assistant administrator would have full line authority over all department heads.
5. An upward line, as for consultants, means their information, recommendations, and so on flow upward. A good rule is that they never consult more than one level below the person they report to; i.e., to the department heads designated by the administrator.

Effective delegation occurs when the lowest person in the echelon who is capable and authorized is making a given decision. This follows the **principle of economy of action**. Without decentralization, department heads could not use their discretion to meet the ever-present, ever-changing situations they face. (Weihrich and Koontz)

Formal and informal organization. Every nursing facility has a formal organization that is diagrammed on the chart of organization. It shows lines of authority and communication that should be followed to promote efficiency. Unfortunately, most nursing facilities have several **informal** organizations. One may be a group of key people, excluding the administrator, who eat or have coffee together, or get together after work and talk business. They have a strong influence on decision making. Often they use authority that is not delegated to them. Such informal organizations can be effective unless they become cliques that keep to themselves, do not cooperate with others, and adversely affect decision making.

The **grapevine** is another example of informal organization. It depends on an employee acting as a "center of information." He collects, or creates, information and feeds it to a few cohorts who in turn tell others. His position depends on his doing this before information is sent out through official channels.

Administrators cannot do away with informal organizations in their facilities. They can use them provided they identify them and know how they operate. Also, management can lessen the authority these groups use. In practice, administrators spend considerable time maintaining balance and cooperation among informal groups. It is best to practice open and frequent communication with staff so grapevines and other informal groups have less power and effectiveness.

STAFFING

The staffing function includes all the things a nursing facility does in recruiting, interviewing, selecting, orienting, training, promoting, demoting, terminating, and retiring employees. This function is discussed in detail in Chapter 6 on Personnel Management.

DIRECTING (LEADING)

The management function **directing**, also called leading, is the process of influencing employees so they will strive willingly and enthusiastically toward achieving organizational goals. (Weihrich and Koontz) It includes all activities required to get employees to do their work, how, and when tasks are supposed to be done. It includes giving instructions, leading, communicating, motivating, coordinating, and representing.

Leaders apparently make assumptions about people, and this affects the manner in which they attempt to lead people. Douglas McGregor developed two sets of assumptions concerning human nature, commonly referred to as Theory X and Theory Y.

1. **Theory X** proposes that some leaders assume the average person:

    a. Dislikes work and will avoid it if he can.

    b. Must be coerced, pushed, controlled, or threatened to get him to work toward organizational goals.

    c. Prefers to be directed and wants to avoid responsibility.

    d. Has little ambition.

    e. Wants security above all.

2. **Theory Y** proposes that some leaders assume:

    a. People feel work is as natural as play.

    b. There are many means of motivating people other than control, threats, and coercion. People will exercise self-control and work toward goals if they are committed.

    c. People are committed to goals in proportion to the rewards offered.

    d. People learn to accept responsibility.

e. People are capable of problem solving with imagination and ingenuity.

Obviously, these two sets of assumptions are very different. Leaders who embrace Theory X handle people quite differently from those who believe in Theory Y. It is apparent all people are not so easily categorized, but McGregor's observations are valuable in managing people. Underlying assumptions that managers make about employee behavior usually leads to a self-fulfilling prophecy. If subordinates are treated as indifferent, lazy, and hostile, they will be conditioned to behave as expected. This leads to widespread suspicion of management intentions and to formation of unions. (Bedelian)

Leadership is the process of influencing employees to work willingly and enthusiastically toward common goals whether managers are present or not. It is not enough to simply get employees to complete their work. Leadership is essential to the success of any organization. It binds work groups together and triggers employee motivation. It is a prerequisite to selecting managers to serve in leadership positions.

Superior/Subordinate relationship The appointment of leaders as administrators, department heads, supervisors and so on creates a superior/subordinate relationship. These managers have superior authority and usually, but not always, superior knowledge in comparison to subordinates. They are not personally superior, only their position in the hierarchy is superior. By nature, this relationship gives rise to problems. When one person has authority over another and can tell him what to do as well as monitor and evaluate his performance, and mete out discipline, it easily gives rise to jealousies and anger. This relationship requires effective leadership abilities on the part of managers at all levels.

Duties of leaders are diverse. They include: (1) goal setting, (2) decision making, (3) giving instructions, (4) listening, (5) representing, (6) problem solving, (7) coordinating, and (8) managing internal conflict.

The **goal-setting** function points the way toward the desired accomplishments of the facility. A goal-oriented administrator keeps the staff aware of the specific goals toward which they will work. Without this, staff may be uncertain or confused about what the administrator believes and wishes to accomplish.

Decision making is perhaps the number one duty of administrators. It is involved in problem solving and goal setting and all his other duties. To leave things hanging without a solution (sleeping on them for a while) promotes uncertainty and confusion. Following these **steps in decision making** can help to ensure quality decisions and solutions to problems.

Step 1. **Identify the problem.** This is possibly the most essential step. Look at the problem from several points of view so that the real problem is identified. Often leaders act on a symptom rather than the real problem, wasting considerable time and effort.

Step 2. **Review all the facts.** Do not make assumptions. Deal with facts and figures. Answer questions of how many, how often, when, where, who. An administrator must do his homework and have the facts on hand when he makes a decision.

Step 3. **Explore the causes**. What is behind the problem? What went wrong? How did it happen in the first place?

Step 4. **Identify possible solutions.** When problem solving with department heads or another staff group, get all their ideas on how the problem can be solved. Don't screen out unworkable solutions at this point. List all possible ways to solve the problem.

Step 5. **Evaluate and decide on a solution or solutions**. Discuss what might happen if a particular solution is tried. Look at the pros and cons of each possible solution, then make a decision.

Step 6. **Develop a plan of action.** Decide who does what, when and where, how other staff will be advised, how reactions will be handled. Make assignments so a step by step plan is developed and implemented.

Step 7. **Develop a plan to evaluate whether the solution works.** How long will the group try the solution before getting together to discuss results? What information will they need to evaluate results? Who will collect the information?

Remember, decisions involving change create a chain of reactions. Change involves the **principle of reciprocal action** which states that no change can be made in any department of an organization but that it affects all other departments directly or indirectly.

Giving instructions involves two steps, the second of which is often overlooked. Step one is to tell the employee what is to be done, how, and when. Step two is to **gain feedback** to ensure that the employee understands. Step two may not be so important when instructing a senior employee who is knowledgeable and well-motivated. Too often the newer employee and the older employee do not have a full understanding of what is expected when a completely new task is assigned.

Administrators develop their own methods of getting feedback, and certainly not by saying, "Now, what did I just tell you?" One must develop phrases like "What is your understanding of what I asked you to do?" Or, "How do you plan to carry out this job" A simple "Do you understand?" achieves no feedback whatsoever.

There are several **types of instructions**: (1) specific or general, (2) formal or informal, and (3) written or oral. **Specific instructions** outline the job in detail stating what, when, where, how, and what feedback is desired. **General instructions** are given in broad terms when the employee already knows the when, where, how, etc. Also, they are given when the employee has judgment and the supervisor can allow variance of the details needed to carry out the instructions.

Formal **instructions** are more of an order to do something. Again, it may allow little leeway.

Informal instructions are those phrased as a request, a suggestion, or a recommendation. The administrator says, "Would you mind doing...?" Or, "Do you have time...?" He may suggest employees take certain actions or recommend ways of carrying out a task. Most employees recognize informal instructions as instructions, and are pleased to act on them. A few will ignore informal instruction.

What type of instructions should one give? This depends on a number of factors:

1. The type of instructions an employee prefers and responds to the best.

2. The type of employee being instructed – experienced or new? Reliable and prompt or a foot-dragger?

3. Urgency of the task being completed.

4. Type of task – requiring accuracy as to procedure and time, or one that can be performed at leisure?

Administrators should especially be aware of the type instructions the employee prefers. Some desire very specific instructions, and some only respond to formal and specific instructions. Others know and take pride in doing their work; they are irritated when specific or formal instructions are given. They prefer informal and general instructions that recognize their ability and knowledge.

Example: The housekeeping supervisor told Ernest to buff the hallway, then proceeded to tell him in detail how to do it. She warned him not to stretch the cord and ruin the electrical plug. Ernest became irritated and said, "I don't need to be told how to do my work. I know how." It was true because he buffed better than anyone and never damaged equipment.

Listening is an important duty of all leaders. Employees need to be heard, "to get their two cents in." Often, when an employee has a problem, listening to him "get it off his chest" is enough. No recommendations are needed or desired. Managers can listen and accept an employee's point of view without having to agree. "Clearing the air" is better than allowing a problem to go unrecognized. (See Crisis Intervention, Chapter 6)

Representing employees properly and adequately is a **must** for leaders. If a supervisor's staff is criticized, he usually protects them or interprets their actions to others in the best light possible. If employees want a change, it is the administrator's duty to take it to the governing body or the ownership and represent his staff's views, even if he knows in advance their request will be denied. Employees respect supervisors who represent them and their point of view, even when they do not obtain desired results.

> **Example**: It was late November. Employees had worked steadily, filling in for each other when needed. Work output and quality of care were excellent. They sent a committee to the administrator requesting that he ask the owners if they could have a half-day off to Christmas shop. Employees would cover for those absent and there would be no problem meeting required nursing hours per resident. The administrator knew the owners feel the six holidays employees already have are one too many. He knew they would deny the request.

How should he handle this? Take it to the governing body (owners) and say that he knows they don't like such requests, but he felt he had to ask them? Tell staff it would be a waste of time as he knows the request will be denied? To maintain staff's confidence in him, he must submit the request with the explanation that staff has worked hard, is deserving, and he recommends the half-day be granted. If the request is denied, his employees, though disappointed, will know he represented them in their best light.

Coordination consumes considerable time for administrators and supervisors. Coordination is getting people to work together toward a common goal so the final result is the quality and quantity desired. Coordination is necessary because of the differences in employees' interest in their jobs, the speed with which they work, their desire to do good work, their attitudes toward authority and working together, and their approach to work. Administrators and supervisors must adjust or coordinate all these differences in order to accomplish goals for quality and quantity of output. Some theorists feel it should be a sixth function of managers.

Conflict resolution requires considerable time for the administrator. It may be two employees who cannot work well together, or a group of employees within a department, or two departments in conflict. There are several problem solving models that administrators should master and utilize. (See Chapter 6)

Also, teams that operate under the TQM style of management are effective in problem solving. Part of continued growth in knowledge and skills is to identify problems and develop solutions to improve quality of performance.

Leadership styles Leaders are concerned about two things: (1) human relations and (2) tasks. **Human relations** involve feelings and attitudes of employees—whether they are happy, enjoy work, or have good morale. **Task** means completing the work according to standards. Leaders have distinct styles of dealing with the human factor and the task factor.

A leader's style largely depends on how he reacts to and handles hostility. In all organizations, hostility develops naturally and flows upward toward the administrator. The mere fact employees are dependent on higher authority for direction, approval, praise, promotion, etc., gives rise to some degree of hostility.

W. J. Reddin observed that supervisors fall into one of eight basic types of leaders. They range from the ineffective **deserter** who is never there or will not make decisions, to the highly effective **executive** who gets the best from all types of employees. Administrators may benefit from reading more on Reddin's ideas or attending a seminar where his concepts are presented.

Hersey and Blanchard advance another theory of leadership. They do not focus on personality traits of leaders as Reddin does. They concentrate on leader behavior which may vary according to the employee and the situation. It is called **situational leadership**. They present four styles of leadership: (1) dictatorial, (2) paternal, (3) democratic, and (4) laissez-faire. The administrator may use all four styles depending on the employee and the situation.

Laissez-faire is a loose, accepting, easygoing, supportive style in which the leader tells his staff what he wants accomplished and leaves them alone. It is believed that 80 to 85 percent of one's employees will respond favorably to this style, complete their work, and accomplish their goals if they receive praise and other rewards. This assumes, however, they are well-trained, motivated, and knowledgeable about their work requirements. Laissez-faire can be effective with this type employee and with professional staff. Management studies show that only 15 to 20 percent of one's employees really cause trouble. This group would be nonproductive under laissez-faire leadership.

Laissez-faire leadership is not strong on human relations or task. Unless this type of leader has a staff attuned to his style, work falls off and job satisfaction deteriorates.

Democratic leadership allows considerable employee input and is a true participative management style. Insofar as possible, the group decides how tasks can best be accomplished. The leader is more like a moderator who seeks to use the knowledge as well as the skills of employees. He believes in involving staff in problem solving. It is very much like the TQM management style, though not as well structured. Of course, a democratic leader cannot surrender all his decision making authority. He must maintain ultimate power of veto in case employee decisions or actions are inappropriate.

Democratic leaders are stronger on human relations than task. Employees may be happy, but work may not be completed properly.

Paternal leadership is a sympathetic, fathering/mothering style that provides many rewards. This style uses a lot of "tell and sell" when instructing employees. The paternal leader is a bargainer who says, "You do right, and I'll take care of you. I'll see you get your raises, leaves, and so on." By the same token he says, "You misbehave and I'll have to punish you." This style is strong on human relations and task; he wants employees to work and to be happy. It seems this leadership style is becoming more popular. However, there can be a problem with paternalism. The actions of the leader may be unpredictable, they may depend on how he feels, whom he likes, and what satisfies him at a given time.

Dictatorial or autocratic leadership is threatening, intimidating, decisive, and uncompromising. This style motivates by fear, an either/or attitude—"Do as I say, or else." The focus is on task. Human relations are unimportant. Dictatorial leaders often say, "I don't care whether employees like me or not, just so they get the work done." And they mean it.

Actually, an administrator might practice all four styles depending on the employee and the situation. He might begin with laissez-faire, but if differences among employees arise, he might shift to a democratic style and say, "Let's do as the majority wants." He could have a good employee who makes an error and handle it in a paternal style. But, if the error is repeated several times, he probably shifts to a dictatorial style and issues an edict that "If it happens again, you are fired."

Administrators may benefit by participating in a seminar on situational leadership to gain an in-depth experience with this concept.

ORGANIZATIONAL COMMUNICATION

In most organizations communication is the number one problem. Too many employees do not get the word, do not understand what they hear, do not retain information, or information is simply not communicated as it should be. Communication breakdown occurs at all levels, usually due to poor communication techniques. People tend to believe others interpret what is said the same as the speaker does. The fact is, each person interprets information in the light of his own experience, thinking, attitudes, education, and beliefs.

Figure 3.2: **Communication Process**

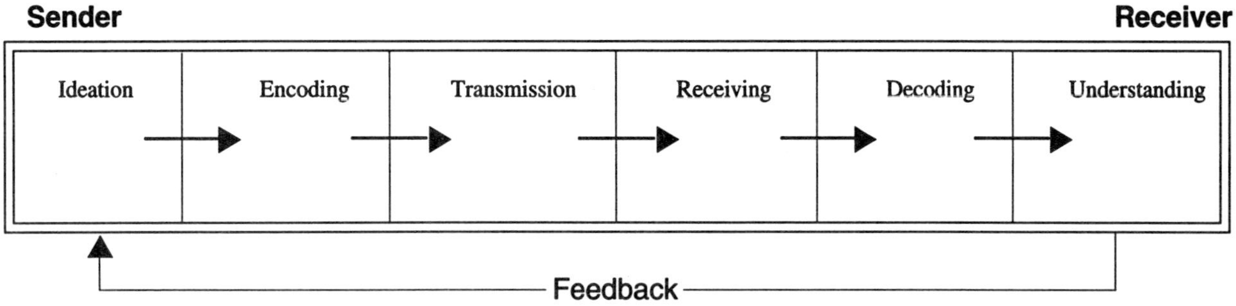

Communication is **defined** as the process of transmitting understood information among two or more people. It involves at least two people – a sender and a receiver. It occurs only when information is received with mutual **understanding** – the sender and the receiver have the same mental picture. (Bedelian)

Communication must be a dynamic and vital process if it is to be effective. Examining the process of communication helps to make communication more effective, as outlined in Figure 3.2.

Ideation means the sender recognizes a need to convey information to another person, or he needs information from someone. This may be facts such as procedures and rules, or opinions and ideas, and so on.

Encoding involves putting the message into oral or written words, diagrams, pictures, charts, and other symbols used to convey a message. This is where barriers to communication begin, for words have many meanings as will be discussed later.

Transmission is the actual sending of the message. It may be oral, either face to face, by cassette, video, telephone or otherwise. Messages may be communicated by gestures, body posture and movements, or by facial expressions. Transmission may be in written form such as memos, letters, manuals, reports, and others.

Receiving means the receiver perceives the message. This requires the attention of the receiver – he must be listening with intent to hear and understand.

Decoding occurs as the receiver interprets the message. This involves both the words and the nonverbal expressions that accompany the message. Decoding will be based on the receiver's background, education, experience, understanding of language, and so on.

Understanding means the receiver has the same mental picture as the sender. He understands the message and what is meant. Communication occurs only when there is **mutual** understanding of the message.

Feedback is necessary for the sender to determine if the message is accurately received and decoded. There is much misunderstanding about feedback. Too often senders ask, "Do you understand?" A yes or no provides no real feedback. It is more appropriate to ask, "What is your understanding of what we discussed?" or "How do you plan to do this task?" or some other appropriate question that provides real feedback on the receiver's understanding. Feedback involves the same process of ideation, encoding, and so on from receiver to the original sender. In fact, they reverse roles during feedback.

Listening is the key to understanding organizational communication. It is , or should be, the most used of the four types of communication: speaking, reading, writing, and listening. Generally, some 40% of a person's communication time is spent listening. In order to be an effective listener, administrators should learn how to do **active listening** which is frequently offered in management seminars on communication. Active listening means to respond not only to the words spoken but to the feelings that accompany the spoken word. This involves **nonverbal** communication – tone of voice (irritation, anger, guilt, or other); body movements that reveal discomfort; gripping the hands tightly or holding on to the chair; facial expressions; fidgeting; and other body movements. By observing the nonverbal as well as the words spoken the listener gains a more complete picture of the message and its meaning.

> **Example:** The dietary manager came to the administrator to discuss a problem. She sat upright, appeared irritated, gripped her hands tightly, and with a tense voice told him some of her employees were giving her a bad time. The administrator responded, "If I hear you correctly, some of your staff are doing some things that really irritate you." Her response, "You are exactly right! They make me so mad I feel like cracking some heads." Feeling understood she openly discussed her problem and a possible solution.

Listening is a skill that can be learned as can speaking, reading, and writing. The problem is that listening skills are seldom taught. Parents, teachers, and others tell children they *should* listen, and the children may be punished if they don't listen, but seldom are they taught *how* to listen. Everyone spends years learning and practicing skills for speaking, reading, and writing, but little time is spent learning and practicing the skill that good communicators use most.

Barriers to communication occur at each step of the communication process. When encoding, some have a problem choosing the right words and phrasing them so they have meaning to the receiver.

Poorly worded messages are the most frequent encoding barrier. To be understood the message must be in words the receiver understands. The speaker must consider the background of the receiver and how he interprets information. Academic jargonese spoken to a group of employees with no more than a high school education certainly will not be understood. Neither will instructions given by a DON in complex medical terminology to a group of nurse aides. Words have meanings according to where people live, their social group, their life experience, their age group, their educational level, and other circumstances.

> **Examples:** In the South when one says a woman has "swallowed a watermelon seed," it means she is pregnant. "The bottom is fixing to fall out" means it is going to rain, unless you are at the stock market on Wall Street. Everyone is aware that teenagers have their own language that changes continuously and that adults seldom understand.

In order to communicate effectively in an organization, managers must be aware of their employees' use of language and their understanding of words. The most **important rule** in communication is to put one's message in the language of the receiver. It is the only way to promote mutual understanding.

There are a number of **transmission** difficulties, often called noise factors. Noise itself can be a barrier – background noise, static on tapes or telephones, and people talking loudly. **Stuttering, mispronounced words**, and **deafness** are barriers. So is a too hot or too cold environment, since people have trouble listening under these conditions. A room that is too crowded or is too large is a hindrance to communication.

A **receiving** barrier is **inattention**, especially when receiving a message while in a group, as some employees tune out and think of something else. They do not hear the message. Others hear a part that interests them, begin thinking about it, and do not hear the remainder of the message. The problem is that people hear and think faster than a person speaks. The average speaker uses about 180 words per minute, whereas the receiver thinks at approximately 300 words per minute. Thinking often gets ahead of listening and becomes a barrier.

Distrust of the sender is a receiving barrier. Employees may have learned that a manager tends to forget what he has told them, or tends to change his mind too frequently. They hesitate to decode, understand and act on a message until they are sure a manager means it and will stand by it. Sometimes employees will ask if he would mind putting his instructions in writing.

Premature evaluation is another receiving barrier. Many people, especially managers listening to a subordinate relating a problem, tend to judge or disapprove what is being said rather than listening so they can understand the speaker's message. Some tend to provide solutions before they have heard all of the problem. American managers are **solution oriented** rather than **problem solving** oriented. They have a solution before full information on the problem is presented. This can be quite frustrating to employees.

Fear of consequences sometimes serves as a barrier. An employee has information useful to managers or to fellow employees but is afraid he may be punished in some way or ostracized if he communicates it.

Poor retention is another major barrier. Individuals tend to retain only a fraction of the information given them, perhaps no more than 30 percent, depending on the message, the timing, and other factors. That is the reason employees often must be told the same thing every few weeks. Several studies show that supervisors retain no more than 50 to 60 percent of the information they receive.

Upward communication has its barriers, too. **Filtering** is a common practice among supervisors. Before passing information upward to their superiors they tend to filter out information that adversely affects them or someone they wish to protect. The lower echelon exercises considerable control over information their bosses receive. Studies show they transmit only enough information to keep their superiors or themselves out of trouble. They are heard to say, "Oh, he does not need to be bothered with those details," and they are not communicated. Or, they say, "He needs to know this. Better tell him right away," and it is communicated appropriately.

The **over/under** barrier affects upward communication. Some supervisors bring a problem to their superior and spend ten minutes relating background details without ever stating the problem. The manager receives far more details than are needed to make a decision. He may feel he is being set up for a bombshell that does not drop. It may be necessary to say, "Give me the bottom line, what is the problem? I'll ask for necessary details as we go along." Fortunate is the administrator who has supervisors that come in and say, "I dropped the ball," then frankly present the facts about a problem.

Change Most frequently, the **purpose** of communication is to effect change that affects employees: changes in schedules, duties, procedures, new skills to be used, further training, and so on. Bedelian contends that "although change is universal and inevitable, it is rarely received without protest. Resistance to change is a natural human reaction." Change is a threat to the *status quo* – the way we always do things. Workers in organizations usually worship at the shrine of the status quo. They want to be left alone with what they already know, with what makes them comfortable. Any threat to "the way we do things now" arouses anxiety. They know how current practices affect them, but they aren't sure what the change will do to their daily routine.

Because of this natural resistance **timing** of a proposed change is important. One should never introduce change and have it begin at 8:00 o'clock tomorrow morning. If this is done, work will slow down, or momentarily cease, until workers determine how the change will affect them. Their time is spent discussing the proposal, asking questions of other departments. What's that going to mean to your group? Does that mean we are going to have to...? How will it affect the way we handle...? On and on the discussions go until workers formulate expectations of how the change will affect their job and security. Meanwhile work performance suffers.

It is more effective to discuss the change with the upper-echelon employees first. Be sure that immediate assistants understand and have their questions answered. Next, introduce the change to department heads and answer their questions, then do the same for line supervisors. Workers get the news last, but their supervisors are now prepared to respond to their questions, help them with their fears and anxiety, and hopefully reduce resistance. Just because the change affects everyone in the organization does not mean they should all hear about it at the same time.

Generally, it is more effective to introduce the proposed change a week to ten days before it is to be effective. This gives time for employees to informally discuss the proposal while continuing to do their work. When the change is implemented employees shrug their shoulders and say, "Well, we knew it was coming; they told us."

The **principle of reciprocal action** is involved in change. As stated earlier this principle indicates no change can be made in any department of a facility that does not affect all other departments directly or indirectly.

> **Example:** A food service worker's schedule was changed so that she came in a half hour early and left early. Within days a nurse aide complained, "I don't know why she gets to come in early. I've been here three years longer than her. I repeatedly asked for an earlier shift, and they wouldn't give it to me."

An effective rule is to allow no change in any department until all department heads are informed and have time to plan for any impact it may have on their department.

Written communication is preferred over oral communication when the information must pass through several levels of management, when employees are new and not well-trained, or when information involves significant change. Writing tends to clarify and to reduce misinterpretation.

Staff conferences held on a regular basis enhance communication and help reduce problems. **Department head meetings** should be held regularly, perhaps weekly, whether management has something particular to discuss or not. Invariably someone has important information of use to all staff. A good format for staff conferences is to have each department head briefly report on the prior week's work and any problems that occurred. Then focus on plans for the coming week and the more distant future. This lessens the impact of the changes departments plan to make.

Face-to-face communication is the most effective. The sender of information can observe reactions, pick up clues on whether it is understood, and obtain other feedback that assures understanding. It offers the receiver an opportunity to ask questions and to have input.

Open door policy Health-care administrators often say they have an open door policy of communication. Any employee at any level can bring a problem to them. This generally is not true nor is it an effective means of management. Usually, a secretary screens people wanting to see the boss. The secretary points out he is tied up for the rest of the day, he has meetings or is involved in other matters that indicate he is very busy. Secretaries are usually quite adept at protecting their bosses' time.

If an administrator does have an open door policy, he is dealing with a myriad of details that should be handled by someone else. Actually, he is doing his supervisors' work and undermining their roles. He doesn't need supervisors if he is going to do their work.

Like Jethro told Moses some three thousand years ago, set up the proper organization and the top executive will deal only with the big problems that no one else can handle.

Directional communication In organizations communication flows downward, upward, laterally, and sometimes diagonally as shown in Figure 3.3

Downward communication occurs when any manager confers with their subordinates in the organization—administration to department head, to supervisor, to worker.

Upward communication occurs when lower echelon confers with their supervisor — worker to supervisor, to department head, to administrator.

Lateral (sometimes called horizontal) communication occurs when people at the same level confer with each other — department head to department head, supervisor to supervisor, employee to employee.

Diagonal communication occurs when a department head confers with a supervisor or worker in another department. Communication in this

Figure 3.3: **Chart of Organization**

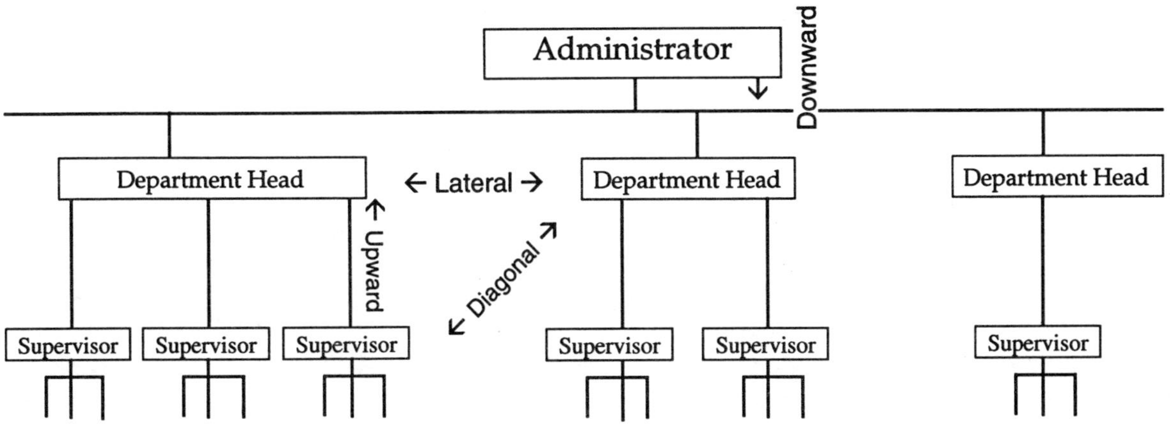

direction is usually discouraged as department heads want information to their staff to come through them. There are exceptions such as an emergency when safety is a factor.

TECHNOLOGY AND COMMUNICATION/INFORMATION SYSTEMS

The computer age Up to this point only processes and features of personal communication within an enterprise have been discussed. With all of the imminent changes in Medicare and Medicaid and the total health care industry there is an increased need for data and information. Other enterprises have already incorporated computer technologies into their businesses, and nursing homes must implement effective computer technologies now. The industry must move from filling out forms and sending out bills, to the era of utilizing computer systems as a timesaving tool. (Jackson) It will not only enhance communication and data handling within the facility but also with other enterprises, including governmental agencies, nursing homes, other health care facilities, banks, accounting firms, and more. Use of computer technologies to promote quality management leads to improved quality care and to greater profitability.

SNF's are already involved with computer technology for they are online with HCFA's mainframe computers in Baltimore. State Medicaid licensing and survey authorities now report survey findings to HCFA's OSCAR system. Surveyors retrieve this information for use in planning their surveys. (See Chapter 11)

An example of how a state can utilize computer technology to enhance communication and disseminate information is the Louisiana Certified Nurse Aide (CNA) Registry. As soon as it receives information verifying that an aide is certified, the information is entered in the Registry's computers. Through a telephone response system it is immediately available to every administrator in the state on a 24-hour, seven-day-a-week basis. Administrators not only determine that an applicant is certified but also receive verification by computer print out via mail. They also have access to certification and disciplinary information on more than 92,000 nurse aides listed in the Registry.

All nursing homes are now required to have a computer that may be largely used to record assessment and care plan data. This is made easier by use of the minimum data set (MDS) and the resident assessment instrument (RAI). HCFA recently modified the RAI partially to make it easier to automate assessment information. Some facilities use this automated data for tracking resident acuity and outcomes, determining staff needs, and generating an array of data on resident characteristics. Some nursing home chains use the information to generate comparative data and measure facilities' performance against quality indicators. They also monitor specialty units such as Alzheimers and acute care. (Wagner)

Facilities that have not moved into the electronic age may expect prodding from government agencies anxious for nursing homes to expand electronic capabilities. HCFA's push to get resident assessments automated is a driving force behind computerization of LTC. The trend is expected to accelerate since regulatory agencies want to build a nationwide database from MDS data. During 1998 HCFA required nursing homes to begin transmitting MDS data electronically to their state office. (See Chapter 12) This will pave the way to a nationwide database of long-term care resident characteristics. (Wagner)

In states with case-mix payment systems, comparative performance data is also generated. States use assessment data to calculate provider payments. Generally, the data is transmitted electronically from providers who receive feedback data based on a set of quality indicators. An example is Vermont, which ranks nursing homes against 29 quality indicators. These include residents who need little help in eating but are underweight, residents who are alert and have low needs for assistance with activities of daily living (ADL) but are incontinent, residents taking antipsychotic drugs, and others.

1. **The Internet** is a huge, rich resource of information stored in thousands of sites and accessible only via a series of computer interfaces. This allows one computer to interface with another to obtain desired information. Simply stated, one computer talks to another. To access the Internet all that is needed is a personal computer, a modem, a communication program, and a telephone line. It can be readily seen that this provides more information more quickly than using the telephone, Western Union, or the Postal Service.

Steven Jaborg reports their Cedar Lake Health Care Center in Wisconsin is on the Internet and finds it helpful in research, communication, purchasing, public relations, fund-raising, employee recruitment, social work, and activities. It has become an integral element in the management of a 415-bed skilled facility. He feels that one of the best features is the ability to enhance nursing home communications.

2. **The World Wide Web** An early problem with the Internet was that the intricacies of not-too-friendly computer interfaces were quite complex, requiring time and patience on the part of the users. The dimensions of the problem can be seen as an estimated 70,000,000 people used the Internet in 1997, and the number steadily increases. The World Wide Web has simplified use of the Internet, making it more user friendly. The Web is defined as a convergence of computational concepts for presenting and linking information dispensed on the Internet in an *easily accessible* way. (December, Randall, and Tatters)

Administrators are referred to *Discover the World Wide Web With Your Sportster* available from Sams.Net Publishing. This publication provides detailed information on the uses of the Web, how it works, how to access and use it, and other valuable data.

The Internet through the Web and several other systems provides a wide range of information (world-wide) of interest to the LTC industry. Government regulatory agencies have information specifically related to nursing homes. So do organizations that disseminate information on arthritis, Alzheimers, and other disorders affecting the elderly. Continuing education for administrators is also available.

Following are a few addresses of Internet sites of particular interest to LTC. There are thousands of others.

a. **HCFA** http://www.hefa.gov/ HCFA often puts information on the Internet a day before it is published by the Federal Register. HCFA also links to other federal health-related servers.

b. **Social Security Administration** http://www.ssa.gov/ Information on Social Security benefits, Medicare, and Medicaid is available.

c. **Code of Federal Regulations** http://www.pls.comi8001/cfr.html All laws are coded, and nursing homes follow the code.

d. **Disability, Aging, and Long-Term Care Policy** http://aspe.os.dhhs.gov/daltcp/home.htm

e. **Long-Term Care Today** http://www.longtermcaretoday.com/index.html Provides news of the LTC industry. It is updated each Tuesday.

f. **Administration on Aging** htt://www.aoa.dhhs.gov/aoa.html

g. **IRS** http://www.irs.treas.gov A good spot to learn about Federal income taxes.

h. **OSHA** http://www.osha.gov This is an excellent site for information of vital importance to facilities located in states where nursing homes are monitored by OSHA.

3. **E-mail** Electronic mail is one of Internet's best contributing features to communications. E-mail provides for transmission of messages from one computer to another in a matter of seconds. One simply enters his own E-mail address, the destination E-mail address, and the message. What an improvement over dictating, transcribing, typing, addressing, stamping, and stuffing envelopes, and getting it to the post office where it will take two to five days for normal delivery. It makes no difference what kind of computer or operating system is used because Internet communication standards function as a universal language understood by all computers. (Jaborg)

News-groups are computerized bulletin boards originally developed for posting news items and notices. Now they are used for live discussion by groups. It's a great place for administrators to share problems and pose questions.

Mail lists are a combination of E-mail and news-groups. An administrator can subscribe to a mail list based on a specific area of interest. Every news-group posting written by people responding to that topic will be automatically routed to his E-mail box. Now he doesn't have to look for information – it comes to him.

Gearing up for automation Facilities that are not already using automation should quickly explore the quickest, best, and most economical means for gearing up. Experts warn that a facility should know it is not easy and it is not quick. First, select the hardware, making sure it will provide the specific service of your facility. Hardware is the tangible part of a computer – the equipment. The next critical step is to carefully evaluate any software vendor it may use. Availability of support and assistance is imperative – hopefully on a 24-hour basis.

In buying software, use an established company that is not likely to go out of business. According to David Patterson, LTC oriented software is on its way. It was developed by NeighborWare Health Systems and Nomad ACE (Accessible Clinical Environment). It addresses the needs of LTC providers and others in health care. Reportedly, this software is the first object-oriented software to be marketed. Object oriented means it is programmed to link together all objects needed to perform a function, such as patient billing or medication management. This software is promoted as being much easier and less expensive than earlier computer programming techniques.

Flexibility in software is important. Can it be simply modified? Adapted to state requirements? Is it user friendly for people who have never used a computer?

Once the vendor and product are chosen, run tests to identify and eliminate any problems. Do a trial run on a fictitious resident. A modem to the software company makes it possible to talk directly with suppliers while the facility and the vendor view the same screen at the same time. This helps to work out problems with the computer. (Wagner)

4. **FAX** (facsimile) technology provides another means of speedy communication between enterprises. The fax machine has its own number, similar to a telephone number, and a separate telephone line. To send, one dials the receiver's number, feeds the written message into the machine, and the receiving fax prints out the message. Administrators may call a government office or other enterprise for information. The office called may say, "Sure, I'll fax it to you." If it's already on paper, there is no typing or any other delay.

The receiving fax machine prints out an image of the document. Older machines use roll paper which tends to fade. It's a good practice to make a copy and file it rather than the fax. Newer machines use regular paper that does not fade.

Again, the value is the speed with which information that needs to be in written form can be obtained or dispersed. Almost all nursing homes now have a fax.

5. **Pagers** The pager has enhanced communication by maintaining contact with the wearer. The caller's number is dialed in and the pager records it. The receiver then returns the call. A drawback to this is the person paged may be some distance from a telephone.

6. **The cellular telephone** A big improvement over the pager is the cellular phone. It may be installed in an automobile or carried by the person. Pocket-sized telephones are now available. The cellular telephone provides immediate contact even if the person called is hundreds of miles away.

7. The **voice response** or **automated answer system** is probably the most irritating communication device in use today. One dials a number expecting a receptionist, or someone, to answer. Instead, he gets a recording that tells him how important his message is and then tips him off that it may be a long process by urging him not to hang up. He then hears a menu of perhaps eight to ten numbers and is advised to punch the desired number *now.* When he punches his number, instead of being transferred to his party he must listen to all the other items on the menu. When his call is forwarded, the system plays a batch of music while he awaits a response. If he is fortunate someone finally comes on the line to tell him his party is on another line or is not available. Then he will likely be transferred to a mail box where he can leave a message.

It is understandable that large enterprises may find this system saves time and money, but it certainly should be programmed so that when one punches in his number, he does not have to listen to the rest of the menu. The personal touch is lost, and management specialists have long taught that the first impression of an enterprise is often the lasting impression. No administrator should install an automatic answer system if he can avoid it. Public relations are too important to a nursing home, and a pleasant-voiced receptionist who can answer most questions – or knows who can – will enhance the facility's public image far more than a recording machine.

The only virtue of the automated answer system for the caller is that if he does not forebear the menu, music and waiting, he will likely spend even more time re-dialing a busy number. With these advances in technology, all telephones should have a redial button.

MOTIVATION

The process by which administrators initiate and direct desired behavior in their employees is called motivation. It is what administrators do to arouse employee interest in work and their desire to do a good job, to cooperate with others, to carry their share of the work load, and to work toward organizational goals. Actually, motivation is more often considered as **internal.** Most employees want to be seen as capable and competent which motivates them toward satisfactory performance. The job of management is to energize, direct, and sustain this motivation. Numerous theories have been advanced on the subject.

Need-hierarchy theory Abraham Maslow developed a need-hierarchy theory that is one of the most popular and widely known theories of motivation. Maslow believed that employees are motivated to meet five needs which are in ascending order of importance. (See Figure 3.4) He contended that a "lower" need must be satisfied before a higher need can be used to motivate desired behavior. Relative satisfaction of a lower need triggers dissatisfaction at the next higher level. When an employee has enough income to support a spouse and to feed, clothe, and shelter a family he begins to look to security and safety needs. Is his job secure? Does it offer adequate health insurance? How safe is the work place? Is it free of threats?

Figure 3.4: **Maslow's Need - Hierachy**

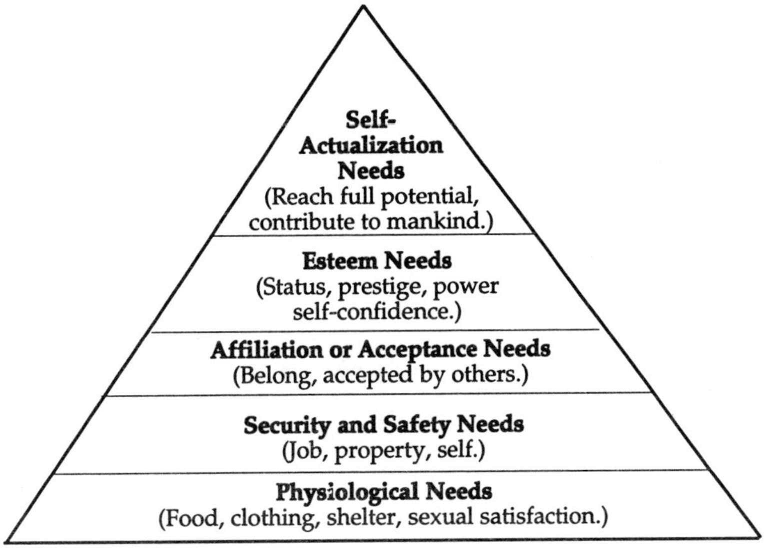

Maslow also thought a person can progress downward as well as upward in the hierarchy. If a safety need such as health insurance is threatened by losing coverage, the employee could shift concern from pursuit of personal recognition to preoccupation with providing health care for self and family. (Bedelian) Actually, research indicates that needs do not progress upward in the hierarchy in the orderly manner Maslow suggested. There is no way of knowing which needs will be dominant once lower-level needs are met. Needs vary greatly so that one person's physiological needs may be far greater than another. Needs change, as does motivation, as the employee gains experience and grows in the job. Some researchers maintain that even when a lower need is met, that need is still important although it may not be dominant at the time.

In spite of questionable validity, Maslow's theory continues to influence thinking about motivation. Bedelian points out these implications to managers:

1. Motivation is determined by multiple needs, not just one.

2. Managers should identify dominant needs and link satisfaction of these needs to performance. As an example, if a need for recognition (esteem) is recognized, work should offer such gratification based on performance. Some nursing facilities do this with such awards as pins, badges, employee of the month parking, and letters of recognition.

3. Managers should be aware that what motivates one employee may not motivate another. Awards as those above may motivate one person but not everyone.

4. Needs are likely to change from time to time, and people are at different levels of the hierarchy at different times.

5. Managers should create a climate that enables employees to meet several different needs within the hierarchy.

6. Failure to provide opportunities for need satisfaction will likely result in frustration, dissatisfaction, and increased turnover.

Two-factor theory In the late 1950's Frederich Herzberg developed a theory of motivation generally referred to as the two-factor theory. It enjoyed popularity through early 1970 but has recently fallen out of vogue. In spite of this, it is briefly presented here since the theory has some management implications that are worthy of consideration. These are identified later in this section.

Herzberg's research showed that factors producing **job satisfaction** were entirely separate from those producing **job dissatisfaction.** He found that although an unpleasant work environment might be a reason given for job dissatisfaction, a pleasant work environment is rarely cited as a reason for job satisfaction. This suggested job satisfaction and job dissatisfaction are not simple opposites. This gave rise to his two-factor theory.

Traditionally, job satisfaction and job dissatisfaction are viewed as opposite ends of the same continuum. Herzberg suggested the opposite of satisfaction is **no satisfaction,** not dissatisfaction. He said factors that promote job satisfaction are **motivators** which are directly related to **job content.** The factors that led to job dissatisfaction were labeled **hygienes** which were related to the work environment or **job context.** (See Table 3.1)

Table 3.1:

Herzberg's Motivators and Hygienes

Motivators Leading to Job Satisfaction	Hygienes Leading to Job Dissatisfaction
1. Achievement	1. Policies and administration
2. Recognition	2. Supervision
3. Work itself	3. Relations with peers
4. Responsibility	4. Working conditions
5. Advancement	5. Pay
6. Personal growth	6. Job security

Based on this dichotomy, Herzberg concluded:

1. To the degree that motivators are present in a job, motivation will occur. When absent, motivators do not lead to dissatisfaction.

2. To the degree that hygienes are absent from a job, dissatisfaction will occur. When present, hygienes prevent dissatisfaction, but do not lead to satisfaction.

In spite of a failure of evidence to support Herzberg's contention that hygienes can prevent dissatisfaction, there is doubt that his theories apply to workers in different settings and questions about his methodology, Bedelian contends the theory merits consideration. His reasons:

1. The two-factor theory suggests an individual can be both very satisfied and very dissatisfied at the same time. A nurse may love her work but be unhappy when she gets her paycheck. Consequently, an employee may be either satisfied, dissatisfied, or both.

2. When managers ask why employees are not motivated, the usual response to solving the problem is to change facility policies and improve working conditions, with little result. Herzberg's theory suggests that hygiene factors may not strike at the root of the problem.

3. The two-factor theory suggests motivation can be increased by designing jobs that provide achievement, recognition, responsibility, advancement, and personal growth. Herzberg's ideas have inspired many enterprises to redesign jobs with excellent results. Job redesign offers the promise of increased motivation for certain jobs and employees.

Reinforcement theory B.F. Skinner advanced the theory that behavior which goes unrewarded tends to extinguish itself. He believed that all positive or desirable behavior of an employee must be rewarded in some way. He calls this **positive reinforcement**. Even if the employee is only doing his routine work, he must be rewarded in some way or he will be disappointed and his work performance will diminish. He may not repeat the desired behavior.

There are many ways behavior can be reinforced. A smile, the "okay" sign, and "I like that" can be just as effective as telling an employee in an interview what a great job he is doing. Praise and recognition for a job well-done may motivate better than an increase in pay. Employees generally want to know they are doing a good job and that they are appreciated. In fact, sometimes a supervisor can promote desired behavior by giving a daily minimum of six "attaboys" to employees. **It can change the whole work atmosphere of the unit.**

Skinner's theory is the most controversial of motivation theories, partially because it was the basis for **behavior modification** programs. When applied in the workplace the basic concept was that behaviors leading to desirable consequences will likely be repeated, and behavior leading to undesirable consequences (punishment) is less likely to be repeated. Criticisms of this theory are listed by Bedelian as:

1. It ignores the human element – people have feelings, desires, motives, and aspirations.
2. It is too rigid and programmed – does not consider individual needs, expectancies, and so on.
3. It overemphasizes external outcomes (pay and promotions) and ignores feelings of accomplishment and recognition.
4. It fails to recognize that reinforcers may initially work, but they lose significance and employees no longer respond.
5. Some people think punishment and behavior modification manipulate employees and may exploit them.
6. It does not appreciate that once manipulated employees learn to manipulate back.

In some 50 years of health-care management, the author finds little evidence to support these criticisms as long as a manager follows six simple rules and acts with sincerity. Never has he observed a person at any level in the management hierarchy who did not appreciate recognition and approval for a job well done. Of course, it cannot stop at this point. It must include opportunities to meet other needs as defined by Maslow and Herzberg. Coupled with the MBWA style, positive reinforcement can be one of the easiest motivational techniques if carried out by these rules. Positive reinforcement must be:

1. **Real** Backslapping, flattery, simulated approval, and false affection are not positive reinforcers. One must know first hand what an employee has accomplished before saying so.

   Example: A large health-care facility had four nursing divisions. A management-training consultant was holding a seminar with the four division heads and the director of nursing. During a break all were standing in the hall when the administrator stopped by and said, "I sure appreciate the fine job all of you are doing. It sure makes my job easier." When he left, the consultant, having noted no change of expression on any face, asked how they felt about the boss taking time to stop and commend them. One nurse said, "I've been here four years, and he hasn't been on my division once. He doesn't even know what I do." Obviously the compliment was not real, and the five nurses knew it.

2. **Earned** Give reinforcement only to those who earn it. Never commend a group of two or more employees when one has not done his part. To do so may anger those who did a good job, since the lazy one received the same reward they did. Get the group together, commend the good workers by name, ignore the one who isn't performing, and watch the result. Usually, the one ignored complains when the administrator leaves; and the others advise that if he did his work sometimes he would be recognized, too.

3. **Timely** Offer reinforcement as soon after good work performance as possible. Do not wait for a week or two, or save up compliments for evaluation time.

   Example: During a very rushed time, a dietary worker0 pitched in to help another worker so mealtime would not be delayed. The food service director was too busy to respond at the time. Ten days later she said to the worker, "By the way, I really appreciate the way you pitched in and helped get the meal out on time the other day." The worker responded, "Oh, that was a long time ago. I didn't think you even noticed." Too late! It was not effective.

4. **Regular** Frequency of reinforcement is more important than the amount. Improvement in employee behavior is not proportionate to the amount of reinforcement he receives. As stated earlier, waiting until performance evaluation time to tell an employee how competent he is, will not be effective.

5. **Consistently given** Supervisors must commend employees each time they do a good job. This may sound like too much of a chore, but if one fails to take note of good performance, generally it slacks off. Failure to do this often results in employees complaining, "It doesn't do any good to work hard around here; nobody notices or cares."

A good example of combining MBWA and positive reinforcement follows:

Example. A male housekeeping aide lazed around, spent much time in the bathroom or outside the building, and did as little work as possible. The administrator could find nothing in the way of positive behavior until he reviewed the aide's attendance record. It was nearly perfect – always present and very seldom late. One morning while on his rounds the administrator stopped and complemented the aide on his attendance. He straightened up, threw his shoulders back, and grinned widely – probably the first compliment he had received on the job. Next morning he was vigorously mopping the hallway when the administrator came in. The administrator commended him on the way he did this work. In two weeks, after regular **attaboys** from the administrator, the aide applied himself enthusiastically to his work. His whole work attitude changed.

Money motivators Money seldom motivates over any period of time. Pay raises motivate only when they are known to depend on high performance and will not be given otherwise. Money may motivate when it is sizeable in terms of what one is accustomed to. An offer of a $50 bonus at Christmas based on no absences during the year will not likely motivate. However, an offer of a $5,000 bonus may motivate employees to report for work even when they are ill. Other examples are the young worker struggling to buy that sports car or to earn the down payment on a house. Money may motivate until one or both are attained and monthly payments level off. After that it may take other needs to motivate.

When employees are well-motivated they identify with facility goals and tend to see them as their own. They often say, "I like my job," or, "I like the way they let me do my work," or, "I like the people I work with." These are measures of well motivated staff and of job satisfaction.

In summary, directing, or leading, is really the essence of management. Many administrators are competent planners and can organize and staff efficiently. However, once staff is hired, trained, and on the job, they have difficulty getting them to perform their tasks when and how they are required. Many are afraid to use the authority vested in them for fear it will make someone angry. To be a competent manager one must realize there is no means of getting employees to do their work properly without making someone angry – some do not intend to "hit a lick more than they have to." Managers must give employees the right to be angry with them, because they sometimes will.

CONTROLLING

Controlling means to measure work performance against original plans to determine if they are being properly carried out and to correct any errors in performance. When work is complete supervisors still have a chore. They must exercise control measures. If work is not monitored and errors corrected, employees think it doesn't matter how tasks are performed.

The **purpose of control** is to maintain harmony between plans and work performance. The **purpose of correcting** errors is to bring about change in the employee's behavior so the error will not be repeated and instead will help him improve his work performance.

Three steps in the control process are: (1) to establish policies, procedures, and rules and to educate all staff, (2) to monitor performance and determine if it is satisfactory, and (3) to correct work errors.

Also, there are **three steps** in correcting errors: (1) review the standards to ensure the employee understands how the task is to be performed; (2) point out the error; and (3) indicate what must be done to correct it. Most supervisors begin an employee interview by confronting him with his mistake. Generally, this makes the employee defensive, and he spends the time trying to defend himself instead of correcting the error. By first reviewing standards, one begins with mutual agreement about what should be done, thus there is less personal defensiveness. In fact, when standards are reviewed first, many employees admit their error before they are told.

Example: An employee arrives for work at 7:45 a.m. instead of his scheduled time of 7:00 a.m. Call the employee in and ask, "What hours did you agree to work when you were hired?" The usual answer is "7:00 a.m. to 3:00 p.m., but..." An excuse or excuses follow, or the person says, "I know I'm late, but I'll work after 3:00 to make it up." The manager's response should be, "You are not needed after 3:00, you are needed at 7:00 as you agreed when you came to work." The manager might add, "We can't pay you when you are not here. Can you be here when you agreed, or do I hire someone else who can?" It is difficult for the employee to make further excuses because the manager reviewed the standard, discussed the error, and indicated the remedy.

There are several important guidelines to correcting errors effectively without promoting defensiveness.

1. **Correct the first error.** Never allow an employee to make even the first error without bringing it to his attention. This does not mean a full conference must be held when a person is late on one occasion. Simply bringing it to attention the first time may be sufficient. If errors are not corrected, employees think their performance is acceptable. Often they say, "I did that several times before, and you did not say anything. I thought it was all right."

2. **Correct the error as soon as possible and in private.** No employee likes being corrected in the presence of coworkers. If supervisors wait too long, the employee may respond, "Oh, that was last week. I had forgotten about that."

3. **Be objective**. Deal with an issue, not the personality. Never tell an employee he has a bad attitude. Deal with the procedure that was not followed. Do not tell him something good, then jerk the rug from under him by saying "but, you . . ." Tell him the good things about his work at the end of the session when he needs a boost.

4. **Be specific**. Deal with one error at a time. General remarks like, "Your attendance is poor" or "Your work has fallen off lately" are interpreted as a criticism of the person. It promotes defensiveness which should be avoided. Pointing out several errors or saying, "This happens too often" also promotes defensiveness.

5. **Stick to the facts.** Do not exaggerate. Never ask an employee what would happen if everyone made the same mistake. That is exaggeration, because everyone is not likely to commit the same error.

6. **Do not react to excuses.** When an employee offers one, simply say, "I understand, but let's

talk about what you can do to ensure that it does not happen again." Focus on solving the problem, not trying to handle excuses.

7. **Be serious.** Do not use sarcasm or joke about an error. If it is serious enough to call to the employee's attention, it is important enough to be serious. Statements like "I thought you knew better" or "I expected better from you" are sarcastic and can promote resentment.

8. **Give the employee a chance to respond.** Let him tell his side. However, just accept his statements with understanding as "I know how you feel" or "I appreciate your feelings." Then focus back on what can be done to solve the problem at hand. Keep the focus on the issue.

9. **Make sure there is a mutual understanding of future expectations.** Ask the employee to give his understanding of the discussion and summarize any decisions that were made.

10. **Let the corrective session be "water under the bridge."** There should be no "I'll be watching you" or "I'll be checking to see how you do." That's a signal the employee is not trusted and is expected to repeat the error. Express confidence that he can handle the situation. At this time point out the things he does well and how it is appreciated. Let him know this error is only a small part of his total performance.

USE OF COMMITTEES

The **committee** is one of the most ubiquitous and controversial devices of organizational management whether it is called a committee, team, task force, or other. Some of the more unkind in management have said, "A committee is made up of the unfit selected by the unwilling to do the unnecessary." Others say the committee is "a place where loneliness of thought is replaced by the togetherness of nothingness." Fortunately, the HCFA requires only the Quality Assessment and Assurance Committee. (See Chapter 12) However, all facilities usually have teams which are much like the committee. This is especially true in facilities where the administrator uses the TQM style of managing.

Much of the confusion about committees is due to the variation in the authority assigned. Does the committee make management decisions, or does it only deliberate on problems and make recommendations? Is their only purpose to receive information? What is the committee's relationship to department heads — can it instruct or does it only recommend? Is it a permanent or an ad hoc committee? (Weihrich and Koontz)

An administrator needs to know some of the advantages and disadvantages in order to use committees and teams. **Advantages** include:

1. **Group deliberation** and judgement brings more experience to bear on a problem. This is the #1 advantage.

2. **Commitment** by members of a committee that makes a decision usually results in the decision being fully implemented.

3. **Coordination** is attained when planning involves several departments.

4. **Splintered authority** can be corrected when no single person has sufficient authority to direct a given activity such as quality and safety.

5. **Transmitting information** is effective by committee.

6. **Motivation** through group participation can be accomplished.

The **disadvantages** include:

1. **Indecisiveness** may occur due to lack of time.

2. **Costs and time loss** can be considerable when five or more department heads deliberate for hours.

3. **Leadership** cannot be provided by a committee. It is a quality of the individual.

The administrator needs to consider **why** he appoints a committee. If it is to obtain loyalty, group judgement, and commitment to decisions, the committee can be valuable. If he is afraid to delegate too much authority to one person, doesn't want to take full responsibility for the decision himself, or just wants the decision deferred, use of a committee is questionable. If the purpose is to meet a government requirement and not to assure maximum utilization of committee knowledge and skills, it may meet the requirement but won't be of further value.

The quality assessment and assurance committee is the administrator's primary concern in using a group to accomplish a goal. He should ensure that its duties and authority are clearly defined and that it is accountable for goals established for it. His best assurance is to be chairman of this committee and have it meet frequently. (See Chapter 12)

RISK MANAGEMENT

Risk Management is a program to reduce occurrences (incidents) that may lead to action that results in damage to the facility and its reputation or in an economic loss. Occurrences include staff performance that results in resident injury or discomfort, injury to an employee, injury to or complaints by family and the public, providing substandard care, and others. Anything that may lead to an occurrence is considered a risk. Some risk factors are:

1. **Administrator** (a) Inadequate policies and procedures for admissions, resident care, safety, handling complaints, and so on; (b) lack of adequate training for all personnel; (c) failure to follow up on accidents, (d) inadequate insurance, and others.

2. **Nursing service** (a) Use of restraints; (b) PRN (as needed) doctor's orders; (c) storage, administration, and disposition of discontinued drugs; (d) confidentiality of records; (e) ambulation of residents; (f) other resident-care practices.

3. **Food service** (a) Improper storage and preparation of foods; (b) lack of proper sterilization of dishes, utensils, pots and pans; (c) grease fires and improper handling of garbage and wastes.

4. **Environmental** (a) Inadequate safety and security measures; (b) lack of infection control; (c) failure to comply with Occupational Safety and Health Act (OSHA), Life Safety Code, Americans With Disabilities Act, and other governmental standards; (d) failure to properly handle and dispose of infectious wastes; (e) lack of preventive maintenance; and other.

There are many other risks than those listed. The **first step** in developing a risk management program is to identify and enumerate the risk factors by department. Then a program for each department should be established and employees in those departments trained to recognize risks and to handle risks with care and judgement.

Examples of some aspects of the program for the business office and administration include (1) adequate general liability insurance in case a visitor is injured; (2) worker's compensation insurance in the event an employee is injured on the job; (3) adequate fire and extended coverage insurance; (4) proper policies with procedures covering every activity of the facility; (5) insuring that all complaints, accidents and incidents are properly investigated and documented; (6) adequate professional liability (malpractice insurance); and many others.

Malpractice insurance is a must because of the legal term **respondent superior** which means let the master answer. The employer is responsible for acts of his employees in the line of duty. The proper amount of malpractice insurance is seen as the most important factor in terms of a nursing home's risk of being saddled with a very large civil penalty that could drive it out of business.

The quality assessment and assurance committee, required by HCFA, is the **key** to a sound risk management program. The committee is to continuously search for risk factors that have a negative effect on the quality of care and the services provided to residents. Properly functioning, it continuously monitors all patient services and ensures that there is proper follow-up and corrective action taken on incidents, accidents, staff behavior, complaints, and other factors that have a risk of damaging the facility's reputation or causing it economic harm. (See Chapter 12 for more detail)

Staff training is another important factor in risk management. Staff must know the risk factors and how to avoid occurrences that have a negative impact, and have some awareness of the total risk management program. They need to know what the program means and the role they play in its success.

MONITORING

Monitoring departmental performance Administrators monitor their facilities in several ways. MBWA provides the opportunity to **observe** performance in each department. Enter the facility by different doors daily, visit all departments, call all employees by name, speak to all residents one encounters, and comment on all positive performance one observes.

Conference is another means of monitoring. Individual conferences regularly with each department head and regular department head meetings are quite useful.

Reports, both oral and written, are useful in monitoring. Determine what reports are desired and how often from each department. Example: What information is needed daily, weekly or monthly from nursing service? Number of residents in restraints? Incidents? Complaints? Medication errors? What reports are needed from dietary? Raw food cost per resident/day? Total food cost per resident/day? Number and type of meals served? Reports from various departments are discussed as their services are outlined in chapters that follow.

GLOSSARY

Active listening A type of listening in which the listener responds both to the message and the feelings of the sender.

ADL The five activities of daily living: eating, dressing, walking, talking, and communicating.

Authority The right or power to act, to decide, and to command others.

Budget A plan expressed in numerical terms—so much money for each category of expenditure for a specified period of time, usually one year.

Case mix A system of reimbursement based on the cost of providing care for a particular disorder.

Chart of organization A diagram that shows all levels of management and the lines of authority and communication within an organization.

CNA Registry A central registry that each state must maintain that includes information on all certified nurse aides in that state.

Communication The exchange or interchange of ideas, information, feelings, etc. with mutual understanding of what has been transmitted.

Consultant A contractual employee who brings expertise in a given area and who advises, recommends, teaches, and problem-solves.

Controlling The management function of measuring work performance against original plans and correcting work errors.

Coordination The art of getting people to work together toward a common goal in spite of their differences in interest, effort, speed, work, or attitudes, etc.

CQI **Continuous quality improvement** that occurs when TQM is used effectively.

Decentralization of authority The tendency to disperse decision-making authority in an organization structure so that departments or units make decisions whenever possible.

Delegation Giving a portion of one's authority to a subordinate(s) who then makes certain decisions.

Departmentalization Setting up units of assigned activities and delegating authority to a supervisor (department head) responsible for performance.

Directing The management function that involves all methods a supervisor uses to ensure that employees perform how and when they have been instructed.

Duties Tasks or work activities that are assigned to an employee.

E-mail A system within World Wide Web whereby one computer sends a message to another computer.

Executive staff Usually the top manager and 3 to 5 assistants found especially in larger organizations.

Fax (facsimile) A machine that sends and receives exact copies of correspondence, drawings, and the like, by means of telephone transmission.

Feedback Securing information from an employee that indicates whether or not instructions have been received with understanding.

Formal organization The organizational structure approved by the governing body of an organization.

Functional authority A relationship in which one person has control over a function but not the people who carry it out. He can tell them how a task must be done but cannot correct errors or discipline.

Goal The end result toward which all effort and activity are directed, sometimes referred to as an objective.

Governing body An individual or group with full legal authority to operate a facility.

Guidelines A term often used interchangeably with standards. Both are all-inclusive terms referring to the plan of operations.

Hardware The tangible parts of a computer which includes such peripheral devices as a printer and storage device that can be attached to the computer.

Informal organization Cliques, grapevines and other loosely organized unofficial groups within an organization.

Internet A huge, rich resource of information stored at many different sites, and available only via a series of computer interfaces.

Leadership The process of influencing employees to work willingly and enthusiastically toward accomplishment of group goals whether the leader is present or not.

Levels of Management Top, middle and line management comprise the management hierarchy.

Line authority An authority relationship in which one person directs, controls, and is responsible for the work of another person(s).

Malpractice Errors in treatment, mistreatment, neglect, and so on that are harmful to a resident; can be classed as malpractice.

Management Getting work done with and through other people. Using knowledge and skill to direct employee effort toward group goals.

MBWA **Management by Walking Around** A style of management in which the administrator daily visits each department of the facility observing the work that is being done and the work environment.

MBO Management by Objectives is a style of management in which objectives are clearly stated, plans established, time limits set, and progress continuously measured.

MDS Minimum data set is a form used in doing an assessment of a resident's functioning in the five ADL's.

Mission (or purpose) The basic task assigned to an enterprise by society.

Modem A peripheral device that connects computers to each other for sending communication via the telephone line. The modem modulates the digital data of the computer into analog signals to send over the telephone line, then demodulates back into digital signals to be read by the computer on the other end; thus the name modem for modulation/demodulation.

Motivation The process of initiating and directing desired behavior in employees.

Need Hierarchy Maslow's theory that basic human needs exist in an ascending order of importance and that once a lower level need is satisfied, it ceases to motivate a person.

Nonverbal communication Expressions, tone of voice, body movements, and gestures used when one communicates.

Open door policy One in which the manager allows any employee at any organizational level to bring problems directly to him.

Organizing The management function of grouping activities and employees, assigning roles, and delegating authority to supervisors in a manner that prevents friction and helps to attain goals.

Participative management A management style in which employees participate in planning and decision making; they have input on how their work should be done.

PERT Program Evaluation and Review Technique The use of a time-event analysis of various events in a program or project.

Planning The act of deciding what is to be done (goals) and developing guidelines (policies, procedures, rules and budgets) to attain the goals.

Policy A broad general statement that primarily guides thinking, decision making, and to some extent, action governing activities required to accomplish a goal.

Positive reinforcement The reinforcement of positive behaviors by some type of reward, as praise, recognition, and approval in order to promote better morale and employee effort.

Principle of the economy of action When a higher paid employee is making a decision that a lesser paid employee can do as well or better it is wasting money.

Principle of reciprocal action A management principle that says no change may be made in any unit of an enterprise that does not affect all other units directly or indirectly.

PRN Pro re nata A physicians order for a medication to be administered as needed.

Problem solving The process of examining a problem situation and helping those involved to select and carry out the best course of action for them.

Procedure A step-by-step guide to action that spells out how activities will be carried out in order to attain a goal.

Program A summation of goals, policies, procedures, rules, work assignments, schedules, etc., to be used to execute an overall plan.

RAI Resident assessment instrument is a form used to assess a resident's condition when they have a special problem, as incontinence.

Rapport Harmony and accord between management and employees.

Reinforcement theory Skinner's theory that behavior that goes unrewarded tends to extinguish itself.

Representing The art of interpreting employee desires, actions, and needs to others, especially to upper management levels.

Respondent superior The legal term for the facility being responsible for acts of its employees while they are on duty.

Responsibility Response to the duties assigned and the authority delegated. It cannot be assigned or delegated, it is exacted.

Risk Management A program that reduces occurrences that may lead to action that damages the facility's reputation or results in economic loss.

Rule A specific guide to specific action that has no exception. It states that certain action shall or shall not be taken.

Scalar chain A method of organizing that shows several levels of management from the governing board down to the line workers.

Site A location where information is stored and accessible via computer.

Software The instructions, called programs, given to a computer that enable it to do things such as locating a web site that contains desired information.

Span of management The number of employees a manager can effectively supervise (direct and control).

Staff authority A relationship in which one person gives advice, counsel and/or recommendations to another person, but cannot enforce decisions.

Staffing The management function of selecting, training, promoting, demoting, terminating retiring, etc. employees.

Standards Another term for the goals, policies, procedures, rules, and other plans used to guide employee behavior and performance.

Strategies General plan of action that focuses largely on long-range goals.

Superior/subordinate relationship The relationship that occurs between the supervisor and his employees in which the supervisor has authority to direct and monitor employee performance.

TQM Total Quality Management A type of management that involves staff in group problem solving with a focus on improving work quality and promoting employee knowledge and skills.

Two-factor theory Herzberg's theory that factors producing job satisfaction are entirely separate from factors producing job dissatisfaction.

Unity of command Insofar as possible an employee has one supervisor who gives him direction and supervises his work.

Voice response system An automated telephone answering system designed to forward telephone calls, to record messages, or to provide information to the caller.

World Wide Web A convergence of computation and concepts for presenting and linking information dispersed across an Internet in an easily accessible way.

REFERENCES

Allen, James E., *Nursing Home Administration,* Third Edition, New York: Springer Publishing Company, 1997.

Aomodt, Michael G., *Applied Industrial/Organizational Psychology,* Belmont, CA: Walsworth Publishing Co., 1991.

Bechler, Curt and Weaver II, Richard L., *Listen to Win,* New York: Multimedia Limited, 1994.

Bedelian, Arthur G., *Management,* Third Edition, New York: The Dryden Press, 1994.

Capezio, Peter and Debra Morehouse, *Taking the Mystery out of TQM,* Second Edition, Franklin Lakes, New York: Career Press, 1995.

Carr, Clay, *The New Manager's Survival Manual,* Second edition, New York: John Wiley and Sons, 1995.

Carr, Clay, *Team Leader Problem Solver,* Englewood Cliff, New Jersey: Prentice Hall, 1996.

Champy, James, *Reengineering Management,* New York: Harper Collins Publishers, 1995.

Crawson, Clay F., *"Governance and Management" in NAB Study Guide,* Washington, D.C.: National Association of Boards of Examiners of Long Term Care Administrators, Inc., 1997.

December, John, Neil Randall, and Wes Tatters, *Discover World Web With Your Sportster, Indianapolis*: Sams.Net Publishing, 1995.

Deming, W. Edward, *Out of the Crises,* Cambridge, MA: Massachusetts Institute of Technology, Center for Advanced Engineering Studies, 1986.

Drucker, P.F., *Management: Tasks, Responsibilities, Practices,,* New York: Harper Collins Publishers, 1973; First Harper-Collins edition, 1993.

Gordon, George K. and Ruth Stryker, *Creative Long-Term Care Administration,* 2nd edition, Springfield, IL: Charles C. Thomas, 1988.

Hersey, Paul and Kenneth H. Blanchard, *Management of Organization Behavior: Utilizing Human Resources,* Englewood Cliffs, NJ: Prentice-Hall, Sixth edition, 1982.

Jaborg, Steven J., "The Internet Comes to the Nursing Home", *Nursing Homes,* Volume 45, No. 1, Indianapolis: Que Corporation, 1996.

Katzenbach, Jon R., and Douglas Smith, The *Wisdom of Teams,* New York: Harper Collins Publishers, Inc., 1993.

Mandell, Steven L., *Computers and Information Processing,* Sixth edition, St. Paul, Minnesota: West Publishing Co., 1992.

Maslow, Abraham, *Motivation and Personality,* New York: Harper and Brothers, 1954.

McGregor, Douglas, *The Human Side of Enterprise,* New York: McGraw-Hill Book Company, 1960.

Patterson, David, "Coming: A New Era of Long-Term Care Software", *Nursing Homes,* Vol. 45, No. 1, Cleveland: MEDQUEST Communications, Inc., 1996.

Peck, Richard L., "HCFA's Software Plans", *Nursing Homes,* Vol. 45, No. 1, MEDQUEST Communications, Inc., 1996.

Pivovarnick, John, *The Complete Idiot's Guide to CD-ROM,* Second edition, Indianapolis: Que Corporation, 1995.

Reddin, William J., *Managerial Effectiveness,* New York: McGraw-Hill Book Co., 1970.

Wagner, Lynn, "Linking Data and Quality in the Age of Computers", *Provider,* Vol. 22, No. 3, Washington: AHCA, 1996.

Weihrich, Heinz and Harold Koontz, *Management,* Tenth Edition, New York: McGraw-Hill Book Company, 1993.

CHAPTER 4

GOVERNING BODY

GOVERNING BODY

LEGAL PROVISIONS

Governing body Until October 1, 1990, SNF's were required to have a governing body which was legally responsible for policies and procedures, appointing a licensed administrator, and for developing a budget and a capital expenditures plan. Federal guidelines provided considerable detail on board duties, specifying that the budget and plan were to be reviewed at least annually.

There was no federal requirement for a governing board in the former ICF's—now called NF's. However, many states developed and imposed the same standards for a governing body in the ICF's as federal guidelines required of SNF's.

ICF/MR's were, and still are, required to designate an individual or individuals to constitute a governing body. Its duties are clearly stated in 42 CFR 483.410:

1. To exercise general policies, budget, and operating direction over the facility.

2. To establish qualifications for an administrator within prescribed guidelines.

3. To appoint the administrator of the facility.

OBRA regulations Effective October 1, 1990, OBRA requires both SNF's and NF's to have a governing body, or designated persons functioning as a governing body. This body is legally responsible for establishing and implementing policies regarding the management and operation of the facility. (42 CFR 483.75) Undoubtedly, this includes procedures, for management practices require any business entity to have step by step guidelines for performing each activity in the business.

A second function of the governing body specified by OBRA is to appoint an administrator licensed by the state where licensing is required. He is responsible for the management of the facility.

Federal guidelines provide no further direction on governing bodies and their duties. Organizations must now use: (1) state laws governing sole proprietorships, partnerships, and corporations; (2) Internal Revenue Code regulations that apply to creating and operating business organizations; and (3) management theories and principles practiced by successful business organizations for defining duties of a governing body.

Sole proprietorships and partnerships may be quite informal, with no written document specifying how they are organized. They have considerable leeway in designating a governing body. The owner(s) is the governing body of this type organization insofar as HCFA is concerned. In the partnership all partners or a selected few are the governing body. A partnership may have up to 50 members. Where owners are a sizeable number, they may choose any member they wish to serve as the governing body. Because of owner liability for business debts, nursing homes are seldom operated as sole proprietorships or partnerships. State laws that govern these two types of organizations are far less rigid than for corporations.

Corporations Every corporation is created under a state law; therefore organizational structure and corporate regulations vary from state to state. Corporate laws are usually specific about structure and duties of governing boards. They are designated as the entity legally responsible for the financial management and operation of the organization. They may not assign or delegate all of their authority to officers of the corporation, to an executive committee, or to their administrator. A major value of operating as a corporation is that shareholders are not responsible for business debts as they are in proprietorships and partnerships. There is an exception; if federal withholding taxes are due, shareholders will pay them.

Articles of Incorporation The state requires a corporation to file **articles of incorporation**, also called a **charter**. It is a relatively simple document that must include the name of the corporation, the street address and name of its registered agent – usually an attorney – the number of authorized shares, and the name and address of each incorporator. The articles **may** include the initial directors and officers, the corporate purposes, powers of the corporation, its board, the shareholders, par value of shares, and provisions required or permitted to be set forth in the bylaws. When the articles, or charter, are filed with the state it becomes the basic governing document of the corporation.

A **closely held** corporation is one that has fewer than 50 shareholders. Frequently, they are family, relatives, or friends. They are usually active in the management and control of the business. They are concerned about whom their fellow shareholders are; consequently, they often impose restrictions upon the transfer of shares which are seldom placed on the market.

Many nursing homes operate as closely held corporations that tend to forgo adherence to corporate formalities such as holding meetings, passing resolutions, and keeping minutes. Some states liberalize provisions of closely held corporations to allow this, but they must conduct business on a corporate basis and provide an adequate financial basis for the business. (Mann and Roberts). On the other hand, there are a number of nursing homes owned by **publicly held corporations** which have a large number of shareholders, and it is widely traded on the stock market. Publicly held corporations tend to be more highly structured with election of officers and a board of directors, regular meetings, minute taking, and extensive bylaws. Many closely held corporations have no bylaws; they simply operate with the articles of incorporation.

The **Internal Revenue Code** has specific regulations governing structure, classification, and operation of corporations. These guidelines specify decisions that must be made by the board, or the board may submit them for corporation member approval. These decisions include certain salaries, dividends, fringe benefits, retirement plans, and so on that will affect federal taxation of the corporation. Many business practices that affect taxes must be approved by the board or the Internal Revenue Service will disallow them for determining the amount of taxes.

IRS requires boards to keep **minutes** on all meetings. These must reflect all official board decisions as documented by passing motions and/or resolutions, if these transactions affect corporate taxes. Without proper documentation, IRS disallows such transactions.

BYLAWS

Constitution and Bylaws Previously the regulations developed by a corporation for its governance were titled constitution and bylaws. More and more the term constitution is omitted. When the corporation is formed the state requires it to prepare **Articles of Incorporation**, but most publicly held corporations also develop **bylaws**. They are the rules and regulations that govern the corporation's internal management. Adoption of bylaws is one of the first items of business at the organizational meeting held immediately after incorporation. They may contain any provision for managing the business and regulating the affairs of the corporation, so long as they are consistent with the law and the articles of incorporation. Bylaws are not filed with the state as is the charter.

The law allows closely held corporations **not** to adopt any bylaws if all information required in the bylaws are stated in the articles of incorporation or in a shareholders agreement. It is considered that the highly structured formalities in typical bylaws can be cumbersome when imposed on closely held corporations. (Mann and Roberts)

Bylaws are required to contain rules and regulations on at least the following:

1. Purpose, mission, or goals of the corporation

2. Membership - active, associate, shareholder, and others

3. Board of directors - number, how chosen, terms, duties

4. Officers of the corporation - how chosen, terms, duties, removal

5. Committees - title, members, how chosen, duties

6. Meetings - membership, board, officers, committees, conduct of meetings, reports, resolutions and motions, voting, minutes

7. Overall financial management of the corporation

8. Indemnification of officers and board members

9. Parliamentary authority

10. Amendments of bylaws

11. Dissolution

Bylaws should be distinguished from **policies and procedures** which the corporation approves for each of its operations. As an example, a corporation may own, lease, or manage a number of facilities. Each will have policies and procedures governing every activity of the facility. These are much more detailed guides to decision making and activities than bylaws, and they are specific to an individual nursing facility. Bylaws serve as an overall guide to developing policies and procedures. They may be written in more general terms that outline **what** the corporation will do. Policies and procedures spell out in detail **how** activities will be carried out in each of its units.

Many small, closely held corporations do not develop a set of formal bylaws since they are not required by law. Their Articles of Incorporation briefly identify members, officers, board, annual meetings, and so on. The corporation then moves directly to policies and procedures or to operational guidelines.

Bylaws are usually approved by the shareholders. **OBRA** mandates that policies in nursing facilities are to be approved by the governing board, but it makes no mention of approving bylaws.

Preparation of policies and procedures generally is the duty of the administrator and his staff. Preparation of bylaws is the duty of the corporate body itself.

TYPES OF BOARDS

Titles of boards vary widely. There are boards of: (1) directors, (2) administrators, (3) governors, (4) regents, (5) trustees, (6) examiners, (7) supervisors, (8) managers, (9) advisors, and others. The two basic types are boards involved with **governance** and those that are **advisory. Governing boards** have authority. By state law they are legally responsible for the facility's **operation** and for its **business** management. Such boards are legally liable for their organization, and they are required to act for the organization using their best judgement.

Duty of Obedience applies to partners, governing bodies, and officers in both partnerships and corporations. In a **partnership** a partner owes his partners the duty to act in obedience to the partnership agreement on all business decisions. Failure to do so may result in that partner being personally liable if anything occurs that results in tort action. **Directors** and **officers** of corporations must act within the authority granted them by the organization. This authority is usually defined in the bylaws, articles of incorporation, and policies and procedures. Directors and officers may be held liable for any unauthorized transactions that result in tort action.

Duty of Diligence Partners and the officers and governing board members must exercise ordinary care and prudence in discharging their duties. Most states require that each discharge his duties:

1. In good faith (adhering to corporate bylaws and other guidelines)

2. With the care an ordinarily prudent person in a similar position would use in similar circumstances, and

3. In the manner he believes to be in the best interest of the partnership or corporation.

Partners, officers, and board members may use poor judgement or make honest mistakes in judgement that result in losses. The partnership or corporation may not hold them liable as long as the individual acted in good faith and with due care. (Mann and Roberts)

The administrator as the **agent** of a sole proprietorship, partnership, or corporate board may also be held responsible for **Duty of Obedience** and **Duty of Diligence**. He must act in the conduct of business affairs only as authorized and obey all reasonable instructions and directions of his employer. The administrator may be held liable for his actions should he: (1) enter into an unauthorized contract that makes the employer liable, (2) improperly delegate authority, or (3) commit a tort for which the employer is liable.

Also, the administrator in his **Duty of Diligence** must act with reasonable care in performing his work, and must exercise any special skill that he has. This means he must at least exercise the skill he represents himself as possessing. The administrator is licensed on the basis he has the knowledge and skill to operate a nursing facility according to federal, state, and local standards. If he fails to do so and tort action results, he may be held liable. (Mann and Roberts)

Advisory boards Generally, advisory boards have no authority. They may be formed to provide an advisory function to an organization that vests its authority in the administrator. Advisory boards offer advice and counsel that are not binding. The top manager still must make the decisions and be responsible even when he follows recommendations of the advisor. Advisory boards often have no legal status. They may be appointed by an owner(s) or an administrator to provide expert advice and to serve a public relations function. Advisory boards provide an opportunity for owners and administrators to interpret the facility to board members and for the members to interpret the facility to the community.

Small facilities often use their board, whether classed as advisory or not, for advice and assistance. They frequently appoint university faculty to their board primarily for advice in areas of accounting, economics, engineering, and management. (Weihrich and Koontz) They may appoint a banker, attorney, or other professional for the same reason.

LTC BOARDS

Henry and Stryker in their publication ***Governance of the Long-Term Care Organization*** point out that governing boards in LTC facilities vary so widely no typical form of governance can be identified. They describe the more common forms of boards, classified in three ways: (1) those that govern a single facility, (2) those that govern multiple facilities, and (3) those with special forms of governance.

1. **Single-facility boards** most often are found in facilities owned by: (a) a single proprietor, (b) a partnership, (c) government, (d) a fraternal organization, or (e) a church. Administrators may benefit by utilizing information regarding boards as presented by Henry and Stryker.

2. **Multiple LTC boards** may be responsible for a few facilities in a local area or many facilities in a state, region, or nationwide. These are usually **corporate** boards that are primarily concerned with **corporate** issues. This means individual facility and local community needs may not be adequately addressed. (Henry and Stryker) Administrators of these facilities might do well to appoint, with corporate approval, local advisory boards whose recommendations the corporate board will probably consider.

3. **Special boards** State owned and operated nursing facilities and veterans homes are examples of special governing boards. It is easy to recognize how complex they can be since state boards are usually politically appointed and may be responsible for many other types of institutions. Most of the veteran's homes have governing boards appointed by the governor. Members are usually representatives of veterans organizations. (Henry and Stryker)

BOARD MEMBERSHIP

Membership of boards and their appointment vary widely. It is readily apparent why people serve on a corporate, sole ownership, or partnership board. They are owners, part owners, or stockholders in the corporation which owns a facility. Their motivation is to ensure that it is properly operated, and in the case of for-profit corporations, to ensure that it generates a fair return on investment.

Size of boards or governing bodies varies widely. In a sole proprietorship the owner may be the entire governing body. In a partnership all partners or a selected few may act as the governing body. No particular number is suggested. The NAB's Board of Governors totals 51. For profit enterprises generally have smaller boards which can more easily convene a quorum and expedite business matters more quickly.

Sitting on boards, especially for a small business, is often attractive to business and professional people since it provides opportunity for **interesting service** and **contribution** to the **free enterprise** system. (Weihrich and Koontz) University professors serve not only because they can offer their expertise, usually for a fee, but also because it affords them opportunity to keep abreast business activities and practices. Members serving on nonprofit boards, especially the charitable organizations, have an opportunity to contribute to a community service.

Most people who are asked to serve on facility boards are successful in the management of some other business such as a bank, farm, construction company, or health-care facility, or a career such as legal practice, teaching, medicine or accounting. Organizations on whose boards they serve hope to utilize their management skills and expertise. (Henry and Stryker)

Appointment Many facility board members are self-appointed. This includes sole ownership, partnerships, closely-held corporations, and other similar organizations. Larger corporations usually elect or appoint board members. This is done by owners, stockholders, or their representatives. In associations and church-owned facilities the general membership usually elects or appoints board members. (Henry and Stryker)

ROLE CONFUSION

The **role** of board members generally is **not well-defined,** and members usually are not trained to be board members. They are trained managers or specialists, but when they sit on a board they do not face **management** problems. Henry and Stryker observe that the **governance** problems they face are different because they have: (1) less clearly defined alternative solutions, (2) no clearly right or wrong answers, (3) incomplete information, and (4) few criteria by which to adjudge success.

> **Example:** A nursing-facility board member was a retail merchant. He was part owner. The administrator discussed a problem he had with his DON. The retailer had an immediate solution, "Fire her!" That's what he did when a store employee failed to perform his duties properly. He had no awareness that RN's were scarce and that the DON was the only one residing within 25 miles of the facility. The manner in which he solved problems in his business was not applicable to nursing homes where professionals are employed.

The authors point out that **role confusion** is further enhanced by the fact that board members often must view the facility as a public, charity-oriented, caregiving institution, as a business enterprise operating on business and economic principles, and as a continuing social interaction among a diverse mix of people. At the same time, it must be operated as a single entity, and board members cannot view the facility from only one of these perspectives. Few board members are faced with this role in their own business or profession.

A third source of confusion identified by Henry and Stryker is the lack of clarity about whom they serve and to whom they are accountable. Most think they serve the **community**, but the term is difficult to define in terms of accountability.

Most people do not fully understand the role of board members. Two **major reasons** are: (1) being a board member is difficult, confusing, and hard to relate to one's occupation, and (2) there is much confusion about the role of governance, especially in contrast to management. This is especially true if one of the owner-board members is the administrator of the facility. A person occupying this dual position must carefully differentiate between his two roles. An effort is made to clarify some of this role confusion in the remainder of this chapter.

DUTIES

Duties of governing boards were listed under legal provisions, but they need further elaboration. Henry and Stryker contend that the major duty of the board is a clear **statement** of the facility's **mission** — the organization's direction and what it is trying to achieve. Since an industry's **mission** is ascribed by society, it appears the board should state it clearly and further delineate the mission into measurable **goals**. How many people of what types do they wish to serve? What types of service will they provide? What percent return on dollars invested do they want? And by what period of time?

The second major duty of the board is to **employ an administrator** who serves as its **agent**. He acts for the board, performing the duties it assigns and exercising the authority it delegates. He serves as the leader within the facility. Boards cannot provide leadership in day-to-day operations of the facility, for leadership is a quality of an individual, not a group. Boards are responsible for governance which essentially includes **planning** and **evaluation**. Boards must **plan** the **right thing** to do whereas their administrators must plan the right **way** to do it.

Evaluation is accomplished both by management and by the board. **Management** evaluation by administrators refers to **efficiency** of management actions. How well did the administrator plan and carry out activities the **correct way**? Did staff provide quality care? Generate adequate income? Stay within the budget?

Evaluation by the **board** means to determine the overall effectiveness of management's actions. It is possible for a facility to be **efficient** without being **effective**. Management may do the right things the right way with little impact on the original mission. When the administrator reports management results to the board, members might well ask "What good did all this do?" Or, "What impact does it have on the mission we set out to accomplish?"

The board must be concerned about the effectiveness of the facility as it carries out the mission. If the board does not clearly state the mission and use it as a **standard** to evaluate effectiveness, the community will not know what to expect from the facility. (Henry and Stryker)

The board also evaluates the **economy** of management. Operations may be highly efficient, but services cost too much. The facility is losing money. The board wants efficiency that is provided by reasonable costs that allow for a fair return on investment. It looks at the **cost effectiveness** of the administrator's management practices.

ADMINISTRATOR'S ROLE

Whether comprised of a single owner, several partners, or a number of elected shareholders, the governing body appoints an **agent** when it selects an administrator. The administrator is **hired** by the board, **acts** for the board, **is responsible** to the board, and **may be terminated** by the board. One of the biggest **problems** in LTC facilities is the lack of clarity and understanding of board/administrator roles. Boards hire administrators to manage, then they often involve themselves in the internal management of the facility, which is damaging both to governance and to management.

A **contract** that delineates the two roles should be detailed in writing, whether in personnel policies and procedures or in the form of a written contract. The first point of clarification should be that the **administrator** is the one person in the nursing facility who **reports** to the governing body. (Pipho and Stryker) This is true whether that body is in a corporate structure or is a sole proprietorships. Administrators simply cannot be effective if department heads or other employees are allowed to report directly to the board.

> **Example:** A food-service worker met a board member in the local grocery store. She asked the member, "What are you going to do about Ms. Smith? (dietary manager) She is driving everybody crazy. If you don't do something, everybody is going to quit." He replied, "I will look into it right away and make sure the problem is corrected." Next day the worker told her co-workers she had talked to the board member and "He told me he was personally going to see that Smith is fired." This created other problems for the administrator.

Members of governing boards should be prepared for this kind of situation. They should listen, then suggest that the *food-service workers* make their problem known to the administrator. Care should be taken that nothing is said which the employee can misconstrue and take back to the facility. The board member should then immediately report the occurrence to the administrator for action.

Other **roles and relationships** that must be clarified are:

1. As agent of the board, the administrator must be delegated the authority to manage the facility for the board.
2. The administrator must have authority to hire and direct his subordinate personnel in order to be effective.
3. Board members listen to employees, when appropriate, but never say anything that can be interpreted as instructions.
4. If an employee brings a problem to a member, the member refers it to the administrator.
5. Any problems with the administrator are handled by the board directly with the administrator and are not discussed with staff.

Number one and two above often are a real problem. Many owners will not delegate sufficient authority to the administrator to hire and fire personnel and properly manage the facility. This is especially true of sole proprietors who sometimes feel they can operate the facility better than a licensed administrator. They inject themselves into daily operations rather than working through their agent.

> **Example:** An administrator terminated an employee whose attendance was quite unsatisfactory. She had been counseled repeatedly about tardiness and failure to call in when absent. The employee went to the owner who said, "Don't worry, I'll take care of it. You report to work tomorrow at your regular time." The owner told the administrator what he had done and directed him to reinstate the employee. The administrator's explanation of the effect it would have on other staff was met with, "You handle that. I want her reinstated immediately."

It is not possible for an administrator to operate a facility properly when owners usurp authority that should be delegated to him. Administrators should clarify at the beginning of employment what authority they have and obtain assurances they will be backed by the owners when justifiable action is taken. The administrator must help owners understand it is his license under which the facility operates and he must have authority to serve in that capacity, otherwise, his license may be in jeopardy.

These roles are usually listed as a requirement of the state Medicaid agency and as a standard of practice by administrator licensing boards. When the owner(s) refuse to delegate adequate authority to the administrator to operate the facility according to proper standards, often the administrator resigns. And well he should, since it is the administrator's license that is at stake. There are frequent resignations that show this as the cause.

Representing the board In Chapter 3 the duty of the administrator to properly represent his employees in requests they make of the board was discussed. He has the same responsibility to accurately represent the board to his employees. Often the bosses want an action taken that the administrator knows is not agreeable. He feels certain staff will be quite upset, and he advises the board of this. The board instructs him to carry out the action anyway.

The administrator should call his management staff together and objectively advise them of the board's wishes. He should allow his supervisors to express their feelings openly and tell them he understands how they feel. Then he should focus on how the instructions can be implemented with the least amount of unsought consequences. An administrator should never tell his supervisors, "I don't agree with the bosses, but..." His stand must be that he represents the board and is obligated to carry out its wishes. The message to his staff is the same — they are expected to implement new instructions even though they may not agree with them.

The method is based, of course, on the assumption that what the governing body wants is not illegal or would require the administrator to do something unethical. In that event he must clarify his position with the board, which could mean resigning as administrator.

The above roles vary to some extent from facility to facility. Sometimes a board wants to approve appointments, especially of key personnel, to review some of the administrator's actions, as employee discipline, or to review in advance the administrator's plan to terminate an employee. This is well and good, so long as it is clarified in the contract before the administrator is employed, and the governing official approaches it through the administrator rather than dealing directly with the employee.

The small town operation It is imperative that the administrator of a nursing home in a small town understand its culture. Everyone knows everyone else and most are related in some way. Community residents don't do things simply because they need doing. They consider who is involved, who may be angered, what possible retaliation may occur, and so on. The administrator must never fire anyone or make a major change without first discussing it with the governing body and getting their reaction and approval. Never should the owners or board learn of an action through a disgruntled employee. Make sure that when the disciplined or fired employee approaches the board, the members know the situation and are prepared to respond appropriately.

Example: A new administrator of a nursing facility in a community of 1,600 people found two department heads that were not performing satisfactorily. He counseled both of them, but they repeatedly failed to improve their performance because they had been doing it their way for the four years the facility had been in operation. The administrator fired them. Rumors began to circulate about the terrible new administrator. An anonymous advertisement appeared in the local weekly paper telling how badly the facility was run and how it would close if something wasn't done. The administrator was *a go-getter* who had improved the facility immensely. Residents were happier, the environment more pleasant, and a survey showed no deficiencies for the first time in the facility's existence. Unfortunately, the disgruntled and their buddies had approached the owner with their terrible (but erroneous) tales. The owner fired the administrator, yet told him he'd done a great job. He had just stepped on too many toes and stirred up too many important people in the community. Had the administrator cleared all proposed changes with the owners first, it could have been a different story.

An administrator who isn't a native of the small town he works in will be seen as an outsider. The natives will not take kindly to his telling them how to do their work, even when they are doing a lousy job. He must take a slow, gentle route to accomplish his goals.

TRAINING BOARD MEMBERS

People serving on boards are almost always well-trained in some occupation or business other than serving as a board member. Whether it is identified as orientation or training, every new board member should have a group session with the president of the board and the administrator. This can help to ensure that both the board and the administrator's roles are clarified and understood. This orientation session should include at least these areas of discussion:

1. Facility ownership

2. Make-up and activities of the board

3. The facility's mission and goals

4. Organization structure, staffing, and lines of communication

5. All policies and procedures including government regulations

6. Duties of the board, including how a board member should handle the problems he may encounter

7. Duties of the administrator

During this session the chairman of the board and the administrator need to help the new member understand the difference between **governance** and **management**. Unless there is full understanding of roles and duties and proper use of communication channels, authority, and procedures, neither the board nor the administrator will be able to function efficiently, effectively, and economically.

GLOSSARY

Advisory Board One that is authorized to meet and advise an organization of plans, programs, and management, but is not authorized to govern the organization; not usually organized under authority of law.

Articles of incorporation The document required by the state that shows incorporators, number of share, addresses, name of agent, and so on.

Board A committee of persons organized to advise, exercise oversight, or control certain matters or to govern an organization. Those authorized to govern are organized under authority of law.

Bylaws Regulations, rules and laws adopted by an organization for governing the board's activities.

Charter This is another name for articles of incorporation.

Closely held corporation A corporation in which a small number of people, usually family members, own all the stock. There can be no more than 50 shareholders.

Duty of Diligence The requirement that a partner, officer, board member, or administrator must carry out his duties in good faith, with care and prudence, and in a manner he believes to be in the best interest of the partnership or corporation.

Duty of Obedience The requirement that partners, officials, board members, and administrators must act within the authority granted them.

Economy Operation of a facility at reasonable costs and as budgeted.

Effectiveness The accomplishment by management of an organization's mission statement.

Efficiency A management principle which means people accomplish objectives with the minimum unsought consequences and costs.

Evaluation To examine performance and end results by an established standard to determine if the mission and/or goals are met efficiently and effectively.

Governance The overall direction of an organization by establishing a mission statement and other guidelines and evaluating management's performance to determine if it is effective.

Governing body A legally designated and/or constituted individual or board which is charged by legal authority to organize, operate, and provide for management of a facility or organization.

Publicly held corporation One that has many shareholders and is traded in the stock market.

Tort A wrongful act, injury or damage (not including breach of contract) for which a civil action can be brought – one can be sued for damages.

REFERENCES

Bedelian, Arthur G. *Management,* Third Edition; New York: The Dryden Press, 1994.

Henry, William, and Ruth Stryker, "Governance of the Long-Term Care Organization" in G. K. Stryker and R. Stryker, editors, *Creative Long-Term Care Administration*, Springfield, IL: C. C. Thomas, 1983.

Mann, Richard A. and Barry S. Roberts, *Smith and Roberson's Business Law, eighth* edition, St. Paul: West Publishing company, 1991.

Pipho, Kathryn, and Ruth Stryker, "Developing the Management Team" in G. K. Stryker and R. Stryker, editors, *Creative Long-Term Care Administration*, Springfield, IL: Charles C. Thomas Publisher, 1983.

State Operations Manual, Provider Certification, Revisions one and two, Springfield, VA : National Technical Information Service, U.S. Department of Commerce, April 1998.

Title 42 Code of Federal Regulations, Public Health, Part 400 to 429, Washington, DC: U.S. Government Printing Office, 1996.

Title 42 Code of Federal Regulations, Public Health, Part 430 to end, Washington, DC: U.S. Government Printing Office, 1995.

Weihrich, Heinz, and Harold Koontz, *Management - A Global Perspective,* Tenth Edition, New York: McGraw Hill Book Company, 1993.

CHAPTER 5

MARKETING AND PUBLIC RELATIONS

MARKETING AND PUBLIC RELATIONS

WHY MARKET LTC?

Marketing of health care services is a relatively new practice first utilized extensively by hospitals. According to the National Research Corporation for Modern Healthcare, hospital administrators made **planning and marketing** their top priorities in 1985. (Jensen and Jackson) A declining census and competition made this necessary, and marketing is now a sizeable expense in most hospital budgets. Frequently this includes a staff trained in marketing.

The same priorities appear to be appropriate for long-term-care facilities since they are also faced with increased competition and a declining census. A considerable portion of the competition comes from hospitals, many of which are opening SNF units and either buying or building nursing facilities. Rural hospitals staffed and operating fewer than 100 beds, exclusive of those for pediatrics and intensive care, may now have some **beds certified for long-term care**. These are referred to as **swing beds** which may be used as acute beds or LTC beds as need dictates.

These developments pose a definite threat to traditional nursing facilities which formerly cornered the long-term-care market. Aggressive hospital-marketing programs have forced nursing facilities to enter the field of marketing and public relations.

High cost of health-care services can be directly related to the recent development of health-care marketing. **Attention of the media** and increased **public consciousness** about health are also factors. High technology and other improvements in health care as well as emphasis on wellness are matters of public expectation. (Weiss)

Increased focus in the 1980's on **health care for the elderly** is another factor promoting health care marketing. Attention is changing from earlier focus on maternal and child health, prevention, mental health and mental retardation to alcohol and drug abuse, and now to services needed by the elderly. This may be partially due to the rapidly increasing elderly segment in the general population and their demand for more and higher quality services. (Lambert and Thanopoulos)

TERMINOLOGY

It is important that administrators and staff understand basic terms used in marketing and public relations. This is especially true since all staff become involved when a facility conducts an effective marketing and public relations program.

Marketing is the act or process of selling or purchasing products or services in the marketplace. Whether it is the stockmarket, a retail outlet, or other business, management is concerned with buying and selling. It includes all the producer does to create demand. It is managing the flow of goods and services from the producer/provider to the user/consumer. As used in this chapter, it means the selling of long-term-care services by the nursing facility.

The **market** is the demand for a given service or product by the people who will purchase. Nursing facilities view this market as the number of disabled, aged, handicapped, and others who need and will pay for the type of LTC service they offer.

Marketable means a service or product is of proper quality and nature to be offered for sale in the market. LTC services are marketable only when they provide what is promised with dependable quality. Both services and products not appropriate for sale are often offered in the market.

To market is to offer or to expose a service or product in the marketplace. It is to inform the buying public what is available and at what price. Also, it is promoting the market potential of a service or product, and developing its sales potential.

The **product/service concept** of marketing means if the service or product that the public needs is made available, people will buy it. The product/service must be of the desired quality.

Market Opportunity Analysis (MOA), also called **Market Analysis** (MA), is a systematic means of developing and maintaining information that reflects the needs and desires of potential consumers and markets. (Lambert and Thanopoulos) This research should precede all marketing.

Market segmentation refers to diversity within the market. Administrators may identify segments of people requiring LTC who have similar needs and might respond more favorably to service specifically designed for them. (Engel, et al.) Examples are an Alzheimer's Unit, day care, and rehabilitation services.

Strategies are planned courses of action used in marketing and public relations to accomplish established goals.

DELICATE NATURE

Marketing of LTC services must be handled with some **delicacy** according to Sue Weiss. In her publication *The Art of Marketing in Long-Term Care* she notes that the American culture is ambivalent toward making money from health and human services. Undoubtedly, this attitude arises from the fact that health-care institutions were operated for centuries by the clergy without charge. Paying for health services rendered by institutions began in the early nineteenth century. It is a relatively new practice.

MARKET OPPORTUNITY ANALYSIS (MOA)

Research in the form of MOA should be carried out before marketing begins and on a continuing basis thereafter. The core of MOA is: (1) market size, (2) market requirements, and (3) competition considerations. These assist in building and maintaining awareness of the marketplace. (Lambert and Thanopoulos)

The **starting point** for planning LTC services should be the needs and wants of residents, patients, homeless elderly, and others who will use nursing-facility services. Orientation to the consumer should be the marketing philosophy, rather than concentrating on the details of providing services. (Lambert and Thanopoulos) Too often owners and administrators adopt early nursing facility concepts about what residents need. They plan and offer services very much on a take it or leave it basis. Changing concepts of LTC dictate that consumer needs and wants be clearly identified before services to meet these needs are planned and marketed.

Market size includes market potential. The administrator becomes aware of the population to whom he can offer services and what percent may need these services. It involves numbers in various age groups and the percent in these groups that may become consumers.

Market requirements delineate the characteristics of the market both in terms of service needed and ability to pay. **Needs of the elderly** are identified in terms of the types of health care in demand such as skilled nursing, nursing facility, day care, and home-health care.

Market opportunity for nursing facilities is dependent upon the extent to which **demand** is being served and on the size and nature of the demand. Lambert and Thanopoulos point out that nursing facilities must be aware of events and forces in the environment in which they operate in order to analyze demand. They list such environmental areas as: (1) social/cultural developments, (2) the economic environment, (3) technological developments, (4) the political-legal environment, and/or (5) relevant ecological concerns. In developing a new facility, its success is largely dependent on an accurate assessment of market opportunity. The same is true of adding a new service; the demand for the service must be sufficient to make its addition economically feasible.

Competition in providing nursing-facility services is identified by MOA. The nature and effect of such competition is analyzed and serves as a basis for planning. (Woodruff) Such analysis includes specific assessment of the **strengths and weaknesses** of local health-care institutions now serving the market in which the nursing facility is interested. Questions should be answered concerning what **services** competing facilities offer, what **unique features** are available, and how they **fail** to meet **demands**. (Lambert and Thanopoulos)

Distribution and Communication The MOA also alerts administrators to the structure of related distribution and communication of services in their target area. (Woodruff) Are institutions and professions coordinating their services? Is there a communication network that enables the consumer to find his way to the needed service? Are there adequate referral mechanisms between facilities? In using the MOA the administrator also concerns himself with how to provide needed **services** more **efficiently**. In addition to providing nursing service, he might consider the economics of providing other needed services, as retirement housing, respite care, day care, sheltered care, subacute care, and assisted living.

Market segmentation recognizes that there is a diversity within a market. Lambert and Thanopoulos apply this concept to LTC, indicating administrators may view the elderly as a single, homogenous group or as having a **diversity of needs**. Diversity of needs permits nursing-home planners to specialize by providing services to segments of the elderly population.

Market diversity in LTC could be identified by first segmenting the care offered on the basis of skilled, extended, convalescent, respite, assisted living, and so on. (Lambert and Thanopoulos) There are many other means of identifying diversity, as economic status, cultural background, sex, health, religion, and recreational interests. By knowing what segments exist, their size, characteristics, and needs, planners can determine what services will meet these needs and which service, or services, they wish to offer on the market.

REFERENT ANALYSIS

Intermediaries are an important part of the MOA. Included in this group are physicians, social workers, nurses, family-service workers, and others who assist people in selecting a nursing facility. They are referred to as **secondary consumers of care**. In the 1977 *National Nursing Home Survey* the Federal Government identified three secondary consumer groups that most often make arrangements for admission to nursing facilities. These were resident's children, other relatives, and non-relative individuals. Now there is a fourth group — HMO's that contract with nursing homes to care for the HMO's insurees.

Lambert and Thanopoulos point out the **value** of the referent analysis as a part of the MOA. It examines the role of intermediaries in the delivery of health care since they are a vital link between the consumer and the provider. They emphasize that **referent analysis** should not only identify intermediaries but also identify means of establishing active relationships with them.

Needs of the sponsor may well be included in the referent analysis. Administrators should know each sponsor's needs, interests, and expectations since the sponsor is the person most likely to move the resident if he becomes dissatisfied. The resident may be content and wish to remain in the facility, but the sponsor frequently initiates removal.

> **Example**: Mrs. Parker had been in the nursing facility for six years. She was semi-ambulatory and could handle most activities of daily living without assistance. She seldom complained. However, her daughter who visited daily filed frequent complaints--her mother's food was served cold, she was late getting her bath, her room was not cleaned early in the day, the aides were rough or they fussed at her. One day the nurse failed to administer a dose of Mrs. Parker's medicine, the only time in six years. The daughter stormed into the administrator's office announcing she was filing a complaint with Medicaid and she was moving her mother. She could not be placated. She found a place in another nursing home and came to move her

mother that afternoon. Her mother was crying and begging to stay. She said, "I know there are a few things wrong, but I like it here. I don't want to move. This is my home." Her daughter moved her anyway.

MARKETING PLAN

Purpose The **basic aim** of all marketing activity is to affect the individual behavior of the potential user. (Johnson) To do so means to change many negative attitudes toward nursing facilities. The attitude that nursing facilities are the place of last resort must give way to the belief that modern, quality LTC is the method of choice for those who cannot be cared for at home. Administrators must sell the concept that resident needs are met, the staff is capable, understanding, and patient; the facilities are comfortable and modern; and food is nourishing and satisfying.

Priorities Most marketing is currently focused on private-pay residents and third-party payment. In many areas of the country owners feel they cannot survive in the LTC industry without 25 to 40 percent private pay. As long-term-care insurance becomes more readily available, residents with this coverage will become a priority. In states where there are few veterans' facilities, nursing facilities are targeting that group for recruitment.

Developing the marketing plan involves many activities beyond routine daily management duties. Administrators would do well to study Sue Weiss' article on *The Art of Marketing in Long-Term Care.* She outlines a formula for successful marketing, creating the service model, and creating the market plan. She points out the need for setting clear, concise objectives in each step. Weiss contends that in developing the marketing plan, the facility should follow these steps

1. Identify the most promising strategies.

2. Determine what resources are available.

3. Place in sequence the strategies that fit in with the overall aims.

4. List strategies according to how and when.

5. Review the experience for total effect and apply it to the problem.

MARKETING STRATEGIES

The **marketing program** may involve a number of strategies, carried out simultaneously, that are designed to attract the interest of potential users. These activities should generate **inquiries** and potential **resident contacts**. Effective techniques for stimulating inquiries about nursing facility-services depend largely on the local market conditions and seasonality. (Johnson)

As soon as the marketing program is developed, the facility will utilize numerous public relations techniques. An ongoing, carefully monitored campaign should be launched to create: (1) a favorable image, (2) visibility, and (3) exposure. (Weiss) This presumes, of course, that the facility indeed has an attractive, affordable, quality service to offer. This kind of service is reflected in the kind of "hospitality" the facility shows. According to Webster's dictionary, hospitality is the "generous and cordial reception of guests." It is an ingredient for success and can be marketable. Hospitality attracts and keeps residents. (Blumenstein and Bernardon)

Following are some strategies that nursing homes have used and are using with considerable effectiveness:

1. **Marketing admission packet** Perhaps the most universally accepted strategy in marketing is the admission packet. It is a valuable, reliable means of informing potential residents and their families of the services provided. Myra Johnson, in her article *Marketing the Nursing Home*, presents an excellent model that administrators might well adapt to their needs.

Johnson's model includes brief descriptions of the services of every department in the facility, resident-care policies, what men and women residents should bring to the facility, visitation and resident leave, facility rules and regulations, transportation, complaints, and other pertinent information. It is brief, to the point, and in understandable language.

2. **Brochure** The two-to-four page letter-size brochure is another favored marketing strategy. It briefly describes the facility and its service and identifies persons to contact. When permissible, they may be left in physicians' offices, hospitals, and clinics. Also, they may be distributed when a facility staff member speaks to a community group. A common error in developing the brochure is to place a picture of a very debilitated resident on the cover. Instead the picture should be that of the most pleasant and attractive resident.

3. **News media** Newspapers, radio, television, and other media accessible to the entire community provide the greatest **exposure**. Letters to the editor, news releases, and feature articles generally are a part of public relations, but at the same time they can be used to attract potential customers.

4. **Paid advertising** Newspaper ads, radio and television commercials, and the yellow pages of the telephone directory are a vital part of marketing. Billboards are increasingly used in health-care marketing. In using community-oriented media as newspapers, radio, and television for whatever purpose, the facility should **highlight** the unique components of its programs. Also, care should be taken in placement of newspaper **advertisements**. They should never be placed near obituaries. (Weiss)

5. **Nursing facility** The sign identifying the facility is often overlooked as a part of marketing. An attractive, well-placed sign promotes a good public impression. The visitor first looks for the sign to identify the facility. It is a factor in creating a good first impression.

6. **Newsletters** Publishing a newsletter is increasingly popular, both as a public relations and a marketing strategy. Effective newsletters are used to arouse the interest of resident and family and to interpret the facility activities. Sometimes, however, they can pose a problem if there are other facilities in the mail-out area. It may be interpreted as recruiting their residents.

7. **Personal contacts** A major part of marketing is personal contact, especially with intermediaries or secondary consumers. A visit with key personnel and distribution of marketing material to hospitals, clinics, physicians' offices, home-health agencies, and others are valuable marketing and public relations tools. Contacts with HMO's which have Medicare contracts and provide managed care are imperative.

8. **Direct mail** The "darling of marketing" is direct mail due to its numerous communication and cost advantages over other forms of paid advertising — newspaper, radio, and television. A facility can obtain a list of names and addresses of direct mail recipients from a number of mail-list vendors. The vendors can customize the list by age, income, and geographic parameters.

There are distinct advantages to direct mail that administrators generally have not recognized. They include (a) one can precisely target the customer group he wishes to reach; (b) one can tell a story about LTC being involved in heath care, housing, and hospitality; (c) recipients are more likely to read and respond to messages received by mail than other forms of advertising; and (d) direct mail is a nonthreatening form of sales. (Thornton) The facility's staff member who coordinates marketing and public relations should fully explore use of direct mail.

There are many other marketing strategies the facility may employ. Suffice to say, marketing LTC is now imperative. Providers can no longer build LTC facilities and expect waiting lists of consumers before the doors open. First, they must know the needs and wants of the population to be served and the demand for that service — how many people need it and will use it?

OPEN MARKET AND RECRUITMENT

Open market In 1977 the courts ruled that no restrictions may be placed on advertising health-care services and prices. To do so could be restraint of trade. This ruling opened the way for marketing and recruitment activities that are sometimes questionable, but they are legal.

Recruitment Licensing boards often receive complaints that one facility is recruiting residents from another. Administrators feel strongly about staff from a competing facility visiting their facility to recruit residents and staff. They frequently request licensing board sanctions against the recruiting administrator. This places the board in an awkward position. It may agree with the complainant, but no board can forbid recruitment from another facility.

These complaints may be difficult to evaluate since it is often a matter of one person's word against another's. Recruiting administrators usually deny that any member of their staff has contacted either a resident or a staff member of another facility. On the other hand, the administrator of the recruited facility insists that contacts were made. Actual proof may be difficult since both resident and family members may deny they discussed a possible transfer with another facility. Even if proof of active recruitment is established, what sanctions can the board bring against the recruiting administrator?

Perhaps the wisest course of action would be for licensing boards to establish and enforce **recruiting ethics** along these lines:

1. No administrator may initiate or allow his staff to initiate contact to recruit a resident from another facility. Initiation must come from the resident or the family.

2. The recruiting administrator must notify the administrator of the applicant's facility before he or a staff member goes to the facility to talk with resident or family who has indicated an interest in a possible change.

3. The administrator must discuss with resident and/or family that the resident's current administrator will be notified that either the resident or a family member initiated a request.

Boards may not tell administrators they cannot recruit, but with a code of ethics they could tell the administrator **how** he can recruit. This could resolve many problems for administrators.

PUBLIC RELATIONS (PR)

Definition Public relations is managing communications between a facility and the public. The essential **difference** from marketing is that marketing seeks to attract residents (customers), while public relations seeks to involve people who have no immediate or long-range need for LTC services. (Mould) PR involves many publics with messages moving to and from them. These publics include news media, government, community, families, employees, and others.

Marketing uses communication as does PR hence in large organizations they do not rely on PR to do all their communications work. Primarily, marketing uses PR for media relations and printed materials, press releases, feature articles, newsletters, photographs, tapes, and films. In nursing facilities the marketing program and public relations program may be one and the same as they generally cannot afford, nor do they need two separate programs.

Why PR? Society has essentially refused to directly address the problem of accepting nursing facility care for the dependent elderly. Society seems preoccupied with youth, so it only learns about LTC when an unplanned crisis occurs. Generally, society does not search out LTC information. Therefore the administrator becomes the responsible person in developing and implementing a communications flow. (Peterson and Thompson)

A major **problem** in PR is that both the facility and the public seldom understand public relations. Facility personnel often do not know how to develop PR programs, and the people may tend to see PR as misleading the public. This further strengthens the concept of the administrator's responsibilities for PR since he represents the provider, and the public is the consumer. As a leader, the administrator is responsible for communication. Most public-relations activities would fall within the administrator's leadership role.

The administrator's commitment to PR and marketing is increasingly important because hospitals are entering the PR arena on behalf of their LTC alternatives and facilities. (Brandt and Allen) They have their own LTC facilities and swing beds, and many operate their own home-health service. Physicians are encouraged to refer to hospital- owned LTC facilities rather than to traditional nursing facilities.

Goals As inferred earlier, the overall goal or objective of PR is to interpret the facility to the public and the public to the facility. The establishment of additional goals is the joint responsibility of the governing board, administrator, and staff. Here again the administrator is the key person since he often must interpret PR needs to the board. Also, the administrator is responsible for the staff's understanding of the PR program and their role in it. The following goals can be attained if the organization adopts and implements an effective public relations program.

1. Increase public awareness of the purpose and progress of the nursing facility.
2. Dispel public misunderstanding of long-term care.
3. Create a positive attitude toward the facility.
4. Strengthen the bonds between facility and community, and involve the two in an interrelationship.

There is no reason why administrators do not develop strong PR programs for accomplishing these goals. Often the term public relations evokes fear in nursing facilities because of the opinion that they should not market and advertise. There is no real basis for this concept because the LTC industry must strengthen its relationships with the community. (Peterson and Thompson)

People must understand what LTC services are, why they are needed, where they are available, how to use them, and what they cost. It is the facility's duty to develop this public awareness as well as the support of the community. The facility must become a resource that the community utilizes and depends on as it does other resources.

Image building is of primary concern in both marketing and public relations. **Image** is what people see or visualize when they think of a nursing facility. The image may be that it is well-run and offers quality service, or it may be the reverse. It is referred to as **public image** when it is the general view people have of nursing facilities. Traditionally, nursing facilities have had a **poor public image**. Often they are seen as dirty, smelly facilities for warehousing the elderly and others who are waiting to die. As one congressman said, "Something between Social Security and the cemetery." Staff is seen as callous and uncaring, and the industry as primarily interested in making a profit.

A **major cause** in the 1970's for this poor image was the publicity and focus on LTC facilities by Congress and the media. A select committee on aging produced voluminous reports identifying examples of resident abuse, financial incompetence, and lack of ethical management practice. These abuses occurred, but only in a small fraction of LTC facilities. The public lost sight of the thousands of well-run facilities offering quality care. (Peterson and Thompson)

Since then medical and nursing care for the elderly has drastically changed for the better, nursing facility administration has significantly improved, and facilities have been upgraded. Still, the public has not seemed to notice that most nursing facilities have dedicated, devoted staff and provide compassionate, quality care.

Governing boards and owners contributed to this poor image when they focused primarily on the "bottom line" — their return on investment. Peterson and Thompson observe that in pre-Medicare years governing boards sometimes judged administrative competence by the relative health of the balance sheet. If the bottom line reflected the desired profit level, the facility was considered successful.

Media coverage of LTC usually is not positive. The 1985 ABC-TV program "Aging in America" focused on hospitals and home health. Their acknowledgment that nursing facilities had improved was attributed to state inspectors, stronger regulations, and stiffer penalties. No credit was given to the **growing professionalism** and dedication to **quality care** that providers, administrators, and staff have developed since 1970. A major **reason** for image-building is that the public still does not recognize that improvements in care are largely due to the professionalism of providers.

The **need** for image-building in LTC is further emphasized by the fact that hospitals, home-health agencies, life-care communities, and community programs for the aging have a far more positive image. Nursing facilities must develop and implement programs that improve their public image to a level equivalent to these competitors. Unfortunately, the LTC industry tends to be **complacent** about its negative public image. Brandt and Allen say this is probably due to several circumstances. The negative image has not hurt the industry's "bottom line." In 1986 occupancy rates were 95 percent, the aging population was rapidly increasing, and most facilities had waiting lists. It is now evident that with increased competition frequent referrals and waiting lists are decreasing.

PR Specialists are moving into the LTC industry and may present themselves as indispensable to an adequate program. Although they may make a significant contribution to developing and maintaining a viable PR program, many facilities feel they cannot afford the costs. In truth, good public relations programs can be planned and operated by administrators and staff without expert assistance. However, there are often media crises when a PR specialist should be called in. This might occur when negative news stories appear in the newspaper, such as a nursing home being fined for being out of compliance, an outbreak of food poisoning, or a staff member abusing a resident. Choose a PR specialist who knows something about LTC. Use them to help develop a step by step program. Usually, PR specialists can talk directly to the press and help to clarify issues and enlist more objective coverage. (Ihle and Shell)

PR Program After goals are set, strategies are selected and implemented and, as already described, most are directed toward building a positive public image. Administrators may find Stephen Mould's **ten commandments of public relations** helpful in promoting this image and maintaining effective public relations. These are:

1. Knowledge of the facility and latest developments, or where to obtain information,
2. Interest in community needs and activities so the facility is not isolated,
3. Visibility to the community,
4. Friendliness, courtesy, understanding, and helpfulness,
5. Sensitivity to others, paying attention to what they say,
6. Honesty in admitting mistakes,
7. Involvement in community affairs,
8. Simple understandable language in speech and writing,
9. Involve as many people as possible in the facility and community activities,
10. Alertness to changing needs of residents, staff, and community.

These ten points can be helpful in all of the following strategies.

1. **Communication** strategy comes first since it permeates every aspect of PR. The **type** of communication **strategy** should depend on the interest in and use of information by the public the facility wishes to reach. Numerous PR specialists have identified five types of public and what should be done with each.

a. When the public has a low probability of seeking or processing information, an effort to communicate is wasted. Nobody listens or acts.

b. If the low probability public is important because it can have severe consequences on the nursing facility, the facility might do the information processing. That segment of the public might retain enough information to recognize a problem which could result in information-seeking.

c. A public that will process rather than seek information requires very different strategies as photos, illustrations, clever writing, catchy phrases, and so on.

d. When the public actively seeks and acts on information, the LTC facility cannot maintain a low profile. It must communicate desired information or the public will obtain information elsewhere and, whether correct or not, it will act on the information.

e. Nursing facilities cannot expect many people to change understanding, attitude, and behavior when information is communicated. Consequently, LTC needs to concentrate on the members of the public who will listen and act and/or who will likely need information on LTC.

2. **Image-building strategies** could make up the entire PR program since a positive image is the primary goal of PR. Before implementing any image-building strategy it is mandatory that the LTC facility provide quality resident care.

   Tour of the facility is considered to be the number one image-building strategy. Getting people in by holding open house, conducting holiday events, and holding wellness fairs can bring the public in. Take them on a tour to see the facility, meet staff, and observe residents in their activities. It is often noted that the people who know most about a nursing home are those who have never set foot inside a facility.

3. **Employee meetings** are the most frequently used image-building strategy according to a 1985 study conducted by the ACHCA. Such meetings familiarize employees with PR goals and strategies and help them understand their role in building good community relations. In many facilities employees are not aware that they are involved in public relations when, in fact, every employee is a part of public relations.

4. **Least used** strategies with great potential identified in the ACHCA survey were **lobbying, letters to the editor, annual reports,** and **health fairs**. Lobbying is obviously important. Legislators want to know the needs of the LTC industry. They need accurate, correct information. Who, better than administrators can provide it?

5. **First impressions** The most important step in PR concerning **residents and families** is to create a good first impression. One will never have a second chance to do so. The key person in creating the desired impression is the receptionist and/or telephone operator. This employee should be well-trained in responding to the social, emotional, and financial stresses family members may experience. That is not to say the employee has all the answers. He knows where to refer people for correct answers.

The **administrator** and all administrative staff are important to creating a good first impression. Administrators should always meet the resident and/or responsible family members before or at the time of admission. It is a time to allay their anxieties, reassure them regarding their decision, and impress them that the staff is interested and understanding.

Arlene Glick and Bill Wojcik in their article *Increasing Public Awareness* suggest several strategies for utilizing **community interaction** to promote public image. Their strategies focus on involving **children** since this will develop the interest of parents or teachers and their pupils, local officials, and community organizations. Also, they suggest that if the facility sponsors an event that raises money, donate it to a charity. This will enhance public image. This can often be accomplished when there is a fair or other community event.

Example: At a Mardi Gras festival in New Orleans an administrator set up a Cajun hamburger stand along the parade route. By Ash Wednesday he had cleared more than $500 which he presented to a local Boy Scout troop at a special ceremony. Newspaper, radio, and television representatives gave it widespread publicity as a community service. The facility message was clear: "We are interested in the community, not just our facility. We want to contribute." It helps the community understand that the nursing facility does not exist just to receive help but to contribute to community well being.

The following strategies, numbered 6, 7, 8, and 9, are suggested by Glick and Wojcik. Refer to their article for details.

6. **Wellness fairs (health fairs)** involve resident, family, staff, and the community at large. They may include such activities as blood pressure monitoring, nutritional advice, lectures by health specialists, educational pamphlets from health organizations, and so on. It is of primary importance to conduct the fair at the nursing facility. The objective is to attract the public to the facility and let them see first hand what it is like. Letting outsiders come in and meet residents and staff and observe programs corrects many false impressions. The wellness fair is one of the most effective means of accomplishing this.

   Example: A nursing facility in a small town conducted a wellness fair inviting students, teachers, community, and government officials. In addition to events listed above they served cookies, soft drinks, and sandwiches outside under a tent. Everyone was invited to take a tour of the facility with an employee as guide. The administrator noticed that a local judge was visiting and shaking hands, but he had not gone into the facility. When the administrator asked, the judge hesitantly said, "No, I haven't been inside." The administrator insisted that he personally take the judge on tour. When they completed the tour and walked out the judge said, "I'm glad you took me around. I have made decisions for years that affected nursing homes but had never been inside one. I think I have a better understanding of what it's like."

7. **Involve churches** by holding a breakfast for ministers, by conducting a training program on the church's role in helping the aging, by providing speakers to church groups concerned with the problems of aging, and other activities of interest to churches. Many churches have Young at Heart and other senior citizen groups that are anxious to know more about aging and elder-care facilities. They welcome speakers.

8. **Holiday events** Halloween, Independence Day, Valentine's Day, and other special days are well-suited for providing programs utilizing their special themes. Resident activity directors often find these useful for involving residents, families, volunteers, and other community groups. They are also a good time to conduct a tour of the facility.

9. **Joint sponsorship** can involve civic clubs, the YMCA and YWCA, the police and fire departments, and other groups in joining the facility in sponsoring events. This is largely an unexplored strategy that offers promise for community involvement.

10. **Community service groups** offer administrators and key staff an opportunity to participate in community service. These include health organizations as American Cancer Society, Alzheimer's, American Heart Association, Diabetes Foundation, and so on. The administrator should: (a) seek to serve on boards and committees of these groups; (b) encourage the groups to use the facility's meeting rooms; and (c) arrange for the facility to sponsor a community service group.

11. **Education programs** are very important. A strong community-education program can dispel myths about nursing facilities and show that the facility is interested in the entire community, that it is not an isolated, final resource.

Education programs should be designed: (a) to utilize the talents of staff members; (b) to conduct courses within the facility for residents, staff, and family; and (c) to conduct classes and disseminate health information on the diseases of the aging for the public. Indeed, the nursing facility should seek to become the **center of geriatric information** in the community. The administrator can enhance the image of his **profession** as well as the long-term-care industry by making the facility a community resource in all matters pertaining to geriatric care. (Peterson and Thompson)

Nursing facilities have not traditionally been considered an important community resource. Peterson and Thompson point out that this is associated with problems such as: (a) the public, other than family and friends, seldom visit the facility; (b) few people are interested in serving as volunteers or board members; (c) people become grudgingly involved but would rather not; and (d) employees seldom have pride and loyalty to the facility because they are aware of negative public attitudes.

Unfortunately for the long-term-care industry, hospitals in many metropolitan areas have developed **centers of geriatric information**. Some use the campus approach which includes the hospital for acute care, one or more nursing facilities, a home-health agency, a day-care facility for elderly, assisted-living units, and an information center. The center provides resident and family counseling and referral. Some will do a full **geriatric evaluation** and assist the family in developing plans for care.

12. **Managing the media** is imperative. It has played a significant role in nursing homes' poor image. As mentioned earlier, this may be a reason for hiring a marketing and public relations specialist to help develop a program. It should include periodic **news releases, but these must be carefully written.** An overlooked practice in news releases is the distribution of the releases to the facility staff, residents, and family. The value is to keep these persons informed of the facility's news and to promote better relations within the facility.

Feature articles attract attention. Almost every facility does something unique or has a resident whose age, background, or current activities make him ideal for a feature story. When feature stories are accompanied by photographs, administrators should consider the impact on the public. Photographs of the most debilitated, depressed, unsightly residents do not help with PR.

Letters to the editor are increasingly highlighted by newspapers. Many place them in a large section of the editorial page where they are not only read but responded to by others. (Pincus) Negative criticism of LTC should never go unchallenged in these columns.

Ihle and Shell list some important do's and don'ts that should be followed in talking with newsmedia.

a. Identify key talking points prior to an interview by the media.

b. Be polite to reporters. They are not enemies.

c. Never say "no comment." It will likely result in a negative report in the news.

d. Always return calls from the media. They can make failure to return a call sound very negative.

e. Don't speak in LTC jargon.

f. Never say anything is "off the record."

g. Never lie.

h. Never let accusations go unanswered.

i. When talking with a reporter try to begin with a key point; don't ramble.

13. **Respite care** is a valuable community service that is easy to provide. When caretakers of an elderly person need a week or two of rest or vacation, the facility can provide the needed care. The facility likely will not make a profit offering short-term respite care, but the PR effect can be valuable. If the person needs

LTC later, the respite care may be good recruitment.

14. **Volunteers** are a voice of the community and they return to the community to share their experiences in the facility. They should be seen as a part of PR. Special events for them can be rewarding. Noting birthdays by sending greeting cards, selecting a volunteer of the month, and celebrating volunteer's day are effective strategies.

15. **Sponsors** are a key target in any successful public relations program. As stated earlier, needs of the sponsor must be considered since they often remove the resident when the sponsor is dissatisfied with services. Many times sponsors are a far greater problem to the facility than the resident.

Other PR strategies are being developed and utilized by individual facilities. These include: (1) a facility-operated **nursery school** for the children of staff and the community; (2) regular **letters** and/or cards to residents' **families**; (3) invitations to family members for a **meal** with their resident; (4) **annual reports** to key members of the public and to families; and many others.

A planned public-relations program and funds to implement it are now imperative to the successful planning and operation of nursing facilities. The administrator must take the lead and make it an integral part of this facility's overall program which should involve all staff.

Written Public Relations Program Most LTC facilities are active in public-relations activities, but they have no written program. They have not stopped to conceptualize what they are doing and reduced it to writing so all staff understands the significance of their activities. Effectiveness is greatly enhanced when the program is written and they are fully aware of their roles. The written program should include goals, strategies, time factors, and staff assignments. Periodically, the administrator and department heads should evaluate the program's effectiveness. At least annually, the administrator should report on the PR program to the governing body.

GLOSSARY

ACHCA **American College of Health Care Administrators,** a national organization for nursing home administrators.

Market The demand for a given service or product by the people who will purchase.

Market diversity The diversity of need within a given market. The LTC market is comprised of many groups with similar needs.

Market segmentation Identifying the diverse groups within a market that may respond to a particular service, such as: skilled nursing, intermediate care, day care, and sheltered housing.

Marketable A service or product that is of the quality and nature to be offered for sale on the market.

Marketing The act or process of selling or purchasing services or products in the marketplace and managing their flow from producer/provider to the consumer.

MOA **Market opportunity analysis** is the systematic means of developing and maintaining information that reflects the needs and desires of potential consumers and markets.

Public image The general view people hold of a service or product concerning its quality, worth, value, and desirability.

PR Public relations is the management of communications between an organization and the many publics with which it is concerned.

Referent analysis Examining the role of intermediaries such as social workers, physicians, nurses, and family who are a vital link between the nursing facility and the consumer.

Respite care Temporary care of a person needing nursing-facility service, usually for a few weeks while family members need a rest.

Strategies Planned courses of action to be used to accomplish established goals.

Swing beds Beds in hospitals operating less than 100 beds that are certified for use as an LTC bed or acute bed as need dictates.

To market Exposing a service or product, offering it for sale in the marketplace, and developing sales potential.

Wellness (health) fair An event involving residents, family, and community, which includes entertainment and such activities as blood pressure checks, nutritional advice, lectures on aging, and others.

REFERENCES

Blumenstein, Wendy and Arthur Bernardon, "Find Creative Ways to Market Hospitality", *Provider,* Vol. 22, No. 4, Washington: AHCA, 1996.

Brandt, Mardell E., and Susan Allen, "Marketing the Image Inside and Out," *Provider*, 12:33-35, March 1986.

Glick, A., and B. Wojcik, "Increasing Public Awareness," *Contemporary Long-Term Care*, 8:25-27, Feb. 1985.

Ihle, Bill and Dianne Shell, 'How to Manage the Media Effectively", *Provider*, Vol. 22, No. 1, Washington: AHCA, 1996.

Jensen, Joyce, and Bill Jackson, "Planning, Marketing are Top Priorities for Administrators in Next 12 Months," *Marketing the Long-Term Care Facility*, ACHCA, pp. 6-7, February 1986.

Johnson, Myra, "Marketing the Nursing Home," *Marketing Long-Term Care*, ACHCA, pp. 12-18, February 1986.

Lambert, Nancy, and John Thanopoulos, "A Dynamic Planning Framework for Nursing Homes," *Marketing the Long-Term Care Facility*, ACHCA, pp. 8-11, February 1986.

Lasek, Alicia, "Getting a Read on Company Publications", *Provider,* Vol. 22, No. 5, Washington: AHCA, 1996.

Luther, William, *The Marketing Plan,* New York: AMACOM, 1992.

Mould, Stephen L., "Ten Ways to Shape Image," *Provider*, 12:51, March 1986.

National Nursing Home Survey: 1977 Summary for the United States, Public Health Service, National Center for Health Statistics, Hyattsville, MD: July 1979.

Peterson, Keith, and John R. Thompson, "The Role of the Administrator" in G.K. Stryker and R. Stryker, editors, *Creative Long-Term Care Administration*, Springfield, IL: C. C. Thomas Publisher, 1985.

Pincus, J.D., "Public Relations: Prescription for an Ailing Public Image," *Journal of Long-Term Care Administration*, spring 1986.

Thornton, Phyllis M., "Direct Mail: The Darling of Marketing," Nursing *Homes*, Vol. 44, No. 10, Cleveland: MARQUEST Communications, Inc., 1995.

Vitale, Joseph, *The Complete Guide to Small Business Advertising,* Lincolnwood, IL: NTC Business Books, 1995,

Winston, William J., Editor, *Marketing Long-Term and Senior Care Services*, New York: The Haworth Press, Inc., 1984.

CHAPTER 6

PERSONNEL MANAGEMENT

PERSONNEL MANAGEMENT

PERSONNEL MANAGEMENT

Personnel management encompasses the staffing function discussed in Chapter 3. It involves determining staffing needs, developing job descriptions, establishing pay schedules and employee benefits, recruiting, interviewing, selecting, orienting, training, promoting, demoting, terminating, and retiring employees. Often this is referred to as **human resource management,** and that's what it is. The administrator's task is to create and maintain a work environment that promotes communications and understanding between management and staff. He must have a plan for managing his human resources just as he does for managing financial, physical, and other resources under his direction.

Purpose The primary purpose or goal of personnel management is to provide quality resident care with efficiency and economy. To do so, facilities must employ a qualified person for each position, create an environment that promotes quality performance, and retain these employees. Failure in any of these areas results in the lessening of efficiency and economy of operations which, in turn, means poorer quality of care.

Personnel management requires extensive knowledge of **government regulations** that affect employment of personnel. In addition to the Health Care Finance Administration's (HCFA's) Medicare/Medicaid personnel requirements, many other government agencies impose standards on hiring, utilizing, and separating personnel from service. These include the Wage and Hour Division, the Equal Employment Opportunity Commission (EEOC), the Immigration and Naturalization Service (INS), the Occupational Safety and Health Administration (OSHA), the Americans with Disabilities Act (ADA), the National Labor Relations Board, the Social Security Administration, the Internal Revenue Service, and state offices of employment security. Regulations that are imposed by some of these agencies will be discussed in this chapter, others in following chapters.

STAFFING

The overall picture There were 1,333,300 full-time equivalent (FTE) employees in nursing homes during 1995 according to the National Nursing Home Survey. (Table 6.1) That means there were 75.3 FTE's per 100 beds, or three-fourth's of an FTE per bed. Several factors influenced the actual number of employees per 100 beds. *Ownership* shows more FTE's per 100 beds in not-for-profit facilities (81.8) than in the for-profit facilities (71.5). Also the smaller facilities - 50 beds or less - had more FTE's per 100 beds (83.7) than the larger facilities - 200 or more beds - which had 75.6 FTE's per 100 residents. Table 6.1 reflects that type of certification, and the census region shows a difference in FTE's per 100 beds.

Nursing hours per resident per day is a significant factor in staffing. HCFA requires that the number of nursing hours/resident/day stipulated to meet the residents' needs be provided. Some states set a specific number of hours, such as 2.65 for SNF's and 2.35 for NF's. Other states hesitate to do this as some nursing homes automatically make this minimum their maximum. These facilities try to hold the nursing hours/resident/day at the required standard for economic reasons, and quality of care suffers.

In practice, no facility can meet resident needs in the minimum set by a state. Note in Table 6.2 that actual nursing hours per resident/day provided in 1997 ranged from 2.9 in Iowa and Kansas to 4.3 in Florida and Hawaii.

In planning his direct-care-staff ratio the administrator should determine if his state sets a minimum number of nursing hours per resident day. In a state with minimum hours, if surveyors found no deficiency in resident care but the facility did not meet the minimum hours required, the state could declare this a deficiency.

Staffing patterns The administrator must first determine staff requirements for a nursing

Table 6.1:

Number of Full-time Equivalent Employees by Occupational Category - 1995 NNHS

	Occupational Category													
					Nursing									
	All FTE Employees		Administrative, medical and therapeutic		Total Nursing		RNs		LPNs		Aides/Orderlies		All Other Staff	
Facility Characteristics	Number	Rate per 100 beds	Number	Rate per 100 beds	Number	Rate per 100 beds	Number	Rate per 100 beds	Number	Rate per 100 beds	Number	Rate per 100 beds	Number	Rate per 100 beds
Total #	**1,333,300**	**75.3**	**20,100**	**1.1**	**913,500**	**51.6**	**129,700**	**7.3**	**185,700**	**10.5**	**600,500**	**33.9**	**399,700**	**22.6**
Ownership														
For Profit	823,000	71.5	13,600	1.2	547,100	49.8	78,000	6.8	118,300	10.3	379,500	32.9	235,300	20.4
Not For Profit	383,100	81.8	4,900	1	254,300	54.3	38,300	8.2	51,500	11.0	164,700	35.2	123,900	26.5
Government	127,200	84.2	1,600	1.1	85,100	56.3	13,300	9.0	15,900	10.5	56,300	37.3	40,500	26.8
Certification														
Medicare/Medicaid	1,055,900	76.6	15,000	1.1	727,900	52.8	105,800	707.0	149,600	10.9	473,900	34.4	313,000	22.7
Medicare Only	52,800	88.5	1,900	302	35,800	60.0	7,400	12.4	7,000	11.7	21,100	35.4	15,100	25.3
Medicaid Only	191,600-	68.4	2,800	1	127,500	45.5	13,600	4.8	24,300	8.7	90,400	32.3	61,300	21.9
Not Certified	33,000	62.8	400	0.8	22,300	42.4	3,000	5.7	4,800	9.1	15,100	28.7	10,300	19.6
Bed Size														
Less than 50 Beds	73,000	83.7	4,700	5.4	49,600	56.8	10,700	12.3	11,100	12.8	29,000	33.3	18,700	21.4
50-99 Beds	320,500	74.5	5,200	1.2	221,400	51.4	29,200	6.8	43,000	10.0	148,800	34.6	93,900	21.8
100-199 Beds	674,500	74.7	8,400	0.9	468,500	51.9	63,700	7.1	96,500	10.7	310,100	34.4	197,600	21.9
200 bed or more	265,300	75.6	1,800	0.5	174,000	49.6	26,100	7.4	35,100	10.0	112,700	32.1	89,500	25.5
Census Region														
Northeast	310,400	81.9	4,200	1.1	214,500	56.6	38,000	10.0	39,300	10.4	136,600	36.0	91,700	24.2
Midwest	388,300	68.8	4,800	0.9	264,300	46.8	40,100	7.1	54,300	9.6	171,600	30.4	119,200	21.1
South	435,100	76.0	6,300	1.1	299,800	52.3	30,200	5.3	65,700	11.5	204,800	35.8	129,000	22.5
West	199,500	78.3	4,800	1.9	134,900	52.9	21,500	8.4	26,500	10.4	87,600	34.3	59,800	23.5

Source: National Center for Health Statistics - 1995 National Nursing Home Survey as printed in Advanced Data, Number 280, January 23, 1997. American Health Care Association

facility – registered nurses (RN's), licensed practical nurses (LPN's or LVN's), physicians, therapists, aides, social workers, dietitians, and others. Secondly, according to facility size and type of resident, he must determine the number of employees that is needed in each category. In a sense, the administrator **forecasts** staffing needs for he is concerned with both present and future needs due to turnover, facility expansion, and other factors.

Table 6.3 should help an administrator determine his staffing. The figure shows a HCFA form 671 that the administrator must complete and make available to surveyors. Note that it includes all categories of employees by service and hours worked by full-time and part-time staff, but not consultants. Numbers of personnel are fairly typical of a 120 bed skilled nursing facility.

Although HCFA does not specify the number of personnel needed to staff a facility, it sets standards for all personnel involved in resident care and for some other personnel. Following are staffing patterns and requirements by department.

Table 6.2:

Average Facility Direct Care Nursing Hours by Position by State per Patient Day - 1997

Hours per Day	Average CNA Hours per Patient Day	Average LPN Hours per Patient Day	Average RN Hours per Patient Day	Average Total Nursing Hours per Patient Day	Number Facility Residents
United States	**2.3**	**0.7**	**0.5**	**3.5**	**88**
Alabama	2.7	1.1	0.3	4.0	102
Alaska	2.6	0.6	0.7	3.9	41
Arizona	2.7	0.9	0.5	4.1	84
Arkansas	2.2	0.8	0.1	3.2	78
California	2.5	0.7	0.4	3.7	76
Colorado	2.3	0.8	0.5	3.7	75
Connecticut	2.3	0.5	0.5	3.4	116
Delaware	2.4	0.6	0.6	3.7	88
Florida	2.7	1.1	0.4	4.3	92
Georgia	2.3	0.9	0.2	3.4	101
Hawaii	3.0	0.6	0.6	4.3	82
Idaho	2.9	0.8	0.5	4.2	56
Illinois	2.1	0.5	0.5	3.1	98
Indiana	1.8	1.0	0.4	3.2	77
Iowa	2.0	0.5	0.4	2.9	65
Kansas	1.9	0.6	0.4	2.9	57
Kentucky	2.5	1.0	0.3	3.8	71
Louisiana	2.3	0.9	0.1	3.3	91
Maine	2.9	0.5	0.7	4.0	61
Maryland	2.6	0.8	0.7	4.0	104
Massachusetts	2.6	0.7	0.6	3.9	91
Michigan	2.6	0.7	0.5	3.7	99
Minnesota	2.3	0.7	0.4	3.4	94
Mississippi	2.3	0.9	0.3	3.6	78
Missouri	2.2	0.8	0.3	3.4	71
Montana	2.7	0.7	0.6	3.9	61
Nebraska	2.2	0.7	0.4	3.3	66
Nevada	2.1	0.9	0.6	3.6	80
New Hampshire	2.7	0.6	0.7	3.9	90
New Jersey	2.3	0.6	0.5	3.5	135
New Mexico	2.4	0.6	0.4	3.4	72
New York	2.1	0.6	0.3	3.0	170
North Carolina	2.6	0.8	0.4	3.9	92
North Dakota	2.6	0.6	0.4	3.6	76
Ohio	2.5	0.9	0.5	3.9	82
Oklahoma	1.8	0.7	0.1	2.6	61
Oregon	2.4	0.4	0.6	3.4	68
Pennsylvania	2.2	0.7	0.5	3.4	109
Rhode Island	2.4	0.4	0.5	3.4	94
South Carolina	2.6	1.0	0.3	4.0	87
South Dakota	2.2	0.3	0.6	3.2	67
Tennessee	2.2	0.9	0.2	3.2	100
Texas	2.2	0.8	0.2	3.3	67
Utah	2.4	0.7	0.6	3.7	62
Vermont	2.4	0.7	0.5	3.6	79
Virginia	2.4	0.8	0.3	3.5	99
Washington	2.8	0.6	0.7	4.2	80
Washington DC	2.6	0.9	0.4	3.9	134
West Virginia	2.5	0.9	0.3	3.7	76
Wisconsin	2.5	0.5	0.6	3.6	99
Wyoming	2.7	0.6	0.6	3.9	68

Source: HCFA - OSCAR Form 671: F41-43, current surveys as of 3/1/98. American Health Care Association

Table 6.3:

FACILITY STAFFING

	No. FTEs	Tag Number	A Services Provided 1	2	3	B Full-Time Staff (hours)	C Part-Time Staff (hours)	D Contract (hours)
Administration	4	F33				3 2 0		
Physician Services		F34						
Medical Director		F35						
Other Physician		F36						
Physician Extender		F37						
Nursing Services		F38						
RN Director of Nurses	1	F39				8 0		
Nurses with Admin. Duties	1	F40				8 0		
Registered Nurses	7.4	F41				1 1 2		
Licensed Practical/ Licensed Vocational Nurses	14	F42				1 1 2 0		
Certified Nurse Aides	39.3	F43				3 1 5 0		
Nurse Aides in Training		F44						
Medication Aides/Technicians		F45						
Pharmacists		F46						
Dietary Services		F47						
Dietitian		F48						
Food Serivce Workers	9.4	F49				7 5 2		
Therapeutic Services		F50						
Occupational Therapists		F51						
Occupational Therapy Assistants		F52						
Occupational Therapy Aides		F53						
Physical Therapists		F54						
Physical Therapy Assistants		F55						
Physical Therapy Aides		F56						
Speech/Language Pathologist		F57						
Therapeutic Recreation Specialist		F58						
Qualified Activities Professional	1	F59				8 0		
Other Activities Staff	1	F60					4 0	
Qualified Social Workers	1	F61				8 0		
Other Social Services Staff		F62						
Dentists		F63						
Podiatrists		F64						
Mental Health Services		F65						
Vocational Services		F66						
Clinical Laboratory Services		F67						
Diagnostic X-ray Services		F68						
Administration and Storage of Blood		F69						
Housekeeping Service	5.8	F70				4 6 4		
Other Maintenance/Laundry	4	F71				3 2 0		

Name of Person Completing Form	Time
Signature	Date

Form: HCFA - 671 (7-95)

* Number of FTEs column added

Administration A **governing body** is mandated by OBRA as discussed in Chapter 4. The **administrator** must be licensed by the state which determines qualifications for licensing. [42CFR483.75 (d)] State Medicaid agencies may add other requirements, such as the administrator position must be his principal occupation, he must be in the facility a certain number of hours per week, he must live within one hour of normal driving time of the facility, and others. Some states require administrators to spend a reasonable and adequate amount of time on site. This causes problems since the Department of Labor rules that administrators are exempt from wages and hours and that only the governing body can specify the number of hours an administrator is to work. A very few states will allow an administrator to direct two nursing homes so long as they are within a specified driving time of each other and of the administrator's place of residence.

Nursing staff (42CFR483.30) Both SNF's and NF's must have sufficient nursing staff to provide nursing and related services for attaining and maintaining the highest practicable physical, mental, and psychosocial well-being of each resident. This level of well-being is determined by resident assessments and individual plans of care. Except as noted later under waivers, **sufficient staff** means the facility provides services of licensed nurses and other nursing personnel on a 24-hour basis. The numbers of each must be adequate to provide nursing care to all residents in accordance with resident care plans. Nursing requirements for a nursing facility follow.

1. **Director of Nursing (DON)** Except as noted under waivers the DON must be a registered nurse, and a registered nurse must be on duty the two days per week that the DON is not on duty. This means that a registered nurse must be on duty eight consecutive hours per day, seven days per week. This requirement may be waived as noted under waivers.

2. **Charge nurse** A licensed nurse (RN, LPN, or LVN) must serve as charge nurse on each tour of duty unless a waiver is granted. The DON may serve as charge nurse only when the facility has an average daily occupancy of 60 residents or fewer.

   Duties of DON's and charge nurses are discussed in Chapter 12 on Resident Care Management.

3. **Other nurses** The facility must determine the number of floor nurses, if any, needed in addition to the DON and charge nurses in order to meet the requirement of providing sufficient nursing staff. The number will largely depend on the size of the facility and the type of residents served. The larger the facility and the more debilitated the residents, the larger the number of nurses required.

Waivers may be granted an NF for the requirements to provide: (a) a registered nurse at least eight consecutive hours per day for seven days per week, (b) a licensed nurse on a 24-hour per day basis, and (c) a licensed nurse as charge nurse on each tour of duty. Waivers may be granted if the following conditions are met:

a. The facility demonstrates to the satisfaction of the state that the facility has been unable, despite diligent efforts, to recruit appropriate personnel. Diligent effort includes offering wages at the prevailing rate for nursing facilities in the community and advertising.

b. The state determines that a waiver of the requirement will not endanger the health and safety of residents.

c. The state finds that for any periods in which licensed nursing services are not available, a registered nurse or a physician is available. This must be an arrangement in which the RN or the physician is obligated to respond immediately to telephone calls from the facility.

Any waiver granted on the above basis to an NF is subject to annual review by the state. In granting or renewing a waiver the state may require the facility to use other qualified, licensed personnel. The state agency granting the waiver must provide notice of the waiver to the state LTC ombudsman and the protection and advocacy systems for mentally retarded and mentally ill. The nursing facility must notify residents, or the appropriate guardians or legal representatives of residents, and members of their families when it is granted a waiver.

Many states, although having the authority, do not grant waivers for DON's or for charge nurses. This regulation is permissive, allowing the state to make the choice.

A SNF waiver of the requirement for a registered nurse for more than 40 hours per week may be granted by the Secretary of DHHS. This may include the director of nursing. This waiver may be granted if the facility meets these conditions:

a. It is located in a rural area and the supply of skilled nursing facility services in the area is not adequate to meet the needs of individuals residing in the area.

b. The facility has one full-time registered nurse who is regularly on duty 40 hours per week. The facility must have only residents whose physicians have indicated through physician's orders or admission notes that they do not require the services of a registered nurse or a physician for a 48-hour period. Instead of this type of physician's orders, the facility could be waived if it has arrangements for a registered nurse or a physician to provide necessary skilled nursing services on days when the regular full-time registered nurse is not on duty.

A facility certified for both Medicare and Medicaid may not be granted a waiver of the SNF provisions for a registered nurse. A waiver of the registered nurse requirements for a SNF of DHHS is subject to annual review by the Secretary. He provides notices of the waiver to the state LTC ombudsman and the protection and advocacy system in the state for mentally ill and mentally retarded. The facility notifies the residents, or their appropriate representatives, and the families of the waiver.

Surveyors must conduct a survey of nursing service if a waiver is requested and if one is granted. They will determine (a) if a continued effort to recruit is being made; (b) how residents needs are met; (c) whether resident-care policies and procedures are followed on each shift; (d) is there a qualified person to assess, evaluate, plan, and implement care plans; (e) is care provided on each shift in accord with professional practice standards; (f) can they ensure that health and safety of residents will not be or is not endangered by a waiver; (g) are there indications of decreased quality of care; (h) is there an increase in hospitalizing residents; and other evidence a waiver should not be granted or be permitted to continue. In the SNF, surveyors will provide information to the Secretary of DHHS when there is a request to continue a waiver.

4. **Certified Nurse Aide (CNA)** The most detailed requirements promulgated by OBRA for nursing facility personnel are for nurse aides. [42CFA483.75(e)] They are **defined** as any individual providing nursing or nursing related services to residents in a facility who is not a **licensed health-care professional**, a registered dietitian, or someone who volunteers to provide such services without pay. Licensed health care professionals include physician, and physician assistant; nurse practitioner; physical, speech, and occupational therapists; physical or occupational therapy assistants; registered professional nurse; licensed practical nurse; and licensed or certified social worker.

The state Medicaid agency must establish a **nurse aide certification program** that meets federal standards for the nurse-aide training and competency program and establish a **certified nurse aide-registry** (CNA Registry). Details of this program are discussed in Chapter 11 on Regulatory Management.

Employing nurse aides The facility must always consult the state CNA Registry before employing a nurse aide. The CNA Registry will show whether the person is properly certified and if there is a record of abuse, neglect, or misappropriation of resident property. Only those on the Registry without a record of violation may be employed. There is an **exception** as the facility can use an individual for up to four months without certification provided the person is undergoing approved training. See Chapter 11 for details.

Medical Director Every nursing facility must designate a physician as medical director. [42CFR483.75(i)] The medical director may be one of the regular attending physicians or the facility may employ a qualified physician, usually on a part-time basis. Many retired physicians are willing to serve in this capacity for a nominal fee. Details of their duties and role in resident care are covered in Chapter 12.

Social worker The facility is required to employ a social worker, or as they are sometimes called a **social service designee**. [42CFR483.15(g)] Facilities with more than 120 beds must employ a full-time **qualified social worker**. A qualified social worker must have at least a bachelor's degree in social work or in a human services field including, but not limited to sociology, special education, rehabilitation counseling, and psychology, **plus** one year of supervised social work experience in a health-care setting working directly with individuals. Facilities with 120 beds or less may employ a part-time person to serve in this capacity. When social workers are properly used by the administration it is advisable to employ them full-time due to the significant role they play in resident care and family counseling. Usually, each state sets the requirements for social workers in facilities with 120 beds or less. They may require certain training and certification in social-service work.

The specific duties of social workers and the role of the social service program in resident care are discussed in Chapter 12 on Resident Care Management.

Resident Activity Director (RAD) The facility must employ a qualified professional to direct the activity program. (42CFR483.15(f) (2)] Preferred qualifications are a **therapeutic recreation specialist** who is licensed or registered, as applicable, and is eligible for certification as a therapeutic recreation specialist. This professional is trained in the use of music, dance, drama, recreation, and other activities in a medical setting. Others who qualify as activity director are (1) an activities professional recognized by an accrediting body, (2) a person with two years experience in a social or recreational program within the past five years, one year of which was full-time in a resident activities program in a health-care setting, (3) a qualified occupational therapist or occupational therapy assistant, or (4) a person who has completed an activities training program approved by the state. Most states approve a training program that certifies activity directors, and smaller nursing homes generally employ directors with this background. States may allow the activity director to be employed part-time dependent on the size of the facility.

Duties of activity directors and the role of their program in resident care are discussed in Chapter 12 on Resident Care Management.

Dietary staffing is discussed in Chapter 9 on Dietary Management.

Dietary, housekeeping, laundry, and maintenance are staffed according to the individual facility's needs. There are no OBRA requirements regarding personnel in these service departments. An important standard practice is that a full-time person be appointed supervisor in each of these departments so some one person can be held accountable for proper performance.

Rehabilitation specialists A facility that provides rehabilitation services must employ qualified specialists. These may include (1) physical therapists, (2) occupational therapists, (3) speech-language therapists, and (4) mental health rehabilitation specialists in mental illness and mental retardation. Each of these are licensed, certified, or registered in accordance with applicable state laws. Many facilities contract for rehabilitation services so they do not employ a specialist on the staff. The administrator is responsible for ensuring that contractual specialists are fully qualified to perform service. [42CFR483.45(b)]

Pharmacists Usually, only very large facilities hire a full-time pharmacist. Most facilities hire pharmacists on a contractual basis. The administrator must ensure that the pharmacist is not only licensed but is also authorized by the Drug Enforcement Administration (DEA) if he is to destroy discontinued scheduled drugs. [42CFR483.60] Details of the pharmacist's duties are discussed in Chapter 12 on Resident Care Management.

POLICIES, PROCEDURES AND RULES (PPR's)

The first step in personnel management is to develop policies, procedures, and rules. Their **purpose** is to serve as guidelines providing information on what employees can expect from management and what management expects in regard to work performance and behavior. **Policies** guide the decision making of the staff, **procedures** guide the actions to carrying out individual tasks, and **rules** specify certain actions to be taken or not to be taken. See Chapter 3 for further details on these organizational plans.

The facility manual must include all personnel PPR's. Since a majority of an administrator's problems usually are with employees, organizations tend to write more PPR's on personnel than on other activities. The manual is a staff guide that should be written in simple language that all employees can understand. Personnel PPR's may be in a separate manual or a chapter in the overall facility manual. Many facilities have a separate **employee handbook** that is even more simply written and covers the more pertinent day-to-day personnel PPR's A copy is given to every employee. The overall personnel manual should include PPR's on all of these activities:

1. Conditions of employment, including rules of conduct
2. Job classifications and descriptions
3. Job application form
4. Pay schedules and allowances
5. Work hours and schedules
6. Fringe benefits, including vacation and sick leave, holidays, insurance, etc.
7. Employment practices
    a. Procurement—recruitment, interviewing, references, examinations, etc.
    b. Selection and placement
    c. Orientation and training
    d. Probation
    e. Promotion
    f. Transfer
    g. Dress requirements
    h. Discipline
    i. Resignation
    j. Retirement
    k. Performance evaluations
8. Employee behavior
    a. Cooperation, working together, conflicts
    b. Solicitations
    c. Grievances
9. Communications
    a. Confidentiality of information and records
    b. Use of telephone
    c. Bulletin boards
    d. Employee handbook
10. Working conditions
    a. Fire and safety, and disaster programs
    b. Care of facility property
    c. Lighting, heating, and cooling
    d. Sanitation
    e. Parking
    f. Packages brought in and taken out

This is not an exclusive list, for others will arise. Frequently, circumstances develop that require a new policy and procedure not included in the original personnel manual.

Job satisfaction is affected by PPR's. Herzberg describes adequate and appropriate personnel PPR's as **positive hygiene factors**. Although valuable to the work climate, they do not motivate. However, if they are inadequate and unfair, they cause job dissatisfaction and adversely affect morale. Management's concern for employees is reflected in personnel PPR's. Adequate and appropriate personnel guidelines indicate to employees that management is interested in their well-being. Also, these guidelines influence the success of organizational goals. Certain policies help to promote employee tenure and to reduce turnover. (Stryker)

Personnel PPR's should be developed by the administrator and his staff and approved by the governing body. When employees participate in developing these guidelines it frequently helps to ensure they will follow them. Employees have more commitment to carrying out plans when they have input as evidenced by the TQM style of management.

JOB TERMINOLOGY

1. **Job** is a term that refers to a collection of tasks that can be performed by an employee as contributions toward providing a certain service. Each job has certain ability requirements as well as rewards associated with it.

2. **Job Classification** is classifying each individual job or position, as nurse, practical nurse, nurse aide, dietary manager, dietary service worker, secretary, housekeeper, orderly, and others. A job class may have more than one level. One may have Nurse Aide I and Nurse Aide II. The Nurse Aide II level requires additional knowledge, skills, experience, and/or training, and involves increased responsibility. The salary paid is higher also.

3. **A job analysis** should be made before a job description is developed. The first step is to determine the activities (or tasks), the employee behavior, and the knowledge and skills necessary to carry out a certain job. Knowledge and skills can be inferred from the description of tasks and behaviors. (Bedelian) If the job requires making patient beds, one can infer that knowledge of bed-making procedures and skills of bed-making are needed.

   A job analysis should utilize the assistance of employees who do that job. Usually, they enjoy being a part of this task and they can contribute significantly to a valid job analysis. One approach in doing this is to have employees write down each task they performed during a day. Then ask that they record tasks that they sometimes perform but did not perform that day. Have them do this for several days. The result will be a complete picture of all tasks performed by a particular job class.

4. **A job description** outlines the duties, authority, and qualifications of each job class. It gives examples of the duties performed and lists qualifications, such as education, training, and experience. If there are special requirements of a job, such as extensive stooping, lifting, and/or standing, these should be included. Some personnel specialists separate **job description** and **job specifications**. But for practical purposes they usually are considered the same in nursing facilities. All job descriptions should be in writing with a copy in the manual and a copy given to the employee. Figure 6.1 provides an outline for writing individual job descriptions.

5. **Job assignment** is the specific assignment of duties to an employee by his supervisor. The assignment may include all duties listed in his job description or only part of them. Job assignments should be made largely on the basis of employees' **abilities and knowledge**. If duties are assigned according to what an employee does best, one may anticipate higher performance. Assignments are best when written, dated, and signed. When supervisors review work assignments with each employee, it can ensure a mutual understanding. Supervisor and employee should sign one copy and place it in the employee's record. Employees often forget what they are

Figure 6.1:

Outline for Job Description

Job Title ______________________________ Salary range __________ to __________

I. Distinguishing Features of Work
- A. Complexity of work. Is work routine? Highly technical? Professional? Clerical? Is there wide variety of duties?
- B. How much judgment is required? Only routine decisions within established procedures? Professional judgment required to make dicisions?
- C. Authority. Does person have authority over anyone? How much? Can they reprimand, send home, discipline, suspend, fire?
- D. Who supervises them? How are instructions received – in specific terms, general terms or both?
- E. How is work reviewed? By observation, conference, reports, etc.

II. Special Demands
- A. Physical. Is it necessary to stoop, lift, stand, walk, climb, etc.?
- B. Other. Is there great deal of pressure, such as angry public, deadlines, long hours, on call?

III. Duties (All duties listed may not be assigned. Some other duties not listed may be added).
- A. Answers telephone and routes calls.
- B. Picks up mail, opens non-personal and non-confidential mail and distributes.
- C.
- D.
- E. Such other related duties as may be assigned.

IV. Qualifications
- A. Education. High school, College, R.N., etc.?
- B. License. Is license, registration, certification required?
- C. Experience. Number of years, type and level of work.
- D. Special. Particular knowledge, or skill in handling people? Work alone or in large group? Pleasant telephone voice, etc.?

told. It is helpful to have this documentation. A second copy of the assignment should be given to the employee.

PROFESSIONAL ETHICS AND STANDARDS

The behavior of a **professional** person is guided by a set of principles or rules that is not expected to apply to the general public. As an example, if a resident curses, screams, or yells at a staff member, the staff member is expected to remain calm and not strike back in any way. Anyone acting in this manner toward a **nonprofessional** in a public setting might bear the risk of being struck by the object of his abuse.

Each professional has a **code of ethics** to follow. Ethical standards are a part of their professional training. Administrators would do well to secure copies of codes of ethics for nurses, physical therapists, dietitians, and other professionals, to review them with staff, and to post them for ready reference.

There are legal provisions available to ensure nursing activities are carried out according to ethics. The Nurse Practices Act, based on constitutional provisions, outlines standards by which nurses must practice. The Act specifies what is included in the *scope of nursing practice.* Any nurse performing a duty not within this scope may be in trouble with her licensing board. (See Chapter 12 for more details.)

Employee conduct must be taught by supervisors. Since nonprofessionals often have little training before employment by a nursing facility, the facility must have its own behavior code in the form of policies, procedures, and rules. Employees must be taught respect for resident dignity and rights, observance of confidentiality, and proper response to residents. With experience they should develop a professional attitude similar to the professionals with whom they work.

EMPLOYEE COMPENSATION

Pay scales for both salaried and wage employees should be identified, clearly written, and made known to employees. This aids the reduction of turnover, the primary purpose of employee compensation, and hopefully will also motivate higher performance. Pay scales are related to level of authority, training required, necessary skill, and supervisory duties. Lower echelon employees who have less training, less skill, and less authority are at the bottom of the pay scale. These may include housekeeping, dietary, and laundry workers who often bring no specific skills to the job, necessitating on-the-job training.

At the other end of the spectrum are the administrator and the director of nursing, both of whom must be trained and licensed. They generally are the highest paid full-time personnel in a facility. The more training required and the more authority delegated to an employee, the higher his pay scale must be in order to attract him to a job.

A minimum wage is imposed by the Wage and Hour Division of the U.S. Department of Labor. It is a part of the Fair Labor Standards Act (FLSA) which imposes other standards on employment. These standards are also administered by the Wage and Hour Division. (See Chapter 11) The current minimum wage is $5.15 per hour. All covered employees must be paid at least this hourly rate. Workers not covered by minimum wage include the following:

1. **Students** in training in a facility where their on-the-job training is part of their regular training program are not considered employees. This includes those in training for registered nurse, licensed practical or vocational nurse, physical therapist, and paramedical jobs.

2. **Externs**, i.e., medical students, working in a nursing facility for short periods of time under the supervision of a licensed physician may not be classed as employees. The key factor in this determination is that the training is predominantly for the benefit of the extern.

3. **Residents who work**, **handicapped workers**, and **full-time students** may be paid a special lower minimum wage provided a **special certificate** is first obtained from the Wage and Hour Division. However, OBRA specifies that any resident asked to perform work must be paid at least the minimum wage. This is in conflict with Wage and Hour laws and possibly could not be enforced if it were tested.

An **increment pay plan** pays new employees at a base wage, then pays increments on a periodic basis. An increment plan provides an increase of perhaps six, ten, or more cents per hour on an annual or semiannual basis. Salaried employees often receive increments of a stated amount per month, usually on an annual basis. Table 6.4 is an example of an increment pay plan providing an hourly increase at six months and annually thereafter.

Table 6.4:

Sample Increment Pay Plan

Classification: Housekeeping aide
Rate of increase: $0.10 per hour

Rate/hour	Eligibility date by year	Pay/40 hr. week
$6.00	entrance	$240
6.10	0.5	244
6.20	1	248
6.30	2	252
6.40	3	256
6.50	4	260
6.60	5	264
6.70	6	268

An increment plan may have more than one basis for granting increases. In a **seniority system**, employees receive pay raises only on the basis of length of service, but there is no reason to believe it motivates employee performance beyond the minimum required. Organized labor often bargains for a seniority system.

In a **merit** raise system pay increases are given solely on the basis of performance usually tied in with periodic job evaluations. A **seniority** increment system is based entirely on longevity. Periodic raises are given, solely on the basis of having done satisfactory work during a specific time, usually one year.

In a **mixed system**, increases are determined by a combination of factors. Frequently, both **seniority** and **merit** are used. Extra increments may also be given for outstanding performance.

Occasionally, employers may pay the same wage to all employees doing the same job without regard to seniority or other characteristics. This is a **job-based** system and is not commonly used. It is very unpopular with senior workers who have worked several years for the facility.

The seniority, merit, and mixed systems tend to promote job satisfaction. Employees have something to work toward. They do not feel their income is frozen. It may help to retain employees, but research indicates it does not motivate an employee to higher performance.

The **key** to a good pay system is to begin with the fair wage standard. If a facility starts line workers at $5.25 per hour when all other health care facilities in the community start them at $5.50, it will never have a good pay system. Unless the facility provides many other benefits it will likely lose the most competent employees to competing facilities that pay more.

Money motivators were discussed in Chapter 3 which states that money motivates only in certain circumstances. In most businesses money is used to keep an adequate staff, not primarily to motivate. It is one reason administrators try to make wages and salaries competitive with other health-care facilities.

Shift differentials are often used to interest employees in working the more undesirable evening and night shifts. Nonsalaried employees may have a slightly higher wage scale per hour than the day shift, and salaried employees may receive a higher remuneration. Generally the night shift is paid a higher differential than the evening shift. For instance, an aide may be paid $6 per hour on the morning shift, while the afternoon shift makes $6.25 and the night shift $6.50.

EMPLOYEE (FRINGE) BENEFITS

Fringe benefits, or employee benefits, are considered a right by employees. However, except for the five benefits required by FLSA, the benefit package is decided by the nursing facility. Fair Labor Standards do not require facilities to provide holidays, vacations, coffee breaks, sick leave, and insurance other than workers compensation and unemployment insurance. Room and board provided an employee who stays in the facility may be considered as income by the Wage and Hour Division of the Employment Standards Administration, U.S. Department of Labor.

Benefits mandated by FLSA are Social Security, unemployment tax (FUTA), workers compensation, and family medical leave. The employer is required to pay at least 50% of Social Security, and 100% of unemployment tax, and workers compensation insurance. (See Chapter 7 for definition of terms)

Family Medical Leave Act of 1993 provides that the employer must grant leave: (1) to fathers in case of a newborn child, (2) for placement of a child for adoption, and (3) to care for the spouse with serious health conditions. This leave is without pay, but the employee must be reinstated to the job upon return. To be **eligible** for family medical leave, the employee must have worked at least 1,250 hours during the past twelve months. This includes any part-time worker employed as much as 60% of the time. Some facilities which provide vacation and sick leave require an employee to take any accumulated leave before being granted family medical leave. The total amount of medical leave per year an employer is required to give is 12 weeks. Not all leave must be taken at one time; leave can be granted for a few weeks at a time at several intervals. This program is monitored by Wage and Hour Division. It has a free brochure available upon request.

Fringe benefits should be clearly outlined in the personnel manual and discussed fully with prospective and new employees. From the beginning employees should have all information in written form and understand what is provided. Fringe benefits usually include five to seven holidays, a specified number of paid vacation and sick leave days, hospitalization and life insurance, and less frequently, disability insurance. Personal liability insurance is seldom included since most nursing facilities carry malpractice insurance covering all employees. Some facilities are beginning to pay personal liability for administrators and nurses. It is sometimes used as a fringe benefit instead of a pay raise so that professional staff pays no tax on the increase.

If paid **vacation and sick leave** are provided, earning it is the right of every employee. Administrators should educate the employee to the fact that taking leave is a privilege. It is to be taken at the convenience of the facility at a time when leave does not disrupt services. Although consideration should undoubtedly be given to an employee's request for a certain time off, employees must know that selecting one's leave time is not part of the employer/employee agreement. Vacation leave is usually the **most costly** fringe benefit.

Monetary value of fringe benefits is important in discussing wages and salaries. Most organizations pay an additional 20 to 40 percent of a person's base pay in fringe benefits. Costs of all benefits provided should be reduced to an hourly rate and explained to all employees. If an employee is paid $6.00 per hour and 25 percent in fringe benefits is provided, that amounts to $1.50 additional per hour. Explain that actually the employee receives $7.50 per hour and does not pay income tax on much of the additional $1.50 per hour.

The **value** of fringe benefits in terms of promoting low employee turnover, morale, and continued productivity is questionable. Many people will not work where fringe benefits are inadequate, but when they are available employees look upon them as a right. Adequate fringe benefits sometimes do improve morale and may increase productivity momentarily, but usually not over a long period of time. Also, adequate fringe benefits may promote management/employee harmony, but there is no guarantee. At best, fringe benefits may help to promote a positive work atmosphere, and may help to reduce employee turnover. (Bedelian)

REGULATORY AGENCIES

Several Federal agencies monitor regulations on employment practices and other aspects of personnel management. Every administrator should be intimately familiar with these regulations since failure to comply may result in civil and criminal penalties and/or tort action against the facility or an employee.

1. **The Fair Labor Standards Act of 1938,** (FLSA) as amended, provides regulations in at least six areas of interest to administrators. Unless otherwise noted herein, all of these are monitored by the Wage and Hour Division, Employment Standards Administration, U.S. Department of Labor. Every facility is required to display the FLSA **Notice to Employees** that outlines basic requirements of the Act. It is provided free by the nearest Wage and Hour Division Office.

   a. **Standard work week** means either 40 hours during a seven-day period or 80 hours in a two-week period. The seven days may be chosen by the facility. It is not necessary to use the calendar week of Sunday through Saturday. Residential health-care facilities, including nursing homes, may use the 8/80 schedule. Although most use calendar weeks, a facility can use any 14-day work period.

   b. **Minimum wages** are enforced by Wage and Hour Division. Currently, it is $5.15 per hour, but an increase is to be implemented soon. In addition to exemptions explained under pay scales in this section professional, administrative, and executive employees are exempt.

   c. **Overtime compensation** must be no less than one and one-half times the employee's regular pay. Facilities using the **40-hour work week** must pay overtime for any hours over 40 worked during the week. An employee may double back and work 16 hours or more during a 24 hour period without being paid overtime as long as time worked during the work week does not exceed 40 hours. Using the **8/80**

schedule an employee must be paid overtime for any hour over 8 during a 24-hour period and for any hour over 80 in the two-week pay period. The 8/80 schedule's **value** is supposed to be that it helps with scheduling and with payroll. This is questionable since an employee cannot double back after working 8 hours and fill in for another employee without earning overtime. (WH Publication 1326)

Premium pay , such as a shift differential, must be included in computing overtime. An example is a CNA whose base pay is $6 per hour, and she is paid $6.50 to work the night shift. If she works 10 hours one day while on the 8/80 schedule, she must be paid $9.75 per hour for the two hours overtime.

Exemptions from overtime pay and minimum wage are executive, administrative, and professional staff. An exempt employee's primary duty must be the management of the nursing home or of a recognized department. An administrative employee must primarily perform office or non-manual work of substantial importance to the management of the nursing home. A professional employee must perform work requiring advanced knowledge in a field of science or learning, such as a nurse, pharmacist, and licensed social worker. They also must be paid a minimum salary determined by Wage and Hour. LPN's are not exempt as they are considered technical employees.

Time of payment is regulated also. Generally overtime must be paid at the pay date following the overtime work. Administrators should keep current on all exceptions.

d. **Child labor** is of interest to facilities that may employ students and individuals under 18 during school hours and in the summer. Minors 14 and 15 years of age may be employed in nonhazardous jobs outside of regular school hours. They may work no more than 3 hours on a school day, 18 hours during a school week, 8 hours on a non-school day, and 40 hours during a non-school week. They may do any type of work other than hazardous duties, including the operation of machines, such as a meat slicer, dishwasher, toaster, milk shake blender, buffer, and a lawn mower. Generally they are not allowed to work in the laundry.

   Students aged 16 and 17 may perform any duty except those declared hazardous by the U.S. Secretary of Labor. They are not allowed to drive for the facility unless it is occasional and incidental to their regular duties. They may be an ambulance helper only if they ride in front with the driver.

   An 18-year-old may operate automobiles and nonautomatic elevators and perform any duty of regular employees even if it is hazardous. Driving is usually ruled out since insurance providers require a minimum age of 25 years.

e. **Record-keeping** is very important to a facility. If employment records are not kept in accord with the FLSA, the facility could be quite vulnerable in case of employee claims. Administrators should obtain a free copy of **Handy Reference Guide to the Fair Labor Standards Act** which contains details of record keeping. (WH Publication 1281) It can be obtained for nonexempt workers and for certain other special employees. **Records** of required information **must be kept for three years.** Some records such as time cards need to be kept only two years. During that time an employee or ex-employee could file a claim against the facility, and the facility must prove the claim is false or the employee wins.

f. **Penalties** may be inflicted after due process for violations of the Act. A fine up to $10,000 and imprisonment up to six months may be given after conviction. No person is imprisoned except after a conviction following a conviction of a prior offense under this Act.

2. **Equal Employment Opportunity Commission** (EEOC) was created in a 1972 amendment to Title VII of the Civil Rights Act. (29 CFR 1600-1699). The **purpose** of EEOC is to prevent any person from engaging in any unlawful employment practice. **Provisions** of this part specify that the commission: (a) receives and investigates complaints, (b) makes a determination of whether an unlawful employment practice has occurred, and (c) by informal methods of conference, conciliation, and persuasion seeks to eliminate the practice. If the state or local government has a law prohibiting the employment practice reported to EEOC, the Commission notifies the state or local government and affords it time, usually 60 days, to act on the matter.

   Administration of EEOC is by the U.S. Department of Labor, and EEOC is a unit of that Department. Enforcement of the provisions of Title VII of the Civil Rights Act of 1964 and its amendments has been transferred to, or created under, the EEOC. Every facility must exhibit a **poster** provided by EEOC which administers the following programs.

   a. **Title VII** forbids discrimination in employment on the basis of race, religion, sex, or national origin. A facility cannot refuse to hire nor can it discharge an individual or otherwise discriminate against an employee with respect to his compensation or to the terms, conditions, or privileges of employment because of any one of the above reasons. Management must not limit, segregate, or classify applicants or employees in any way that would deprive or tend to deprive an individual of employment opportunities, or adversely affect his status because of race, color, religion, sex, or national origin. This includes wage increases, benefits, and other job practices.

   b. **The Equal Pay Act of 1963,** as amended, prohibits **sex discrimination** in payment of wages to men and women performing substantially equal work in the same establishment. This law covers employees in nursing facilities and other private industries as well as state and local governments and educational institutions. The Act provides that one may be paid more than the other based on longevity, merit, or other conditions as long as the employee's sex is not considered.

   c. **The Rehabilitation Act** of 1973, as amended, provides for discrimination on the basis of handicap. Its purpose is to eliminate discrimination on the basis of handicap in any program or activity receiving federal financial assistance. Provisions in Section 504 of the Act are that no qualified handicapped person may be, on the basis of handicap, excluded from any activity, denied benefits of, or subjected to discrimination under any programs which receive or benefit from federal financial participation. Section 503, in addition to prohibiting job discrimination, requires employers who hold federal contracts to develop **affirmative action** programs to employ and promote the handicapped.

      Vietnam Era and **disabled veterans** are covered in Section 402 of the Vietnam Era Veterans Readjustment Assistance Act of 1974. Employers with federal contracts must operate affirmative action programs to employ and advance qualified Vietnam Era veterans and disabled veterans. For details on how these programs operate refer to 29 CFR 84.1 and 84.61.

   d. **Sexual harassment** Discrimination on the basis of sex was further clarified under Title VII in 1980. **Provisions** are that sexual advances, requests for sexual favors, and other verbal or physical conduct of a sexual nature constitute sexual harassment when: (a) submission to such conduct, made either explicitly or implicitly, is a term or condition of employment, (b) submission to or rejection of such conduct by an individual is used as a basis for employment decisions affecting such individuals, or (c) such conduct has the purpose or effect of unreasonably interfering with the individual's work performance or creating an intimidating, hostile, or offensive working environment. (29 CFR 1604.11) This is an area of increasing concern to administrators. Frequency of complaints are increasing. A number of these were filed with EEOC by female employees who had been fired by a male administrator. An important practice is that an administrator must take every complaint seriously. He should investigate, take corrective action and document each instance; otherwise, EEOC may find him equally liable if they find harassment has occurred and the administrator took no action.

e. **Age discrimination in Employment Act of 1967** as amended. Purpose of the Act is to abolish discrimination in employment on the basis of age. It is designed to protect older individuals. Provisions are that an employer may not discriminate in hiring or in any other way by giving preference because of age for individuals aged 40 and older. Hiring, promotions, and other practices must be based on factors other than age. Help wanted advertising may not use items such as young, college students, age 20 to 35, or any other age group. Involuntary retirement may be done only when it is part of a bona fide retirement plan. Administration of the program was transferred to EEOC within the Department of Labor in 1978. (29 CFR 1625)

f. **Pregnancy Discrimination Act of 1978** is an amendment to Title VI. Purpose is to prevent discrimination in employment on the basis of pregnancy, childbirth, and related medical conditions. Provisions are that disabilities caused or contributed to by pregnancy, childbirth, or related medical conditions shall be treated the same as disabilities caused or contributed to by any other medical condition under any health or disability insurance or sick leave plan available in connection with employment. All employment practices must treat disability due to pregnancy the same as other disabilities. If the facility has a sick leave plan, it applies to leave due to pregnancy.

Administrators must be careful about discrimination during maternity leave. One facility's maternity leave period was nine weeks during which her job was held by a temporary employee. The pregnant employee was to be reinstated to her job if she returned within the nine weeks period. When the facility allowed three and one-half months leave to another employee to complete a course in college and reinstated him, the pregnant employee asked for the same amount of leave. EEOC ruled the facility must grant it and reinstate the pregnant employee after three and one-half months.

g. **Title VI of the Civil Rights Act** prohibits discrimination in providing services in a nursing facility. Management may not exclude anyone from participation in any activity or deny him any benefits on the basis of race, color, or national origin when the facility receives federal aid. This includes **bed assignments to** residents. Management may not segregate in any form, placing minorities in rooms together or in less desirable rooms or sections of the facility. This does not mean a white and a member of a minority race must be placed in every room. The facility must assign rooms to residents on the basis of their medical needs without regard to race, color, or national origin. (45 CFR 80.3-80.6)

Administration of this program is by EEOC and the states. Federal funds are granted to states which match them according to a designated formula. The state designates a civil rights agency that provides information to nursing facilities including a **poster** which must be exhibited. The poster may also be obtained from EEOC. The state licensing and certification agency can direct administrators to the proper state agency participating in handling provisions of Title VI.

h. **Americans with Disabilities Act of 1990 (ADA)** will eventually affect all types of businesses including government. **Purpose** of the Act is to prohibit discrimination against qualified disabled individuals in employment, housing, public accommodations, education, and transportation. It is to provide clear, strong, consistent, and enforceable standards addressing discrimination against people with disabilities. It ensures that the federal government will play a central role in enforcing standards established under the Act. Nursing facilities are affected primarily by Title I and III of the Act—employment and public accommodations.

Who is protected? Individuals with a physical disability of any type, and those with a mental or psychological disability—retardation, depression, etc. The term "handicapped" is no longer used; it is "disability." Individuals who are current alcoholics and illegal drug users, homosexuals, bisexuals, AIDS patients, kleptomaniacs, and others are not protected under the Act.

Title I-Employment specifies no "covered entity" shall discriminate against a qualified individual with a disability because of the disability, including job application procedures, hiring, promotions, discharge, employee compensation, job training, and other terms and privileges of employment.

Reasonable accommodations must be made by an employer for an applicant with a disability, except when the accommodation would impose undue hardship on the operation of the business. This includes modified work schedules, necessary equipment, training materials, alterations and so on. However, extensive renovations may not be a reasonable accommodation. In recent developments it has become apparent that a facility should submit a proposed renovations plan to EEOC for approval. EEOC may declare it a reasonable accommodation in spite of the cost, as it did in the following case not requiring renovations.

Example: A facility interviewed an applicant, who was wheelchair bound, for a clerical position that included operating a word processor. She was the best qualified applicant, but the facility had no desk or table that would accommodate a wheelchair. Also, it used only four-drawer filing cabinets which meant the applicant could not reach the two top drawers. EEOC considered that buying the proper desk and using two-drawer file cabinets, or having the other clerk do the filing, were reasonable accommodations.

What the employer can do in considering an applicant with a disability:

1. Make pre-employment inquiries about ability to perform job functions.

2. Describe job tasks, have an employee demonstrate them, or show tasks by video cassette and ask applicant how he would do tasks; let applicant decide when there are tasks he could not perform.

3. Require medical examination after offer of employment provided it is required of all employees. It must be performed before employee starts to work, and may be a condition of employment on outcome of the exam.

4. Determine illegal use of drugs – a drug test is not considered a medical exam.

What the employer **cannot do** in considering an applicant with a disability:

1. Require pre-employment medical physical.

2. Make inquiry to determine nature and severity of disability.

3. Tell applicant they cannot hire a disabled person.

4. Focus the interview on the disability, must focus on ability to perform tasks.

5. Refuse to hire because insurance cost will increase.

6. Use the term handicapped - must say disabled.

Enforcement is by several government agencies. However, complaints should be directed to EEOC or the U.S. Attorney General. It is a complex program that will take years to fully clarify and implement. One attorney described the program as 300 pages of legalese that involved four different agencies. **Money penalties** are being awarded. Size of the penalty depends on the number of people the enterprise employs. Administrators must become familiar with ADA and carefully plan for compliance for it is obvious the courts, especially a jury, will rule in favor of the disabled complainant if there is any evidence of discrimination.

EEOC investigates when an employee files a complaint in any of the programs EEOC monitors. It will make a determination of whether discrimination has occurred. If EEOC determines there has been discrimination, the complainant may file tort action in court in an effort to recover damages. Since EEOC has made a determination in the complainant's favor, many of the cases are settled out of court.

Administrators need to know that findings of the EEOC in sexual harassment cases are not available to anyone other than those involved. EEOC will not provide a report or any type of information on its decision to either the facility or to a state agency unless the facility or agency is considered at fault. If the accused is an administrator, the state board of examiners that licensed him cannot secure information from EEOC. Neither are EEOC's records subject to subpoena by a state board that has subpoena powers.

In recent years EEOC has entered suit in behalf of complainants, especially those that had no resources or the case was unique and EEOC wanted a court interpretation. One such case provided clarification of who is covered by ADA:

> **Example:** An obese lady weighing 349 pounds applied for a job in an ICF-MR. The physician ruled she was not able to carry out duties involving active mental retardates due to her weight. He advised she must lose at least 49 pounds before she could be employed. EEOC brought suit in her behalf under ADA regulations. The court ruled she had been discriminated against since the facility had not determined whether her obesity was due to eating too much or to endocrinological problems. She was awarded damages.

Administrators need to be forewarned that some attorneys are sending people with a disability to apply for work. They hope the applicant will be denied a job so they can enter suit.

3. **Citizenship** The Immigration and Naturalization Service (INS) requires that employers complete Form I-9 on every employee hired after Nov. 6, 1986. The **purpose** is to verify employment eligibility. Only American citizens and aliens who are authorized to work may be employed. It is interesting to note that in order to establish a person's eligibility for employment, the facility must require the applicant to bring at least two documents for review - birth certificate, driver's license, or other. These documents include much of the information that EEOC and Wage and Hour Division consider discriminatory information, as birth date, nationality, height, weight, and sex. Every employee's personnel record must include a copy of Form I-9. To ensure compliance obtain a copy of the *Handbook for Employers* from the INS. It includes the employment verification forms and information on completing them.

EMPLOYMENT PRACTICES

Employment practices, or selection procedures, refer to the activities used in recruiting, interviewing, checking references, evaluating, and employing staff. These practices are to be clearly stated in the manual, and they must conform to federal regulations enforced by the Equal Employment Opportunity Commission (EEOC), the

Wage and Hour Division, the Immigration and Naturalization Service, and the Americans With Disabilities Act. (ADA)

Recruitment practices must be free of discrimination on the basis of race, religion, sex, national origin, age, and disability. Administrators may advertise for applicants, use employment agencies, job fairs, posters, and community agencies that may be willing to refer applicants. Recruiting by **word of mouth** is not considered proper as it lends itself to discrimination by sending out information for a particular type of employee.

It is interesting to note that current employees are usually one of the best **sources of recruitment**. Generally, they only recommend good employees as they know that if the applicant does not do his work it will reflect on the referral source. Also, it may mean the referring employee must pitch in and do more work.

Labor pools are a resource, especially for nurses; however there are distinct disadvantages. Using a labor pool affects continuity of care, quality of care, and staff morale. Often recruits from a pool are not knowledgeable in long-term care and they certainly are not familiar with facility policies and procedures. Residents may complain about staff that comes in for a day then are never seen again. Regular staff may tire of explaining to the temporary employee how work is to be done. This interferes with their regular work. **Cost** is also a factor. At one time an employee from a labor pool cost less than a regular employee who had benefits. This is no longer true. Perhaps the best that can be said for using a labor pool is that it will provide the warm body to meet nursing-hour requirements. **Employment agencies** are a recruitment resource. Often they do the initial screening, indicating that the applicant the agency refers meets personnel standards and usually has a good work record.

Advertising is an external recruitment device, but it has restrictions. It is not permissible to use terms as *young*, *college student*, *male*, *female*, *healthy*, or words that may be construed as discriminatory. (29 CFR) As an example, advertising for a "healthy, female student to work part-time" is considered discriminatory. Advertisements referring to height and weight may not be used unless they are a specific requirement of the job. Example, an ad for a "female, under five feet in height, to model female children's clothes" might be considered acceptable. Generally, EEOC would accept the fact that a taller person could not model small children's clothing and a male would not be an acceptable model of girl's clothing.

Job posting is a method of internal recruitment. When a position is vacant it is posted on the bulletin board so all staff may learn of it. Any interested employee may apply. An example would be the vacancy of the housekeeping supervisor's job. When posted, employees from dietary service, nursing, or laundry could apply.

References are important to assess potential applicants. Best references are those from previous employers when applicants have a work history. Contact prior employers, at least by telephone, and obtain information on applicant's performance. Employers frequently hedge their statements, especially when written, because of the threat of law suits should they release erroneous information that might prevent employment. Always check at least two references, preferably prior employers, and document and file information received. The prior work record, that is, length of time on a job, is one of the best **indicators of success** of new employees. Ask the former employer if he would rehire the person if a job became available. If he hesitates or hedges his response, you have your answer — he probably would not rehire.

Application forms must conform to the requirements of the EEOC and Fair Labor Standards regulations. Check these regulations before constructing an application form. The facility may include only those questions that relate to the specific job for which the applicant applies. Listed below are some items of information which can or cannot be requested on an application for employment, based on what EEOC and the Wage and Hour Division may consider discrimination.

Acceptable information

1. Name
2. Address
3. Telephone number
4. Education
5. Special job training
6. Work history
7. Licenses when required
8. References
9. Citizenship
10. Felony conviction relating to the job
11. Have they ever abused or neglected a resident or misused resident property?

Information not to be requested

1. Age or birthdate, except whether they meet required minimum age
2. Race or color
3. Religion
4. Marital status, except one may ask "Mr., Mrs. or Miss" provided the inquiry is made in good faith for a nondiscriminatory purpose.
5. Arrest record (This is being changed.)
6. Birthplace
7. Sex, except when it is a bonafide qualification for the particular job
8. Height, weight, or handicap unless it relates to job
9. Length of residence
10. Welfare benefits

A problem is developing regarding an applicant's criminal record. Some states have enacted new laws that require administrators to make a criminal background check before hiring anyone, or at least any unlicensed person, to work in a health-care facility.

Even with these restrictions, application forms are quite useful. When the applicant fills out the form alone at the facility it provides a measure of his ability to read and write. Having him sign the application frees the facility to contact references the applicant has listed. The application form is considered one of the most valid predictors of success since applicants tend to give more accurate information than they do in interviews.

Interviewing job applicants must adhere to certain federal guidelines. Following are a list of items with an explanation of information that may and may not be requested during pre-employment interviewing without it being considered discriminatory.

Information needed	What regulations allow
1. Name	May secure person's legal name. **May not** ask questions about titles that refer to race, color, religion, sex, handicap, or national origin.
2. Address	**May** ask how long at present address. **May not** ask questions on foreign addresses as this could refer to national origin.
3. Age	**May** ask if they meet the minimum age requirement (16, 18 or 21), if job so requires. **May not** ask about birth or baptismal certificates, or birthdate.
4. Race	**May not** make any inquiry.
5. Birthplace	**May not** inquire about applicant's or ancestors' birthplace.
6. Religion	**May not** ask questions on religious background or preference. **May not** obtain references from pastors.
7. Sex	**May not** ask if male or female, unless it is a bonafide occupational qualification for the particular job. **May not** ask questions of one sex, but not of the other sex.
8. Citizenship	**Must** ask if citizen, if legal resident, and if applicant intends to become citizen, and if spouse is citizen. **May not** ask questions regarding whether applicant or parents are native born or naturalized.
9. Arrests	**May not** inquire about arrests. (This is being changed.)
10. Convictions	**May** ask about convictions of specific crimes relating to job for which application is made. This includes misdemeanors involving resident abuse, neglect, and misuse of resident property. (OBRA-87)
11. Education	**May** ask nature and extent of education and training, and ability to read and speak a foreign language. **May not** ask questions on how language ability was acquired.
12. Organization	**May** inquire into organizational memberships and offices held, except those that by name might indicate race, religion, etc.
13. Photographs	**May not** require photograph until person is hired.
14. References	**May** require personal work references only. **May not** request references from clergy or any other source indicating race, religion, etc.
15. Work schedule	**May** ask if willing to work the required schedule. **May not** ask about working religious holidays.
16. Pregnancy	**May not** ask about pregnancy.
17. Marital status and children	**May not** ask about marital status or children. If applicant volunteers that they have children, may not ask about child-care plans.
18. Health	**May** inquire about health as it relates to job and advise applicant if a health certificate is required for the job.
19. Height and weight	**May not** inquire unless there is specific requirement for the job.
20. License	**May** ask to see current license certificate if job requires license.

Applicants may volunteer information of any type; however, as noted under number 17, it may be considered inappropriate to explore this information.

The **purpose** of these regulations is to ensure that no person is denied employment on the basis of any type of discrimination. However, when a person is employed administrators are required to obtain much of the above excluded data and to include it in personnel records. Refer to the section on records in this chapter for details.

Interview methods There are numerous methods of interviewing but three are most commonly used.

1. **Non-directive** interviewing is used to elicit information from the applicant without unduly influencing his responses. It uses open-ended questions that cannot be answered by a yes or no. Questions may begin with **how, what, when,** or **why.** Examples are "What did you like (or dislike) about your last job?" "Why do you feel you would like to work in a nursing home?" During this type interview the interviewer observes the applicant's feelings and attitudes that accompany his answers.

2. **In-depth** interviewing has a little more structure than non-directive. Questions might focus on how the applicant would perform certain tasks, how he would respond to certain situations, what he considers he is most skilled in, etc.

3. **Patterned interviews** are very structured. The interviewer asks detailed questions regarding all aspects of work to be performed, attitudes, and so on. Usually the interviewer uses a full schedule of written questions and records the responses. (Allen)

Interview techniques are important and administrators should follow certain steps in interviewing in order to assess an applicant's qualifications. The following steps are recommended.

1. **Become familiar with the job description.** Learn the duties and requirements of the job.

2. **Put applicant at ease** with small talk in a private office.

3. **Ask applicant questions that draw information from him** about prior work experience, the type of work he is interested in, and what he wants from a job. Never describe the job available until enough information is elicited to do an initial assessment of the applicant. Should one provide job information first, the applicant may tailor all his information to what he thinks is desired.

   Describe hypothetical situations that may occur on the job, and ask how he would handle them. Review his application and ask appropriate questions. Ask open-ended questions that will elicit answers which reveal the applicant's interests, feelings, attitudes, and approach to work. Use the **how, what, why,** and **when** described above. **Examples:** How would you respond if a resident cursed you? What would you say if your supervisor asked you to help another employee with his work?

4. **Describe the job** to the applicant. If he is interested, discuss wages or salary and fringe benefits. Briefly discuss the **employer/employee** agreement which tells what is expected of him, who instructs and supervises him, and what he may expect from the facility. (See Figure 6.2)

5. **Answer any questions** the applicant may ask. Be sure there is a mutual understanding of what is discussed.

6. **Wrap up the interview by reviewing what has been agreed upon** and what the next step is. Express appreciation for applicant's time and interest.

Tests In addition to application forms, reference checks, and interviews tests are often used as a predictor measure. Test batteries may include **personality, interest, ability,** and **work sample**. Standardized personality, interest, and ability tests are available; however, they must be administered and scored by a qualified examiner in order to obtain accurate results. On the other hand, work-sample tests may be conducted at the

Figure 6.2:

The Employer-Employee Agreement

Every employee enters into an agreement (or contract) with his employer, no matter how verbal. This agreement is:

Employers give instructions ---------->
Employees carry them out!
and
The agreement (Er ----------> Ee) cannot
be reversed (Er <---X---- Ee). Employees
cannot tell Employers what they will
do or how they will do it.
and
The agreement does not apply between
two people at the same level.
Supervisor ----X-----> Supervisor
Employee ---X----> Employee
nor
Does it usually apply between a Supervisor
in one department and employee in another department.

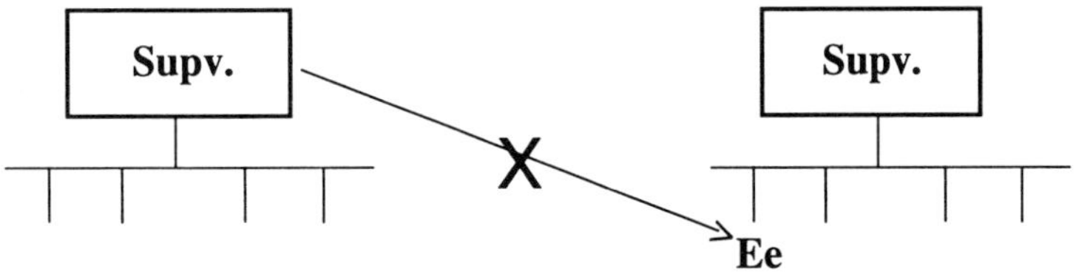

facility. A secretary may be given a typing test or asked to demonstrate her ability to operate a computer. A nurse aide may be required to demonstrate giving a bed bath or other nurse aide chores.

Personality and interest tests are seldom good predictor measures. Ability tests, if properly geared to the work situation, are reasonably valid predictors. Work-sample tests have much greater validity as success predictors. A much needed test that is seldom used in nursing facilities is a **reading test**. All workers must be able to read and understand procedures and instructions, yet this is often not measured. As explained earlier the application form can be developed at the desired reading level, and if filled out at the facility, the information will reveal whether applicants can read and comprehend at the desired level. No tests may be given that have an adverse impact on minorities or women. If it is determined an adverse impact occurs, the facility should modify or eliminate the testing. Such testing is unlawful under Title VII unless it is justified by business necessity.

Validity requirements are concerns to personnel management theorists. They insist that whatever screening devices are used they should have both **content validity** and **construct validity**. Content validity means assessment devices must actually measure the employee traits and behavior the employer is looking for. Construct validity means the tools used must actually measure skill, knowledge, and performance requirements.

Medical examinations Pre-employment medical examinations may be required only after a job offer has been made. EEOC's *Technical Assistance Manual* specifies that the physician's role be clear. He is only to provide findings regarding the applicant's health, not to make employment decisions. The administrator must make his decisions based on the physician's findings and other available objective data.

Drug and alcohol testing Generally pre-employment drug and alcohol testing are permissible, but the administrator should obtain written consent of the applicant. Costs of testing and examinations must be borne by the facility. Before performing tests or medical examinations the administrator should determine state statutes and refer to Americans with Disabilities Act (ADA) restrictions monitored by EEOC.

Selection of the first well-qualified applicant interviewed is a frequent **error**. If there are several applicants, interview them all before making a selection. Even though the second or third applicant may be just what is needed, the fifth or sixth may be even better qualified.

Selection of supervisors is considerably different from hiring line workers and professional staff. Often a supervisor is selected because they have a high level of competence in carrying out technical tasks. Administrators may say, "You are good at doing your work, you should be good at getting others to do it." This infers that it takes the same knowledge and skills to get others to perform a job as it does to perform the work oneself. The truth is it takes an entirely different body of knowledge and set of skills to plan, assign, monitor, and evaluate work of others rather than doing the job oneself.

Two important skills to look for in a supervisor are to be (1) a good communicator and (2) a good problem solver. A person competent in these two areas can learn how to plan others' work, give instructions, delegate, monitor, correct errors, and other related skills. In interviewing an applicant for a supervisory position notice their communication skills. Can they listen attentively? Express themselves clearly and in simple terms? Respond openly and easily to the interviewer's questions? Give them examples of a problem with one employee, with two employees, and with a group of employees. Ask them how they would handle these problems. Explore how they would handle anger or other strong feelings, and how they handle a situation that requires a behavior change in an employee.

Administrators should evaluate an applicant's desire to be a supervisor, their honesty and integrity, and their past experience as a manager. (Weihrich and Koontz) If they have had experience, ask what kinds of problems they have encountered, how they were handled, and what the applicant liked and disliked about being a supervisor.

Selection of nurse supervisors may be particularly problematical. Few have had administrative nurse training. Clinical and bachelor's degree programs often offer only two weeks in administration. This calls for plans to offer management training to DON's and charge nurses.

Hiring a DON Kenneth Cohen and his Professional Placement Specialists, Inc., have developed what they call "The 12 Deadly Sins of Hiring." They feel these practices should particularly be avoided in employing a DON.

1. **Employer oversells** the job by exaggerating its positive aspects, describing the good points and masking some of the challenges to be faced.

2. **Candidate oversells** self to employer by the manner in which questions are answered – usually trying to say what he thinks the employer wants.

3. **Good paper match** between resume and job description that overemphasizes training, knowledge, and experience. The focus should be on what the applicant is likely to do in given situations.

4. **Overreliance on generic job** descriptions which do not differentiate unique needs of similarly titled jobs in different settings.

5. **Resumes are deceptive.** Many are professionally prepared to make a person appear qualified. This is another "looks good on paper" situation that is easy to buy into. Often DON's hire an expert to rewrite their resume.

6. **Hiring decisions** are made at the gut level; i.e., subjective impressions held by the interviewer. It's better to evaluate training, experience settings, and the applicant's demonstrated ability to work in a setting where they have few peers. A nursing home isn't like an acute care setting where there are many co-professionals.

7. **Hiring decisions** are made on first (and lasting) impressions. Some candidates may be anxious and a bit uncertain in the initial interview, and most administrators dismiss them at that point. They should consider all factors, for first impressions in hiring are not always the most accurate.

8. **Hiring decisions** are made in the first four minutes of the interview. This type administrator then tries to elicit information that will support his decision. He is not open for information that contradicts his decision.

9. **Interviewers hire people** they like. It is important to like employees, but likeable supervisors often encounter staff resistance that requires another stance. Evaluate ability rather than likability.

10. **Interviewers hire people** like themselves. They often favor people with a background similar to theirs--same college, common social or sport interests, from the same area, and so on. This is a trap. New managers should **supplement** the administrator's style, not imitate his strengths and weaknesses.

11. **Interviewers "hang hats"** on applicants by attributing characteristics that may not be factual. Sometimes it's because the applicant reminds them of someone else—good or bad.

12. **A warm body will suffice** concept may pervade due to urgency to fill a position. The first available is hired, often leading to much concern later when the misfit must be terminated.

Cohen points out that the wages of these Deadly Sins are the manager's department goes into a tailspin, work suffers, complaints occur, valued employees may leave, and quality care diminishes. The administrator is left to wonder why the supervisor did not succeed since he was so well qualified.

A **probationary period** for all new employees provides the opportunity to observe and evaluate performance before they are employed on a permanent basis. Probation also provides the new employee an opportunity to determine whether he really wants to continue in the job. Three months probation is used by many facilities. At the end of this period the employee usually is hired on a permanent basis, or is terminated.

A **promotion policy** is very important to staff. Although there is little opportunity for promotions in nursing facilities unless there is employee turnover, employees like to feel promotion is possible. If the policy is to promote from within, state it clearly and explain it fully. Many organizations have a policy of promoting from within unless they are able to hire someone from the outside who is better qualified. Employees tend to interpret **policy** as a **rule**, thinking the promotion from within policy is strictly followed and no outsider is ever hired for a higher level position for which a current employee qualifies.

> **Example**: A facility established a **policy** of promoting from within. The housekeeping supervisor resigned due to ill health. She had four housekeeping aides, one of whom was her assistant. This assistant and the other workers fully expected the assistant to be promoted. The facility hired an executive housekeeper from a local hospital. She had far higher qualifications than the assistant. The facility was organized by the Service Employees International Union, so the assistant took her complaint to the union steward. The administrator had a difficult time convincing the union that it had a promotion **policy** not

a **rule.** It was resolved, but from that point on the facility carefully differentiated policy, procedure, and rules for the staff.

Transfer policy also needs to be clear and well-understood. Often an administrator wishes to transfer an employee who is not performing well to another department because he feels the supervisor of the new department can "straighten the employee out." Seldom can one change a problem employee by transfer unless it is clearly a personality conflict between supervisor and employee. If his performance cannot be improved in one department, it probably will not improve in another. Occasionally a department head believes he can work with a problem employee and welcomes the transfer. In this case the transfer may work.

Dress requirements for personnel must be decided. Of course nurses as professionals may furnish and wear uniforms. If nurse aides, orderlies, housekeeping, and dietary personnel are required to wear different colored uniforms, the administrator must refer to provisions of the Wage and Hour Division. If buying a uniform the first week of work causes an employee's hourly rate to fall below the minimum wage, the facility must reimburse him. Some facilities pay enough above the minimum wage to avoid this problem.

Some facilities require employees in each department to wear a simple smock over street clothes. This is a uniform. Unless it is furnished and laundered by the facility, the facility could have a problem. It is wise to check with the Wage and Hour Division before making a decision to require uniforms. A facility can, however, require employees to dress appropriately, **not wear** blue jeans, earrings, and so on. They cannot be told **what** to wear for then it becomes a uniform.

COMMUNICATION STRATEGIES

Administrators often overlook the fact that communication problems will develop, and PPR's covering communications are needed. They should be taught during orientation and training and reviewed at least annually.

Confidentiality is the most important aspect of communication. All information regarding residents and their families is confidential. To protect resident privacy and rights all employees should be taught not to reveal any resident information except as officially authorized. This is important since employees are likely to come into contact with confidential information in reports, resident records, and when overhearing physician's comments.

Use of telephone frequently becomes a problem. PPR's should spell out which telephone may be used, for how long, and for what type of calls. Incoming personal calls to employees can be disruptive to work performance. Unless properly trained, employees often take liberties and use the telephone excessively. This should be grounds for discipline, such as reducing pay for the period of time an employee uses the telephone to excess.

Bulletin boards may be widely used by a facility. To be useful and effective, what is posted on them should be controlled. A special employee bulletin board located near the dining room may be used by employees to post for sale, rent, car pool, and other personal notices. The value of bulletin boards can be enhanced by assigning to an individual(s) the task of rearranging notices on each board daily. Bulletin boards with the same notices in the same place, often outdated, are seldom read.

An **employee handbook** discussed earlier in this chapter greatly enhances communications. It should contain a simplified version of personnel PPR's. Present a copy to each employee and direct each supervisor to review the handbook periodically with his employees.

ORIENTATION AND TRAINING

Requirements For some unexplained reason OBRA removed 42CFR 442.314 which required facilities to conduct staff orientation and in-service training programs and to maintain records documenting them. New OBRA regulations found in 42 CFR 483.75 require in-service training only for nurse aides. After January 1, 1990, facilities were required to provide both performance review and in-service training to ensure that nurse aides are competent to perform their duties. The training program must include training for nurse aides who provide nursing and nurse-related services to residents with **cognitive impairments**. Interpretive Guidelines found in the *State Operations Manual* indicate adequacy of the in-service education program will be measured by demonstrated competency of nurse aides to apply interventions needed to meet residents' particular needs. OBRA requires 12 hours per year of in-service training for CNAs.

When **surveyors** identify deficiencies that may be attributable to inadequate training of any staff they will check training records. By this means, OBRA indirectly requires training for all staff. Also, records of properly trained staff are invaluable when administrative or legal problems arise regarding personnel and resident complaints. No facility that expects to be successful will operate without a fully adequate in-service program for **all personnel**.

The **administrator** is the key person in orientation and training since the success of these two activities is primarily his responsibility. A training director may be appointed and an adequate program developed, but it will probably fail unless it has full support of the administrator. Support is shown by participating in part of the program, holding regular conferences with the training director, reviewing reports of training sessions, ensuring there are adequate time, space, and materials, and occasionally checking to ensure there is adequate documentation.

Orientation means providing the information that employees need to carry out their work properly. It never ends because employees always have questions, especially when problems occur and when change is introduced. Supervisors sometimes feel frustration when they must repeat instructions, but it is to be expected and it is necessary. Employees simply do not retain all the information they receive from supervisors.

Initial orientation of new employees should include: (1) a tour of the facility, (2) introduction to all departments, their duties, and how they interrelate, (3) introduction to the work area, coworkers, and the new employee's general duties, (4) a discussion of personnel policies and procedures, and (5) fire and disaster procedures. Initial orientation does not include lectures or other types of training in resident care or other procedures to be used in the new employee's work. How to perform tasks is a part of **job training**. The administrator may find it prudent to do a part of the initial orientation, especially the discussion of personnel policies and procedures. If left to each department head to interpret, there may be diverse understanding of what is expected of employees.

Document orientation with a **check sheet** that shows the date each topic is covered and by whom. Have both supervisor and employee sign the check sheet and file it in the employee's personnel folder. These records may be required to document that employees have been adequately oriented to the facility and to their work. It may be invaluable when an employee offers an excuse that no one told him something covered in orientation or training.

Organization The facility should have a training director or coordinator with assigned duties to plan, schedule, coordinate and document the training program. This person should be assisted by a **training** committee made up of representatives of the major departments. When a committee develops a plan its members are more often committed to ensuring it is implemented. **Schedules** for training should be posted, showing dates, topics, participants, and instructors. The coordinator and the training committee can best decide on scheduling.

Training staff Trainers or instructors may be recruited from the staff. Also, all the facility's consultant staff should be involved in training. Immediate supervisors are usually best for training new employees. Since it involves in-depth discussion of duties, where materials are located and how to use them, and specific job skills and work procedures, the supervisor is not only best prepared to teach but can ensure that new information is incorporated into practice.

Supervisors sometimes resist training of their employees. They **fear** if they send employees to training sessions they may return knowing more than the supervisor. Involving supervisors in the training of employees offsets this fear.

Content areas Content of training depends on the duties an employee is required to perform. If an employee must lift or help ambulate residents, he needs training in proper lifting and how to fall with a resident when a fall cannot be prevented. No matter how much training in job skills an employee may have when employed, he must still be trained in the specific skills the facility requires. In addition to job skills, employees need training in several other areas.

1. **Attitude training** is extremely important since most facility employees are not professionals. This is especially true of attitudes toward older people. If an employee has a stereotyped attitude toward the aged, thinking all older persons are alike, it is better to try changing the employee's attitude through training and experience than to bring in another person who may possess the same or more destructive attitudes.

2. **Resident rights** All new employees should be trained in resident rights and in the consequences of not abiding by these rights. The facility should ensure that they understand the meaning of abuse, neglect, and misuse of resident property, and that a violation will result in discharge and possible court action. This is best accomplished by the administrator or other professional who can fully explain the meaning and the reasoning behind resident rights. All employees should review the rights annually.

3. **Fire prevention and control** It is imperative that all employees be fully trained in fire prevention and control. Lack of knowledge of how to prevent fires and the employee's duties when fire occurs can result in catastrophe. It is the **number one priority** for overall staff training. No employee should be allowed on duty until he has at least been walked through his duties in case of fire.

4. **Prevention and control of infection** All staff, but especially dietary service, nursing, housekeeping, and laundry should be carefully trained in procedures for preventing infections and in control measures when infection occurs. This training is **top priority** in dietary service where certain diseases can so easily spread through food handling. There should be at least an annual review of infection prevention and control measures by all staff.

5. **Accident prevention** Housekeeping, nursing, and resident activity personnel should particularly be trained in safety and accident prevention. However, all staff should be trained in avoiding such hazards as obstacles in hallways, liquids on floors, use of smoking materials, and so on. At least an annual review is indicated to ensure preventive measures are followed. Specific information to include in this training is discussed in Chapter 7.

6. **Communication with residents** Since nurse aides generally have more contact with residents than other staff, aides particularly should be trained in how to communicate with them. Learning how to handle a resident's anger, insults or hurtful remarks, demanding behavior and crying are important to quality care. Some nurse aides have a knack for handling unpleasant resident behavior while others are hurt and become angry or unsympathetic. Aides can be trained how to respond and to communicate in a helpful way.

   Example: Ms. C's condition was slowly deteriorating. She was losing bladder control, needing help with ambulation, and unable to sleep well. When staff entered Ms. C's room and she started to cry, they teased her, "Don't start crying, now. It won't help a thing. Give us a big smile like you used to." This only intensified the crying. An aide trained in communication entered the room and when Ms. C began to cry she sat down, took her hand, and said, "Go ahead and let it out. A good cry sometimes helps." Ms. C cried for a few minutes, then began to talk about how she felt about her worsening condition. Slowly, she brightened up and said, "I'm glad somebody here appreciates the way I feel." When the aide left Ms. C said, "Come back to see me real soon."

7. **Other areas** for training include **confidentiality** of resident information, **preservation** of **dignity**, and protection of resident **privacy** which are discussed more fully under resident rights.

Documentation of all training should be done by way of a central training record or in each employee's personnel folder. Such records serve as objective data for evaluating performance. They provide evidence of what the employees should know and be held accountable for. They are proof the administrator seeks to have qualified personnel that are kept up to date on new knowledge.

Training methods Sometimes supervisors required to do training are despaired by their teaching role because they usually are not trained for it. They think in terms of lesson plans, lectures, and demonstrations. Currently, there are many prepared programs utilizing video cassettes that can be helpful. Such visual aids make it much easier on the supervisor. Another popular method is to assign new employees to a senior worker who coaches them in proper procedures. Daily coaching by senior workers and supervisors is highly recommended. Demonstrations followed by practice is a useful method. It really isn't necessary for supervisors to be trained teachers to do an effective job of helping employees learn proper procedures and develop adequate skills.

Effectiveness Both employees and supervisor must be motivated in order for training to be effective. The employee must also be capable of learning. No training program can be effective if an employee has neither motivation nor ability. However, a good program may be successful with a capable employee who is not well-motivated, and with a highly motivated employee that is not too capable. Some borderline retardates are so highly motivated that once they learn a skill the task will always be carried out properly.

Neglected training Currently, housekeeping, laundry, and dietary service personnel tend to have the least training. Formerly, the least trained were supervisors, but training in this area has improved. However it is not enough and should still be a priority. Lower echelon personnel must have training in more than procedures and work skills. Housekeeping, laundry, and dietary service workers need to be trained in taking **pride in their work** and understanding **their contribution** to the facility goal of quality care.

Legal liability The legal term **respondeat superior** is extremely important to administrators. It means the facility is responsible for work errors of employees when on duty. The administrator must know that every employee is fully trained to handle any work assignment before that assignment is made. No one should ever be allowed on the job unless they are fully qualified to perform their assigned duties.

HUMAN RELATIONS

Administrators and supervisors are concerned with human relations as well as tasks (getting the work done). Employees who feel understood, appreciated and valued, who are listened to, and who have some input into decision making, usually experience a higher degree of job satisfaction (morale).

The **superior/subordinate relationship** between supervisor and the supervised was discussed in Chapter 3. Since this relationship often gives rise to anger, supervisors must be able to give employees the right to have these feelings. When an employee does not like instructions, let him express himself. A supervisor may even encourage an employee to identify his feelings and bring them into the open by saying, "I don't believe you like what I just said." It is healthy if the employee can say, "Well, I don't like it. I don't like it at all." A supervisor may respond by expressing appreciation of the employee's feelings. It's not necessary to agree. Just expressing anger may clear the air. Both the supervisor and the employee may then focus on the task at hand and the fact that it must be carried out.

Employees need to be **listened to**, to be heard. It is one of the strongest needs they bring to the job. Employees feel understood when they really need to talk and their supervisor listens. Supervisors must be accessible and available as needed throughout the employment of subordinates, not just during orientation and training programs. Subordinates want reassurance from time to time that all is well between them and their supervisors. This is provided when supervisors are available when needed, give required information, take time to listen, and show interest in each employee and his work.

Some organizations seek to promote the **management/employee relationship** through planned activities of a social nature. Picnics, cookouts, and other outings that include both management and employees afford the opportunity for each to be with the other outside the work environment. This may break down barriers and allow all staff to recognize qualities in each other that enhance the working relationship.

Employee/employee relationships in nursing facilities often receive little attention. Administrators may assume that people working together are adult enough to know they must get along, that people know how to accept each other's points of view, and how to resolve their differences. Frequently employees do not possess these characteristics. Differences, petty jealousies, and antipathy may develop between two or more people within a department, or between departments. Such problems are destructive to the teamwork concept and to the coordinating of all efforts toward facility goals.

Differences between individual employees are generally not difficult to resolve through **creative problem solving**. Supervisors who master the following problem solving model frequently experience considerable success in resolving employee conflict.

Step 1 Call the two employees together and tell them **we** have a problem.

Step 2 Wait until they ask what it is, or what do you mean.

Step 3 Identify the problem and describe its effect on their work and the department.

Step 4 If they start accusing each other or trying to deny the problem, stop them.

Step 5 Set ground rules that each employee can express personal opinions without interruptions.

Step 6 When one employee presents his side of the story, have the other employee repeat what has been said before he presents his own point of view. Sometimes the problem is settled at this point, particularly if the problem is primarily one of poor communication. Once employees are involved in a situation in which they are required to listen, it is not at all unusual to hear one employee exclaim, "Oh, I didn't know that's what you meant. I thought you..." The problem is solved.

Step 7 If the problem is not resolved at this point, there is generally conflict of values. Repeat each person's point of view, recognize that they have differences, and focus on the job.

Step 8 Ask what they can do to ensure that this difference does not affect their work. Involve them in identifying specifically what they will do to resolve the problem and work together.

Step 9 If they do not enter into problem solving, take a firm confrontation approach. Tell them it is recognized that they have differences, but that these must not interfere with their work. Advise that the concern is not with how they feel or act toward each other when off the job, but at work they are required to communicate, to work together.

Step 10 Ask them firmly if they can work together or is it necessary to hire someone else who can.

Using this approach it is surprising to see many differences quickly resolve and the antagonists learn to work together harmoniously. Don't make the mistake of exploring feelings or allowing too much ventilation of feeling. Focus on the job, how their differences affect performance, how this cannot be tolerated, and what they can do to work together.

> **Example**: In a large health-care facility two men in maintenance disliked each other so much they asked their supervisor to let them put up a partition between their work benches so they wouldn't have to see each other. Using creative problem solving he called the two together and advised that they have a problem. They would not enter into problem solving with him. The supervisor moved to **Step 9** and said, "I know you do not like each other and when you leave the facility you can fight it out if you want. Let's get one thing clear, as long as you are here you will talk to each other, you will work together, and you will do your work as required. Now, can you do this or do I hire someone who can?" The two looked at each other for the first time and hesitantly agreed they could work together.

Interdepartmental relationships often are a greater problem than individual employee relations. Sometimes departments lose sight of overall goals and develop a **functional orientation.** They are oriented only to their department's function which promotes the attitude that they are working harder than anyone else. It is recognized in the expression, "If everyone else around here worked as hard as we do, things would be easier." This is only a step from seeing other departments as their enemy: "Looks like everyone else around here just tries to make our work harder. They never cooperate or help out."

Two approaches to this type of employee problem are: (1) **preventive** and (2) **problem solving**. To prevent development of poor relations between departments, communications must be kept open and common goals stressed. One department may not know what another department really does. Periodic department **open house** can help. Having one department tell and demonstrate what they do in their department is often an eye-opener to the employees in other departments. Usually, employees have little knowledge of the nature and extent of work in other departments or how work in one department affects employees in another. This approach may help them identify common goals toward which they are to work together.

At least weekly **department head meetings** promote communication and may prevent problems. Each department head should briefly report on their week's work, problems they have encountered, what they did about them, and their plans for the coming week.

Require that **no change** be made in any department before these changes are fully discussed with all department heads. The management **principle of reciprocal relations discussed in Chapter 3** describes how no change can be made in any department without affecting all other departments, either directly or indirectly. Consequently, all department heads must know in advance about proposed changes and when they are to be implemented. Give them time to plan for the impact on their department. This helps to offset the fact that solving one problem creates at least three new problems; hopefully the new problems are not as serious as the one solved.

When poor interdepartmental relationships exist, deal with the situation by **group problem solving** using the following model. Properly used it can be a very effective management tool.

Step 1 Have each department designate two or three representatives.

Step 2 Meet with all the representatives as a group and state the purpose of the group.

Step 3 Have them write down problems they have with the other department.

Step 4 Have them list the problems they think the other department has with them.

Step 5 List problems on a slick board or flip chart for all to see.

Step 6 Have them decide which problem they want to deal with first. Select only one problem, something very specific and solvable.

Step 7 Have participants write down possible solutions to the problem selected.

Step 8 List solutions on the board and have them select the best solution for implementation.

Step 9 Help them develop a plan of action: What is to be done, who will do it, when, where, and so on. Make specific assignments.

Step 10 Meet with them a week later and have them report on the results.

In nursing homes, problems frequently occur between nursing service and dietary service. When this problem solving model is used, usually the list of problems nursing thinks the dietary service has with nursing is almost identical to dietary service's list of problems they have with nursing, and vice versa. Just listing problems and recognizing that both are aware of them often brings about laughter and moves the two groups toward working together.

After leading the group in the solution of one or two specific interdepartmental problems, the problem of relationships begins to clear up. It is difficult to deal with the whole problem of relationships. One can effectively deal only with one element at a time. Other elements begin to fall into place and soon the overall problem is resolved. One of the most important needs in development of employee relationships is a **problem-centered approach**. Too often managers deal with problems by telling and selling solutions to their employees. It is more effective when employees have input as this tends to make them more committed to making the solution work.

Reading signals as a measure of relationships is often overlooked in nursing homes. Department heads frequently stick their heads in the administrator's office in the morning and say something like, "How's it going today?" Generally, they do not mean "How are you?" They aren't asking about well-being; they are checking to see how their relationship is with the boss, what mood he's in. If the administrator stops what he's doing and gives a cheerful greeting, usually the department head goes about his work. If the administrator is grumpy or shows disinterest in communicating, the department head is likely to pause and ask other questions or remark on some aspect of work. The department head leaves wondering what is wrong, and frequently whether they had anything to do with his unpleasant attitude. They pass the word around, "Better leave the boss alone; he's not in a good mood today." One can be sure the department head will not take a problem to the boss that day, unless it is unavoidable.

Signal reading takes many forms. A supervisor with a problem often checks with his secretary before talking with the administrator, asking, "How's he feeling today? Do you think this is a good time to tell him...(about a problem)? Following is another form of signal reading.

> The maintenance worker stops by the administrator's office each morning and asks him questions about some maintenance task to be done. He asks questions about how it should be done, but the administrator is aware the worker knows far more about the task than he does. One day he told the worker, "You know far more about how to do that job than I do. You waste a lot of time coming in and asking me about it. Why don't you just go ahead and do the work then show it to me later?" The employee had always completed his work on a timely basis and with skill. After the conversation with the boss he began to mope around and drag his feet; his work performance was well below par. When the administrator realized what he had done he said to the worker, "You haven't been by to see me in a long time. Hope you're not mad at me or something." Next morning the worker stopped by for a chat. The administrator stopped what he was doing and gave full attention. He gave a "pat on the back" for something well done the day before. The worker's performance resumed its high quality, and he was all smiles. With the individual

attention the administrator gave him, the employee's visits dropped from ten to fifteen minutes to three to five minutes, and his performance was first rate.

It is readily seen that the maintenance worker was not seeking advice or instructions. He just wanted to ensure that all was well between him and the boss, that the boss would listen, and that he was appreciated. His work performance continued to be very satisfactory, and gradually his morning visits became less frequent.

If an administrator wishes to test this theory, one morning when he gets up on the wrong side of the bed he should come in, go to his office without saying anything, and slam his door. Momentarily work will cease as the word gets around that the boss is in a foul mood today, better stand clear. Further time is wasted while employees wonder what's wrong and speculate on whether they had anything to do with his mood. Is he mad at them?

The correct way to do when one is in a bad mood is to walk in, tell staff in the office he is not in a good mood, and assure them it has nothing to do with them. He should say, "Give me a little time to cool off, and I will be available." The signals are clear, staff continues their work, and no time is lost.

Staff/resident relationships are the key to quality service in the facility. No matter how much technical knowledge the staff may have regarding chronic disorders and the aged, the feelings, attitudes, and behavior of the facility's personnel toward residents will determine whether the residents are happy and receive quality care.

Pepper points out that as a group, residents in nursing facilities are unique; problems of aging are different from other health problems. Unfortunately, staff seldom listens to residents. Too many professionals in the health-care field do not like residents who are communicative and articulate. Perhaps it is a reflection of the staff's sense of inadequacy in their ability to cure the aged and to cope with their own anger toward their failures. Pepper suggests one approach toward better understanding and relationships is use of **resident groups** in the treatment program. Residents are usually very interested in these programs, and their suggested courses of action should be heard. Resident/staff groups develop mutual confidence as communication improves. Such groups focus attention and conversation on improvement rather than limiting residents to talk about each other, the food, and the facility.

Most resident-care staff come to the facility with little understanding of what it is like to be old and/or infirm. They know little about the physical and physiological changes and the aged's emotional reactions to losses in hearing, sight, taste, smell, and mobility. It can be beneficial to design training programs that help staff to gain understanding and develop appreciation of the older person's situation. During a training session, request staff to put on a pair of work gloves, insert ear plugs, place a clothespin on the nose, and don a pair of glasses covered with enough margarine or vaseline so they can hardly see. Let them eat while wearing this paraphernalia. Also, let them try three other basic activities of living—walking, dressing and toileting while hampered with some of these or similar devices. Put the staff members in wheelchairs for a while and direct them to participate in resident activities. Nursing facilities who have tried these techniques and other related methods find staff develops a much greater appreciation of the problems of aging. Some administrators use other methods to gain insight into residents' feelings.

Example: New administrator P. Tulane Patterson checked himself in as a resident of his own facility, "to find out what it is like on the other side of the bedrail." He checked in with a fictitious name, disguised himself as aged, and used a wheelchair. Experiences ranged from lengthy, inadequate paperwork in a cooped up office, to feeling of loss of independence when he gave up his car keys, being "tagged" with a wristband warning device, loneliness of staying in a sterile, cold, uninviting room with nothing to do, boredom of hanging around the nurses station and other discomforts. No one asked how he liked his meals, if he wanted more, or attempted to make his experience more pleasurable. Needless to say, he made a number of changes in the operation of his facility.

All staff should be trained to present a **positive approach** to residents. Teach them to relate to residents on pleasant, cheerful topics rather than complaints and unpleasantries such as discomforts, pain, depression, and inabilities.

When greeting a person in public with "How are you?" There are a few standard replies: "Fine, thank you," "Okay," "Holding my own." Seldom does anyone interpret this greeting as an invitation to tell how he really feels. Not so in the nursing facilities. Ask a resident, in his room or elsewhere, how he feels today, and he will likely expound on his symptoms, complaints, and miseries.

Every resident gives clues to what is important to him and what is safe to discuss —a photograph on the bedside table, a painting on the wall, a colorful bedjacket, bedspread, robe, or new pair of slippers. How different the response if staff comments on these rather than ask, "How are you feeling today?" Asking if the photograph is his daughter when it is obviously a granddaughter elicits a smile and sets the stage for pleasantries. "What a lovely bedspread! Who made that for you?" "I love your painting. Did someone do that just for you?" Such remarks can lead to a pleasant discussion of those things pleasing to the resident. The resident can also exhibit pride, and it increases the self-esteem of the elderly to know his "favorite things" can be shared and appreciated by others.

> **Example**: Mrs. LeBlanc, aged 85, kept many mementos in her room. One was a color picture of a beautiful teenage girl. The administrator entered her room, spoke, then said, "Mrs. LeBlanc, is that a picture of your daughter?" Her response, "Aw, shucks, that's my great-granddaughter!" She then proceeded to tell the administrator how the great-granddaughter was a cheerleader at school, made straight A's, and was president of her class. She was so pleased to share something important to her and to see the administrator enjoy the exchange.

When the resident is alert and responsible and has fairly good contact with reality and the environment, everyone should use this approach — administration, nursing personnel, housekeeping, and any one else who comes into frequent contact with residents. Once a relationship is established on this basis the resident may put complaints and disagreements in proper perspective and discuss them in a more realistic manner.

Without first relating to positive things, ask a resident how he likes the food, and he will likely explode with a diatribe on the "slop" served at the facility. All his irritations, dissatisfactions, and unhappiness may focus around the subject of food. But, if a positive relationship is established before asking about the food, one may get a different response "Oh, it's not too bad. It could be improved, though. I wish they would..." Most likely one will hear a more accurate assessment of the food, the services, and what's important to the resident.

Gentle teasing can lead to positive relationships with residents. An example is a physician who used his keen sense of humor to cheer geriatric residents while giving them gentle, very competent care. To a female resident he might say, "My, you look pretty today. You must be looking for a new boy friend!" To one who was sad and crying he would remark, "Now, just look at you. All those tears are ruining your makeup. We're going to have to send you back to the beauty parlor." Invariably, some of their discomforts subsided and the residents departed feeling more cheerful, often smiling and laughing.

To understand the aged and their problems is to appreciate the elderly and how they feel. It is imperative to lay the groundwork for meaningful relationships that will lead to excellent care. All staff must be well-trained in developing relationships.

Staff/family relationships Not enough attention is given to staff/family relationships, especially where the nursing service staff is concerned. The support of the family is necessary for the staff to provide adequate care. How to obtain family support and cooperation is often not well understood.

Staff can be trained to empathize with family members who place someone in a facility. Beyond offering sympathy and reassurance, staff may not know how to relate and develop rapport with family members. They may interpret family complaints and suggestions as criticism of resident care and staff performance. More often the staff reacts to family anger with anger of their own. Staff/family relationships can be enhanced by **involving family** in the facility programs. Regular group meetings of staff and family representatives can be productive. In these meetings department heads discuss the role of their unit in providing care. Suggestions from families are welcomed and wherever possible adopted and implemented.

Stryker reports that families also can be an ally in **staff recruitment.** When there is high employee turnover and staff often works shorthanded, share this information with the family group. Ask for their assistance. Some facilities have had very gratifying results.

Meetings between a family representative and the nursing staff who personally care for the resident are a second means of involvement. Family members should know and have frequent conversations with nurses, aides, activity coordinators, and social workers. Once the staff and family are acquainted and have established a relationship, family members may be less likely to criticize and complain. Family and staff may help each other to understand the resident and his needs.

EMPLOYEE GOALS AND ATTITUDES

There are at least three sets of goals in every organization: (1) organizational, or overall, (2) departmental, and (3) personal. The **overall goals** for a nursing facility should be clearly stated, taught, and available to all supervisors. They are the guideline for developing other goals.

Department goals are derived from the overall goals. If the overall goals are not stated clearly, then each department's goals become primary to them. Departments will develop the aforementioned functional orientation in which they see their work as being an end within itself. Department employees will not see that meeting their goals is an integral part of the facility attaining its overall goals.

Every employee brings **personal goals** to the job. There are certain things he hopes to attain at or from work. Some are constructive and some destructive. Constructive goals may rather closely follow Maslow's hierarchy of human needs. When asked, employees may identify several of these fairly typical goals:

1. To get a good job and keep it (survival)
2. To earn money and help support the family and to have good benefits, especially insurance
3. To get ahead, that is, to improve their current financial situation, to be able to buy things they cannot now afford
4. To have a good job, meaning one that is pleasant, secure and offers raises
5. To get ahead in the sense of being promoted or improving themselves occupationally
6. To have fair and consistent supervision in the sense of being treated like everyone else—no discrimination
7. To help sick or aged people
8. To work with other people in a social environment
9. To receive recognition, praise, and other rewards

Unfortunately, employees bring destructive personal goals to the job. Some appear facetious, but they are goals that are often verbalized and frequently acted out.

1. To get by with as little effort as possible
2. Not to "hit a lick" more than anyone else
3. To make sure no one gets anything they don't
4. To show up weaknesses of other employees
5. To tell everybody else what to do
6. To get everything possible out of the employer

There are many personal goals, some of which fall somewhere between constructive and destructive as the following:

1. To have something to do

2. To get out of the house

3. To get away from the kids

4. To gather all the gossip

Personal goals are usually reflected in **work attitudes**. Employees with constructive personal goals that are in harmony with organizational goals will generally be regular in attendance, apply themselves diligently, show interest in their work, complete their tasks, and cooperate with co-workers. Their attitudes may be reinforced or they may lessen, according to how well the individual's personal goals are met. If an employee wants recognition, praise, and approval, and these goals are not met by management, attitudes change and work performance drops in quality and quantity.

Employees with **destructive** personal goals, not in harmony with facility goals, can be a disruptive influence. These employees' attitudes reflect disinterest in doing a good job, applying themselves fully, or cooperating with others. They are the "hiders" that seldom can be found when there is work to do, or the troublemakers who frequently fail to do work properly, or they promote trouble among staff.

Insofar as possible, personal goals should be considered and met by the employer. How does one know what their specific goals are? Ask them. Some administrators explore the goals of each employee, what they hope to attain from the job, and what they want to do in the future. Doing this about once each year can be very meaningful and will improve attitudes and performance.

Of course, the **number one** goal of most organizations and of every employee is **survival**. If the facility doesn't generate sufficient income to cover operational costs, it can forget other goals. The survival need is activated in employees when a change is introduced in the organization. Every employee momentarily stops work to determine if the change will affect his job. It is only when he is reassured that his job is safe that he resumes work.

Harmony of objectives (goals) means that organizational goals and the goals of employees are in harmony, not in conflict. Administrators and all supervisors spend a great deal of time in maintaining this harmony.

Teamwork comes about through proper handling of personal goals, fair and equal treatment, expressed confidence in employees by supervisors, and competent supervisory leadership. When supervisors and employees establish goals and make decisions together on how tasks should be performed and when supervisors give competent employees some latitude in decision making, teamwork occurs. Teamwork is a group approach that establishes group goals and considers strengths and weaknesses of each employee. It teaches cooperation and creates a work environment in which everyone pitches in to complete the total job and to help each other. The essence of **teamwork** is for administration and employees to share knowledge and maintain open communication. It is a major component of participative management. TQM is an example of the team approach.

Job satisfaction, or morale, has received much attention and study. Some management specialists point out that job satisfaction seems to depend on the employee's evaluation of his job and the environment surrounding it. The employee's evaluation is based on his actual experiences (compensation, supervision, work conditions) as compared to what he wants from the job. Three components greatly affect job satisfaction and promote a positive work environment.

1. **Organizational policies, procedures** and **practices** are a major factor. Personnel practices are particularly pertinent. Such things as compensation, promotions, and job security fall into this category. When employees feel they receive a fair wage and adequate benefits, when there is opportunity for growth and promotion, and when the job is secure as long as their work is satisfactory, job satisfaction is promoted.

2. People need to work in a **social environment**. If co-workers are pleasant, congenial, and cooperative, job satisfaction is enhanced. This includes supervisors who must treat employees with fairness and consistency, which does not mean treating everyone alike. Treating everyone alike is neither fair nor consistent. People are too different in their reactions to supervision. Some must be dealt with gently while others require very positive direction just to get their attention. Employees cannot be treated the same, they must be individualized.

3. The **work** itself must be something the employee has knowledge about and the skill to do. An employee should derive satisfaction from doing his job and feel a sense of accomplishment upon completion. Quantity of work is a part of this factor. Employees who feel they are **overworked** tend to slow down and do less. Fairness of work load assignment is important to job satisfaction.

Rewards are important to both job satisfaction and motivation. Job satisfaction from hygienic work conditions and the ability to do a job is not enough. Employees must be willing to work toward certain goals, and this is motivation. People are stimulated to action by their own needs (personal goals) and by rewards that may satisfy these needs.

Organizational rewards take many forms—pay increases, fringe benefits, work scheduling, advancement, and job security. Using ingenuity, administrators develop other material rewards that may be cherished—longevity pins, letters of commendation, employee of the month with a special parking space, and goal achievement bonuses. Some facilities show originality in the latter category.

> **Example:** A facility placed a chart on the bulletin board in the nursing service. All CNA names were listed. Each time a CNA received a compliment from a resident or a family member a gold star was placed by the aide's name. The aide with the most stars at the end of the week received a $20 bonus. Relationships between CNA's and residents and family began to improve immediately.

Rewards from the **work itself** may be great motivators. A worker's feelings of satisfaction, achievement, and accomplishment arising from what he actually does are positive rewards the job can provide. Employees who say, "I like my job; I enjoy my work," are motivated by the job itself. A spin-off from his work performance is it improves morale of other employees. They appreciate others who do their part well.

Social rewards come from the other employees in the facility. Supervisors can provide recognition, praise, and appreciation. Co-workers may provide approval and give status to persons in their group. (Heneman, et al.) The organization can control the rewards given by it and by the supervisors, but rewards given by co-workers cannot be controlled by management. They express those to each other privately and in their co-worker relationships.

SCHEDULING

The standard 40-hour work week and the 8/80 scheduling method for health care facilities were discussed earlier. There are other aspects of scheduling to be considered. Wage and Hour Division established regulations for a person working a 24-hour schedule and a person on call. The scheduling methods are complex. Administrators should refer to the W. H. Publications 1318 and 1326 for more detail.

MONITORING PERFORMANCE

The manner in which administrators and supervisors monitor performance is important to goal achievement. Certainly, administrators depend on written reports from department heads, verbal reports in staff meeting, and individual conferences. However, **regular visits** to each department and **observance** of daily activities and the physical environment are essential (MBWA). Asking specific questions about residents, materials, employees, equipment, and space utilization indicates his interest and his knowledge of work performance. Department heads and supervisors can be so wrapped up in detail they sometimes overlook important matters that an administrator's trained eye can detect.

This is extremely important to maintain adequate standards of care.

Accountability is a valuable monitoring factor. It means to hold each employee accountable for the work assigned to him, for what he does, and how he does it. When employees fail to perform up to standard there is a strong tendency to blame someone else or the organization. Regular monitoring of work keeps management in touch with employee performance and corrects deficiencies before they are magnified out of proportion or their proper perspective.

Regularity of monitoring varies with the type of work and the employees involved. Some tasks are simple enough that checking the final product is adequate. Other activities are so complex and require such a high degree of control that the entire process must be monitored daily. An example is the handling of Schedule II drugs. Not only should the director of nursing monitor this activity daily, but both the administrator and the pharmacist should check regularly to ensure the standards are met.

Monitoring the performance of **individual employees** varies with many things—the employee's training and experience, his reaction to monitoring, and the complexity of the job. Simple tasks handled by experienced employees may need little monitoring. In fact, monitoring too often and too closely gives the feeling the supervisor is constantly looking over the employee's shoulder. It may be interpreted as a lack of confidence in the worker. On the other hand, **infrequent monitoring** may be interpreted by some employees to mean the work is not important and that a high level of performance is not necessary.

Predictability in monitoring is important. Employees should know *what* is expected, *how* it will be checked, and by *whom.* Generally, employees do not need to know *when* work will be monitored. Surprise monitoring may be necessary when work performance is substandard, or when certain inappropriate employee behavior is suspected. Unannounced and unexpected visits by the supervisor may solve a problem that is not easily identified.

EMPLOYEE TURNOVER

Management specialists generally agree that there are two major reasons employers have a serious problem keeping their staff working: (1) absenteeism and (2) turnover. **Absenteeism** simply means a person temporarily stays away from work, while **turnover** means he leaves permanently. Voluntary absenteeism refers to unscheduled absences. Involuntary absenteeism are absences due to illness or other reasons beyond the employee's control. **Voluntary turnover** means the employee leaves on this own. **Involuntary turnover** means the employer initiates the action.

Turnover rate Staff turnover rate in nursing homes is appalling as can be seen in Chart 6.1. A 100 per cent turnover in CNAs, and a 50 percent turnover in RNs and LPNs is obviously unacceptable. **Negative features of such high turnover are:** (1) financial costs, (2) poor or inadequate resident care, (3) disrupted personnel relations, (4) training staff tires of training people, only to see them leave, (5) staff works short-handed, and (6) residents dislike such frequent changes in personnel who care for them. Management specialists believe a 35 percent turnover in one year is a real problem.

Judy Parker-Tursman reports that research shows turnover now ranges between 60 percent and 80 percent per year. She cites Vetter Health Services, Inc. in Omaha whose systemwide rate was 77.6 percent in 1990 and fell to 59.8 percent in 1995 due to a program designed to reduce turnover. The rate of turnover is computed simply by dividing the number of positions the facility has into the number of employees who leave in a given period.

> **Example:** 80 positions divided into the 35 who left the facility results in: 35 ÷ 80 = 43.5 percent turnover rate.

Cost of turnover can wreck the facility's bottom line. A survey by the Tennessee Health Care Association and Vanderbilt University showed the cost of recruiting, interviewing, checking references, hiring, orienting, and training one CNA ranges from $800 to $2,600. If a facility has 15

Chart 6.1:

Staff Turnover Rate — by position 1994-1996

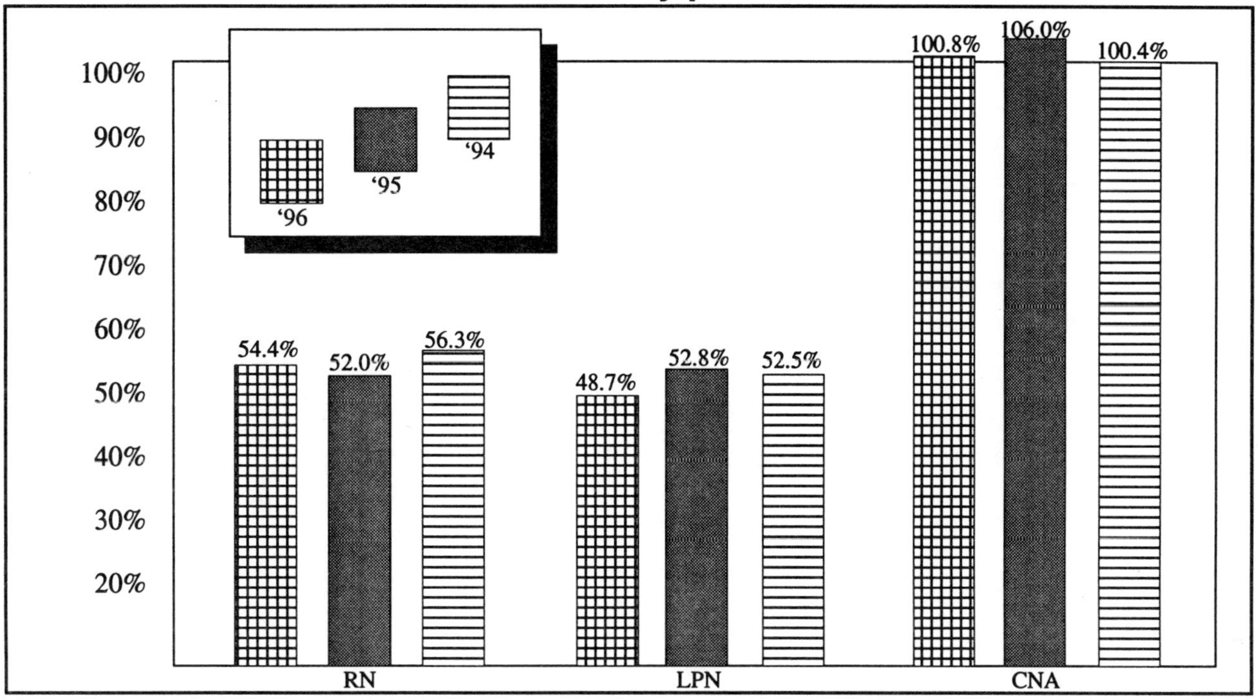

Source: American Health Care Association and Buck Consultants

CNA's and seven leave (46.9 percent) and it costs $1,200 to train one aide, total cost for new CNA training would be $8,400. Using a very conservative cost figure of $603 per employee lost through turnover, Table 6.5 shows total turnover costs for 25 to 200 employees who leave within a year. Administrators need to interpret to owners that turnover costs often far exceed the cost of a raise, better benefits and other factors that tend to reduce turnover.

Exit interviews are the starting point in resolving turnover problems. The administrator should interview every person leaving his employ to determine why they leave and from which department. Findings of these interviews should be documented and analyzed preparatory to developing a program to reduce turnover.

The Consolidated Omnibus Budget Reconciliation Act (COBRA) provides that every facility having *health insurance* must offer an employee who leaves the opportunity of staying in the program for at least 18 months. The exit interview is a good time to discuss this and document whether the departing employee wishes to remain in the program. Of course, he would have to pay the entire fee plus a small amount for handling, if the facility wished to charge. The **purpose** is to ensure no one is suddenly without insurance coverage.

Table 6.5:

High Cost of Absenteeism

How Much Will You Lose This Year?

Number of Employees	Average Annual Loss
25	$15,075.00
50	$30,150.00
75	$45,225.00
100	$60,300.00
125	$75,375.00
150	$90,450.00
175	$105,525.00
200	$120,600.00

Source: The 1996 Commerce Clearing House Unscheduled Absence Survey. Actual costs are 10-25% higher when related expenses are included.

Reasons for leaving are varied, but studies show that most often the major reason for leaving is the feeling of not being appreciated. In other words, job satisfaction is lacking. This is such a broad statement that administrators should determine its specifics. Do they leave because of the pay? Poor supervision? Poor working conditions? Difficulty with other staff? Lack of reinforcement when work performance is of top quality? Are procedures not well understood? Do they have input in decisions made on their work? All of these, and others, contribute to job satisfaction or dissatisfaction.

In areas where facilities start line employees at minimum wage, the problem is that basic physiological needs–food, clothing, shelter, etc.– cannot be met with that rate of pay. Often, new employees receive their first pay checks, look them over, and say, "I can do better than that on welfare." And they are right, for public assistance reportedly equals $8 to $15 per hour when the value of food stamps, medical care, housing, and cash is tabulated. For them, work is a losing proposition.

Solutions to turnover should not be too difficult when administrators know why employees quit. The following ideas may be of value to owners who want to provide quality care.

1. **Better pay, less welfare** is one solution to turnover. It should be helpful if facilities set up an increment pay plan when they are using the new minimum wage. There should be entrance pay, then an increase in three to six months, followed by annual increases closely tied to meritorious work performance. Gradually, longevity means something to employees who do their work well. Of course, this increased pay will come out of owner profits. With many owners making a 20 percent to 35 percent profit on operations costs, they should sacrifice some of it for better satisfied workers and higher quality care.

Government is now reducing welfare benefits by offering workfare, more training, job placement, and limiting the length of time an individual can remain on public assistance. When these programs are fully implemented they should have impact on employee turnover rates.

Block grants to states to operate Medicaid and public assistance programs appear to be on their way. This could have a tremendous impact on turnover as some state legislators are already addressing the high profit margins realized by some–but not all, by any means–providers. If this occurs and facilities receive the same rates for Medicaid residents, there will be no place for savings on profits to be expended except for better wages and materials for higher quality care.

2. **Training and advancement** opportunities are attractive to employees and should be a part of the staff retention program. The Sombrillo Nursing and Rehabilitation Center in Los Alamos has developed a program in which CNA's are offered an additional, more advanced training program. Upon completion they are promoted to CNA II and given a 50-cents-an-hour pay hike. The program costs little and provides great benefits to the facility. It no longer employs temporary workers who cost a lot of money, do not know the residents, and give inferior service. Some of the CNA's are using this program to move up to LPN training or to an associate degree in nursing. (Packer-Tursman)

3. **Improving worker's lives** will help meet Maslow's identified physiological needs which will reduce turnover. Providers can bring a variety of resources to bear on helping employees reduce costs of housing, food, child care, medical care, and transportation. (Packer-Tursman) Examples are:

    a. Making an agreement with a landlord for an **apartment building.** The provider could pay a monthly note for all units, whether occupied or not, in return for below-market-value rents. All units could be rented to employees at a significant savings.

    b. **Day care** for employees' children in a building that is proximal to the nursing home has demonstrated value. One facility had such a building and developed it into day care. Benefits accrued to both employees and residents. The latter thoroughly enjoyed watching children play and having some interaction with them.

c. **Bulk food buying** could be arranged through an employee-run food cooperative.

d. **Transportation** could be provided for employees with the facility van since it is not in constant use. If a group of employees lived some distance, they could carpool and have the van pick them up at a convenient point.

e. **Health insurance** could be provided through a group policy. Premiums could be shared by the provider and the employees, or employees could pay the entire premium with the facility withholding and remitting premium payments.

4. **Promoting job satisfaction** can offset leaving when an employee does not feel appreciated and the job is not interesting or challenging. Later in this chapter under employee health and safety, note the recommendations for reducing work-related injuries/illnesses. The same program can be used for job satisfaction which is a major reason for turnover– employees must feel appreciated and properly rewarded.

Nurses – particularly the younger ones – frequently want to do "hands on" nursing, and they may leave if it isn't provided. A change in nursing-resident ratio provided more job satisfaction for nurses in the Northwood Health-care Center in Bedford, NH. It offered nurses higher pay, more hands-on care, and heightened responsibility for residents' well-being. The number of RN's and LPN's was increased and the number of CNA's reduced, with the total nursing personnel remaining the same. This primary nursing program has significantly reduced turnover, provided job satisfaction, and promoted career development. (Packer-Tursman)

PERFORMANCE EVALUATIONS

Two major **purposes** in evaluating, or appraising, employee performance are: (1) to help the employee improve his performance and (2) to help management evaluate its own policies and procedures. Evaluations (or appraisals) are done periodically, either quarterly, semi-annually, or annually, and usually by the immediate supervisor. The immediate supervisor is more familiar with an employee's performance and behavior and, therefore, usually best qualified to conduct the evaluation.

An **evaluation form** is most often used. It lists characteristics and behaviors, such as (1) knowledge of job, (2) level of skill, (3) work completion, (4) attendance, (5) cooperation, (6) initiative, and (7) job interest. Many evaluation forms are available, but no one has developed a form that is universally satisfactory. Such forms can be helpful in seeking to standardize evaluations so that all employee performance is measured by the same fair and unbiased scale.

Generally, the supervisor seeks to measure an employee's work performance by determining how well he followed procedures and attained the goals established for his particular job. Employees are seldom compared to each other in evaluations. Measurement of work performance is far more difficult in health-care facilities than in certain businesses where both volume and quality of output are easily identified. Some businesses can measure performance by the number of satisfactory units produced or the volume of sales made. Measuring work performance for **services** rendered is far less objective.

Objectivity in evaluation is important, but much of evaluation is subjective. Objective measures are written reports, attendance records, work completion, volume of materials used, and number of documented errors. **Subjective** measures include the supervisor's observations and opinions of work quality, employee attitudes, and cooperation. Managers must remember they are evaluating performance, not personalities.

Methods of evaluation vary widely. Two methods frequently used in nursing facilities are: (1) The supervisor fills out the evaluation form and discusses it with the employee; and (2) the employee and the supervisor each fill out a form and the employee evaluates himself with the supervisor. Studies show that in using the second method employees tend to score themselves lower than their supervisors do. This is not always the case as shown by the following.

> **Example:** At evaluation time Ms. M, who was housekeeping supervisor, scored herself superior in all 12 content areas on the evaluation form. Two weeks later the facility was surveyed, and housekeeping had more deficiencies than all other departments combined. Ms. M was not aware there were many things she did not know. This is not an admirable quality in a supervisor. She was terminated and counseled to seek training as an executive housekeeper. She undertook this training, secured a job in another facility, and became a most capable supervisor.

The second method may not work with **nurses** and other **professional staff**. They are fully trained, consider themselves to be knowledgeable enough to make professional decisions, and usually do not underestimate their performance.

Whichever method is used, an employee should not be confronted with anything new at evaluation time. If monitoring of work and correcting of errors are properly carried out, the evaluation becomes a summary of what has transpired during the evaluation period.

Documentation of performance evaluations is imperative. The form must be dated and signed by both the supervisor and the employee. If the employee wishes to add comments to the evaluation, let him do so. The employee should be assured that signing the evaluation does not mean he agrees, it means it has been discussed with him. If an employee refuses to sign, the supervisor should note on the form that the employee chose not to sign.

Performance evaluations are a complex management tool that is often improperly used, and this subject cannot be adequately dealt with in this publication. It is prudent and certainly advantageous for administrators to attend seminars on performance evaluations, employ a consultant to help develop a system appropriate to the facility, and carefully train supervisors.

Recent developments Some personnel management specialists now recommend that performance evaluations be discontinued because they tend to emphasize the negative aspects of work performance. This should not be true since a proper evaluation deals with both positive and negative performance.

DISCIPLINE

Discipline is action taken when an employee disregards a procedure or rule that specifically indicates disciplinary action will be taken, or when an employee fails to respond to repeated correction of errors. The **purpose** of discipline is to change employee behavior from unacceptable to acceptable and to help them improve work performance. Several types of discipline may be utilized and all should be carefully outlined in the personnel PPR's, and in the employee handbook.

1. **Oral reprimand** is warning an employee he must terminate certain action or behavior to avoid more severe measures. Any oral reprimand should be documented by the supervisor.

2. **Written reprimand** means to conduct a formal conference with an employee. The conference must be documented, dated, and signed by both supervisor and employee and made a permanent part of the employee's record.

3. **Docking pay** is a reduction of the regular eight-hour work period by the number of minutes or hours an employee failed to work. This is used for tardiness and other forms of absenteeism.

4. **Suspension** means not allowing a person to work for a specified period of time. Suspension may be with or without pay.

5. **Termination** is removing an employee from his job on a permanent basis.

Fairness and consistency in discipline are mandatory. Wage and Hour Division officials and EEOC will not permit discrimination. If a nurse and an aide are guilty of the same offense, management cannot be more lenient with the nurse simply because nurses are in greater demand.

Example: The DON made a surprise visit to the nursing home during the night shift. She found the LPN charge nurse asleep on a couch and an orderly asleep in a vacant room. The orderly was terminated, but the nurse was suspended two weeks without pay as nurses were in short supply. The orderly filed a complaint with Wage and Hour Division. After a hearing the facility was ordered to reinstate the orderly with back pay because of unfair and discriminatory employment practices.

The **most severe** disciplinary action is likely to be taken when employees abuse or neglect residents, misuse resident property, report to work under the influence of alcohol or illicit drugs or fight on the job. Generally, there is a rule that these and some other offenses are grounds for dismissal on the first offense.

Techniques of discipline are important. An employee may be publicly reprimanded, embarrassed, reproached, penalized, or subjected to any one of a dozen hostile, aggressive approaches to discipline, and there will be no effective positive change in behavior. The employee, however, will be angry and defensive. All his energy will be directed toward defending himself rather than dealing with his problem. A **problem-solving** approach is a far more effective technique. Try using these steps.

Step 1 Decide if an effort will be made to try to salvage the employee or if the problem is one that must be solved at all costs.

Step 2 If the decision is to try salvaging the employee, call him in for a private conference. Do the homework and have all the facts available.

Step 3 Tell the employee, "We have a problem," and wait for his response. If his response is "You may have a problem, I don't," shift to a firmer stance.

Step 4 Tell him, "I didn't ask you whether we have a problem. I said we have a problem and you are part of it." Usually, the employee will respond by asking what that means

Step 5 Briefly identify something specific he has done and how it affects his performance, his co-workers, and the supervisor.

Step 6 If he starts making excuses or blaming others, say "You want to talk about..., I want to talk about what you just did."

Step 7 Shift immediately to problem solving by asking "What can you do to make sure this does not happen again?" Do not spend time exploring reasons or asking why. That is an ineffective approach. Maintain focus on the problem and its solution.

Most employees will problem-solve with their supervisor and arrive at solutions. If they do not, then shift to the firm confrontation technique described earlier in this chapter. It may mean termination.

Document all disciplinary action. If it is oral, simply make a note of it for the record. If it is written, date and sign it and ask the employee to sign. File it in his record. Such documentation is invaluable if the employee is finally terminated for any reason and he tries to collect unemployment benefits.

Abuse, neglect and misappropriation of resident property requires specific action by the administrator. [42CFR 483.13(L)] Refer to Chapter 10 in Legal Management for a clear legal definition of these terms. HCFA mandates that a facility develop and implement policies and procedures that prohibit mistreatment, neglect, and abuse of residents and the misappropriation of resident property. **Purpose** of the regulation is to ensure that the facility has an effective system, regardless of source (staff, other residents, visitors, and others), that prevents these forms of mistreatment. This system does not guarantee a resident will not be abused. It simply assures the facility will do everything in its power to control and prevent any form of mistreatment of a resident or mishandling of resident's property.

An **occurrence** of any incidence of mistreatment, abuse or neglect, or misappropriation of property must be handled in this manner.

1. Report it immediately to the administrator and to the state Medicaid agency, and others as required by state law.

2. Fully investigate and document the incident.

3. Report findings to the state Medicaid agency, and in case of a CNA, report it to the state CNA Register, both within five working days.

4. Ensure that the incident cannot reoccur while the investigation is in process.

5. If the alleged violation is verified, take appropriate corrective action. Any staff member found guilty can never be employed in a nursing home again.

UNEMPLOYMENT INSURANCE

In some states one of the administrator's biggest personnel problems is unemployment insurance. Employees are terminated for valid reasons, such as abuse, neglect, sleeping on the job, absenteeism, and fighting only to have the state's employment security office declare them eligible for unemployment benefits. Every administrator should secure publications from his state employment security office and carefully study this program which can be costly to the facility.

Unemployment insurance is a program that provides temporary weekly benefits for workers who have lost their jobs through no fault of their own, are able to work, are available for work, are actually seeking suitable employment, and who have earned sufficient base period wages from covered employers to qualify for benefits. (Sherman and Bohlander) This state program must follow regulations of the Federal Unemployment Tax Act (FUTA) and the Social Security Act. Funding of the program is discussed in Chapter 7 on Financial Management.

Unemployment benefits are paid, usually for up to 26 weeks, from the tax paid to the state. The 26-week period is often extended when certain extenuating economic conditions exist. The state costs for administering the benefits program is paid from FUTA funds, provided the state program is in compliance with FUTA and SSA regulations.

Objectives of the program are admirable and if properly attained, they have an impact on the economy. Following is a list of one state's purposes.

1. To assist the prompt employment of persons seeking work and to help employers obtain qualified employees

2. To lessen hardships to the involuntary unemployed

3. To stabilize purchasing power, halting the spread of unemployment and the economic disruption it causes

4. To lessen the need for public relief and charity

Admirable though these purposes are, in some states administrators feel the program has become a form of relief and charity. The office of employment security in these states considers the only justifiable basis for terminating an employee without benefits being paid is misconduct. It is difficult to obtain a clear definition of what the state considers misconduct.

> **Example**: An LPN walked off the job just before scheduled medications pass. She was the only nurse on duty so she was terminated for neglect of her patients. She applied for unemployment benefits and they were granted. The facility requested a hearing in which the state ruled the LPN had just cause for leaving. No consideration was given to her neglect of patients and the fact she could have given and hour or two notice so a replacement could be called in.

Administrators often complain that the office of employment security is vague about what constitutes adequate documentation. They say the state frequently rules a facility has not properly documented misconduct yet they provide no clear guidelines to follow.

> **Example**: The DON visited the nursing home at 11:30 PM and found a nurse aide asleep and snoring in a lounge chair. She awakened the aide and terminated her for neglect of duty by sleeping on the job. The state ruled she

was eligible for unemployment benefits because the facility had not properly handled and documented the case. At the end of the hearing the administrator asked the state to please advise what would be satisfactory documentation for similar cases in the future. The state's answer: "You should write out the dismissal and place it in the employee's lap so she will see it when she wakes up."

Many similar cases are cited by administrators' who contend that the program amounts to public welfare. They should be concerned about these practices because they not only cost the facility in unemployment taxes but in hiring costs for new employees. Also, when ordered to reinstate an employee, the facility is faced with an untenable personnel problem in the form of an employee who feels he can get by with most anything. But the problem is not with the state; it is with the administrator who in every case he loses has not kept adequate records or handled the problem properly. The state offices of employment security do not want ineligible employees to draw unemployment benefits either. The problem is they must follow the law, so when the administrator is in error the state must rule in favor of the employee. Most states employment security offices have an educational team that will conduct seminars, at no expense, for nursing homes and any other employers. They describe in detail what must be done and provide clearly written guidelines that will help administrators avoid error.

UNION ACTIVITIES

In recent years organized labor has lost membership in industry and business to the extent that it now focuses heavily on the service fields, especially government employees and health-care workers. **Unionization** of employees means personnel/human resource activities are jointly determined by management and the union, i.e., wages, hours, schedules, and benefits. Activities are carried on by management, subject to monitoring by the union. (See Chapter 11 for details on the Fair Labor Standards Act (FLSA) and Federal regulations)

Conditions favoring unionization include: (1) poor supervision, which is the primary cause, (2) job dissatisfaction, (3) low wages and fringe benefits, (4) lack of grievance procedures, and other inadequate management practices. It has often been said that labor cannot organize a group of satisfied employees. There must be a sufficient degree of dissatisfaction with management for unions to organize. Some contend that the employees most susceptible to unionization are friends of union members. This may be generally true, but there are exceptions in which union members advise health-care employees not to unionize.

Example: A union attempted to organize a large health-care center in a heavily industrialized city. More than 80% of the center staff were women and the majority of these were married to industry employees. As the administrator planned his program to discourage unionizing, he became aware of this situation. He learned that husbands were advising their wives to vote against the union – it was good for them in industry, but they did not think it would help a health-care center. At the close of employee meetings where unionizing was discussed, management reminded married employees, "Listen to what your husband says." The election went two and one-half to one against the union.

Signs of union activity can be noted by the administrator. When small groups are seen talking in hallways and lounges, and they disperse when the administrator appears, it can be a sign of efforts to organize. Another sign is that these same employees tend to avoid the administrator; or they speak but continue doing their work, obviously not wanting to talk. Often a stranger may be seen talking with one or more employees, and they stop or walk away when the administrator appears. Unions do not always come to the administrator to let him know of their interest in trying to organize his staff.

Unions try to develop an in-house organizing committee with whom they meet at restaurants, taverns, and other gathering places–usually at night and on weekends. At this point it is no secret and activity begins to spill over into the facility as noted above. (Bedelian)

Things to do When **labor** attempts to **organize** the first thing to do is confer with a labor relations specialist, frequently an attorney, and develop a plan of action. Labor relations are too complex for most administrators to deal with alone. After conferring with a labor relations specialist, call all supervisors together and advise them of the facility's stand. It is usually wise to clearly state that while management is not against organized labor, it does not believe a union will help the employees or the facility. Supervisors should be informed that they are a part of management and are expected to represent management's stand on unions. If a supervisor supports the union and this stance is not resolved at this point there can be trouble.

> **Example:** An administrator did not clarify early in a union organizing campaign the role and support expected of supervisors. He did not indicate they were a part of management and were expected to support management's point of view. Several employees told the administrator the dietary manager was encouraging her staff to join the union effort. The administrator called her in for a conference and confronted her. She said she believed the union would be helpful. The administrator told her she was expected to support his stance against unionizing. She said she could not do that, so he terminated her. She advised the union organizers who reported the situation to the National Labor Relations Board. (NLRB) The Board ruled the administrator was harassing her and indirectly threatening other employees by sending the unspoken message, "You see what happened to her; she was for the union, and I fired her." The facility had to reinstate the manager.

It may be advantageous for a labor relations consultant to conduct training sessions to teach supervisors what management can and cannot do and to indicate what actions they are to take. These are some things management **can** do.

Step 1 Conduct employee meetings and tell them the disadvantages of unions, using specific instances concerning employees who organized and were later dissatisfied.

Step 2 Invite administrators whose facilities have been organized to speak to employees and enumerate actual disadvantages of the union.

Step 3 Discipline employees who discuss the union or hand out literature while **on the job**.

Step 4 Tell employees what collective bargaining is, that the union cannot guarantee them anything, that they may lose benefits as bargaining may start at minimum wage with no fringe benefits.

Step 5 Tell employees that if they organize, a labor union representative will act for them when they have a complaint and individuals will not be able to bargain directly with management.

Step 6 Advise all employees that the supervisor who favors a union does not represent or speak for management.

Step 7 Tell employees that signing a card now does not mean they must vote for or join the union if the facility is organized.

Step 8 Tell employees if they go out on strike they can be replaced and cannot be guaranteed their job when the strike is over; i.e., if a strike is for better wages or benefits.

Step 9 Forbid labor representatives and off-duty employees to pass out union literature in resident-care areas. Inform them it is allowed only in nonresident-care locations when employees are off duty.

Some **things the administrator cannot do** when the union attempts to organize are defined as tips:

TIPS

1. **Threaten** to fire or demote an employee who supports the union.

2. **Interrogate** employees by asking if they are for or against the union, have they signed a card, or do they attend union meetings.

3. **Promise** a raise, promotion, or any other benefits if they vote against the union.

4. **Surveillance** of employees by watching to see who attends meetings, discusses unions or passes out union literature on their own time, and, an **administrator can never try to attend** a union meeting himself.

Card signing and the hearing If 30 percent of the employees sign union cards and the union submits them to the National Labor Relations Board (NLRB), an election may be called. Most unions do not submit at the 30 percent level. They get more signatures first. A Board hearing is conducted to determine who is **eligible to vote**. Management is often surprised by the NLRB list, as many supervisors are not considered a part of management. Whether a supervisor is classified as management depends largely on the degree of authority delegated to him and the number of people he supervises. If he cannot hire, discipline, and fire, the supervisor will generally be classified as a worker eligible to vote.

Election After the hearing the NLRB decides whether an election is to be held and who will be in the voting unit. The election is usually held at the facility and presided over by an NRLB representative. Both the union and the facility appoint election watchers who observe the voting. **If 50 percent plus one** of the employees who vote, vote for the union, the union will be established. The administrator should ensure that all employees that are against unionizing cast their votes.

Bargaining When the union is established, bargaining will begin. Before going to the bargaining table, the administrator should determine what the union will request and decide what concessions, if any, he will agree to regarding wages, fringe benefits, and other matters. He has employees who will share this information with him. The administrator should always be accompanied to the bargaining table by his labor relations specialist. The specialist should be fully apprised of anticipated requests and what concessions the facility will make. Remember the labor union representatives are professionals at bargaining. The administrator will likely be overwhelmed without help of an expert bargainer.

Negotiation begins at the bargaining table where a **labor/management contract** must be developed. Steps in negotiation are:

1. The union presents a list of its demands. This should be in written form.

2. The employer obtains the list and usually spends a day or more studying the demands.

3. Management and labor return to the bargaining table to take up each demand.

4. Management presents its counter demands, usually one by one.

5. Negotiation begins. It is a give-and-take action. The union usually agrees to less than its original demands, and the employer agrees to somewhat more than his counter-demand offer. On some counter-issues the employer will not agree at all, so the union loses this demand. Or the union may threaten to take employees out on strike if an acceptable degree of the demand is not approved.

As each demand is settled, if there is agreement, it is reduced to writing. It becomes the labor/management contract which management and labor both sign. Each is bound to abide by provisions of the agreement during that period.

Demands The first demand of the union is usually a check off for union dues. They ask management to deduct union dues from employee paychecks and remit the total to the union since it is often difficult for the union to collect individual dues. The administrator must do his homework and determine ahead of time what this will cost the facility. He will not likely get by with saying, "We cannot do that; it will cost too much". The union officials will have already familiarized themselves with the facility's margin of profit. The administrator must have his accountant determine ahead of time what the cost to the facility will be. If the administrator can say, "That will cost us $3,250 per year, and we cannot afford to make that contribution to the union," he then has a strong bargaining point.

Length of the contract An administrator should never sign a labor/management contract for longer than one year, though his employees through the union may request two or three years. The reason is that both management and labor are bound by the agreement for the period specified in the contract. Employees often become disillusioned with the union and want to terminate the agreement.

> **Example:** A nursing home entered into a three-year contract. Employees were disappointed in the union and wanted out. The administrator advised that they could sign a petition and present it to the NLRB for consideration.

Decertification If they want out, employees who are union members may sign a decertification petition and present it to the NLRB. The Board will conduct a decertification election at the end of the current contract period. In the example above that would be two and one-half years later.

Representation Unions seek to become the bargaining agent for employees. After the election that results in establishing a union, stewards are selected to represent employees in their demands of management. When an employee has a problem, a steward takes it to management rather than the employee himself. Negotiation skills are a must for administrators in these matters. The facility may have policies and procedures that call for termination of the employees, whereas the union feels that a written reprimand is sufficient. Through the give and take of negotiation the administrator may find it best to amend policy and settle for a ten-day suspension without pay. The result is typical of negotiation in which both management and the union won a little and lost a little — the true win-lose situation.

OTHER EMPLOYEES

In addition to full-time and part-time employees, the Fair Labor Standards Act regulates certain other employees as discussed earlier in this chapter. Wage and Hour Division advises that a **resident** becomes an employee when he performs work of any consequential economic benefit to the nursing facility. This does not include such activities as voluntary personal housekeeping of the resident's own room, provided the physician has approved it as an appropriate activity for the individual resident and it is included in the resident's plan of care. Nor does it include making craft products as long as the income from sales goes to individual residents or is used to purchase materials consumed in making the craft products.

Private duty nurses and sitters are private contractors employed by the resident, family, or other responsible party. A facility may not specify who the nurse or sitter will be, what rate will be paid, what resident they will care for, nor when the work will be performed. All private duty nurses and sitters should be oriented to the facility and its policies and procedures. They should be instructed that while on duty in the facility they are to abide by the facility practices concerning behavior and work performance. With proper orientation and development of staff relationships, private duty nurses and sitters can be of considerable assistance in providing excellent resident care.

EMPLOYEE COUNSELING

Employee counseling involves considerable skill. When employees bring problems or complaints to management the most important action is to listen. Do so without criticism or advice until the employee presents his case and gets the negative feelings off his chest. Do not make hasty decisions or give advice prematurely. Responses such as, "I don't think it is that bad," and "Maybe you are overreacting," are not appropriate. To the employee it is that bad and they do feel strongly. Speak with **low affect** — without showing strong feeling — so the employee will not become defensive. Accept the employee's anger by simply saying, "I understand how you feel" or "I can see this is upsetting."

Problem Solving Techniques should be used. If an employee brings a problem to his supervisor, these steps should be followed:

1. Let the employee unload his feelings — irritation, anger, and others. (See crisis intervention, next paragraph)

2. Employees usually ask for a solution — "What do you want me to do about this?" Do not give one.

3. Say, "Let's start with what you have done already. How have you handled it up to now?"

4. Employee will describe what he's done.

5. Help him evaluate his efforts — "How did it work? What do you suppose went wrong?"

6. Help him to identify a new approach — "What else could you do to handle this?"

7. If he comes up with a solution that will cause new problems, ask "What kind of reaction do you think we will get if we try that course of action?" Often the employee will see it is not a workable solution.

8. If he cannot identify a workable solution and you have one, ask, "Have you ever thought about (state the solution)?" Plant the idea and leave it. Often the employee will pick up on it in a few minutes as if it is his own idea, especially if it is a supervisor.

9. When a solution is decided on, ask "How do you plan to implement this action?" Anticipate reactions of the staff and how, they will be handled.

10. Plan evaluation — "How long do you want to try this before we get back together to see how it is working?" Decide a specific date and time.

Using this technique, the administrator or supervisor has effected a true win-win solution. He has won since he helped his employee solve a problem. The employee has won because he developed his own solution. Some theorists call this a **nondirective technique** of counseling. You do ask open-ended questions that cannot be answered with a yes or no, but the technique is called **creative-problem solving**. It results in more workable solutions because the solutions are those of the employee who is much more committed to implementing and insuring his success.

Crisis intervention uses some of the above skills but is somewhat different. Periodically, everyone loses emotional equilibrium. One becomes so angry, irritated, anxious, or defensive he cannot use the knowledge and skill for which he was employed. A person cannot think things out, cannot make a decision, and cannot listen with his usual understanding. Strong emotion is literally blocking his ability to do his work properly. That person needs to ventilate, to get it off his chest. He needs a listener, not someone to instruct him. Sometimes a person in this situation will say to the other, "I need your ear, not your tongue." It's literally true. The individual needs to explode.

> **Example:** A DON walked into the administrator's office and said, "You've just got to do something about the night shift!" The administrator put his pen down, gave full attention and said, "Tell me about it," The DON poured out irritation and anger about some of the night personnel who half did their work, slept on the job, or left the building to go to a fast food store. The DON said, "I feel like cracking some heads!" After about five minutes of ventilating she slowed down, stopped, then took a deep breath. She got up, said, "Thank you," and walked out. The administrator had done nothing but listen–no advice, no suggestions, nothing. The DON told the administrator several days later how she worked the problem out.

It is obvious what had happened. The DON ventilated her feelings and gained access to the knowledge and skills she normally used. She did not want the administrator to do anything, nor to give her any instructions. This scenario was repeated several times during the ensuing months with the explosive session lasting only three to five minutes. One day after she ventilated, took the deep breath, and stood up to leave the administrator asked, "By the way, how do you plan to handle that?" Her response, "I don't know exactly, I just have a feeling I can do it." That's crisis intervention, letting a person get feelings out of the way so they can perform their usual duties.

The administrator with department heads, supervisors with their employees, social workers with family members, and anyone else who listens until a person regains his emotional equilibrium does crisis intervention. The signal of success is the deep breath after which the person becomes quiet, is ready to leave, changes the subject, or enters into problem solving if he really wants assistance in deciding what action to take.

Occasionally, a person feels guilty or a bit uncomfortable after ventilating and starts to apologize. The listener should respond in some way that alleviates the guilt, such as, "I think you were quite justified in feeling that way," or "I can see how that would upset anybody"–some expression to indicate it's quite acceptable, apologies not needed.

The **key person** in handling employee problems and grievances is the immediate supervisor. His ability and style of handling problems when they first appear are singularly important. Some supervisors seek to squelch problems or they distort the circumstances as they pass them up the administrative hierarchy. This only creates new problems. An understanding supervisor who deals openly and frankly with employees can resolve many problems before they reach the grievance stage.

Negotiation Some personnel management theorists advance the concept that management must be good negotiators with their staff. In practice it is seldom used with the same effectiveness of creative-problem solving. Outside of negotiating a union contract, management seldom negotiates, especially with employees. Occasionally, he might have to negotiate a salary with a DON or other professional employees. But even then it is a win/lose technique. Both management and the employee must give up something — each compromises which by nature is always a win/lose experience. There is no way to make it a win/win approach.

GRIEVANCE PROCEDURES

Grievance procedures are designed to ensure that employees have opportunity for due process when they believe management has not acted fairly. The procedures allow employees access to superiors to air their opinions and feelings. Several methods are used, including **direct anonymous** access to top management to report complaints. An employee registers an anonymous complaint that must be investigated and remedial action taken when indicated. (Heneman, et al.) Some means of getting feedback to the anonymous employee must be devised, and that may be difficult, especially when no action is indicated.

The **ombudsman** method uses a designated employee who hears complaints and has certain authority to investigate, counsel, and make some decisions. Sometimes this method creates resentment on the part of supervisors unless the ombudsman is an unusually skilled counselor. Supervisors feel he is usurping their authority, and to a degree this may be true.

Some health-care facilities use an **employee review board**. The members of the board hear complaints and seek to act impartially in resolving major grievances. Sometimes the board is made up of employees at the same organization level as the grievant. Employees usually favor this method, feeling they will get a fairer hearing from co-workers. In practice the co-worker board often makes harsher decisions than management.

A more **traditional method** is movement of a grievance up the administrative hierarchy when it cannot be resolved at a lower level. This method uses procedures which usually require the complaint to be written and reported first to the immediate supervisor. If not settled, it is moved to the department head. If the grievant is still not satisfied, it goes to the administrator or a grievance committee. In this method, no supervisor has authority to prevent an employee from taking a grievance to a higher authority.

All facilities need some type of grievance procedure to ensure that employees feel they will be heard. When no grievance program is used, employees often say, "It doesn't do any good to complain when something is wrong. Nobody is interested." Often this is the kind of employee dissatisfaction that sets the stage for unionizing.

Employee complaints Every employee's complaint should be fully investigated by the supervisor, the administrator or by another grievance method. When complaints go unnoticed or are squelched, employees experience frustration and often feel management doesn't care about them. Following the investigation, the employee should be given feedback on the findings and what action, if any, will be taken. It may be the complaint is unfounded or the desired action cannot be taken; but, the fact that the complaint is taken seriously, the employee is heard, and he receives feedback, greatly contributes to a positive work atmosphere.

PERSONNEL RECORDS

Although HCFA does not require that **personnel records** be maintained on each employee, no facility can operate efficiently without them. All data kept in the record should be accurate and confidential. More than half of the states have legislation holding private employers responsible for the accuracy of data in personnel files, and granting employees the right to periodically inspect and, if necessary, to correct information in the files. Management must check carefully to ensure that data is correct and updated at all times. However, it should be noted that the U.S. Department of Labor has no regulations granting an employee the right to access his record or to obtain a copy.

Agencies other than HCFA do require personnel records. Some of these are EEOC, Wage and Hour Division, IRS, Social Security, and Immigration and Naturalization Services.

Only job related information should be kept. This includes:

1. Personal data, such as name, date of birth, sex, address, social security number, and minority group
2. Recruitment and selection data, application, interview summaries, references, and so on
3. Work experience data, jobs held since employed by the facility, and specific skills
4. Compensation data, and record of pay and increases
5. Performance evaluations
6. Benefit plan data, vacation and sick leave records,
7. Attendance record
8. Health/safety/accident data
9. Orientation and in-service training data, dates and training topics
10. Disciplinary action, reprimands, suspensions, demotions, etc.

All data must be factual. Opinions and references to personality should be omitted. Much of this identifying data may be obtained only after the individual is employed.

The same regulations apply to personnel records relating to prospective-employee interviews. There can be no documentation of information concerning religion, politics, or arrests and convictions unless the latter are related to the individual's job. As noted earlier, arrest and conviction record keeping is changing as some states now require a criminal record check before employment.

Personnel records are **confidential**. The employee handling these records cannot discuss content with anyone except as authorized by the administrator. Personnel records should be kept under lock and key, available only to authorized staff, usually the record clerk, supervisor, the administrator, and the individual employee if the state provides for it. Following is an example of problems the lack of confidentiality may cause.

Example: A facility operating a general hospital and an adolescent psychiatric unit employed an RN who later developed agoraphobia. She took sick leave days to undergo psychiatric treatment. Her leave request showed the name of her physician, and the personnel records clerk recognized the physician as a psychiatrist. She passed the word through the facility grapevine. Later, the facility closed its general hospital unit converting it to adult psychiatry. The RN, who worked in the general hospital applied for the new unit after being terminated. She was denied reemployment by the DON who told her they did not think she had the emotional stability to work with psychiatric patients. The RN called her attorney who conferred with the administrator. The RN was rehired next day with back pay. The administrator recognized she had grounds for tort action.

Value Personnel records serve as an objective source of data for decision making on personnel matters. They may be checked by EEOC, the Wage and Hour Division, the state licensing and certification agency, and other appropriate authorities who require certain data to be included or excluded from the records.

EMPLOYEE HEALTH AND SAFETY

OBRA mandates that facilities provide a safe and healthy environment for residents, personnel, and the public, and OSHA requires a safe and healthy workplace for staff. And well they should, as nursing homes in 1994 had the second highest incident rate of on-the-job injuries and illnesses among industries reporting 100,000 or more cases. (See Table 6.6)

Table 6.6:

WORK-RELATED INJURIES/ ILLNESSES 1994

Industry	Total cases	Incidents per 100 full-time employees
Motor vehicles and mfg.	171,400	18.2
Long-term care facilities	217,200	16.5
All private industry	6,800,000	8.4

Source: Bureau of Labor Statistics

The Service Employees International Union (SEIU) used this data in an organizing effort. The union was able to get stories in the newspaper emphasizing that nursing homes were more dangerous to work in than mining and other industries considered dangerous by the public.

Leslie Nier in the *Provider* quotes extensive studies made on work-related injuries. The only two factors that showed significant correlation were a history of lower back injury and job dissatisfaction. One of these studies conducted by the National Institute of OSHA identified "unhealthy stress as the cause of occupational injury and disease." Robert Rosen, a specialist in workplace health improvement, found several factors can lead to unhealthy stress among workers.

1. Too much or too little responsibility
2. Not being able to use personal talents and abilities effectively
3. Lack of control or authority over job decisions
4. Poor supervision
5. Tense work relationships
6. Impaired communications and lack of opportunity to voice opinions
7. Confusion about one's job or role within the organization
8. Inadequate rewards and recognition

It is readily seen that nursing homes cannot do anything about a history of lower back injury, but much can be done about work dissatisfaction. Most of these have been discussed in this Chapter and in Chapter 3. Nier makes these suggestions:

1. Use Total Quality Management that utilizes employee knowledge.
2. Provide proper supervisory-training opportunities.
3. Clearly define goals and expectations for employee performance and show them how their work contributes to overall goals.

4. Assign duties and delegate authority in a way employees have more control over job decisions.

5. Provide ongoing skill training and job knowledge for all employees.

6. Reward work performance and job dedication.

Another aspect of employee health and safety is a program that investigates and takes corrective action, and documents all work-related accidents in accord with OSHA standards. (See Chapter 8) Also, it provides proper training for lifting, turning and other behaviors that are hazards to safety. This type of training is now promoted by OSHA and is offered by this agency on a limited basis.

GLOSSARY

Absenteeism Temporarily staying away from work whether for 15 minutes or for days.

Accident Unintentional occurrences of physical damage to an object or an injury to an individual.

Accountability Holding an employee answerable for work results and behavior.

ADA Americans with Disability Act that provides standards for employing individuals who have a disability.

Confidentiality Communicated in confidence, treated as private, to be revealed only as authorized.

Creative problem solving A form of individual or group problem solving in which an individual solves a problem or group members reach a consensus and no one is placed in a win/lose situation.

Discipline Action taken to correct an employee who disregards a procedure or rule, or who fails to respond to repeated corrections of errors.

DEA Drug Enforcement Administration that regulates handling and disposition of scheduled drugs.

Discrimination The act of making a distinction in favor of or against a person or thing based upon a group, class, or category.

Documentation To reduce to writing facts concerning any activity and to file the document.

EEOC Equal Employment Opportunity Commission, the federal agency that monitors employment in order to prevent any type of discrimination.

Employee turnover An employee permanently leaving a job either voluntarily or by action initiated by the employer.

8/80 Scheduling A special two-week scheduling period provided for health-care facilities by the Fair Labor Standards Act in which overtime is paid for all hours worked over eight in one day and/or all hours over 80 in a two-week pay period.

Employer/employee agreement The verbal and written agreement, in the form of PPR's, that tells an employee what is expected of him and what he can expect from management.

Employment practices Activities used by an employer in recruiting, interviewing, checking references, and employing staff.

Family Medical Leave Act Legislation regulating the granting of leave when there is a newborn child, an adoption, or a spouse needs care during a serious illness.

Fringe benefits Extra remuneration or benefits provided in addition to regular and overtime pay by an employer, such as holidays, paid leave, insurance, and other.

FTE Full-time equivalency The number of employees needed to equal 8 working hours per day 5 days per week.

Grievance An employee complaint against management when he believes management has not acted fairly.

Grievance procedure A method by which an employee may have the opportunity for due process when he believes management has not acted fairly.

Handbook A guidebook for employees that contains personnel PPR's in a simplified, abbreviated form.

Harmony of objectives When objectives (goals) of management and employee are not in conflict and both are working together toward the same end results.

INS Immigration and Naturalization Service operated by the federal government.

Increment pay plan A plan that pays a base wage rate to new employees then pays increments (raises) on a periodic basis.

Job A collection of related tasks that can be performed by an employee as contributions toward providing a certain service.

Job analysis A method used to determine the tasks, the employee behaviors, knowledge, and skills necessary to carry out a certain job. It is sometimes referred to as a job appraisal.

Job-based system A pay system in which all employees doing the same job are paid the same wages without regard to seniority or other characteristics.

Job classification Classifying each individual job providing a title, as nurse, nurse aide, secretary, dietary manager, or other.

Job description An outline of duties, authority, and qualifications of each job class.

Job satisfaction The feelings of satisfaction an employee derives from the work he performs and from the work environment. It is also called morale.

Manual A written document containing official guidelines in the form of policies, procedures, and rules, and approved by the governing body of the organization.

Merit system A pay plan in which pay increases depend on job performance.

Mixed system A pay plan in which pay increases depend on both seniority and merit.

Monitoring Action in which supervisors check the work and the performance of subordinates to determine if they measure up to standards.

Negotiation A win/lose approach to reaching agreement in which both parties compromise by give and take techniques.

NLRB National Labor Relations Board which, with the general counsel, administers the National Labor Relations Act.

Non-directive counseling A method by which the counselor asks open-ended questions to secure the counselee's feelings, ideas, and suggestions for solutions to problems.

Objectivity Unprejudiced, unbiased judgment based on facts rather than opinion.

Office of Employment Security The state office responsible for unemployment insurance program. (Title of office may differ according to state.)

Ombudsman One who makes observations and speaks or acts in behalf of another, usually a person who is not in a position to speak or act effectively for himself.

Orientation Providing information on duties, goals, procedures, materials, and so on that employees need to carry out their work assignments.

OSHA Occupational Safety and Health Administration, the federal agency that monitors business and industry in order to ensure a safe and healthy workplace.

Overtime Hours worked beyond the standard 40-hour work week; or in 8/80 scheduling, hours worked beyond eight in one day and beyond 80 in a two-week work period.

Overtime pay The minimum of one and one-half times base pay which must be paid wage employees for overtime worked.

Performance evaluation Systematic measurement, or appraisal, of employee performance whereby both employee and employer learn how effectively the job is being performed.

Positive approach A human relations method in which employees initiate contact with a resident by commenting on and discussing pleasant topics of special interest to the resident.

Positive hygiene factors As identified by F. Herzberg, such things as company policy and administration, supervision, working conditions, pay, security, and other factors that are necessary to prevent job dissatisfaction, but do not necessarily motivate employees.

Positive work atmosphere A work atmosphere created by management in which employees feel understood, appreciated and valued.

PPR's Policies, procedures, and rules.

Professional One who is guided by a set of principles or rules that is not expected to apply to the general public.

Promotion policy One that states whether vacancies above the beginning-worker level will be filled by promoting employees within the organization or by recruiting outside prospects.

Reciprocal relations A management principle describing how a change in one unit of an organization affects all other units either directly or indirectly.

Rewards Pay increases, benefits, advancement, job security, recognition, status, praise, sense of achievement, and other things that meet employee needs.

Salaried employee One who is exempt by wage and hour standards from workweek requirements and overtime pay.

Seniority system A pay plan in which raises are given only on the basis of seniority, a favorite plan of organized labor.

Shift differential Added pay for working on more undesirable shifts in the evening and at night.

Sick leave Paid leave that an employee earns and may take when too ill to work.

Suspension Temporary removal of an employee from his job with or without pay for a specified period of time, usually a disciplinary action.

Teamwork A positive working relationship that occurs when management and employees share goals and knowledge and maintain open communication.

Termination Discharging an employee for any one of a variety of reasons.

Transfer Lateral transfer of an employee from one unit to another with no increase or decrease in pay.

Unionization Personnel/human resources activities are jointly determined by management and a union, and activities are carried out by management subject to monitoring by the union.

Vacation leave Paid leave that an employee earns and can take upon mutual agreement with management.

Wage and Hour Division A unit of the U.S. Department of Labor that carries out provisions of the Fair Labor Standards Act.

Wage employee An employee covered under minimum wage, overtime, and other regulations of the Wage and Hour Division.

REFERENCES

Allen, James E., *Nursing Home Administration*, Third edition, New York: Springer Publishing Co., Inc., 1997.

Bedelian, Arthur G., *Management,* Third Edition, New York: The Dryden Press, 1994.

Cohen, Kenneth R., "The 12 Deadly Sins of Hiring," *Nursing Homes,* Vol. 45, No. 3, Cleveland: MEDQUEST Communications, Inc., 1996.

Facts and Trends - The Nursing Facility Handbook, Washington: American Health Care Association, 1998.

Fair Labor Standards Act of 1938, as Amemded, WH Publication 1318, Washington: U.S. Department of Labor, 1991.

Handbook for Employers, Instructions on Completing Form I-9, Washington: U.S. Dept. of Justice, 1987.

Handy Reference Guide to the Fair Labor Standards Act, WH Publication 1282, Washington: U.S. Department of Labor, 1994.

Heneman, Herbert, G., III, Donald P. Schwab, John A Fosswm, and Lee D. Dyer, *Personnel /Human Resource Management*, Homewood, IL: Richard D. Irwin, Inc., 1983.

Herzberg, Frederick, Mausner, B., and Syncherman, B., *The Motivation to Work*, New York: John Wiley and Sons, Inc., 1959.

Hospitals and Residential Care Establishments under the Fair Labor Standards Act, W.H. Publication 1326, Washington: U.S. Department of Labor, 1975.

Nier, Leslie, "On-the-job Injury Tied to Job Satisfaction," *Provider, Vol.* 22, No. 6, Washington: AHCA, 1996.

Pacetta, Frank, *Don't Fire Them, Fire Them Up,* New York: Simon and Schuster, 1995.

Packer-Thursman, Judy, "Reversing the Revolving Door," *Provider, Vol.* 22, No. 2, Washington: AHCA, 1996.

Patterson, P. Tulane, *What Do Residents Really Need?* Perspectives, Washington: ACHCA, July 1997.

Pepper, Nathan H., *Fundamentals of Care of the Aging, Disabled, and Handicapped in the Nursing Home*, Springfield, Illinois: Charles C. Thomas Publisher, 1982.

Regulations, Part 541: Defining Terms Executive, Administrative, Professional and Outside Sales. W.H. Publication 1281, Washington: U.S. Department of Labor, 1993.

Regulations, Part 778: Interpretative Bulletin on Overtime Compensation, W.H. Publication 1262, Washington: U.S. Department of Labor, 1983.

Sherman, Arthur W., Jr. and George W. Bohlander, *Managing Human Resources*, Cincinnati: Southwestern Publishing Co., 1992.

State Operations Manual, Provider Certification, Revisions One and Two, Springfield, VA: National Technical Information Service, U.S. Department of Commerce, 1998.

Title 42 CFR, Public Health Title Part 400 to 429, Washington: U.S. Government Printing Office, 1992.

Title 42 CFR, Public Health Title 430 to end, Washington: U.S. Government Printing Office, 1993.

Weihrich, Heinz and Koontz, Harold, *Management - A Global Perspective,* Tenth Edition, New York: McGraw-Hill Book Company, 1993.

CHAPTER 7

FINANCIAL MANAGEMENT

FINANCIAL MANAGEMENT

FINANCIAL MANAGEMENT

Financial management is the process of ensuring that all materials and other resources of the facility are bought and used efficiently and economically. Proper financial management helps to attain the facility's goals. The **primary value** of financial management is that it provides accounting information the administrator can use to make decisions and manage the facility. Financial information also serves as a control device. It provides a set of standards by which the administrator can measure performance.

The continued advances in computer and communications technology are revolutionizing the manner in which finances are managed and financial decisions are made. Even the individual nursing facility which has a contractual accountant service managing the actual bookkeeping and accounting, has quicker access to more accurate information needed to manage finances. Companies with a number of nursing homes have the capabilities of linking each facility's computer to its mainframe computers and perhaps with those of suppliers. It is much easier to access and analyze data without cumbersome paperwork. (Brigham)

ADMINISTRATOR'S ROLE

Owners hold the administrator responsible for the financial operations of his facility and for attaining a satisfactory return on investment. The administrator need not be an accountant, but certainly he must understand financial planning, cost management, and the use of financial information in making decisions. This requires knowledge of financial terminology, basic bookkeeping procedures, purchasing techniques, and proper allocation and management of funds and other resources.

The administrator's role varies considerably dependent upon the ownership pattern of his organization and the owner's wishes. Some organizations delegate full authority to the administrator to supervise budgeting, purchasing, payroll, accounts receivable and payable, payment of taxes, ect. In this arrangement owners may reserve the right to review and approve the budget, increases in pay, purchase of capital outlay items, and some other activities. Administrators with this system usually contract with a fully qualified accountant who supervises bookkeeping, verifies accuracy, develops financial reports and statements used by the administrator and those required by government, closes out accounts at year's end, etc.

Multi-nursing home enterprises (called chains) may assign a very different role to administrators. They may have a central office main line computer that accesses each of their nursing homes' computers. Most business matters may be handled by central office accounting. This may include budgeting, billing, payment of bills, payroll checks, and other. Whether a part of a chain or an individual ownership nursing home, every facility must now have a computer, and they are fast moving towards electronic accounting procedures entirely.

It is imperative that the administrator clarify his role in financial management, obtaining a clear mandate from the ownership as to what his duties are and exactly what he is responsible for. This is especially true where he is expected to sign all checks drawn on the facility account.

> **Example:** An owner presented his administrator an invoice for a new auxiliary generator and told the administrator to sign the check in payment. Later, an investigation revealed the generator had not been purchased but was billed to Medicaid. The invoice was a fake. The administrator was fined and his license revoked by his state licensing board. Both he and the owner were prosecuted for fraud.

FORMS OF BUSINESS ORGANIZATIONS

Accounting serves all three basic forms of business organization: single (sole) proprietorship, partnership, and corporation. The corporation is the most significant form of business organization in terms of volume of business. However, virtually the same accounting concepts apply to all three forms of organization. (Hermanson, et al.)

A **sole proprietorship** is an unincorporated business owned by an individual. Frequently, it is managed by the same individual. No legal formalities are required to organize this form of business. There is no legal distinction between the business and the owner as entities. The owner is responsible for both personal and business debts. There is, however, an accounting distinction. The financial activities of the business are kept separately from the proprietor's personal financial activities. (Hermanson, et al.)

The important **advantages** of the proprietorship are: (1) it is easily and inexpensively formed, however, they nearly always must be licensed by a governmental unit, (2) it is subject to few government regulations, and (3) the business pays no corporate taxes. There are three important **limitations**: (1) it is difficult to obtain large sums of capital, (2) the proprietor has unlimited liability for business debts, and losses could exceed what is invested in the business, and (3) the life of the business is limited to the life of the individual who creates the proprietorship. (Brigham)

Few nursing facilities operate as a single proprietorship. The risk of personal financial loss is too great since the owner has unlimited liability for his firm's debts. Some begin as a sole proprietorship and then convert to a corporation when disadvantages of the proprietorship outweigh the advantages.

A **partnership** is a business owned by two or more persons associated as partners and is usually managed by one or all of the partners. Terms of the partnership agreement should be in writing, but they can be oral. Such an agreement should be drawn up by an attorney to ensure that all necessary terms are included. (Hermanson, et al.) Formal agreements should be filed with the secretary of state in order to protect the partners and reduce misunderstanding. Disadvantages are similar to sole proprietorships: (1) the unlimited liability for business debts, (2) limited life of the organization, (3) difficulty of transferring ownership, and (4) difficultly in raising large amounts of capital. There are still the advantages of no corporation taxes, ease and inexpensive formation of the business, and few government regulations to deal with. (Brigham)

A **limited partnership** consists of one or more **general** partners who are responsible for the operation of the business, and one or more **special** partners who contribute a specific sum of capital to the common stock, but who **are not liable** for partnership debts beyond the amount of funds contributed. They are referred to as limited partners. Unlike general partnerships, limited partnerships are statutory creations. The limited partnership is attractive as it has tax advantages and limited liabilities.

A **corporation** is a form of business owned by a few persons or by thousands of people. It is incorporated under the laws of one of the states. Major owners often serve as officers of the corporation, but the business is usually managed by persons other than the owners. Shares of stock are issued and their owners are called shareholders or stockholders. A corporation is a separate legal entity from its owners. (Hermanson, et al.) There are several types of "C" corporations and there is an "S" corporation.

Since the corporation is a separate entity, stockholders usually are not personally responsible for the debts of the organization, except unpaid payroll taxes. The Internal Revenue Service has collected payroll taxes from stockholders of bankrupt corporations.

Most nursing facilities are organized as **C** corporations. Some **advantages** are: (1) ease of transfer of ownership through selling shares, (2) limited liability by stockholders as explained above, (3) professional management, (4) centralized authority, and (5) limited legal exposure since stockholders are not agents of the corporation. Of course there can be **disadvantages**, too, as: (1) government regulations, (2) taxation, (3) entrenched management, and (4) lack of access to management. (Hermanson, et al.) Double taxation is the major disadvantage. The corporation pays income tax and stockholders pay personal income tax on dividends.

S corporations were made possible by The Revenue Act of 1958. A corporation qualifying as an S pays no corporate taxes with some exceptions regarding long-term capital gains. **Profits**, including long-term capital gains, pass to stockholders, who individually show their portion of the profit on their personal income tax returns. **Losses** also pass to the stockholders. They can apply them as their personal business losses on their individual tax returns. The **advantage** is the **S** corporation avoids double taxation.

Eligibility for S corporations specifies, among other things there should be only one type of stock, and not more than 35 stockholders. The **purpose** of this type organization is to benefit the small business corporations.

There are numerous special rules regarding distribution of profits and allocation of losses. One needs to consider many factors, as: (1) the stockholders' tax brackets, (2) the need to take money out of the corporation, (3) likelihood that the corporation will have losses, and (4) special situations concerning the corporation's status. Discuss with an accountant the advantages and disadvantages of an S corporation for a nursing facility business.

Profitability refers to the ability of a business to generate sufficient revenues to realize a profit. In **for profit** corporations this profit may be distributed as dividends to its stockholders. Dividends are a means of rewarding stockholders for providing capital. A **nonprofit** or **not-for-profit** business may not pay dividends to owners. Owners may be paid salaries, expenses, and certain allowances, but no dividends. Some states allow nonprofit organizations to generate income over total expenses, but such profits must be utilized within the business for replacement of equipment, improvements, etc.

FISCAL YEAR AND BUDGETING

The **fiscal year** is the twelve-month period a facility uses as its business year. Accounts are opened at the beginning of the year and are balanced and closed at the end of the twelfth month. The fiscal year is the tax reporting period required by Internal Revenue Service. The fiscal year is determined by the type of business organization. The Internal Revenue Code specifies the fiscal year as follows:

1. Sole proprietorships must use the calendar year.

2. Partnerships generally use the calendar year. Exceptions can be identified by a CPA or by referring to the Internal Revenue Code.

3. S corporations must use the calendar year unless they meet certain IRS requirements and obtain IRS approval.

4. C corporations may use any twelve-month period they choose.

Budget As explained in Chapter 3, a budget is a plan expressed in numerical terms, usually dollars and cents. It is a plan that deals with the future allocation and utilization of various resources to different activities over a given period of time – usually one year. Most frequently, especially in nursing homes, they are thought of in financial terms, but they can also be used for allocation and utilization of labor, floor space, machine hours, raw materials, and others. (Bedelian)

The value of budgeting is that (1) it expresses in financial terms the **goals and programs** of the organization, (2) it describes how resources will be allocated to attain these goals, (3) it provides criteria for the evaluation of performance, and (4) it serves as a control device. (Cirn) Since the budget includes anticipated revenues by service and anticipated expenditures by category, the administrator can determine at any point whether expected revenues are generated, whether expenditures are within planned limits, and whether profit goals are being met. The budget provides a standard by which the administrator can compare actual performance to the planned performance of his facility.

Budget formats The most commonly developed budgets are (1) capital, (2) cash, and (3) operating. Some organizations develop a master budget, but most administrators conduct business primarily by an operating budget.

1. A **capital budget** includes real estate, buildings, and equipment. It includes a list of equipment to be purchased and major improvements to be made during the fiscal year. Capital expenditure items are defined by Medicare as those costing more than $5000 each and having a useful life in excess of one year. If they cost less than $5000, they can be expensed out as supplies or maintenance and repairs.

2. A **cash budget** is a forecast of cash receipts and disbursements for each month during the budget year. It projects cash outflows for all expenditures – utilities, taxes, payroll, supplies, and so on – according to due dates. It shows a schedule of cash inflows and payments of obligations. Its **value** is that the facility can plan for periods when inflows exceed outflows and short-term investments can be made. Also, it shows the periods when expenditures will exceed cash inflows and working capital must be expanded to meet this need.

3. An **operating budget** includes details of anticipated revenue by service and anticipated expenditures by category. Generally, this is the budget of most interest and concern to the administrator since the governing body expects him to operate by it. Its **value** is that it helps to continuously study and control finances. The administrator can determine if revenue is received as expected and expenditures kept within planned limits.

4. A **master budget** includes the cash budget, the capital budget, liquidity ratios, and proforma financial statement. This budget format is less often used by administrators. It is comparable to what Cirn calls an **integrated budget** which projects all capital and operating costs and all revenues, and consolidates this information in a meaningful way in a single document.

Budget methods Preparation of budgets varies according to the organizational structure of the enterprise and the wishes of the owner(s). Nursing home chains use several methods of preparing the budgets for its facilities.

1. Central office develops a budget and presents it to the facility. The administrator has no input. He is advised to operate by the budget plan. It is sometimes called the "top down" method.

2. Central office develops a budget, sends it to the facility which makes recommendations and returns it to central office. The administrator and central office negotiate changes. This method is used more frequently.

3. The administrator develops a budget and sends it to central office, which may make changes or may negotiate changes with the administrator. This method is rarely used.

The most difficult of these methods for the administrator is number one. It may not take into consideration local differences in vendors, delivery, availability of personnel, wages, and so on. Central purchasing may take care of part of this, but availability of personnel, especially nurses and rehabilitation specialists, is another matter. The administrator should make every effort to gain input into budget preparation for his facility. Participation in the budget process by the administrator and his staff can be the beginning of cost management.

1. **Timing** Begin budgeting well before the beginning of the budget year. A frequent error is that budgets are thrown together just before the beginning of the fiscal year. They reflect inadequate planning and are often unrealistic as they are based on inappropriate data and hurried judgement.

2. **Basis** Budgets are based on past years' experience, historical trends, and expectations for the future, except in the zero-based method. Regular budgeting involves forecasting. In forecasting revenue and expenditures for the next budget year, the facility must decide on whether services will continue at the

present level or be reduced or expanded. Will new services be added, as an Alzheimers unit or subacute care? Then prior years' experience must be considered, especially occupancy rates, average daily census, and total patient days by level of care, payer, etc. A trend analysis is helpful in projecting the future. It should consider such possible changes as reimbursement rates, needs for various levels of service, trends in the economy, inflation, increased or decreased competition, and manpower needs.

Forecasting the **cash budget** requires establishing timetables for payment of all obligations – mortgages, taxes, payroll, utilities, insurance, supplies, dividends, and other. An important factor in this budget is the lag time between billing for services and receipt of payment. Planners must be attuned to any lag in Medicare, Medicaid, and insurance reimbursement and in private pay remittances.

3. **Participatory method** Proper budgeting involves all department heads in the facility. They learn the steps in budgeting, how their department needs fit into overall goals, what it takes to operate their department, and assumptions to use in budgeting. Participating in the budget process can be the beginning of cost awareness and result in greater cooperation in regard to cost management.

4. **Revenue/cost balance** A basic budget planning principle is to keep anticipated revenues and costs in balance. Suffice to say, no one should start a budget year with an anticipated deficit unless it is a start-up facility in which first year revenues will be low. Even then the lack of revenues is covered by other sources of capital funds. Inflating anticipated revenues to cover anticipated high costs can result in problems.

5. **Zero-based budgeting** This method involves evaluation of costs and benefits of all activities in comparison to alternative expenditures, then ranking and choosing from these alternatives in terms of how they fit with overall priorities. This is different from building on previous budget categories and amounts and deciding what resource allocations of the past should be continued. Since the latter method is simpler and easier, it is frequently used instead of zero-based budgeting.

6. **Sharing the budget** Whether budgets are handed down as fiat by the owners or are developed by the facility and approved by the governing body, the administrator should share the budget with those affected. Department heads cannot be expected to stay within the budget when they have no idea of the allocation of resources, or what it should cost to operate their departments. (Jacobs)

Regulatory requirement Until October 1, 1990, Medicare required SNF's to have the **governing body** approve an annual facility budget. OBRA discontinued this requirement. However, sound financial management dictates that the governing body review and approve an annual budget. As discussed in Chapter 4 it is legally liable for facility management, and certainly should have the final say.

ACCOUNTING SYSTEMS

Financial accounting is the process used to identify, measure, record, and report information (mostly financial in nature) about activities of a business or societal entity. It provides statements which describe a firm's financial position, changes in position and the profitability of operations. The financial accounting information is historical as it reports what has happened. The information must conform to certain standards called "generally accepted accounting principles." (GAAP) The Financial Accounting Standards Board (FASB) issues Statements of Financial Accounting Standards which guide accounting practice. The board is widely accepted as a major influence in developing financial accounting standards. (Hermanson, et al)

A **cash basis** of accounting system means that expenses and revenues are not recorded until cash is received or is paid out, except for depreciation expense. Generally it can be used only in **small businesses**. Because of the potential mismatching of revenues and expenses, cash basis accounting is generally **considered deficient**. (Hermanson, et al.)

An **accrual** basis of accounting records revenues and expenses when they are incurred rather than when cash is received or is paid out. When a service is rendered, the revenue to be derived from it is recorded as income even though it may not be paid for 30 days or more. When the facility incurs an expense it is recorded although payment may await a bill from the vendor. The **accrual** basis of accounting is **required** by Medicare. States generally require accrual accounting for Medicaid reporting.

An **annual uniform cost report** is required of Medicaid facilities by each state. It includes revenues by source and expenditures by category and is used as one factor in establishing Medicaid reimbursement rates. The state provides a report form listing categories as it wishes them reported. As a result, in designing the facility's accounting system there is an **advantage** in tailoring it to the annual uniform cost report. This report becomes a public document and is available to the public upon request.

Cash flow is often a problem, especially during the start-up period of a nursing facility. To offset this, the administrator may want to develop a **cash flow statement** to identify his financial position at a given time. A cash flow statement shows cash receipts and disbursements leading to a net change in cash in a given period. In preparing the statement, each item in the earnings statement is examined together with related changes in current asset, current liability, or other balance sheet accounts to determine the cash flow from the item. The cash flow statement provides information for planning short-range cash needs. An analysis of cash flow shows whether the facility's cash flow from operations will enable it to pay debts promptly. The cash flow statement is an important management tool. (Hermanson, et al.)

Value of accounting The primary value of accounting information is to aid the administrator in decision making. Administrators use it to determine what to buy, when, and at what price as well as how they will invest. Accounting also has value as a **control measure**. The performance of the facility and its units are measured against the established standard, the budget. In decentralized organizations operating several nursing facilities it serves well as a control device and as a basis of comparing the performance of different facilities.

BASIC ACCOUNTING PROCEDURES AND RECORDS

The nursing facility engages in hundreds, or perhaps thousands, of transactions that must be classified and summarized. Although the administrator is not likely to enter a transaction in these records, he needs to understand them and how they can be used. The facility's accounting system will include at least the following records.

1. **An account** is a means used to summarize changes in assets, liabilities, stockholders' equity items, revenues, and expenses. (Hermanson, et al.) Each account is assigned to an appropriate category which has been given a title that describes the nature of the items included within it, as: (a) equipment, (b) utilities, (c) auto expense, (d) salaries, and others.

2. **A chart of accounts** is a complete listing of the names of all the categories in the ledger. The chart may include account numbers if they are used. A chart of accounts is somewhat like a table of contents, it lists all accounts receivable and accounts payable. (Hermanson, et al.) The chart of accounts is standardized by nursing homes for ease in preparing state cost reports.

3. **A journal** is a book of original entry. It contains in chronological order the financial transactions of a business. In a sense, an entry in the journal is a set of instructions that directs the entry of a dollar amount as a debit in a specific account and as a credit in another specific account. (Hermanson, et al.) This involves **double entry** accounting in which there is an equal debit and equal credit in each transaction.

4. **A ledger** is a complete listing of all accounts, both payable and receivable. This is called a general ledger and may be the only one used by a nursing facility.

5. **Basic accounting procedures** involves three steps:

   a. Making journal entries

   b. Posting to the ledger

   c. Tabulating the account balances at specified intervals. (Cirn)

6. **Financial statements** are needed to determine whether a business meets its primary financial **goals** of **profitability** and **solvency**.

   a. A **trial balance** is a listing of all accounts and their debit and credit balances, with the exception of accounts with a zero balance. The total of debit balances equals the total of the credit balances. A trial balance may be prepared at any time — after a day, month, quarter, etc. (Hermanson, et al.) Trial balances are used in preparing the other financial statements. It has no particular value to the administrator.

   b. A **balance sheet** summarizes assets, liabilities and stockholders' equity at a given point in time. In a small business it may show **net worth** rather than stockholders' equity. The balance sheet shows that assets equal liabilities plus stockholders' equity, or net worth. This financial statement reflects the firm's **solvency**. Like the trial balance, it may be prepared at any time — end of the day, end of the week, end of the quarter, end of the year. The balance sheet is used extensively by the administrator to determine if finances are progressing as planned in the budget.

   c. An **earnings statement** compares revenues with expenses incurred to produce the income. It shows a profit or a loss and is sometimes referred to as a **profit and loss statement**. The purpose of this statement is to reflect **profitability** for a stated period of time.

   d. A **retained earnings statement** explains the changes in retained earnings that occurred between two balance sheet dates. The changes usually consist of the addition of net earnings or the deduction of net loss, and the deduction of dividends. (Hermanson, et al.) When cash dividends are paid, it reduces cash and retained earnings. The earnings are no longer retained.

   e. A **statement of changes in financial position** shows flows of funds into and out of the business. It is derived from analysis of the other three statements and ties together the financial activity of the organization into a **single report**. (Hermanson, et al.) This statement answers many more questions on financial activity than the first three statements.

   f. **Bank statements** are prepared monthly by the bank. Statements list balances at the beginning of a time period, usually one month, deposits, all checks the bank paid, bank charges, interest earned (if any), daily balances, and ending balance.

These business financial statements should not be confused with a **personal financial statement** although they have similarities. The personal statement summarizes assets and liabilities and stocks and bonds, real estate owned, life insurance, and debts. It reflects one's net worth and is used by lending institutions to determine eligibility as a borrower.

RATIO ANALYSIS

Big businesses and industry often further analyze financial statements to determine relationships between certain items on the balance sheet and on the earnings statement, as well as pairs of items on different statements. This is computed by a **ratio analysis**. Apparently, ratio analysis is rarely used in nursing homes, for in 25 years of teaching nursing home administrators this writer has never met an administrator whose facility computed ratio analysis. However, such analysis would be valuable to large nursing-home chains with highly sophisticated finance officials. It could be a means of not only measuring efficiency of operations in a given facility but also to compare financial operations of a number of facilities.

Ratio analysis is a method of analyzing the strength and profitability and the efficiency of operations. The ratios are often broadly classified as (1) liquidity ratios, (2) tests of equity positions and solvency, (3) tests of profitability, and (4) market tests. (Hermanson, et al) Although most administrators may never see a ratio analysis, and certainly never compute one, it may be helpful to understand this concept and its value.

1. **Current or working capital ratio Working capital** is the excess of current assets over current liabilities. It reflects the facility's ability to pay its bills (solvency). The dollar amount of working capitol, however, does not provide an adequate index of the ability to meet obligations. The **current ratio** provides a better index. It is computed:

$$\textbf{Current ratio} = \frac{\textbf{current assets}}{\textbf{current liabilities}}$$

   In terms of dollars, if current assets are $100,000 and current liabilities are $75,000, the ratio is 1:33 to 1. This is a figure that the facility's short-term creditors are particularly interested in as they expect to be paid promptly. On the other hand, investors in the facility are more interested in long-range earnings. (Hermanson, et al)

2. **Quick or acid test ratio** is concerned with what are called **quick assets** (cash, accounts receivable, and marketable securities) and their relation to current liabilities. Inventories and prepaid expenses are excluded since they generally cannot be readily converted to cash.

$$\textbf{Acid test ratio} = \frac{\textbf{quick assets}}{\textbf{current liabilities}}$$

   This relates ready cash and immediate cash inflows to immediate cash outflows. Again, facility vendors are interested in this ratio.

3. **Equity ratio** is equal to the proportion of the owners' equity to total equity (or total assets) at the end of a given period.

$$\textbf{Equity ratio} = \frac{\textbf{owners' equity}}{\textbf{total equity}}$$

   Again this method is more applicable in business and industry where there are numerous stockholders.

4. Other ratio methods are quite numerous, such as those that show **profitability, equity debt, earnings per share, dividend yield,** and **payment ratios.** The latter ratios involve dividends per share, earnings per share, yield on preferred stock, and **return on investment** (ROI). The ROI is of particular interest to owners as they expect a certain percent return on funds invested. Also, owners often use it as a measure of the administrator's success in managing the facility. Lack of an adequate ROI can cost an administrator his job.

Meaning of ratios A current ratio of 1 to 1 indicates the facility can pay its debts and perhaps have a surplus. At first glance a ratio of 2 to 1 appears much better. That may not be the case since too much money might be tied up in current assets that are not liquid. (Allen) A *quick* or *acid* test ratio may be more meaningful because it relates cash, accounts receivable, and other liquid assets to current liabilities. A *quick* ratio of 2 to 1 means the facility has adequate assets to meet obligations and a sizeable surplus that can possibly be invested until needed.

ACCOUNTS RECEIVABLE - MEDICARE

Billing systems Multi-facility enterprises sometimes do all billing for each of its facilities. The facility sends its billing information electronically to central offices where bills are made up and mailed. This appears to be duplication of effort, and its economy is questionable. Other corporations require each facility to send billing information to the central office, bills are made up and returned to the facility for changes where indicated, then mailed by the facility. Payments are usually made to the facility where they are receipted and deposited.

Individual nursing homes and some of the smaller chains do all billing and receiving within each facility. Again the system used depends on the owners and their wishes.

Prospective Payment System (PPS) The Balanced Budget Act of 1997 (BBA97) provides a new payment system for SNFs. The Act has two new rules: (1) phasing in the new PPS beginning July 1, 1998, and (2) requiring consolidated billing.

PPS establishes new rules for assessment of Medicare residents, and for determining the amount to be paid a SNF. It sets a per diem rate for resident care similar to the diagnosis related groups (DRGs) in hospitals. These rates are based on resident classifications as determined by an assessment program described in Chapter 12.

Consolidated billing creates significant changes in billing for Medicare services. The SNF will bill all Part A services provided to a Part A resident. (See Chapter 11 for definitions of Part A) The per diem payment covers cost of all services provided in a Part A stay, except for physicians' services and some others. Also, the SNF must bill for all Part B services, with some exceptions, which are reimbursed on a fee basis. Outside service providers will no longer bill Medicare for services rendered a Medicare resident in a SNF.

The basics of these two rules are well presented in the AHCA's publication "PPS - 1 2 3, What You Need To Know." An administrator will find this brochure helpful in getting acquainted with the new complex changes in nursing home care.

Per diem rate PPS established 44 separate per diem rates based on resident classification which is determined by assessments. (See Chapter 12 for specifics on assessments and their frequency) HCFA used nursing-home costs data for fiscal year 1995 to determine the level of payment for each classification. The payment includes: (1) routine costs, (2) ancillary costs, and (3) capital-related costs.

1. **A routine cost** is defined as costs for which daily charges are made. Included are room and board, nursing service, medical and psychiatric social services, minor medical supplies, and use of specified equipment and facilities for which there is no separate charge.

2. **Ancillary costs** are physical, occupational and other rehabilitation services and laboratory tests that are directly related to a resident's care.

3. **Capital-related** costs are costs of real estate, buildings, and equipment. Also included are interests payments on any of these that are financed.

Eligibility has not changed, but AHCA points out some changes in what Medicare pays for. To be eligible for SNF care under Medicare Part A the resident must: (1) have had a medically necessary hospital stay of three consecutive days, (2) be admitted to the SNF within 30 days of hospital discharge, (3) require skilled-nursing or skilled-rehabilitation services that must be performed by or under supervision of skilled professionals, (4) need these services on a daily basis, and (5) require these services on an inpatient basis.

Urban and rural rates There are two sets of rates depending on geographical location of the SNF. The Federal Office of Management and Budget sets up the classifications.

1. **Urban SNF rates** are for SNF's located in an area classified as a Metropolitan Statistical Area (MSA) and those located in a New England County Metropolitan Area (NECMA).

2. Rural SNF rates are paid to SNFs located in any area not classified as MSA or NECMA.

HCFA publishes a table of per diem rates for each fiscal year. Using this table, a SNF's rate is adjusted to the urban or rural rate. Currently, urban payment rates range from $384.21 to $117.15 per day, while rural rates range from $408.19 to $116.85 per day.

Parts of per diem The per diem rates have two parts: (1) labor and (2) nonlabor. Slightly more than 75 per cent of total SNF costs are considered labor-related. These costs are adjusted according to wage differences in various geographic areas. HCFA indicates these figures will be adjusted annually to allow for inflation. (AHCA)

Intermediary HCFA makes no direct payments to nursing homes. These are handled by an **intermediary** appointed by HCFA. SNFs bill the intermediary as directed. Currently, most billing is done electronically, and all billing will eventually be electronically processed. This type billing reputedly reduces payment from 28 to 14 days, there are fewer errors, and errors are more easily corrected. PPS will obviously affect SNF billing in the near future.

Keeping in touch There is still much to be decided in terms of Federal procedures, and questions have already arisen during PPS's transitional periods. An example is billing for ambulance service. HCFA has already ruled that ambulance cost will not be included in consolidated billing if the ambulance services are not included in a resident's plan of care, such as an emergency trip to the hospital. (Hawryluk) Administrators must stay in close touch with HCFA as rate setting proceeds. The **Federal Register** can be accessed by computer at www.thomas.loc.gov. The facility's intermediary is also a source of official information. AHCA, other trade associations, and journal publications are informed sources available to facilities. (Kruger)

ACCOUNTS RECEIVABLE - MEDICAID

Medicaid billing Each state selects a Medicaid fiscal **intermediary** who reimburses facilities for Medicaid services. Per diem reimbursement rates are set by the state. Some states have only two or three levels of care with a rate for each; whereas, states using case-mix may have as many as eleven levels of care, each with a separate reimbursement rate.

Usually by the middle of the month the intermediary sends each Medicaid certified facility a list of Medicaid residents that were in the facility at the end of the prior billing period. In states where this is used it is referred to as a turnaround document (TAD). The facility adds any new Medicaid residents showing date of admission, and identifies any resident who was discharged, and the date. Administrators return this to the intermediary as soon after the end of the month as possible. Many deliver the TAD by hand. Time between billing and receipt of payment varies from state to state.

Electronic billing is used by intermediaries in some states. No reports of the advantages or disadvantages were found by this writer, but it can be presumed the value is in faster payment, fewer errors, and easier correction of errors, since this has been the experience with Medicare.

ACCOUNTS RECEIVABLE - OTHER

Private pay billing Chain nursing homes sometimes have private pay data sent to the corporate office where billing is made up and returned to the facility. Generally, this is not an economical practice because residents and their families generally bring a check or cash to the facility business office. A standard practice is to make payment of bills as convenient as possible. Consequently, payments are usually accepted, receipted and deposited as they are paid. This practice, especially payments by cash, require very tight internal controls and close monitoring of the staff responsible for carrying out procedures covering private pay.

Aging accounts Nursing homes are beginning to age their accounts receivable much as other businesses have done for some time. If an account is not paid by the next billing date, the billing or statement should show amounts currently due, amounts past due, and the period of time past due. If numerous accounts are past due, the facility should set up an accounts aging schedule, such as that shown in Table 7.1.

Table 7.1:

Analysis of Accounts Receivable
January 31, 1996

Customer	Balance Due	No. of Days Past Due 1-30	31-60	61-90	91-120
Jones	$2,400	$1,200			
Smith	$2,700	$1,200	$600	$600	
Black	$3,000		$1,800	$600	$600
Lowe	$1,900	$900	$500	$500	
TOTALS	**$10,000**	**$3,300**	**$2,900**	**$1,700**	**$600**

Values of aging accounts are twofold. It is a reminder to customers (residents) that their accounts are not paid up to date and need attention. Aged accounts are used by the facility to estimate the percent of the accounts that are uncollectible. Generally, one percent of accounts not yet due are uncollectible. This uncollectible amount increases sharply as the account ages. Accountants have determined that uncollectibles are: (1) five percent of accounts 1-30 days overdue, (2) 10 percent of accounts 31-60 days overdue, (3) 25 percent of accounts 61-90 days overdue, and (4) 50 percent of accounts 91-120 days past due. The need to regularly work accounts receivable is readily apparent. Not only do they affect cash flow, but the greater the age the less likely they will be collected.

Estimating past due income is relatively easy, and it helps to plan for cash flow. Tables 7.2 and 7.3 demonstrate how estimated total income on past due accounts can be determined.

Table 7.2:

Income Past Due by Days

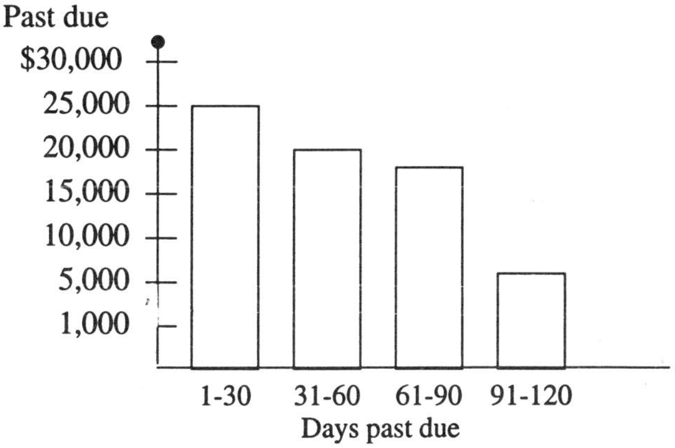

Table 7.2 shows total past due accounts receivable of $67,500. Table 7.3 shows the amount the facility will probably be unable to collect, calculated by using percentages listed above.

Table 7.3:

Estimated Uncollectible Accounts Receivable

$25,000 x 5%	=	$1,250
20,000 x 10%	=	2,000
17,500 x 25%	=	4,375
5,000 x 50%	=	3,500
Uncollectible		$10,125

Of the total $67,500 past due this facility would lose $10,125, leaving an anticipated income on these accounts of $57,375.

One administrator had an effective approach to discussing past due bills with residents and families. He taught his business staff to approach the payee by saying, "We need your help." When the resident or family responded, they were told, "Your account is past due, and we can't pay our staff and buy the supplies to provide the service you want." Usually, it was quite an effective approach.

Billing by invoice Billing is done by invoice. Sequentially numbered invoices are best. An invoice states (1) items or services sold, (2) number of units, (3) cost per unit, (4) total costs, (5) terms of payment, and (6) age of accounts. A **statement** shows the status of an account:

(1) balance at the beginning of the month, (2) new charges (3) amount paid, (4) balance at the end of the month, and (5) age of accounts. Some facilities have combined the two. The invoice or statement shows all of the above. Computerized accounting makes this a convenient, economical process, and with the proper program items on the statement can be automatically computed.

Receiving and receipting In the past, facilities often used a sequentially numbered, duplicate receipt book. All income was receipted, one copy given to the payee if they wanted it, and the duplicate stayed in the receipt book. With computers this has changed. The amount of each receipt is entered on the proper resident account, and the software package automatically posts it and does the aging.

Delinquent accounts Some delinquent accounts appear uncollectible and may require more drastic action. **Collection agencies** may be a resource, but care should be exercised in their use. They can be a public relations factor. Before turning any account over to a collection agency, the nursing home should suggest to the responsible party that they obtain a loan and pay their account. The facility would benefit, and the responsible party might have longer to repay a loan.

Some delinquent accounts may involve potential legal action and require an attorney's help.

> **Example:** Mrs. Owens used up her eligibility for Medicare and qualified for Medicaid. She was bedbound and could not very well handle her affairs. She received a $725 month Social Security check which was to be applied to her account with the nursing home. Family members were very vague about the check which was never brought to the nursing home. After months of delinquent notices and telephone calls, the administrator investigated and learned the check was cashed each month and used by the family. He called the facility attorney who contacted the family and advised the $7,200 delinquent bill was to be paid, and in the future the check was to be brought to the nursing home. If not, he was filing theft and criminal neglect charges under state law against family members. They paid up, and arranged to have the Social Security check mailed to the facility.

False Claims Act False billing claims have been a problem for both Medicare and Medicaid for several years. Estimates by the federal government are that 10 percent to 25 percent of Medicare billing involves fraud, abuse, and waste. This includes billing for services not rendered, for unnecessary services, for services not covered, and for duplicate billing. To combat these losses the federal government has resurrected the False Claims Act that dates back to the War for Southern Independence (Civil War). The statute was designed to deter contractor fraud, but is now the preferred method to recoup significant payments for false billings in Medicare and Medicaid. (Richards and Lucas)

The Department of Justice and other government officials have notified providers that they are being investigated under this Act. They warn that violators may face significant penalties, among which is an automatic $10,000 fine for even small errors in billing. In the past two years there has been a significant increase in claims under this Act against Medicare/Medicaid facilities. Many claims involve honest billing mistakes for which administrators paid the $10,000 fine rather than pay high legal fees to defend themselves, and still face the chance of losing. (Hawryluk)

Fortunately, Congress is considering a bill that will offer some relief if it is enacted. It will require that a claim exceed a minimum amount and that facilities not be held responsible for billing errors that are due to vague government instructions. Also, it will provide that claims show clear and convincing evidence of wrongdoing.

Every administrator should obtain information on this recovery/prosecution program from his attorney or other sources. He should develop a preventative program that ensures the facility is in compliance. Carefully established policies and procedures, monitoring billing practices, and keeping abreast of regulatory procedures are necessary to avoid false claim actions. The facility should keep employees advised on what the government is targeting. This is released through "fraud alerts."

BANKING

Deposits Receiving payments offers the first opportunity for the loss of funds. The facility should have strict procedures on receipting and depositing. Deposits should be made at the end of each day. No monies should be kept in the facility overnight. Although it is not always a feasible practice in nursing homes, the person receiving revenue and entering transactions into the computer should not make up the bank deposit slip. This provides a second opportunity for loss of funds.

Savings and checking accounts The standard of practice that directs that no funds be idle, make them work for the enterprise is often overlooked in banking. The facility should have its savings account and one or more checking accounts. If the receivables amount to $200,000 by the fifth of a month, and much of this will not be needed until late in the month, or even later, the money should be drawing interest. A common practice is to maintain in the checking account only the funds needed for a day or two, and keep the remainder in savings. Some administrators stop by the bank almost daily and transfer to checking only the amount needed for a few days. It is a sound business practice that will become easier as facilities move to electronic funds-transfer procedures.

Bank statement reconciliation Each month when the bank statement is received it should be reconciled immediately. It is a relatively simple procedure and it is the only way the facility will know its cash position. First, enter any bank charges for NSF checks, service, etc., in the check book. Check off in the check book each deposit listed on the statement and each check that has cleared the bank. Add to the ending balance on the statement any deposits made that are not shown on the statement to obtain a total balance. Add amounts of all checks written that have not cleared the bank. Subtract the latter total from the total balance. This figure is the current check book balance. Should the balance in the check book differ from the correct balance on the bank statement reconciliation, verify any discrepancies. It is a good idea to go back to the last corrected balance and check all figures entered afterward to determine where the mistake occurred. It is essential to edit the figures in the check book to reflect the correct balance. If the amount written differs from the number amount on a check, the bank uses the written amount. This fact may help in reconciling the statement.

The bank statement should be reconciled by an employee other than the one who prepared the bank deposits. Proper internal controls dictate that a different employee should handle each of these money transactions. Due to limited staff some facilities have the person receipting funds received do the bank statement reconciliation which provides some control as a second person makes bank deposits.

ACCOUNTS PAYABLE

Payment by invoice Vendors usually send the facility a numbered invoice including items as shown earlier under accounts receivable. At the end of each month vendors usually send the facility a statement showing status of its account. **Payment** of bills should always be by invoice. If one pays by statement on an open account–one which is charged to on a regular basis–vendors usually ask which invoices are being paid. Always return a copy of the invoice with the check issued in payment. This adheres to the principle that every check be backed by an invoice.

Discounts Many vendors offer a discount of two percent or more when accounts are paid within a specified period, usually 10 days or so. Take advantage of all discounts, as this is a means of helping cash flow.

Credit period Vendors list a payment due date on each invoice. As an example the invoice may be dated the first of the month, and the due date is 30 days later. Pay it on the 29th or 30th day. Paying earlier does nothing for one's credit record at the credit bureau. All the bureau enters in the file is whether the bill is paid or not. Using the full credit period is another means of maintaining a healthier cash flow.

Safe Harbor rules It is imperative that administrators know and practice Safe Harbor regulations published by the Office of the Inspector

General (OIG) in July 1991. These regulations are a guide to complying with the federal prohibitions against illegal payment for services or items reimbursed under Medicare and Medicaid. Safe Harbor regulations define what business practices do not violate the federal Anti-Kickback Statute and are thereby a Safe Harbor. All nursing facilities must take a close look at the impact of Safe Harbor regulations because of their widespread application and the expansive definition given to those in a position to influence referrals and business. (Cohen and Currier)

A Safe Harbor is a joint venture or business that meets all standards issued by OIG. It is clearly legal under the Anti-Kickback Statute and is immune from criminal prosecution or civil sanctions under the statute. Arrangements made by a nursing home that are not Safe Harbors are subject to increased risks of investigation. Investment interests, space and equipment rentals, personal services, and management contracts are the most applicable Safe Harbors to nursing facilities.

Investment interests regulations are very concerned with **interested investors,** which means investors in a position to influence referrals, furnish items or services, or otherwise generate business for the facility. This is a complex area of Safe Harbors that the administrator should become fully knowledgeable about. The standards covering the area of Safe Harbors cannot be covered in detail in this publication. One needs to secure a copy of the regulations to use as a guide.

Space and equipment rentals may not be in compliance with the Anti-Kickback statute if the lessor is in a position to make referrals or otherwise generate business for a nursing facility. Before entering into any type of rental agreement, the administrator should ensure that the lessor meets all Safe Harbor regulations, such as the lease must:

1. Be in writing and signed by all parties,
2. Specify the premises or the equipment leased,
3. Specify whether the lease is full time or periodic,
4. If periodic, specify the schedule of their length and rental amounts, and be not less than one year duration, and
5. Set out in advance the aggregate rental price, consistent with fair market value.

There are other regulations governing rentals that the administrator must use to determine if a transaction qualifies as a Safe Harbor. Never should an administrator enter into a lease without ensuring it meets all standards.

Personal service and **management contracts** must comply with a number of regulations which include:

1. The agreement must be in writing and signed by the parties thereto.
2. Services must be specified.
3. If not full time, the service agreement must specify the schedule of intervals, their length, and compensation by interval.
4. The term must be for at least one year.
5. The aggregate compensation must be set out in advance and be consistent with fair market value, and not related to the volume or value of referrals or business generated by the lessee.

Again the administrator must obtain and abide by Safe Harbor regulations which provide the detail he must follow in contracting. An effort is made here only to call attention to what the administrator must look for and abide by. He should clear every contract with the facility's attorney to ensure it is in full compliance. (Cohen and Currier)

OTHER ACCOUNTING PROCEDURES

The **journal** entries and posting to the **ledger** discussed earlier involve two terms administrators should know: (1) debits and (2) credits. A **debit** is an entry on the left side of an account.

Debits increase assets and expense accounts. They decrease liability, owners' equity, and revenue accounts.

A **credit** is an entry on the right side of an account which increases liability, owners' equity, and revenue accounts. A credit decreases asset and expense accounts.

Do not confuse the facility's use of debit and credit with the bank's use of the same terms. The bank uses them in an entirely different manner as noted on the monthly bank statement.

Adjusting entries may be done by the accountant when an administrator is particularly concerned with **profitability**, say for a month. In order to be sure the accounts reflect all operations for the month and the financial status at month's end, he must analyze accounts and make updated adjustments when required. These adjustments are referred to as adjusting entries. (Hermanson, et al.)

Adjustments in basic bookkeeping transactions are made in the general journal. An example is sending a bill to a resident's family and recording it as accrued income. Two months later it is determined the bill is uncollectible, so it is written off to bad debt. Also, the facility may make a $500 purchase and record it as an accrued expense. When the vendor sends the bill it indicates a two percent discount if paid within 10 days. If the bill is paid within 10 days a $10 adjustment must be made as the vendor is paid $490. If an error is noted during the audit, an adjustment is made in the general ledger.

Break-even analysis is the method by which management determines the break-even point in operations by analyzing **variable expenses** and **fixed expenses**. It is the point at which revenue equals expenses – the facility is not making a profit, but it is able to pay its bills. It is referred to as a **marginal return**. The assumption is made that fixed expenses will stay the same regardless of the volume of business and variable expenses will change in direct proportion to volume. Revenues and expenses do not always develop according to expectations, but an administrator needs to identify his break-even point.

One **procedure** for determining the break-even point is to divide fixed costs by revenue minus variable costs for the number of days in the period, then multiply by the number of resident days service provided during that period:

$$\frac{\$600{,}000\ \textit{(fixed cost)}}{\underset{\textit{(revenue)}}{\$400{,}000} - \underset{\textit{(variable cost)}}{\$100{,}000}} = \frac{2 \times 9{,}000}{\textit{(days service)}} = \underset{\textit{(days needed to break even)}}{18{,}000}$$

In facilities with a computerized accounting system this can be easily calculated as computer software packages are available to perform a number of break-even calculations. If this service is not available, accountants generally determine the number of residents (daily census) required to break even. Refer to the Percent Occupancy section of this chapter.

Advantages of break-even analysis are: (1) It enables management to study information concerning volume of service and expenses in an integrated manner; (2) expenses can be more closely controlled; (3) decisions on size of facility and expansion can be carefully considered; and (4) it provides the administrator with an easy-to-read reporting device that summarizes data contained in various income statements.

Disadvantages are: (1) difficulty in obtaining reliable estimates of revenue and expenses, (2) assumptions made in the analysis, and (3) determining availability of residents and their use of the facility.

ACCOUNTING PROCESS

In summary, the accounting process begins with **invoices**, both accounts receivable and payable. Information from these original records is entered in the **journal**, usually cash disbursements and cash receipts journals. From the journal it is posted to the **ledger, and periodically accounts are balanced**. At specified periods of time a **trial balance** is developed. From this are developed the **balance sheet** and any **other financial statements** needed by management. At the end of the fiscal year the books are closed and year end financial statements developed.

Following this, states require a Certified Public Accountant (CPA) audit. Facilities certified for Medicaid then prepare the annual uniform cost report for the state.

ACCOUNTING TERMS

In order to use accounting information properly, administrators must understand a number of accounting terms. The principal terms most frequently encountered are:

1. **Accounting** is a process that includes bookkeeping but involves much more. It includes budgeting, financial reports, special studies, auditing, and designing accounting systems.

2. **Assets** are things of value, things owned, such as cash, equipment, real estate, and accounts receivable. Assets can be measured and expressed in money terms.

   a. A **current asset** is cash or other short-lived assets expected to be converted to cash or used up in business operations, usually within one year. In addition to cash, current assets include accounts receivable, notes receivable, and certificates of deposit. (Hermanson, et al.)

   b. **Fixed**, or **long-lived**, assets are buildings, land, equipment, etc. to be used in the business on a long-term basis. They are also referred to as **capital assets**.

   c. **Tangible assets** are those with physical characteristics. They can be seen and touched. Tangible assets include buildings, equipment, and other resources. (Hermanson, et al.) They will wear out or deteriorate and are depreciable.

   d. **Intangible assets** are noncurrent, nonphysical assets including leaseholds, copyrights, patents, and goodwill. Goodwill may be an intangible asset to a nursing facility that produces superior service and earnings and has high resident loyalty. (Hermanson, et al.) Goodwill is marketable when a nursing facility is sold. Accounts receivable are nonphysical assets, but they are current; they are to be collected. They are not considered an intangible asset.

3. **Book value** is the cost of a depreciable asset less accumulated depreciation. It is the net amount of an asset. Book value (per share) means a stockholder's equity per share. It is the amount stockholders would receive per share if the business were liquidated as is. (See depreciation in this chapter)

4. **Bookkeeping** is the initial recording of business transactions. It is very mechanical and is usually done by a clerk. It is only a part of accounting.

5. **Capital** is a term embracing funds acquired from several different sources. (Hermanson, et al.) It includes funds invested, income from sale of shares, a donation of cash or land, and retained earnings. Under certain circumstances, determined by the federal government, real estate, buildings, and certain equipment may be included.

   a. **Investment capital** refers to the cash used to purchase real estate and equipment and to construct the buildings in which the business operates. These are operating assets which management actively uses to produce operating revenues.

   b. **Working capital** is the excess of current assets over current liabilities. It is a measure of the facility's ability to meet its obligations.

   c. **Capital expenditures** are expenditures that increase the book value of plant assets. Capital expenditures are added to the asset account or charged to the accumulated depreciation account. For example, after using an auxiliary generator for four years, it is reconditioned at a cost of $1,750. This increases the life of the machine four years for a total of 14 years. The original life estimate was 10. This capital expenditure increases the accumulated depreciation account by $1,750.

d. **Revenue expenditures** must be differentiated from capital expenditures. Revenue expenditures are immediately expensed out. They are recurring and minor repairs that neither add to the quality of service-rendering abilities of the asset nor extend its estimated life. (Hermanson, et al.) For example, regular maintenance of the auxiliary generator as replacement of a fan belt is charged to maintenance expense, a revenue expenditure.

6. **Consignee** is a person or party to whom merchandise is consigned or shipped.

7. **Deficit** is a debit balance in a retained earnings account. It occurs when no profit has been realized resulting in no increase in shareholders' equity.

8. **Earnings** refers to generated revenue (income) which is generally not recognized until all activities to create it have been completed.

   a. **Gross earnings** refers to total revenues, or income, generated.

   b. **Net earnings**, or **net profit**, equal revenues (including gains) minus expenses (including losses and taxes). It is the amount by which the revenues of a period exceed the expenses of the same period, the amount available for distribution or retention. Determining net earnings is the primary focus of financial accounting. (Hermanson, et al.)

   c. **Gross profit** amounts to the net sales less cost of goods sold. The term is used frequently in sales organizations.

   d. **Operating profit** is gross profit from sales less operating expenses. It measures effectiveness of management operations for a given period of time.

   e. **Dividends** are earnings distributed to stockholders. They are a means of rewarding stockholders for providing capital.

   f. **Retained earnings** are accumulated net earnings less dividends distributed to stockholders. It is the revenue (income) remaining after all expenses, taxes, and dividends are paid. Only limited earnings may be retained without IRS levying taxes.

9. **Equities** are interests in or claims upon the assets by owners of a business. Equities equal the amount contributed (capital stock) plus retained earnings.

10. **Expenses** fall into two basic categories: (a) fixed and (b) variable. Figure 7.1 shows how they may be represented graphically.

    a. **Fixed expenses** are those that remain constant without regard to volume of business. They include rent, depreciation, property taxes, certain types of insurance, etc. No matter what percent occupancy the facility has, these usually do not vary.

    b. **Variable expenses** are those that change in direct proportion to the change in volume of services, as supplies, materials, labor, and perhaps utilities. As the occupancy rate increases, more food, medical supplies, and utilities are used. At certain predictable occupancy levels more staff is added.

Figure 7.1:

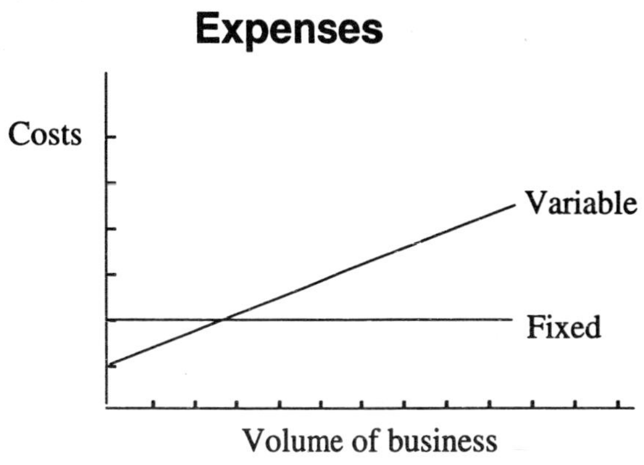

11. **Gross income** is a term used to describe taxpayer's income from services such as wages, fees, dividends, interest, proprietorship earnings, and partnership earnings. A few types of income such as capital gains,

interest on municipal and state bonds, and workers compensation insurance benefits may also be included as gross income. (Hermanson, et al.)

12. **Internal controls** are all the financial procedures and actions taken to:

    a. Protect or safeguard assets against theft and waste, the **primary** purpose of controls

    b. Ensure compliance with policy and procedure and federal laws

    c. Evaluate performance and efficiency

    d. Ensure accurate, reliable data for accounting reports

    Examples are the handling of funds as described earlier in this chapter and the use of purchase requisitions, internal audit, purchase orders, invoices, receiving reports, etc.

13. **Liabilities** are debts or obligations owed by a business. Typically, liabilities are a known amount to be paid on a certain date. Liabilities include notes, and accounts payable, accrued interest, taxes, and so on.

    a. **Current liabilities** are debts, usually due within one year, that normally require use of current assets. Examples are accounts and notes payable, federal withholding tax, FICA taxes, dividends payable and unemployment tax (FUTA).

    b. **Long-term liabilities** are those not due for a relatively long period of time, usually a year beyond the balance sheet date, and bonds payable when evidenced by formal printed certificates sometimes secured by property liens or mortgages. (Hermanson, et al.) Long-term debt in the form of a mortgage or note payable is an example.

14. **A lien** is a claim or charge on particular property for payment of a debt or obligations. (Black) The debt or claim is secured by the lien on the property which cannot be sold without satisfying the debt. A mortgage is a type of lien, but there can be differences. A lien can be placed on property by court order, while mortgages are voluntary agreements.

15. **Liquidity** denotes how quickly an asset can be converted to cash without appreciable loss. Cash is the most liquid asset, and marketable securities are highly liquid assets. Land and equipment tend not to be liquid. When there is a problem of liquidity management has difficulty raising necessary cash to pay obligations as they come due.

16. **A marginal return** occurs when revenues (income) equal expenses, the break-even point.

17. **A mortgage** is a conditional transfer of title to property by a borrower to a lender to secure payment of a debt or loan. All mortgages should be recorded with the clerk of court in the jurisdiction in which the property is located.

18. **Net profit** may refer to income over expenses before taxes and dividends are paid, but it has other meanings. The term is infrequently used in corporate accounting.

19. **Net worth** refers to total assets less total liabilities.

20. **A note** is an unconditional written promise to pay a definite sum of money at a certain or determinable date, usually with interest at a specified rate. (Hermanson, et al.) A note is a legal document and is sometimes secured by a lien or a mortgage. If the note is given to the facility, it is a note receivable. If management signs a note to secure funds, it is a note payable. A **cosigner** is a person who signs a note along with the borrower, making him equally liable for payment.

21. **Operating expenses** are those incurred in the normal operation of a facility. They include salaries, fringe benefits, utilities, materials and supplies, depreciation, rent, etc.

22. **Par value** is the value amount printed on a stock certificate, the amount per share at which par value stock is recorded in the accounts. In some states the par value of the issued shares is the legal capital of the corporation; it is the amount of capital which must be maintained unless, by formal procedure, it is reduced. (Hermanson, et al.)

23. **Revenue** refers to the inflow of assets from the sale of products or rendering of services to customers. (Hermanson, et al.) Nursing facility revenues are derived largely from payment for resident-care services, sales from vending machines, and employee and visitor meals. The term **income** is often used when referring to revenues.

24. **Revenue center** is a unit of the facility that generates income. Examples are nursing service, food service, barber shop, and vending machines.

AMORTIZATION

Hermanson describes **amortization** as the estimate of services or benefits received from an *intangible* asset in a given period. The upfront cost of the asset is allocated over a specific period of time. All **noncurrent**, intangible assets, as patents, copyrights, franchises, and goodwill are amortized if they are acquired at a specific cost. If there is no cost they should not be reported on the balance sheet.

The estimate of services from an intangible asset during a given period is debited to an amortization account and credited to the intangible asset account or to an accumulated amortization account. The Accounting Principles Board requires that intangible assets be amortized over a period of 40 years using the straight line method.

Usually the only intangible asset a facility encounters is goodwill. If it has high occupancy, a healthy ROI, and high resident/family loyalty, the owner may add a sizeable price for goodwill if he sells the facility. However, the buyer will not likely want to pay it as goodwill since it requires bookwork to amortize it. The buyer usually asks that it be added to the basic purchase price, as an additional amount per bed. In this way it does not become an intangible asset.

DEPRECIATION

Depreciation is the allocation of the cost of a long-lived tangible asset (buildings, equipment, automobiles, etc.) over a number of years. The original cost of the depreciable asset is distributed over the asset's estimated useful life. Depreciation is one of the costs of operating a business. Use of a depreciable asset in a facility represents the change from asset cost to operating expense. Depreciation is a noncash cost because there is no actual cash outlay. (Hermanson, et al.)

Food for preparation, medical supplies, housekeeping materials, and other supplies are current assets and cannot be depreciated. Buildings, computers, laundry equipment, emergency generator, and other similar equipment can be depreciated. The cost of the depreciable asset, less any salvage value, is distributed over the asset's estimated useful life.

The **causes** of depreciation are use, wear and tear, action of the elements, and obsolescence. The latter refers to equipment that may be in good condition but is out of date or obsolete. Word processors and computers are examples of assets that may quickly become obsolete. Improvements are made so rapidly that new models with greater capabilities at lower prices are placed on the market almost yearly.

Use of depreciation allows management to recover the initial investment in buildings, equipment, and other long-lived assets. The most frequently used is the straight-line method.

The **straight-line method** distributes the same dollar amount of depreciation to expense each year (or period) in the asset's assigned life. This method assumes that wear and deterioration occur at the same rate over the period of the asset's life. If the facility's kitchen range and oven have an estimated life of ten years, depreciation is determined by dividing their cost by ten. Each year 10 percent of the original cost is charged to expense

Table 7.4:

Straight-line Depreciation Schedule for $10,000 Equipment with 10-Year Useful Life

Year	Book Value 1st of Year	Amount of Depreciation	Book Value End of Year	Accumulated Depreciation
One	$10,000	$1,000	$9,000	$1,000
Two	9,000	1,000	8,000	2,000
Three	8,000	1,000	7,000	3,000
Four	7,000	1,000	6,000	4,000
Five	6,000	1,000	5,000	5,000
Six	5,000	1,000	4,000	6,000
Seven	4,000	1,000	3,000	7,000
Eight	3,000	1,000	2,000	8,000
Nine	2,000	1,000	1,000	9,000
Ten	1,000	1,000	0	10,000

until they are fully depreciated in ten years. **Medicare requires** the straight line method to be used, and most states require the same for Medicaid facilities. Table 7.4 is an example of a depreciation schedule.

If there is **salvage value**, it is subtracted from the original cost before depreciation is calculated. If the $10,000 equipment item in Table 7.4 has a salvage value of $1,000, depreciation in the first year would be calculated on $9,000. Depreciation for each year would be $900 rather than $1,000. Book value at the end of 10 years would be $1,000 since the item may be sold or traded in for that amount.

Accelerated depreciation methods allocate larger amounts of depreciation in the earlier years of an asset's useful life than in later years. In earlier years Medicaid and Medicare allowed this method to be used by nursing facilities. Federal guidelines specified the percent of depreciation in the earlier years. It was the preferred method because increased depreciation in the early years, when less revenue was probably generated, reduced taxable earnings. (Hermanson, et al.)

Double-declining balance is an accelerated method that allows management to double the straight-line rate and to apply the doubled rate to the declining balance of the asset. (Hermanson, et al.) If an equipment item costs $8,000, management may double the 10 percent straight-line depreciation rate, thereby expensing out 20 percent of $8,000 which is a $1,600 first-year depreciation expense. At the end of the second year the depreciation formula is: $8,000 - 1,600 = $6,400 x 20% = $1,280, which is the amount to be depreciated. The original cost minus previous depreciation times 20 percent is applied each year thereafter. This method is often called simply "declining balance." LTC facilities certified for Medicare may not use this method.

Other depreciation methods used in business are:

1. **Production-unit** can be applied when the asset is used directly in producing a specifically identifiable product, such as units of goods or miles driven. When you purchase an asset it is assumed a certain number of units of service has been acquired.

2. **Service-hours** is similar to the production-unit method. The depreciable cost is allocated to the number of times the item was in use.

3. **Sum-of-the-year's digits** applies a **declining** rate to the depreciable cost in order to compute depreciation. It is another **accelerated** method that results in high depreciation charges in the early life of an asset and low depreciation charges in the later life.

4. **Group depreciation** is used when the facility purchases several units of a particular item. If

depreciated separately management must deal with an **average** figure, whereas some units wear out before the assigned useful life and others last longer. By depreciating the items as a group, the losses on the items retired early are offset against gains on the assets that last beyond the average life.

5. **Composite depreciation** depreciates groups of **unlike** assets. It uses weighted-average useful life (composite) for all fixed assets. It is difficult to apply and sometimes considered unjustifiable.

Accumulated depreciation is the total depreciation taken to date on depreciable assets. Accumulated depreciation is determined by adding depreciation taken each year to date. It is used in determining **book value** of an asset. The terms "reserves for depreciation" and "allowance for depreciation" are occasionally used instead of accumulated depreciation. The total amount of all depreciation allocated can never exceed the original cost of the item depreciated.

INVENTORY CONTROLS

Inventory in nursing facilities refers to the amount of goods and materials on hand which are to be currently used in producing services or held for sale. Medical, office, housekeeping, and other supplies are examples of inventory to be used. Vending machine products and food for employee and visitor meals are examples of inventory held for resale. Proper and accurate measurement of ending inventories is necessary to reflect net earnings for a particular period.

1. **Physical inventory** means the actual counting of goods and materials on hand at a given period of time, usually the end of a fiscal year. The value of the goods and materials is subtracted from the cost of all goods and materials during that period to determine total cost of goods and materials used or sold.

2. **Perpetual inventory** is an inventory control system in which all purchases, requisitions filled, and balances on hand are recorded and reorder levels used. This system reflects **cost** based on **actual usage**. Computers are extremely helpful in a perpetual inventory system. They can be programmed to print out purchase orders when reorder levels are reached. Table 7.5 is an example of how a perpetual inventory is kept either by computer or by hand using a card system.

3. **Turnover** rates are important to inventory control. The facility should determine the

Table 7.5:

Perpetual Inventory Record

Item:	Underpads (medium)	**Vendor:**	ABC Supply Co.
Order Units:	30 cases of 60	**Address:**	4000 Highland Ave.
Cost/unit:	$35.00		Monroe, LA 71045
Reorder level:	12		

Received/On Hand		Issued		Balance cases
Date	**No. Cases**	**Date**	**No. Pads**	**On Hand**
2/2/94	/34	2/3/94	180	31
		2/4/94	240	27
		2/5/94	270	22.5
		2/6/94	270	18
		2/7/94	240	16
		2/8/94	240	12
		2/9/94	180	9
		2/10/94	240	5
2/11/94	30/35	2/12/94	240	31

number of times an inventory of given items are replaced during the year. If the turnover rate is slow for an item used extensively this indicates an excessive amount is being ordered. A very rapid rate of turnover indicates too few are ordered too frequently; a larger order is indicated.

4. **Valuation** of existing inventory must be made at the end of the fiscal year. It is necessary in order to calculate net earnings. Ending inventories should be valued at the lower of these: (1) actual cost when purchased, (2) cost if currently purchased. Cirn describes three valuation methods that may be used.

   a. **Average cost** method is used to determine a unit cost for each item in stock every time new stock is added. This is accomplished by adding the cost of old stock to the cost of new stock received and dividing the total by the total quantity on hand, old and new.

   b. **First-in, first-out (FIFO)** is a method that assumes older supplies in stock are used first. If inflation occurs, the value of the remaining goods in stock is **higher** than goods already used. This method is often used in operations as a means of using up certain inventories to prevent spoilage. It is often used in the kitchen as well as in the pharmacy where an item may have a short shelf life.

   c. **Last-in, first-out (LIFO)** method assumes that new inventory will be used first. This makes the value of goods remaining in the inventory **lower** than the value of goods already used to provide service.

Whatever inventory method is used, including perpetual, there is still the need to periodically do a hand count of items. It is often said, "Nobody in a nursing home steals, but somehow certain items take wings and fly."

In practice most nursing homes do not calculate value of inventory on the basis of the lower cost when purchased or cost if purchased now. They use cost when purchased as this is less paper work and requires less staff time.

TRANSPORTATION COSTS

When equipment or other goods are purchased, often there is a delivery cost. Several freight terms are used to identify payment of cost. **Freight** is the property carried by the transporter. Also freight refers to the **cost** of transporting goods. There are several methods of paying freight.

1. **F.o.b. shipping point** means "free on board" at the shipping point. The buyer pays all transportation costs after the goods are loaded at the point of shipment.

2. **F.o.b. destination** means the seller pays all costs of transporting the shipment to its destination.

3. **Freight prepaid** means the seller pays the freight before goods arrive at the destination.

4. **Freight collect** means the buyer pays the freight upon arrival of the goods. (Hermanson, et al.)

AUDITING

Auditing refers to the checking, reviewing, testing, and verifying the accuracy of accounting records and procedures by a third party. Generally it includes expression of a professional opinion on the fairness of the audit information. (Hermanson, et al.) Auditing is usually carried out by a certified public accountant (CPA) who must be licensed in some states. When seeking loans, financial statements must be furnished. Banks and other institutions give more credibility to financial statements that are properly audited by a CPA.

Compliance audit In addition to checking accuracy of the accounting records, some facilities do a compliance audit. This involves determining whether all financial procedures were adhered to during the fiscal year. Included are purchasing procedures involving requisitions, receiving reports, and packing slips; payroll accounting procedures involving withholdings and their remittance; receiving and depositing funds and reconciling bank statements; handling of resident funds; billing; paying bills; and all other financial transactions. This kind of audit provides information on how well the facility's internal financial controls are followed. It is usually a more expensive audit.

PERCENT OCCUPANCY

The percent occupancy or occupancy rate is the ratio of the actual number of resident days to the total bed capacity. (1) Multiply the total number of beds by 30 days, or total days in the month, to determine the total resident days possible. (2) Multiply the number of beds actually occupied by 30 days, or total days in the month, to determine actual number of resident days for the month. (3) Divide the number of actual resident days by the number of possible resident days to determine the percent occupancy. Example:

175 total beds x 30 days = 5,250 possible resident days
150 beds filled x 30 days = 4,500 actual resident days
4,500 divided by 5,250 = 85.7% occupancy

The percent occupancy is a key factor in determining the financial status of a nursing facility. It can be used to determine the break-even point. If 85.7 percent occupancy, as shown above, is the break-even point, the facility begins to realize a profit on the 151st resident. When a goal is established to achieve a given amount of profit within a predetermined time period, it is also necessary to calculate the required occupancy rate. If management determines 95 percent occupancy will meet its goal, the facility must maintain an average of 168 residents.

Daily census, preferred by some administrators, converts percent occupancy to an actual head count, i.e., a daily census. This means to maintain an 85.7 percent occupancy, the facility must have an average of 150 residents. When resident census falls below 150 it loses money. When resident census is maintained at 168, it attains the desired profit.

RETIREMENT SYSTEM

All organizations, whether for profit or not-for-profit, are required to participate in the Social Security program unless specifically exempt. Only organizations with their own government-approved retirement systems and which meet several other tests may be exempt. This, too, is in process of change. Employees in government funded retirement programs are sometimes required to pay that part of Social Security that makes them eligible for Medicare. Other changes are imminent. In order to be **tax** exempt a retirement system must include all employees, and each level in the hierarchy must be treated equally.

A nursing facility may set up a retirement system that takes its employees out of Social Security or the facility may set up a system to supplement Social Security. Before considering any type of system, contact the Internal Revenue Service for guidelines, for Congress is in the process of making major changes in Social Security.

GARNISHMENTS

A **writ of garnishment** is a legal proceeding which directs an employer to withhold a designated portion of an employee's wages, and to remit those funds to the designated government agency which in turn settles with the third party to whom the employee is indebted. (Black)

The Federal Wage Garnishment Law (Title III of the Consumer Credit Protection Act) provides that no employee may be discharged because of garnishment on any one indebtedness. The term "one indebtedness" is complex and can lead to problems. Action should never be taken against an employee who has a garnishment without first seeking legal advice.

This law also restricts the amount of an employee's earnings that may be deducted in any one week through garnishment. It does not change most state garnishment procedures or affect state laws that provide greater restrictions on garnishment than federal law. Administrators must honor a writ of garnishment by withholding and remitting as directed.

PAYROLL ACCOUNTING

Payroll accounting is an extremely important part of a general accounting system. Generally an owner-manager or an administrator of a nursing facility cannot handle the entire payroll procedure alone, or even directly oversee the performance of a payroll accountant. In an effective payroll accounting system timekeeping, preparing the payroll, keeping payroll records, and handing out paychecks may be handled by different individuals or units of the business.

The purposes of payroll accounting are:

1. To process data such as names, Social Security numbers, hours worked, rates of pay, and deductions for taxes, health insurance, union dues, etc.

2. To provide accurate paychecks when due.

3. To explain to each employee his gross pay, deductions, and net pay, sometimes including year-to-date figures on each item.

4. To provide employee earning records, withholding statements, and government reports.

5. To protect against fraud by paying more than earned, making checks to fictitious employees, preparing duplicate checks, and overstating deductions. (Hermanson, et al.)

When one employee handles all payroll accounting it is easy to issue and cash checks to fictitious or former employees, arrange kickbacks, issue overpayments, prepare and cash duplicate checks, and overstate deductions, and thus to embezzle funds. People handling these functions should be **bonded**, and the administrator should review payroll.

Procedures must be established whereby hours worked are recorded by time-cards or sign-in records showing date and time of sign in and sign out. Wage and Hours Division recommends that **records** of attendance, earnings, pay periods, etc. should be retained at least three years. The statute of limitations allows employees to file claims regarding minimum wages and overtime pay up to two years after the date of occurrence and for three years in cases of willful violation by an employer. Procedures must include **documentation** of all withholdings, Social Security numbers, each employee's earnings, and periodic payroll reports to federal and state governments. Generally, these records must be made available to surveyors for determining proper staffing.

1. **Payroll taxes** on an employee's gross earnings generally include federal, state, and local (where applicable) income tax, Social Security and Medicare taxes. Other deductions may be authorized by an individual when appropriate, as insurance, union dues, credit union payments and deposits, and retirement. Employers must follow the Employer's Tax Guide issued annually by IRS.

   a. **Federal income taxes** are withheld according to the IRS schedule. Employees must sign an Employee's Withholding Allowance Certificate (Form W-4) accurately stating the number of exemptions to which they are entitled. A W-4 Form must be kept on file for each employee. State and sometimes local income taxes are also withheld according to the appropriate schedule.

   At the end of the calendar year each employee must be provided a Wage and Tax Statement (Form W-2) by the following January 31. It is a summary of gross earnings and income tax , Medicare, and Social Security tax withheld. The employee must attach a copy of the W-2 Form to his income tax return as required by federal and state laws.

   b. **Social Security** tax was created by the Federal Insurance Contributions Act (FICA). The employer is required to withhold a sum stipulated by federal law from an employee's pay. A like or similar amount is paid by the employer, i.e. 50 percent.

   c. **Medicare** tax is now separate from Social Security. Organizations that have an approved retirement program and are exempt from Social Security tax are required to withhold, match, and remit Medicare tax. Currently, the rate is 2.9 percent of a person's total earnings. The employee and employer each pays 50 percent of the tax.

Deposits of withholdings are regulated by Internal Revenue Service. Refer to the above mentioned Employer's Tax Guide for most recent regulations that were imposed January 1, 1993. Basically, the new regulations involve a **lookback period** - a three month period during the past tax year. If the facility paid less than $50,000.00 total payroll tax, it now must deposit each month's withholdings by the 15th of the following month, instead of quarterly. The remittances are reconciled quarterly on IRS Form 941. Beginning in 1996 the IRS made available its 941 ELF program. Through the Electronic Data Interchange (EDI) format, businesses depositing monthly payroll tax can file their Forms 941 electronically. Advantages of using the EDI are:

1. Reduced chance of duplicate or erroneous returns,
2. Acknowledgment within 48 hours of receipt,
3. Information available sooner to clear up questions quicker and easier, and
4. Individual can file by personal computer.

EDI transmitted software is available through local **software stores.**

Facilities that paid more than $50,000 in payroll taxes during the prior year's lookback period **are required to** make their depository tax payments by **electronic fund transfer** (EFT). They can no longer make payments with a Federal Tax Deposit (FTD) coupon. They are required to use the Electronic Federal Tax Payment System (EFTPS). Facilities must enroll in the EFTPS before they can initiate any electronic payments. Enrollment applications are available from IRS. When a facility applies for enrollment, IRS sends information on steps to follow in making electronic tax deposits.

Administrators should be extremely careful about payroll taxes if they sign the remittance checks. IRS has held the administrator responsible for unpaid payroll taxes when a facility took bankruptcy. They ruled that the person signing remittance checks is responsible for payroll taxes being paid. In one instance IRS filed a $100,000.00 lien against the administrator's properties when the facility he directed went bankrupt, even though he had no ownership interest. Congress is supposed to correct this kind of inequity.

Pay checks Many facilities contract with a CPA firm that makes up payroll checks. When this system is used all payroll information is sent to the contractor. It includes names, regular and overtime hours, hourly rate of pay, SS, Medicare and FWT withholdings, and other authorized deductions including a garnishment when it is ordered by the court. Usually this information is sent electronically. Checks are computed, made up, and a computerized signature placed on each. Checks are then returned to the facility for distribution.

Before handing out or mailing checks, or depositing them electronically when authorized by the employee, the payroll and checks should be reviewed. Sometimes errors are made that can be costly to the facility.

> **Example:** Payroll was sent electronically to the contracting firm. A group of employees made $7.50 per hour. It was entered as $75 per hour, checks were made up, and distributed. Those who worked 80 hours during the pay period received checks amounting to $6,000 instead of $600. When the error was discovered funds were recovered from all employees except one. He skipped the country.

One of the best ways to handle this problem is the two-signature check. One signature can be computerized, but one must be written by hand. The signer, often the administrator, should review the payroll and the checks before signing. Upon reviewing the check of an employee who made $600 during a pay period, the reviewer would have certainly noted that the amount was $6,000 instead.

2. **The Federal Unemployment Tax Act (FUTA)** is funded totally by the employer in most states. The amount of the federal taxation varies from year to year. Since this is a federal-state program, taxes are also paid to the state. The percent of state tax varies from state to state. States usually require new employers to pay the state's maximum rate for a period of time, often three years. It is paid to the state's office of employment security or to an office by another name but having the same functions. A facility can earn a reduced rate based on taxable wages, taxes paid, and claim record. The fewer dismissals qualifying for unemployment compensation the better the chance of earning a lower rate.

   Most states levy their portion of the unemployment tax against the employer only. Currently, 5.4 percent of taxes paid to the state may be credited toward the federal payroll tax (FUTA). In order to receive credit for taxes paid to the state, the fourth quarter tax must be paid before January 31st. The federal government bills the employer in January for the amount due above that paid to the state.

   If a nonprofit facility wishes to be **self-insured**, application must be made to the official state agency handling unemployment compensation. This agency determines eligibility and supplies the needed information. If the agency qualifies and benefits are due any of its ex-employees, the state agency pays the benefits and bills the agency for reimbursement.

   It is necessary that all nursing facilities contact their appropriate state agency for information, directions, and the forms used to comply with FUTA requirements. Even so, the program can create a serious problem for employers as noted in Chapter 6 on Personnel Management.

3. **Workers Compensation** is a type of insurance paid entirely by the employer. It is to protect the employee and his dependents in the event of injury or death in the course of employment. This insurance is discussed further under financial planning later in this chapter. It is generally considered a payroll tax, though it is insurance.

4. **An employee earning record** is frequently maintained for each employee by employers. Federal laws dictate how funds will be withheld from employees' paychecks, the minimum rates of pay and overtime payment, and how payroll taxes will be paid by employers. To ensure compliance with these laws adequate payroll records must be kept on each employee. These records indicate employee's name, Social Security number, address, phone number, date employed, date of birth, sex, marital status, number of exemptions, pay rate, and present job. The number of hours worked during each pay period, gross pay, deductions, and net pay are logged on each employee's earning record. The cumulative total of gross pay helps determine when to stop deducting Social Security and employer's payroll taxes. (Hermanson, et al.) This record is invaluable when a claim is filed by an employee or a question arises regarding payroll matters.

OTHER TAXES

Nursing facilities may be required to pay a number of taxes in addition to payroll tax. The levying of taxes varies greatly from state to state. In some states there is a state, county, and local tax on the same item. Since accountants must be knowledgeable in tax matters, they are able to advise on taxes to be paid and amount of taxes. Following are examples of taxes a facility might pay: (1) sales, (2) property (real estate), (3) federal and state corporate income, (4) occupational, and (5) business.

UNIFORM COST REPORTS AND REIMBURSEMENT

Federal regulations require the states to provide for the filing of **uniform cost reports** (mentioned earlier) by each nursing facility certified and enrolled in Title XIX. States base these on the facility's individual fiscal year. Each state has its own cost reports program which provides all facilities with information on how and when to report.

Usually facilities are notified shortly after enrollment, and cost report forms are sent to them. If the accounting system is tailored to accommodate cost report forms, it is much easier to compile reports at the end of the year. Generally, cost reports are due 90 days following the end of the fiscal year.

The single state agency responsible for the Medicaid program arranges for an **audit** of annual cost reports. Only **costs related to resident care** are allowable. These are the common and accepted costs in the field of provider activity. They include nursing, administrative, and maintenance costs, depreciation, interest expense, cost of employee pension plans, and others. A facility may also have **costs not related to resident care**, as cost of meals sold to visitors, cost of operating a gift shop, etc. These costs are not allowable on the annual cost report.

Reimbursable costs There are a number of reimbursable costs that administrators must be knowledgeable about in order to be properly reimbursed. **Allowable costs** are those related to resident care and certain indirect costs computed by the state. **Direct costs** are those chargeable to a specific revenue center such as dietary service. Food, kitchen and dining room supplies, and dietary workers salaries are examples. **Indirect costs** are those incurred for the benefit of two or more departments, such as administrative, housekeeping, and maintenance costs. **Ancillary charges** are for supplies, drugs, laboratory tests, and others not included in the basic per diem cost billed to residents or the intermediary.

Cost-related reimbursement rates are determined by the state using information on annual cost reports and other criteria as cost-of-living and wage index. The state establishes a **per resident day** rate for each level of care in a Medicaid facility. These rates allow for a margin of profit and they vary widely from state to state. **Profit** is realized by providing proper care to residents with efficiency and economy. The more efficient the operation, the greater the amount of profit.

Cost per resident day is a measure of the efficiency of operations. It means the average costs involved in caring for one resident for one 24-hour period. Management may wish to calculate its per resident day costs monthly, quarterly, semiannually, annually, or for other periods of time. Cost per resident day is calculated by dividing the total costs of operations for a given period of time by the total number of resident days realized in that time period. For example, the following total annual operational costs are divided by the total resident days for the year to determine cost per resident day because it is simple and easy to determine.

$1,620,000 ÷ 30,000 = $54 cost per resident day
(total cost) *(total resident days)*

If the per resident day reimbursement rate is $60 the facility realizes a $6 profit per resident per day. There are other methods of determining income over total expenses, but administrators often use per resident day costs as a basis for calculations.

PETTY CASH FUND

A facility establishes a **petty cash fund** primarily for convenience and to reduce check writing. Although it is desirable that all disbursements be by check, small items are often needed immediately and the purchase handled more quickly by using petty cash. Most facilities establish a petty cash fund of $50 to $100. The fund should contain a sufficient amount for a reasonable amount of time, such as one month. (Hermanson, et al.)

Proper **controls** must be maintained for the fund to serve its purpose. This may be accomplished by appointing a petty cash cashier who is responsible for the fund, and by requiring each petty cash expenditure to be supported by a receipt.

Replenishing Most petty cash funds are set up on an **imprest** basis which means that petty cash is only periodically reimbursed out of general cash. When the fund is relatively low on cash, receipts are grouped according to category of expenditure: postage, office expense, and so on. Each category is totaled and that amount entered in the proper account. All categories are then totaled, and a check made to petty cash for this amount. The check is cashed and the money placed in the fund. This amount plus cash left in the fund when expenditures were totaled should equal the original amount of the fund.

Example: A total of $100 is placed in a petty cash fund. When the balance in the fund is $10, categories are totaled: stamps $10, office expense $30, resident activities $20, delivery charges $20, other charges $10 — a total of $90 spent. A check is drawn for $90, cashed, and the money added to the $10 remaining in the fund for a total of $100. The total for each of the categories is posted to the appropriate account.

One check was written for petty cash whereas 15 or more would have been written for small amounts without a petty cash fund. The value is convenience in payment of small items, the reduction of check writing, and not cluttering accounts with numerous entries of small amounts.

RESIDENT FUNDS
[42 CFR 483.10 (c) (1-8)]

A resident has the right to manage his/her financial affairs. The facility cannot require a resident to deposit funds with the facility. The facility must, however, protect and manage residents' personal funds whenever the resident desires. Previously, the facility was required to handle resident funds only if the resident was unable to manage them and there was no responsible party. OBRA 87 requires that upon **written authorization** of a resident, the facility now must hold, safeguard, manage, and account for personal funds.

Receiving The facility should install a resident fund system governed by policies and procedures that provide adequate financial controls. Each resident must have a separate account in which all funds received and paid out are recorded. When funds are received a duplicate receipt should be completed, one kept by the facility, and the other given to the resident or responsible party.

Funds paid out should be documented with receipts that are initialed by the resident and the facility employee handling the transaction. In case of funds withdrawn for the vending machine where no receipt is received, both the resident and the employee should initial the withdrawal. Proper financial controls dictate that one employee should receive funds and another pay them out. This is seldom economically feasible in a nursing facility.

Deposits A resident's funds in excess of $50 must be deposited in an interest bearing account separate from facility funds. Earned interest must be credited to the resident's account. Funds of $50 or less must be kept in a noninterest bearing account, an interest bearing account, or in a petty cash fund.

Accounts The facility must maintain full, complete, and separate accounting records for each resident who deposits funds. Records must be kept according to generally accepted accounting principles. There can be no **co-mingling** of resident funds with facility funds, but all resident funds may be kept together. The individual record must be available through quarterly reports and on request to the resident or his legal representative.

Notices The facility must notify each Medicaid resident when his account balance is $200 less than the Supplemental Security Income (SSI) resource limit for one person, and that the resident may lose eligibility for Medicaid or SSI if the amount of his account plus the value of his other exempt resources reaches the SSI limit for one person.

Conveyance at death Should a resident with funds deposited with the facility die, the facility must convey the resident's funds and final accounting of those funds to the person administering the resident's estate within 30 days.

Financial security OBRA further requires the facility to purchase a surety bond or provide evidence of self-insurance that ensures security of resident funds. The bond or other assurance must be at least equal to the total resident funds in the care of the facility. Alternative assurance must be satisfactory to the Secretary of the US

DHHS. It can be provided by another institution or by the facility. If the facility provides the assurance, there must be adequate facility funds irrevocably dedicated to repayment of resident funds in case of loss.

Charges No charges may be made against a resident's personal funds for any item or service for which payment is made under Medicaid or Medicare. The facility may charge the resident for requested services that are more expensive than or in excess of covered services. Medicare and Medicaid facilities may not charge a resident for the following categories, items, and services:

1. Nursing services required under 42CFR 483.20
2. Dietary services required under 42CFR 483.20
3. Activities program required under 42CFR 483.20
4. Room/bed/maintenance services
5. Routine personal hygiene items and services required to meet resident needs, including but not limited to, hair hygiene supplies, comb, brush, bath soap, disinfecting soaps or specialized cleansing agents when indicated to treat special skin problems or to fight infection, razor, shaving cream, toothbrush, toothpaste, denture adhesive, dental floss, moisturizing lotion, deodorant, incontinence care and supplies, sanitary napkins and related supplies, towels, washcloths, hospital gowns, over the counter drugs, hair and nail hygiene services, bathing, and personal laundry.

Surveyors will examine monthly statements to residents to determine if this regulation is followed.

COST MANAGEMENT

Cost management is an ongoing, active program of managing costs in every unit of the facility. Its objectives are fourfold:

1. To avoid waste which means buying what is necessary and saving what one can — **cost effectiveness**
2. To be **cost efficient** by producing more results with the required costs
3. To enhance quality and productivity
4. To implement voluntary cost reduction by staff (Jacobs)

Cost management involves a **cost benefit analysis** to determine if the facility gets its money's worth. It also utilizes a **sensitivity analysis** for the **purpose** of anticipating changes in variable costs so controls may be planned. Jacobs discusses these in detail.

Example: Floods in California destroyed 80% of the vegetable crop in farming areas that shipped their produce to markets suppling the health-care and restaurant industries in the state. Nursing-home administrators had their accountants do a sensitivity analyses to determine approximately when and in what amount their food costs would rise due to expected shortages. Knowing this, they could plan for cost containment.

Employees are the **biggest cost control problem** as they may waste or misappropriate assets. By the same token, they are the only solution to cost management. Administrators must teach them to be cost conscious and to practice efficient, economic use of materials and supplies.

According to HCFA labor-related costs in nursing homes can be as much as 75 percent of the budget. The other part of the budget for purchasing equipment, supplies, and contractual services is also extremely important. The **key to good purchasing** is: (1) **standardize** both products and vendors well before one plans to purchase, (2) **centralize** purchasing into one department, and (3) **minimize** the number of employees authorized to purchase. The advantages are increased purchase power which may mean lower prices, lower shipping costs, larger orders, fewer deliveries, and fewer invoices to process. (Jacobs)

Example: A turnaround specialist took over a large nursing home that was about to collapse financially due to a huge indebtedness. One of the first activities he investigated was purchasing. He found each department head purchased for his department. As a result he determined numerous gratuities were clandestinely given to department heads. These department heads bought more supplies than were needed and some items that were never used. The new manager changed purchasing procedures to those suggested by Jacobs, and instituted a rule that "no employee may accept anything from a vendor that he cannot eat or drink at the time." Purchasing costs nose-dived 30% the first month.

Jacobs' publication *Cost Management in Long-Term Care Facilities* has many practical suggestions that administrators can use. Proper cost management in every unit of the facility is covered.

FINANCIAL PLANNING

Financial planning begins with budgeting, but there are many other planning activities an administrator must carry out in order to do an efficient job. Understanding terms and procedures previously discussed is necessary to enhance planning. Some areas of planning follow.

Excess funds When a facility has funds that may not be needed for awhile they should be put to work earning revenue. No funds should remain idle. An **interest-bearing checking** account keeps funds very liquid but usually generates the least amount of interest. Placing funds in a **savings account** keeps them just as liquid and generates slightly more interest. It is wise to maintain a small balance in checking and place as much as possible in savings. Frequent trips to the bank to transfer from savings to checking is worth the time, as noted earlier.

A **money market** account keeps all deposited funds actively generating interest. These accounts are quite liquid and usually generate more than savings and often more than a short-term **certificate of deposit** (CD). The CD is not as liquid as the money market account since the latter can be available in 24 hours. Usually, the best investment of funds that must remain liquid is the money market fund.

Compound interest It is important to understand compound interest when using funds to generate revenue. Interest on funds invested may be compounded daily, weekly, monthly, quarterly, semiannually, or annually, dependent on what is allowable and practiced by a given financial institution. Interest is compounded when interest is paid on accumulated interest. This occurs when interest for one period is added to the base investment and interest paid on the total during the second period. An example on $2000 invested at five percent per year is:

	1st year	2nd year	3rd year
	$2,000	$2,100	$2,205
	5%	5%	5%
Interest earned	$100	$105	$110.25

Generally, financial institutions will provide an interest table which facilitates computing the future worth of monies invested at a given rate. (Hermanson et al.)

Planning insurance Proper insurance coverage, especially **liability**, is quite important to a facility's survival. This includes **general** and **professional** liability. **General liability** covers injuries to nonresidents and other losses that occur in the facility, except for staff when on duty. **Professional liability**, commonly called malpractice, covers injuries, improper treatment, neglect, and so on involving residents.

Several factors should be considered in planning liability insurance. Most important is the possible **size** of a loss. What are the trends in courts granting awards in the area where the facility is located? Recently, a Texas court awarded $39 million to the children of a woman who died in a nursing facility. She was in restraints, partially slid out of bed, and choked to death. One such loss can put a facility out of business.

A second consideration is the **probability** of a loss occurring. This means to know the statistics on the number of accidents and incidents that generally occur in a nursing facility and to be aware of the thoroughness of the facility's resident care practices and safety programs and the attitudes of the clientele served toward seeking recourse should something happen to a resident.

Some communities tend to resort to tort action very quickly, while others tend to seek solutions with the facility.

Workers compensation, discussed earlier, is largely controlled by state laws. Depending on the individual state law, employers have several options: (1) a payroll-based state insurance system, (2) insurance through a private carrier, or (3) self-insurance. Premium rates depend on risk class of the occupations involved, the claims-experience rating of the facility, and any state regulations. Rates are computed on the total payroll, including full-time and part-time employees. (Hermanson et al.) In planning workers compensation insurance, employers must compile data on the incidence rate and the cost of accidents. This insurance program must be closely related to the facility's safety program.

Property insurance In addition to the above insurance and FUTA, a facility needs fire and extended coverage insurance. Standard policies and the broad-form policy do not adequately cover the facility, since neither covers resident property. Adequate insurance would include a special provision covering loss of resident properties, as jewelry, wheelchairs, or other valuables. The only alternative would be to require residents to carry their own insurance or to work out a legal arrangement whereby the facility is not responsible for resident property.

In considering **premium rates**, deductibles are a major factor since they significantly reduce rates. The facility must determine the extent of loss it can absorb before insurance pays. A $5,000 deductible has a much lower rate than a $1,000 deductible. Rating and reputation of the insurance company is another factor to consider in planning. Insurance should never be purchased from an unrated company or one with a poor claims settlement record. A company's rating can be determined by calling the state insurance department.

Recovering costs Vendors offer enticing deals on equipment and materials that supposedly represent savings. Usually these offers involve a sizeable upfront investment. The administrator must plan carefully in this area by determining payback on investment. An example is a new type of bed linen which has a long, useful life and maintains its quality. The vendor offers a new laundry setup plus a large supply of the new linens guaranteeing a certain savings per year, dependent largely on the size of the facility and volume of linens needed. Before making a decision the administrator should compute the payback period in order to evaluate whether there is an actual savings. If the laundry/linen program has an initial cost of $12,000 and a savings of $1600 per year, payback would be calculated as follows: $12,000 ÷ $1600 = 7.5 years. Payback period is calculated simply by dividing the original cost by savings per year. The facility will recover its cost a second time through depreciation, but it is not considered in calculating the payback period.

Cash flow requires careful planning, too. At all times the administrator should know how much working capital he has, since that determines whether bills can be paid. Frequently, there is a **lag time** between billing and collecting. This can occur with residents as well as the fiscal intermediary. The solution is to increase the working capital so there is cash for operations. There are several methods for doing this.

1. The **best method** is to work **accounts receivable**, collecting income already earned. In fact, the amount of working capital generated from operations is one of the most important financial figures. A successful facility acquires plant and other assets, retires long-term debt, and pays dividends from working capital generated by operations. (Hermanson, et al).

2. Another favored method is to **pledge accounts receivable** to the bank. This generates immediate capital, and as the A/R's are collected the money goes to the bank to cover the amount advanced. The bank charges interest only on the amount of funds advanced to the facility.

3. **Securing a line of credit** is often used. It is an agreement with the bank which extends credit to the facility up to an agreed upon maximum. Interest is charged only on funds actually used.

4. Another method that is quick but not too efficient is to increase **long-term debt**. This supplies immediate working capital but incurs interest costs over the life of the debt. **Borrowing** is usually necessary for nursing facilities, but it must be carefully planned. Long-term loans for equipment, automobiles, and building and loans for unforeseen emergencies are made by most enterprises. It is considered good business practice. Borrowing, however, to pay current bills is usually a bad practice and may indicate real financial problems. Two accounts are affected when loans are made: cash and notes payable.

5. **Issuing shares of stock** is another method of generating working capital. Most closely held corporations do not wish to use this method. Chain enterprises often use it.

6. Using **retained earnings** is a sixth method. This, too, can be an economical means as corporations usually pay dividends from working capital generated by operations.

7. Another method often not possible in nursing facilities is to sell **noncurrent assets**. Most facilities simply do not have this type asset to sell.

8. Not-for-profit corporations have still another method. If they qualify under IRS, they may raise capital by securing **grants**.

Energy costs Many facilities are concerned about utility costs at some point. Cost management planning is essential in this area. Energy costs tend to increase steadily and any sudden rise in utility bills is cause for concern. When a facility is faced with this problem the first step is to conduct an **energy audit**. Hire a maintenance engineer to do this and to set up an energy-saving program. This will entail the monitoring of energy use by all systems, equipment, and staff on a continuous basis, usually by one person, the maintenance worker. Maintenance engineers will usually guarantee a savings the first year that will more than pay for the audit and program planning.

As mentioned earlier, immediate planning is necessary to cope with the impact of **managed care.** If this type of health-care delivery continues to expand at the rate of the past four years, nursing facilities have little time to plan for the impact of managed care's objective to purchase services at the lowest possible price. Also, in some areas managed care enterprises have warned nursing homes they are planning to provide less expensive care in the patient's own home or in assisted living units.

> **Example:** In a community with four nursing homes, managed care executives met with the four administrators. They outlined details of their plans and advised administrators they must provide less expensive care or managed care would not place residents in their facility. The executive's parting shot was, "There are four of you now; in about three years, there will probably be only two in operation."

Lower break-even point Particularly in a new business the owner often becomes impatient with the ROI. He cannot take any money out as profit since the break-even point has not been reached. It is possible to lower the break-even point by taking certain actions.

1. **Increase prices** wherever possible. Of course, this cannot be done with Medicaid residents, but it can with private pay. Also, the price of meals for staff and guests, the prices at vending machines, and prices at any other revenue center can be raised.

2. **Reduce fixed costs**, largely by refinancing long-term debt and paying less per month.

3. **Reduce variable costs** by careful cost management practices and maintaining lower inventories.

Surety bond Any employee regularly handling facility funds should be bonded. A **surety bond** is a form of insurance designed to compensate the employer for losses incurred when an employee fails to carry out his fiduciary duties in the proper manner. Surety bonds are for specific amounts, not like liability insurance. Cost of the surety bond depends on the freedom and latitude the bonded employee has in handling funds. Tight internal financial controls will mean lower premium rates. Administrators can obtain additional information from their insurance agents.

GLOSSARY

Accelerated depreciation A method of depreciation which allocates a greater portion of cost to the early years of the life of an asset. Double-declining balance and sum-of-the-year's digits are two types of this method.

Accounting The process used to identify, measure, record, and report financial information.

Accounts payable Amounts owed to suppliers for goods or services purchased on credit.

Accounts receivable Amounts due from customers or residents.

Accrual basis of accounting Income is recognized when earned rather than when cash is received, and expenses are recognized as incurred regardless of whether payment is made.

Accumulated depreciation Total depreciation taken to date on a depreciable asset.

Allowable cost Cost related to resident care and certain indirect costs allowed by Medicaid.

Amortization The allocation of the original cost of a noncurrent intangible asset over a period of time specified by the Accounting Principles Board.

Ancillary cost Cost that is not part of a daily charge and is related to an individual resident.

Anti-Kickback Statute A federal law prohibiting the payment of kickback for referrals, leases, and contracts.

Asset Things of value, things owned as cash, equipment, buildings, and accounts receivable.

Audit Checking, reviewing, testing, and verifying the accuracy of accounting records by a third party.

Balance sheet Financial statement summarizing assets, liabilities, and retained earnings or net worth.

Bank statement Periodic statement from bank summarizing deposits, checks paid, bank charges, balances, etc.

BBA97 Balanced Budget Act of 1997 that changed the way Medicare pays for SNF services.

Bond A surety bond is a type of insurance covering employees who handle money.

Book value Cost of a depreciable asset less accumulated depreciation

Break-even analysis Determining the break-even point when revenues equal expenses.

Capital Funds acquired for use in a business.

Capital-related costs Cost of land, buildings, and equipment, including interest if they are financed.

Cash basis of accounting Revenues and expenses are not recognized until cash is received or paid out, except for depreciation expense.

Cash flow statement Financial report showing cash receipts and disbursements leading to a net change in cash in a given period.

Chart of accounts Complete listing of the names of all the categories in the ledger.

Consignee A person or party to whom merchandise is consigned or shipped.

Consolidated billing The requirement that SNFs bill Medicare for Part B services received by residents.

Corporation A business owned by either a few persons or thousands, and incorporated under the laws of a given state.

Cost management An ongoing, active program of managing costs in a facility.

Cost-related Those costs in a nursing facility related to providing resident care.

Credit An entry on the right side of an account which increases liability, owner's equity, and revenue accounts.

Current liability Debts generally due within one year that usually require use of current assets.

Debit An entry on the left side of an account that increases assets and expense accounts and decreases liability, owners' equity, and revenue accounts.

Deficit A debit balance in a retained earnings account.

Depreciation The allocation of the original cost of a tangible asset over the period of anticipated useful life of the asset.

Direct costs Costs chargeable to a specific revenue center.

Dividends Earnings distributed to stockholders.

Double-declining balance A method of accelerated depreciation in which the percent used in the straight-line method is doubled.

Double-entry Accounting procedure in which each financial transaction is recorded so that each entry has equal debits and credits.

DRGs Diagnosis-related groups by which hospitals are paid according to resident diagnosis.

Earnings Generated revenues which are generally not recognized until all activities to create them have been completed.

Earnings statement Compares revenues with expenses incurred to produce the income (also called profit and loss statement).

Electronic billing Billing by computer rather than by hard copy.

Equities Rights of the owners in the assets of a business.

Expenses Cost of operating a business, including capital, administrative, and other operating expenditures.

False Claims Act An act of Congress now used to pursue investigation and prosecution of false claims in Medicare and Medicaid.

FASB Financial Accounting Standards Board which establishes standards to guide accounting practice.

FICA Federal Insurance Contributions Act that established the Social Security program.

Fiscal Intermediary A federal or state designated agency named to reimburse Medicare and Medicaid providers for services rendered.

Fiscal year The twelve-month period for which budgets are compiled and expenditures authorized, and at the end of which accounting books are balanced.

Fixed assets Long-lived assets to be used in a business on a long-term basis, including land, buildings, and equipment.

Fixed expenses (costs) Those that remain constant without regard to volume of business, as rent and mortgage note payments.

Freight The property carried by a transporter. Also the cost of transporting goods.

FUTA Federal Unemployment Tax Act that established the unemployment insurance program.

GAAP Generally accepted accounting principles used by accountants.

Garnishment Legal proceedings that direct employers to withhold a designated portion of an employee's pay and remit it to the proper government agency.

Goodwill An intangible asset resulting from the provision of superior services and earnings and from high resident loyalty.

Gross income A taxpayer's income from services such as fees, wages, dividends, and interest.

Indirect costs Cost incurred for benefit of two or more departments not involved in direct resident care.

Intangible asset Noncurrent, nonphysical assets such as leaseholds, copyrights, patents, and goodwill.

Inventory The amount of goods and materials on hand which are to be currently used in producing services or held for resale.

Invoice A document prepared by the seller of merchandise or services and given or sent to the buyer.

Journal A book of original financial entries.

Ledger A complete listing of accounts payable and receivable.

Liability Debts or obligations owed by a business.

Lien A claim on particular property for payment of a debt or obligation.

Limited partnership One in which there is one or more special partners who are not liable for partnership debts beyond the amount of funds contributed.

Liquidity Denotes how quickly an asset can be converted to cash without appreciable loss.

Long-term liability An obligation not due for more than one year.

Marginal return The point at which income equals expenses, the break-even point.

Master budget One that includes cash budget, capital budget, liquidity ratio, and proforma financial statement.

Medicare Part A Inpatient services rendered by hospitals and SNFs and reimbursed by Medicare.

Medicare Part B Outpatient services rendered by providers and reimbursed by Medicare.

MSA Metropolitan Statistical Area as classified by the office of Management and Budget as urban.

NECMA New England County Metropolitan Area classified by the office of Management and Budget as urban.

Net profit Income over expenses before taxes and dividends are paid.

Net worth Assets less liabilities.

Note An unconditional written promise to pay a definite sum of money at a certain date.

Open Account One that is used regularly with periodic payments and charges.

Operating budget One that includes anticipated income by source and anticipated expenditures by category.

Partnership A business owned and usually operated by two or more persons associated as partners.

Par value The value amount printed on a stock certificate, the amount per share at which par value stock is recorded in accounts.

Per diem rate The established rate that Medicare pays for Part A services under BBA97.

Petty Cash Fund A fund maintained to provide quickly available funds to make small purchases that may be urgently needed.

Posting Transfer of a journal entry to the ledger.

PPS Prospective Payment System by which SNF's are reimbursed under BBA97.

Profit The same as earnings.

Profitability The ability of a business to generate revenues (income) to pay all expenses and realize a profit.

Proprietary Exclusive ownership of property or a business. A term commonly used to mean a profit-making enterprise.

Ratio Analysis A method used to analyze financial strength and profitability of a business and to determine the degree of management efficiency in operation.

Real estate Property in the form of land, buildings, and hereditaments.

Reconciliation To make consistent as by adjusting differences between a bank statement and a check book.

Reimbursable costs Costs that Medicaid will reimburse such as allowable, direct, indrect, and ancillary.

Resident funds Personal funds of the residents within a facility which they may place in a facility maintained resident account.

Retained earnings Accumulated net earnings less dividends distributed to stockholders.

Revenue The inflow of assets from the sale of products or rendering of service. (Also called income.)

ROI Return on Investment is a method of ratio analysis used to determine the rate of return on dollars invested, often considered a measure of the facility's success.

Routine costs Medicare costs for which daily charges are made as room and board, nursing service, and other.

Rural SNF A SNF that is not located in an MSA or NECMA.

Safe Harbor A business whose practices do not violate the Anti-Kickback Statute.

S corporation A corporation that pays no corporate tax since profits pass to stockholders who individually pay tax on their portion of the profit.

Sole proprietorship An unincorporated business owned by an individual who usually manages it.

SSI Supplemental Security Income is federal assistance to a needy person who has not worked under Social Security but is aged 65 or older or is disabled, or to a person who draws less than $406 per month Social Security and meets the age or disability requirement.

Straight-line depreciation A method in which the same dollar amount of depreciation is allocated each year of a depreciable asset's assigned life, required by Medicare.

Tangible asset One that has physical characteristics and can be touched, as equipment, land, and buildings.

Trial balance Listing of all accounts and their debit and credit balances, except for accounts with a zero balance, in which debit balances equal credit balances.

Uniform cost report Reports required by each state to be filed at the end of each fiscal year on forms furnished by the states, and showing all costs related to patient care in a facility.

Urban SNF A SNF located in an area classified as an MSA or NECMA.

Variable expense (cost) Those that change in direct proportion to the change in volume of services, as supplies, materials, and food.

Workers compensation insurance A type of insurance that protects an employee and his dependents in the event of an injury on the job.

REFERENCES

Allen, James E., *Nursing Home Administration*, Third edition, New York: Springer Publishing Co., Inc., 1997.

Bedelian, Arthur G., Management, Third Edition, New York: The Dryden Press, 1994.

Black, Henry C., *Black's Law Dictionary*, Sixth Edition, St. Paul, MN: West Publishing Company, 1991.

Brigham, Eugene F., *Fundamentals of Financial Management*, Fort Worth: The Dryden Press, 1992.

Cirn, John, *Financial Management*, in NAB Study Guide, Third Edition, Washington: National Association of Boards of Examiners of Long Term Care Administrators, Inc., 1997.

Cleverly, William O., *Essentials of Health Care Finance*, Third Edition, Rockville, MD: Aspen Publications, 1992.

Cohen, Gerald M., and Marcia Currier, "Complying With Safe Harbor Rules Decreases Risks by Providers," *Provider*, Vol. 22, No. 3, Washington: AHCA, 1992.

Hawryluk, Markian, "Newscurrents," *Provider*, Washington: AHCA, 1998.

"Here At Last," Cover Feature, *Nursing Homes*, November/December 1998.

Hermanson, Roger B., James D. Edwards, and Roy H. Garrisson, *Financial Accounting*, Second Edition, Plano, TX: Business Publications, Inc., 1994.

Internal Revenue Code of 1986 as Amended, Paramas, NJ: Prentiss Hall, Inc., 1990.

Jacobs, Michael, *Cost Management for Long Term Care Facilities*, Bossier City, LA: Professional Printing and Publishing Co., 1986.

Kruger, Patricia E., "Frequently Asked Questions About PPS," *Balance*, ACHCA, March 1998.

Medicare Provider Reimbursement Manual, Publication HIM 15-1, HCFA, Washington: U.S. Department of Health and Human Services.

Mills, Daniel Q., *Labor Management Relations*, New York: McGraw-Hill Publishing Company, 1993.

PPS-1,2,3, What You Need To Know, Washington: American Health Care Association, 1998.

Reporter–A Newsletter for Employers, Internal Revenue Service, Washington: U.S. Government Printing Office, Summer 1996.

Richards, Dorothy, and Albert J. Lucas, "Beware the False Claims Act." *Nursing Homes*, Vol. 45, No. 6, Cleveland: AHCA, 1996.

Title 42 Code of Federal Regulations, Public Health—Part 400 to 429, Washington: U.S. Government Printing Office, 1995.

Title 42 Code of Federal Regulations, Public Health–Part 430 to end, Washington: U.S. Government Printing Office, 1996.

Weihrich, Heinz and Harold Koontz, *Management–A Global Perspective,*, Tenth Edition, New York: McGraw-Hill Book Company, 1993.

CHAPTER 8

ENVIRONMENTAL MANAGEMENT

ENVIRONMENTAL MANAGEMENT

The **physical environment** in which care is offered requires a great deal of the administrator's time and attention. Most facilities cannot afford a maintenance engineer or even a fully-trained maintenance worker. This fact requires the administrator to be quite knowledgeable about housekeeping, laundry, maintenance, safety, and many other aspects of maintaining the proper physical environment. OBRA specifies that nursing facilities must be designed, constructed, equipped, and maintained to protect the health and safety of residents, personnel, and the public. (42 CFR 483.70)

BUILDINGS AND SAFETY CODE [42 CFR 483.70 (a)]

Standards for construction and access to nursing facilities were established by two private organizations: (1) The National Fire Protection Association (NFPA), and (2) the American National Standards Institute (ANSI). Standards of both organizations were adopted by the Federal Government. They were incorporated by reference in the February 7, 1985, *FEDERAL REGISTER*. Notice of changes in either of these standards will be published in future issues of the *FEDERAL REGISTER*. More recently, the Americans with Disabilities Act (ADA) has imposed additional standards designed to meet needs of employees with disabilities.

The **Life Safety Code** (LSC) was developed and published by the NFPA. The **purpose** of the code is to ensure that there is a reasonable degree of safety from fire in all buildings used by the public. The *Life Safety Code Handbook* establishes classifications of occupancy and degrees of hazard of the contents and identifies fundamental requirements for all buildings used as places of assembly, schools, hotels, health-care facilities, apartment buildings, rooming houses, family dwellings, stores, businesses, industry, storage, and many more. It is a very detailed publication which contains regulations governing egress, fire protection, utilities, heating and cooling, elevators, incinerators, alarm and communication systems, extinguishing equipment, and many other features of buildings. (Lathrop) The NFPA also publishes *Standards for Health Care Facilities*, in which chapter 8:4 identifies standards for residential-custodial-care facilities. Two separate electrical systems are required: (1) emergency and (2) critical. Specifications for their installation and operation are listed in the standards. (NFPA)

The state licensing and certification agency, the state fire marshal, and/or other state and local regulatory agencies monitor compliance with the Life Safety Code. Each state designates its monitoring agency(ies). Some states designate a LSC specialist within the monitoring agency.

Life safety from fire With certain exceptions, facilities must meet applicable provisions of the 1985 edition of the Life Safety Code. One exception is a facility which on November 26, 1982, complied, with or without waivers, with requirements of the 1967 or 1973 editions of the Code and continues to be in compliance with those editions. A second exception is a facility which on May 9, 1988, complied, with or without waivers, with the 1981 edition of the Code and continues to remain in compliance with that edition.

Other waivers If the state survey agency finds that rigid application of specific provisions of the Code would result in an undue hardship, a waiver may be granted, provided such waiver does not affect the health and safety of residents. HCFA makes the decision on waivers for SNF's. The state decides on waivers for NF's. The Code is not applicable in a state where HCFA finds that a fire and safety code imposed by state law adequately protects residents and personnel in long-term care facilities.

New construction and renovations Plans for construction of new nursing homes or for major renovations must be submitted to the state Medicaid agency and the agency that monitors Life Safety Code for prior approval. For this reason, the architect and engineer who design the buildings or renovation must know and be able to abide by all regulations governing building structure and space. It is not necessary for the administrator to know every detail of the LSC.

Code regulations The Code regulates all aspects of the building and its contents. Regulations are so extensive all of them cannot be included in this publication. Only the major Code regulations are briefly listed.

1. **Building materials** must all be fire-rated dependent on the number of stories in the building. The code specifies which materials must be two-hour and one-hour fire-resistant or less.

2. **Sprinklers** New facilities must have an approved sprinkler system that is automatically activated when there is smoke or heat.

3. **Exits** No room shall be more than 100 feet from an exit in the facility. Exits used for **egress** must have **lighted exit signs** of a specific size.

4. **Doors** The width of doors is regulated by the Life Safety Code. The 1991 edition of the Life Safety Code on health-care facilities (12-2.3.5) states that all doors, except bathrooms and toilets, used by occupants (residents) of a nursing home must provide a clearance of at least 41.5 inches. The overall door size, frame and all, may be 44 inches or more, but LSC is concerned with clearance only. Doors to bathrooms and toilets used by residents must have a clearance of at least 32 inches. Doors to areas not used by residents–medicine room, storage, kitchen, etc – must have at least a 32-inch clearance. All doors used for entrance/exit must open outward (egress).

5. **Locks** When clinical needs of a resident require specialized security arrangements, locks may be installed on resident-room doors. Staff must be able to unlock the door from the corridor, and all staff working in the area must have keys. Doors used for egress may not be equipped with a lock that requires a key or tool to open from the inside. There can be outside locks only.

6. **Fire doors** Fire doors are required in corridors. They must have automatic hold-open devices activated by the manual fire-alarm system so they close when the alarm goes off.

7. **Corridor walls** The corridor walls must extend continuously to the roof deck of the next floor. They may not stop at a suspended ceiling. Materials must meet fire and smoke ratings, and the finish must also meet flame-spread requirements.

8. **Heating, ventilating, and air conditioning** All equipment to provide heating, cooling, and ventilation must be installed according to the Code. This involves so many regulations, the administrator should refer to the Code itself.

9. **Fire alarms** Both the Code and ANSI require flashing and audible fire alarms for the benefit of residents with hearing and sight deficiencies. The alarm must be one that's automatically activated by **smoke** or **fire**. The preferred alarm system is connected to the local fire department so it is automatically alerted when a fire occurs. The Code also requires facilities to install approved smoke detectors.

10. **Furnishings** All carpets, drapes, bedding, and other furnishings must meet the fire rating required by the Code. The administrator should keep the fire-rating records on each of these items when purchased since Life Safety Code inspectors may ask to see them during their survey.

11. **Smoking** Smoking regulations must be in writing and carefully enforced. The most frequent cause of fire in nursing facilities is improper handling of smoking materials. The program must include:

    a. **Smoking areas** clearly marked and containing only noncombustible ashtrays. Metal containers with self-closing covers are required, and ash trays are emptied into them.

    b. **Prohibited smoking areas** include **resident rooms** and beds, areas where oxygen is used or stored, areas in which flammable liquids are used or stored, areas containing combustible gases, and other potentially hazardous areas. These areas must have **no smoking** signs prominently displayed.

c. **Smoking materials** should never be emptied into regular lined or unlined waste containers, but emptied only in the above mentioned metal containers.

d. **Residents** deemed "not responsible" should be allowed to smoke only when supervised by a staff member.

e. **Disciplinary** measures should be spelled out for all to know and understand.

Only the more pertinent regulations of the Life Safety Code have been listed. There are many others covering stairways, ramps, towers, vertical openings in multi-storied facilities, and more. State and local building codes are often more strict than the Life Safety Code, consequently, the administrator should confer with the appropriate local and state agencies to determine details of regulations for his area.

Surveyors Frequently the state Medicaid agency responsible for the survey of nursing facilities does not conduct the Life Safety Code survey. The state fire marshal's office or some other office may be assigned to monitor building regulations. The administrator should determine who surveys for Life Safety Code and try to secure a checklist of all items this agency will monitor. The official state agency designed to do the Life Safety Code surveys must coordinate its report with the state Medicaid agency.

ANSI/ADAAG REGULATIONS

Building regulations developed by the American National Standards Institute (ANSI) and the Americans with Disabilities Act Accessibility Guidelines (ADAAG) are the same. **Purpose** of ANSI regulations were to make buildings accessible to and usable by the visually and physically handicapped. These are the non-ambulatory, semi-ambulatory, blind, deaf, and uncoordinated. There are no provisions for the mentally handicapped–retarded and the mentally ill.

Purpose of ADAAG is to make buildings accessible to and usable by employees with a disability. The Americans with Disabilities Act discussed in Chapter 5 has two titles that affect nursing homes. Title I of the ADA established guidelines for hiring individuals with a disability. Title III of the ADA deals with making the workplace accessible to and usable by people with disabilities.

ANSI or ADAAG? Each state has authority to choose which set of regulations it will follow in monitoring nursing homes. Some have chosen ADAAG, others still try to implement both. The states that have adopted ADAAG still must use ANSI standards for buildings that are not covered by ADAAG. An example of a health-care facility not covered by ADAAG is assisted-living units.

Publications ANSI standards may be found in the publication *American National Standards for Buildings and Facilities–Providing Accessibility and Usability for Physically Handicapped People.* It is an 84-page publication which may be obtained from ANSI, 1430 Broadway, New York, NY, 10018. Order number is ANSI A1171-1986.

ADA Accessibility Guidelines are published in the *ADA Handbook.* It is issued by EEOC and the U.S. Department of Justice, and published by BNI Publications, Inc., in Los Angeles in 1990. The Handbook contains guidelines and regulations for Titles I and III of the ADA, the two titles that concern nursing homes.

Monitoring As noted in Chapter 5, the EEOC and U.S. Department of Justice monitor Title I of ADA. Both ANSI and Title III of ADA are monitored by an agency within the state. This may be the state fire marshal, department of public safety, Medicaid certification and survey agency, or other agency as determined by the state. It is usually the same agency that monitors the Life Safety Code. If the monitoring agency is other than the state's Medicaid agency, it must coordinate its findings with the Medicaid agency as noted earlier.

ANSI/ADAAG regulations Regulations established by these two are the same for nursing homes. Some of these two standards are listed, but administrators should determine from their states which standards to follow. Unless specifically noted following standards are the same for ANSI and ADAAG.

Standards Space does not permit a full discussion of ANSI and ADAAG standards, but they are all included in the ANSI and ADA publications listed above. Some of the standards most pertinent to nursing facilities are listed. These may be more stringent than OBRA standards, and in that event, ANSI/ADAAG standards must be followed. Standards change from time to time, but usually the state monitoring agency notifies facilities.

1. **Accessible routes** One accessible route from the handicapped parking spaces to the building is required. The accessible route must continue to any part of the building that a person may use. Both standards specify width, height, passing space, surface texture, etc.

2. **Wheelchair passage width** The minimum clear width or passage is 32 inches for doors and 36 inches elsewhere. All space used by residents and all activities must be accessible and usable by wheelchair residents.

3. **Gratings** When located on walking surfaces, gratings must have spaces no greater than one-half inch in one direction. If openings are elongated, the long dimension must be perpendicular to the dominate direction of travel.

Figure 8.1:

Outside Grating

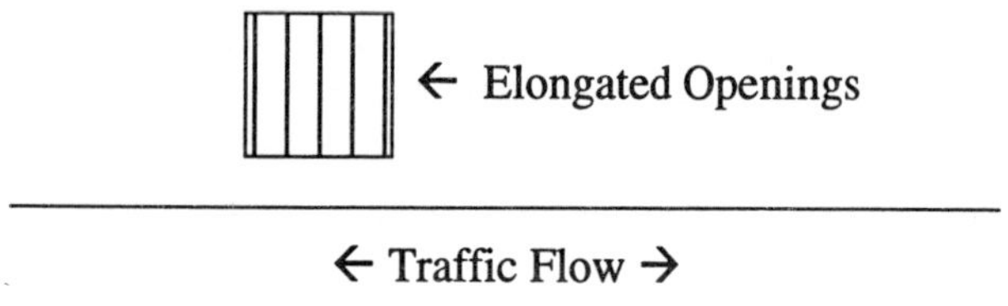

4. **Parking** Handicapped parking spaces are to be located on the shortest possible route to the building. Spaces shall be 13 feet wide — eight feet for the vehicle, and five feet for an aisle. The five feet aisle may be used for two parking spaces, one on each side. Parked vehicles may not overhang the sidewalk to the extent they reduce the clear width of an accessible route. Spaces must have reserved signs that are not obstructed.

Figure 8.2:

Handicap Parking

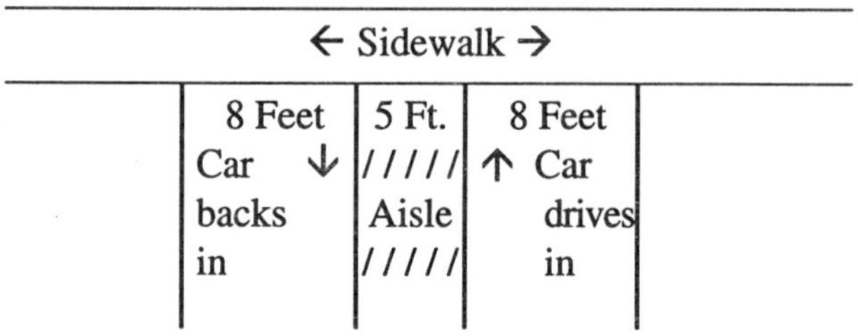

5. **Ramps** Whether inside or outside, ramps shall have the least possible slope. Any part of an accessible route with a slope greater than 1:20 inches shall be considered a ramp. The maximum rise of any ramp is 30 inches. The slope on new construction shall be 1:10 inches.

Figure 8.3:

Ramp

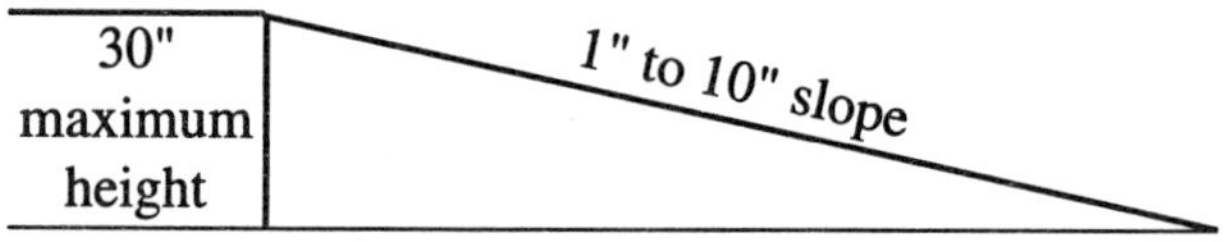

6. **Water fountains** Spouts of a fountain for handicapped can be no more that 36 inches from the floor. Flow of water must be at least four inches in order to fill a glass. Wall-mounted units shall have a clear knee space of 27 inches from the bottom to the floor, and 17 to 19 inches deep.

7. **Telephones** The coin slot shall be accessible using forward/side reach principles. The dial must be push-button if available. Handset

cord length must be at least 29 inches. To assist the hearing impaired they must be equipped with a receiver generating a magnetic field in the area of the receiver cap, but no braille is required for the blind.

8. **Reach** Maximum high forward reach is 48 inches. Minimum low forward reach is no less than 15 inches. Maximum high side reach is 54 inches; the low side reach is no less than 9 inches above the floor.

9. **Toilets** ANSI regulates every aspect of a toilet for the handicapped. Doors may open in or out, but if they open inward, floor space must be five by four and one-half feet. Grab bars must be 33 to 36 inches from the floor and the toilet seat 17 to 19 inches from the floor. The size of toilet stalls, height of urinals and mirrors from the floor, and all dispensers — paper, soap, and towels — are regulated. Proper signs are also required. Toilets are of particular concern as some residents cannot use standard toilets. When they cannot, the facility must arrange for nearby handicapped facilities accessible and usable by residents. Generally, five percent or more of the toilets in a nursing facility must conform to ANSI standards for handicapped.

10. **Handrails** ANSI requires that all ramps and stairs have handrails measuring 30 to 34 inches from the ramp or stair tread. ADAAG specifies 34 to 38 inches for all handrails. They must be on both sides and continuous. Both standards require handrails to extend 12 inches beyond the last stair tread in stairwells. OBRA requires handrails in all corridors, but specifies no height; consequently, ADAAG's standard would apply for handrails in corridors, but the individual state regulates the exact height.

11. **Alarms** Emergency warning systems shall include both audible and visual alarms for the blind and the deaf. ANSI sets standards for the level of sound and the frequency of flashing. Tactile warnings near hazardous areas are required, as well as some means for the blind to identify their rooms.

ANSI and ADAAG promulgate numerous other standards regulating buildings, such as curb ramps, stairs, elevators, windows, doors, entrances, bathtubs, shower stalls, and storage. Since facilities are surveyed at least annually in most states, it is imperative that the administrator or another staff member be familiar with standards used by the state in which their facility is located.

EMERGENCY POWER
[42 CFR 483.70 (b) (1) (2)]

An emergency electrical power system must supply power adequate at least for: (1) lighting all entrances and exits; (2) equipment to maintain the fire detection, alarm, and extinguishing systems; and (3) life support systems in the event the normal electrical supply is interrupted. OBRA requires that nursing facilities abide by Life Safety Code Standards which are more detailed.

Emergency generator When life support systems are used, the facility must provide emergency electrical power with an on-site emergency generator as defined in *NFPA 99, Health Care Facilities*. In practice, many states require an on-site generator for all nursing facilities, especially those states subject to tornadoes, hurricanes, and other natural disasters. In order to ensure the emergency generator is operable, these three things must be fully documented because they will be monitored by surveyors:

The Generator Must:

1. Start and transfer power within 10 seconds of loss of normal power,

2. Be started at least weekly, and

3. Be tested monthly with a full load for 30 minutes.

The NFPA requires that the generator supply power to at least:

1. Life support system

2. Nurses station

3. Medicine preparation area

4. Alarm system

5. Boiler (power) room

6. Communication system (including resident call system)

Battery backups In facilities without an emergency generator, the electrical power system **should** have battery backups for the fire life-safety detection and alarm system. The system **must** have, as a minimum, battery operated lighting for all entrances and exits. For these purposes an exit is a means of **egress** (door opening outward) which is lighted and has three components: (1) an exit access (corridor leading to the exit), (2) an exit (a door), and (3) an exit discharge (door to the street or public way). HCFA defines an **entrance** as any door through which people enter the facility. If it also serves as an exit, the three components listed above **must** be lighted. A **waiver** of lighting for exits and entrances is not permitted.

SPACE AND EQUIPMENT [42 CFR 483.70 (c) (1)]

The facility must provide sufficient space and equipment in dining, health services, recreation, and program areas. **Sufficient** means enough to enable staff to provide residents with needed services as required by OBRA and as identified in each resident's plan of care. This is further interpreted to mean areas large enough to accommodate comfortably the maximum number of persons who ordinarily occupy that space. This includes wheelchairs, walkers, and other ambulation aids. These types of aids require more than standard circulation spaces. Space must be adequate to promote full physical and social participation of residents. Residents should have access to adequate space and their functioning must not be limited when they gain access to the area. It cannot be off-limits because of a resident's functional limitations.

Nurses station requirements are not mandated by HCFA. The structure of facilities vary so greatly, dependent on type and number of services offered, that space requirements for a nurses station is left to the states.

Rehabilitation space Areas in which resident groups engage in activities to develop manipulative skills and hand-eye coordination should have sufficient storage space. It is needed to house their supplies and "works in progress." Physical therapy areas should have space for storage of exercise equipment, and the equipment should be in working condition and adequate to promote resident activity and involvement.

Recreation areas must also be provided. These may be either inside or outside, such as balcony, porch, patio, courtyard, and solarium. Purpose of these areas is to provide space for residents to sit and to enjoy fresh air. The inside areas should be used primarily for activities organized by the facility and large enough for residents to pursue activities identified in their care plans.

Surveyors, in examining these group areas, will determine if they are attractive to residents and whether space is adaptable to a variety of uses and residents' needs. They will determine if space is used for multipurposes, as the dining area for resident activities at nonmealtime hours. Also, they observe whether there is crowding, easy passage for residents using mobility aids, and full use of available space.

DINING AND ACTIVITIES SPACE [42 CFR 483.70 (g) (1-4)]

The facility must provide one or more rooms designated for resident dining and activities. These rooms must be:

1. Well-lighted,

2. Well-ventilated,

3. Adequately furnished, and

4. Large enough to accommodate all activities.

Lighting Well-lighted means that levels of illumination must be suitable to tasks performed by the resident. Tasks performed in this area may include: (1) dining, (2) religious services, (3) birthday and other parties, (4) bingo and other games, and (5) other group activities. Lighting will not be the same for all of these. There should be no glare, and no sharp contrasts of light and dark.

Ventilation Well-ventilated means good air circulation with no drafts at floor level. There must be adequate exhausts for smoke removal. Temperature, humidity, and odor levels must be acceptable. **Nonsmoking** areas must be identified by signs in accordance with state law regulating smoking policy and/or facility policy.

Adequately furnished To meet this requirement, the dining area must accommodate physical and social needs of residents, including those in wheelchairs. An adequately furnished lounge area allows residents to control seating arrangements. An organized activities area is adequately furnished when it accommodates the specific activities offered. Furnishings must be structurally sound and functional. Chairs must be of varying sizes and some must be movable by residents. Wheelchairs must fit under the dining room tables.

Sufficient space This means there is enough space to accommodate all activities, and that it is adaptable to a variety of uses and resident needs. There must be maximum flexibility in moving tables and arranging furniture to accommodate residents using walkers, wheelchairs, and other mobility aids. There will be no crowding if space is sufficient. Space must not limit resident access to the area.

MAINTENANCE
[42 CFR 483.70 (c) (2)]

Facilities are required to maintain all essential mechanical, electrical, and resident-care equipment in safe operating condition. OBRA's interpretation of **essential equipment** is the boiler room, refrigerators in the nursing/medication areas, kitchen refrigerator/freezer units, and laundry equipment. To accomplish this, the facility needs an organized, **preventive** maintenance program. Preventive maintenance means to inspect all systems and all equipment on a scheduled basis, to make necessary repairs, to service, and to document these actions. In addition, preventive maintenance should include: (1) all systems — water, heating/air conditioning, sewerage, and electrical; (2) physical therapy equipment, water fountains, hair dryers, wheelchairs, and all other equipment used by residents; (3) kitchen equipment as stoves, ovens, and dishwashers; and (4) the entire building structure—roof, windows, screens, doors, floors, and ramps. (Roffmann)

Regular inspection of the building itself is often overlooked in spite of the fact that the roof is the most important asset the facility has. It protects all other assets. In some climates, roofs depreciate rapidly, due to action of the elements, and must be repaired or replaced often. When there is a leaky roof, it is usually discovered only after considerable damage has occurred.

A **log** is frequently used to document preventive maintenance. Each item to be checked is listed, usually in alphabetical order and by location. Space is provided for date checked, remarks, and initials of the person conducting the inspection. A **card** system may also be used. A card is made for each item to be checked, providing space for date of inspection, remarks, and initials. These are usually kept in alphabetical order with a "tickler" system to identify dates items are to be checked. When an item is replaced a new card is made.

Manufacturer's manuals on each equipment item serve as guides for scheduling inspections and determining what should be done each time. Some items must be checked daily, others only weekly, monthly, or quarterly.

Many facilities **tag each item** when checked so preventive maintenance dates can be determined simply by observation. A hand-operated label maker that uses plastic strips with adhesive backing is very efficient for making tags on the spot. This system is especially useful for all pieces of equipment, electrical outlets, and light switches. It enables the administrator to walk through his facility and immediately determine if preventive maintenance is being done.

The major **purpose** of preventive maintenance is to ensure that all equipment is safe and operable for resident care. Harold Roffmann lists many other values which include:

1. To save time
2. To save money
3. To reduce energy consumption
4. To extend useful life of equipment
5. To ensure no disruption in service to residents

Reducing downtime of equipment that has broken down is quite important. This is the period between equipment break down and becoming operative again. Administrators who plan adequately can realize benefits for residents by reducing downtime.

Example: A facility has under-window air conditioning/heating units. It maintains two or three extra units in good working order. When a unit goes down, maintenance simply brings a working unit to replace it. The down unit goes to the maintenance shop for repairs.

Money is saved by making minor repairs as needed since these are less expensive than major repairs. This also extends useful life of equipment, and in some instances reduces energy consumption.

Maintenance **costs** can be staggering. In fact, maintenance engineers insist that the lifetime maintenance costs for poorly designed and planned buildings will equal the original cost of construction. They recommend that building plans consider both quality service and maintenance needs and costs.

Types of maintenance The typical nursing home operates with an onsite maintenance worker and contracts with specialists for major repairs to its equipment, building, and systems. The advantages of this arrangement are:

1. Cost control is under direct supervision of the administrator.
2. The facility has use of more specialized services.
3. There is less investment in measurement devices and repair equipment.
4. Less salary and benefits than are required by a full-time engineer.

Unfortunately, there are also disadvantages in using outside maintenance specialists, such as:

1. There is more waiting time for specialists to do the work.
2. Contractors sometimes do not perform their work properly, resulting in fix-up charges at more cost to the facility.
3. Contractors sometimes bill for repairs not made.

Work Orders Maintenance needs work orders to operate efficiently and economically. Work orders are simple written requests indicating the problem and its location. The primary value of work orders is the scheduling of work to be done. It saves time and duplication of effort. Without them, maintenance may make repeated visits to one area of the facility; with work orders all needed tasks can be handled in one trip. Work orders are also useful in the housekeeping department. They too find them helpful in scheduling and carrying out their work.

RESIDENT ROOMS
[42 CFR 483.70 (d) (1-3)]

Resident rooms must be designed and equipped for adequate nursing care, comfort, and privacy of residents. Four residents is the maximum that may occupy one room.

Specifications OBRA specifications for resident rooms and other aspects of the physical plant sometimes vary from the Life Safety Code. Facilities must abide by both OBRA regulations and the

Code. Where there is a difference in OBRA and Life Safety Code specifications, it will be noted in this publication.

Room size Federal regulations require at least 80 square feet per resident in multi-bedded rooms. At least 100 square feet is required for single rooms. Minimum width of rooms may be established by the state, whereas federal regulations formerly required it to be 10 feet. **Surveyors** carry a tape measure to take measurements of any room that appears too small. Their measurements will be based upon the usable living space in the room. Minimum square footage excludes toilets and bath areas, closets, lockers, wardrobes, alcoves, or vestibules. If, however, the height of the alcoves or vestibules reasonably provides useful living area, their floor area may be included in the calculations.

The typical room has two beds against one side wall — one close to the window, the other close to the door. It would be more functional if rooms were designed for placing beds against the window wall with both facing the door. This eliminates trying to get around one bed to reach the other, and nurses can see both residents from the doorway.

Access Each room must have direct access to a corridor. The door providing access to the corridor must open inward (ingress), as explained earlier.

Exceptions Regulations provide certain exceptions to the number of occupants and the room size. Variations may be permitted for two types of facilities in individual cases in which the facility demonstrates, in writing, that the variations:

1. Are required by special needs of the resident; and

2. Will not adversely affect the residents health and safety.

If the facility is Medicare, HCFA decides whether the variations are approved. The state makes this decision when the facility participates only as a Medicaid nursing facility.

Privacy Resident rooms must be designed or equipped to assure full visual privacy for each resident. Full visual privacy means that residents have a means of completely withdrawing from public view while occupying their beds. Equipment to provide privacy may be a curtain or moveable screens. A private room has adequate privacy without a curtain or screen. Any facility initially certified after October 1, 1990, must provide ceiling-suspended curtains for each bed in a multi-bedded room. The curtains must extend around the bed so that they, in combination with adjacent walls, provide total visual privacy.

Windows OBRA regulations require at least one window to the outside in each room. Life Safety Code requires a window or a door. Since OBRA regulation is stricter it must be followed.

Floors Resident room floors must be at or above ground level of the building. If they or any other floors are carpeted, the fire-rating of the carpet is regulated by the Life Safety Code, and the facility must have documentation of the fire-rating on file. The rating is not always easily obtained.

Furnishings Rooms must be provided with adequate furnishings for each resident which include:

1. Separate bed of proper size and height,

2. Clean, comfortable mattress,

3. Bedding appropriate to weather and climate,

4. Dresser or chest of drawers,

5. Night table,

6. Comfortable chair, and

5. Individual in-room closet space with racks and shelves accessible to the resident.

The furniture must be functional and appropriate to the resident's needs. It should be structurally sound and designed so a resident can attain the highest practicable level of independence and well-being. The chest of drawers may be built in.

Toilet facilities [42 CFR 483.70 (e)] Each resident room must be equipped with or located near toilet and bathing facilities. Toilet facilities mean a space that contains a lavatory with mirror and a toilet. **Located near** means a toilet on the unit that residents who are able to use a toilet independently, including chair-bound residents, can routinely use. Federal guidelines do not specify the number of toilet facilities for residents, nor the maximum distance from the farthest resident room. States have authority to determine these standards, except for those noted under the ANSI/ADAAG section of this chapter.

Bathing facilities Bathtubs or showers are not required in resident rooms. They, of course, must be provided for proper resident care. The number of residents per bathroom/toilet may be established by the state. **Bathroom/toilet floor** surfaces should be nonslip material. Asphalt tile is generally considered the best nonslip covering.

Resident call system [42 CFR 483.70 (f)] Each nurses station must be equipped to receive resident calls through a communication system. The system must register calls from every bed, toilet, and bathing facility. Cords must be accessible to residents. The best system is one which cannot be turned off until the resident's call is answered. In some systems the call signal can be turned off only at the location where the call originated.

OTHER ENVIRONMENTAL CONDITIONS [42 CFR 483.70 (h) (1-4)]

The facility must provide a safe, functional, sanitary, and comfortable environment for residents, staff, and the public. This obviously involves numerous environmental factors.

Water Procedures must be developed to ensure that water is available to essential areas when there is a loss of the normal water supply. This may be accomplished by a contract with a business that will bring in tanks of water along with the necessary equipment for connecting to the regular water system. [42 CFR 485.70 (h)(1)] Water **temperatures** are regulated by the state. The administrator should ensure that the **automatic control valves** on the water heaters are checked regularly. A malfunctioning control valve may allow water temperature in the resident areas to rise to a point of burning residents. It has happened in several facilities.

> **Example**: An orderly placed a male paraplegic in a tub for his bath. The resident had no feeling from the waist down. The orderly checked the temperature of the running water and found it comfortable. He left it running when the nurse called for him. The orderly was gone longer than he anticipated, and when he returned steamy water was pouring from the faucet. The control valves on the water heater had broken, and the water was extremely hot. The resident had third degree burns.

A better method of control is the heat-control device that is inserted into the water faucet. They are produced to expand and cut off the water supply at the temperature desired. If maximum temperature is 105°, the insert that shuts off water at that temperature should be used.

Ventilation All areas must be ventilated to the outside of the building. This may be accomplished by windows or mechanical ventilation or a combination of the two. There must be good air movement and acceptable humidity and temperature levels. These are determined by the state.

Surveyors will inspect ventilation to determine that temperature, humidity and odor levels are acceptable. They grade the facility on an ABC scale.

A = Good air movement. Temperature, humidity, & odor levels are all acceptable.

B = Little air movement. Temperature, humidity, and odor levels less than acceptable to residents who appear slightly uncomfortable due to heat, excess humidity, or smoke.

C = No air circulation. Temperature, humidity, or odor levels unacceptable. Residents & staff appear distressed due to these factors.

Corridors Corridors must be equipped with handrails firmly secured on each side. Specifications are discussed under ANSI/ADAAG regulations. Life Safety Code regulates the length of dead-end corridors. In older buildings no corridor may exceed 30 feet without an exit door. New construction may not have any dead-end corridors. All must have an exit door at the end.

Isolation room When the infection control program determines that a resident needs isolation to prevent spread of the infection, the facility must isolate the patient. [42 CFR 483.65 (b)] Federal guidelines do not specify standards for an isolation room. Standards of practice in health care dictate that it have these characteristics:

1. Single occupancy,
2. Ventilated to the outside,
3. Contain a private toilet,
4. Have hand-washing facilities, and
5. Identified by signs when in use.

Neither bathtub nor shower is indicated since the resident can be given bed baths.

Pest Control The facility must maintain an effective pest-control program so that it is free of insect pests and rodents. There must be an effective program that controls roaches, ants, mosquitoes, flies, mice, and rats. [42 CFR 483.70 (h)(4)] States set the specific standards to follow. Most states forbid use of anything that may be hazardous to residents, such as open traps, above ground poison bait, and sticky flypaper. Some states do not allow any type of aerosol spray, whereas all allow staff to use pressure sprayers of the pump-up type.

An effective pest control program involves all staff and usually an outside contractor. It requires a planned program that is strenuously enforced. Effective controls include at least these measures:

1. Properly fitting covers for all garbage containers which must be leakproof;
2. Emptying garbage containers as often as needed, and in the kitchen, at least after every meal;
3. Maintaining clean garbage containers, often accomplished by using plastic liners;
4. Regular policing of outside garbage bins to ensure that bins are clean, lids are closed and fit properly, and contents are not accessible to rodents, flies, and roaches;
5. Continuous monitoring to ensure food is kept only in containers and areas not accessible to pests;
6. Enforcing rules on the quantities and types of food brought in by families, usually only the amount that can be consumed at that time or properly stored at the nurses station;
7. Scheduling the use of appropriate pesticides by contractors;
8. Storing canned goods and other foodstuff in boxes so they are off the floor and far enough from walls to allow cleaning and prevent hiding places for roaches and rodents;
9. Frequent monitoring of vending machines to ensure empty bottles are removed regularly and no bits of food are left on the machines or on the floors;
10. Checking screen doors and windows and doors for damage and for proper closing;
11. Disciplining any employee who fails to comply with pest control measures; and
12. Regulating and carefully inspecting radios, televisions, boxes, and other items brought to residents.

An administrator should check with his local heath unit to determine what sanitary and pest control procedures have been developed for facilities. The local health unit will have a regular schedule of inspections.

Advantages Using a pest-control contractor provides specialists who are usually licensed and trained in the use of pesticides. In many states only a licensed pest control agent may purchase and use certain pesticides. They know how to rotate various chemicals to prevent the buildup of resistance by insect pests.

ENVIRONMENTAL QUALITY [42 CFR 483.15 (h) (1-7)]

Regulations thus far in this chapter deal with the physical aspects of the environment. These quantitative aspects are designed to enhance quality of the physical structure. OBRA goes beyond this and establishes regulations requiring the facility to provide a **safe, clean, comfortable, and homelike** environment. The facility must allow residents to use their personal belongings to the extent possible as discussed under resident rights in Chapter 11.

The **safe** environment is discussed fully under the safety program in this chapter. The **comfortable** environment must provide: (1) adequate and comfortable lighting levels, (2) comfortable and safe temperature levels, and (3) comfortable sound levels discussed later in this section.

A **homelike** environment de-emphasizes the institutional character of the facility to the extent possible. It allows the resident to use those personal belongings that support a homelike atmosphere. His room should show individualization and continuity with his past. The resident's pictures, paintings, chair(s), and other favorite objects should be in evidence. By observing the room the surveyor should be able to gain an understanding of the resident's life. A personalized, homelike environment recognizes the individuality of the resident. It provides an opportunity for self-expression, and encourages links with the past and with family members. It meets a territorial need that all humans seem to have; everyone wants at least some space that is his own. In monitoring this regulation **surveyors** will look for family photographs, books and magazines, bedspreads, knickknacks, mementos, and furniture belonging to the resident. These objects may look like **clutter** to the staff, but each has a special meaning in the resident's life, and staff are required to respect resident belongings.

Room arrangement is important to the homelike atmosphere. Some facilities permit residents to arrange their furniture any way they desire as long as it is not a safety hazard and does not interfere with staff providing service.

> **Example:** An 80-bed nursing home comprised of double rooms suggested that residents arrange their own room furniture. Some placed beds head to head, others foot to foot, and some against opposite walls. There was a wide variety of arrangements that residents enjoyed. They were pleased that they could rearrange their rooms at any time.

Surveyors will look for cleanliness of the room, expecting clean floors, a lack of dust, and walls without fingerprints or stains. They will also determine if objectionable odors from urine, feces, and so on are present. If any odor is present, the surveyor will determine if it is preventable. Surveyors will determine the homelike atmosphere by evaluating whether resident possessions tell them about the person, his past, and his interests. If a resident is demented and the room shows no homelike atmosphere, they determine whether this is a part of the plan of care. Also, when a room is not personalized by the resident, they determine if it is a facility practice or the choice of the resident.

Lighting Adequate lighting means levels of illumination suitable to the tasks the resident chooses to perform, or the facility staff must perform. **Comfortable** lighting minimizes glare and provides as much resident control of lighting as possible. The resident should be able to specify the intensity, location, and direction of illumination insofar as is feasible. This is especially true of the visually-impaired who need their own levels of lighting to enhance independent living. An example is the resident with glaucoma who needs a lower level of lighting.

Administrators often overlook the values of lighting and the effect of colors on the elderly. There is much that can be done with wall colors, curtains, and shades to promote restfulness and reduce tension. Interior decorators and some architects are especially helpful in planning in this area.

Surveyors will carefully note lighting levels and the amount of resident control over lighting. They not only monitor lighting in resident rooms, but also in hallways and group activity areas.

Temperature **Comfortable** and **safe** temperature levels mean that ambient temperature should be a relatively narrow range. Facilities initially certified after October 1, 1990, must maintain this range at 71-81°F. This narrow range should minimize residents' susceptibility to the loss of body heat and risk of hypothermia, respiratory ailments, and colds. The state may establish a more specific room temperature within the OBRA range.

Exceptions Temperatures may exceed the upper range of 81°F for facilities in geographic areas where that temperature is exceeded only during rare, brief episodes of hot weather. These areas are primarily in the northernmost or high altitude parts of the country. Of course, this exception is allowed only when it does not affect resident health and safety. The exception helps in cold climate areas where air conditioning is rarely needed. Facilities can avoid the expense of purchasing this seldom used, but costly equipment. In these areas facilities are expected to use fans and other temporary cooling devices.

Another exception is the relatively rare individual whose health requires higher temperatures for comfort. There are instances in which the resident becomes chilled when temperatures drop lower than 85°F. In these instances, the physician should document the need in the medical record.

In making his rounds the administrator might observe that while standing in a resident's room the temperature is either too cool or too warm. He should measure the room temperature at three feet above the floor level to determine if it is in the proper range. This is what surveyors do, and when they find temperatures that place residents at risk they will investigate the status of the air conditioning/heating system.

Sound levels Comfortable sound levels do not interfere with residents' hearing. Such levels enhance privacy when privacy is desired, and encourages social interaction and participation when these are desired. Unwanted background noise should be under the resident's control. This means if the facility uses a centrally operated music system, residents must be able to regulate it in their area. Sudden, loud noises are particularly objectionable. Background noises of sufficient volume that residents or staff must raise their voice to be heard is also unpleasant and unacceptable.

Sound levels often must be considered in assigning residents to a room. If one likes continuous, blaring television, and the other prefers soft music and quietness, the latter is certainly not comfortable. They will not be compatible roommates. Hearing deficiency should also be considered. Placing a resident with considerable hearing loss in a room with a resident with normal hearing can result in much irritation and stress.

HOUSEKEEPING
[42 CFR 483.15 (h) (2)]

Housekeeping is one of the most important environmental services since it plays a major role in providing a healthy, comfortable environment. OBRA requires housekeeping services necessary to maintain a sanitary, orderly, and comfortable interior. This service makes a significant contribution to facility-wide sanitary practices and the prevention and spread of disease-causing organisms.

An **orderly** interior means an uncluttered physical environment in which residents and staff can function safely. Orderliness involves not only housekeeping, but also nursing and maintenance. It includes: (1) equipment and supplies properly stored and not in corridors, (2) proper handling of spills, and (3) no peeling paint, visible water leaks, and plumbing problems. Orderliness may be involved in making a room homelike. The resident may prefer a cluttered room. This can be allowed so long as the clutter does not represent a fire hazard, a threat to safety, or impediment to staff performing their duties. Resident and staff safety take precedent over a resident's choice.

Personnel A full-time person should be named supervisor and held responsible for carrying out established procedures for housekeeping. OBRA does not address staffing requirements for housekeeping, but administrators may want to employ an executive housekeeper or supervisor since they are trained in housekeeping in health facilities.

No nursing service employees should be assigned any housekeeping duties other than bed-making. This duty is too closely related to resident care to allow an untrained housekeeping aide to make beds occupied by a severely debilitated resident. Nursing staff combines giving bed baths and making beds.

Administrators may need to work closely with their housekeeping supervisors to develop and teach proper housekeeping policies and procedures. They need to inspect regularly two aspects of housekeeping: (1) cleanliness of overhead lights, door facings, wall shelves, and cabinet tops, and (2) handling and storage of cleaning materials. In nursing facilities housekeeping personnel tend to never "look up." They may thoroughly clean floors, tables, window sills, and equipment if they normally can see the top, but fail to dust overhead lights and other areas they must reach up to clean.

Cleaning materials should never be left on unattended carts nor in unlocked closets where residents have access to them. Residents have ingested poisonous cleaning materials. This is discussed further under OSHA regulations in this chapter.

Safety measures need to be clearly stated in policies and procedures and housekeeping aides carefully monitored to ensure they are carried out. At least the following safety measures should be included.

1. When mopping hallways, do one side at a time; place *wet floor* signs so they are readily visible; develop a plan to ensure that ambulatory residents in rooms on the side being cleaned do not walk on wet floors.

2. Establish procedures on handling of antiseptic cleaning materials and train staff in their use, their dangers, and what to do in case a problem develops.

3. Carefully store any used aerosol spray cans since their propellants are potentially explosive.

4. Establish a rule that any employee who discovers a wet spot on the floor — whether a spilled liquid or urine — is not to leave the spot until he summons someone to bring cleaning materials for cleaning the area.

5. Never leave carts or equipment in corridors where they can be a hazard. The housekeeping supervisor should be trained to observe contents of all containers of cleaning solutions and disinfectants. The pH content should be noted. The supervisor should know the norm is 7.0, and be aware of whether it is possibly too alkaline or too acid. All disinfectant containers must show strength and toxicity levels of the contents. (See OSHA Standards in this Chapter)

Equipment storage The administrator periodically needs to monitor storage of housekeeping materials and equipment. If he does not, equipment is likely to be stored improperly and/or without proper cleaning. Buffing machines should never be stored on their pads as that reduces useful life.

Mike Jacobs offers a number of other helpful suggestions on cutting costs of housekeeping. Administrators can benefit from his publication.

LINEN SUPPLIES AND LAUNDRY

Previously, Medicare and Medicaid specified the minimum amount of bed linens a facility should have. Under OBRA, the state establishes any regulations it may deem advisable. Facilities will be expected to provide an adequate supply of sheets, pillow slips, towels, and so on to provide for the comfort and care of the residents. Generally, three sets of bed linens per bed are considered to be the minimum needed to accomplish this goal. Federal standards require that the facility provide clean bed and bath linens that are in good condition. Noticeable holes, threadbare spots, and objectionable stains are not acceptable. Bed linens must be of proper size with no double-bed sheets used on single beds. [42 CFR 483.15 (h) (3)]

Soiled linen Personnel must handle, store, process, and transport linens in a manner that prevents spread of infection. It must be handled so that waste products are contained. Storage for soiled linen must be well-ventilated and maintained under negative air pressure, insofar as possible. The laundry should be designed so that soiled and clean linen do not cross paths in transporting. [42 CFR 483.65 (c)] **Improper handling of soiled linen** is the major cause of exposure to infection by residents and staff.

Specific standards for handling soiled linens may be set by the state. If not, the facility will need to develop and enforce its own. This should be a part of the infection control program, particularly in handling bed linens, bed clothes, and all other items used by a resident with a communicable disease. (See infection control in this chapter)

Laundry Standards for the laundry are set by individual states. The facility may have its own laundry or contract with an outside laundry. If the facility has its own laundry it must establish procedures for collecting soiled linens, transporting them to the laundry, operating the laundry, handling clean linens, inventorying, and so on. The facility will need to secure state guidelines on the physical layout of the laundry and its operation.

Equipment Maintenance Proper care of the washer and dryer machines should be an integral part of preventive maintenance. Regular monitoring of their use, immediate attention to minor repairs, and replacement of filters and worn belts can extend useful life. Age of laundry machines is important. Maintenance engineers maintain that a **guideline** to keep in mind is that after ten years the maintenance cost of machines usually justifies replacement. This does not mean that when the age of laundry equipment reaches ten years it should be replaced. If after ten years it begins to break down, it is time to consider replacement.

Monitoring of the laundry by the administrator is important to its efficient, economic operation. Administrators can monitor a number of operational procedures periodically that will reveal both efficiency and economy.

1. **Use of bulk soap**, according to maintenance engineers, is a waste of money. Use an automatic feed system for detergents so that the correct amount is dispensed for each load.

2. **Overloading and underloading** are poor practices. Underloading a machine is not economical since it costs as much to run a half load as a full load. Overloading may increase wear and tear of machinery, reducing useful life of the machinery.

3. **Overdrying** is expensive. Many items need only 15 minutes to dry, while most items require 30 minutes or more. Separating quick-dry items from regular items and drying separately is more economical.

4. **Cleaning** filters regularly is imperative to economy. Washers and dryers operating with clogged filters use significantly more electrical power, and it increases wear of the machine.

5. **Proper water temperature** is important. Water that is too cool does not clean properly. When water is too hot it wastes energy. Some states set the water temperature in washing machines. Roffmann in his *Maintenance Management for Health Care Facilities* discusses many other aspects of laundry equipment and operations that will benefit the administrator.

Theft of linen is a common nursing facility problem that requires administrator attention. The following practices often prove helpful in reducing theft:

1. Use colored rather than white linen since many facilities find white linen is more frequently stolen, even when stamped with the facility's name.

2. Inventory linen once per week and make this practice prominently known in the facility.

3. Require personnel receiving clean linen from the laundry to sign for it and verify the amount.

4. Require laundry personnel to sign for dirty linen and verify the amount.

5. Regularly check rooms for linen hidden by residents who fear they will not receive an adequate supply.

Administrators may need to develop clear, concise policies and procedures for handling, processing, storing, and issuing linens. They usually have no laundry personnel capable of doing this themselves. Jacobs offers a number of other ideas that contribute significantly to efficient and economic laundry operations.

SAFETY AND INFECTION CONTROL

Safety [42 CFR 483.70(a)] Medicare and Medicaid mandate a safe, healthy environment to protect residents, staff, family, and visitors. **Infection control** is also mandated by Medicare and Medicaid. [42 CFR 483.65(a-c)] A facility's safety and infection control programs are an integral part of the risk management program discussed in Chapter 3. In addition, the Occupational Safety and Health Administration (OSHA) mandates a healthy and safe **work** environment for employees. This involves both the safety and the infection control programs. The administrator's role in safety is to ensure that a proper safety program is planned and implemented that will do two things:

1. Reduce work-related illness, injury, and death among staff; and

2. Reduce accidents and injuries among residents, families, and visitors.

A **safety committee** is not required by federal standards. OBRA anticipates work of the safety committee will be accomplished by the assessment and quality assurance team. Administrators may still want a smaller safety committee, perhaps made up of representatives of administration, nursing, housekeeping, food service, and maintenance. Whichever organizational arrangement is used, the group that plans and monitors the safety program should be assigned at least these duties:

1. Plan a safety program involving all departments,

2. Receive and review all accident reports,

3. Investigate each accident with a view toward identifying high risk areas,

4. Review each accident with the supervisor in whose area it occurs, and

5. Establish measures to prevent recurrence of accidents.

Goals The primary goals of both the OBRA and OSHA mandates for safety and infection control are to prevent **accidents**, to reduce work-related **illness,** and to prevent **death** in staff, residents, and visitors. An **accident** is unexpected, unintentional damage to an object or injury to a resident, employee, family member, or other person. If it is intentional, it is not an accident. Accidents are caused by **unsafe behavior** or **unsafe working conditions**. Most resident accidents are from falling which may be unsafe behavior or unsafe environment. Most employee accidents are from lifting which is usually unsafe behavior. (See Employee Safety in Chapter 6)

Accident hazards are physical features in the nursing facility that can endanger a resident's safety. Some features that are potential hazards are necessary to resident care, such as bedrails, wheelchairs, and walkers. Two things make them hazardous: (1) misuse, or (2) poor conditions due to lack of maintenance. Other accident hazards include:

1. Bathrooms with nonslip surfaces,

2. Wet floors from mopping or spills,

3. Excessively hot water in sinks,

4. Extension cords on the floor,

5. Frayed electrical wires,

6. Unattended cleaning carts,

7. Restraints, and

8. Electrical adapters that are not grounded.

Federal guidelines require that each resident receive adequate supervision and have necessary **assistive devices** to prevent accidents. An example is a resident with ambulation problems. He must have assistance in walking and/or a cane or walker.

Recordkeeping Every facility needs OSHA's booklet "What Every Employer Needs to Know About OSHA Recordkeeping." It is available from any OSHA office. The Form OSHA No. 200 is a log and summary of occupational injuries and illnesses that must be used by every facility unless it has fewer than 10 employees. It is important to record on Form 200 **only** those injuries and illnesses that OSHA classifies as **recordable** and **work related**. Resident incidents and accidents are not recorded on Form 200.

Work-related injuries and illnesses that occur in the work environment, which includes all areas of the employer's premises, such as worksite, cafeteria, or parking lot must be recorded. Work-related fatalities must be recorded, as well as all work-related illnesses, work-related injuries that require medical treatment, or involve restriction of work or motion, or transfer to another job. An incident involving a fall in which only first aid is needed is not recordable. Detailed descriptions of these are included in the above mentioned booklet, as are instructions on recordkeeping.

Reportable Any accident that results in death or the hospitalization of five employees or more is reportable to the OSHA area director within 48 hours. Hospitalization of a single employee is not considered reportable. Reports may be made orally or in writing.

Retaining records for five years is required. The record must show any changes in outcome of an injury or illness. These records must be accessible to OSHA monitors and must show that they are current. OSHA must be able to trace a recordable incident back for five years if it occurred within that time frame.

Training The safety committee or quality assessment and assurance committee should ensure that each department has a safety program that includes preventive measures, documentation, and training. Resident-care personnel need special training in body mechanics, avoiding back fatigue, making resident transfers, and lifting. All staff should be oriented to both their departmental and the facility-wide safety programs and practices.

Hazard Communication Program (29 CFR 1910.1200) Every administrator should secure from OSHA a copy of *Fact Sheet No. OSHA 93-26* which provides a general description of OSHA's Hazard Communication Standard (HCS). Information contained therein can be the beginning of developing the facility's Hazard Communication Program (HCP). The **purpose** of the HCP is that hazards of all chemicals are evaluated, and information concerning their hazards is transmitted to employers and employees. Evaluating the potential hazards of chemicals, and communicating information concerning hazards and appropriate protective measures may include but is not limited to: (1) developing a hazard-communication program for the facility, including lists of hazardous chemicals present, (2) labeling of containers of chemicals in the facility, (3) preparation and distribution of **material safety data sheets** (MSDS) to employees, and (4) development and implementation of employee-training programs regarding hazards of chemicals and the protective measures. OSHA requires chemical manufacturers and importers to assess the hazards of chemicals which they manufacture or import, and to provide this information to employers. This information may be distributed by means of labels, the MSDS, or other forms of warning.

Every **container** in a facility must be **labeled.** The label must include (1) the identity of the product, (2) the identity of hazardous chemicals, (3) appropriate hazard warnings, and (4) the name and address of the chemical manufacturer. For every hazardous chemical in a facility, there must be a corresponding material safety data sheet. These sheets identify the hazardous chemicals in the product, the description of the product, and precautions for safe handling and use.

Chemicals found in nursing homes that are classed as hazardous include any product that has a **warning** or **caution** label. Cleaning compounds, Clorox, furniture polish, pine oil, and detergents are examples.

Written program The facility's HCP must be written. It must reflect what employees are doing in a particular work area, list the chemicals used at that site, indicate who is responsible for various aspects of the program in that facility or area, and where materials will be available to employees. It must describe how the requirements for labels and other forms of warning, MSDS's, and employee information and training will be met in the facility.

Lockout/Tagout Also of concern to OSHA is the control of hazardous energy. To protect employees from hazardous energy, OSHA set up guidelines for a Lockout/Tagout program. The **purpose** is to require employers to establish a program and utilize procedures for affixing appropriate lockout or tagout devices to energy-isolating devices, and to otherwise disable machines or equipment to prevent unexpected energizing, start-up or release of stored energy in order to **prevent injury** to employees. (29 CFR 1900.147) There must be in-service training for any employee whose job requires him to operate equipment that poses an electrical hazard. OSHA requires that a person be authorized to **monitor** the lockout/tagout program. In nursing facilities, the person usually is the maintenance supervisor.

A **lockout device** is some type of lock, either key or combination type, that will hold an energy-isolating device in a safe position that prevents energizing the machine or equipment. For example, if an electrical outlet is malfunctioning, an authorized employee should install a *tagout* device on the outlet to prevent anyone energizing tools from that outlet. The authorized employee should also install a *lockout* device on the circuit breaker that disengages the malfunctioning outlet. The lockout/tagout policy applies to any device that isolates energy, which includes mechanical, electrical, hydraulic, chemical, thermal, or any other energy source. The **key** to the lockout device is an important safety factor. Where should it be kept? OSHA does not specify how the key should be handled. Undoubtedly, the key should be in the possession of the employee designated to monitor the program — usually the maintenance person. This would ensure that no unauthorized person could use the key before the malfunctioning equipment is repaired.

A **tagout device** is to be used when an energy source is not capable of being locked out. In such case, a prominent warning device, such as a tag that can be securely fastened, should be attached indicating that the energy-isolating source is not to be used until the tag is removed. An example is the above mentioned electrical outlet.

Right-to-know laws Many states have right-to-know laws that specify procedures for handling potentially hazardous materials. OSHA's HCS preempts all state and local laws relating to issues covered by HCS. The only state worker right-to-know laws accepted by OSHA are those established by states that have OSHA-approved state programs.

Consultation is supposed to be available from OSHA. Monitors will do a trial run survey in a facility and offer consultation on what is needed for compliance. No penalties are levied on deficiencies noted in this type survey.

OSHA surveyors will observe whether the facility has a complete safety program for protecting employees. They check accident reports and the accident log. They determine if the facility has a written HCP, and whether it has been implemented and maintained. Surveyors inspect containers for labels and corresponding MSDS's. Generally, they randomly select an employee and ask, "Where is the MSDS book? What is the purpose of MSDS Sheets?" Failure to answer correctly may result in a fine or other penalty. Surveyors also check policies and procedures for the lockout/tagout program, examine locks and tags, and ask for examples of their use. OSHA makes it clear they are interested only in employee accidents and illnesses.

Penalties may be enforced for any finding that OSHA considers a hazard to employee safety and health. The minimum penalty is a $1,000 fine per deficiency. This may be multiplied seven times dependent on the severity of the deficiency. For instance, if the surveyor notes a condition that has a base penalty of $2,000, he can increase it up to $14,000 if it is an extremely hazardous situation. However, OSHA's concept of the degree of hazard can be quite subjective.

Example: An OSHA surveyor found no deficiencies in a large nursing home. He commented to the administrator that the facility couldn't be perfect. He again searched for a deficiency and finally found a remote electrical outlet with a minor crack in the plate on the wall under a table. It was never used, but he fined the facility the basic $1,000 times seven for a total of $7.000. Upon appeal it was reduced to $4,000 which the facility had to pay.

The President and Congress have requested that OSHA scale back on penalties, imposing smaller fines. OSHA continues to do research to support the basis for stringent standards and to direct more attention to compliance and enforcement measures related to workplace safety. OSHA has agreed to dramatically reduce fines and penalties for enterprises that agree to cooperate with OSHA and their employees on eliminating job-site hazards.

Medicaid/Medicare Surveyors will review accident/incident reports for the three months preceding the first day of a survey. They will note the number of accidents for all shifts and determine *why*, if more occur on one shift. Surveyors will monitor the types of accidents and any resident repeatedly involved in accidents. If they find this type of resident, surveyors determine if the resident has been assessed for being at risk. Do they have properly fitting, properly used assistive devices, and are drugs affecting balance and ambulation involved?

Safe Medical Devices Act (SMDA) The Safe Medical Devices Act of 1990 requires health-care facilities to **report** any **incidents** that reasonably suggest a medical device caused or contributed to the death or serious illness or injury of a resident or an employee. **Medical devices** are thermometers, catheters, pacemakers, contact lenses, restraints, hearing aids, wheelchairs, blood glucose monitors, gerichairs, beds, infusion and feeding pumps, whirlpool and whirlpool chairs, suction machines, and any other apparatus used in diagnosing, treating, and caring for a resident, or preventing disease, or is intended to affect the body's function and structure without chemical or metabolic action within the body. **Serious illnesses** or injuries are those that (1) are life threatening, or (2) result in permanent impairment to body structure or functioning, or (3) need immediate medical or surgical intervention to prevent permanent illness or injury.

Medwatch Administrators should secure a copy of FDA's "Medwatch" packet which also includes regulations on reporting problems with **drugs**. The packet contains all instructions and forms a facility needs for the program. It includes information on reporting to FDA by computer.

The SMDA **program** must include policies and procedures that (1) guide activities of the staff, (2) designate a person to whom incidents are reported, (3) identify who and how reports will be made, and (4) specify how and when the incidents are reported to the Food and Drug Administration (FDA) and the manufacturer. Any employee witnessing or discovering an incident must report it to the designated staff member within 24 hours. Within **ten days** the designated staff member **shall report** the incident to the FDA and to the manufacturer if known. The program must include a system for review and evaluation of events that may require reporting, training of personnel in responding, and **documentation** of all incidents and reports. These **records** must be maintained for **two years** from dates of filing with the FDA or manufacturer.

Enforcement and penalties The FDA generally is empowered to seek **imprisonment and fines** for violation of the Federal Food, Drug, and Cosmetic Act (FFDCA). Indications are enforcement action can be taken for (1) failure to have a written program or to make written reports, (2) refusal to allow access to records by FDA, (3) refusal to allow compliance inspections by FDA, and (4) failure to provide information or material required by the FFDCA. The SMDA program became effective and user penalties went into effect July 1, 1996, but no regulations are available. FDA now contacts facilities to determine if their program is in place.

Infection control [42 CFR 483.65] HCFA specifies that nursing homes must establish and maintain an infection-control program designed to provide a safe, sanitary, and comfortable environment and to help prevent the development and transmission of disease and infection. OSHA establishes the same standards to ensure safety and health of employees. Facilities are not required to develop two separate programs. They may have one program that encompasses standards of both regulatory groups.

Figure 8.4:

HCFA Standards For Infection Control

The HCFA standards for infection control may be outlined as follows:

1. Investigate, control, and prevent infections in the facility.
2. Decide on procedures, such as isolation, to be used in individual cases.
3. Document incidents and corrective actions.
4. Isolate an infected resident to prevent spread of infections.
5. Allow no employee with communicable disease or skin lesions to have contact with residents or their food.
6. Require staff to wash hands after direct resident contact according to accepted professional practice.
7. Handle, process, store, and transport linens in a manner that prevents spread of infection.

OSHA standards are far more specific, so usually the nursing home designs its program to embrace both OBRA and OSHA standards. Although an Infection Control Committee is not required by either standards, administrators may find that a Committee is the best approach. OSHA requirements follow.

1. **Standard (formerly universal) precautions** is an approach to infection control. It assumes that all human blood and certain body fluids are to be treated as if they are infectious for HIV, HBV, and other bloodborne pathogens. Other potentially infectious materials are vaginal secretions, semen, cerebrospinal fluid, synovial fluid, pleural fluid, pericardial fluid, peritoneal fluid, saliva, and any body fluid contaminated with blood, and other potentially infectious material. The procedures for handling infectious body fluids are developed by the Centers for Disease Control (CDC) and are usually available through local health units. All facilities are required to use these precautions. Standard precautions is an approach to infection control and is primarily designed to control and prevent transmission of bloodborne pathogens. **Handwashing** is a key procedure in standard precautions. It means the facility provides an adequate supply of running, potable water, soap, and single use towels or hot air drying machines. Handwashing or changing gloves is **necessary** at mealtime, after providing personal care, and when performing tasks among individuals who provide opportunity for cross-contamination to occur. Handwashing facilities must be available to staff, and they should be trained in their proper use. The facility should follow *Guidelines for Handwashing and Hospital Environmental Control*, 1985 edition, developed by the CDC. **Spread of infection is best controlled** by a set of control procedures which includes proper handwashing and are followed by all employees.

2. **Bloodborne Pathogens** (BBP) are pathogenic microorganisms that are present in human blood and can cause disease in humans. These pathogens include, but are not limited to, **hepatitis B virus** (HBV) and **human immunodeficiency virus** (HIV). (29 CFR 1910.1310) All facilities must have a Bloodborne Pathogen training program in

which employees are taught how to handle blood spills and materials that may be infected with bloodborne pathogens. It must include training in procedures to handle an **exposure incident** which is a specific eye, mouth, or other mucous membrane, non-intact skin, or parenteral contact with blood or other potentially infections materials that result from the performance of an employee's duties.

HBV program Hepatitis is an inflammation of the liver caused by **hepatitis B virus**, medications, or toxins. There are several types of infections of hepatitis (A, B, non-A / non-B and delta), but hepatitis B is the greatest risk to health-care workers. It can be transmitted by sexual contact, contaminated blood or blood products, and needle sharing, for example. OSHA mandates practices for protection against **occupational exposure** to both HBV and HIV. These include standard precautions, proper handling and disposal of contaminated sharps and other material, and use of personal-protective equipment. The facility must provide HBV **vaccinations** for all staff at no cost to the employee. The vaccination is especially important to employees who are at risk of acquiring HBV infections. If an employee refuses the vaccine, the facility must have employee sign a waiver the text of which is found in the OSHA regulations.

Personal protective equipment (PPE) must be used by employees with a potential for occupational exposure to BBP's and to other hazards. The facility must provide the equipment at no cost to the employee. PPE's include, but are not limited to gloves, gowns, laboratory coats, face shields, eye protection, mouth pieces and resuscitation bags, pocket masks, or other ventilation devices. Normal work clothes are not included. Employees must be **trained** in the use of PPE's, their decontamination or disposal, use of needles and syringes and their disposal, and cleaning blood spills.

Contaminated sharps require special attention. These are any contaminated object that penetrates the skin, such as needles, scalpels, broken glass, broken capillary tubes, and exposed ends of dental wires. Nursing facilities are primarily concerned with needles and the attached syringes. They require **engineering controls** that isolate or remove the BBP hazard from the workplace. Generally, they are called **sharps containers** that must be properly installed on the wall in the **nursing area** where they are used and in the **laundry**. The facility must have a written procedure on emptying these containers including specific dates.

Regulated waste includes contaminated sharps. It also means liquid or semi-liquid blood or other potentially infectious materials in a liquid or semiliquid state if compressed; items that are caked with dried blood or other potentially infectious materials; and pathological wastes containing blood or other potentially infectious materials. Employees must be trained in the handling and disposal of these wastes in accord with OSHA guidelines.

Contaminated linens and bedclothes require special handling by OSHA. They must be properly contained in color-coded bags and cleaned and sterilized, or disposed of, according to OSHA standards. Some facilities now use a bag that is placed in the washer without emptying it, and it dissolves in the wash.

OSHA Compliance and Exposure Control Plan Checklist is a **must** for administrators (29 CFR, 1910-1030). The checklist is compiled to assist administrators in ensuring that their facility is in compliance with OSHA rules. It is available from OSHA and serves as an excellent guideline for setting up an exposure-control program.

3. **Isolation** An infected resident is to be isolated only to the degree needed to isolate the infecting organism. As an example, the acquired immune deficiency syndrome (AIDS) virus spreads through intimate contact with blood, semen, saliva, and other visibly blood-tinged body fluids. Handwashing is required after each direct resident contact for which accepted professional practice indicates it is needed. The facility should prevent contact of these fluids by residents, family, and staff. It should not isolate the AIDS resident unless there is bleeding or passing of blood-tinged body fluids. Usually isolation is to protect

others, but the AIDS resident should be isolated for his protection if a secondary infection of a contagious nature occurs in the facility, such as influenza. This is sometimes referred to as **reverse isolation.** When a facility has proper infection control and isolation techniques in place it can safely provide service to residents with AIDS. When staff adhers to proper infection-control measures there is no chance of their contracting AIDS from an infected resident.

4. **Employee infections** No employee with infected skin lesions can be allowed to work in dietary service or any other place where resident contact occurs. Lesions of this type are defined as open skin wounds with purulent drainage, or that are red and hot without purulent drainage. State law defines communicable diseases for purposes of defining facility policy. State and local health departments will supply any information on infection control needed by a facility.

5. **Aseptic cleaning** When a resident is no longer infectious the isolation area needs to be cleaned aseptically according to infection control procedures. This includes floors, walls, furnishings, and so on.

6. **Uniforms** Procedures for wearing gowns and other PPE into isolation areas and their disposal should be established and followed as outlined in the facility's standard precautions.

7. **Post-exposure procedure** The facility must have a written plan for post-exposure evaluation and follow-up. Following an exposure incident described earlier in this chapter, the individual from whom the blood or other potentially infectious material came shall be tested for hepatitis B and HIV viruses, unless it is already known that the source individual is infected. **Consent** must be obtained prior to testing; however, OSHA states that if consent is not required by state law, the testing should be done anyway. The blood of the exposed person must be tested also, but only after consent. OSHA has no provision on what to do if the person refuses to consent. OSHA does require that the exposed employee be examined by a physician and that the physician prepare a report. The testing and examination must be done immediately after the exposure, and it must be held confidential.

There are other activities the infection control program should monitor, such as: garbage and waste disposal, pest control, visitation procedures, etc. Any of these can be a potential for disease spread.

Medicaid Surveyors will review procedures to determine if the CDC handwashing procedures are followed, and whether residents who are isolated really need to be. They observe whether staff uses proper isolation procedures, properly handles visitors in infectious-disease cases, prohibits persons with infected skin lesions from working, and whether any employee has developed a communicable disease while in the facility.

OSHA surveyors determine whether policies and procedures governing exposure control are in place, whether there are written programs for employee safety, BBP and standard precautions, and hazard communication. They look for documentation that employees are trained and knowledgeable. They select employees and ask such questions as: "Where are the material safety data sheets?", "What handwashing procedures do you use?" or "What would you do if a resident's blood got on your clothing?"

DISASTER AND EMERGENCY PREPAREDNESS [42 CFR 483.75 (m)]

A facility must have detailed written plans and procedures to meet all potential emergencies and disasters. This includes fire, severe weather, missing residents, chemical spills (where applicable), and so on. The disaster program is tailored to the facility's location and types of residents it serves. If it is located near industrial plants, the facility should have plans in case of explosion. If located near a major trucking route or a railroad, plans should be developed for chemical spills. In some areas they plan for hurricanes and floods; in others they plan for tornadoes, snow storms, and wild fires.

An effective plan would include:

1. Assistance of qualified fire, safety, and other appropriate experts in planning and maintaining the program;
2. Procedures for prompt transfer of casualties and records;
3. Instructions on the location and use of alarm systems, signals, and fire-fighting equipment;
4. Information available on methods of containing fire;
5. Posted specifications for evacuation routes and procedures;
6. Emergency procedures for care of the resident;
7. Procedures for notifying the attending physician responsible for the resident;
8. Procedures for arranging transportation, hospitalization, and other appropriate services;
9. Training all employees; and
10. Regular unannounced drills.

Special emergency plans for **cardiac cases** should be developed. Standard operating procedures for their care are needed. They should be reviewed and rehearsed regularly in order to be effective.

The **disaster plan** must be quite complete because it may involve moving the entire resident population and staff a considerable distance to another city. Arrangements must be made for housing of residents and staff, perhaps for several days. Nursing must be prepared to move appropriate records, medications, and treatment and assistive devices. The facility must plan not only for transporting from the endangered area, but also for returning them to the facility, which is not always well-planned.

> **Example**: In Louisiana hurricane Andrew, which struck the coastal areas, caused evacuation of nursing home residents to central Louisiana, 145 miles away. Families, staff, and transportation companies helped transport residents out of the area. The hurricane destroyed all telephone lines. When it was over, the nursing-home staff could not contact families or transportation companies to return residents home. They had to stay in the central state area three days longer than planned.

Periodic review of disaster plans is required. Review intervals are determined by the facility based on its unique circumstances. Any change in the physical plant, change external to the facility, change in the type of resident served, or other notable change should indicate a review of the plan.

Training All staff must be trained in emergency procedures when they begin work. No employee should be allowed to go on duty without first being walked through his duties in case of emergency. This is especially true in the case of fire since time is such an important factor. Also, there must be periodic review of procedures by the staff.

Drills Regular drills in which staff carry out emergency procedures are required. This applies to disasters as well as fire. Facilities decide on the frequency of disaster drills, unless the state sets standards. Frequency of fire drills is determined by the Life Safety Code which is discussed later.

Surveyors will review disaster and emergency plans to determine if they meet standards. They will ask two staff persons in each department what they do when the fire alarm goes off. They also ask what the employee would do if he/she discovered a resident is missing.

Fire prevention and control Medicare/Medicaid regulations require plans in case of fire and specify that fire drills are to be conducted periodically. The Life Safety Code establishes regulations for building materials and plans to prevent fire, as discussed earlier.

Planning In developing fire prevention and control plans, there is a distinct **advantage** in utilizing the assistance of the local fire department. By visiting the facility and helping to develop plans, the firemen become familiar with the facility layout, the fire-control equipment, and location of cutoffs and hookups. Firemen are usually quite willing to assist with both planning and staff training since a large portion of their time is spent waiting for calls.

A major factor to consider in planning is that **smoke inhalation** is the principal cause of death in fires. This necessitates a plan that includes closing all doors primarily to contain the smoke. Staff often think that closing doors is to contain the fire, but this is secondary to smoke containment. Another important factor is **time**. Most fires are out of control within five minutes of their start. A fire out of control is referred to as a **flashover**. In summary, the three most important factors in fire prevention and control planning are **time, smoke,** and **closed doors.** Staff should be well-trained in understanding these factors.

The plan should specify that in case of a fire or disaster, the highest ranking staff member on duty is in charge. In the event of fire this person is in charge until the firemen arrive to take over.

Fire drills Whereas Medicare and Medicaid require fire drills, the Life Safety Code outlines the specifics. The Code requires one fire drill on each shift per quarter, a total of 12 per year. Generally, this is not sufficient. Because of high turnover and the education level of many employees, fire drills at least once per shift per month, for a total of 36 per year, seem indicated. The facility is certainly better prepared by using this frequency of drills. The Code requires that fire drills be properly documented for easy reference by inspectors.

Fire drill steps The most commonly used guide to action that must be taken is RACE:

R **Remove** any resident from danger.

A Pull the fire **alarm.**

C **Control** the fire if possible, but be sure to use the correct extinguisher.

E **Evacuate** adjacent areas, if indicated.

In practice, actions taken do not necessarily follow these steps. Following are the most commonly used steps in nursing facilities.

1. **Call for help**. The employee who discovers fire may detect smoke far down the hall. He should call for help as he moves toward the fire location. The call is usually in code, such as: **code red, doctor red, or code 13**. A facility is wise to have the person finding the fire add its location. An example, "code red, 101," which means fire in room 101. If the facility has an intercommunication system, the person nearest the microphone should sound the code with the location. In this way everyone knows why the alarm sounds and where the fire is located.

2. **Sound the alarm** if the detector does not automatically trip the alarm. This may be done by the person nearest an alarm device. Also, someone should be designated to call the fire department.

3. **Close the door** to the fire area to prevent smoke spread.

4. **Remove any resident** in the fire area, and close the door to that room.

5. **Close all doors** between residents and the fire. This includes closing doors to all resident rooms.

6. **Contain the fire** by using fire-control equipment, but be sure the correct equipment is used.

7. **Evacuate the building** only when necessary. This is the last step to be carried out when it is evident the fire has reached the **flashover** stage and cannot be contained.

In practice, several of these steps may be taken simultaneously.

Example: One resident was known to hide matches and on occasion start a fire. He had been moved to room 201, nearest the nurses station. The two nurse aides made their rounds at 9:30 p.m. As they completed their room check and came out of the last room at the end of the corridor they smelled smoke. They knew where it was. One called out, "Code red, 201," and pulled the nearby fire alarm. The other hastily took the fire extinguisher from its niche in the wall and they raced toward 201.

The charge nurse and station manager were around the corner from the nurses station when they heard the code called out. The station manager rushed to the station and announced, "Code red, 201," on the intercom and called the fire department. The charge nurse reached 201 at the same time as the two aides. She literally picked up the resident, whose pajama legs were ablaze as he stood in his burning bed, and handed him to the station manager in the corridor with instructions to put out the pajama-leg fire. The charge nurse began removing an oxygen tank from the room as the aide with the extinguisher very competently put out the fire. Actually, the door to the room was not closed until the incident was over since the action moved so rapidly. The automatic fire doors in the corridors closed properly, but other staff was still closing doors to resident rooms when the firemen arrived.

Control of fires must be carefully planned with the local firemen. There are several types or classes of fire. Each must be controlled or extinguished according to type.

1. **Class A** is paper, wood , rubber, plastic, linen, wool, etc. These may be controlled by use of water or water-based extinguishing agent. Many of these occur in wastebaskets and are easy to extinguish with a container of water, by covering the wastebasket with a solid object that cuts off the oxygen supply, or by a Class A extinguisher.

2. **Class B** is grease and flammable liquid fires that frequently occur in the kitchen. They may be extinguished, if on the cooking range, by pulling down the hood and cutting off the oxygen supply, or by a Class B extinguisher that uses CO2 or dry chemicals.

3. **Class C** are electrical fires which can only be controlled by a Class C extinguisher. It must be identified by the letter C. Water can never be used as it conducts electricity and may injure the person using the water.

Fire extinguishers must be properly placed. The Life Safety Code specifies that Class A extinguishers be placed no more than 75 feet apart. Class B and C extinguishers may be no more than 50 feet apart. The Code further identifies the location in which each type should be installed.

Inspections The state fire marshal or other office responsible for LSC enforcement conducts regular inspections to monitor the facilities compliance in these areas:

1. Servicing of fire extinguishers
2. Operability of fire alarms
3. Exit lights
4. Auxiliary generator
5. Automatic fire doors
6. Smoke detectors
7. Smoking procedures
8. Oven hood
9. Fire drills

The LSC inspection report must be coordinated with the state Medicaid agency's survey reports in those states where the Medicaid agency does not do LSC inspections itself, as noted earlier.

Reporting fires States set standards for reporting fires in nursing homes. They often require that all fires, no matter how small, be reported to both the state Medicaid agency and to the fire marshall. The fire marshall in many states does an inspection after any significant fire in a nursing home.

SECURITY

Security is a broad term generally referring to measures taken to ensure protection and safety of residents, staff, and visitors. Security means not only physical protection, but protection from theft. Although there is no specific federal requirement, the proper security program should be written with clear policies and procedures covering each activity that is designed to provide security. **Location** of the facility is a prime factor in security planning. If the facility is located in a high crime area, more numerous measures are required.

1. **Well lighted** building and parking areas are advisable. Every entrance to the building should be adequately lighted to discourage anyone from lurking outside or trying to clandestinely enter the building. Staff should be discouraged from going to their cars in the parking lots at night, except during shift change.

2. A **security** guard is often needed in high crime areas, especially at night. The guard should make regular rounds outside the building in order to be visible to possible offenders. Regular rounds inside the building should be made to check entrances, door locks, and other security measures. When shifts change the guard should be on watch in the parking areas.

3. **Entrances** should all be locked from the outside, and if a security guard is on duty, only he should admit anyone to the building after curfew. If there is no security guard, two staff members should go to the door and require identification and an explanation for the visitation before opening the door.

4. **Local police** should be alerted to the facility's security needs and plans. Usually, they are quite willing to review the facility's security measures and to make recommendations. If prowlers are seen, they will promptly respond to a call. Some nursing homes encourage police to drop by at regular intervals on the night shifts by providing them coffee and a snack.

5. **Drug abusers** can be a major threat because they are aware nursing homes have drugs. In addition to the above procedures to ensure safety, nursing staff will want to pay particular attention to the narcotics key, ensuring that it is properly protected. Unfortunately, if a drug abuser gains entrance and demands narcotics, and a security guard or policeman is not present, it is best to give him what he asks. Generally, they are ruthless and will attack or kill without hesitation. This area of security requires careful planning by the staff.

Internal security must be planned also. Security of resident valuables has already been discussed, as has the security of wanderers. Alarm devices for the latter and procedures to follow in case a resident disappears must be used. Each staff person must know what to do in case a resident walks away. A **third** area of internal security involves residents who may be dangerous to others. If a resident tends to be argumentative and/or assaultive, staff must ensure that devices these residents can use to injure are not readily available to them.

> **Example**: A semi-ambulatory resident went about the facility in a wheelchair or with the use of a cane. Even when in a wheelchair he always kept his cane handy. One evening he became enraged with three male friends. While in his chair he struck one resident on the head, killing him with the cane. He injured the other two so badly they were hospitalized. The facility had allowed him to keep his father's walking cane because it meant so much to him. The fallacy of this decision was that the walking cane was made of seasoned hickory. It was truly a lethal weapon. The facility was sued and damages paid because it had not provided adequate security to other residents.

AUDITING

Environmental management is easier to audit than some other domains of practice. MBWA is the best method because the administrator can observe housekeeping, monitor the laundry, determine if equipment is working, examine doors, locks, and other security measures, determine if employees know what to do in case of fire, disaster, or a hazard communication problem. Other means of auditing are (1) checking the accident log, (2) examining the preventive maintenance log, (3) monitoring infection control measures, (4) evaluating security practices, and (5) requiring follow-up reports on theft and missing resident valuables. Personally conducting fire drills and checking fire-control equipment provides first hand information on the fire prevention and control program.

The **quality assessment and assurance committee** is a second major factor in monitoring the environment. It should regularly review all aspects of the physical environment observing and correcting any problem that is a detriment to resident care. The committee should regularly report its findings and actions to the administrator unless he serves on the committee and obtains his information first hand.

GLOSSARY

ADA Americans with Disabilities Act that provides standards, employment, and accessibility of buildings for disabled.

ADAAG Americans with Disabilities Act Accessibility Guidelines which are the ADA standards.

AIDS Acquired Immune Deficiency Syndrome, a relatively new disease in the United States that attacks the body's immune system.

ANSI The American National Standards Institute which establishes standards for making public buildings accessible and usable by the handicapped.

Aseptic cleaning Procedure for cleaning an isolation area by using cleaning materials that destroy bacteria.

Assistive devices Any device used to assist a resident to eat, walk, or carry out any other activity of daily living.

Bathing facilities A bathtub and/or shower stall equipped for residents to bathe themselves.

BBP Bloodborne pathogens are microscopic pathogenic organisms present in human blood that cause disease.

CDC Centers for Disease Control and Prevention located in Atlanta, Georgia.

Communication system A self-contained, two-way system by which staff and residents may communicate with each other from resident rooms to the nurses station.

Contaminated linens Bed sheets, pillow slips, and bedclothes that have been exposed to human excreta, blood, or other potentially hazardous material.

Contaminated sharps Contaminated needles, scalpels, broken glass, etc., that can penetrate the skin.

Disaster plans Written plans including step-by-step procedures on action to be taken in case of fire, explosion, flood, or other disaster.

Emergency power A source of electrical power that can be used in case of a municipal-power failure.

Exposure control plan The facility's plan of prevention and control of exposure to bloodborne pathogens.

Exposure incident A situation in which a person has come in contact with contaminated sharps, regulated waste, contaminated linen, or other potentially infectious material.

FDA U.S. Food and Drug Administration that monitors the Safe Medical Devices Act.

FFDCA Federal Food, Drug, and Cosmetic Act that empowers FDA to seek penalties against violators of SMDA.

Fire prevention Actions to be taken by staff, residents, and visitors to prevent fires.

Fire rating The period of time material will resist fire as determined by Life Safety Code Standards.

Fire resistive material Walls, doors, carpets, drapes, and other materials that are proven to resist fire for an approved period of time, usually one hour or more.

Hazard communication program A program mandated by OSHA to protect staff from hazardous chemicals used in a facility.

Housekeeping Activities required to keep a facility clean and orderly.

Infection control A program to prevent the spread of any type infection.

Isolation room A room designated and used for the purpose of isolating residents who have a communicable disease.

Life Safety Code Standards for grounds and buildings established by the NFPA to ensure that the structures are accessible, safe for public use, and fire protected.

Lock out, Tag out A safety requirement of OSHA in which equipment being repaired is properly locked or labeled so staff cannot use.

Log A written record documenting actions taken, by whom, and on which date.

Maintenance Actions taken to keep equipment in working order and buildings in good repair.

MSDS Material Safety Data Sheets that indicate hazardous chemicals in a product, describing the product, and giving precautions for safe handling and use.

Multipurpose room A room in a facility that is used for more than one activity, such as dining, meetings, and recreation.

NFPA National Fire Protection Association that develops the Life Safety Code and the National Electrical Code.

Nurses station An area on a nursing unit that serves as a focal point for nursing activities.

OSHA Occupational Safety and Health Administration, a federal organization that monitors employee safety and health conditions in business and industry.

Pest Control Activities carried out to reduce the presence of cockroaches, flies, rodents, mosquitoes, and other pests.

Physical environment The building and grounds that comprise a nursing home, including electrical, heating, cooling, lighting, water, sewage disposal, parking, and other systems.

Post-exposure procedures Written program to examine and evaluate blood of the exposed employee and the course person and to follow up.

PPE Personal protective equipment which is used to protect against chemical hazards and infections.

Preventive maintenance Regular checking and servicing of equipment, buildings, and systems to prevent breakdowns and other operational problems.

Regulated waste Contaminated needles, syringes, scalpel blades, liquid or semi-liquid blood, or other potentially infectious materials.

Security Measures taken to protect residents, staff, visitors, and property.

SMDA Safe Medical Devices Act that requires a facility to report to the FDA any incident that reasonably suggests a medical device or a drug contributed to death or a serious illness or injury of a resident or employee.

Standard precautions Procedures developed by the CDC for handling of body fluids of residents in order to prevent disease spread. (Previously called universal precautions)

Toilet facilities Flush type commodes and/or urinals.

Work orders A written request for corrective action on a piece of equipment, an electrical or other system, or the building itself.

REFERENCES

ADA Handbook, EEOC and U.S. Department of Justice, Los Angeles: BNI Publications, 1990.

Jacobs, Michael, *Cost Management for Long-Term Care Facilities*, Bossier City, LA: Professional Printing and Publishing, Inc., 1986.

Lathrop, James K., editor of *Life Safety Code Handbook*, Quincy, MA: National Fire Protection Association, Inc., Fifth Edition, 1991.

Roffmann, Harold, *Maintenance Management for Health Care Facilities*, Bossier City, LA: Professional Printing and Publishing, Inc., 1988.

Specification for Making Buildings and Facilities Accessible and Usable by the Physically Handicapped, New York City: American National Standards Institute, A112-1986.

Standards of Health Care Facilities, NFPA 99, Quincy, MA: National Fire Protection Association, Inc., 1996.

State Operations Manual, Provider Certification, U.S. Department of Health & Human Service, Springfield, VA: U.S. Department of Commerce, National Technical Information Service, 1992.

Title 29 Code of Federal Regulations, Part 1900-1010.13,, Washington: U.S. Government Printing Office, 1989.

Title 42 Code of Federal Regulations, Public Health, Part 400 to 429, Washington: U.S. Government Printing Office, 1995.

Title 42 Code of Federal Regulations, Public Health, Part 430 to end, Washington: U.S. Government Printing Office, 1996.

Title 45 Code of Federal Regulations, Part 84, Washington: U.S. Government Printing Office, 1989.

CHAPTER 9

DIETARY MANAGEMENT

DIETARY MANAGEMENT

THE ADMINISTRATOR'S ROLE

The **administrator's role** in developing and maintaining a quality dietary department is the focus of this chapter. No effort is made to present in-depth concepts or recommendations of the type a consulting dietitian provides for operation of a dietary service. Rather, some indicators are identified that the administrator may use to ensure that his facility meets standards and provides quality food. First and foremost is the administrator's **visibility** in showing his interest in his dietary service. Adequate interest cannot be shown by sitting in his office and having his dietary manager report to him. Neither is it sufficient to make an occasional visit to the dining room and observe the finished product. His visit may be on a day when all goes well and one of the more appetizing meals is served.

The administrator needs to be seen in dietary service, regularly asking questions, commenting on activities, chatting with employees, and checking the environment. When he does this, he sends a message, loud and clear: "I am interested in what goes on; I want everything to go according to standards." During these visits a few words of praise regarding specific performance of individuals may be an effective motivator. Employees like to know they are appreciated and that their boss notices how they perform their work.

Problem area Dietary service is generally the second biggest problem area in the facility. The majority of complaints originate in nursing service. This is expected since many residents are in pain or do not feel well, are taking several medications, and are undergoing various treatments that may be unpleasant. The second area on which residents and family focus their complaints is food. The administrator will need to plan carefully in order to lessen these complaints.

Cost/revenue center Dietary service is a high-cost area where cost management must be planned, implemented, and practiced if the facility is to prosper. It is also a revenue center that helps to ensure a satisfactory ROI. The administrator cannot expect dietary service to operate efficiently and effectively on its own. His attention is required on a continuing basis.

Organization The administrator should pay particular attention to the organizational structure of his dietary service. So much depends on the size of the facility and the personnel available. A wide variety of activities must be performed by a relatively small number of employees, including purchasing, receiving, storage, menu planning, food preparation, tray assembly and delivery, cleaning, garbage disposal, and reporting. The dietary manager will need the administrator's assistance in grouping and assigning activities so that work is performed efficiently. Purchasing is often handled by the manager, but with his many other duties it may be a problem. Purchasing and production functions may have to be separated. (Dougherty) The administrator should maintain close contact, open communication, and frequent conferences with the dietary manager. This is the key to a well-run dietary service.

MEDICARE/MEDICAID STANDARDS

OBRA makes no distinction between dietary services in SNF's and NF's. Until October 1, 1990, there were some differences in standards which Medicare and Medicaid facilities were required to meet. Title 42 CFR 483.35 specifies standards that all nursing facilities must abide by now. The facility must provide a nourishing, well-balanced diet that meets the daily nutritional and special dietary needs of each resident. The former federal standards provided that the facility could contract with an outside dietary-management service. The new standards (OBRA) make no reference to such arrangements. It is presumed contracts are still permissible, provided the vendor and service are in full compliance with standards.

In practice, administrators often choose to operate their own dietary service rather than contract because they believe: (1) It is less expensive, (2) the administrator retains control over the final product, and (3) staff shows more loyalty as facility employees. Frequently, administrators make decisions against contracting without adequate planning or knowledge of the advantages and disadvantages of contracting. Herman Zaccarelli describes the steps that administrators should take to determine whether to contract the dietary service. Many who have used his methods have developed contracts with food-management companies. Administrators may find his helpful suggestions in the "Handbook for Health Care Food Service Management."

STAFFING

OBRA established standards, including qualifications, for personnel in dietary service. [42 CFR 483.35 (a) (b)]

1. **Dietitian** The facility must employ a qualified dietitian either full-time, part-time, or on a consultant basis. A qualified dietitian is one who is qualified by either registration by the Commission on Dietetic Registration, the American Dietetic Association, or by education, training, or experience in identification of dietary needs, and planning and implementation of dietary programs. Qualification by education, training, and experience means the following are included.

   a. Assessing needs of geriatric and physically impaired persons,

   b. Developing therapeutic diets,

   c. Developing regular diets to meet special needs of geriatric and physically impaired persons,

   d. Developing and implementing continuing education programs for dietary and nursing personnel,

   e. Participating in interdisciplinary care planning,

   f. Budgeting and purchasing food and supplies, and

   g. Supervising institutional food preparation and service.

2. **Dietary Manager** If the facility does not employ a full-time dietitian, it must employ a full-time, qualified dietary manager. The manager must have frequent, regularly scheduled consultation from a qualified dietitian. Qualifications are not specified by OBRA; however, standards of practice dictate that a qualified dietary manager is one who:

   a. Is a dietitian as identified above; or

   b. Is a dietetic technician registered or eligible for registration with the Commission on Dietetic Registration of the American Dietetic Association; or

   c. Is a certified dietary manager or eligible for certification with the certifying Board for Dietary Managers; or

   d. Is a graduate of a Dietary Managers Association approved dietary-manager training program; or

   e. Is a graduate of a state-approved course that provided 90 or more hours of classroom instruction in dietary-service management and has experience as a supervisor in a health-care institution with consultation from a qualified dietitian.

The Dietary Managers Association is comprised of members who work in nursing facilities, hospitals, school systems, and restaurants. Its basic management-training program leads to a credentialing examination which has two parts: (1) Competency in nutrition and dietary-service operations, and (2) dietary-service sanitation and safety. Upon meeting all requirements the Dietary Managers Association awards trainees a Certified Dietary Manager (CDM) certificate. A person with these qualifications has valuable knowledge of nutrition and dietary-service operations and should be included in developing all standards for a professional dietary service. In addition to its basic-training program, the Association conducts continuing-education programs to ensure continued growth of its members. The administrator **should require** his dietary manager to be a member of this association or a similar organization, and be a CDM.

Surveyors will carefully check to determine if resident nutritional needs are met. If they find problems in this area, surveyors will determine what practices of the dietitian or dietary manager contributed to these nutritional problems. They will then determine the education, training, and experience qualifications of the facility's dietitian to determine if they meet the above listed requirements. If surveyors find no nutritional problems they are not likely to examine qualifications.

3. **Other Staff** The facility must employ **sufficient** support personnel competent to carry out the functions of the dietary service. There are no federal guidelines specifying how many cooks, salad makers, dishwashers, and other personnel the facility should employ. **Sufficient** support personnel means enough to prepare adequate meals at proper temperatures and at appropriate times. In order to do this most dietary services have an early shift and a late shift of employees whose schedules overlap during the midday when work load is heaviest. Generally, there must be personnel on duty at least 12 hours per day in order to meet residents' nutritional needs and maintain the required meal schedule.

Surveyors are to observe the kitchen and food preparation. They determine two things: (1) whether food is prepared in scheduled time frames and at the proper temperature, and (2) whether food leaves the kitchen in scheduled time frames. It is no longer their role to check routinely the staffing patterns, policies and procedures, condition of equipment, and so on, unless they identify resident nutritional problems.

THE CONSULTING DIETITIAN

The typical nursing facility employs a consulting dietitian part-time rather than full-time. Careful thought must be given to selecting the dietitian, developing the contract, and using his time. Frequent errors are made by employing a dietitian simply because one is qualified, available, and willing to work for a reasonable fee.

1. **Qualifications** In addition to meeting federal qualifications, the dietitian should have a strong **administrative orientation**. The clinical aspects of dietary work will probably be handled with ease. The dietetic service needs proper organization, policies and procedures, supervisory direction, economic purchasing, inventory control, work scheduling, and other administrative practices that promote efficiency, economy, and quality. Unless the facility has an unusually well-trained and competent dietary manager, the consultant may be required to do considerable consultation in these areas.

   Knowledge of **consulting** methodology is necessary. Many dietitians know how to manage dietary services, evaluate performance, and give instructions, but are weak in problem solving. They do not know how to help the manager find and implement solutions to which he is committed. Consultants must know their job is to evaluate, problem solve, make recommendations, and teach.

2. **Duties** Duties of consultant dietitians are not identified by federal guidelines. It is the administrator's duty to develop a job description that clearly outlines the dietitian's duties. It is generally accepted standards of practice that the following duties are assigned:

   a. Ensuring that residents' nutritional needs are met according to physician's orders,

   b. Liaison between medical and nursing staff,

   c. Guidance to the dietary manager and staff,

   d. Counseling residents on food needs and eating habits,

   e. Approval of menus,

   f. Preparation and/or approval of therapeutic diets,

g. Assisting with development of policies and procedures,

h. Assisting with the training of dietary-service personnel, and

i. Written and verbal reports to the administrator.

3. **Authority** The dietitian's contract should clearly define the extent of authority the consultant role involves. The contract should specify that the consultant does not have authority to give orders, to reprimand or otherwise discipline, or to terminate employees. His role is primarily problem solving. Problems are identified, discussed with the dietary manager, and together they decide on solutions that will accomplish the goals of the dietary service and meet the required standards. The consultant may make recommendations, give suggestions, and teach. When the dietary manager fails to make needed corrections or to follow proper procedures, and the problem-solving approach does not work, the consultant reports it to the administrator. Only the administrator has authority to use disciplinary action with his employees. He may ask the consultant's opinion on appropriate actions or may solicit suggestions, but he decides whether these will be followed and assumes responsibility for these actions.

4. **Frequency of visits** Each state determines the minimum amount of time per month or quarter that consulting dietitians must spend in a facility. The facility is sometimes permitted to decide on the frequency of visits. Weekly visits of at least two-hours duration appear to be the bare minimum, especially when therapeutic diets are involved.

5. **Reporting** The consulting dietitian is no longer required by federal guidelines to give written reports to the administrator. Sound management practices do require it. The dietitian, and any other consultants, should report to the administrator after each visit. A verbal report after each visit should be very specific. Reporting that, "Everything is okay. I found a few problems, but cleared them up," or, "You have a very good dietary service," is neither acceptable nor helpful. The same is true of a written report that should follow each visit.

The administrator needs to agree with the consultant on a standard report form, both verbal and written. As a minimum these items should be included: (1) time, date, and duration of visit; (2) what the consultant did during the visit, such as: counseled with 10 residents, observed food preparation, reviewed menus, etc.; (3) problems identified, what action was taken, and what the administrator should do to follow-up; (4) staff reactions to solutions and recommendations; and (5) plans for the next visit. This kind of documentation is useful to the administrator in keeping track of dietary-service operations. It is especially valuable when **surveyors** find problems in resident nutritional status. The reports show how the administrator has expressed interest and given direction, and the reports may help identify the source of the specific problem noted by the surveyors. It is also an established procedure for correcting the noted deficiency.

The administrator may find it helpful to have the dietary manager present during consultant reports at the end of visits. This demonstrates that the consultant is not telling the administrator anything that was not discussed with the manager. Certainly, a copy of written reports should go to the dietary manager.

MENUS AND NUTRITIONAL ADEQUACY [42 CFR 483.35 (c) (1-3)]

Menus must meet nutritional needs of residents in accordance with the recommended dietary allowances of the Food and Nutrition Board of the National Research Council, National Academy of Sciences. They must be prepared in advance and followed in planning individual meals. Menus may be prepared by the dietary manager, but they should be approved and regularly reviewed by the dietitian. Most facilities use rotational menus, so there is no concern about how long menus are **retained**. Such menus are a matter of written records for several months or longer. States may establish and monitor a regulation that provides a schedule of menu retention, but there is no longer a federal standard.

Recommended Dietary Allowances (RDA's) Menus should contain the RDA's which are the recommended amounts of vitamins, minerals, and other elements needed per day to maintain health. These are recommended and are not a binding requirement, although every facility will certainly provide recommended dietary allowances if it is to be successful.

There are five basic-food classes which provide the required RDAs. Figure 9.1 shows these classes and the basic per-day quantities. The pyramid shown in this figure is an outline of what to eat each day. Its not a rigid prescription, but a general guide that lets a person choose a healthful diet that is right for that individual. The pyramid calls for eating a variety of foods in order to get the nutrients and right amount of calories. It should be a guide for dietary service managers.

These are basic and will vary according to a person's size, age, activity level, health, and so on. It behooves the administrator to learn something about these food classes, such as, meats provide proteins to build body tissue, and residents are more likely to develop **hypersensitivity** and **allergies** to dairy products, fish and seafood, eggs, walnuts and peanuts, and glutens (proteins in wheat, rye, oats, barley, and malt). Hypersensitivity in some people is in the form of anaphylaxis. (Smathers) The administrator must make sure staff is aware of allergic reactions and how to handle them. Often there isn't much time to cope with a reaction as the smell of certain foods may trigger an allergic reaction within 60 seconds.

Figure 9.1:

Food Guide Pyramid

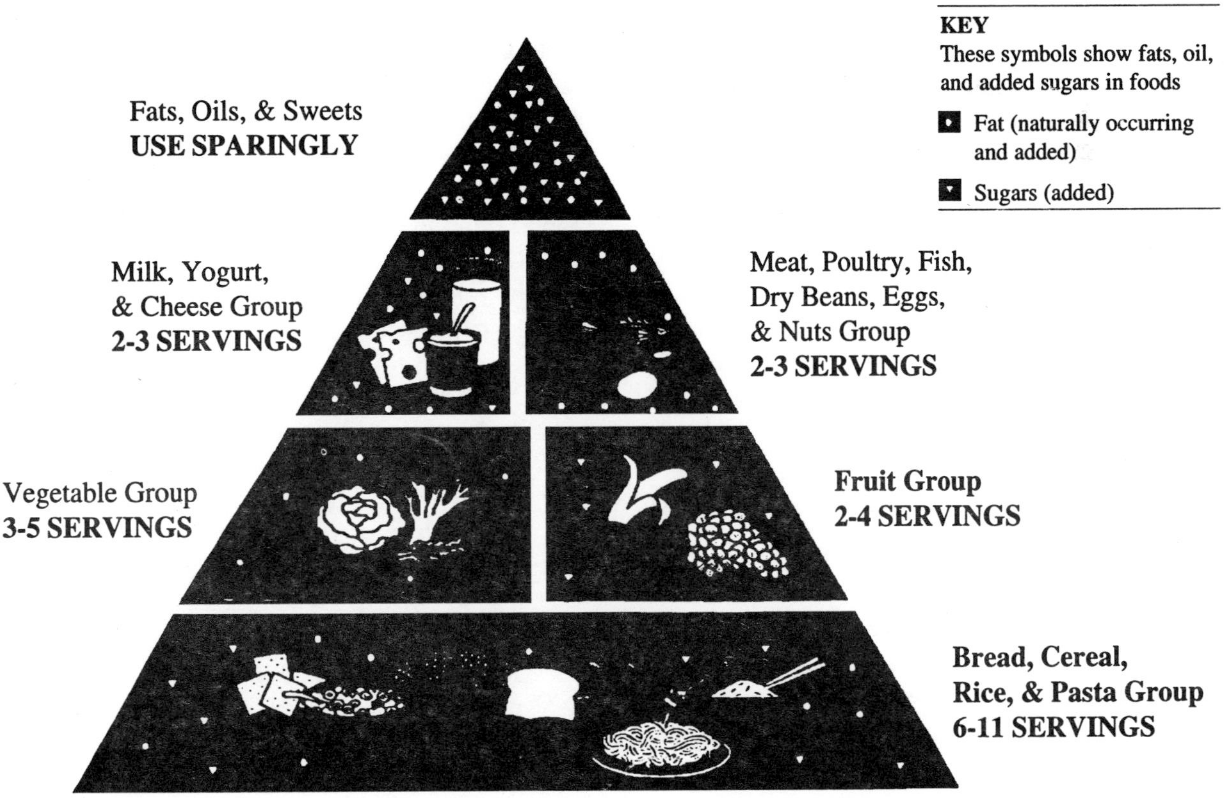

Source: American Dietetic Association

Surveyors, in determining whether menus meet standards and are nutritionally adequate, will observe whether residents are maintaining usual body weights, and whether there are acceptable nutritional values in the food served. If food intake appears inadequate based on their observation of meals being served, or if the residents' nutritional status is poor based on **Quality of Care** review, surveyors will determine if the menus meet the caloric and nutritional intake needs of residents. If surveyors find that dairy food, vegetables, and fruit are missing from the resident's daily diet, they will expect to find alternative means of satisfying the resident's nutritional needs. Also, they will determine whether the menus supply the RDA's. Surveyors will measure **percentages** of food eaten by determining the overall percentage of the food that is eaten by the end of the meal. Measurements are as follows:

Figure 9.2:

Measurement of Food Eaten

A = Resident eats 75 percent or more.

B = Resident eats between 50-75 percent.

C = Resident eats 25-50 percent.

D = Resident eats less than 25 percent.

In determining whether menus are followed, surveyors look for dated cycle menus for both regular and modified diets. They will obtain documentation from diet cards, record review, and interviews with the dietary manager or dietitian to support reasons for deviating from the written menu.

FOOD AND FOOD PREPARATION [42 CFR 483.35 (d) (1-4)]

This section of the CFR sets standards for food and its preparation. Food preparation methods must conserve nutritive value, flavor, and appearance. Preparation procedures must ensure that vitamins are not destroyed. Unacceptable practices are shown in Figure 9.3:

Figure 9.3:

Unacceptable Food Preparation Practices

- Prolonged food storage
- Too much exposure to light
- Prolonged cooking in a large volume of water
- Addition of baking soda
- Overcooking to attain soft texture

Food safety A number of facilities have experienced a large scale outbreak of foodborne illness caused by undercooked beef as was served by a popular hamburger chain. Others have had contaminated ice cream in their freezers. Cost of foodborne illness is high in terms of human suffering, litigation, lost revenue, and damaged reputations. (Sambataro)

The administrator may want the **Hazards Analysis Critical Control Point** (HACCP) as an effective means of preventing foodborne illness. This system traces how, when, and where contamination can occur in food manufacturing and in his own facility. Both food-processing and food-use enterprises use it, reaping safety benefits from the quality assurance measure. It is a systematic approach that uses seven principles standardized by the National Committee on Microbiological Criteria for Foods. HAACP uses **seven principles** to attain desired results.

1. Determine the hazards and risks with all aspects of the product being produced with respect to the end-use of such products.
2. Identify the critical control points (CCPs) required to control the hazards identified.
3. Establish limits which must be met at each CCP to control the hazards.
4. Establish monitoring procedures for each critical limit established at each CCP.

5. Establish corrective action to be taken if a critical limit is met or exceeded during monitoring. This corrective action is designed to bring the hazard back under control.

6. Establish a record-keeping system which provides positive documentation that critical limits are being met, and when not met, that corrective action has been taken to bring the system back under control.

7. Establish verification procedures that demonstrate the HAACP system is functioning as planned.

Paul Sambataro recommends that every facility develop a written plan that incorporates these seven principles, along with sanitation operations principles with current Good Manufacturing Practice (GMP) guidelines, and specific regulations covering cooking and cooling practices. The Food and Drug Administration (FDA) outlines HAACP and sanitation procedures in its 1993 Code Manual. A well-qualified dietary manager can implement this program with the encouragement and assistance of the administrator.

Administrators should not be surprised if the government soon requires HAACP. They should begin to prepare for it now. It's a strong element of a good **risk management** program.

Nutrition [42CFR 483.25 (i)] Based on a resident's comprehensive assessment, the facility must ensure that the resident maintains acceptable parameters of nutritional status. This includes body weight and protein levels. Of course, if the resident's clinical condition demonstrates this is not possible, or there is any other nutritional problem, the resident must receive a therapeutic diet. Unfortunately, ideal body weight charts for the institutionalized elderly have not been validated. Consequently, surveyors will look at weight loss or gain as a guide in determining nutritional status. This analysis will be accomplished by comparing weight loss or gain to the resident's former lifestyle as well as the current diagnosis.

OBRA suggests parameters for evaluating significance of unplanned and undesired weight loss in residents as follows in Table 9.1.

Table 9.1:

Degree of Weight Loss

Intervals	Significant Loss	Severe Loss
1 month	5%	Greater than 5%
3 months	7.5%	Greater than 7.5%
6 months	10%	Greater than 10%

Percentage of weight loss is determined by using this formula:

$$\frac{\text{usual weight less actual weight}}{\text{usual weight}} \times 100 = \%\text{ of weight loss}$$

$$\frac{150\text{ lbs} - 100\text{ lbs}}{150\text{ lbs}} = .33 \times 100 = 33\%$$

In checking weight loss, surveyors will consider whether the resident was on a diet, or if he is newly admitted and obese, or on a normal diet with less calories than prior to admission. Also, they will note if resident was edematous when weighed and with treatment no longer has edema. Surveyors will determine whether the resident refused food. All of this should be well documented if and when it occurs.

Surveyors check appearance of food to determine if it has an appetizing aroma and/or appearance, such as the use of garnishes, and a variety of color while it is on the plate. Flavor is checked to ensure food is not too sweet or salty. Then the surveyor determines if preparation destroys vitamins for any of the reasons listed above. Food must be palatable, attractive, served at the proper **temperature**, and prepared in a form to meet individual needs. Substitutes must be offered that are similar in nutritive value when a resident refuses food. **Appropriate temperatures** means that potentially hazardous foods leave the kitchen or steam table at or above 140° F and cold foods at 41° F or below. Food is to be cut, chopped, or ground to meet individual resident's needs.

Surveyors observe residents, looking for potential indicators of malnutrition such as pale skin, dull eyes, swollen lips or gums, swollen and/or dry tongue with scarlet or magenta hue, poor skin turgor, cachexia, bilateral edema, and muscle wasting. They note whether risk factors are present, as drug therapy, poor oral-health status, depression, lack of access to culturally acceptable food, slow-eating pace, etc.

THERAPEUTIC DIETS [42 CFR 483.35 (e)]

OBRA requires that **therapeutic diets** be prescribed by the attending physician. As a matter of fact, all diets are prescribed by the physician. When the physician designates a regular diet he has in essence prescribed it for that specific resident. Generally, it is considered that a qualified dietitian should plan and write these diets. In practice, well-qualified dietary managers often plan and write therapeutic diets. The dietitian approves them and consults on their preparation. A therapeutic diet manual should be available for reference by physicians, nurses, dietary managers, and dietitians. The consulting dietitian provides information on obtaining this manual. Major **types** of therapeutic diets include those that follow:

1. **Low sodium** These are prescribed for people with heart problems, especially congestive heart failure and high blood pressure. Many salt substitutes are available to add taste to food without the sodium content. Residents often dislike these because the taste is not the same as regular salt.

2. **Low fat** (low cholesterol) Low-fat diets are for people with high cholesterol levels.

3. **High protein** This diet is used for many types of problems which require rebuilding of body tissue. Meats and other proteins are referred to as the **building blocks** for body tissue.

4. **Diabetic diets** These diets are prescribed for individuals with a diagnosis of diabetes. Often, they are not completely prescribed, for the prescription must include the number of calories and the food groups to be served.

5. **Low residue** (low fiber) Persons with intestinal inflammation and other digestive disorders may be placed on this diet.

6. **Liquid diets** These are transition diets used in some surgical cases, especially gastric surgery. They are likely to be used in hospitals more frequently than in nursing facilities.

7. **Bland diets** These diets are primarily for residents with gastritis, ulcers, and other gastric conditions. As the name indicates, they are bland, without much flavor or taste, and not popular with residents.

Increasingly, questions are raised about the value of therapeutic diets for the elderly. Low sodium sometimes disturbs other biochemical balances and is used less due to the problems it creates with medication. A low-fat diet probably will not reduce an older person's cholesterol level. Diabetic diets are almost impossible to enforce. Families bring in sweets and often insist the resident have what he wants. Bland diets are almost passe'. Before taking a stance on enforcement of therapeutic diet plans, the administrator should confer with his consulting dietitian and with the attending physicians.

Cost of therapeutic diets is an important economic factor. The administrator should closely monitor these costs as they can sharply affect budget. The facility should determine the number of therapeutic diets it can provide without increasing operating costs to an unacceptable level. One administrator discovered his food costs were 50 percent beyond budget. The reason was that 75 percent of his residents were on therapeutic diets. The facility could not finance this number of special diets and generate a profit.

MEALS [42 CFR 483.35 (f) (2) (4)]

Frequency OBRA established standards for meals and bedtime snacks. The facility must provide at least three meals daily at regular times comparable to normal mealtimes in the community. There can be no more that 14 hours between a substantial evening meal, and breakfast the following day, unless a nourishing bedtime snack is served. In that event 16 hours between the evening meal and breakfast is allowed. However, a resident group must agree to this meal span and the snack.

A **substantial** evening meal offers three or more menu items at one time, one of which includes a high-quality protein such as meat, fish, eggs, or cheese. The meal can represent no less than 20 percent of the day's total nutritional requirements. Many residents prefer a light evening meal. Even with a nourishing snack, this will not qualify for the 16-hour span. The evening meal and the snack must include the required RDA's in order to use the 16-hour span.

Nourishing snacks are made up of single items or a combination of items from the daily food guide. They must be offered unless the physician rules otherwise.

Surveyors will check to determine whether proper mealtime hours are observed, whether nourishing snacks are offered, and whether individuals eat and enjoy bedtime snacks. They will also determine whether any groups who want to do so, influence meal schedules. This is accomplished by resident interviews and by evaluation of the overall nutritional status of residents.

ASSISTIVE DEVICES
[42 CFR 483.35 (g)]

The facility must provide special eating equipment and utensils to residents who need them. The **purpose** of assistive devices is to maintain or improve a resident's ability to eat independently. These devices include: (1) silverware with enlarged handles for residents with impaired coordination; (2) plate guards for residents with tremors; (3) postural supports for the head, trunk, and arms; (4) sectional plates for the visually deficient; and many others. In addition, a written feeding plan must be developed for the severely visual-deficient and blind. The dietitian, or a well-trained dietary manager, can provide information on devices needed and where they may be obtained.

Surveyors will observe whether assistive devices are readily available. They select a sample of residents, review their comprehensive assessment for eating abilities and observe these residents while they eat. This is part of the surveyor Dietary Service System Assessment.

SANITARY CONDITIONS
[42 CFR 483.35 (h) (1-3)]

Procurement The facility must procure food from sources approved or considered satisfactory by federal, state, and/or local authorities. **Surveyors** will check to ensure this is being done by observing fluid milk and milk products, dry milk and milk products, fresh and frozen stocked shellfish, eggs, canned goods, fresh produce, meat, poultry, and fish.

Sanitary conditions Storage, preparation, distribution, and serving of food must be accomplished under proper sanitary conditions. The purpose is to prevent food-borne illnesses. These preventive measures focus on potentially hazardous foods subject to continuous time/temperature controls for preventing either the rapid, progressive growth of infections or toxigenic microorganisms. **Potentially hazardous** foods are animal products toxicogenic (milk, butter, cheese), eggs, poultry, fish, meat, and synthetic food ingredients. Some fruits and vegetables (i.e. baked potatoes and cantaloupe) and specialty foods, as garlic and oil, are potentially hazardous.

Storage Surveyors observe food storage rooms and food storage in the kitchen. They determine whether food is stored off the floor and on clean surfaces in a manner protecting it from contamination.

Refrigerator and freezers are inspected to determine whether they have readily visible, workable thermometers. They will use their own thermometer to check internal temperatures in questionable equipment. **Temperatures** in refrigerators are to be at or below 41°F. Federal standards say foods are to be stored as follows:

1. Potentially hazardous foods at 41°F or below
2. Frozen foods at 0° F or below

Food preparation Surveyors use a sanitized bayonet thermometer to evaluate food temperatures. In addition, they examine the manner in which staff treats leftovers, and how they thaw frozen foods. The **purpose** is to determine whether staff properly handles and cooks potentially hazardous foods. Surveyors not only examine temperatures and handling, but also how it is transported to the dining room and to resident rooms.

Dishwashing There is no federal standard on methods to be used for sanitizing food preparation equipment, dishes, and utensils. In practice, facilities endeavor to destroy potential disease-carrying organisms by using chemical or heat sanitizing methods. If heat is used, the water temperature in the dishwasher wash cycle must be 140°F and 180°F in the dishwasher rinse cycle. When chemicals are used, water temperature should be according to the manufacturer's instructions. There must be a safe water source that provides sufficient hot and cold water under pressure. Both the potable and nonpotable water systems must be in accord with state and local regulations. Administrators should check water temperatures and the sanitizing equipment on a periodic basis.

Surveyors will determine if temperatures or chemical solutions are adequate to destroy disease organisms. They will also determine if there are poorly-equipped **handwashing** facilities for dietary service personnel. They will observe whether toxic materials such as insecticides, detergents, and polishes are properly labeled and stored away from food preparation and storage areas. The administrator should have a firm rule that no **poisons** may be stored, even momentarily, in the dietary service. Toxic items (insecticides, detergents, polishes) must be properly labeled, used and stored.

Sewage All sewage, including liquid waste, must be properly disposed of by a public sewerage system, or by a sewage disposal system constructed and operated in accordance with state and local laws.

Garbage disposal The disposal of garbage may be a problem, especially in regions where cockroaches and flies are abundant. All garbage containers should be lined, have covers that fit properly, and not leak. Containers should be emptied as needed, but at least after each meal. The entire facility should operate by strict procedures designed to keep it free of roaches and flies.

When using d**umpster** service, a special problem may arise. Keeping the large dumpster bins clean and lids closed is a continuing problem Dumpsters should be located as far from the dietary service as possible, and strict procedures set up for their use. Both the administrator and the dietary manager must spend time monitoring garbage disposal if the facility is to be kept free of insect pests.

Infection control As noted earlier, dietary service personnel are a key factor in infection control and should be regularly trained and retrained in the facility's control program.

HYGIENE OF STAFF

Formerly, federal guidelines required that dietary personnel be free from communicable diseases. They were required to have periodic examinations to ensure that no one with a contagious condition could work in the dietary service. Apparently, Medicare and Medicaid now leave these requirements to the states, although they will be checked if problems on nutritional status are noted. In practice, individual states set the specific standards for dietary service personnel's checkups. Some states require annual stool, tuberculin, and other exams by a designated state agency that issues each employee a health card. Other states have abandoned this practice. In these states the facility is required to develop its own policy for health examinations. Some require only an annual tuberculin test which the facility may administer and record. Individual facilities set their policy, and the state licensing and certification agency monitors it to ensure compliance.

Housekeeping The dietary service does its own housekeeping, and usually all dietary service personnel participate in some aspect of cleaning. Personnel from resident-care areas are not allowed to work in both resident care and dietary service. The dietary service has its own brooms, mops, scrub buckets, and other cleaning equipment and materials. They are used in dietary service only, and neither equipment nor cleaning materials may be borrowed from the resident care area. Many facilities allow house keeping personnel to do the cleaning in the dining room but not in other dietary-service areas.

DINING AREA

OBRA requires the facility to provide an adequate dining area, large enough to accommodate comfortably the maximum number of people who usually occupy that space. [42 CFR 483.70 (c) (1)] This space is described more fully in Environmental Management, Chapter 8.

All residents who are ambulatory, semi-ambulatory, and wheelchair cases should be encouraged to eat in the dining room unless their physician orders otherwise. It can be a time of relief from the confines of one's room, and a time for pleasant socializing. Staff should make a special effort to ensure that it is. Of course, there are special problems in this plan. Some residents simply do not wish to eat with other residents with whom they have little in common. Those who have trouble eating—dropping food, spilling liquids, drooling—may make it uncomfortable for those who have no eating problems. It may be necessary to assign those who have difficulty to a special area of the dining room. Some private nursing facilities have separate dining rooms for the severely handicapped and for those without problems. Both groups seem happy with this arrangement.

The **administrator** makes a great difference in resident relationships when he regularly visits during meals. Speaking to everyone, calling them by name, commenting on their appearance, clothes, hairstyle, and so on, promotes cheerfulness and friendliness. Commenting on food is often inadvisable, but just recognizing residents, gently touching those who appreciate it, and being highly visible tells residents the administrator is interested and he cares.

FOOD NEEDS OF THE ELDERLY

Although administrators depend on their dietitians and dietary managers for specifics, they need to know something of the food needs and practices of the elderly. Such knowledge helps administrators monitor the efficiency and adequacy of their dietary service.

Value of food For some of the elderly, food is their only significant enjoyment. Food becomes increasingly important to them and may be a focus of enjoyment, or of contention. Food habits need to be considered in menu planning. If the facility has a significantly large population of Hispanic, Asian, African-American, European, or other ethnic group, certainly the group's food preference should be considered. Also, people of different socioeconomic status and background may have different food preferences. (Gilbert)

Some elderly have experienced little in life other than work, caring for family, and paying bills. They have had no significant social or recreational life. When they become debilitated and must enter a nursing facility, they have neither the drive, energy, nor the interest in developing new social skills and recreational interests. Food is the one thing they enjoy. They may become obese, and the physician urges them to lose weight. With no other joys in life than food, the questions arise, "Why diet? Why deny the one thing that brings pleasure?" Nurses frequently express this point of view.

Taste changes Taste buds usually diminish in number as people age. Taste for salt and for sugar become less acute. Heavily salted or sugared foods may not taste salty or sweet to the aged. Taste buds for bitter foods tend to remain acute and may sometimes be a factor when taking medication. Psychologists have observed that as a result of these changes, the elderly tend (a) to heavily season their food in order to recapture desired tastes, (b) to eat very little and become malnourished, and (c) to complain that nothing tastes good anymore.

Dentures Most elderly in nursing homes have either partial or complete sets of dentures. This can be a factor in residents not eating enough and is often overlooked. **Poor dentition** is a **major cause** of malnutrition among the elderly. Staff should be attuned to this factor when there is an eating problem.

COST REPORTS

The dietary service, as a major **cost center**, is of vital concern to the administrator. Since he expects efficiency and economy, he needs regular reports of revenue and expenditures. The dietary managers should provide a weekly, or at least monthly, report to the administrator that analyzes a number of income and cost factors. The report should include:

1. Number of meals served, broken down into resident, staff, guest, and so on,
2. Total raw food costs, and
3. Raw food cost per resident per day.

Calculating raw food cost per resident per day is determined by dividing the number of resident days into total raw food cost during a specific time period, usually once a month.

> **Example:** A facility has a daily census of 100 residents during a 30-day month which means a total of 3,000 resident days. Total raw food costs for the month was $9,000.

$9,000 ÷ $3,000 = $3 raw food cost/resident/day

The administrator must establish a range for raw food costs per resident/day, especially if he is expected to generate an acceptable return on investment. The range will vary according to the area in which his facility is located. It may be $3 to $4.50 per day, or higher, or lower. But, he should know what the facility can afford and keep close watch on this cost.

Using these figures along with salaries, utilities, and other dietary costs, his accountant may make further analyses, as total cost per meal per day, cost of feeding one resident for one year, and total annual food service costs. This is valuable information for comparison to prior year's costs and in measuring performance in relation to the current budget. Generally, information is available so the facility's costs may be compared to those of comparable facilities in the area. It is only with this type of financial data that the administrator can ensure efficient, economical operations that provide quality service, meet the required standards, and generate an acceptable ROI. As the use of computers reaches dietary service, data will be readily accessible and fully analyzed.

SAFETY AND ACCIDENT PREVENTION

Accidents According to the National Safety Council, accidents in the food service industry are almost twice as frequent as the average in all of industry. They are costly in terms of pain, worker's compensation, time lost, and sometimes court costs. Accidents do not just happen. There are causes, and usually they can be prevented. (Puckett)

Administration is responsible for developing and monitoring a safety program to ensure a reduction in accidents as discussed in Chapter 8. It cannot be left to the dietary manager alone.

Resident safety Some states have enacted laws requiring dietary-service personnel to be trained in the Heimlich Maneuver, a type of first aid for choking. In nursing facilities it is particularly appropriate that all personnel coming in contact with residents at mealtime be properly trained in this first-aid procedure.

SECURITY

Loss through **theft** in dietary service is a common problem. It may range from consuming a carton of milk when no one else is present to a plan for regularly removing food from the facility. Costs of loss by theft may range up to five percent, which a facility can ill afford. (Connell)

A carefully designed security program that covers purchasing, receiving, storage, and issuing helps to reduce theft. Some facilities find it effective to have a dressing area where dietary-service personnel can leave their coats, sweaters, and purses in lockers. They must put on their uniforms before entering dietary service. They also ensure that no large bags are taken into the kitchen area or taken out. One facility allows no one to go out to employee cars without permission, which enables someone to observe whether anything is taken to their cars. Every employee needs to be trained in security procedures and to be fully aware of the consequences of theft. Both the dietary manager and the administrator's monitoring of security is important. Perhaps no action is more effective than the administrator being seen regularly checking the security systems, asking questions, and showing a personal interest in what goes on in dietary service. His visibility is a big factor in ensuring proper controls.

GLOSSARY

ADA The American Dietetic Association which approves various dietetic training programs and registers qualified dietitians.

Administrative orientation Knowledge and skill in planning, organizing, staffing, and other management functions used in organizations.

Assistive devices Special silverware, plates, plate guards, and other devices to assist the handicapped when eating unassisted.

CCP Critical Control Point in keeping foods safe.

CDM Certified Dietary Manager is a person who has undergone required training and passed a competency and sanitation and safety examination given by the Dietary Manager Association.

Consulting methodology A method of problem solving in which a specialist assists another person in developing workable solutions and plans.

Dietary Managers Association Organization of dietary managers that establishes professional standards.

Dietary service The department in a facility responsible for the production of meals, snacks and therapeutic diets; also, called food service.

Dietitian A person trained in dietetics and eligible for registration in the ADA or other certifying organization.

Food guide pyramid A figure showing the five food classes and basic amount of servings to provide proper nutrition and RDAs.

Food service management company An organization that specializes in food preparation and enters into a contract to administer the dietetic service of a facility.

Four basic foods The four foods required in a balanced diet—meats, vegetables, milk, and fruits.

GMP Good Manufacturing Practice is a program providing guidelines to ensure food-borne pathogens are not involved in any aspect of food processing.

HAACP Hazard Analysis Critical Control Point is a program using seven principles to discover hazards and set up controls for insuring foods are safe from foodborne disease organisms.

Heimlich Maneuver A type of first aid administered to individuals who are choking.

Menu A selection of the foods contained in a meal.

Raw food cost The cost of foods at the time of purchase before costs of storage, preparation, and serving are considered.

RDA The recommended dietary allowances of the amount of vitamins, minerals, and other elements needed per day to maintain health.

Special eating equipment Self-help devices as specially designed forks, spoons, sectional plates, and other utensils to be used by a resident who has difficulty feeding himself.

Stool examination A laboratory examination of a food handlers' feces to determine if he is infected with or carrier of a communicable disease.

Therapeutic diets A special diet prescribed by a physician, and at least approved by a qualified dietitian, and designed to correct a patient's condition or to prevent further problems.

Tuberculin test A patch test administered to the skin to determine if a person may possibly have tuberculosis.

REFERENCES

Connell, Bert C., "Controlling Theft," in James C. Rose, editor, *Handbook for Health Care Food Service Management*, Rockville, MD: Aspen Systems Corporation 1984.

Dorner, Becky, "Dignity in Dining: Feeding Techniques for Elderly and Disabled Clients," *Dietary Manager,* Vol. 5, No. 3, Itasca, IL: Dietary Managers Association, 1996.

Dougherty, Darlene A., "Options in Developmental Organization," in James C. Rose, editor, *Handbook for Health Care Food Service Management*, Rockville, MD: Aspen Systems Corporation, 1984.

Gilbert, Robert A., "Menu Planning," in James C. Rose, editor, *Handbook for Health Care Food Service Management*, Rockville, MD: Aspen Systems Corporation, 1984.

Hisel, Eileen, "The Resident as Customer: Assuring Quality in Food Service," *Dietary Manager*, Vol. 5, No. 4, Itasca, IL: Dietary Managers Association, 1995.

Puckett, Ruby P., "Playing it Safe," *Contemporary Administrator for Long Term Care, 7:6,* June 1984.

Sambataro, Paul, "HAACP Implementation–An Effective Way to Ensure Safety," *Dietary Manager,* Vol. 4, No. 6, Itasca, IL: Dietary Managers Association, 1995.

Smathers, Jamie, "Food Allergies: What You Should Know," *Dietary Manager,* Vol. 5, No. 2, Itasca, IL: Dietary Managers Association, 1996.

State Operations Manual, Provider Certification, Revisions One and Two, U.S. Department of Health and Human Services, Springfield, VA: National Technical Information Service, U.S. Department of Commerce, 1998.

Title 42 Code of Federal Regulations, Public Health, Part 400 to 429, Washington: U.S. Government Printing Office, 1995.

Title 42 Code of Federal Regulations, Public Health, Part 430 to end, Washington: U.S. Government Printing Office, 1996.

Zaccarelli, Herman E., "Cost Effective Contract Food Service: The How-To Guide for Health Care Administrator and Food Service Director," in James C. Rose, editor, *Handbook for Health Care Food Service Management*, Rockville, MD: Aspen Systems Corporation, 1984.

CHAPTER 10

LEGAL MANAGEMENT

LEGAL MANAGEMENT

CHOOSING AND USING LEGAL COUNSEL

Administrators must understand certain basic legal concepts. It is wise to have an attorney on retainer or at least establish a working relationship with an attorney who has an understanding of long-term care. Some attorneys have special knowledge of nursing facilities and Medicaid and Medicare laws and regulations. Usually it is wise to use an attorney with this background since he will not need to research every problem as an attorney in general practice would. His special knowledge can save time, money and trouble.

Early in their practice administrators should confer with an attorney for help in anticipating trouble areas. Attorneys can also alert administrators to possible occurrences in their practice that should be discussed at the first indication of a problem. When a complaint is filed against an administrator or the nursing facility, the administrator should confer with his attorney immediately. He should never try to dismiss the complaint as trivial or unimportant. It is always advisable to seek an attorney's advice on the proper course of action.

BASIC LEGAL TERMS

In the course of practice an administrator will need to know a number of basic legal terms. Most of the following are taken from *Black's Law Dictionary*, Sixth Edition. This publication is no ordinary dictionary. It cites cases, explains conditions under which terms apply, identifies origins of terms, and discusses their applicability. The definitions given are not all-inclusive. Legal terms may have meaning according to the context in which they are used. Unless otherwise noted, all definitions are from Black.

Abuse The term abuse as used in nursing facilities generally refers to resident abuse, and it is doubtful anyone understands exactly what is meant. Resident abuse statutes are very unclear and they create a situation in which almost the slightest turning aside from total and complete performance of one's duty could be considered resident abuse. (Johnson) Certainly, striking a resident, pulling someone's hair, shoving, or any other willful harm is abuse. But what about serving food or coffee that could cause harm to a resident? Is operating a facility with deficiencies abuse? The whole issue of abuse is unclear and confusing.

In one section of OBRA, regulations define abuse as conduct amounting to at least **simple assault** under the criminal laws of the state. It provides that allegations of emotional and verbal abuse are not to be reported to any law enforcement authority unless state law requires it.

Another OBRA section provides that residents must be free of verbal, sexual, physical, and mental abuse, as well as corporal punishment and involuntary seclusion. [42CFR483.13(b)] Residents must not be subject to abuse by anyone, including facility staff, other residents, consultants, volunteers, staff of other agencies serving the resident, family members, legal guardians, friends, or others. This section of OBRA defines **abuse** as the willful infliction of injury, unreasonable confinement, intimidation; or punishment with resultant physical harm, pain or mental anguish; or deprivation by an individual, including a caretaker, of goods or services that are necessary to attain or maintain physical, mental, and psychological well-being.

Verbal abuse refers to any use of oral, written or gestured language that includes disparaging and derogatory terms to residents or their families; or within their hearing distance, to describe residents, regardless of their age, ability to comprehend, or disability. Although this definition is clear and concise there are instances when an accusation of abuse would not stand up in court or when the court would not entertain action against the accused.

Example: Ms. Day, an 81 year old white lady, was irritable and crotchety most of the time. She ordered black nurse aides out of her room on occasion and frequently made derogatory remarks to them. Two nurse aides working in Ms. Day's area referred to her as "that old biddy in 171". They did not do so with hostility or anger, but more as pet name the two used when talking to each other. A family member overheard the two aides refer to "the old biddy" and reported it to the administrator. He counseled with the two aides who admitted use of the term, but denied any intent to be abusive. The administrator called the State Complaints Office who referred them to the Medicaid Fraud Control Agency. The Agency attorney advised that if this were the only evidence of abuse, it should be handled as a personnel matter. He was sure the agency could not interest the courts in prosecuting anyone for use of the term "old biddy."

Sexual abuse includes, but is not limited to, sexual harassment, sexual coercion, or sexual assault. It does not include sexual contact by mutual consent, even if it involves an employee and a resident.

Example: An administrator filed a complaint with the state Medicaid agency when two male attendants had sex with a female resident during the weekend. It was referred to Medicaid Fraud Control which investigated. The agency advised the administrator they found no evidence of abuse as the act was by mutual consent, and no evidence the orderlies had neglected the lady's needs, and no evidence they had misused her property. The agency suggested the incident be handled as a personnel matter by the facility.

Physical abuse includes hitting, slapping, pinching, kicking, and other physical hurt. It also includes controlling behavior through corporal punishment. Even though there is evidence of physical abuse such as bruises, redness, swelling, or scratches, these cannot always be established unless there are eyewitnesses.

Example: Shortly after the 3:00 p.m. shift came on duty the nurse noticed that Mrs. Williams had red marks on her throat. By 5:30 p.m. these marks were turning blue. They appeared to be finger marks. When asked how the marks occurred Mrs. Williams said the aide had choked her. Staff immediately investigated and reported it to the State Medicaid complaints program. Their investigation revealed Mrs. Williams often abused herself by scratching, pinching or hitting herself around the face. She often yelled, "Stop! Stop!" when no one was in her room. Also, she was taking a medication that caused easy bruising and skin discoloration. The accused aide had no history of abuse and was a valued employee. Medicaid Fraud declared the case nonprosecutable as they found no conclusive evidence of employee abuse.

Mental abuse includes, but is not limited to humiliation, harassment, threats of punishment or deprivation. The administrator must be very alert to this type abuse as it can easily go undetected. Mild threats as, "If you don't take your medicine, you won't get any supper," are often heard in some homes. However mild the threat, it can be classed as abuse.

Involuntary seclusion means separation of a resident from other residents or from his or her room against the resident's will, or will of the legal representative. Emergency and short term separation is not considered involuntary seclusion. It may be permitted if it is used for a limited period of time as a therapeutic intervention to reduce agitation until a plan of care can be developed to meet the resident's need. Any type of seclusion must be carefully documented and must be fully justified to protect the resident or others.

Surveyors will review any complaints in their presurvey planning so they can focus their on-site review on actual incidents and on predisposing factors to abuse or neglect. They ask residents if they are aware of any abuse or neglect, if anything happened how soon would a staff member give help, how does staff react to people who often ask for help, and how does staff react when a resident complains of pain. They question residents about loss of personal items and how staff reacts when they report an item missing. They especially examine incidents of a resident frequently separated from others on a temporary basis. They note what symptoms or behavior prompted the separation, and what caused these symptoms.

State laws may differ in their definitions of abuse, as well as enforcement by the State Medicaid Fraud Control Agency. Administrators should determine definitions and gain understanding of both laws and practices in their states.

Affidavit A written or printed declaration or statement of facts, made voluntarily, and confirmed by the oath or affirmation of the party making it, taken before an officer having authority to administer such oath.

Agent A person authorized by another to act in his behalf; one entrusted with another's business. A responsible party is an agent for a resident. The administrator is an agent of his governing body.

Aggrieved A person who has suffered loss or injury, such as a substantial grievance, a denial of personal or property right, or the imposition of a burden or obligation upon a person. A resident or a family member filing a complaint is an example.

Assault An intentional, unlawful **offer** of corporal injury to another by force, or force unlawfully directed toward another person under such circumstances that create well-founded fear of imminent peril, coupled with apparent present ability to carry out the attempt, if not prevented. Intention to harm is the essence of assault, but it includes malevolence and recklessness. If a member of the staff intentionally threatens a resident, whether in anger or not, it may be considered assault. It also includes reckless operation of machinery and almost any act that disregards human life and safety. Assault is a form of verbal abuse under many state laws.

Assignment Transfer of rights of property, real or personal, to another person.

Battery Any unlawful beating, or wrongful physical violence or constraint, inflicted on a human being without his consent. The offer, or threat, to use force to injure another is **assault**; the use of it is **battery,** which always includes assault. It is important to remember that unlawful touching of another person is included. If an employee only slightly touches a resident, without his consent, in a rude, insolent, or angry manner, it could be classed as battery.

Civil Action A personal action which is instituted to compel payment or the doing of some other thing which is purely civil. This includes court actions in which a person or organization is sued for a specific sum of money. It is also referred to as **tort** action.

Claimant One who claims or asserts a right, demand, or claim. There are other, more restricted definitions, but the definition cited seems most applicable to nursing facilities.

Code of Federal Regulations (CFR) The CFR is a publication containing codified laws and all rules and regulations of federal agencies responsible for monitoring the law. There are many parts of the Code. *Title 42 Public Health, Part 400 to 429* and *Part 430 to end* concern Medicare and Medicaid. From these parts of the Code, the U.S. Department of Health and Human Services (DHHS) develops its federal guidelines which govern operations of nursing facilities.

Competent Duly qualified, legally fit, having sufficient ability and authority, and the mental capacity to understand the nature of his act. Determining competence is a part of the **interdiction** process.

Complainant One who applies to the courts for legal redress. Also, one who instigates prosecution or who prefers accusation against a suspected person. A resident or family member filing charges against a facility and/or staff is an example.

Contract A promissory agreement between two or more persons that creates, modifies, or destroys a legal relation. The agreement is to do or not to do a particular thing. In essence resident and family enter into a contract with the facility. They agree to pay a certain fee and to abide by certain policies in exchange for certain services.

Criminal charge An accusation of crime, formulated in a written complaint, information, or indictment, and taking shape in a prosecution. This type action is instituted to punish for an infraction of the criminal laws. A resident, family member, Medicaid Fraud Control, or other entity may accuse a facility of criminal action, which means the action was contrary to law.

Curator As used in civil law, a person who is appointed to take care of anything for another, a **guardian**. One appointed by the court to take care of the estate of a person regarded by the law as **incompetent** to administer it for himself. The definition of curator may vary to some extent from state to state. Administrators often must work with the curator of a resident.

Decedent A deceased person, especially one who died recently. The word denotes a person who **is dying,** but it is used in law to signify any deceased person, testate or intestate.

Deed A written, signed conveyance of title to real estate transferred from one person to another.

Defamation The offense of injuring a person's character, fame, or reputation by false and malicious statements. The term seems to include both libel and slander.

Deposition The testimony of a witness taken upon interrogatories (questioning), but not in open court, and reduced to writing and duly authenticated, and intended to be used in a court trial. It is sometimes used as synonymous with **affidavit** or **oath,** but its technical meaning does not include such terms. Depositions are frequently used when the witness cannot be present at the trial due to health or other reasons. Many courts now video tape depositions so a jury can view the person as he gives a deposition.

Endorsement (or indorsement) The act of a holder of a bill, note, check or other negotiable instrument, assigning or transferring ownership to another by signing his name upon the back of the negotiable instrument.

Executor A person appointed by a **testator** (one who dies leaving a will) to carry out the directions and requests in his will, and to dispose of the property according to his testamentary provisions after his death.

Executrix A woman appointed by will to execute such will and testament.

Felony A crime of a graver or more atrocious nature than those designated as misdemeanors. Felony crimes have many classifications. For example, in some states felony thefts mean the illegal taking of something valued at $500 or more. A felony usually is punishable by imprisonment in a penitentiary and/or fine.

Fraud The act of deceiving, tricking, or using other means to gain an unfair or dishonest advantage over another person, thereby cheating him of a legal right or out of something valuable. A typical act of fraud is a facility billing for a service not actually provided.

Ground of action The basis of a suit, the foundation or fundamental state of facts on which an action rests; the real object of the plaintiff in bringing suit. This is sometimes expressed as grounds for action referring to a real basis for filing a charge.

Incompetency Lack of ability, legal qualification, or fitness to discharge the required duty. When a person is declared legally incompetent, a curator or guardian is appointed. A resident who is comatose, mentally ill, or mentally retarded may be declared incompetent during an interdiction. Generally, a person is considered incompetent when they are unable to understand or comprehend the nature and effect of an agreement, a contract, or an act in which they are involved. (Mann and Roberts)

Informed Consent **Consent** means a voluntary agreement by a person of sufficient mentality to make an intelligent choice to do something proposed by someone else. **Informed consent** means that one consents with full knowledge of the activity he agrees to participate in and with full understanding of possible consequences, both positive and negative. **Informed consent** is a basic principle by which physicians practice. It is required when residents participate in any type of drug study or other form of research. It can only occur when the person is competent.

Interdiction In civil law an interdiction is a judicial decree by which a person is deprived of the exercise of his civil rights. (Black) In nursing facilities it is sometimes used when a resident is not physically or mentally capable of managing his affairs, yet important decisions relative to self or property must be made. The court may declare the person incompetent and appoint a **guardian, curator,** or **conservator** to act for him. Interdictions are complex as they are governed largely by state laws and these vary from state to state. Legal definitions of guardianship often are vague. They are sometimes limited and/or temporary. (Johnson)

An interdiction is different from the authority to act for another through power of attorney, since the latter is granted voluntarily. In an interdiction a person may not be capable of agreeing to the action taken, or even aware it is being taken.

When an administrator is confronted with the situation in which a resident is incapable of acting for himself, he should enlist the assistance of the facility's attorney.

Intestate Without making a will. A person is said to die intestate when he dies without making a will, or dies without leaving anything to testify what his wishes were regarding the disposal of property after his death.

Law That which is established by a governmental body. It must be obeyed and followed by all citizens, subject to legal consequences imposed by a court which decides all questions of law.

Liable Bound or obliged in law or equity, responsible, chargeable, answerable, compellable, to make satisfaction, compensation, or restitution. The nursing facility may be liable in case of an accident, an employee's mistake, or negligence.

Legal guardian A commonly used term for curator. A person appointed by the court to take care of anything for another person as a child of minor age, a spendthrift, or a mentally incompetent.

Libel A method of defamation expressed by print, writing, pictures, or signs. In a most general sense, any publication that is injurious to the reputation of another. Libel includes anything in written or printed form against the character of a person which affects his reputation. Libelous statements frequently lead to civil suits.

Malpractice Bad, wrong, or injudicious treatment of a resident, professionally and in respect to the particular disease or injury, resulting in injury, unnecessary suffering, or death to the person, and proceeding from ignorance, carelessness, want of proper professional skill, disregard of established rules or principles, neglect, or a malicious or criminal intent. (Black) Administrators should be especially familiar with this term and teach their staff the meaning and implications of malpractice. It is mandatory that resident care procedures be developed and taught to the staff and their performance monitored. **Ignorance** of what should be done in a given situation can be malpractice, and the facility may be liable.

In today's suit-minded culture, one must be careful to ensure that resident needs are met by a staff of well-trained, knowledgeable personnel. A malpractice suit seeks to establish that the facility and/or the staff are at fault. It is then that compensatory damages may be sought.

Misdemeanor Offenses lower than felonies and generally those punishable by fine or imprisonment other than in a penitentiary. (Black) They may include libel, conspiracies, and attempts and solicitations instigated to commit felonies. **Resident abuse, neglect** and **misappropriation of property** are often classed as misdemeanors. However, serious acts involving any of these offenses may be classified as a felony.

Neglect Neglect may mean to omit or fail to do what one should or is required to do. It may mean the absence of care or attention in what one does. It may also mean refusal or unwillingness to do one's duty. The term is used in some aspects of the law as synonymous with **negligence.** (Black) OBRA regulations define neglect as "the intentional or grossly negligent acts or omissions of an employee that either have, or might reasonably be expected to cause the death of, or serious bodily injury to, a resident. It shall also mean the deliberate refusal of an employee to carry out any assigned duties relating to the care of a resident." As in the case of abuse, the wisest course of action for the administrator is to determine the definition of neglect in his state law and as used by the state's Medicaid Fraud Control Agency.

Negligence Doing something or failing to do something that a person in a given situation should or should not do; failing to carry out a necessary act or exercising proper caution in resident care. There are many types of negligence for which a person is legally liable. It can be readily seen that neglect and negligence may mean the same thing under the law.

Negotiation The deliberation or discussion of terms of a proposed agreement, or the act of settling or arranging terms of a business transaction. Negotiations may take place in settling any dispute, usually involving **give and take** by each party. Administrators may negotiate wages or a union contract.

Nonprosecutable Complaints wherein Medicaid Fraud Control feels there is inadequate evidence to convict, such as one person's word against another's and circumstantial evidence only. This is often the case when it is a nurse aide's word against that of a resident and there are no witnesses.

Notary public A public officer whose function is to administer oaths, to attest and certify by his hand and official seal, certain classes of documents, in order to give them credibility and authenticity in foreign jurisdiction. Notaries may have other duties as defined by the state in which they are licensed. In some states a notary needs only to sign a document; he is not required to affix his seal to the notarized document. If the document is to be used out of state, he must affix his official seal. Administrators need a notary on many occasions, but usually an attorney is a notary and can serve this function.

Power of attorney An instrument authorizing another person to act as one's agent or attorney. This power may be given to someone other than an attorney-at-law. It may be a family member or a friend. It is conveyed by a written statement which may be called *Letter of Attorney* or *Power of Attorney*. It conveys the right to another to speak, sign, or otherwise act in a person's stead.

Power of attorney may be **special** if the agent's authority is limited to particular acts, as signing one act of sale, paying certain bills, or buying a certain item. **General and durable power** authorizes the agent to act generally in behalf of the principal. However, questions often arise, and must be clarified by the court, as to whether the agent may make decisions regarding health matters, such as use of surgery and certain treatments, participation in research, and use of life-support systems. Administrators may often work with persons who have power of attorney for some of their residents.

Privileged communication A communication made to an attorney, a counsel, or other professional in confidence, and which he is not permitted to divulge. In most states it includes privileged relations as husband/wife, physician/patient, nurse/patient, and any other professionals whose licensing law provides for privileged communication. The courts may not require such communication to be revealed except when alleged child abuse or certain other conditions exist. Generally, privileged communication does not exist between administrator and resident, family, or staff. It is not included in the administrator's licensing law.

Respondeat superior Let the master answer, which means the master (nursing facility) is liable in certain cases for wrongful acts of its employees, provided the wrongful acts occurred in the course of employment. This is a very important legal concept for administrators to understand. Because of this provision administrators should never allow an untrained or inadequately trained person to perform duties.

Seizure To take possession of forcibly, to grasp, to snatch, or to put in possession. Administrators may be faced with seizure of certain records, especially when it involves a potentially serious Medicaid or Medicare complaint. An officer of the law may appear without notice and demand certain records. He has the right to take them provided he has a court-approved warrant. Administrators should confer with their attorneys beforehand to determine if they have the right to make and keep copies of any records seized. In the case of resident records they may be needed long before they are returned. Regardless of the reason which precipitates the removal of records from the facility, a copy should be made, if it is at all permissible.

Courts often accept a certified copy of a resident's record rather than requiring the original record. Administrators should always determine whether the court will accept a copy so the resident's original record remains in the facility.

Slander Speaking base and defamatory words tending to prejudice another in his reputation, office, trade, business, or means of livelihood. Such words must be spoken in the presence of someone other than the person slandered and that person must understand the language which is spoken. Slander may be grounds for civil suit. Staff should be trained in the importance of respecting others and never uttering defamatory statements. Actually, this could be declared a form of verbal abuse.

Statute of limitations A statute prescribing limitations to the right of action, declaring that no suit shall be filed on a course of action unless it is brought within a specific period of time after the action occurred. Statutes apply to both civil and criminal matters. Limitations vary according to federal and state laws and to the type of action under consideration.

It is imperative that administrators confer with an attorney on all matters that may lead to civil or criminal action. The attorney can advise on the statute of limitations of the particular action under consideration. This is important in terms of action taken by employees as well as residents. The statute of limitations is the guideline for length of time to keep resident records, payroll records, and others.

Subrogation Substituting one person for another with reference to a lawful claim, demand, or right. The person substituted succeeds to the rights of the other in relation to the debt or claim and its rights, remedies, or securities. There must by an **assignment** or **agreement** for subrogation. This action cannot apply to a volunteer who pays a debt for someone else.

An example of subrogation may be found in an insurance claim against a nursing facility. The facility's insurer may ask for an assignment of subrogation which gives the company the right to decide how the claim will be settled within bounds of the law. The insurer could contest the claim in court, settle it out of court, or declare it void which would require the claimant to file suit if he is not satisfied. In many cases the facility may not want to assign subrogation as the insurance company may be willing to settle out of court when the facility is confident they can win the case.

Subpoena A process to cause a witness to appear and give testimony before a court or magistrate therein named at a time therein mentioned to testify for the party named under a penalty therein named. Subpoena literally means **under penalty.** To ignore a subpoena is to be in contempt of court.

Subpoena duces tecum A process by which the court commands a witness, who has in his possession or control some document or paper that is pertinent to the issues of a pending controversy, to produce it at the trial. This is used to require administrators to present such documents as a resident's record, the facility financial records, or a written defamatory statement. Upon receiving this type of subpoena, make a copy of the documents before presenting them to the courts. They may be needed before the court releases them, especially in the case of resident records.

Testament A disposition of **personal** property to take place after the owner's death, according to his desire and direction. **Will, testament,** and **will and testament** are commonly used as meaning the same. Strictly speaking, testament refers only to **personal property** and does not include real estate. Today, testament is seldom used except in the heading of a person's "last will and testament."

Testator One who makes or has made a will; one who dies leaving a will. Testate means the same as testator. A person who dies leaving a will is said to have died **testate.**

Theft The fraudulent taking of personal property belonging to another, from his possession, or from possession of some person holding the same for him, without his consent, with intent to deprive the owner of the value of the same, and to appropriate it to the use or benefit of the person taking. Theft is a popular name for larceny.

Misappropriation of property is the term OBRA uses to mean theft of a resident's property. OBRA specifies the term does not include negligent handling of property. Apparently, this means that a staff member in a facility that breaks, damages, or misplaces a resident's property is not guilty of misappropriation. Again, the wisest action by the administrator is to determine the definition of misappropriation included in his state's law and used by the state's Medicaid Fraud Control Agency.

Tort A private or civil wrong or injury. A wrong independent of contract. This is used frequently and may need to be clarified with an attorney. There are many types of torts — personal, property, maritime, willful, etc. The word itself means twisted or wrested aside. In order to be a **tort action,** there must be a legal duty from defendant to plaintiff, a breach of this duty, and damage as proximate result. A legal wrong committed in a nursing facility could be a tort.

Trespass Performing an unlawful act or a lawful act in an unlawful manner which results in injury to another person or his property. It may involve force or violence or be in the nature of a tort.

Warrant This term has many different meanings, too numerous to include here. The definition most often needed by an administrator is: A writ or precept from a competent authority in pursuance of the law, directing the doing of an act, and addressed to an officer or person competent to do the act, and affording him protection from damage, if he does it. Examples are an arrest warrant that requires an officer of the law to arrest a person and bring him before a magistrate or court, and a search warrant directing an officer of the law to search a specific place for a specific item(s).

Warranty This term also has many meanings, according to the context in which it is used. The definition most applicable to nursing facilities is: A promise that a proposition of fact is true. The warrantor (the person who makes a warranty) enters into a legal agreement that expresses or implies assurance or promise that certain action will be taken. Warranties are especially important in purchasing equipment. They should be carefully examined and the warrantor questioned about any unclear statements. Fine print should be read to ensure understanding of what the seller guarantees to do in a given period of time.

ESTATE PLANNING AND WILLS

Estate means everything a person owns or has a right to or interest in — both real estate and personal properties.

Estate planning refers to developing plans for the disposition of one's real and personal properties after his death. One can take advantage of all federal and state laws governing succession of estates. Also, one can maintain some degree of control as far as distribution of his estate, especially if he sets up a trust(s). Many banks have estate or trust departments which help people plan without charge. Some attorneys specialize in estate planning.

A **will** is a legal expression or declaration of a person's mind or wishes regarding the disposition of his property to be performed or to take effect after his death.

A **holographic will** is one entirely written, dated, and signed by the hand of the testator himself. It may not require witnesses or signing under oath. Statutes differ from state to state, but most states honor this type of will.

A **nuncupative will** is an oral will declared and indicated by the testator before witnesses and afterward reduced to writing. In nursing facilities this may occur when a resident who has no written will is faced with death. When the resident's desire is made known to the facility, staff should know how to proceed in assisting the resident in carrying out his wishes.

The **living will or advance medical directive** is relatively new and is of special interest to administrators. It is a legal document that specifies a person may instruct family and professional staff that he is not to be kept alive by mechanical or heroic means. When there is no quality to life, the living will may specify that life support systems are not to be used to keep a person alive. It may also specify that in the event of heart failure, stroke, etc., no cardiopulmonary resuscitation (CPR) is to be used. This type case would be listed as **no code,** meaning customary emergency treatment measurers will not be used. (Refer to notice of legal rights in this chapter).

Many states have enacted laws providing for the living will, but its legal status and meaning are unclear. Some states have recently revised their laws in an effort to clarify them. Much controversy surrounds a person's right to die, or to refuse treatment. Federal law now requires health-care facilities to inform patients/residents of state laws concerning their right to make decisions concerning his or her care. The **value** of the living will is that professionals are not required to make certain decisions when a resident is terminally ill.

There are many other types of wills such as **ambulatory, joint, mutual,** and **nonintervention.** These generally require assistance of an attorney as each must meet specific provisions of the law.

A **probated will** means its validity has been proven in probate court. The court gives the executor a copy of the will under seal of the probate court and a certificate showing the will has been proved. This can be an expensive process in which court cost must be paid and a sizeable bond posted by the executor. One of the values of the holographic will is that bond may be avoided and costs significantly reduced.

If the opportunity arises, administrators may want to ask the family if a resident has a will. They should never probe or pry into family business or personal affairs. Simply raise the question. The administrator may indicate that he and his spouse have wills and cite the advantages of a will for every adult person. It makes settlement of their estate much simpler and less expensive. In case of large families or numerous claimants to the deceased's property, settlement can become very difficult. Perhaps nothing can alienate family members quicker than the division of the properties of the deceased.

Discussing a will is often upsetting to people. Usually these feelings are dispelled by the administrator's relaxed attitude about his own will and the wisdom of having a will.

ARBITRATION

Arbitration is submission of a disputed matter for determination by an unofficial person or persons (arbiters) selected in a manner provided by law or agreement. The two parties agree in advance to abide by the arbiter's decision or judgment rendered by a court.

Arbitration is often used in disputes between organized labor and management when they cannot agree on a certain matter. It may be compulsory, if one party's consent is enforced by statutory provisions, or it may be voluntary, if by mutual consent. If ever involved in arbitration, the administrator should have his attorney present to represent him.

POTENTIAL PROBLEM AREAS

Administrators must be aware of potential legal problems and plan for their prevention when possible. It is unwise to wait for an occurrence which can result in civil or criminal action and then seek legal counsel.

Medicaid fraud in financial management is an area of obvious concern. Billing for materials not used and for services not rendered has been practiced. Several administrators have been fined and/or sent to prison for billing Medicaid for hours not worked by staff members.

Example: the DON, being short of nursing staff, included nurse hours on the time sheets that were not worked. The administrator was held liable by the courts since he made no effort to verify hours before signing claims for reimbursement. He simply accepted the DON's word. He was fined and spent time in federal prison.

Example: An administrator billed for an additional day after residents were discharged. He felt no one would ever know, but a disgruntled employee reported him. The administrator's license was revoked, and the courts fined him and placed him on probation. HCFA banned the administrator from participation in Medicare or Medicaid for five years.

It is extremely important for administrators to verify the accuracy of Medicaid/Medicare claims. One can rest assured that sooner or later there will be an audit and any discrepancies identified. Medicaid Fraud Control prosecutes the case and in most instances are successful in attaining conviction.

Resident funds is another danger area. The administrator must ensure that there is proper accounting for all residents' personal funds. They may never be intermingled with facility funds or used for anything not specifically approved by the resident. A number of administrators have been fined, placed on probation, and their licenses revoked for improper handling of resident funds.

Example: An administrator wrote a personal check on the resident fund for $9,000. He cashed the check. When Medicaid Fraud Control started investigating he replaced the funds with interest. The administrator claimed he borrowed the money and used it for the facility with interest to be paid. Medicaid Fraud Control did not feel they could obtain conviction as the funds were returned with interest. The administrator's Board of Examiners revoked his license for co-mingling resident and facility funds.

Resident valuables Facilities may be liable when there is neglect in handling resident valuables. It is not sufficient to have a policy against bringing expensive watches, necklaces, bracelets, rings, and other valuables to the facility. There must be clearly stated procedures for all to follow in the handling of valuables. Staff must be trained and periodically reviewed in these procedures. Supervisors must monitor them regularly. Careful documentation is necessary or the facility may be held liable.

Wanderers Residents who wander are a potential legal problem. In a number of cases residents have left a facility unnoticed and have been injured, killed, or died from exposure.

Example: A female resident walked away from a nursing home in a small town. A concerted search by law enforcement with bloodhounds was fruitless. Eight months later her skeleton was found in a dense wooded area one mile from the facility. The family sued for negligence. The court ruled in the facility's favor, but legal expenses were significant.

Wanderers in a facility require very careful planning for monitoring their activities. It is important to include family in both the planning and the monitoring of the resident. This sends a strong message that the facility is aware of the problem and it is making extra effort to provide proper care.

Abuse, neglect, and misappropriation of property As noted earlier in this chapter, OBRA regulations concentrate on preventing abuse, neglect, and misappropriation of resident property by staff. It focuses on nurse aides, requiring them to be properly trained and certified by the state. The state maintains a Certified Nurse Aide Registry that records any abuse, neglect, or misappropriation of property by an aide. The administrator is responsible for policies and procedures that clearly define the offenses and what action is to be taken. He must ensure that aides are properly trained and that all violations of procedures are reported to the proper state authority. In some states an administrator may lose his license for failure to report these violations. (Johnson)

From experience to date, it appears that many states will deal with hundreds of offenses. The purpose of OBRA's program is to reduce these offenses by prohibiting guilty individuals being employed by nursing facilities. Ultimately and ideally, in the near future such offenses will be eradicated completely or at least held to minimum.

As a means of ensuring that this goal is reached, OBRA forbids the employment by a nursing facility of **any person** guilty of any of these offenses. This regulation is not limited to nurse aides; it clearly states **any person.** This requires a background criminal check on employees, but there is much controversy in this area. Many states have enacted legislation requiring background checks, but some provided no funds. As for new gun control laws requiring record checks, local law enforcement has refused to cooperate due to lack of staff and lack of funds. Some states with the required legislation have placed criminal background checks on hold until this practice can be financed. Other states have fully implemented background checks.

Resident health and safety Violations of federal or state regulations that immediately jeopardize the health and safety of residents is now of vital concern to the administrator and the facility because all states have implemented OBRA's proposed penalties. OBRA regulations authorize the state to remove the jeopardy and correct the deficiency by one or several actions. These include: (1) denial of payment for new admissions, (2) civil-money penalties assessed and collected, (3) appointment of temporary management, and (4) termination of a facility's participation under the state plan.

> **Example:** An older facility had trouble with its air-conditioning system and temperatures exceeded 100 degrees Fahrenheit in resident rooms during August. After a second citation the facility was fined $44,000 by the state Medicaid agency in a state that had enacted OBRA's proposed regulations.

There are many other violations for which a facility may be fined depending on state laws. These penalties are imposed by the state without going to court. The facility may ask for an administrative review, but if the decision is confirmed, the only recourse is to appeal to the courts. The likelihood of winning is minimal since it involves health and safety of residents. Health and safety precautions go beyond actions of the staff as discussed in Chapter 8 on Environmental Management.

The state may impose penalties for violations that do not directly involve health and safety. One facility failed to notify its state Medicaid agency of a change in DON's. Beginning the eleventh day after the new DON was appointed, a fine of $100 per day was imposed for a total of $4,400. One of the first actions a new administrator should take is to determine what sanctions his state may impose on his facility, and for what reasons.

Americans with Disabilities Act discussed in Chapter 6 can be a problem area. EEOC is interpreting provisions of this Act very broadly as discussed in Chapter 11.

Only a few of the potential problem areas have been mentioned. Administrators may find it helpful to participate in seminars on legal aspects of health-care management, and to secure a copy of a publication that identifies additional problem areas and recommends appropriate planning.

NOTICE OF LEGAL RIGHTS [42 CFR 483.10 (b) (7)]

OBRA requires the facility to furnish residents a written description on their legal rights including at least the following areas:

1. **Personal funds** The facility must provide a description of the manner for protecting personal funds. This is more fully discussed in Chapter 7 of this publication.

2. **Medicaid eligibility** Residents must be given a description of requirements and procedures for establishing eligibility for Medicaid. This includes the right to request an assessment which determines the extent of a couple's nonexempt resources at the time of institutionalization. Also, it includes information on

the community spouse's equitable share of resources which cannot be considered available for payment toward the cost of the institutionalized spouse's medical care in his or her process of spending down to Medicaid eligibility levels.

3. **Advocacy groups** Residents are to be informed of agencies and groups that they may contact to exercise their rights. Names, addresses, and telephone numbers of all pertinent state client advocacy groups **must** be posted. These include the state licensing office, state ombudsmen program, protection and advocacy network, and Medicaid fraud control unit. The network refers to Developmental Disabilities Assistance and Bill of Rights Act and the protection and advocacy for Mentally Ill Individuals Act.

4. **Filing complaints** The written description must include a statement that a resident may file a complaint with the state survey and certification agency concerning resident abuse, neglect, and misappropriation of resident property in the facility.

5. **Advance medical directives** The facility must have written policies and procedures in regard to advance medical directives. Residents must be educated regarding their right under state law to formulate an advance medical directive and the facility's policy regarding implementing such directive. The facility is not required to implement an advance medical directive if state law allows the provider to refuse on the basis of conscientious objection. Neither is it required to provide care that conflicts with an advance medical directive.

In addition to a facility providing information on advance medical directives, they are generally expected to provide forms if the resident wishes to formulate a directive. This directive is often referred to as a **living will.** It should be placed in the resident's record when signed, or documented in the record when the resident chooses not to formulate an advance medical directive. The facility may not discriminate against any resident which chooses not to formulate a directive. It must ensure that staff is educated in policies and procedures in this area and provide a community education program. This program must include (1) information on the rights under state law to formulate an advance directive, (2) the facility's policies and procedures on implementation of these rights, and (3) the limitations the facility has with respect to implementing this right on the basis of conscience.

Other Notices [42 CFR 483.10 (6) (8 and 9)] In addition to these legal notices the facility must also provide other notices to residents.

1. **Physician** The facility must inform each resident of the name, specialty, and method of contacting the physician responsible for his or her care. Most residents will already have this information, but the facility should not make this assumption. It should document verification that each resident has this information.

2. **Application for benefits** The facility **must** prominently display written information to both applicants for admission and residents on how to apply for and use Medicare and Medicaid benefits, and how to receive funds for previous payments covered by such benefits. In addition to posting or displaying, this information must be available to the individual in oral and written form.

Surveyors will request a copy of the written information that is provided residents. They do this at the entrance conference and review the document to determine if it addresses the specified requirements for these notices. Surveyors will determine whether regulations on advance medical directives are followed, whether staff, resident, and family are educated on facility policies and procedures in this area, and whether the facility conducts the proper community education program.

GLOSSARY

No glossary is included for this chapter since definitions are included in the chapter itself.

REFERENCES

Black, Henry Campbell, *Black's Law Dictionary, Sixth Edition*, St. Paul, MN: West Publishing Company, 1991.

Federal Unemployment Tax Act, Washington: U.S. Government Printing Office.

Johnson, Sandra H., *Long Term Care and the Law*, Owings Mill, MD: National Law Publishing Corporation, 1983.

Mann, Richard A. and Barry Roberts, *Smith and Roberson's Business Law, Eighth Edition*, New York: West Publishing Co., 1991.

Pozgar, George, *Legal Aspects of Health Care Administration, Fifth Edition*, Rockville, MD: Aspen Publications, 1993.

State Operations Manual, Provider Certification, Revision One and Two, U.S. Department of Health and Human Services, Springfield, VA: National Technical Information Service, U.S. Department of Commerce, 1998.

Title 42 Code of Federal Regulations, Public Health, Part 400 to 429, Washington: U.S. Government Printing Office, 1995.

Title 42 Code of Federal Regulations, Public Health, Part 430 to end, Washington: U.S. Government Printing Office, 1996.

CHAPTER 11

REGULATORY MANAGEMENT

REGULATORY MANAGEMENT

Public laws enacted by the U.S. Congress are the bases for federal guidelines. All laws are coded and are used by the monitoring federal agencies. Federal legislation in an area of services, products, or activities is given a title and published as a part of the Code of Federal Regulations (CFR). For example, *Title 42 Code of Federal Regulations, Public Health, Part 400 to 429 and 430 to end* contains the Medicare and Medicaid regulations. The U.S. Department of Health and Human Services (US DHHS) uses these in monitoring health-care facilities.

Roman numerals are used to identify the laws themselves, as Title XVIII for Medicare and Title XIX for Medicaid. These titles are part of the Social Security Act (SSA), as amended. Titles VI and VII are part of the Civil Rights Act, as amended.

Arabic numerals are used to identify a specific section of the Code of Federal Regulations. Examples are Title 42 CFR for Public Health, and Title 29 CFR for Occupational Safety and Health.

In summary, Roman numerals refer to laws (Acts of Congress), and Arabic numerals refer to the Code of Federal Regulations.

The US DHHS issues its interpretation of the meaning of the CFR. This serves as an interpretive guideline to the state monitoring agencies and to the facilities. In the past these guidelines were called *Conditions (Standards) of Participation and Interpretive Guidelines and Survey Procedures.* They were also referred to as *Federal Care Guidelines.* Until April 1992, states used the *Self-Instructional Manual for an Outcome Oriented Survey of Long-Term Care Facilities.* In the April 1992 State Operations Manual, Provider Certification was issued as Transmittal No. 250. Since that date, Transmittals No. 251 through 274 have been issued as supplements. Revisions one and two were issued in 1998. Every facility should have a copy of this manual and most of the supplements. Call HCFA to ensure which transmittals are necessary to form a complete set of guidelines because some later transmittals cancel out earlier transmittals. These new regulations are a part of the Omnibus Budget Reconciliation Act (OBRA) mentioned in earlier chapters of this publication.

In addition to the US DHHS, several other federal agencies issue regulations which affect nursing facilities. These include the Occupational Safety and Health Administration (OSHA) discussed in Chapter 8, the Equal Employment Opportunity Commission (EEOC) discussed in Chapter 6, the Drug Enforcement Administration (DEA) to be discussed in this Chapter and in Chapter 12, the Wage and Hour Division of the US Department of Labor discussed in Chapter 6, and the National Labor Relations Board (NLRB). Also included are the American National Standards Institute (ANSI) and the National Fire Protection Association (NFPA) discussed fully in Chapter 8. Some others are discussed in this Chapter. Individual states may establish stricter regulations than those in the federal guidelines. In this instance, the stricter regulation must be followed.

A part of the national licensing examination, distributed by the National Association of Boards of Examiners of Long Term Care Administrators, is based on these federal guidelines. The examination does not include state standards as they may differ from state to state, especially as they relate to Medicaid.

SOCIAL SECURITY ACT

Of the several federal programs established by acts of Congress affecting health care facilities and professional caregivers, Title XVIII and Title XIX of the Social Security Act, as amended, have greatest impact on nursing facilities. They outline procedures for the construction, licensing, certification, staffing, operation, and monitoring of nursing facilities. Both programs establish payment schedules for all health-care providers, although Medicaid rates vary from state to state.

1. **Title XVIII of the SSA** Medicare is the federal health-insurance program for the aged and disabled. To be **eligible** a person must be aged 65 or older, or handicapped, or have end-stage renal disease. Income is not a factor in determining eligibility, since it is a form of insurance. Anyone who paid Social Security is automatically eligible for Part A without cost. However, he must pay the Part B premium.

Nonpayers of Social Security Anyone aged 65 or older is eligible for Medicare whether or not they have paid Social Security during their working days. The nonpayer may subscribe to Medicare Part B and pay the regular monthly rate which changes in January each year. If the nonpayer subscribes to Part A, he is required to take Part B also. At this writing, Part A premium is $309 per month. Enrollment periods are three months prior to the 65th birthday and three months after the 65th birthday. If a person does not enroll during this period, he may enroll during January through March of any year. For this group, the Part A rate is $309 plus 10 per cent for 15 years. After that date they pay the regular Part A rate. Enrollment can be arranged through the local office of the Social Security Administration.

Administration of the Medicare program is by the Health Care Finance Administration (HCFA) which is part of DHHS. States participate by licensing facilities, doing certification surveys for HCFA, and monitoring hospitals, nursing facilities, and home-health agencies that provide services to Medicare patients.

Medicare Part A pays for the hospital, SNF, home health, and post-hospital rehabilitation services. Since it is insurance, Medicare specifies an amount to be paid to hospitals based on **diagnosis related groups** (DRG). Currently, there are 497 separate DRG categories. Hospitals are paid a specific amount for each category of illness no matter what diagnostic and treatment procedures are used or how long the patient stays.

There are limitations on the number of days that Medicare will pay a SNF, currently 100 days for a single spell of illness. Also there are certain deductibles and coinsurance amounts for which the patient is responsible. (42 CFR 409.20) This poses a problem to facilities since residents tend to believe they have up to 100 days without regard to their condition. When a resident attains maximum benefits of SNF care and is ready for discharge, he is no longer eligible. Also when a resident is not improving and is not expected to improve according to his plan of care, he is no longer eligible. In the latter instance he may still need skilled care, but he is now identified as needing a maintenance level of care which Medicare does not provide in the SNF. Residents and families often are upset by this. They have difficulty understanding why, if one still needs skilled care, one is no longer eligible under Medicare.

Medicare Part B pays for the supplementary medical insurance program that includes physician's services, home health, outpatient diagnostic and treatment services, and certain durable medical equipment and prosthetics. Prosthetics that may be paid for do not include hearing aids or batteries, dentures, and eyeglasses — except after cataract surgery. Part B includes physician's services while in a hospital or a SNF, or while an outpatient.

Both Parts A and B pay for home health, whereas neither pays for regular physical checkups, private duty nurses, or medications when not hospitalized. Considerable effort is now exerted to include outpatient prescription drugs, but this requires Congressional action.

Providers are institutions, agencies, and individuals who provide inpatient or outpatient health-care services to Medicare participants. Physicians, hospitals, SNF's, and home-health services are in this group.

Application by a SNF to participate in Medicare begins with **licensing** by the state licensing and certification agency. HCFA designates a fiscal intermediary for the facility. A **fiscal intermediary** is an insurance company providing hospital and health insurance. The fiscal intermediary has several duties:

a. Conduct a pre-certification survey of the SNF, supervised by auditors, and check the facility's record-keeping capabilities

b. Determine allowable costs and set an individual rate for each SNF

c. Process Medicare claims from the SNF and reimburse the facility, with no payments for SNF care being made to the patient or his family

In the meantime, the state licensing and survey agency has the SNF complete an application for **certification** and conducts a pre-certification survey. Results of the survey are directed to the appropriate DHHS regional office. If the facility meets all standards, HCFA certifies it as a provider.

Deductibles Both Part A and Part B have deductibles that change yearly. Part A's deductible applies to the first hospitalization during a given year. The patient pays this deductible to the hospital. For Part B charges, Medicare approves a certain amount. It pays eighty percent of the approved amount. The provider may bill the patient for the other twenty percent, or he may bill for the remainder of the original charge, i.e., the amount not approved by Medicare. The provider is required to file each patient's Medicare bill. The provider can accept payment or the check is sent directly to the patient, and the physician may bill the entire charges to the patient.

2. **Title XIX** The medical assistance program (MAP), is referred to as **Medicaid**. It provides medical assistance to low income persons aged 65 or over, blind, disabled, or members of families with dependent children. The program is jointly financed by federal and state governments. It is **administered** by the states. Within broad general federal regulations, each state decides eligibility, types and range of services, payment level for services, and administrative and operating procedures. (42 CFR 431)

Medicaid's major distinction from Medicare is that Medicaid is a form of public medical assistance based on financial need. Whereas Medicare is a type of health insurance available to eligible persons without regard to financial status, Medicaid requires that a "means test" be applied in determining financial eligibility. The **means test** is computed by local units of the state Medicaid agency. A nursing home applicant may have maximum income determined by the state with HCFA approval. If it does not exceed the maximum, Medicaid will pay the balance of a state approved daily rate over and above the applicant's income. A certain amount of personal income determined by the state is kept by the resident for personal needs. Additional resources include liquid assets - cash, CD's, and so on - up to an amount determined by the state with HCFA approval. Usually this is $2,000 or more, depending on the state's rule. Also, an applicant may possess a house and an automobile; however, the house may not be rented or lived in unless the tenant helped care for the applicant. Spousal allowances are a complex factor in the means text. Administrators should secure eligibility requirements from their state agency which includes spousal allowances.

Administration Currently the Medicaid program is administered by the state. It operates under federal and state laws and federal and state policies and procedures. The state develops its Medicaid program, and it is approved by HCFA. The state compiles a set of standards and issues a document, approved by HCFA, that serves as a guideline for nursing facilities.

Nursing facilities with Medicare beds follow the same standards as those with Medicaid beds only. State surveyors monitor both types of facilities, although the states have nothing to do with Medicare funding and payments.

Funding Medicare funds are provided by the federal and state governments using a formula established by HCFA. The poorest states provide fewer funds than the states with higher per capita incomes. For instance, a poorer state may provide 30 percent of funds and the federal government 70 percent. A wealthier state may abide by a funds ratio of 40 percent state and 60 percent federal. These are essentially considered grants to the states (42 CFR 430.30).

Audits are regularly compiled by HCFA to determine if programs are operated in a cost-efficient manner and funds are properly expended.

Payments may be withheld by HCFA after giving a state reasonable notice and an opportunity for a hearing when the plan no longer complies with provisions of the Act. The federal government may disallow certain claims or any portion of a claim for federal financial participation (FFP). When claims are paid by HCFA and later found not to be in compliance, it may also require repayment. Under certain conditions this may be done on an installment basis.

Services may vary widely from state to state. They include inpatient and outpatient hospital care, laboratory and X-ray, SNF and NF, home health, private-duty nursing, dental, physical and occupational therapy, prescribed generic drugs, and others. Refer to 42 CFR 440.1 through 440.270 for details on all services provided.

STATE ORGANIZATION

Single state agency (42 CFR 431.10) Title XIX requires states to designate a single state agency for the Medicaid program. A state plan must be developed for the administration or supervision of the entire Medicaid program including institutional care, Medical assistance, Aid to Families with Dependent Children, and others. A **state plan** is a comprehensive written statement to HCFA by the designated state agency that describes the nature and scope of its Medicaid program and gives assurance it will be administered in conformity with requirements of Title XIX and other regulations issued by USDHHS. The plan contains all information necessary to determine whether the plan can be approved to serve as a basis for federal financial participation (42 CFR 430.10).

Standard setting and survey agency (42 CFR 431.610)States must also designate agencies or authorities responsible for establishing and maintaining health and other standards for private or public institutions participating in Medicaid. This must be the same state authority used by HCFA to determine qualifications of institutions and providers of services to participate in **Medicare**. In other words, the state licensing and certification agency must be the same for both Title XVIII and Title XIX. The agency must set standards, in accord with federal guidelines, and license and participate in certification of nursing facilities, hospitals, home health agencies, and certain other health-care facilities.

The requirements for establishing and maintaining standards do not apply to **Christian Science sanatoriums** operated, or listed and certified, by the First Church of Christ Scientist, Boston, Massachusetts.

The **state plan** must show the relationship between the single state agency responsible for the Medicaid program and the state agencies and authorities responsible for the various institutional standards. In addition to the state licensing and certification agency, these may include state agencies regulating fire and safety, sanitation, communicable and reportable diseases, postmortem procedures, and other relevant health and safety requirements. (42 CFR 431.610)

Licensing nursing facilities The state is required to license all nursing facilities that are certified for Medicare and Medicaid. Most states also license private nursing facilities that do not accept Medicare or Medicaid patients, using the same licensing agency and state minimum standards that must be met for licensing. That agency also furnishes copies of federal standards, or advises where they may be obtained.

Certification of nursing facilities The state licensing and certification agency provides forms for facilities to apply for Medicare and/or Medicaid certification. After the agency licenses a facility, it conducts a certification survey. If the facility applies for Medicaid certification, the state approves the certification. For Medicare facilities the state forwards its certification report and recommendations to DHHS which certifies all Medicare facilities.

1. **Distinct part** In addition to regular nursing homes, some hospitals have long-term care beds certified as a distinct part. The unit operates under the hospital's license. NF's may also have beds certified as a SNF distinct part without having to secure a separate license.

2. **Free standing** Hospitals may operate a long-term care facility which has a separate license and certification from that of the hospital. These free standing facilities must all be directed by a licensed nursing home administrator.

3. **Swing beds** Rural hospitals operating fewer than 100 beds may have some beds certified for use as acute or long-term care. When the physician certifies that a patient no longer needs acute care but needs skilled nursing and cannot be transferred to a SNF, the bed may be designated long-term care. The hospital bills and is reimbursed for the appropriate long-term care rate. Every five days the physician must determine if the patient can be moved to a regular skilled facility in order for the bed to remain eligible for long-term care. Should the patient's condition worsen, the bed may swing back to acute care.

   Some states require that hospitals with swing-beds must have a licensed nursing home administrator. Many states do not. The swing-bed program is not a popular program with nursing homes as they feel the hospital is holding patients who should be in a regular nursing facility.

Provider agreement The single state agency provides facilities with provider agreement forms. When the state determines a facility is eligible by licensing and certification for Medicaid, it signs the provider agreement with the facility and issues a provider number. DHHS signs the provider agreement with Medicare facilities and issues the provider number. This number must be used in billing for services rendered.

Disclosure of ownership Title 42 CFR 483.75 (p) provides that a facility must comply with the disclosure requirements of 42 CFR 420.201 and 455.104 (Medicaid). Information in Figure 11.1 must be disclosed to the state and to the Secretary of DHHS on HCFA Form 1513 before entering into a contract with Medicare or Medicaid.

Figure 11.1:

Ownership Information

1. Name and address of each person with an ownership or control interest in the facility, or in any subcontractor in which the entity has direct or indirect ownership interest, totalling five percent or more;

2. Whether any two persons named are related to each other as spouse, parent, child, or sibling; and

3. Any of the related persons' interest in another facility that must file disclosure of ownership papers which means other certified facilities, not a nonparticipating facility.

Updated The facility must give written notice to the state Medicaid agency at the time that any change occurs in the following:

1. Persons with an ownership or control interest as defined above,

2. The officers, directors, agents, or managing employees,

3. The corporation, association, or other company responsible for the management of the facility, or

4. The facility's administrator or director of nursing.

The notice must include the identity of each new individual or company.

Failure to comply Administrators must initiate notices of the changes. States establish a deadline for receipt of the notice following the change. Federal financial participation is denied to a provider who fails to disclose ownership or control information as required.

Licensing administrators The state Medicaid plan must provide for licensing of nursing home administrators as outlined in Chapter 1 of this publication. It is the only health-care profession for which the Federal Government mandates licensing. The state licensing program must provide that only nursing facilities supervised by an administrator licensed by the state may operate within the state. (42 CFR 431.700 through 431.715) As stated in Chapter 1, this may change when the Secretary of DHHS promulgates minimum standards for administrators.

Hospital based Medicare SNFs operating as a **distinct part** are not licensed as a nursing home. Consequently, federal regulations do not require that it be under direction of a licensed nursing home administrator. However, this does not prevent the state form requiring the hospital to have a licensed NHA. Some states require both the **distinct part** and **swing beds** to be under direction of a licensed NHA.

NURSING FACILITY STANDARDS

Prior to October 1, 1990, minimum standards for Medicare and Medicaid nursing facilities were not the same. Medicare standards were promulgated by DHHS, and Medicaid standards by each state. Of course, the state standards had to be approved by DHHS. The states were expected to establish Medicaid guidelines that closely tracked Medicare.

OBRA standards which went into effect on the above date are essentially the same for Medicare and Medicaid. Although 42 CFR 405 governing Medicare was not removed, DHHS states that Medicare facilities will abide by the new 42 CFR 483 along with Medicaid facilities. There will be a few differences which DHHS proposes to make known before the OBRA regulations are fully implemented. Administrators will need to keep in contact with their state agency in order to keep abreast of any difference in regulations.

SNF/NF The title **skilled nursing facility** still applies to facilities qualified under Medicare. The title **nursing facility** applies to facilities that qualify under Medicaid. It simply replaces the former term intermediate care facility (ICF). A Medicaid NF may have an SNF **distinct part**. In this case, the facility must have a separate provider number for the SNF, and SNF requirements for nursing staff, physicians' visits, and so on must be met.

State standards Based on federal guidelines, each state establishes Medicaid standards as stated earlier in this chapter. Generally, the state develops minimum standards governing all nursing facilities, Medicaid and private. Some states develop a separate set of regulations governing Medicaid facilities. It is sometimes referred to as the **standards for payment**. Standards for payment incorporate and elaborate on federal standards. It is the primary guideline used by all Medicaid facilities.

Some federal government regulations are referred to in almost every chapter of this publication. Other regulations are discussed in some detail in this chapter.

Administration (42 CFR 483.75) A facility must be administered in a manner that enables it to use its resources effectively and efficiently to attain or maintain the highest practicable physical, mental, and psychosocial well-being of each resident.

Surveyors will fully review this requirement if there is a Level A deficiency in resident rights (483.10), resident behavior and facility practices (483.13), quality of life (483.15), or quality of care (483.25). These regulations are fully discussed in other parts of this publication.

Licensure [42 CFR 483.75 (a)] A nursing facility must be licensed under applicable state and local law. All applicable licenses, permits, and approvals must be available to inspectors within the facility. This includes evidence that the administrator holds a valid license.

Surveyors, upon finding any problems with quality of care, will monitor this requirement. Licenses, permits, and approvals must be available to them upon request. This includes verification of licenses, permits, or approvals of licensed personnel providing or supervising care in the facility. Current reports of inspections by various state and local authorities should be on file. Notations must be made to reflect action taken by the facility to correct deficiencies.

Compliance [42 CFR 483.75 (b)] The facility must be in compliance with federal, state and local laws, regulations, and codes relating to health, safety, and sanitation. Its operation and services must meet these standards and the **accepted professional standards and principles** that apply to professionals providing services in the facility. Accepted professional standards and principles include practice acts and scope of practice regulations of the state for physicians, nurses, administrators, and other health-care professionals. Also included are commonly accepted health standards established by national organizations, boards, and councils, such as the American Medical Association, American Nurses Association, American Dietetic Association, and Centers for Disease Control and Prevention (CDCP).

Other DHHS regulations [42 CFR 483.75 (c)} In addition to compliance with the regulations listed above, facilities are obliged to meet applicable provisions of other federal regulations. These include, but are not limited to those pertaining to nondiscrimination on the basis of:

1. Race, color, or national origin (45 CFR 80),
2. Handicap (45 CFR 84),
3. Age (45 CFR 91),
4. Protection of human subjects of research (45 CFR 46), and
5. Fraud and abuse (42 CFR 455).

These regulations are not in themselves considered requirements under Part 483. However, violation may result in the termination or suspension of or refusal to grant or continue payment with federal funds. If agencies monitoring these regulations found a facility out of compliance to the extent they felt a need to report it to Medicare and Medicaid officials, they could take appropriate action.

Surveyors If during a survey problems relating to compliance and relationships with other agencies are noted, surveyors are to forward this information to the HCFA Regional Office which will forward it to the appropriate agency. When appropriate, they refer problems to other state agencies as the Office of Civil Rights, the Ombudsman, or other advocacy group.

Governing body regulations [CFR 483.75 (d)] covering its makeup, authority, and duties are discussed fully in Chapter 4.

CERTIFIED NURSE AIDE (CNA) PROGRAM [42 CFR 483.150 through 483.156 and 483.75 (e)]

During 1990 DHHS established a program covering requirements for nurse aides and penalties for infraction of regulations governing care of residents and their property. A facility must not use any individual working as a nurse aide for more than four months on a full-time basis unless that person meets established requirements shown in Figure 11.2.

Figure11.2:

CNA Requirements

1. The individual is competent to provide nursing and nursing related services; and
2. The individual has completed a training and competency evaluation program approved by the state as meeting the requirements of 42 CFR 483:151 through 154; or
3. The individual has been deemed or determined competent as provided in 42 CFR 483.150 (a) and (b).

Volunteers are not nurse aides and do not come under nurse aide training provisions. Private-duty nurse aides are not employed by the facility on a contract, per diem, lease, or other basis and do not come under the nurse-aide training provisions. [42 CFR 483.75(e)]

Facilities may use as nurse aides, any individual who has successfully completed a nurse-aide training and competency evaluation program or a competency evaluation program. However, if the individual has not completed a program at the time of employment, a facility may only use that individual as a nurse aide if the individual is in a nurse-aide training and competency program (not a competency evaluation program alone) and that individual is a **permanent employee** in his first four months of employment in the facility. A permanent employee is one who is expected to continue working on an ongoing basis.

Nonpermanent employee A facility cannot use on a temporary, per diem, lease, or other basis than permanent any person who does not meet the requirements listed above. Failure to adhere to this regulation places the facility in a vulnerable position regarding liability, especially if the employee should err in his duties.

Competency A nursing home must not use any person who has worked less than four months as a nurse aide in that facility unless the individual (1) is a full-time employee in a state-approved training and competency evaluation program, (2) has demonstrated competence through satisfactory participation in a state-approved nurse-aide training and competency evaluation program or a competency evaluation program, or (3) has been deemed or determined competent as provided in 42 CFR 483.150 (a) and (b).

Certified Nurse Aide-Registry Each state must develop and maintain a CNA Registry. Information in Figure 11.3 must be maintained on each CNA and regularly updated in the Registry.

Figure 11.3:

CNA Registry Information

1. Name and address,
2. Social Security number, and identification numbers, if different,
3. Date of birth,
4. Name of training and competency evaluation program,
5. Date completed training and competency evaluation, and
6. Documentation of specific findings of resident neglect, abuse, or misappropriation of property; date and result of any hearing; and statement of CNA disputing findings, if applicable.

Fees The state may not charge a CNA any fee for certification, placing his name in the registry, or for recertification. A state may charge nurse aides a fee for a certificate, which is an official state document, and make certain other charges as approved by HCFA, provided it is in compliance with state statutes.

Registry verification Administrators must verify with the CNA Registry that a nurse aide is registered and in good standing before allowing any individual to serve as a nurse aide. **Exceptions** are: the individual is a full-time employee in a training program approved by the state, or (2) the individual can prove he has successfully completed a training program and competency evaluation program approved by the state and has not yet been placed on the register. Facilities must follow up to ensure that such person becomes registered. Some states issue certificates or certification cards to CNA's. The facility may not accept this as evidence a nurse aide is qualified because he could have been proven guilty of abuse, neglect, or misappropriation of resident property since the card was issued. Calling the register for verification of eligibility is the only safe course of action.

Multi-state registry verification When a nurse aide was trained or worked in other states before applying to a facility, the facility must ensure they are fully certified before employing the individual. State registers are developing **reciprocity** agreements in which a state determines if it will endorse a nurse aide's certification in another state. This means the register must check with all states in which the nurse aide professes to have been certified. The reason is the aide could have violated OBRA standards in one state then obtained certification in another.

Recertification Each CNA must reregister at least every two years on a schedule established by the state. **Regular in-service education** is required for recertification. The facility must complete a performance review of every nurse aide at least once every twelve months and must provide regular in-service training based on the outcome of the reviews. This in-service must meet criteria listed in Figure 11.4.

Figure 11.4:

CNA In-Service Requirements

1. Be sufficient to ensure the continuing competence of nurse aides, but must be no less than **twelve hours** per year;

2. Address areas of weakness as determined in the nurse aides' performance reviews, and may address the special needs of residents as determined by the facility staff; and

3. For nurse aides providing services to residents with cognitive impairments, address care to the needs of the cognitively impaired. It is the facility's duty to ensure that its nurse aides meet these requirements and are properly recertified according to the state schedule.

Required retraining Nurse aides who are not employed as a nurse aide or to provide related services for a continuous 24 month period following completion of their most recent training and competency evaluation program, must be retrained. Such individuals must complete a new training and competency evaluation program or a new competency evaluation program in order to be certified again. The purpose is to ensure that they keep abreast of new knowledge and skills in their field.

Proficiency of nurse aides The facility must ensure that nurse aides are able to demonstrate competence in skills and techniques necessary for resident needs. This means the needs as identified in resident assessments and as described in the plan of care. This includes competence in communication and personal skills, basic nursing skills, personal-care skills, mental health and social-service needs, basic restorative services, and resident rights.

Some states are establishing money penalties to be assessed administrators who fail to use the registry when employing nurse aides. It is entirely possible that state Medicaid fraud control agencies will file criminal charges against administrators who do not use the registry and who employ a person guilty of any of these offenses against residents. This action will depend on individual state law.

Surveyors will determine whether individuals employed as nurse aides are properly trained and certified. The facility must have documentation the surveyor can examine. Surveyors will ask nurse aides where they received training, length of training, and how long they have worked in the facility as a nurse aide. They observe nurse aides performing their duties to determine if there is evidence they are properly trained. Other areas surveyors check are whether there is a review of performance, whether in-service training addresses areas of weakness, whether it includes training to deal with cognitive impairments, and with resident rights.

STAFF QUALIFICATIONS
[42 CFR 483.75 (g)]

The facility must employ on a full-time, part-time, or consultant basis those professionals necessary to carry out the provisions of OBRA requirements. All professional staff must be licensed, certified, or registered in accordance with applicable state laws. Simply asking to see licenses and certification or registration papers may not always be adequate. Frequent forgeries, which appear very authentic, occur especially for registered nurses and licensed practical nurses. If there is any doubt regarding an applicant's papers, check with the appropriate board. Boards may normally respond to a request in two or more weeks, but most will do an immediate search if the administrator tells the board they suspect forgery.

> **Example**: An LPN presented a forged license that appeared authentic. The facility contacted her last employer who verified she had worked as an LPN for six months in their hospital. After a few weeks the DON began to suspect an irregularity when the LPN showed a lack of knowledge and skill in some basic nursing practices. When questioned about her performance the LPN disappeared. When the administrator contacted the LPN board the board verified the license as a forgery.

Outside Resources If a facility does not employ a qualified professional to furnish a specific service to be provided by the facility, it must arrange for that service by a person or an outside agency. Examples are the dietitian, pharmacist, medical director, medical records administrator, and rehabilitation therapists. The arrangement must be in compliance with section 1861(w) of the Social Security Act, or with an agreement as follows.

Agreement The facility must have a written agreement with each professional and agency which provides a needed service to the facility. It must specify that the facility is responsible for obtaining services that meet professional standards and principles which apply to professionals providing services in the facility. Time to be spent in the facility, and whether the professional is on call should be specified. Before employing any outside person or agency, the facility must ensure that the provider meets professional standards. The facility should examine licenses, certificates, and so on, and document that the provider is properly qualified.

Consolidated billing Rehabilitation therapists offering services to Medicare SNF residents will be affected as the facility must bill for Part B Medicare services offered to its residents. The agreement between the facility and rehabilitation therapists must include this feature which begins no later than January 1, 1999.

LABORATORY SERVICES [42 CFR 483.75 (j)]

The facility must provide or obtain laboratory services to meet the needs of its residents. It is responsible for the quality and timeliness of the services. **Laboratory services** or tests are defined as any examination or analysis of human body materials for purposes of providing information for diagnosis, prevention, or treatment of any disease or impairment of, or the assessment of the health of human beings. If a facility provides its own laboratory services, it must comply with 42 CFR 493. The facility must apply to HCFA, or have obtained a certificate of waiver or certificate of registration. An application for waiver may be applied for if the facility only performs the tests on the waiver list, i.e.:

1. Dip stick or tablet reagent urinalysis (nonautomated for: bilirubin, glucose, hemoglobin, ketone, leukocytes, nitrate, pH, protein, specific gravity, and urobilirubin),
2. Fecal occult blood,
3. Erythrocyte sedimentation rate, nonautomated,
4. Hemoglobin - copper sulfate, nonautomated,
5. Blood glucose by blood glucose monitoring devices cleared by the FDA specifically for home use,
6. Spun microhemocratic, and
7. Urine pregnancy tests - visual color comparison tests.

If the facility performs any laboratory service or test other than these, it must apply for a certificate of registration. Administrators who have questions concerning application of these requirements should contact the state laboratory consultant or the Regional Office of HCFA.

If the facility provides **blood bank** and **transfusion services,** it must meet the requirements of laboratories specified in 42 CFR 493.

Referring specimens If the facility's laboratory wishes to refer its specimens for testing in another laboratory, the referral laboratory must be approved in the appropriate specialties and subspecialities of services in accord with requirements of 42 CFR 493. This means it is approved for participation in Medicare.

Outside laboratory services If the facility does not provide on-site services, it must have an agreement with a hospital or an independent laboratory to provide these services. The hospital and/or the independent laboratory must be approved for participation in the Medicare program. (42 CFR 493) This is extremely important as Medicare will not pay for services unless the laboratory is approved and accepts Medicare payment levels. The laboratory cannot charge Medicare residents an additional fee. When the facility uses outside laboratory services it must follow OBRA requirements:

1. The facility provides the services only when ordered by the attending physician.

2. The attending physician is promptly notified of the test results.

3. If the resident needs assistance in making transportation arrangements to and from the source of service, the facility must give that assistance.

4. The signed and dated clinical laboratory reports containing the name and address of the testing laboratory are filed in the resident's medical record.

Consolidated billing Since laboratory services for Medicare SNF residents falls under Part B, the agreement with certain laboratories must include an arrangement for the facility to do the billing for these services. Administrators will need to keep updated on this new aspect of the PPS described in Chapter 7.

RADIOLOGY AND OTHER DIAGNOSTIC SERVICES [42 CFR 483.75 (k)]

A facility must provide or obtain radiology and other diagnostic services to meet the needs of residents. The same standards listed in this chapter for laboratory services apply for radiology and other diagnostic services. This includes timeliness, quality, compliance of the providers with Medicare, and the four courses of action the facility must follow.

If a facility provides its own diagnostic service, as a hospital might do for its nursing facility, the services must meet the applicable conditions of participation for hospitals contained in 42 CFR 482.26. If the facility does not provide its own diagnostic services, it must have an agreement to obtain these services from a provider or supplier that is approved to provide these services under Medicare. The facility must meet the standards set forth in Figure 11.5.

Figure 11.5

Facility Requirements for Use of Radiology and Other Diagnostic Services

1. Provide or obtain radiology and other diagnostic services only when ordered by the attending physician.

2. Promptly notify the attending physician of the test results.

3. Assist the resident in making transportation arrangements to and from the source of service, if needed.

4. File in the resident's medical record the signed and dated reports of X-ray and other diagnostic services.

Consolidated billing Since radiology and other diagnostic services are usually Medicare Part B, these services will also be offered by PPS. Facility agreements with agencies offering these services to a Medicare SNF unit must include this new regulation.

Surveyors will observe whether, for any type of diagnostic service, there are delays in transporting residents to and from the service. They also will determine if there are delays in interpreting test results. A key factor will be whether there is prompt notification of the resident's physician so there is no delay in changing needed treatment or the care plan.

CLINICAL RECORDS [42 CFR 483.75 (l)]

The facility must maintain **clinical records** (commonly called medical records) on each resident in accordance with accepted professional standards and practices. Records must be complete, accurately documented, readily accessible, and systematically organized. A complete clinical record contains an accurate and functional representation of the actual experience of the individual in the facility.

Frequency of documentation of resident's progress is determined by the facility. This documentation takes place apart from the annual comprehensive assessment, periodic assessments when change in status occurs, and quarterly monitoring assessments. For functional and behavioral goals, the clinical record should document any change toward achieving these care-plan goals. There is no **required frequency** or format for reporting progress. There should be, however, a unique reporting schedule for charting a resident's progress in maintaining or improving functional abilities and psychosocial status. The facility should be more concerned with whether staff has sufficient information to work with residents and less with how often that information is gathered.

Exceptions on when to record include medication passes and physicians visits and orders. These are recorded each time they occur, not at the end of a shift, end of the day, or at any other time.

Surveyors will be more concerned about the staff having sufficient progress information to work with the residents than how often that information is gathered. They will examine whether there is enough documentation for staff to conduct and revise care programs. Also, surveyors monitor the use of the clinical record in managing the resident's progress.

Retention Clinical records must be retained for the period of time required by state law. If there is no state law, they must be retained for five years from the date of discharge. For a resident who is a minor, records must be retained for three years after the individual reaches legal age under the state law. States generally have laws requiring retention for a period that at least covers the statute of limitations for tort action against the provider.

Loss and Confidentiality The facility must safeguard clinical record information against loss, destruction, or unauthorized use. Written records must be properly stored under lock and key and available only to authorized staff. Information in the form of video or audio must be properly stored and protected. Computerized information will require special security and protective measures. The facility must have proper entry codes for authorized staff. Computers must have proper protection devices to prevent loss of information during power surges, extreme heat changes, and certain types of inclement weather.

Keeping records confidential means safeguarding their content and **releasing information** only with the informed consent of the resident or his legal representative. Staff and professional consultants should have access only to the information that is necessary to provide needed services. Information too confidential to place in the record may be family financial status and sensitive medical data. This type information should be retained in a secure place within the facility, such as a locked cabinet in the administrator's office. The clinical record should note the location of this type information.

Release of information All clinical record information must be kept confidential, regardless of the form or storage method of the records. Information may be released by written permission of the resident and when required by:

1. Transfer of the resident to another health care facility,

2. A court order such a subpoena duces tecum, and

3. A third party contract including Medicare/Medicaid officials which includes surveyors.

Ownership and Accessibility [42 CFR 483.10 (b) (2)] The courts have ruled that clinical records belong to the facility. However, each resident must be able to inspect his record upon request even though the physician has given instructions otherwise. When this occurs it places nursing staff in a dilemma. Proper action is to call the physician, explain that regulations require that the resident has access to his record, and determine whether the physician wishes to talk with the resident and/or family before honoring the resident's request. Upon oral or written request the resident must have access to his records within 24 hours.

Copy(s) of the record must be provided to a resident within two working days after written request from the resident. A photocopying charge, not to exceed the amount customarily charged in the community, may be made. Again, it is wise to confer with the resident's physician so that he is fully aware of the transaction.

If a facility is sold, the records become the property of the new owner who must comply with state regulations regarding retention of old records. Often this is a problem because the new owner does not wish to be responsible for records of residents who are no longer in the facility.

Contents OBRA regulations require that the clinical record contain the information listed in Figure 11.6.

Figure 11.6:

Clinical Record Information

1. Sufficient information to identify the resident,
2. A record of the resident's assessments,
3. The plan of care and services provided,
4. The results of any pre-admission screening conducted by the state, and
5. Progress notes.

Discharge summary The state imposes regulations on closing records of deceased and discharged residents. Usually, a discharge summary is required. It includes (1) a recap of resident's entire stay, (2) a summary of resident's status, and (3) a post-discharge plan. An administrator should periodically check on closed records to ensure the procedure was carried out correctly. Such action can avoid deficiencies during surveys.

Staff A full-time staff member should be designated as the clinical records clerk. With consultation from a qualified medical records consultant, this employee should be responsible for:

1. Setting up a record on each patient,
2. Ensuring that all required information is in the record,
3. Supervising the checking in and out of records and accounting for their location,
4. Ensuring their proper filing and security,
5. Releasing no information without proper authority, including consent forms, and
6. Disposal of records at appropriate times.

Few facilities can afford a full-time **medical records administrator** (MRA) or an **accredited record technician** (ART). If the facility does not have a full-time professional, it should employ a medical records consultant. As discussed under outside resources, this person must meet educational and licensing or certification requirements of his professional field. He should consult with the clinical records clerk and other staff on the above duties and the federal requirements for maintaining records. States usually specify a minimum number of hours that the consultant should work at the facility.

Legal liability for the clinical record is borne by the physician. Courts have ruled the attending physician is responsible for content of the record; consequently he should review notes of the nurses, social workers, rehabilitation specialists, and other staff who make entries in the resident record.

Surveyors will take a sample of clinical records and determine if there is sufficient documentation to develop and implement a plan of care, to revise the program when needed, and to respond to a resident's changing status. They will determine how the record is used in managing a resident's progress in maintaining or improving his status. Should there be information too sensitive to include in the clinical records, as family finances and sensitive medical data, surveyors will note if it is kept elsewhere in a secure place. Also, surveyors select a sample of records (five in a 120 bed facility) of recently discharged residents and determine if the their records are properly closed.

TRANSFER AGREEMENT [42 CFR 483.75 (2) (n)]

Paragraph 1861(1) of the Social Security Act provides that a facility must have a written transfer agreement with one or more hospitals. The hospitals must be approved for participation under both the Medicare and Medicaid programs. Nursing facilities located on an Indian reservation are excepted. The agreement must provide reasonable assurance that residents will be transferred from the nursing facility to the hospital and admitted on a timely basis. The transfer must be medically appropriate as determined by the attending physician. Some facilities, when the hospital has emergency room services, include in their agreement that these services may be used. This is especially helpful when a resident emergency occurs and the attending physician and his backup are not readily available. However, facilities must not come to depend on emergency rooms for physician's services.

When information is necessary to determine whether the resident can be adequately cared for in a less expensive setting than either the hospital or the nursing facility, medical and additional information needed for care and treatment of the résident will be exchanged between the two institutions.

Exception There are instances in which hospitals will not enter into a written transfer agreement. In this event, the facility documents that it attempted in good faith to effect an agreement with a hospital close enough to the facility to make transfer feasible. Documentation must include date efforts were made, the proposed agreement discussed with the hospital, and the name of the person responding to the facility's request.

OMBUDSMAN PROGRAM [42 CFR 483.10 (j) (1) and (3)]

The Older Americans Act of 1965, as amended, provided for establishment of an office of **long-term care ombudsman** in each state and identified its role relative to nursing facilities. Section 201 of the Act requires states to develop an ombudsman program on a full-time basis. Its primary **duty** is to investigate and resolve complaints made by or on behalf of older individuals who are residents of long-term care facilities. They are to investigate any action, inaction, or decisions made by providers of long-term care services which could adversely affect the health, safety, welfare, or rights of residents. The Developmental Disabilities Assistance and Bill of Rights Act provides that a state agency be responsible for protection and advocacy for mentally disabled and other developmentally disabled persons. Also, the Protection and Advocacy for Mentally Ill Individuals Act mandates that an agency be responsible for protection and advocacy for the mentally ill.

Notification Medicare and Medicaid requires that each state Medicaid agency notify the ombudsman program of any survey findings of noncompliance that would affect the elderly as noted above. Also, the state must notify the program of any action taken against a nursing facility under the state's enforcement regulations.

Access and visitation Medicare and Medicaid also specify that the ombudsman and advocacy representatives have immediate access to any resident in a facility. They further require that, with the resident or legal representative's consent, an ombudsman may examine the resident's clinical records. Access must be consistent with state law. [42 CFR 483.10 (j)]

Notice of transfer appeal rights When a facility notifies a resident of the right to appeal a proposed transfer, the facility must include in the notice the name, mailing address, and telephone number of the state ombudsman.

Notice of facility waiver Whenever DHHS or the state grants a facility waiver of licensed nursing requirements, the state ombudsman must receive notice of the waiver This information is useful to the ombudsman when he receives a complaint that relates to a problem which the waiver affects. He may be able to help.

Resident right to contact ombudsman As stated under residents' rights in this chapter, a resident must be able to receive information from agencies acting as client advocates. Residents must be afforded the opportunity to contact these agencies which include the state ombudsman, and the agencies for mentally disabled and mentally ill.

Survey participation The state Medicaid agency must contact the long-term care ombudsman to discuss a scheduled facility survey and afford the ombudsman the opportunity to observe the exit conference. The ombudsman may suggest families to interview and be present during resident interviews.

In practice, the ombudsman reports significant deficiencies observed in a facility to the state Medicaid agency. If he observes apparent substandard practices of facility administrators, they may report these to the state's board of examiners for nursing-home administrators for possible disciplinary action.

RESIDENT RIGHTS [42 CFR 483.10, 483.12, 483.13, 483.15]

All residents in nursing facilities have rights guaranteed to them under federal and state law. Each resident has a right to a dignified existence, self-determination, and communication with and access to persons and services inside and outside the facility. The facility must protect and promote each resident's rights and closely adhere to OBRA - 87 guidelines that follow.

Exercise of rights Each resident has the right to exercise his or her rights as a resident of the facility and as a citizen or resident of the United States. **Exercising rights** means that residents have autonomy and choice, to the extent possible, over how they wish to live their everyday lives and receive care. This is subject to the facility's rules affecting resident conduct, and those regulations governing protection of resident health and safety. [42 CFR 483.10 (a) (1)]

Residents have the right to be free of interference, coercion, discrimination, or reprisal from the facility in exercising their rights. The facility cannot hamper, compel by force, treat deferentially, or retaliate against residents for exercising their rights. This does not include the facility's efforts, as documented in the assessment and care plan, to encourage residents in participation that helps to attain care planning goals.

Facility practices considered to limit autonomy or choice in exercising rights are those such as: (1) reducing the group activity time of a resident who tries to organize a resident group, (2) requiring residents to seek prior approval to distribute information about the facility, (3) discouraging residents who want to hang religious ornaments above their beds, (4) isolating residents in a prejudicial manner during activities, and (5) purposely assigning inexperienced aides to a resident with **heavy care** needs because he exercised his rights.

The rights of a resident adjudged **incompetent** by a state court are exercised by the person – guardian, curator, conservator — appointed by the court. There must be clear documentation of the assignment of these rights to a court named individual. Pertinent consent forms and documents must be signed by the appointed guardian. The right to make health-care decisions is included in the duties of the incompetent resident's legal representative. However, the facility should ensure that this authority is within the courts ruling for sometimes the court-appointed conservator only has power to make financial decisions. Even when the resident has been declared incompetent, if he can understand the situation and expresses a preference, his wishes should be respected to the degree possible. The involvement of a legal representative does not automatically relieve the facility of its duty to protect and promote the resident's interests. The right of the representative to reject treatment may be subject to state law limits. [42 CFR 483.10 (a) (3) &(4)]

Notice of rights Prior to or upon admission, and during the resident's stay, each resident must be informed both orally and in writing of resident rights and the facility's rules. It must be in language the resident understands. The receipt of this information, and any amendments to it, must be acknowledged in writing. For hearing-impaired who communicate by sign language, the facility must provide an interpreter. Large print texts of resident rights and the facility's rules should be available for the visually deficient.

The facility should explain the agreement, and have residents sign, attesting to their understanding that it is a two-party agreement. The resident has rights, but the facility has rules the resident must abide by or action to discharge may be taken. The facility must inform the resident any time federal or state laws pertaining to resident rights are changed.

The facility must discuss in detail the following broad areas of resident rights and ensure that they are practiced. Also, it must ensure that residents who are mentally competent understand their rights. [42 CFR 483.10 (b) (1)]

1. **Records** In the section on clinical records in this chapter it was noted that residents have a right to information in their clinical record. Title 42 CFR 485.10 (b) (2) extends this right to all records. Residents have a right to inspect and purchase copies of all records pertaining to them.

2. **Medical Care and treatment** Residents have the right to be fully informed in a language they can understand of their **total health status**. This includes, but is not limited to, their medical condition. It also includes functional status, medical and nursing care, status of nutritional and oral health, psychosocial status, and sensory and physical impairment. [42 CFR 483.10 (b)(3)] Residents have a right to freedom of choice, insofar as possible, in matters pertaining to their care and treatment. Unless adjudged incompetent, or otherwise found to be incapacitated under state law, residents should be offered the opportunity to participate in planning their care and treatment or in effecting changes in care and treatment. [42 CFR 483.10 (d)(3)]

Choosing the physician Residents have the right and must be given the freedom to choose their personal, attending physician. Generally, if the resident is unable to choose an attending physician, the court-appointed person exercises this right. The facility must inform each resident of the name, specialty, and way of contacting the physician responsible for managing his plan of care. This does not include other physicians the resident may see from time to time. [42 CFR 483.10 (d) (9)] If the resident's chosen physician fails to fulfill a given requirement, such as those for use of unnecessary or antipsychotic drugs, the facility has the right, after informing the resident, to seek other physician participation to assure appropriate and adequate care and treatment. This is a situation in which the medical director should confer with the attending physician and action taken to secure alternative physician services only when differences cannot be mediated by the medical director. The facility should assist the resident, when requested, in selecting an alternate physician. [42 CFR 483.10 (d)(1)]

Informed in advance Residents have the right to be informed in advance about their care and treatment, and how the treatment may affect their well-being. This means staff discusses with the resident and/or his legal representative treatment options and alternatives. The resident has the right to be involved in the discussion of diagnosis, treatment options, risks, and prognosis — all the assessment and care planning process. Again, this must be in a language the resident understands. The resident then has freedom to select and approve the specific plan of care before it is implemented. Of course, this may not apply to emergency procedures in life-threatening situations unless an advance medical directive is in effect.

Refusal of treatment The resident must be allowed to make choices based on the information just described. The resident has the right to refuse treatment. Refusal must be documented in the resident's record. Discussion with the resident regarding the consequences or risks of the refusal and any alternative treatment available must be documented. If the resident's refusal is persistent and consistent, discharge on the grounds that the resident's needs cannot be met by the facility is permissible. However, if the refusal and the discussion brings about significant change, the facility should reassess the resident and institute care-planning changes. All criteria of 42 CFR 483.12 (a) (1-2) must be met if discharge is actually effected. In the meantime the facility must provide care.

Refusal of research Residents have the right to refuse to participate in experimental research. This includes developing and testing clinical treatment, such as a new drug or new therapy that involves both treatment and control groups. If a resident is considered for research, the facility must fully inform him of the nature of the experiment and possible consequences of participating. The resident or legal representative's written consent must be on file before participation. This must be informed consent. [42 CFR 483.10 (b) (4)]

Notification of change [42 CFR 483.10 (b) (11)] Except in an emergency, or when a resident is incompetent, the facility must: (1) consult with the resident immediately, (2) notify the resident's physician, and (3) if known, notify the family member or legal representative when any change involving the resident occurs. This must be done within 24 hours in the instances shown in Figure 11.7.

Figure 11.7:

Instances Requiring Notification of Change

a. An accident that results in injury that has the potential for requiring physician intervention,

b. A significant change in physical, mental, or psychosocial status such as deterioration in life-threatening conditions or clinical complications,

c. A decision to alter treatment significantly such as the need to discontinue a present form of treatment due to adverse reactions or to begin a new form of treatment, and

d. A decision to transfer or discharge the resident.

The facility must notify the resident and, if known, the resident's legal representative or interested family member when there is to be: (1) change in the resident's room or room mate, and (2) federal or state law or regulations make a change in the resident's rights.

Also, the facility must periodically update the address and telephone number of the resident's legal representative or interested family member. The facility needs this in order to know who is to be informed in case of significant change. **Significant change** means deterioration in physical, mental, or psychosocial status in either life-threatening conditions or clinical complications. **Life-threatening** means heart attack, cancer, and so on. **Clinical complications** means, for example, a stage II pressure sore (refer to Chapter 12), onset or recurrent periods of delirium, recurrent urinary tract infection, and depression.

Self-administration of drugs Each resident has a right to self-administer drugs, provided the interdisciplinary team has determined for each resident that this practice is safe. If the resident wants to self-administer medications, the team must assess the resident's cognitive, physical, and visual ability to carry out this responsibility before the resident can exercise this right. The team must also determine who will be responsible, resident or nursing staff, for storage and documentation of the administration of drugs. Also, the team must determine where the medication will be stored - resident's room, nurses station, or activities room. Appropriate notation of these determinations should be in the resident's care plan. If medications are required before the team has completed an assessment and care plan, they may be administered by a nurse or another person qualified under state law. [42 CFR 483.10 (n)]

Surveyors will not count errors in self-administered drugs as a medication error. They will question the team's judgment in allowing self-administration in those cases. It is anticipated this will be a controversial area. Experience shows that some residents who are very much in contact will flush medication down the toilet, yet report it was taken. Elderly residents often do not remember whether they took their medicine. If the dose is missing, how will the staff know whether another resident did not take it? Certainly, this is a right that the team must evaluate and reevaluate with considerable frequency in order for the right to be exercised appropriately.

3. **Resident funds** [42 CFR 483.10 (c) (1-3)] the resident has the right to manage his or her financial affairs, and the facility may not require residents to deposit their personal funds

with the facility. If a resident chooses to have the facility handle his personal funds, the facility cannot refuse; however, the facility is not required to know about a resident's assets that are not on deposit with it. The resident who desires the facility to manage personal funds must request it in writing so they may have ready and reasonable access to their funds. The facility must hold, safeguard, manage, and account for personal funds deposited by the resident in accord with procedures outlined in Chapter 7 on Financial Management.

4. **Privacy and confidentiality** Residents have a right to personal privacy and to confidentiality of clinical records. Right of privacy means residents have the right to privacy with whomever the resident wishes to be private. This privacy includes full visual and auditory privacy, to the extent desired, for visits or other activities. Personal privacy includes accommodations, medical treatment, written and telephone communications, personal care, visits, and meetings of family and resident groups. This does not require a private room, for privacy may be created by use of the dining room between meals, an office, a treatment room, a vacant chapel, resident's own room, a cordless telephone, etc. Visual privacy in multi-bedded rooms is provided by the explicit OBRA requirement of privacy curtains.

Privacy of the body must be observed as staff works with residents. Staff must plan for and observe privacy as residents use bathrooms and attend to other activities of personal hygiene. Only staff directly involved in treatment should be present when treatments are given, unless the resident consents to others being present.

Personal and clinical records may not be released without the resident's consent, except as noted under clinical records in this chapter. Financial and other records must be handled with the same confidentiality.

5. **Grievances and complaints** [42 CFR 483.10 (f)] A resident has the right to voice grievances and register complaints. They have the right to voice grievances regarding the treatment or care provided, or the staff's failure to provide it. There can be no discrimination or reprisal for voicing grievances. Facility staff must make prompt efforts to resolve grievances, including those that involve behavior of other residents. Too often residents have been afraid to voice grievances because they were fearful of retaliation. There are documented instances in which staff has warned residents to keep quiet or they will suffer the consequences. OBRA's **purpose** is to terminate this practice. Facility administration must take grievances seriously and promptly investigate, document, and give feedback on actions taken, including those relating to the behavior of other residents.

Surveyors will question residents about whether they have complained, to whom, what about, whether the complaint was written, and how staff responded. They will ask if the complaint was resolved and were they satisfied. If the problem was not resolved, surveyors will ask the staff if they explained the reasons to the resident.

6. **Survey results** [42 CFR 483.10 (g) (1-2)] Residents have a right to examine results of the most recent survey of the facility and any plan of correction in effect concerning the facility. Survey results must be available for examination by residents. They must be unaltered by the facility and in readable form, as in a binder. They must be placed where residents have ready access to them without asking staff, and the facility must post a notice of their survey.

Residents must also be able to receive information from agencies acting as client advocates and be afforded the opportunity to contact these agencies. Posting of names, addresses, and telephone numbers of these advocates was discussed earlier.

7. **Work** the resident has the right to refuse to perform services for the facility. However, he has the right to perform services, if he chooses, under circumstances shown in Figure 11.8.

Figure 11.8:

Requirements For Allowing Residents To Work

a. The facility has documented the need or desire for work in the plan of care.

b. The plan of care specifies the nature of the services performed and whether the services are voluntary or paid.

c. Compensation for paid services is at or above prevailing wage rates.

d. The resident agrees to the work arrangement described in his plan of care.

All resident work, paid or unpaid, must be part of the plan of care. Each of the four conditions above must be carefully documented. The therapeutic work assignment must be medically appropriate. The resident has the right to discontinue or to refuse work as a part of the treatment program. (42 CFR 483.10 (h)]

Practicing administrators relate numerous examples of resident-work activities that proved valuable to the individual, other residents, and the facility. Witness the 83 year old retired engineer who had lost his ability to function in the community but maintained the knowledge and skills of 55 years of practice. He helped the maintenance worker develop a highly efficient maintenance program. And the retired postal-service employee who volunteered to handle the facility's resident mail needs. He established a system that drew accolades from residents, families, and staff. There are many other examples.

8. **Mail** [42 CFR 483.10 (i) (1-2)] The resident has a right to privacy in written communication, including the right to send and promptly receive mail that is unopened. The resident must have access to stationary, postage, and writing materials at his own expense. **Promptly** means within 24 hours of mail delivery to the facility and sending outgoing mail to the post office within 24 hours. Sometimes this right is questioned by the family.

   Example: A 75-year-old gentleman with beginning Alzheimers received some mail that was very upsetting to him. Family members were concerned and his daughter requested that they be allowed to intercept the letters that upset him. Staff reviewed the situation carefully and found that some letters did upset him for a short period of time, but he eagerly looked forward to receiving mail, even that which upset him. The administrator discussed the situation with the facility attorney. He advised that unless the mail was unduly disturbing and interfered significantly in his care plan, his mail should not be intercepted by anyone unless he had been declared incompetent.

9. **Access and visitation** The resident has the right, and the facility must provide **immediate access** (24 hours per day) to the resident of any of the following:

   a. Any representative of the Secretary of the US DHHS,

   b. Any representative of the state,

   c. The resident's physician,

   d. The state long-term care ombudsman, or

   e. The agency responsible for protection and the advocacy system for the developmental disabled and for the mentally ill.

The facility must provide reasonable access to any resident by an entity or individual who provides health, social, legal, financial, or other services to the resident. Reasonable access means during the day time, evening, or weekend hours at times that do not disrupt resident programs. The resident has the right to deny or withdraw consent at any time. Immediate family or other relatives are not subject to visiting limitations or other restrictions not imposed by the resident. However, the facility may change location of visits to assist care giving or protect privacy of other residents. For instance, the family might ordinarily visit late in the evening which prevents the resident's room mate from sleeping.

10. **Telephone** [42 CFR 483.10 (k)] The resident has the right to have access to the private use of a telephone. This means auditory privacy, and to the extent possible, visual privacy. Telephones in occupied offices and at an occupied nurses station do not meet provisions of this agreement. Telephone equipment must accommodate the hearing impaired and wheelchair bound residents.

11. **Personal property** [42 CFR 483.10 (l)] Residents have a right to retain and use personal possessions. This includes some furnishings and appropriate clothing as space permits. Use of personal possessions must not infringe upon the rights or health and safety of other residents. Staff must treat the possessions with respect without regard to the apparent value of the possessions. They are of great value to the resident and they help to promote the homelike environment already discussed. Staff should be willing to share in the pleasures these objects bring to residents, not to treat them as so much "clutter". Each item is a milestone in their existence, having special meaning they would like to share.

    Example: Mrs. Young complained to the aide about her food and was not eating much. She had begun to be irritated and fuss about minor things that had not bothered her before. The DON knocked on her door, asked to come in, and was invited in. She noted Mrs. Young wore a new, brightly colored bed jacket that was obviously handmade. The DON commented on its beauty and wondered who made it for her. Mrs. Young brightened, smiled and told how her daughter was gifted in making clothes. She told how the daughter won many prizes at the county fairs. After Mrs. Young further shared her joy in her daughter's talents, the nurse asked her about her food. Mrs. Young said, "Well, I don't know that it is so much the food, I just haven't had much appetite lately. Nothing seems to taste good any more." They were able to explore the problem in a pleasant, amicable manner.

Facility responsibility for lost or damaged personal property of residents should be outlined in policies and procedures that establish reasonable preventive measures. These include counseling resident and families about the risks in bringing valued and valuable personal items into the facility. Residents' belongings should be labeled, and storage space provided in closets with properly closing doors. All loss of, or damage to, resident property should be fully investigated and documented. As noted in Chapter 7, if this is not properly handled, the facility could be liable for losses and damage.

12. **Married couples** (42 CFR 483.10 (m)] Husband and wife have a right to share a room provided both spouses consent to this arrangement. If no room is available the facility is not compelled to relocate another resident in order to accommodate a spouse. Facilities sometimes learn that husband and wife sharing a room is not a desirable arrangement as both parties fare better when they reside in separate rooms and see each other during the day. The facility must respect resident's wishes in regard to the spousal arrangement, insofar as it is possible.

Facilities that have a clearly stated policy are not required to grant the right of sharing a room to unmarried, consenting adults. However, in case a resident has a friend of the opposite sex who visits, and they wish to have uninterrupted privacy for a reasonable period of time, many facility attorneys advise administrators to honor the request. They explain residents may not be denied intimacy simply because they reside in a nursing facility.

Example: A 42-year-old paraplegic female was visited regularly by a male friend. She asked for and was given privacy in the treatment room during each visit where she and her friend had sex. Nurse aides were required to give her a bath, dress, and return her to her room after each visit. They grew tired of this practice and complained to the DON. When the facility's attorney was consulted, he advised that the facility could not deny this right and that the nurse aides needed to understand this resident's right.

13. **Transfer and discharge** [42 CFR 483.10 (o)] A resident has the right to refuse transfer to

another room in the facility if the purpose is to relocate: (a) a resident of a SNF from the distinct part of an institution that is a SNF to a part of the institution that is not a SNF, or (b) a resident of a SNF, from the distinct part of the facility that is a NF to a distinct part that is a SNF. A resident's exercise of the right to refuse transfer does not affect his eligibility for Medicare or Medicaid benefits These provisions allow a resident to refuse transfer from one room to another for purposes of obtaining Medicare eligibility. However, the move is appropriate if requested by a resident.

Example: A Medicare eligible resident is paying for his care in a facility that also operates a Medicare distinct part unit. He asks for transfer to the distinct part of the facility since he believes such transfer will result in Medicare paying for his care. The transfer was granted.

Transfer and discharge as used in 42 CFR 483.12 includes movement of a resident to a bed outside of the certified facility, whether that bed is in the same physical plant or not. Transfer and discharge does not refer to movement of a resident to a bed within the same facility.

The facility must permit each resident to remain in the facility and not transfer or discharge the resident unless standards set forth in Figure 11.9 are met.

Documentation The basis for transfer, as outlined in **a** and **b** of Figure 11.9, must be entered in the resident's clinical record by the resident's physician. OBRA regulations provide that any physician can document the basis of transfer under **d**. The facility also needs to document that appropriate interdisciplinary measures have been tried and have failed before discharge of a resident for violent behavior, although this is not required.

Figure 11.9:

Valid Reasons For Resident Transfer

a. The resident's welfare and needs cannot be met by the facility.

b. The resident's health is improved sufficiently that the resident no longer needs services provided by the facility.

c. The safety of individuals in the facility is endangered.

d. The health of individuals in the facility would otherwise be endangered.

e. The resident has failed, after reasonable and appropriate notice, to pay for a stay at the facility. Only charges allowable under Medicare and Medicaid may be considered allowable in this instance.

f. The facility goes out of business or ceases to operate.

Notice Before a facility discharges or transfers a resident, it must notify the resident and the family member, if known, or the legal representative that action is to be taken. The facility must document reasons in the clinical record, and include in the written notice these items:

a. Reason for transfer or discharge,

b. Effective date of transfer or discharge,

c. Location to which resident is to be transferred or discharged,

d. Notice of right to appeal the action to the state, and

e. Name, address, and telephone number of the state ombudsman, the advocacy agency for developmental disabilities, or the advocacy agency for the mentally ill, as is appropriate for a given resident.

Timing The timing of the notice is important. Except when health of individuals in the facility would be endangered, notice of the transfer or discharge must be made at least 30 days before actual transfer or discharge. Notice may be made as soon as practicable, and the 30-day period does not apply under these circumstances shown in Figure 11.10.

Figure 11.10:

Valid Reasons For Immediate Transfer

a. Safety of the individuals in the facility would be endangered.

b. Health of individuals in the facility would be endangered.

c. Health of the resident improved sufficiently to allow a more immediate transfer or discharge.

d. Immediate transfer is required by the resident's urgent medical needs.

e. The resident has not resided in the facility for 30 days.

The requirement that the resident reside in the facility for at least 30 days is important. Frequently, a person is admitted under Medicaid, but in two or three weeks he wants to go home, and the family is willing. If this person is discharged before the first 30 days are up, Medicaid will not pay for the stay. Facilities should give residents and families this information in writing at admission, otherwise, families often refuse to pay for the services the facility rendered.

Orientation A resident must be oriented to the proposed transfer or discharge. There must be sufficient preparation and orientation of residents to ensure a safe and orderly transfer/discharge. Transfer and discharge must be a planned event. Staff should handle the transfer/discharge in a way that minimizes the resident and family's anxiety. Trial visits by the resident to the new location, asking the family to assist, giving attention to personal belongings, and orienting the new staff to the resident's daily patterns may help to reduce the trauma of change.

Bed-hold policy Bed-hold means how many days the facility will hold the resident's bed while the resident is in the hospital or on therapeutic leave. The allowable days are determined by the state with approval by HCFA. The facility will be paid up to the maximum days established by the state–usually about five days for hospitalization, and nine to 14 days for other leave. Before a facility transfers a resident to a hospital or allows a resident to go on therapeutic leave, the facility must provide written information to the resident and a family member, or the legal representative. Information includes:

a. The duration of the bed-hold policy under the state plan, if any, during which the resident is permitted to return and resume residence in the facility, and

b. The facility's policies regarding bed-hold periods.

Notice At the time of transfer the facility must provide to the resident and a family member, or legal representative, written notice which specifies by date the duration of the bed-hold policy. This is in addition to the written information shown above.

Readmission The facility must establish and follow a written policy under which a resident whose hospitalization or therapeutic leave exceeds the bed-hold period under the state plan. Such resident must be readmitted immediately upon the first availability of a bed in a semiprivate room shared by a resident of the same sex. This is applicable if the resident requires services provided by the facility and is eligible for Medicaid nursing-facility services.

Surveyors will examine records of transferred residents to determine if transfer/discharge was handled correctly and properly documented. They may do a closed-record review to determine whether staff planned the move and oriented the resident ahead of time. [42 CFR 483.12 (a-d)] All resident rights will be examined much closer than in previous types of surveys. Surveyors have more specific guidelines to follow. In doing so they are expected to gain an accurate picture of what staff observance of resident rights contributes to the quality of care.

14. **Restraints** [421 CFR 483.13 (a)] The resident has a right to be free from any physical restraints or chemical restraints imposed for the purpose of discipline or convenience, and not required to treat the resident's symptoms. **Physical restraints** are any manual, physical or mechanical device, material, or equipment attached or adjacent to the resident's body that the resident cannot remove easily, or that restricts freedom of movement or normal access to one's body. These include leg and arm restraints, hand mitts, soft ties or vests, wheelchair safety bars, and gerichairs. Also, included are tucking a sheet so tightly a bedridden resident cannot move, bedrails, or chairs that prevent rising, or placing wheelchairs so close to the wall that a resident cannot stand up. **Bedrails** are not considered a restraint when they are used to assist a resident to turn over, but this should be well documented in the clinical record. Wrist bands or devices on clothing that trigger alarms to warn staff of resident's whereabouts do not restrict freedom and are not considered a restraint. Any belt, sash, or other device used to hold a resident in a chair is a restraint unless the resident can release it himself. Proper use of restraints is discussed in Chapter 12.

Chemical restraints means a psychopharmacologic drug that is used for the purpose of discipline or convenience and not required to treat medical symptoms. These are further discussed under psychoactive drugs in Chapter 12.

Discipline is any action taken by the facility for the purpose of punishing or penalizing residents for their behavior. **Convenience** is any action taken by the facility to control resident behavior or maintain residents with the least amount of effort by the facility, and not in the resident's best interest.

Example: An NF had several semi-ambulatory residents who were not fully responsible for themselves. Most of their time was spent in wheelchairs in the corridor near the nurses station. Some would get out of their chairs and wander aimlessly, sometimes falling and injuring themselves. During a survey it was noted that staff had lined this group up, all facing the wall and so close to the wall they could not stand up. When the surveyor asked for reasons the response was, "Well, it's a lot easier to handle them that way."

15. **Abuse** [2 CFR 480.13 (b)] The resident has a right to be free from verbal, sexual, physical, or mental abuse, corporal punishment, and involuntary seclusion. The facility must develop and implement written policies and procedures that prohibit mistreatment, neglect, or abuse of resident. In order to be effective these must be clearly written, very detailed, and easily understood. Only by careful training, frequent review, and immediate attention to violations can the facility maintain an abuse-free environment. It is the facility's duty to ensure the residents are not subjected to abuse by staff, other residents, consultants, volunteers, staff of other agencies serving a resident, family members or legal guardians, friends, or other individuals. This is a far-reaching OBRA regulation that may require administrators to go beyond usual boundaries of protecting residents from abuse.

Verbal abuse refers to any use of oral, written, or gestural language that includes disparaging, demeaning, or derogatory terms to residents or their families. It refers to describing a resident within hearing distance of the resident or family, without regard to the resident's ability to comprehend. **Sexual abuse** includes, but is not limited to, sexual harassment, sexual coercion, or sexual assault. **Physical abuse** includes hitting, slapping, pinching, kicking, pushing, pulling hair, handling in a rough, angry manner, and other related acts against a person. It also includes corporal punishment used to control behavior. **Involuntary seclusion** means separation of the resident from other residents, or from his room against the resident's will or the will of his legal representative. Temporary monitored separation used as a therapeutic intervention to reduce agitation is not considered involuntary seclusion, provided it is determined by the professional staff and is part of the plan of care. **Mental abuse** includes such actions as humiliation, harassment, threats of punishment or deprivation, etc.

Employment of individuals who have been convicted of abusing, neglecting, or mistreating individuals is not permitted. This regulation does not specify the offense must occur in a nursing facility. The regulation seems to indicate administrators should check the criminal record of applicants. Particularly, the administrator must check with the Certified Nurse Aide Registry to determine that applicants in this category are free of conviction of an offense. As noted in Personnel Management, most states now require a criminal background check of unlicensed applicants for employment.

Reporting and investigating The facility **must** ensure that all alleged violations involving mistreatment, neglect, or abuse, including injuries of an unknown source, are reported immediately to the administrator. He, in turn, must ensure that alleged violations are thoroughly investigated, and **must** prevent further potential abuse while the investigation is in progress. The facility **must** have established procedures for documenting the alleged violation and findings of the investigation. Documentation must include: (a) who committed the abusive act, (b) the nature of the abuse, (c) where it occurred, and (d) when it occurred. It should include evidence that the incident was addressed immediately. Results of all investigations must be reported to the administrator or his representative. The administrator **must** ensure it is reported to the proper state authority within five working days of the occurrence.

16. **Activities** Residents have the right to self-determination and participation in activities and other contacts. Individual residents have their right to choose activities, schedules, and health care that is consistent with the resident's interests, assessments, and plans of care. This has to do with their sleep schedule, whether they are awakened at night, eating schedule, choice of clothes, grooming, visitation with others, short leaves from the facility, and freedom to spend some time as they like.

Residents have the right to interact with members of the **community** both inside and outside the facility. They have a right to make choices about aspects of their lives in the facility that are significant to them. As an example, if the facility institutes a "No Smoking" policy, it must allow residents who smoke to continue smoking in the appropriate no smoking areas and according to procedures. This may be an outside area when weather permits. Residents admitted after the policy is changed must be notified before admission that they are not permitted to smoke.

Participation A resident has the right to organize and participate in **resident groups** in the facility. A resident's family has the right to meet in the facility with families of other residents. Residents and families may also organize a resident/family group. Staff or visitors may attend these meetings only by the group's invitation. A staff person designated by the facility must provide assistance and respond to written requests from these groups. The facility must listen to and act upon grievances and recommendations made by a resident council or family group. This refers to matters concerning policy and operational decisions affecting resident care and life in the facility. Residents may not be required to organize a resident or a family group. If either group wishes to organize, the facility must allow and recognize the organization. It must provide space, privacy, and staff support for the meetings. The designated staff person will normally be the only staff member attending meetings, and only when the group requests assistance. Resident and family groups may meet regularly and often they serve as a support group. They must be able to plan resident and family activities if they desire, and to participate in educational or any other activities. [42 CFR 483.15 (c) and (d)]

Surveyors will convene a resident group if one is organized. If there is no group they will question residents on whether they have attempted to form a group and what happened. Also, they will ask about recommendations and the staff's response, whether the group has difficulty with staff attending meetings, what staff person assists the group(s), has space been provided, and so on. [42 CFR 483.15 (c)]

Other activities A resident has the right to participate in social, religious, and community activities that do not interfere with the right of other residents in the facility. To the extent possible, the facility should accommodate a resident's needs and choices on how the individual's time will be spent, both inside and outside the facility. [42 CFR 483.315 (d)] Further discussion of an ongoing activity program is found in Chapter 12 on Resident Care.

17. **Accommodation of needs** [42 CFR 483.15 (e)] A resident has the right to reside and receive services in the facility with reasonable accommodations of individual needs and preferences. This right does not apply if the individual needs endanger the health and safety of the resident who has the needs, or of other residents. **Reasonable** means adaptations of the facility's physical environment and staff behaviors to assist residents in maintaining independent functioning, dignity, and well-being. It does not mean modifying interior design of a resident's room to satisfy esthetic preferences. Reasonable does include adaptations and arrangements that help residents to maintain unassisted functioning. It also includes furniture and adaptive equipment that gives proper support to stand or to transfer without assistance and to maintain body symmetry. Grab bars, and elevated toilet seats, safeguards from undue danger for wanderers, and measures to reorient and remotivate residents are reasonable adaptations. Preferring a tub bath to a shower, or a bath at a different time or on a different day, being uneasy about the nurse aide who attends him, worried about falling, and so on represent needs the staff should consider and make adjustments for in the care plan.

Roommate change A resident has the right to be notified before the resident is to change rooms or roommates. Special consideration should be given to roommate changes, trying to avoid placement of a resident who likes quietness with one who prefers blaring television, or with one who has numerous loud-talking visitors. Placing a meticulous resident in good contact mentally in a room with an incontinent person can also be problematic.

Example: Mrs. A, an active, well-groomed, mentally alert lady was placed in a room with Mrs. B who was incontinent, essentially bed ridden, and out of contact with reality. Mrs. B had frequent bowel movements, and until she could be changed the odor in the room was extremely unpleasant. One day Mrs. B's daughter noted her mother's nose was discolored and bruised as if it had been pinched. She accused a CNA that she felt was responsible. However, later at an appropriate time, the administrator asked Mrs. A, "Why did you pinch Mrs. B's nose?" Mrs. A replied unhesitatingly, "Because I got tired of her stinking up our room."

Surveyors will monitor signs of resident neglect due to absence of reasonable accommodations of individual needs and preferences. They observe how the staff handles these needs, what interaction occurs when residents make requests or they refuse something, both of which are statements of preference. They will note to what extent the staff adapts the physical environment to help residents meet such needs as standing independently, transferring without assistance, maintaining body symmetry, and participating in preferred activities. Also, they will note measures used to enable residents with dementia to walk, to reorient and remotivate, and to promote mobility and independence so disabled residents can use the bathroom. If any of these are found, surveyors will carefully monitor the physical environment and staff behaviors to determine if there are adequate adaptive actions taken.

FINANCIAL AFFAIRS
[42 CFR 480.10 (b) (5-7)]

Per diem rates The facility must inform in writing each resident who is entitled to Medicaid benefits at the time of admission to the facility or, when the resident becomes eligible for Medicaid of:

1. The **items** and **services** included in the facility's services under the state plan and for which the resident may not be charged.

2. The other items and services that the facility offers and for which the resident may be charged, and the amount of the charges. This includes such items as brand name drugs which Medicaid generally does not pay for.

The facility **should** advise residents and families in writing that if the resident does not remain in the facility a full 30 days, Medicaid will not reimburse the facility. The resident will be liable for full charges.

Changes in rates The facility must fully inform each resident when any change is made in the items and services provided by the facility. This should be done in advance so residents will anticipate the change in their bills. The facility must inform residents before, or at the time of admission, and periodically during the resident's stay, of services available in the facility and of charges for those services, including any charges for services not covered by Medicare or by the facility's per diem rate.

Notice of legal rights The facility must furnish each resident a written description of their rights in four areas relating to financial affairs:

1. The manner of protecting personal funds described earlier in this Chapter;

2. The requirements and procedures for establishing eligibility for Medicaid, including the right to request an assessment which determines the extent of a couple's nonexempt resources at the time of admission and attributes to the community spouse an equitable share of resources which cannot be considered available for payment toward cost of the institutionalized spouse's medical care in his or her process of spending down to Medicaid limits;

3. A posting of names, addresses, and telephone numbers of all pertinent state client-advocacy groups such as the state certification and survey agency, the state licensing office, the state ombudsman program, the protection and advocacy network, and the Medicaid fraud control unit; and

4. A statement that the resident may file a complaint with the state survey and certification agency concerning resident abuse, neglect, and misappropriation of resident property in the facility, and noncompliance with the advance medical directives requirements.

THE FACILITY SURVEY

Survey agency The state survey and certification agency surveys all Medicare/Medicaid nursing facilities at least once per year in most states. An administration should be thoroughly familiar with what the survey team expects and how their survey is conducted. He should inform his staff on survey procedures so they will be more comfortable about being monitored by state officials. Detailed survey information can be found in the *State Operations Manual,* Provider Certification, Transmittal No. 150. Revisions in the survey process may be found in Transmittal No. 274 issued in 1995. New revisions are currently in process.

OBRA's new survey guidelines represent a dramatic change from prior survey methods. Instead of a checklist guide to compliance with every federal/state regulation and the monitoring of every management, resident care, dietary service, physical resource, and other facility procedure, the survey now focuses on the quality of care actually provided. The focus has changed from **paper compliance**, which indicated the facility's potential ability to provide service, to the **outcome** of the facility's efforts to provide service.

Figure 11.11

Goals Of Surveys

1. To improve the quality of care in nursing facilities,

2. To make information gathering more resident centered and more outcome-oriented,

3. To improve accuracy of the survey by correctly identifying any problem that exists, and

4. To make the documentation of problems and the determination of deficiencies more reliable by improving surveyor performance.

The standard nursing-facility survey has the same subtasks as the former long-term care survey:

1. Information gathering,
2. Identification of problems,
3. Determination of deficiencies, and
4. Communication of those deficiencies orally in an exit interview, and in writing through a statement of deficiencies.

The **standard survey** was a resident-centered, outcome-oriented inspection which relies on a case-mix stratified sample of residents to gather information about the facility's compliance with certification requirements. In 1995 the standard survey was changed to provide a **focus** on certain areas of operations when the survey begins. Surveyors use the OSCAR system to determine areas of concern in a facility. The system provides data on past compliance as well as recent problem areas. In the process of focusing on these areas the surveyors assess:

1. Compliance with resident rights,
2. The accuracy of residents' comprehensive assessments and care plans based on these assessments,
3. The quality of services furnished as measured by indicators of medical, nursing, rehabilitative care and drug therapy, dietary and nutritional services, activities and social participation, sanitation, and infection control, and
4. The effectiveness of the physical environment to empower residents, accommodate resident needs, and maintain resident safety.

The standard survey procedures are used for surveys of all SNF's and NF's, whether freestanding or distinct part. The standard survey is not used for ICF-MR's, swing-bed hospitals, or skilled-nursing sections of hospitals that are not separately certified as distinct parts. There are separate survey procedures for these facilities.

Extended survey Based on the resident-centered tasks of the standard survey, if it appears a facility has provided **substandard care** that indicates a Level 4 deficiency, surveyors conduct an **extended** or **partial extended** survey to ensure that administrative requirements related to the problem which caused the citation of a Level 4 are reviewed. A **Level 4 deficiency** is defined as one that involves immediate jeopardy to the health and safety of a resident(s). They may occur in four areas that will require an extended survey: (1) resident rights, (2) resident behavior and facility practice, (3) quality of life, and (4) quality of care.

The extended survey includes: (1) a review of facility policies and procedures pertinent to the areas of deficiencies, (2) an expansion of the review of resident assessment, and (3) a review of staff in-service training. If the extended survey is conducted because of a Level 4 deficiency in **quality of care**, surveyors will do an in-depth review of the accuracy of the comprehensive assessment.

Partial extended survey This type survey is conducted when there is a deficiency in any Level 4 requirement other than the four areas listed above. It consists of a review of those structural requirements that are pertinent to the deficiency cited. The surveyors review requirements indicated for an extended survey that could be related to the cause of the Level 4 deficiency.

Follow-up survey The follow-up survey is for the **purpose** of reevaluating the specific care and services that were cited as deficient during the original standard, extended, or partial extended surveys. Surveyors determine the status of corrective actions being taken on all deficiencies cited, focusing on care of residents. Scope of the follow-up is dictated by the nature of the deficiencies.

Survey tasks Survey procedures for long-term care facilities involve several tasks surveyors must perform.

Phase I There are four tasks in this phase.

1. Off-site preparation consists of an analysis of OSCAR system information and determining the areas the survey will **focus** on.

2. **Entry conference** with staff includes a request for any records surveyors will need.

3. **Orientation tour** is made, during which other areas of focus may be noted.

4. **Sample selection** is made dependent on the areas of focus. As noted earlier, residents selected will be on a case-mix stratified basis.

Phase II The survey is carried out by six tasks.

1. **Environmental assessment** involves checking the physical features of the facility and evaluating environment management.

2. **Quality of care** of service assessment determines how resident outcomes are related to the care given.

3. **Closed-record review** determines appropriateness of transfer/discharge and quality of care provided before this. Surveyors do an indepth review of a number of records – five in a 120 bed facility.

4. **Resident rights** assessment is done in the areas of focus to determine how rights are protected, whether they are exercised without problems, whether residents can influence facility policy.

5. **Dietary assessment** determines any deficiencies affecting nutrition in the focus areas.

6. **Medication pass** observes appropriate number of drugs passed and talks to residents about administration of their medications. The focus is on the error rate, number of unnecessary drugs, and number of psychotropic drugs.

Information analysis When all tasks are completed the survey team analyzes the data and determines any deficiencies and their levels and scope.

Deficiency levels When deficiencies are noted, they are classified by the level of harm involved as shown in Figure 11.12.

Figure 11.12:

Levels of Deficiencies

1. **Level 1** No actual harm thus far but there is a potential for minimal harm; minor negative impact on residents. Examples are problems with diet, food choices, and so on.

2. **Level 2** No actual harm with potential for more than minimal harm. Examples are medication error rate, harm of short duration as falls, lacerations and others that are easy to remedy.

3. **Level 3** Actual harm that is not immediate jeopardy, negative outcome that has compromised resident's ability to maintain or reach his highest level of functioning. Examples are pressure sores, and urinary tract infections after admission.

4. **Level 4** Immediate jeopardy to health and safety of residents. Immediate corrective action is necessary because noncompliance in one or more requirements have caused or is likely to cause serious injury or harm, impairment, or death. Examples are fire alarm system not working, resident call system not operating, and lack of staff.

Deficiency scope The next step is for surveyors to determine the scope and severity of the deficiency, using three categories as shown in Figure 11.13.

Figure 11.13:

Scope of Deficiencies

1. **Isolated** means one or a limited number of residents or staff are affected. Deficiency occurs occasionally in a limited number of locations.

2. **Pattern** refers to whether more than a limited number of staff or residents are affected. If there are repeated occurrences, they are not throughout the facility.

3. **Widespread** means pervasive in the facility. It is systematic and affects a large portion or all of the facility.

The level and scope of the deficiency is charted on a grid which makes classification of the deficiency automatic. The level of the deficiency is recorded.

The exit interview is conducted with the administrator and designated staff. The ombudsman is invited to attend, and the administrator should request representatives of families and residents to participate. **Purpose** of the interview is to inform the facility of the surveyors' observations and findings. These are in writing on the Statement of Deficiencies.

Action of the survey agency depends on the level of the deficiency.

1. **Level 4** deficiency requires the state to send a letter to the agency putting it on fast track (23 days) in which deficiencies must be corrected.

2. **Level 3** deficiency must be corrected within 60 days.

Plan of correction (POC) Immediately after the exit interview the facility must develop a POC showing:

1. **How** corrective action will be taken for residents affected by the deficient practice.

2. **How** the facility will identify other residents having potential to be affected.

3. **What** measures or changes will be made to ensure nonrecurrence.

4. **How** corrective action is to be monitored to ensure nonrecurrence. No consultation may be given by surveyors or by HCFA.

Informal Dispute Resolution (IDR) The facility may request the informal resolution process. It must include in its written request what findings by tag number it wishes to contest. This must include the time period specified by the state for the correction to be completed.

Revisit Only one survey revisit may be made to determine compliance. If corrections are not completed under certain circumstances a facility may be given further chance to correct the deficiencies. When this does not apply, penalties are assessed.

CIVIL PENALTIES AND INCENTIVES (Public Law 100-203)

Congress amended the Social Security Act in 1987 by enacting P.L. 100-203. This law provides that states must impose penalties when nursing facilities have certain deficiencies. These are deficiencies found in any type of survey. States will be required to establish criteria as to how each remedy is to be applied, the amount of money penalties, and the severity of each remedy. It further provides that states may establish a program of rewards for facilities that provide the highest quality of care to residents.

Implementation This law was implemented in 1995. States have established penalties approved by HCFA.

Immediate jeopardy to health and safety If a state finds that a facility's deficiencies immediately jeopardize the health and safety of residents, the state must take immediate action to remove the jeopardy, and correct the deficiencies. Remedies under this finding include: (1) appointment of a temporary manager, or (2) terminating the facility's participation in Medicare/Medicaid. The second remedy may include further remedies of denial of payment and imposing civil money penalties.

1. **Temporary Manager** The temporary manager is to oversee the operation of the facility and to ensure the health and safety of the facility's residents. While this is being done, the temporary manager oversees the orderly closure of the facility, or improvements to bring the facility into compliance. The manager continues to serve when there is an effort to bring the facility into compliance until the state determines the facility has management capability to ensure continued compliance.

2. **Termination of participation** States also establish criteria for termination of a facility's participation in Medicare and/or Medicaid. In

essence, this means closing the facility when it has a predominance of Medicare/Medicaid residents. States may take different means of imposing this penalty. Some states set up a 30-day and/or a 90-day deadline for facility compliance. If the facility has not attained compliance during the specified time frame, termination of participation is effected. The state may also impose the penalty of denial of payment for new admissions, or impose a civil money penalty, or transfer residents to other facilities.

No immediate jeopardy If the state determines a facility's deficiencies do not **immediately** jeopardize the health and safety of residents, the state may still terminate the facility's participation in Medicare/Medicaid, or impose penalties of denial of payment, fines, transfer of residents, or both. There is considerable flexibility in the state's decision regarding the imposition of established penalties.

1. **Denial of payment** If a facility has not complied with requirements within three months of the date the state found the facility out of compliance, the state must deny payment for any resident admitted after that date. The purpose of this remedy is to assure prompt compliance.

2. **Civil money penalty** States must establish a money penalty for each day a facility is out of compliance with requirements specified in P.L. 100-203. The state imposes and collects these penalties in accordance with its established regulations. Funds collected are to be applied to the protection of the health or property of residents of nursing facilities that are found deficient. This may include payment of the cost of relocation of residents to other facilities, maintenance of operation of the facility pending correction of deficiencies or closure, and reimbursement of residents for personal funds lost.

3. **Closure and/or transfer** In the case of emergency, the state may close a facility, transfer the residents to another facility or both. This is and should be a last resort due to effects on the aged when moved. Frequently their conditions worsen and some do not live long after a transfer.

Administrators must determine from their state Medicaid agency the regulations that has been established, and what penalties are in effect.

Incentives States may establish a program of rewards to facilities that provide the highest quality of care to residents who are entitled to medical assistance. Rewards may be through public recognition, incentive payments, or both. State expenses incurred in carrying out such a program are considered to be expenses necessary for the proper and efficient administration of the state plan. An incentives program could be an important motivating factor for nursing facilities. Properly used, it could have distinct advantage over negative measures, such as penalties and bad publicity, by encouraging facilities to stay in compliance and to provide quality care.

Federal role It should be noted that the Secretary of DHHS has the same authority as the state to impose penalties on nursing facilities. If the Secretary and the state do not agree on a finding of noncompliance, P.L. 100-203 establishes special rules that must be adhered to when it is implemented.

COMPREHENSIVE DRUG ABUSE PREVENTION AND CONTROL ACT

Five schedules of drugs were established by the Comprehensive Drug Abuse Prevention and Control Act of 1970. Its **purpose** is to classify and set standards for use and control of substances that have an abuse potential. (21 CFR 1308)

Schedule I Substances are drugs with no accepted medical use in the United States and with a high abuse potential. Heroin and other opium derivatives, LSD, marijuana, and other related drugs are included. To sell, possess, or use these drugs is a criminal offense.

Schedule II Substances are drugs with a high abuse potential and with severe psychic or physical dependence liability. These drugs require a written prescription from a physician. These prescriptions may not be refilled nor can the medication be transferred to a person other than the patient for whom it is prescribed.

Three classes of Schedule II Substances are:

1. **Narcotics** Including morphine, codeine, cocaine;
2. **Stimulants** Including amphetamines and Ritalin; and
3. **Depressants** Including Seconal and Nembutal.

Schedule III Substances are drugs having less abuse potential than Schedule II or compounds containing limited quantities of certain narcotics. They require prescription by a physician. Prescriptions may be refilled, if the physician authorizes, up to five times in six months. After six months a new prescription is required. Examples are Empirin with codeine and paregoric.

Schedule IV Substances are drugs with less abuse potential than Schedule III. They are dispensed on the same basis as Schedule III drugs. Examples are Librium, Valium, Equanil and Dalmane.

Schedule V Substances are drugs with less abuse potential than Schedule IV. They are preparations containing limited quantities of certain narcotic drugs designed for use generally as antitussive and antidiarrheal preparations. Examples are Robitussin AC and Parapectolin. Some states require a prescription, whereas others require the patient to sign for the drug when dispensed by the pharmacist. If dispensed by physician's prescription, refills are on the same basis as Schedules III and IV.

A **cautionary statement** must be placed on any scheduled drug dispensed by the pharmacist, as follows:

CAUTION: Federal law prohibits the transfer of this drug to any person other than the patient for whom it was prescribed.

Other cautionary statements may be placed on any type of drug. These include such precautions as do not use with alcohol, wine, cheese, or must be taken with food or milk.

Schedules II, III, IV, and V are referred to as controlled substances. In the facility all must be stored under double lock and key and destroyed as described in Chapter 12 on Resident Care Management. The Drug Enforcement Administration (DEA) monitors this program.

Destruction of drugs The Act provides for destruction of discontinued drugs as outlined in Chapter 12.

NATIONAL LABOR RELATIONS ACT (NLRA)

Four major federal laws regulate employer and/or labor union conduct in labor-management relations. These are the: (1) Norris-LaGuardia Act (1932), (2) Wagner Act (1936), (3) Taft-Hartley Act (1947), and (4) Landrum-Griffin Act (1959). The Norris-LaGuardia Act set the stage for the National Labor Relations Act (NLRA) of 1936. It provides that (1) **yellow-dog** contracts in which employees agree not to join unions in return for continued employment are forbidden and (2) federal judges are forbidden from issuing injunctions against lawful labor activities unless there is danger to life or property. The NLRA should not be confused with the **Labor Management Relations Act (LMRA)** monitored by the Department of Labor. It concerns the internal operations of labor unions only.

Organizing requirements stipulate that at least 30 percent of a facility's employees must sign cards or by other actions indicate their desire for an election to organize. Usually the evidence submitted is signed cards. If the NLRB decides requirements have been met, it will conduct an election. If the majority of employees who vote (50 percent plus one), vote for the union, the NLRB certifies the union as the bargaining agent for the employees. (Twomey) Generally, labor unions do not submit cards to NLRB when only 30 percent have signed. Since they need at least 50 percent of those who vote before an election can be won, the union submits its request to the Board after they have more than 30 percent of employees signing cards. (See Chapter 6)

Purpose of the NLRA as established in the Act is: (1) to define and protect the rights of employees and employers, (2) to encourage collective bargaining, and (3) to eliminate certain practices on the part of labor and management that are harmful to the general welfare. **Provisions of NLRA** include: (1) defining the rights of employees to organize and to bargain collectively with their employers through representatives of their own choosing, (2) ensuring that employees can choose their own representatives by secret ballot election conducted by the National Labor Relations Board (NLRB), and (3) defining certain unfair labor practices of employers and unions.

Administration and enforcement are principally carried out by the NLRB and the general counsel through 45 regional or other offices. The general counsel and his regional office staff investigate and prosecute unfair labor practice cases and conduct elections to determine employee representatives. The five-member NLRB decides cases involving charges of unfair labor practices and determines election questions including which employees are eligible to vote in union elections. (NLRA Guide.)

Collective bargaining is the key provision of NLRA. It is defined as the employer and the representative of his employees meeting at reasonable times, conferring in good faith about certain matters, and putting into writing, if requested, any agreement reached. The parties must confer in good faith on wages, hours, and other terms or conditions of employment, the negotiations of an agreement, or any questions arising under an agreement.

It is an unfair labor practice for employers or organized employees to refuse to bargain collectively with each other. However, neither party is compelled to agree to a proposal made by the other, nor to make a concession to the other. **Changes** in a collective-bargaining agreement also are governed by very strict guidelines. (NLRA Guide.)

Rights of employees are: (1) To self-organization; (2) to form, join, or assist labor organizations; (3) to bargain collectively through representatives of their own choosing,; (4) to engage in other concerted activities for collective bargaining or other mutual aid or protection; and (5) to refrain from any or all such activities except to the extent such right may be affected by an agreement requiring membership in a labor organization. Examples of employee rights are:

1. Forming or attempting to form a union,
2. Joining a union whether the union is recognized by the employer or not,
3. Assisting a union to organize employees,
4. Going out on strike to secure better working conditions, and
5. Refraining from activity in behalf of a union.

Collective bargaining agreement If a facility is organized, union representatives and the facility work out an agreement. It is a legal document that sets forth conditions and standards for labor/management relations. It is hammered out through negotiations at the bargaining table. Administrators should be extremely careful about the period covered by the agreement. Generally, it is for one year, but it can be for two, three, or more years. Reason to exercise care is that if employees become dissatisfied they may want to vote the union out. In order to do so, employees who are members of the union must petition NLRB for a decertification election. This election can only be held at the end of the current bargaining agreement.

> **Example**: A facility signed a collective bargaining agreement with a labor union for three years upon insistence of employees who voted to organize. In 6 months members of the union were disillusioned and angry with the union. It had kept none of its promises and gained no benefits for employees. They wanted to vote the union out. NLRB advised they could sign a decertification petition and an election would be called. However, the union could not be voted out until the end of its contract one-and-a-half years later.

Strikes by employees are carefully regulated by the Act. As an example, picketing at any health-care institution can be done only after a 10-day written notice to the institution and to the Federal Mediation and Conciliation Service. (NLRA Guide) **Economic strikers** are those who strike to obtain higher wages, shorter hours, or better working conditions. They cannot be discharged, but may be replaced by bona fide permanent replacements. The employer is not required to reinstate strikers when they apply. They are entitled to reinstatement when jobs for which they qualify become vacant. During the past several sessions of Congress organized labor has pushed legislation that would require employers to reinstate strikers who went out for economic reasons. Should this legislation be enacted, nursing facilities may well find themselves at the mercy of organized labor.

Unfair labor-practice strikers cannot be discharged nor permanently replaced. When the strike ends they are entitled to reinstatement. (NLRA Guide)

For more detail on the very complex activity of unionizing, secure a copy of *A Guide to Basic Law and Procedures under the National Labor Relations Act.*

The Federal Mediation and Conciliation Service (FMCS) was established under the Taft-Hartley Act. This agency has two major duties: (1) to receive notifications of contract expirations and to offer to assist parties in developing new contracts without work stoppage and (2) to maintain a list of arbitrators qualified to decide on interpretation of current contract language when labor and management cannot agree on the interpretation.

The FMCS makes government facilities available for conciliation, mediation, and arbitration of labor-management problems. **Conciliation** means to bring together, to win over, to placate and/or to reconcile differences. **Mediation** means a third party is brought in to help settle differences, but neither party is bound by his decision. **Arbitration** means a third party is brought in, or assigned by a government authority, to settle differences in which both parties have agreed to abide by the arbiter's decision. It is sometimes referred to as **binding** arbitration.

Other federal provisions for monitoring nursing homes were discussed in Chapters 6 and 8. They include EEOC, FLSA, OSHA, Civil Rights, ADA, and Safe Medical Devices Act.

PROFESSIONAL LICENSING BOARDS

State licensing boards Licensing of professional personnel and registration of other allied health personnel are a prerogative of states. The federal government licenses no one. State boards of examiners, or a comparable legal entity, are responsible for setting standards, examining, issuing licenses, monitoring, and disciplining of practitioners. In a few states they have a department of licensing which administers examinations, issues licenses, investigates complaints, and disciplines. Their boards only certify applicants' eligibility and carry out any other assigned duty. Most states have an individual board for each profession; it handles all aspects of licensing in its particular discipline.

In the health-care field there are boards for physicians, pharmacists, nurses, licensed practical nurses, social workers, psychologists, dentists, chiropractors, and others. Physical, occupational, and speech therapists, physicians assistants, medical technologists, X-ray technicians, and others are often registered or certified by a state agency. Some health-care professionals are not licensed by the state; they are certified by their national association, as the American Dietetic Association, and the Dietary Managers Association.

Scope of practice All licensed, registered, and certified professions have regulations covering scope of practice and ethics. Some of these are statutory, as the Nurse Practices Act. Others are regulations promulgated by the board as authorized by law, especially a profession's code of ethics.

Complaints In a nursing home, when a licensed or state registered employee performs an act not within the scope of practice of his field or violates his board's code of ethics, it should be fully documented. The administrator should file a complaint with the appropriate state board or agency; otherwise, he may be declared equally liable. There is a temptation not to report it if a DON is involved in an area where nurses are not readily available. No matter the circumstances, it should be done, and the state board of nurse examiners will decide what action should be taken.

Example: A facility in a semi-rural area had several residents needing podiatric care. The DON called the podiatrist newly arrived in the community. He treated eight residents for in-grown toenails, bunions, etc. Three of these contracted severe infections, one losing a toe, another a foot, and the third hospitalized. The DON had not called the residents' physicians, although the facility policy clearly stated "no health-care professional is to provide service to a resident without the nursing staff first notifying the resident's physician."

Staff physicians were quite upset and told the facility owner he should fire the administrator for allowing this to happen. The administrator had immediately notified the state Medicaid agency which conducted an investigation. Investigators ruled it was not only improper for the DON to ignore facility policy, but it was extremely poor nursing practice to allow the infections to occur and to become so severe before calling the resident's physician. The administrator reported it to the state board of nursing which took disciplinary action. When the owners and the physicians learned the full story, they realized the administrator was not at fault. The DON was terminated and the administrator saved his job as well as avoided possible tort action against him.

THE LEGISLATIVE PROCESS

All administrators need to know something of the legislative process. There are times when they must work with their state legislators and their congressmen to procure proper nursing-home legislation. Fortunately, there are several organizations at the state and national levels that keep nursing homes apprised of proposed legislation that has been introduced in their state and in Congress. At the state level these include the state Nursing Home (or Health Care) Association and the state Association of Homes and Services for the Aging. At the national level the American Health Care Association and the American Association of Homes for the Aging, plus several other private organizations interested in long-term care are the watchdogs for legislation introduced in Congress.

Administrators should particularly understand the legislative process at the state level as they may be called upon to support legislation through lobbying efforts. Most legislatures require bills to be prefiled, while others encourage prefiling but also allow filing bills after the legislature convenes. All bills are referred to a committee for review and approval or disapproval. The committee decides whether a bill will reach the floor of the house and senate to be considered for passage.

Lobbying efforts focus on passing or killing a bill at the committee level. In case of long-term-care legislation this is nearly always the health and welfare committee. Administrators through their state health-care association have their bills introduced in either the house or the senate, or both, by a legislator(s) who is willing to support the bill.

Homework The key to favorable action on a bill is for the nursing-home industry to do its homework. Usually administrators are asked to contact their local legislators and request they support the legislation. They must know the bill by number and the value of the legislation. Senators and representatives are often not too interested in the details of a bill, because they expect the organization to explain this in committee. Before a bill is brought up in committee, the LTC organization should know how the vote will go. Be sure the legislator knows what opposition there may be and by whom. Sometimes he may have a commitment on something else to the opposition. Don't let the legislator be surprised and embarrassed in committee.

If the state allows it, some organizations have their bill filed after the legislature convenes, especially if there is opposition. It gives the opposition less time to prepare its proposals against the bill. Make sure legislators know of this plan and the opposition.

Committee appearance When called to testify on a bill before the committee, be prepared to make a very short presentation — three or four sentences at most — then offer to answer any questions of the committee. Never go before a committee with a mountain of information and data, planning to educate the committee. Many lobbyists lose their case with this approach. Legislators don't have time for lengthy presentations; it often irritates them. The less said before a committee the better. Homework should already have accomplished the LTC purpose.

When committees vote, it is often to defer rather than kill the bill, especially if the legislator who offered the bill testifies. Deferment usually means the bill is killed, but by deferring, it is less embarrassing to the author. Sometimes when there is heavy opposition, the committee will defer the bill, ask the opposing parties to work out their differences and return for another hearing. If the parties can reasonably agree, the committee will rehear the bill, and it may be reported out favorably.

Legislation When favorably reported out of committee, the bill goes to the legislative chamber in which it was introduced for further action. There may be floor debate so the organization backing the bill should contact as many legislators as possible to ensure a friendly reception of the bill. Amendments can be made on the floor of the chamber. Unless the sponsoring organization has done its job, unfriendly amendments can make the bill ineffective.

When a bill is passed it goes to the governor. The sponsoring organization should have previously determined whether the governor will sign. This is often done through a friend who has the governor's ear or through a governor's assistant. The governor usually has several options dependent on his state laws. He may sign, or veto, or allow the bill to become law or a pocket veto by not acting on it within a prescribed period of time.

Codifying In most states when the bill passes, the legislation is then codified much as federal legislation is placed in the Code of Federal Regulations. The legislation, with some detail on how it is to be carried out, is advertised in the state or federal *Register* as a proposed rule. Comments are invited for a specified period of time–usually 30 days–then it is advertised in the *Register* as a rule that is now in effect. If there is opposition that cannot be reconciled within the 30-day hearing period, the rule may be dropped or it may be revised and re-advertised.

The approved rule then becomes the guideline of operations rather than the law itself.

GLOSSARY

ADA Americans with Disabilities Act.

Case-mix management A system of reimbursement in which payment is based on the diagnosis and the cost of providing services to each diagnostic group.

Cautionary statement A warning placed on prescription drugs as required by law or as prescribed by the physician.

Certification The process of determining that a nursing facility meets federal standards for operation and the issuance of a certificate authorizing it to participate under Medicare and/or Medicaid.

CFR Code of Federal Regulations that describe procedures for carrying out provisions of federal laws.

Civil rights Rights that belong to every citizen of the state or country, including rights of property, marriage, protection by the laws, freedom of contract, trial by jury, and others.

Collective bargaining The employer and the representative of an employee union meeting at reasonable times, conferring in good faith about certain matters, and putting into writing, if required, any agreement reached.

Controlled substance Drugs that are classified and controlled by standards set forth by the Comprehensive Drug Abuse Prevention and Control Act.

DEA Drug Enforcement Administration that sets standards for controlling certain drugs.

Distinct part A long-term care unit operating under a hospital's license but certified for Medicare/Medicaid.

DRG Diagnosis related groups into which all types of illnesses are classified to determine payment to hospitals by Medicare.

Extended survey A survey conducted when the standard survey identifies a substandard case indicated as a Level A deficiency.

Fiscal intermediary — Medicaid An agency designated by an individual state to process claims and make payments to providers under the Medicaid program.

Fiscal intermediary — Medicare An agency designated by DHHS to process claims and make payment to providers under the Medicare program.

Form HCFA-1513 The disclosure of ownership form used by nursing facilities participating in Medicaid and/or Medicare.

FMCS Federal Mediation and Conciliation Service that makes government facilities available for settling labor-management contract problems.

Follow-up survey One that reevaluates specific care and services that were cited in the standard survey but are not supposed to be corrected.

Free standing facility A long-term care unit operated by a hospital, but the nursing facility has its own license and certification.

Governing body Person or persons legally responsible for the operation and direction of an organization or business, usually a board of directors.

HBV Hepatitis B virus that infects the liver and is highly contagious through fresh or dried blood, saliva, nasal mucus, seminal fluid, and menstrual discharge.

Heavy-care resident One who generally requires extensive staff assistance in transferring/mobility, using the toilet or catheter care, and eating.

Human subjects Individuals who participate in any type of research to test drugs, a type of treatment, or other activity.

Level A deficiency One that is a threat to the health and safety of resident(s).

Light-care resident One who may need assistance in grooming and dressing, but functions relatively independently in transferring/mobility, using the toilet or catheter care, and eating.

Mediation Using a third party to help disputing parties reach an agreement; disputing parties are not bound by any decision.

Medicare Part A The hospital, SNF, home health, and post-hospital rehabilitation services insurance program.

Medicare Part B The supplementary medical insurance program that includes physician's services, outpatient diagnostic and treatment services, and certain durable medical equipment and prosthetics.

Medication pass The administration of medications by the nursing staff.

MDS Minimum data set is an instrument used to examine in depth the history and assessment of each resident.

NLRA National Labor Relations Act which regulates relations of organized labor and management.

NLRB National Labor Relations Board created by the NLRA to decide cases involving charges of unfair labor practices and to determine union election questions.

Partial extended survey One that is conducted when there is a deficiency in a Level A requirement other than substandard care.

Plan of correction A document showing how each deficiency will be corrected and by what date.

Prosthetics Artificial parts added to the human body as a leg, arm, eye, or other.

Provider An individual, agency, or institution that provides health services to individuals.

Provider agreement An agreement executed under Medicaid and Medicare stating terms of services and payment to the providers.

Provider number The number assigned to Medicaid and Medicare providers which must be used in all transactions concerned with the two programs.

Resident rights The rights of the individual resident that federal law requires nursing facilities to protect and respect.

Resident sampling Selection of a stratified sample of residents for conducting a survey of individual resident rights, quality of care, environmental quality, and dining assessments.

Scheduled drugs Drugs that the DEA classified into five schedules according to abuse potential.

Sexual harassment Certain sexual advances, request for sexual favors, and other verbal and physical conduct in the work place as described under Title VII of the Civil Rights Act.

Single state agency The agency designated by a state to administer or supervise the Medicaid program.

Standards of participation Standards used under Title XVIII and Title XIX for the operation of health-care facilities participating in Medicaid and Medicare until OBRA became effective.

Standard setting and survey agency The agency designated by a state to license, participate in certification, and monitor operations of health-care facilities.

Standard survey A new survey procedure under OBRA that is resident centered and outcome oriented rather than focusing on the provider's potential for offering care.

State plan The plan developed by the single state agency for operation of the Medicaid program within the state.

Statement of Deficiencies A form on which facility deficiency is listed and related to the standard with which it is not in compliance.

Strike A walkout by employees in protest of an economic condition, such as low wages, poor employee benefits, and poor working conditions, or of unfair labor practices by management.

Substandard care Services of poor quality that result in a Level 4 deficiency.

Swing bed A bed in a rural hospital that may be used for either acute or long-term care.

REFERENCES

Mills, Daniel Q., *Labor-Management Relations, Fifth* Edition, New York: McGraw-Hill, 1993.

Pharmacist Manual, An Informational Outline of the Controlled Substances Act of 1970, Washington: Drug Enforcement Administration, U.S. Department of Justice, 1986.

State Operations Manual, Provider Certification, Revisions one and two, U.S. Department of Health and Human Services, Springfield, VA: U.S. Department of Commerce, National Technical Information Service, 1998.

Twomey, David P., *Equal Employment Opportunity Law*, Second Edition, Cincinnati: Southwestern Publishing Company, sixth edition, 1989.

Twomey, David P., *Equal Employment Opportunity Law,* Third Edition, Cincinnati: Southwestern Publishing Company, 1994.

U.S. Government Printing Office, Washington, D.C., all the following are available:

1. *A Guide to Basic Law and Practices Under the National Labor Relations Act,* 1976.
2. *Fair Labor Standards Act of 1938*, as amended, W.J. Publication 1318, 1985.
3. *Hourly Reference Guide to FLSA*, W.H. Publication 1282, 1983.
4. *Interpretive Bulletin, Part 785: Hours Worked under the FLSA of 1938*, W.H. Publication 1312, 1979.
5. *Overtime Compensation Under the FLSA*, W.H. Publication 1325, 1982.
6. *Records to be Kept by Employers under the Fair Labor Standards Act of 1938,* W.H. Publication 1261, 1986.
7. *Title 21 Code of Federal Regulations, Food and Drugs, Part 1308*, 1989.
8. *Title 29 Code of Federal Regulations, Labor, Parts 500-899*, 1989.
9. *Title 29, Code of Federal Regulations, Labor, Parts 1600-1699* (Equal Employment Opportunity Commission); *Parts 1900-1999* (OSHA), 1989.
10. *Title 42 Code of Federal Regulations, Public Health, Part 400 to 429*, 1995.
11. *Title 42 Code of Federal Regulations, Public Health, Part 430 to end,* 1996.

The Medicare Handbook, Publication HCFA 10050, Baltimore: U.S. Department of Health and Human Services, 1990.

Worker Exposure to AIDS and Hepatitis B, (OSHA 3102) Washington: U.S. Department of Labor, 1988.

CHAPTER 12

RESIDENT CARE

RESIDENT CARE MANAGEMENT

THE MISSION

Proper care of residents is the mission society has assigned to nursing facilities. Specifically, they are to develop and provide long-term care for the aged, disabled, and chronically ill who cannot be properly cared for at home or in a nonmedical environment.

Nursing facilities are relatively new on the service-providing scene. They have had far less time to perfect services and their delivery than schools with their mission to provide education, hospitals with their mission to provide acute care, and hotels with their mission to house and feed the traveler. Gerontology still has much to learn about the processes of aging and how to make people's senior years more healthful, comfortable, and rewarding. Much of what is known about gerontology and geriatrics has not yet been incorporated into LTC practice.

All that has been discussed previously in this publication leads to and supports the accomplishment of the LTC mission. Providing a comfortable and safe environment, a sound financial structure, a staff of trained, competent people, a nourishing, tasteful food supply, and a solid legal base for operations point to one thing—the delivery of adequate, proper and quality resident care. No matter how well the above needs are met, success is measured almost entirely in terms of the care given to the individual resident. Resident care is the focal point of the industry. It is the most sensitive aspect of any nursing facility operation. More dissatisfaction and complaints arise from resident care than any other activity in the industry. It is understandable, since far less is known about long-term care than about building, housing, maintaining, feeding, financing, training, and managing.

THE ADMINISTRATOR'S ROLE

Although there is much to learn about long-term care, a vast body of knowledge exists. The administrator's duty is to ensure this knowledge is available to a staff which is properly trained to use this knowledge with skill, and that a suitable environment in which to practice is provided.

Although the administrator is a manager charged with hiring a trained and skilled nurse to direct resident care, he himself must be knowledgeable in certain aspects of health care. Unless he is already a nurse, pharmacist, medical technologist, physician, or other health-care specialist, he probably knows little of the language or the practices used. Consequently, he should learn basic health-care terminology, diagnostic categories, drugs and medications, techniques for working with various disabilities, nursing, and other resident-care practices, and government regulations covering resident care. Without this knowledge he cannot communicate adequately with his resident-care staff, help them to solve their problems, and properly monitor their performance. He needs this knowledge to determine the quality of care his facility provides.

Basic resident-care information that administrators need to learn is presented in this chapter. Mastering this knowledge can be the beginning of their continuing education in long-term care, together with how to provide this knowledge efficiently and economically.

HEALTH CARE TERMINOLOGY

There is a tremendous number of health-care terms that nurses, pharmacists, physicians, dietitians, medical-record administrators, social workers, and other health-care personnel use in conferring with the administrator. The terms will be used with the assumption the administrator fully understands them. Without learning these basic terms, an administrator runs the risk of embarrassment in repeatedly asking his staff what they mean. He cannot pretend to understand a term because the risk is too great. He might underestimate the seriousness of what he is told, or he may make a wrong decision. Also, his staff will probably feel he is not very well-informed. The terms used in this publication may be found in Taber's Cyclopedic Medical Dictionary, 14th edition, or other medical dictionary. The terms which follow are but a beginning. They are only a sample of those more commonly used in nursing facilities.

1. **Prefixes** In health care there are many prefixes combined with a great number of medical terms. When used by two persons who understand them it enhances and saves time in communication. Although the administrator probably will not know them all, he will find prefixes helpful in understanding his staff's messages. Following are some of the **prefixes commonly used in nursing facilities.**

Ante- Before, as in anterior

Anti- Against, as antidote or antiseptic

Auto- By ones self or itself, as autonomic nervous system

Bi- Two, double, or twice, as biceps

Cardi- Pertaining to the heart, as cardiac arrest

Derm- or Derma- Pertaining to the skin, as dermatitis

Endo- Inner or within, as endoscopy - examination of lower intestinal tract

Gastro- Pertaining to the stomach, as gastroscope

Hemi- One half, as hemiplegia (hemiparalysis)—paralysis of one side of the body including one arm and one leg

Hemo or hema- Blood, as a hematoma — bleeding in a tissue or organ

Hydro- Referring to water, as hydrotherapy

Hyper- Above, excessive or beyond, as hyperactive

Hypo- Less than, below or under, as hypothermia—lowered body temperature. Hypo is also used to mean a hypodermic injection by needle—from "hypodermic", literally meaning "under the skin."

Mono- One or single, as monocular which refers to one eye

Myo- Pertaining to the muscle, as myositis - inflammation of muscle

Naso- Pertaining to the nose and nasal passages, nasogastric

Nephro- Pertaining to the kidney, as nephritis

Neuro- Pertaining to nerves, as neurological

Osteo- Referring to bone, as osteomyelitis – infection of bone marrow or bone structure

Oto- Pertaining to the ear, as otology

Para- Two like parts, such as both legs, as paraplegia—paralysis of both legs

Patho- Suffering or disease, as pathological and pathogen

Peri- Around, as pericardial

Pneumo- Pertaining to lungs, air, or respiration, as pneumonia or pneumatic

Procto- Rectum or anus, as proctoscopy — examination of interior of rectum

Quadra- Involving four, as quadriplegia — paralysis of all four limbs

Semi- Partial, not full, as semiconscious

Thoracic- Pertaining to the chest or thorax, as thoracectomy

Tri- Three, as triceps—a muscle with three heads

Uro- Pertaining to urine, as urology

2. **Suffixes** Numerous suffixes are used in health care, sometimes combined with one of the above prefixes. Others combine with medical terms that describe resident conditions or constitute a diagnosis.

-algia Pain, as in neuralgia

-ectomy Removal of any organ or gland, as appendectomy

-emia Pertaining to condition of blood, as hypoglycemia – low blood sugar

-ism Abnormal condition from excess of something, as alcoholism or botulism

-itis Infection of, as tonsillitis or appendicitis

-mania Madness or passion for, as kleptomania — compulsive stealing

-ology Study of, as neurology – study of nervous system

-osis Abnormal or diseased condition, as osteoporosis – bone disease

-otomy Incision of, as tracheotomy

-paresis Partial or incomplete paralysis, as hemiparesis

-pathy Indicating disease or morbid affection, as psychopathy

-philia A liking or affinity for, as hemophilia—a bleeder

-phobia Unreasonable fear or dread, as claustrophobia — fear of closed rooms or spaces

-plegia Paralysis, as hemiplegia—paralysis of one side of the body

-rrhage Abnormal or excessive discharge or flow, as hemorrhage — bleeding

-rrhea Discharge, as in diarrhea

3. **Common medical terms** The following medical terms are used to describe a resident's condition, a symptom, a technique, or something relating to health care. The terms listed are those especially used in long-term care.

Activities of daily living The five basic everyday activities residents engage in — eating, dressing, walking, toileting, and communicating

Acute Intense, usually a painful and/or serious condition, often fatal, as an acute illness

Ambulatory Able to walk about, not bedridden

Amputation Surgical removal of a limb, part, or organ

Aseptic Free from disease producing organisms. Also, referred to as asepsis.

Aseptic techniques Precautions used to kill or exclude pathogenic bacteria, as aseptic cleaning of an isolation room.

Atrophy The wasting away of an organ or tissue as brain cells in Alzheimer's

Autopsy Examination of organs, tissues, and cells of a dead person

Bedridden Confined to bed, unable or not allowed to sit, stand, or walk

Benign Not recurrent or progressive, nonmalignant, good prognosis

Blood Pressure The pressure of the blood on the walls of the blood vessels, measured as systolic and diastolic and recorded as 130/80.

Bypass Surgically installing an alternate route for blood to bypass an obstruction in a main or vital artery

Chemotherapy Treatment of a disease with chemical compounds, as thiazides and coumarins

Chronic Prolonged, of long duration and/or recurring, as a chronic disease

Colostomy Opening of a portion of the colon onto the abdominal surface to divert the flow of feces from the colon and anus

Coma A state of profound insensibility caused by disease, injury, or poison; totally unconscious

Comatose Relating to or like a coma; in a coma; lethargic

Communicable Capable of spreading from one person to another, as a communicable disease

Congenital Existing at, or dating from birth, not inherited, as a congenital deformity

Contagious Communicable by contact, spreading from one person to another, as a disease; or charged with disease germs, as contagious material

Contusion A bruise in which the skin is not broken

Convalesce To gather strength after sickness; to recover health gradually

Cytotoxic Destructive of white cells as in patients treated with radiation, chemotherapy, and immunosuppressants

Decubitus ulcer A bedsore, frequently called pressure sore

Degenerative Deterioration of a tissue or an organ in which vitality is diminished

Dehydrated When body tissues lose too much water

Delirium A state of mental confusion characterized by disorientation of time and place

Delusional A false belief or misconception regarding the self, as delusions of persecution or being poisoned

Diagnosis Determined by examination using both clinical and laboratory methods; also, the decision reached, as pneumonia, carcinoma, etc.

Dialysis Removing impurities from the blood by machine when kidneys fail to function

Edema Condition in which body tissues retain an excessive amount of fluids

Equilibrium State of balance, contending forces are equal

Etiology Cause of a disease

Gangrene Necrosis or death of tissue, usually due to deficiency in blood supply

Geriatrics A medical specialty concerned with care and treatment of the aged

Germicide A disinfectant which destroys disease germs; used to control the spread of disease

Hallucination Having a sensory experience—feeling, hearing, smelling, seeing, or perceiving — when there is no basis in reality nor any exterior stimuli, as hearing voices when no one speaks

Hematoma A swelling that contains blood; blood under the skin or in tissues

Hemorrhage Any discharge of blood from blood vessels; it may be internal or external

Hepatitis Inflammation of the liver which is of viral or toxic origin

Hereditary The transmission of genetic characteristics from parent to offspring

High Blood Pressure (HBP) Blood pressure that measures above the normal for an individual, usually one in which the diastolic (lower) approaches 100

Hypertrophy Enlargement or overgrowth of a part of the body

Incontinent Lack of proper bladder and/or bowel control

Inflammation Tissue reaction to injury; changes which occur in living tissue when it is injured; not the same as infection with which it is often confused

Intramuscular In the muscle, as an injection

Jaundice Yellowness of the skin and whites of eyes, mucous membranes, and body fluids due to deposit of bile pigment in the blood

Laceration A tear, irregular cut, or mangled condition of the body—a wound in which there is bleeding.

Malignant Virulent, resisting treatment, tending or threatening to produce death, as a malignant tumor

Malnutrition Deficiencies in nutrition, usually characterized by both weakened body condition and resistance to disease.

Metastasis Spread of bacteria or body cells to other organs, as in a malignancy

Modality A mode or type of treatment or procedure, as diathermy and hydrotherapy; previously used only in physical therapy

Morbidity The incidence of disease, known cases of a disease, usually expressed as rate per thousand or hundred thousand population

Mortality Death rate, usually expressed as rate per thousand population

Nausea Sickness of the stomach with a desire to vomit

Neurosis A disorder of the thought processes not due to any disease of the nervous system. It is probably caused by unresolved internal conflicts and may be characterized by fatigue, phobia, nervousness, hypochondria, compulsiveness, and/or depression.

Nosocomial Infection contracted while in facility, as MRSA — methicillin-resistant staphalococcus aureus

Obese Extremely fat, at least 20% above weight for height, build, age, and sex.

Paranoid Suspicious, has delusions of persecution, projects blame on others, may be suicidal

Pathogenic Causing disease, as streptococcus organisms

Pathological Due to disease, as pathological tissue

Phobia Any persistent abnormal fear

Prognosis Probability of outcome, outlook for future or recovery of patient, as prognosis is guarded

Prone Lying horizontal with face and palms downward

Psychosomatic Physical conditions resulting from mental causes

Ptomaine Illness from eating filthy food; is not a true food poisoning

Renal Dialysis Treatment for end stage renal disease in which impurities normally removed by the kidney are removed by a dialysis machine

Senescent Tendency of older people to become forgetful and less perceptive

Sharps Objects that can penetrate the skin as needles, scalpels, broken glass, broken capillary tubes, and exposed ends of dental wires

Spasm An involuntary and unnatural muscle contraction

Spasmodic Intermittent, lacking in continuity, as spasmodic headaches

Subcutaneous Under the skin, as subcutaneous injection

Suicidal Appears to want to, or intends to voluntarily take his own life

Supine Lying on back with face, palms, and feet facing upward

Symptoms Any perceptible change in the body or its functions

Thorax The chest, that part of the body between the neck and the diaphragm

Toxic Poisonous to a person's system

Trauma A wound or injury; in psychiatry, a horrifying or shocking experience

Tumor An abnormal growth of noninflammatory tissue that has no physiological function

Vaginal discharge A drainage of blood or secretions from the vagina

Vertigo A term used for dizziness, light headedness, and giddiness

Vital signs Body temperature, pulse, respiration, and blood pressure

Ulcers Open sores of the skin or mucous membranes accompanied by sloughing of inflamed necrotic tissue

4. **Abbreviations** Several abbreviations are used by medical and nursing staff to save time and enhance communication. The following are only a few examples.

BID Twice daily used in prescriptions

BMR Basal metabolic rate is the rate of metabolism under basal conditions as 12 hours of fasting, after restful sleep, no exercise or activity preceding test, and so on; seldom used today.

BP Blood pressure

ECG and EKG Electrocardiogram, a record of the electrical activity of the heart

EEG Electroencephalogram, a tracing of electrical activity of the brain

HBV Hepatitis B virus that infects the liver, is highly contagious

HPB High blood pressure

Hypo Short for hypodermic injection

I. M. Intramuscular, as injection of medication into the muscle by needle and syringe

I.V. Intravenous, as injection of medication or other fluids into the vein

I.V. Push Administration of medication intravenously by quick forcible injection

MRI Magnetic resonance imaging, a diagnostic procedure in which the patient's body is placed in a magnetic field providing images of body organs and systems

PRN As necessary, used in prescription and order writing

QID Four times daily

SOB Shortness of breath

Stat Immediately

TID Three times daily

TPR Temperature, pulse, and respiration refers to the measurement of each of these.

COMMON DIAGNOSES

A working knowledge of diagnoses common to the aged and disabled is important to administration. Diagnostic terms are used all too freely by the nursing staff, with a resident sometimes referred to and related to as a diagnosis rather than as a person. Certain diagnoses may arouse fear, impatience, rejection, or hopelessness in some of the nursing staff. This may, in turn, affect their attitude, behavior, and handling of the resident. This may be especially true of terminal cases which may cause staff to feel helpless since they cannot promote healing.

By knowing the meaning of diagnoses and understanding something of their characteristics, the administrator can help to lessen adverse reactions on the part of the staff and sometimes the residents' families. As an example, a diagnosis of cancer is synonymous with death in most people's minds. Understanding that each cancer is individual and that many people live out their days in relative comfort may assist the administrator in helping his staff to develop proper attitudes and practices with cancer cases. The following diagnoses, medical conditions, and comments are often useful to an administrator in carrying out his role as a leader and shaper of constructive resident-care attitudes.

AIDS Acquired immune deficiency syndrome that results in a person having little or no immunity to disease.

Alcoholism A chronic, progressive, potentially fatal disease characterized by physical dependency and/or pathological organ changes due to ingestion of alcohol.

Alzheimer's disease A form of presenile dementia due to atrophy of frontal and occipital lobes of the brain. This is an increasingly prevalent disorder among the elderly. It's cause is yet unknown. It is a progressive deterioration of the intellect. It is a classic, chronic disease of the elderly that interferes with social and vocational functioning.

AMD Age-related macular degeneration is a disorder of the eye characterized by inability to see anything that requires straight ahead vision, often resulting in blindness.

Angina pectoris Severe pain about the heart, usually radiating to the left shoulder and down the arm

Anorexia Loss of appetite

Aphasia Absence or impairment of the ability to communicate through oral and/or written language; it often occurs after brain damage in accidents and from strokes.

Apnea Temporary cessation of breathing, a serious symptom sometimes occurring in the aged during profound sleep

Arteriosclerosis Thickening, hardening, and loss of elasticity of the walls of arteries; it is the most frequent metabolic disorder of the aged.

Arthritis Inflammation of a joint, usually accompanied by pain, and frequently by changes in bone and joint structure

Atrophy A decrease in size of an organ or tissue

BDA Benign disequilibrium of aging, a very common disorder in which the balance centers of the inner ear fail to function properly causing imbalance while walking

Botulism Food poisoning caused by toxin of a bacillus that may infect preserved foods, sausage, and canned meats

Carcinoma A new growth or malignant tumor that tends to give rise to metastasis; it is synonymous with the term cancer.

Cataract Opacity (darkening) of the lens of the eye or its capsule or both; very common in the aged

Cerebrovascular Pertaining to the blood vessels of the brain, especially to pathological changes

Cerebrovascular accident (CVA) A cerebrovascular condition resulting from a hemorrhage, a stroke – may result in paralysis

Congestive heart failure A condition characterized by weakness, breathlessness, abdominal discomfort, and edema in the lower portions of the body due to reduced outflow of blood from the heart

Coronary heart disease Myocardial damage due to insufficient blood supply, caused by pathological changes in the coronary arteries

Cystitis Inflammation of the bladder, usually following urinary tract infection

Dementia Impairment of mental powers due to organic causes

Depression An emotional condition, an affective disorder characterized by feelings of hopelessness, sadness, and inadequacy. It is the most frequent mental problem in nursing facilities. Residents may withdraw, isolate themselves, lack motivation, and/or show agitation.

Diabetes A general term for disease characterized by many symptoms, one of which is excessive urination. There are many types, but it usually refers to diabetes mellitus (sugar diabetes) in which there is a deficiency of insulin.

End-stage renal disease A permanent failure of the kidneys to perform essential functions that results in a need for dialysis

Epilepsy A recurring paroxysmal disorder of the brain characterized by sudden, brief convulsive seizures, altered consciousness, motor activity, or sensory phenomena.

Glaucoma Disease of the eye characterized by increase in pressure within the eye; may result in blindness. It can be controlled but generally has no cure.

Heart attack Descriptive term for a clinical condition caused by occlusion of a coronary artery(s), characterized by heavy pressure or squeezing pain in the chest that may spread to the shoulder and arm. There may also be sweating, nausea, vomiting, and shortness of breath.

Hemiparesis Partial or incomplete paralysis of one side of the body

Hemiplegia Paralysis of one side of the body

Hypertension A condition in which a person has higher blood pressure than normal

Hemophilia Hereditary blood disease in which there is greatly prolonged coagulation time for blood; abnormal bleeding occurs.

Herpes A general term used for a variety of infections of nerve endings caused by a number a different herpes viruses.

Multiple sclerosis A chronic, slowly progressive disease of the nervous system, with many symptoms, that is degenerative

Nephritis Inflammation of the kidney

Obesity Abnormal amount of fat on the body, usually 20 to 30 percent over the average weight for a person's age, sex, and height

Osteoporosis Disease of the bone characterized by a reduction in bone density associated with loss of calcium

Paraplegia Paralysis of lower portion of the body and of both legs

Parkinson's disease A chronic nervous disease characterized by a fine slowly-spreading tremor, muscular weakness and rigidity, and peculiar gait; common in the aged.

Pressure sore (decubitus) Bed sores that occur on pressure points of the body.

Pulmonary conditions Disorders of the lungs and bronchial tubes, as pneumonia, lung cancer, and bronchitis

Quadriplegia Paralysis of all four limbs and usually the trunk of the body

Senile dementia Deteriorative mental state due to organic brain damage occurring in the aged, characterized by loss of memory

Shingles Acute inflammation of peripheral nerves in the trunk of the body, and sometimes elsewhere, by a herpes virus

Stroke Sudden loss of consciousness followed by paralysis caused by hemorrhage into the brain, formation of a blood clot, or rupture of an artery in the brain; a cerebrovascular accident

Syndrome A group of signs and symptoms that collectively characterize or indicate a particular disease or abnormal condition, as Down's Syndrome

HEALTH CARE SPECIALISTS

Resident rights specify that the resident choose his own physician. If a resident is unable to make this choice, his legal representative makes the choice. But, there may be times when a physician is needed; however the resident's attending physician and his backup cannot be contacted, and the legal representative is not available. In this event, if the resident cannot make a choice, the administrator must choose for the resident. The following health-care specialties are often involved in caring for nursing-home residents.

1. **Physicians** A Doctor of Medicine (MD) and a Doctor of Osteopathy (DO) may admit residents to nursing facilities, attend residents, and prescribe medications. The following list shows disorders in which they specialize.

Allergist Allergic disorders, as to pollen, dust, chemicals, certain foods, etc.

Anesthesiologist Administers anesthesia for surgery and related medical procedures

Cardiologist Diseases of the heart and blood vessels

Dermatologist Diseases of the skin

Endocrinologist Disorders of the endocrine (ductless) glands and their functions

Gastroenterologist Disorders and diseases of the digestive tract

General practitioner Physician who specialized in family practice

Geriatrician All aspects of aging, including diseases and emotional and other problems, sometimes used synonymously with gerontologist

Gynecologist Problems and diseases of the female reproductive system

Hematologist Study of blood

Internist Internal medicine, and treating internal disorders

Nephrologist Disorders of the kidney

Neurologist Disorders and diseases of the nervous system, interprets electroencephalograms (EEG's)

Obstetrician Pregnant women and delivery of babies

Oncologist Tumors, especially cancer, and use of radiation therapy

Ophthalmologist Examination and treatment of disorders of the eye, including treatment of glaucoma, an oculist

Orthopedist Bone, joint, muscle, and other supporting structures of the body

Osteopath A doctor of osteopathic medicine

Otologist Hearing problems and diseases of the ear

Otolaryngologist Diseases of the ear, nose, and throat; an ENT specialist

Pathologist Diagnosing morbid changes in body tissues removed in operations and postmortem examinations

Pediatrician Children's diseases

Physiatrist Physical medicine, works with physical and occupational therapists, directing various physical rehabilitation therapies

Proctologist Disorders of the colon and the rectum

Psychiatrist Specialist in emotional and mental disorders who does psychotherapy or counseling

Primary physician A physician in charge of one's overall care in a managed-care organization; he makes referrals to specialists and orders tests.

Radiologist Specialist in diagnosis and treatment by use of X-ray and other radiant energy

Rheumatologist Specialist in rheumatic disorders, arthritis

Surgeon May specialize in general surgery or a special branch of surgery, as cardio, cosmetic, neuro, ortho, thoracic

Urologist Disorders of the urinary tract

2. **Dentists** These are Doctors of Dental Surgery (DDS) who may attend residents in nursing facilities, but cannot admit them.

Oral surgeon A dentist who specializes in corrective surgery involving teeth and/or jaws

Orthodontist A dentist who specializes in abnormality and malfunctions of the teeth and jaws; applies braces and may do corrective surgery

Periodontist A dentist specializing in diseases of the gums

3. **Other health-care professionals** There is a number of other health-care professionals with whom administrators need to be familiar. They may provide services to residents, but they cannot admit or serve as attending physicians.

Anesthetist An R.N. trained to administer anesthesia

Chiropractor A doctor of chiropractic who may attend residents but cannot admit them to nursing homes. He is not a doctor of medicine.

Gerontologist One who studies and describes the aging processes and problems and endeavors to increase understanding of how to work with the aged. He may or may not hold a doctor of medicine degree.

Licensed Practical Nurse or Licensed Vocational Nurse Graduate of a practical nursing school who is licensed to practice

Optometrist A doctor of optometry examines and diagnoses problems of the eye, prescribes and fits eyeglasses, but cannot treat diseases of the eye or do surgery. He can attend residents in nursing facilities but cannot admit them or prescribe medication. He is not a doctor of medicine.

Pharmacist A person duly qualified by training and licensing to fill prescriptions, review medications, and serve as a consultant to nursing facilities.

Podiatrist A doctor of podiatric medicine who specializes in diagnoses and treatment of problems of the feet. He can attend residents in a nursing facility but cannot admit. He can write prescriptions. He is not a doctor of medicine.

Psychologist A specialist in determining mental abilities and diagnosing and treating mental and emotional disorders through counseling. He cannot prescribe medications. They are licensed in many states.

Registered nurse A graduate of a registered nurse school and is licensed to practice

Social Worker A person with at least a bachelor's degree in social work trained to counsel people on social and emotional problems. They are licensed in many states.

Family counselor Some states license family counselors whose work is much like psychology or social work.

EQUIPMENT AND SUPPLIES

Knowledge of equipment and supplies, their cost, and their use is important to administrators. Otherwise, they could be persuaded to purchase equipment or material that is only minimally used or not necessary. Equipment and materials are sometimes improperly stored or misused unless the administrator is knowledgeable and monitors these activities.

The following resident-care equipment and supplies are some of the most commonly used in nursing facilities.

1. **Aspirator** An aspirator is used to withdraw fluids from the body by suction, more frequently the stomach and the lungs. This equipment should be used only under direct supervision of a nurse.

2. **Autoclave** An autoclave is used to sterilize instruments and various materials by use of steam and heat. Autoclaves are not required in a nursing facility, but the facility must have some means of sterilizing. Frequently, this is done by using a table-model water bath in which instruments may be placed and boiled. Alcohol may be used to sterilize thermometers and other small instruments. Due to increased use of disposables, sterilizing equipment is used less frequently.

3. **Bathing systems** Most facilities find that the automatic, whirl-type bathing system is extremely valuable in resident care. It is a large, relatively expensive tub into which residents are placed. Water temperatures and levels are automatically controlled. The tub must be in a room where privacy is possible. Some facilities install it in their therapy room.

   Strict procedures must be established, taught, and practiced. Since many residents using the tub are nonambulatory or semiambulatory, they cannot be left unattended at any time. Procedures for cleaning the system must be strictly enforced since a large number of individuals may use the tub daily. Temperature and water level controls need frequent preventive-maintenance monitoring to ensure safety of the resident and to prevent overflow and flooding.

4. **Disposables** Many medical supplies are now available as disposables: bedpans, emesis basins, water pitchers, drinking glasses, underpads, egg crates, hypodermic needles and syringes, and so forth. The administrator with his director of nursing must evaluate their advantages over reusables, comparative costs, required equipment for cleaning and storage, potential overuse, possible theft, proper disposable procedures, and so on. **Underpads**, as an example, are frequently misused. Instead of placing one or two, as needed, under the resident, aides sometimes cover the entire bed with them—an expensive, unnecessary practice. **Needles and syringes** must be controlled by rigid procedures and/or rules as discussed in Chapter 8. They are sometimes stolen, before use, and removed from the facility. On occasion they have been removed from the facility after being used.

5. **Egg crates** Foam rubber pads called egg crates, are placed on the top of mattresses to provide a softer surface. The name is derived from the indentations on one surface which look like an egg crate. Administrators need to establish a policy concerning their use. If prescribed by the physician, the facility must have a policy on whether it furnishes them free, furnishes them and charges the resident, or requires the family to purchase them and bring them to the facility in the unopened container.

6. **Emesis basin** An emesis basin is the crescent-shaped container placed under a resident's chin when he vomits or expectorates. The plastic type is frequently used as it can be cleaned and reused by the same resident. This type cannot be used by more than one resident. Emesis basins and bedpans are a frequent problem since staff tends not to keep them properly cleaned and stored. The state establishes and monitors procedures covering this activity.

7. **Medical supplies** The state specifies certain basic medical supplies that Medicaid facilities must furnish as a part of the resident-day cost. DHHS determines these for Medicare SNF's. These include dressings, wipes, needles and syringes, etc. Administrators must determine from their state agency that authorizes Medicaid payments, or their state licensing and certification agency, which medical supplies they must furnish without additional charge. Medicare SNF administrators may obtain this information from DHHS or their Medicare intermediary.

8. **Nasogastric (Levin) tube** Nursing facilities often have residents who are unable to swallow and therefore require a nasogastric tube. It is inserted in the nose, through the nasal cavity, down the esophagus into the stomach. The tube is used both for feeding and for aspirating fluids from the stomach. Extreme care must be exercised both in inserting the tube and in feeding through the tube.

9. **Oxygen** Use of oxygen in the nursing facility requires carefully followed procedures that the administrator as well as his director of nursing should monitor. When it is ordered, nursing facilities generally use oxygen in tanks. **Use** of oxygen must be accompanied by strict rules. Signs must indicate no smoking and oxygen in use. No oxygen tank should ever be left free standing. Because of its **weight**, if the tank falls over, it can easily break a leg or foot.

While in use tanks must be securely fastened to an oxygen truck (dolly) or to the wall. **Storage** of oxygen tanks is equally important. When not in use they must be stored outside, away from any electrical equipment or hazardous area. Also they must be securely fastened in an upright position to the building or placed in an enclosure where they cannot topple over. Administrators should check further with their local fire marshal on regulations for handling oxygen.

10. **Sphygmomanometer** The sphygmomanometer, generally called a cuff, is used to take blood pressure. With his director of nursing the administrator should determine whether the floor model with wheels is preferable and more efficient and economical than other models.

11. **Thermometer** An instrument used to measure body temperature. They are produced in a variety of models. Some are used for oral and some for rectal temperatures and some for ears.

STAFFING

Standards of health-care practice dictate that a facility must be adequately staffed to provide the services that it offers to the public. OBRA regulations specify certain minimum levels of staffing which it considers necessary to provide quality service to residents. These levels of staffing include physicians, nurses, social workers, activity directors, rehabilitation specialists, and the required health-care consultants. Administrators often find that the required minimum staffing is not adequate.

Qualifications of some professionals and paraprofessionals are specified by OBRA regulations. Others are required to meet standards established by states. Qualifications of some staff continues to be under discussion by the Federal Government, and these should be clarified when OBRA is fully implemented. Current qualifications are discussed in Chapter 6 on Personnel Management.

The required staff and their number and their qualifications are discussed in Chapters 6 and 9. Duties are discussed in this chapter under the appropriate service. Information is based on current OBRA standards. Administrators must keep alert to possible changes.

MEDICAL DIRECTOR [42 CFR 483.75 (i)]

The facility must have a physician who serves as medical director. There is an insufficient number of interested physicians and few facilities are large enough for there to be an organized medical staff as it exists in hospitals. Those that do have an organized medical staff are fortunate, since this staff elects a medical director. Most facilities have an attending physician to serve in this capacity. Some physicians serve as medical director without pay, while some facilities have a contract with a physician who serves as medical director for a fee. This is especially true in areas where medical residents are trained. Often a resident agrees to serve in this capacity for a nominal fee. Also, many retired physicians are now available to serve as medical director.

Duties The medical director is responsible for implementation of resident-care policies and the coordination of medical care in the facility. Policies include those on admission, transfer, resident's discharge, infection control, and physician privileges and practices. Also included are policies relating to the duties and responsibilities of nonphysician health-care workers, such as nurses, rehabilitation therapists, dietary services in resident care, emergency care, and resident assessment and care planning, In addition, the medical director is responsible for policies related to accidents and incidents, laboratory, radiology, pharmacy services, use of medications, use and release of clinical information, and overall quality of care.

The medical director is also responsible for coordination of medical care in the facility. The coordination role means the medical director shares responsibility for ensuring appropriate care is provided by monitoring and ensuring implementation of resident care policies, and providing oversight and supervision of physician services. When possible inadequate medical care is noted, he is to evaluate the situation and take appropriate steps to correct the problem. This may involve consultation with the resident, the family, and the attending physician. The medical director role includes assuring the support of essential medical consultation as needed. If his sole function is to approve resident-care policies that will not meet OBRA requirements.

The medical-director role may be enhanced by the administrator arranging regular luncheon or dinner meetings for all the attending physicians. All staff physicians should know the medical director and his duties. The medical director can often be helpful when the facility has a problem with an attending physician who does not visit his residents as required and/or fails to properly document.

PHYSICIAN SERVICES
[42 CFR 483.40]

As discussed under resident rights in Chapter 11, each resident chooses his own personal physician as long as the resident is capable of doing so. If the resident is not capable of choosing, his legal representative chooses the physician. In case of emergency when neither the physician nor backup physician are available, the administrator may be required to decide who attends the resident.

Qualifications The administrator should ensure that each physician attending residents is licensed to practice in the state in which the facility is located. This may be accomplished by contacting the state board of medical examiners or the local medical society. Most state medical examining boards publish a list of licensed physicians.

The **purpose** of determining qualifications is to ensure that no unlicensed person attends a resident in the facility. This has occurred, much to the facility's embarrassment.

Admission Each resident must be personally approved for admission in writing by a physician. Actually, the physician recommends admission. The facility decides whether to admit on the basis of availability of a bed and the facility's ability to provide the appropriate services. Should the physician recommend admission, and the facility believes the admission is not appropriate, staff should confer with the physician before a decision is made. The facility should explain its inability to admit the resident and plan with the physician for an appropriate placement. If the resident is admitted, the physician's admission orders for immediate care are accepted as his approval of the admission.

Supervision of each resident's medical care must be by a physician. OBRA further requires that the facility know who the **backup physician** is, and how he can be contacted when the regular physician is not available.

Supervision of medical care by the physician includes:

1. Participating in initial assessment and care planning
2. Monitoring changes in the resident's medical status
3. Providing consultation or treatment when called by staff
4. Prescribing any new therapy
5. Ordering resident's transfer to a hospital when necessary
6. Conducting required routine visits, or delegating and supervising follow-up visits by nurse practitioners or physician assistants.

Surveyors In monitoring these requirements, surveyors will determine if there is a deficiency in resident rights, resident's behavior and facility response, quality of life, or quality of care. If there is a deficiency, the regulation involved will be fully reviewed. Surveyors will also observe how the physician was involved in assessment and care planning, how the physician responded to a notification of change in his resident, whether the backup physician responded if the regular physician was not available, and whether residents were routinely sent to hospital emergency rooms because the facility had no physician on call.

Physician visits OBRA regulations require the resident's physician to visit the resident and to conduct the following activities during each required visit: (1) review the resident's total program of care, including medications and treatments, (2) write, sign, and date progress notes for each visit, (3) sign and date all orders.

Physician recording If the facility maintains computerized clinical records instead of hard copy, **electronic signatures** of physicians are acceptable. This is a convenience for both the physician and the facility, and it can represent a savings of time and money. When records are not computerized, physician's orders may be transmitted by a **fax machine** provided the physician has signed and retained the original copy of the order, and it is available upon request. The original may be sent to the facility later and substituted for the fax copy. The facility should **photocopy** the faxed order if its machine uses roll paper which fades over time. The original fax copy may then be destroyed. The facility should establish adequate safeguards for this system so it will not be subject to abuse. Should the fax copy be kept in the record, the physician is not required to resign it.

Rubber stamp signatures may be authorized by facility management; however, the individual whose signature the stamp represents must place in the facility's administrative office a signed statement that he is the only one who has the stamp and uses it. Under proper safeguards the facility must maintain a list of computer codes and signatures. They must be readily available to surveyors.

Total program of care includes all care the facility provides a resident to maintain or improve his highest practicable mental and physical functional status, as defined by the comprehensive assessment and care plan. Care includes medical services and medication management, physical, occupational, and speech/language therapy, nursing care, dietary interventions, social-work service, and activities to maintain or improve psychosocial functioning. The physician records a resident's progress and problems in maintaining or improving functional status. The physician is required to review the total plan of care during required visits, but he need not do so during other visits.

Frequency of visits are specified by OBRA regulations for SNF's and NF's. The resident must be seen at least once every 30 days for the first 90 days after admission. Thereafter, the resident must be visited at least once every 60 days. A physician's visit will be considered timely if it occurs within 10 days after the date they are required. The 10 day slippage of a due date does not affect the due date of the next visit. All **required** physician visits must be made by the physician personally, except after the initial visit. After the first visit, the visits in a SNF may alternate between personal visits by the physician and visits by a physician assistant or nurse practitioner. This practice is more fully discussed under delegation of tasks in a later paragraph.

Emergency care by a physician is the duty of the facility. Each facility must provide for or arrange physician services on a 24-hour a day basis in case of emergency. Each resident's physician should designate a backup physician to take his calls when he is not available. The facility should contact this physician when the resident's physician is not available.

When physician's services are not available from either of the above sources, the facility must assign a physician, or it may use a hospital emergency room or other medical facility. Some facilities in areas where medical residents train have an agreement with a resident physician to provide services in this type of emergency. Others have arrangements with the medical director in these instances. [42 CFR 483.40(d)]

Surveyors will note whether the facility has an on-call physician for medical emergencies, and whether this physician responds to calls. They also observe whether the handling of an emergency affected the resident's maintaining or improving his functional abilities.

Delegation of tasks may be used in a SNF by assigning certain tasks to a physician assistant, a clinical nurse specialist, or a nurse practitioner who meets qualifications in 42 CFR 492.1. Since these practitioners are regulated by individual states, they must act within the scope of practice as defined by their state law. Also, they must practice under supervision of the resident's physician. A physician may not delegate a task when regulations specify it is to be performed personally by the physician. No task may be delegated if prohibited by state law or the facility's own policies. [42 CFR 483.40 (e)] Administrators must determine whether physician assistants and nurse practitioners are allowed to practice as described herein before permitting any delegation of physician services regarding a resident in their facilities.

In a NF performance of physician tasks may be delegated to a nurse practitioner, a clinical nurse specialist, or a physician's assistant so long as they are not employed by the facility but are working in collaboration with a physician, provided state law permits it. This includes tasks that regulations specify must be performed personally by the physician.

Surveyors will monitor frequency of physician visits as they relate to any quality of care problems. Also, when nurse practitioners or resident assistants performs a physician's visit, surveyors will note whether the physician promptly followed-up when it was determined a personal visit was indicated.

DENTAL SERVICES
(42 CFR 483.55)

The facility must assist residents in obtaining **routine 24-hour emergency** dental care. These services must be provided by the facility, or obtained from **an outside source** in accord with 483.75 (h). This is a dramatic change from former Medicare and Medicaid regulations. Previously, an advisory dentist was required, and the facility only arranged for dental services as needed by each resident. Now the facility is directly responsible for dental care needs of residents. The facility must ensure that a dentist is available for residents, either by employing a staff dentist or contracting with a dentist to provide services. **Routine dental services** means inspection of the oral cavity for signs of disease, diagnosis of dental disease, dental radiographs as needed, dental cleaning, new fillings and repair of fillings, minor dental plate adjustments, and smoothing of broken teeth. It also includes limited prosthodontic procedures, such as taking impressions for dentures and fitting dentures. **Emergency dental services** include services needed to treat an episode of acute pain in teeth, gums, or palate. It also includes broken, or otherwise damaged teeth, and any other problem of the oral cavity appropriately treated by a dentist and requiring immediate attention.

Payment Although SNF's and NF's are responsible for providing or obtaining dental services, they are not required to pay for the services. SNF's are not obligated to pay for services to a Medicare resident. NF's are required to pay only for those services that will be reimbursed under the state's Medicaid plan. The facility may charge Medicare residents for both routine and emergency dental services. If the resident does not have funds to pay for needed dental care, the facility should have its social worker explore alternative means of having that care provided. The facility is obligated to provide access to dental care, but payment is the obligation of the resident, except for the Medicaid portion.

Qualifications In entering an outside resource agreement, the administrator must select dentists who are fully qualified and licensed in the state. He must ensure that dentists provide services in accordance with professional standards of quality and timeliness, as required under agreements with outside sources.

Prompt referral When residents lose or damage dentures the facility must promptly refer them to the dentist. This means as soon after dentures are lost or damaged as feasible. It does not mean the resident must see the dentist at that time, but it does mean an appointment (referral) is made, or the facility aggressively works toward replacing the dentures.

Appointments and transportation If a resident needs assistance with making appointments, staff must provide whatever assistance is needed. If necessary, the facility arranges transportation to and from the dentist's office. Arranging transportation means determining if family can provide it, securing nonemergency medical transportation, or if none is available, to provide it.

Since poor dentition is a major factor in malnourishment, the facility should have an active dental hygiene program. One of the dentists should assist with training nursing staff in helping residents to maintain proper oral hygienic practices, such as proper brushing and flossing their teeth, care and use of dentures, and early attention to dental needs.

Surveyors will select a sample of residents with dentures and determine whether they use them. They check a sample of residents with missing teeth to determine if dentures are needed. Also, they monitor a sample of residents who have problems eating and maintaining nutritional status because of poor oral health or hygiene. Surveyors will question individual residents on whether the facility has helped them to see the dentist and to deal with lost or damaged dentures. They will note how long it takes to get dentures repaired or replaced.

NURSING SERVICE
[42 CFR 483.30]

Both SNF's and NF's must have sufficient nursing staff to provide nursing and related services for attaining or monitoring the highest practicable physical, mental, and psychosocial well-being of each resident. This level of well-being is determined by resident assessments and individual plans of care. Staffing patterns, qualifications, and waivers for nurses were discussed in Chapter 6 on Personnel Management.

Nursing hours per resident day are established by the state with federal approval. Currently, many states have established a minimum of two and one-quarter nursing hours per resident day for SNF residents and two hours for residents in an NF. This is subject to change, especially if case-mix management is adopted by HCFA. In any event the two and one-quarter hours for skilled residents is a bare minimum that will not meet required needs if the facility has severely debilitated residents.

Duties Duties of the **director of nursing** and of the charge nurses are not listed in OBRA regulations as they were in previous Medicare/Medicaid regulations. The following duties for the DON, some of which were in prior federal guidelines, are useful to the administrator in developing a proper job description. They are based on standards of practice.

1. Develop and periodically update statements of philosophy and objectives that define the type of nursing care the facility proposes to provide. The objectives identify the importance of integrating both the plan of medical care and the plan of resident care.

2. Develop and maintain nursing-service policies and procedures to implement the program of care.

3. Ensure that the total nursing needs of residents are met by assigning a sufficient number of qualified supervisory and supportive nursing personnel for each tour of duty.

4. Participate in coordination of resident-care services through use of the interdisciplinary team's assessment and care plans.

5. Cooperate with the administration in planning a staff development program that will upgrade the competence of the personnel. Specific attention is given to improve supervisory skills of the charge nurses and the multi-disciplinary approach to resident care.

6. Ensure that all nurses' notes are informative and descriptive of the nursing care provided and of the resident's response to care.

7. Participate in planning and budgeting for nursing service.

8. Review the nursing requirements of each resident admitted to the facility and assist the attending physician in planning for the resident's care.

9. Assume responsibility for maintaining her own professional competence through participation in programs of continuing education, e.g., nursing seminars and short-term training courses.

10. Ensure that the philosophy and objectives are understood by nursing personnel.

11. Establish a procedure for ensuring that nursing personnel, including private-duty nurses, have valid and current licenses as required by the state in which the facility is located.

12. Assign duties and monitor and evaluate work performance of subordinate nurses and other nursing staff as indicated.

Charge Nurse OBRA does not specify duties for charge nurses; however, standards of practice indicate the following list is fairly characteristic of practice in nursing homes.

1. Make daily resident visits to observe and evaluate physical and emotional status.

2. Review medication cards for completeness of information, accuracy in the transcription of physician orders, and adherence to stop order policies.

3. Participate in resident assessment and care plans for appropriate resident goals, problems, approaches, and revisions based on nursing needs.

4. Assign duties for the direct care of specific residents to the nursing staff based on the needs of the facility and the capability of the staff, monitor performance and complete employee evaluations.

5. Arrange schedules to allow time for supervision and evaluation of performance of all nursing personnel on the unit.

Surveyors will monitor adequacy of nursing personnel in each unit by observing whether staff is available when needed and whether resident needs are being met. They will determine if there is sufficient staff to meet direct-care needs, do assessments planning and evaluations, and provide supervision. Surveyors will observe whether all the following activities are met: (1) staff are responsive to resident needs for assistance, (2) resident call bells are answered promptly, (3) nursing staff are always nearby or responsible, (4) there is little delay in answering resident calls or needs for assistance, (5) residents seeking staff have little difficulty locating a staff member when the need arises, and (6) residents do not have to call repeatedly for assistance.

In making these observations, surveyors will consider what the staff is doing when resident requests and calls are made. They will consider whether staff is attending need of another resident, sitting in the lounge, or simply chatting with other staff. Also, surveyors will consider the nature of the resident's request. If there is urgency, such as the resident is cold, wet, or needs assistance with toileting, surveyors expect the response to be prompt.

Training The administrator and the director of nursing should plan a regular program for updating nursing staff on geriatric care. With so much new knowledge being developed regarding Alzheimer's, arteriosclerosis, AIDS, and the aging process, nursing staff needs continuing education. OBRA only requires such training for aides, but all nursing staff need it. If surveyors find deficiencies in resident care, they will monitor the training program.

Performance of the nursing-staff duties are reflected in the Resident Care Practices section of this Chapter.

SOCIAL SERVICE
[42 CFR 483.15 (g)]

Regardless of size, all facilities must provide medically-related social services to attain or maintain the highest practicable physical , mental, and psychosocial well-being of each resident. In order to accomplish this, both SNF's and NF's with more than 120 beds must employ a full-time social worker as described under social-work qualifications in Chapter 6.

Duties Social-worker duties are not specified in OBRA regulations. Certainly, the social worker should not be an assistant to the DON nor to the activity director. Administrators should assign specific duties that will enhance resident assessment and care plans. A well-trained social worker will bring knowledge and skills of counseling with residents, family, and staff regarding social and emotional needs. Services provided by the social worker, which amounts to duties, might include those that follow.

1. Participate as a member of the interdisciplinary team responsible for resident assessment and development of the care plan. They should identify and seek ways to support resident needs and preferences, customary routines, concerns, and choices.

2. Identify and develop a file of all community services and help the resident and family utilize them when needed. Figure 12.1 lists some examples.

Figure 12.1

Community Resources

Resource	Service
• Lions Club	eyeglasses
• Speech & Hearing Foundation	hearing aids
• Cancer Society	support groups other
• Alzheimers Society	support groups
• Non- emergency Transportation	transportation
• Council on Aging	depends on local council
• Library	talking books bookmobile, etc.
• Hospice	counseling support service
• Children's Day Care Center	child visitation
• High schools	teen adoption of residents
• Churches	religious services

3. Compile social histories to assist in understanding resident's background, family resources, history of illness, interests, and so on.

4. Maintain contact with resident and family regarding the resident's problems and his rights, reporting changes in health, encouraging resident and family to participate in care planning, and planning for discharge.

5. Assist the family in planning when there are financial, legal and other problems, and refer to mortuaries when preplanning arrangements are indicated.

6. Assist residents in utilizing individual and group activities to their best advantage, and finding options to meet emotional and physical needs.

7. Observe, record, and notify staff of changes in affect, behavior, or personality, especially depression, anxiety, withdrawal, and uncontrollable aggression, and confer with families on change of health status, needs for transfer, and so on.

8. Develop and use skills of interviewing, nondirective counseling, crisis intervention, and communicating with community resources, especially if specialized counseling is needed, and counseling during the grieving process.

9. Maintain contact with the family regarding resident's problems and rights.

10. Record all pertinent social data about medically related personal and family problems in patient's medical record.

11. Make arrangements for obtaining adaptive equipment, clothing, and personal items.

12. Help the staff to understand emotional needs and how to provide support to residents, including dignity and individuality.

13. Helping staff to understand resident behavior, what residents are trying to communicate, and what needs the staff should try to meet.

Counseling Social workers should have special training in counseling techniques. Those with master's degrees and licensed, when applicable, are trained in these techniques. Many of them are trained in psychotherapy, but social workers in nursing homes generally do not practice psychotherapy. More often they refer residents to mental-health centers or private practitioners for this form of treatment.

Social workers should give particular attention to helping provide services when there is (1) a lack of family/social support systems, (2) a psychotic episode or depression, (3) chronic or acute pain, (4) difficulty in personal interaction and in social skills, (5) abuse of alcohol or drugs, (6) changes in family relationships and living arrangements, (7) a need for restraints, and (8) chronic, disabling medical or psychological conditions as multiple sclerosis, Alzheimer's, schizophrenia, or others.

Evaluation How does an administrator determine whether he has an effective social-service program? He should regularly audit the program through conferences with his social worker and reports. The social worker's community resource file should be reviewed to ensure all resources available to residents are on record. The program is effective when it links social supports, physical care, and the environment with resident needs.

Surveyors look for evidence that social-service interventions successfully address residents' needs and link social supports, physical care, and physical environment with residents' needs and individuality. They will note how social work monitors resident progress and how care plans link goals to psychosocial functioning and well-being. Surveyors also observe whether social-work staff has established and maintained relationships with the residents' families or legal representatives.

RESIDENT CARE POLICIES AND PROCEDURES

As discussed earlier, sound management practices dictate that a facility have policies and procedures covering **every activity of the facility**. This is especially true of resident care as it involves safety and health of the consumer the facility serves. Nursing service alone may have as many as 100 individual procedures covering every aspect of nursing care from giving bed baths to administering narcotic medications. Such procedures are needed as a guide to nursing staff in providing care to the resident in a manner that ensures all services are equal to, or exceed, standards of practice. In addition to nursing procedures, a facility should have clear, concise procedures on admission, social service, resident activities, pharmacy and medications, rehabilitative services, medical and dental services, clinical records, discharge, and others. Every aspect of resident care should be in writing, updated regularly, and reviewed and approved at least annually by the governing body.

OBRA regulations make few references to policies and procedures since the Federal Government expects facilities to adhere to sound management practices and professional standards of practice. It is the administrator's duty to ensure that the facility has proper resident care guidelines. The administrator cannot expect the director of nursing, the social worker, and other department heads involved in direct resident care to develop proper policies and procedures by themselves. Every administrator must take an active personal interest by helping to develop policies and procedures and by observing how they are followed. Resident care departments heads can be expected to draft both policy and procedure, but it is the administrator who must put them in final form and present them to the governing body for review and approval.

OBRA regulations specify that the **medical director** is responsible for ensuring that resident care policies and procedures are implemented. [42 CFR 483.75 (i)] In practice, it is obvious that although the medical director is responsible, the director of nursing is the most active person in ensuring implementation of resident-care guidelines. It is a day-to-day duty of the DON. The administrator is equally responsible in this activity. Resident care is largely delegated to the DON, but the administrator must indicate continued interest in how well care guidelines are carried out. This may be accomplished by frequent visits — daily is best — to the resident care areas and observing staff's efforts and the results. The administrator's visibility sends a strong message to staff, residents, and families that he is interested in resident care and that he is supportive of staff efforts. Guidelines for evaluating policies and procedures are discussed in Chapter 3.

PREADMISSION SCREENING [42 CFR 483.20 (f)]

OBRA requires preadmission screening of any new resident who might have some form of mental illness or mental disability that prohibits admission. A person who is mentally ill or mentally disabled may not be admitted to a SNF or NF unless the facility provides **specialized services** and all other care and services needed. As an alternative, some states provide for ICF-MR facilities to provide specialized services to mentally disabled and do not admit them to SNF's or NF's.

Mentally ill Definition for mental illness is a person who has a serious mental illness (as defined by the secretary in consultation with the National Institute of Mental Health), and does not have a primary diagnosis of dementia (including Alzheimer's disease or a related disorder), or a diagnosis (other than a primary diagnosis) of dementia and a primary diagnosis that is not a serious mental illness.

Mentally disabled A person is considered mentally disabled if he has been diagnosed as mentally disabled, or if he has a related condition. Guidelines for determining mental disability are available from local associations of mentally disabled people and other sources.

Specialized Services The term specialized services, formerly referred to as active treatment, means a continuous program for each person with MR or MI which includes aggressive, consistent implementation of a program of specialized and generic training, specific therapies or treatments, activities, health services, and related services as identified in an individualized plan of care. For an MI, the plan must be developed and supervised under direction of a physician. The prescribed components of active treatment must be provided by a physician or other qualified mental-health professional. For an MR, the program plan must be developed and supervised by an interdisciplinary team that represents areas that are relevant to identifying the individual's needs and to designing programs that meet these needs.

Preadmission screening is provided by professionals or agencies qualified to perform physical and mental evaluations, and not by the state mental health authority. The administrator should contact his state Medicaid agency and secure information on its admission-screening program. This agency will provide information on when screening is indicated and how it is accomplished. Facilities should pay close attention to this process because it will receive no funds if a resident needing to be screened is admitted without it. It is a sound practice to consult the prescreening unit about any applicant taking a psychoactive drug, even the milder ones like valium, sleeping pills, and antidepressants. More often a nurse can screen the latter cases through review of records and a conversation with the physician.

EQUAL ACCESS, ADMISSIONS, CHARGES [42 CFR 483.12 (c-d)]

Equal access to quality care A facility must establish and maintain identical policies and practices regarding transfer, discharge, and provision of services under the state plan for all individuals without regard to source of payment. All services must be provided according to each resident's needs as determined by assessments and care plans. A facility may charge any amount for services furnished to non-Medicaid residents consistent with notices under 42 CFR 483.10 (b)(5)(i) and (b) (6). Each resident must be notified of what services and materials are included in the basic rate. No state is required to offer additional services on behalf of a Medicaid resident other than services included in the state plan. The state plan, having been approved by the federal government, is the guide in regard to payment of services provided to Medicaid residents by a facility.

Admissions Neither SNF's nor NF's can require a third-party guarantee of payment to the facility as a condition of admission. Neither can this type guarantee be required in order to expedite admission, or to ensure continued stay in the facility. A third-party **guarantee** is not the same as a third-party payer. The facility may obtain information from Medicare, Medicaid, or private insurance regarding a resident's eligibility. The facility is prohibited, however, from requiring a person other than the resident to assume personal responsibility for any cost of a resident's care. However, a third party could **voluntarily** make payment for a resident.

OBRA prohibits a facility's requiring residents or potential residents to **waive their rights** to Medicaid or Medicare. If a resident is Medicaid or Medicare eligible, and the facility provides the service needed, the facility must accept the resident under the program for which they are eligible. Neither can the facility require a resident or potential resident to give **oral** or **written assurances** that he is not eligible for, or will not apply for, Medicare or Medicaid benefits. A state or political subdivision may apply even stricter standards to prohibit discrimination against individuals entitled to Medicaid benefits.

A facility may require a person to **sign a contract** if he has legal access to a resident's income, or resources available, to pay for the resident's care. Although the contract assures that the person will pay for the resident's care out of resident funds and resources, that individual does not incur personal financial liability for payment of any type.

Additional charges An NF may charge a resident who is eligible for Medicaid for items and services, requested by the resident and provided by the facility, that are not covered in the state plan under nursing-facility services.

The facility must give proper notice of the availability and cost of these services to the resident. The residents admission and continued stay cannot be conditioned on the request for and receipt of additional services.

Contributions A facility may solicit, accept, and/or receive a charitable, religious, or philanthropic contribution from an organization, or from a person unrelated to a resident or potential resident. However, the contribution cannot be a condition of admission, expedited admission, or assurance of continued stay in the facility for a Medicaid eligible resident.

A facility should exercise care in accepting contributions, since it may be considered income. Unless the facility has a specific Internal Revenue Service classification that places it in the proper charitable status, any contribution may be taxable as income.

Surveyors will question residents about whether the facility required their families to guarantee payment if the residents did not have funds to pay. Also, they will ask if the facility suggested ways to speed up admission. Surveyors will review state-covered services and compare the list of items for which the facility charges to determine if the facility is charging for covered services.

RESIDENT ASSESSMENT
[42 CFR 483.20 (a-c)]

The facility must conduct, initially and periodically, a comprehensive, accurate, standardized, reproducible assessment of each resident's functional capacity. **Admission orders** by the physician are the beginning of assessment. The physician must provide orders at admission for the immediate care of the resident. These are written orders that the facility staff need to provide essential care to the resident, consistent with the resident's physical and mental status at admission. Admission orders, as a minimum, include dietary, drugs, and routine care required to maintain or improve the resident's functional abilities until staff can conduct a comprehensive assessment and develop an interdisciplinary care plan.

Interdisciplinary team Assessments must be made by an interdisciplinary team that is coordinated by a registered nurse. The team includes, to the extent indicated by the resident's physical, mental, and psychosocial condition, a physician, rehabilitation therapists, activity director, social worker, dietitian, and other professionals such as MR, MI, and developmental disabilities specialists. Others may be involved dependent on the resident's status and needs.

Uniform data set The comprehensive assessment is based upon a uniform data set specified by HCFA. The uniform data set is also called minimum data set (MDS). **Comprehensive** means that the information enables staff to plan care that allows the resident to reach the highest practicable level of physical, mental, and psychosocial functioning. Forms for this procedure are available from the state.

The assessment describes the resident's capability to perform the activities of daily living (ADL) and notes any significant impairments in functional capacity. It describes the resident's physical and mental deficits and his strengths. Also it includes the equipment and staff assistance needed by the resident. Risk factors associated with possible decline in functional ability should be identified. Resident objectives for maintaining and improving functional abilities are to be included.

Content It is important that administrators have some knowledge of the content of the assessment. Obviously, details of the assessment process and content are duties of the registered nurse coordinator. A comprehensive assessment includes information in all the following areas:

1. Medically defined condition and prior medical history before admission, which includes resident's description of current medical diagnosis. It includes history of mental disability and current mental illness, if applicable;

2. Medical status measurement of resident's physical and mental abilities including vital signs, laboratory findings, diagnostic tests, etc.;

3. Functional status, both mental and physical, in terms of ability to perform activities of daily living, including need for staff assistance, assistive services, and equipment to maintain or improve these abilities;

4. Sensory and physical impairments, such as decrease in vision and/or hearing, paralysis, and bladder incontinence;

5. Nutritional status and requirements, which means weight, height, hemotological and biochemical assessments; nutritional intake, eating habits and preferences; and dietary restrictions;

6. Special treatments or procedures **not** needed by independent residents, such as treatment for pressure sores, nasogastric feeding, specialized rehabilitation services, and respiratory care;

7. Psychosocial and mental status, meaning ability to deal with life, interpersonal relationships and goals, and indicators of behavior and mood;

8. Discharge potential which means the facility's expectation of discharging the resident within the next three months;

9. Dental condition, such as condition of teeth, gums, and other structures of the oral cavity that may affect nutritional status, communication abilities, or quality of life; and need for or use of dentures or other dental appliances;

10. Activity potential, meaning the ability and desire to undertake activities which maintain or improve physical, mental, and psychosocial well-being activities outside of activities of daily living;

11. Rehabilitation potential, the ability to improve independence in functional status through restorative care programs;

12. Cognitive status, the ability to problem solve, decide, remember, and be aware of and respond to safety hazards; and

13. Drug therapy, which means all prescription and over-the counter medications taken by the resident, including why prescribed, dosage, frequency of administration, and recognition of potential side effects. Information on drug therapy need not appear in the assessment itself. If not included, it must be in the residents clinical record.

All this information is incorporated in the MDS which forms the core of each state's resident-assessment instrument (RAI). Additional assessment information is also gathered using triggered resident-assessment protocols (RAPS). The RAPS are used when there is a particular problem as constipation, incontinence, or others. The RAPS include information on how to handle the special problems the resident may have upon admission.

Frequency Medicaid and private pay assessments must be completed no later than 14 days after admission for an initial or return stay. If a resident is readmitted after being hospitalized or returns from a off-site visit or therapeutic leave, and there is a prior RAI on file, a new assessment is not required unless significant change has occurred. An MDS/RAI need not be completed on a person who stays less than 14 days. Assessments must be made promptly after a **significant change** in resident's physical or mental condition, and in no case less than once every **12 months**.

Significant change includes, but is not limited to, any of the following:

1. Deterioration in two or more ADL's, in cognitive abilities or communication that appears permanent,

2. Loss of ability to ambulate freely or to use hands to grasp small objects to feed or groom self,

3. Deterioration in behavior or mood to the point where daily problems arise or relationships become a problem,

4. Deterioration in health status where this change places resident's life in danger, such as CVA, heart disease, and cancer, and

5. Improvement in behavior, mood or functional status to the extent the plan of care no longer addresses needs of the resident.

Short-term or insignificant decline in physical, mental, or psychosocial well-being does not require reassessment or a change in the care plan. Examples are (1) side effect of a psychotropic drug while determining dosage level, (2) short-term acute illness such as a cold from which resident is expected to recover, (3) well-established symptoms associated with previously diagnosed conditions, such as depression when resident was diagnosed with bipolar disease, and (4) if resident continues to make steady progress under current care, then assessment is required only when the condition has stabilized.

Medicare assessment is different. New rules under the Prospective Payment System (PPS) require SNFs to keep assessment results on computer, using special **grouper software.** A copy of this software, which is called **RAVEN,** can be obtained from HCFA's web site at http:/ www.hcfa.gov/medicare/hspb/mdszo. It may also be purchased from a software vendor, but it must meet HCFA standards.

SNF facilities must use the MDS 2.0 to screen and assess residents. The form contains all data needed to classify a resident for purposes of determining into which of the 44 Resource Utilization Groups (RUGs) the resident will fit, thereby determining the per diem rate that will be paid for services provided. (See Chapter 7)

Frequency of Medicare assessments also differs from Medicaid. Table 12.1 outlines frequencies; however, the facility should note that the day of admission counts as day one.

Accuracy of assessments This **interdisciplinary** team must conduct all assessments; however, a registered nurse must **coordinate** the assessment and **certify** its completeness. The initial comprehensive assessment serves as the baseline data for ongoing assessments of resident progress. Each professional completing a portion of the assessment must **sign** and **certify** the accuracy of his portion of the assessment. **Accuracy** means the appropriate health professional has correctly documented the resident's medical, functional, and psychosocial problems and identified strengths to maintain or improve status in these problem areas.

Penalties for falsification Any individual who wilfully and knowingly certifies, or causes another to certify, a material and false statement

Table 12.1:

Medicare Assessment Schedule

Medicare MDS assessment type	Reason for Assessment (AA8b code)	Authorized for reference date	Number of days Applicable Medicare coverage & payment	Payment days
5 day	1	Days 1 - 8*	14	1 through 14
14 day	7	Days 11-14**	16	15 through 30
30 day	2	Days 21-29	30	31 through 60
60 day	3	Days 50-59	30	61 through 90
90 day	4	Days 80-89	10	9 through 100

* If a patient expires or transfers to another facility before day 8, the facility still must prepare an MDS as completely as possible for the RUG-III Classification and Medicare payment purposes. Otherwise, the days will be paid at the default rate.

* * RAPs follow Federal rules; RAPs must be performed with either the five-day or 14-day assessment.

Source: Federal Register, May 12, 1998

in a resident assessment is subject to civil money penalties. Use of independent assessors may be imposed if a state determines there has been certification of false statements. The state may require, for a period of time specified by the state, that resident assessments be conducted and certified by professionals who do not work for the facility. They must be approved by the state. If this does occur, the state is to notify HCFA Regional Office which will request the Inspector General's Field Office to further investigate Medicare facilities. For Medicaid, the state requests the Inspector General's Office to further investigate.

Exception A facility may amend assessment information collected during the 14-day period until the 21st day after readmission, if: (a) staff has no way to complete an item by the fourth day because information is not available, or (b) further observation and interaction with the resident reveals the need to alter the initial assessment in cognitive patterns, communication patterns, potential for self-care improvement, psychosocial well-being, mood and behavior patterns, or activity pursuit patterns.

Coordination The facility must coordinate assessments with any state-required preadmission screening program. This is to be done to the maximum extent possible to avoid duplicative testing and effort. Reports of required portions of the assessment that were performed in the preadmission screening should be entered in the appropriate form. This portion of the assessment should not be repeated by the facility unless significant changes have occurred between the preadmission screening and the resident's admission to the facility.

Quarterly review Facility staff must examine each resident once each quarter, and as appropriate. This is for the purpose of revising the resident's assessment to ensure continued accuracy of the assessment. The assessment results are **used** to develop, review, and revise the resident's comprehensive plan of care.

Surveyors monitor the facility's review process and whether staff acts on results of the review. They will note whether it is reviewed quarterly, and whether the assessment is used as the basis for developing care plans.

Electronic reporting Beginning in 1998 HCFA required facilities to electronically transmit assessment data on the MDS form, and the RAPS form when used, to the state Medicaid agency. The state agency must have a **repository** for this data on all residents in certified facilities — both

Medicare and Medicaid. This data is accessible to HCFA which means it will have information on every resident in every certified facility in the United States.

COMPREHENSIVE CARE PLAN [42 CFR 483.20 (d)]

The facility must develop a **comprehensive care plan** for each resident. It must include measurable objectives and timetables to meet a resident's medical, nursing, and psychosocial needs that are identified in the comprehensive assessment. The plan must deal with the relationship of items or services ordered to be provided, or withheld, to the facility's responsibility for fulfilling other requirements of OBRA.

Timing The care plan must be developed within seven days after completion of the comprehensive assessment, which means within 21 days after admission. The care plan must be periodically reviewed and revised by an interdisciplinary team after each assessment. It may also need review and revision after the quarterly review of assessment plans.

Contents Participants should develop objectives for the highest level of functioning the resident may be expected to attain, based on the assessment findings. These objectives should be measurable or quantifiable. For example, the resident cannot stand or walk. From the assessment it appears that with the aid of a walking cane he could learn to walk, the ultimate objective.

Intermediate steps could be established along with intermediate objectives such as to stand alone in three weeks, take up to 30 steps with assistance of staff in four weeks, walk alone holding a handrail in six weeks, ambulate using a walker in eight weeks, and walk steadily using a cane in ten weeks. These goals are measurable, and they would be used by the staff to measure the resident's progress.

Team members An interdisciplinary team must prepare the care plan. Staff members required to serve on this team were listed earlier in this chapter. The **resident** and the **resident's family**, or legal representative, are to participate to the extent possible. This is one of the best means of dealing with family complaints. If they are active in setting goals for their resident, helping to select treatment modalities, and assisting with the decision on the steps for reaching these goals, they should feel very much a part of the resident's care.

Family participation is especially important when family members tend to "dump" the resident, expecting the facility to assume full responsibility for all of the resident's care without any family participation. This type family often shows little interest, seldom visits, and complains about the care given. Often, they are the type who will sue the facility in case anything goes wrong — accident, elopement, and so on. The facility should insist the family take an active role in care planning and activities, as appropriate, listed in Figure 12.2.

Figure 12.2

Family Role in Resident Care

1. Visit regularly
2. Brings "goodies"
3. Take resident for wheelchair rides
4. Take resident for auto rides
5. Take resident for walks
6. Take resident out to lunch
7. Have lunch with resident at facility
8. Read to resident

When family participates, and a part of the care plan is not working, staff can remind family that what "we" planned is not productive. They can explore with family what changes might be helpful. Make family a part of the care-plan team.

Surveyors will determine if care plans reflect assessment findings and are oriented toward preventing decline in functioning and/or functional level, and attempting to manage risk factors.

They monitor whether care plans build on the resident's strengths, reflect current standards of professional practice, and contain measurable goals. Also, surveyors observe whether services provided in carrying out the plan are in accord with the written plan itself. Surveyors examine care plans to determine if the treatment approach endeavors to maintain or improve functional abilities. For example, are they designed to maintain or improve eating abilities? Does the speech therapist work to improve swallowing and the dietitian determine optimum textures and consistency of nutritionally adequate food? Do occupational therapists design adaptive equipment? Does the nursing staff reinforce speech therapy exercises during meals? The ways in which residents and families are involved in care planning will be noted. If surveyors find any problem with quality of care and/or life, or with resident rights, they will determine if this could be due to lack of staff qualifications.

PHARMACY SERVICES AND PROCEDURES [42 CFR 483.60 (b-e)]

The facility is responsible for either supplying drugs and biologicals or obtaining them through an agreement with a qualified outside source. The facility must have procedures that ensure the accurate acquiring, receiving, storing, dispensing, and administering all drugs and biologicals needed to meet the needs of each resident. The complete pharmacy services program is primarily to **protect** the resident, but it also provides liability protection for the physician, the facility and its staff.

Pharmacist The facility must have a licensed pharmacist either full-time or as a consultant as described in Chapter 6. One pharmacist may perform both the consultation and the other pharmacist duties. If one pharmacist does both, time must be fully allocated to give consultation on all aspects of pharmacy services. In essence he performs duties formerly handled by a pharmaceutical services committee. OBRA no longer requires this committee. If the same pharmacist performs these duties and reviews drug regimens, the facility must document the amount of time spent in the consultation role. States determine the minimum time that must be spent in this capacity.

Drug regimen The drug regimen of each resident must be reviewed at least once a month by the licensed pharmacist. It may be necessary to review a regimen more frequently as indicated by a resident's condition and the drugs he is taking. Any **irregularity** must be reported to both the physician and the director of nursing. Reporting to both depends on the severity of the drug therapy circumstance, whether physician's action is necessary, and which of the two is responsible for correcting the irregularity. For example, a small overdose of antacid or caution not to crush certain tablets before administering may be handled by the director of nursing. If the pharmacist feels a certain laboratory test is needed to determine blood-level of a drug, the physician is involved. Neither DON nor physician must agree with the pharmacist, but they must document their decision, and sign their names.

Prescribing The resident's attending physician or the staff physician prescribes all medication. Standard medical practice requires that these procedures be followed.

1. The order may be oral or written.
2. Oral orders must be given by the physician to a licensed nurse, pharmacist, or other physician.
3. The person receiving the oral order must record and sign it immediately and have the physician sign it in a manner consistent with good medical practice. The order and signature can be faxed as explained earlier, except for Schedule II drugs.

DEA has now ruled that the physician may fax orders for a Schedule II drug to the pharmacist. Even in an emergency it may not be faxed to the nursing home. In any event, the facility should have procedures for the **original** order to be placed in the resident's record.

Dispensing This means to fill the prescription by taking two or more doses from one container, placing them in another container, and labeling the second container. Only a pharmacist may fill prescriptions, and thus dispense drugs. A physician may give a patient sample drugs, but this is not permitted in many nursing homes. A nurse may place one dose of medicine in a second container and label it, but this is not considered dispensing. She may do this on physician's order when a resident is leaving on a visit.

Labeling Medications are labeled by the pharmacy from which they are ordered in accordance with accepted professional principles. Labels must include appropriate accessory and cautionary instructions, as well as expiration dates when applicable. In long-term care facilities it is critical that the **name** and **strength** of the drug is on the label. OBRA does not require that the name of the resident and his physician be on the label of the package, but it must be identified in a manner that ensures the drug is administered to the right resident. Pharmacy standards require that each resident's individual drug container bears his full name, the prescribing physician's name, and the name, strength, and quantity of the drug dispensed. Appropriate accessory and cautionary statements are included, as well as the **expiration date** when applicable. This means the statements must be on all drugs used in LTC facilities unless state law stipulates otherwise. Standard health-care practice requires that if a medication with a **marred label** is delivered by a pharmacy, the facility should return it to the pharmacy. The same is true of a medication on which a label becomes marred in the facility. Only the pharmacist may relabel drugs.

Storage Professional and legal standards for storing drugs must be followed. Federal and state standards require separately locked compartments with proper temperature controls, and only authorized personnel may have access to keys. OBRA identifies compartments as drawers, cabinets, rooms, refrigerators, medicine boxes, and carts. The facility must provide separately locked, permanently affixed compartments for storage of controlled drugs listed in Schedule II of the Comprehensive Drug Abuse Prevention and Control Act of 1970, and other drugs subject to abuse. If the facility uses single unit package drug distribution systems in which the quantity stored is minimal and a missing dose can be readily detected, these storage regulations need not apply. **Separately locked** means the key to Schedule II drugs is not the same as the key used for other drugs. It should be kept on a separate key ring.

Standard pharmacy and medication procedures for storage require that:

1. Drugs and biologicals are stored in the containers in which they are received. Transfer between containers is performed only by the pharmacist.

2. Drug containers with illegible, incomplete, makeshift, damaged, worn, soiled, or missing labels are returned to the dispensing pharmacist for proper labeling.

3. No discontinued, outdated, or deteriorated drugs or biologicals are available for use in the facility. Such drugs are disposed of in compliance with federal, state, and local laws.

4. Drugs for external use, as well as poisons, are stored in separate areas from other medications.

5. Antiseptics, disinfectants, and germicides used in resident care have legible, distinctive labels that identify the content and strength, and include instructions for use.

6. Compartments containing drugs and biologicals are locked when not in use, and trays or carts used to transport drugs and biologicals are not left unattended.

Administration of drugs Medications are administered as ordered by the physician with emphasis on administration at the prescribed times. Drugs are administered only by physicians, licensed nursing personnel, or by other personnel who have completed a state-approved training program in medication administration. Some states have medication aides who complete the state-approved course and are allowed to administer medications. On the other hand, some states still have some licensed practical (vocational) nurses who cannot give medications since they were "grandfathered" under old licensing laws before LPN and LVN training programs included the required state-approved course.

Steps in administration In order to minimize errors, nurses should follow steps outlined in Figure 12.3.

Figure 12.3

Steps in Medication Administration

1. Review physician's order
2. Identify the drug and required dosage
3. Identify the resident
4. Administer immediately after preparation
5. Administer as ordered

The reason for identifying the physician's order and the drug first is that pharmacists sometimes err in filling prescriptions. On one occasion the physician ordered Zantac, but the pharmacist sent Xanax. The nurse should note the form of the drug. If the medication normally comes in tablet form, but the pharmacist sends capsules, the nurse should call the pharmacist for clarification. The drug is to be administered as soon as possible after preparation for administration by the person who prepared the drugs. It is to be accurately recorded. The administration should ensure that the following management and healthcare practices are adhered to:

1. The facility's records show that all personnel whose assignments include administration of medication have successfully completed a state-approved program and have had additional orientation to the facility's policies and procedures.

2. Registered nurses and licensed practical (vocational) nurses are deemed to meet the requirement for completion of a state-approved program in medication administration.

3. Drugs are administered and monitored on an individual basis, and records are adequately maintained. To improve communications, written procedures are posted.

4. The charge nurse provides ongoing supervision of personnel administering medications that include: (a) regular observation of performance in actual preparation and administration, and (b) review of medication records for accuracy and conformance with orders.

5. Administering drugs and biologicals "as soon as possible after doses are prepared" means that drugs are prepared only for one medication pass at a time, e.g., the drugs prepared (poured) for administration at 8 a.m. should be administered and recorded before the 12 noon or subsequent doses are prepared.

6. Written procedures for the administration of drugs and biologicals should include the following instructions:

   a. Recording in the patient's record method of administration, name and dosage of drug, site of injection (if applicable), medication errors, adverse reaction, and corrective action taken, name or initials of persons administering the drug or biological,

   b. Recording and reporting to the prescribing physician when prescribed drugs are not given or are refused, and

   c. Reporting immediately to the attending physician medication errors and adverse drug reactions.

7. A list of approved drug abbreviations and/or names is made available to appropriate personnel in the facility.

8. Drugs brought to a facility by the patient should be used only when in compliance with policies established by the facility on recommendation of the pharmacist. If such drugs are permitted, they are positively identified as to name and strength, stored in accordance with standards listed herein, and administered only upon the written orders of the attending physician.

9. A system of resident identification is established and implemented to assure that drugs prescribed for one person are not administered to another.

10. Current reference materials on the use of drugs are readily available to each nursing unit. The most commonly used drug reference is the *Physicians Desk Reference.* Many pharmacists contend it is not the best reference, since it is published by drug companies and does not always contain desired information. These pharmacists usually recommend *Facts and Comparisons* which contains full information on all drugs used in a facility.

Medication error Administration of the wrong drugs or failure to administer a dose requires immediate staff attention. The facility must ensure that it is free of significant medication error rates of five percent or greater, and residents are free of any significant medication errors. **Medication error** means a discrepancy between what the physician ordered and what the nursing staff administers to a resident. A **significant** medication error is one that causes a resident discomfort, or jeopardizes his health and safety. The **medication error rate** is determined by calculating the percent of errors. This is accomplished by dividing the total number of doses given, plus doses ordered but not given, into the total number of errors made. An example: 78 doses were given, two ordered were not – a total of 80. In addition to the two not given, two wrong medications were administered – a total of four medication errors. By dividing the 80 ordered doses into four medication errors the medication error rate is determined to be five percent as shown below.

$$\frac{\text{4 errors}}{\text{80 opportunities}} = .05 \times 100 = 5\% \text{ error rate}$$

Significant medication error rate means that in a sample of residents surveyors choose for observation of medication administration, a number of errors were made. The surveyor determines whether there is a significant error rate. A five percent or more error rate may indicate a significant error rate exists, especially if individual medication errors are significant. The facility must remain free of significant medication error rates. There are general rules for determining significance, and the administrator should expect his director of nursing to be fully knowledgeable about these. He should also require the DON to know the methodology surveyors will use in medication error detection, dose reconciliation, and writing deficiencies for medication errors. [42 CFR 483.25 (m)] Perhaps the easiest means of reducing medication errors is to institute the **unit-dose system.** When used, it significantly reduces the error rate.

Automatic stop order Procedures must cover this practice. There must be a provision for the control of drugs not specifically limited as to time or number of doses when ordered. The nurse must call the physician prior to the last dose so he may decide whether to continue, alter, or discontinue use of the drug. Stop order procedures formerly were developed by the pharmaceutical services committee. Since it is no longer required, the pharmacist and medical director should establish these procedures. When stop orders exist on a particular drug, they must be carefully followed. Only a physician may override a stop order for his resident.

Discontinued drugs (Dc'd) OBRA regulations do not address disposition of drugs that have been discontinued. This is controlled by other federal, state, and local regulations that require all discontinued drugs to be destroyed. These are drugs left when a person dies or is discharged and when the physician orders discontinuance of a drug. In the event the physician should reorder the drug, some state regulations permit **retention** of a discontinued drug for 60 days when the resident is still in the facility or has been transferred to a hospital. **Destruction** of discontinued drugs should be under supervision of the pharmacist. He will possess a copy of the Drug Enforcement Administration's *Pharmacist Manual* which includes specific procedures on destruction of controlled substances. The pharmacist may be authorized by DEA to destroy certain substances. It is necessary that he use the DEA Form 41. Procedures may vary to some extent from one DEA district to another. In some states the pharmacist, with another health-care professional as a witness, may destroy controlled drugs. In other states they must be forwarded to a specified location where the DEA witnesses their destruction. The facility must have documentation of all Dc'd drugs. Nurses are allowed to destroy nonscheduled drugs and document the type, amount, and date of destruction.

Taking medications home When the resident is discharged, he takes medications home only on written orders from the physician. If a resident goes home on a visit with physician's orders, the nurse may send one dose of medication in a new container. If more is needed the physician would need to order that the entire container be sent with the resident, provided the physician feels it is safe.

Commonly used drug terms All commonly used drugs are terms which should be well-known to administrators. The following may be used extensively in nursing facilities.

Analgesic A drug that relieves pain but does not cure illness. Two types are (a) opiates as codeine, morphine, and Darvon and (b) nonopiates as aspirin, Tylenol and Advil.

Antibiotic A drug that kills or inhibits the growth of pathogenic microorganisms within the body. Examples are penicillin, doxycycline, and Keflex.

Anticoagulant An agent that prevents or delays coagulation of blood as Coumadin, given orally, and heparin, which is injected.

Anticonvulsant A drug used to prevent or control convulsions as Dilantin, phenobarbitol, and intravenous Valium.

Antidepressant A medication given to relieve depression, as Prozac, Zoloft, and Paxil.

Antidote A medication or other substance given to offset the effect of a poison or another drug. Milk is the universal antidote for poisons, whereas antidotes for drugs are specific to the individual drug.

Antihistamine A drug used in certain allergy cases and to dry out nasal tissues to reduce postnasal drip, as Benadryl and Chlortrimeton.

Antipsychotic A drug given for mental disorders, as thorazine, loxitane, and mellaril.

Antiseptic A drug that destroys or inhibits the growth of microorganisms in the environment.

Antitoxin An antibody produced in response to and capable of neutralizing a specific biologic toxin, as an antitoxin for gangrene and tetanus.

Antitussive A drug given to control coughing, as Robitussin and Phenergen expectorant.

Decongestant A drug that constricts blood vessels in the nose and relieves nasal congestion as Sudafed and Afrinol.

Diuretic A drug that increases volume of urine output and reduces body fluids as Dyazide, Lasix, and Diuril.

Generic substitution A different brand or an unbranded drug product substituted by the pharmacist for a trade-name drug product prescribed. The drugs are exactly the same chemically and in the same dosage form, but distributed by different drug companies. Examples are Rufen brand of ibuprofen for Motrin brand ibuprofen, and unbranded ampicillin for Polycillin brand of ampicillin. Brand name drugs begin with a capital letter that distinguishes them from generic drugs.

Laxative A drug used to relieve constipation as Dulcolax, Doxidan, and Metamucil.

Palliative A drug that relieves pain without curing, as aspirin and Tylenol.

Parenteral A drug or solution given by subcutaneous or intravenous injection.

Placebo An inactive medication having no physical healing effect. It is usually given to satisfy the patient. Placebos are also used in drug studies to determine the effectiveness of another drug. They may be given orally, by injection, as a suppository, or topically.

Psychotropic See antipsychotic drugs that follow in this section.

Sedative A medication which exerts a soothing or tranquilizing effect. They may be general, local, nervous, or vascular. Examples are Valium and Dalmane.

Suppository A semisolid substance for introduction into the rectum, vagina, or urethra where it is dissolved and absorbed. It contains medications such as laxatives, and aspirin or Tylenol to reduce fever.

Topical medication A medication applied to an area of the skin, as ointments and lotions.

Tranquilizer A drug which acts to reduce mental tension and anxiety without interfering with normal mental activity, as Librium, Thorazine, and Equanil.

Unnecessary drugs [42 CFR 483.25 (l)(1)] Each resident's drug regimen must be free from unnecessary drugs. An **unnecessary** drug is any drug used (1) in excessive doses (including duplicate therapy), (2) for excessive duration, (3) without adequate monitoring, (4) without adequate indications for use, (5) in the presence of adverse consequences which indicate the dosage should be reduced or discontinued, or (6) any combination of the above reasons. This is a very complex area of resident care that the administrator will likely need to rely on the DON for specific information. It involves a long list of drugs, such as long-acting Benzoidiazepine, other anxiolytic and sedative drugs, sleep inducing drugs, hypnotic drugs and antipsychotic drugs.

Antipsychotic drugs [42 CFR 483.25 (l)(2)(i)] Based on a comprehensive assessment the facility must ensure that residents who have not used antipsychotic drugs are not given these drugs unless antipsychotic drug therapy is necessary to treat a specific condition as diagnosed and documented in the clinical record. Residents who use antipsychotic drugs must receive gradual dose reductions, and behavioral interventions, unless clinically contraindicated, in an effort to discontinue these drugs. Antipsychotic drugs are given for the purpose of modifying types of behavior seen in schizophrenia, delusional disorders, acute psychotic episodes, Tourette's disorder, organic mental syndromes (dementia and delirium), and other mental disorders. They should never be given for wandering, poor self-care, restlessness, impaired memory, anxiety, depression (without psychotic features), insomnia, and other similar behavior if it is the **only** indication of need for medication.

Aging process and drugs Aging affects the manner in which the body reacts to, metabolizes, and disposes of drugs. Generally, the elderly become more sensitive to drugs, and drugs tend to affect them longer and more intensely. The elderly usually change eating, drinking, and activity patterns, all of which affect the discharge of drugs from the body. Since unutilized drugs are discharged through urine, feces, breathing, and perspiration, changes in these patterns may affect the means of discharge. Usually, these changes in the elderly indicate reduction of dosages of medications. However, the American Association of Retired Persons did a recent study that showed one of the most frequent problems among the elderly living in the community is toxicity to prescribed drugs. The study found that people over age 65 included in the study were taking an average of 7.2 different drugs per person.

Medication problems Frequently problems arise due to medications a resident takes. The administrator should be alert to this, and frequently check with his DON. **Side effects** of certain drugs is a risk factor. Clinical records are tagged in a manner that known reactions are noted when the chart is opened. A resident's reaction to a new drug will not be known so the nursing staff should be alert to possible side effects.

Multiple medications often cause undesirable side effects. Pharmacists caution that any elderly person taking **four** or more different drugs should be closely monitored for imbalance, a frequent side effect. The drugs themselves may be compatible but some tend to affect balance when taken in combination.

Emergency drug kit Standards of practice require that each nursing facility have an emergency drug kit approved by the state pharmacy board. It might be kept along with a first aid kit.

Contents of the emergency kit should be decided by the pharmacist, medical director, and director of nursing. The kit should belong to the pharmacist who should inspect it regularly and replace any items as necessary. The emergency kit should be either locked or sealed. If the nurse finds the seal broken, or the lock open, she should call the pharmacist immediately. He should inventory the contents of the kit to determine if anything is missing.

Surveyors will observe a drug pass and note whether all needed medications are available. If they find a problem related to drug therapy or distribution, surveyors will determine if the pharmacist periodically reconciles controlled drugs. If all controlled drugs are not properly accounted for, the surveyors are to report it to the local DEA, to the state nursing-facility licensing authority, and to the state board of pharmacy. Surveyors will also monitor whether the pharmacist has notified the physician and/or director of nursing when there is a need. This includes drug irregularities, and whether appropriate action was taken. In observing environmental quality, surveyors will note whether drugs and biologicals are properly stored.

RESIDENT ACTIVITY PROGRAM [42 CFR 483.15 (f)]

As a part of quality of life, the facility must provide a full activity program for its residents. It must be an ongoing program of activities designed to meet, in accordance with comprehensive assessment, the interests and the physical, mental, and psychosocial needs of each resident. This is an important program that often gives direction to the resident's life. It can be the difference between a resident vegetating with little interest in life or developing interests that keep him active and relatively happy.

Staff OBRA regulations require that the activity program be directed by a capable, competent person. No specific number of activity directors is required, nor does OBRA specify that they be full-time. Requirements in these areas may be established by the state. Refer to Chapter 6 on Personnel Management for qualifications of activity directors. Previously, there were detailed federal guidelines for resident activities. However, OBRA apparently expects facilities to develop and carry out their program according to standards of practice in the recreational therapy field.

Definition Activities in a nursing facility refer to taking part in social, recreational, religious, and other activities in order to promote quality of life. These are activities over and above modalities use to maintain or enhance performance of activities of daily living. As an example, having a staff member take a resident for a walk to improve ambulation is not an activity; it is a part of therapy.

The **administrator's role** in activities is largely ensuring that the activity director has materials, equipment, space, and so on to conduct a quality program. The administrator should ensure that the facility has one of the many publications that can assist the activity director in planning and carrying out the program. A good example is *Activity and Volunteer Service Policies and Procedures* by Pamela Sander, listed in this chapter's reference. The administrator should also visit and observe activities in progress. It indicates his support and interest, which residents and staff appreciate. A major advantage is that he sees residents while they are involved in pleasant activities and are not seeking him out with problems. The administrator can share a positive experience with residents.

Planning Activities are an integral part of the assessment and plan of care for each resident. As such, it fulfills a medical as well as social need and helps residents with goal-attainment. Activities are to be **based** on each resident's needs and interests, as identified in the comprehensive assessment. Activities should be those from which the resident derives personal satisfaction, social contacts, creative expression, recreation, and/or spiritual gratification. Activities are not necessarily to develop skills, although this may be an important part. They are not to emphasize the finished product. Again, this may be a goal that provides personal satisfaction, but participation and enjoyment are the focus. Activities should provide stimulation or solace, promote physical, cognitive, and emotional health, enhance mental and physical status, promote self-respect, and allow for self-expression, personal responsibility, and choice. Activities may not involve *useful service* to the facility, as explained in resident rights, except under very specific circumstances. These circumstances are explained under the resident's right not to perform work except by choice and the approval of the physician.

Program content A fully planned program with a **monthly schedule** usually provides direction to the activity program. Residents come to expect bingo or some other favored game at certain times each week. Religious services are provided on a regular basis that residents may anticipate. The program should include use of community resources that will bring music, entertainment, or some type event to the facility. It should also include regular planned trips for residents to engage in community recreation, entertainment, celebrations, and other activities. The program should reflect interests of various groups, interests that tell about their background and social and emotional needs. It should provide for resident, resident/family, and other types of groups discussed in Chapter 11 under resident rights.

Handicapped Severely handicapped residents may not be able to participate in group activities, or to be present as an observer. They cannot be neglected as each resident must have a program designed to meet his needs. Staff must plan activities that the handicapped can enjoy. These may be bedside activities rather than groups.

Volunteers The activity program is a principal means of using services of volunteers. The administrator should ensure there are policies and procedures governing their activities. In this way volunteers are aware of their role and the limitations on what they may do with residents. Administrators should recognize the use of volunteers is more than a service to the activity program. It is good public relations, since they bring ideas from the community and take back positive information to the community. It is one means of strengthening the bonds between facility and community. The administrator should ensure there are means of recognizing volunteers and their contributions to the facility. Pamela Sander advances helpful suggestions in this regard.

Measurement How does the administrator know the activity program is successful? One means is to observe any increase in the number of residents who participate, either actively or as observers. Also, the administrator needs to know how many residents do not participate and are exercising their right not to be involved. The administrator's observance of activities, along with his occasional participation, will provide first-hand knowledge of the success of the program.

SPECIALIZED REHABILITATIVE SERVICES
[42 CFR 483.45 (a-b)]

Provision of services When specialized rehabilitative services are required in the resident's plan of care, these services must be provided by the facility, or obtained from a qualified outside resource. Services include, but are not limited to, physical therapy, occupational therapy, speech/ language therapy, and services to the mentally ill and mentally disabled. The typical facility does not employ full-time rehabilitation specialists. These services most often are obtained through agreements with clinics or professionals in private practice. The facility must be aware that by whatever means these services are provided, the facility itself is responsible for the care given its residents. This is the reason administrators must be quite sure that all rehabilitation specialists providing services to the facility are fully qualified, as noted under staffing in this chapter.

Specialized rehabilitative services should be distinguished from rehabilitative measures used by nursing and activities staff. **Rehabilitative nursing** includes exercises such as range of motion, ambulation, and breathing exercises. Certain activities may contribute to maintenance or improvement of eye/hand coordination, dexterity, and ambulation. Also, activity directors often conduct exercises that promote relaxation and maintain muscle tone. The major focus of the occupational therapist is work with upper and lower extremities. Their goal is to maintain or improve dexterity, coordination, range of motion, strength, and other abilities. Activities often have some of the same objectives. Sometimes the occupational therapist may differ from the activity staff only by a higher degree of training and knowledge.

Planning programs Specialized rehabilitative therapy is a part of assessment and the care plans that result. It must be provided under **written order** of a physician. (See Figure 12.4)

Figure 12.4

Planning Rehabilitation Therapy

1. Physician's order
2. Assess resident's need
3. Set goals
4. Select treatment modalities
5. Identify resources needed
6. Implement treatment
7. Report progress, or lack thereof

The **first step** the therapist uses in developing a rehabilitation plan is to **assess** the residents needs. **Goals** are then established, based on findings of the assessment. The goal of all rehabilitation is to help the resident to live at his **fullest potential**. It may not be to improve sufficiently to live independently and to return to his home. It may be just to feed or dress himself, to bathe and toilet without assistance, to walk with the use of an assistive device, or to communicate with others.

When goals are established, the therapist then **selects modalities** to be used in treatment. Although specialized rehabilitation therapists may not carry out therapy without the physician's order, they have considerable discretion in selecting treatment modalities. After modalities are selected, the therapist **implements** them using the resources the facility must provide. As a member of the interdisciplinary team they **report progress,** or the lack of it, to the team and participate in the periodic reassessments.

Surveyors will monitor a sample of residents needing physical therapy services to determine if it improved muscle strength, balance, use of less restrictive assistive devices, and/or if resident's participation in physical activity increased. They will note whether occupational therapy decreases the assistance residents need; if it improves motor coordination, sensory awareness, and body integration; whether it decreases inappropriate behavior; and so on. For speech/language therapy surveyors will note what is used to improve auditory comprehension, speech production, and expressive behavior. For the hearing impaired, surveyors will monitor what is done to improve functional abilities of moderate to severe hearing impaired residents. They will observe whether there is improvement in compensating for hearing loss, such as eye contact, preferential seating, and use of the best ear. If surveyors find problems in quality of care related to functional abilities, they will examine whether they could be attributable to the qualifications of the therapists.

RESIDENT CARE PRACTICES [42 CFR 483.25]

Resident-care practices utilized by staff must reflect **quality of care** which promotes the highest practicable physical, mental, and psychosocial well-being. The overall resident-care management system should use a **holistic** approach, since it must address the total needs of an individual. **Highest practicable** means the highest level of functioning and well-being that can be expected considering the resident's functional status at the time, and his potential for improvement, or to reduce the rate of functional decline. This is determined through assessment and care planning.

Some knowledge of resident-care practices is vital to the administrator's role. Generally, he cannot know the details of resident-care practices as well as the staff, and it is not necessary that he does. However, since administrators will have resident contact and will monitor resident care, they should know something of how to approach various types of residents and what modalities the staff should use.

Staff attitudes The most significant aspect of resident-care practices are staff attitudes toward residents. Earlier, negative stereotyping of the elderly resulting in low expectations for improvement was discussed. Gustafsen points out that if negative attitudes can be said to influence or even create negative results, then the converse can be true. Staff attitudes seem to be the factor in some LTC facilities that produces more independent and capable residents than others. She observed that through positive attitudes and emphasis on rehabilitation, many elderly can be returned to independent living settings, with appropriate therapy. (Gustafsen) The administrator will do well to obtain additional information on how staff attitudes affect the disability and progress, or lack of it, in residents.

1. **Accidents** As discussed in Environmental Management, the facility must ensure that the environment is as free of accident hazards as possible. An accident as described earlier is an unintended event, but it does not include adverse outcomes associated as a direct consequence of treatment or care. It may be an unintended side effect of care, as when an aide causes a skin tear while turning a resident, or drops the resident; that is an accident. A burn secondary to a topical treatment of a resident's skin is **not** an accident. The facility should have clearly stated procedures, and teach them to staff, which identify steps to follow when a resident is injured. All staff should know whether to move the resident, or to call the charge nurse for directions. Each resident must receive adequate assistive devices and supervision to prevent accidents. [42 CFR 483.25 (h)(2)]

2. **Activities of daily living** (ADL) Based on the assessment, OBRA specifies the facility must ensure that the resident's activities of daily living do not diminish unless the resident's condition demonstrates that diminution is unavoidable. Should the resident, or family, or legal representative, as appropriate, recognize the resident's abilities are deteriorating due to illness, and refuse aggressive treatment to maintain or restore them, this should be documented. ADL's include the following:

   a. **Bathing, dressing, grooming** Bathing refers to washing and drying the body (excluding shampooing hair and washing the back), a full sponge bath, and transferring into and out of a tub or shower. *Dressing* means selecting, obtaining, putting on, fastening, and taking off all items of clothing. This includes putting on or removing braces and artificial limbs. **Grooming** means maintaining personal hygiene. It includes preparation and activities of combing hair, brushing teeth, and, when applicable, shaving and applying makeup.

   b. **Transfer and ambulate Transfer** means moving between two surfaces, such as to and from bed, chair, wheelchair, and standing position. It does not include transfer to and from bath and toilet. **Ambulation** means how resident moves between locations in his room and adjacent corridor on the same floor. If they move only in a wheelchair, it refers to self-sufficiency once they are in the chair.

   c. **Toileting** This is interpreted to mean use of the toilet room, bedpan, bedside commode, or urinal, transferring on and off the toilet, cleaning self after elimination, changing sanitary napkins/incontinence pads/ external catheters, and adjusting clothing prior to and after toileting.

   d. **Eating** This refers to eating and drinking adequate liquids, regardless of skill, once the meal is prepared and liquids made available.

   e. **Communicating** To communicate means use of speech, language, or other functional communication systems to communicate requests, opinions, urgent problems, and social conversation. This includes use of speech, writing, sign-language, assistive devices as appropriate, gesturing, or a combination of these.

Each resident must be given appropriate treatment and services to maintain or improve his abilities in each of these activities. If a resident is unable to carry out activities of daily living, the staff must provide services to maintain good nutrition, grooming, and personal and oral hygiene. These services may include hand, tube, or syringe feeding, or total parenteral nutrition through a central intravenous line. They may include total care in terms of dressing, bathing, and grooming. Oral hygiene will include brushing teeth, cleaning dentures, cleaning mouth and tongue with a gauze sponge, and other care to keep the oral cavity clean and healthy.

Type of care In regard to ADLs residents are classified into two categories of care:

a. **Heavy care** refers to residents who generally require extensive staff assistance in transferring/mobility, using the toilet or other care, and in eating.

b. **Light care** is a term used to denote residents who may need assistance in grooming and dressing, but they can function relatively independently in transferring/mobility, using the toilet, and eating.

Charge nurses should consider these categories in making nursing staff assignments. A nurse or CNA assigned a larger number of heavy-care residents may be carrying more than her share of the workload.

Surveyors will include residents from each category and examine three things: (1) Has the resident's ability in a given activity changed since admission, or during the past six months? (2) Was decline in any ability unavoidable? (3) Is there evidence an ability could have improved with proper services in residents whose ability had been maintained? Surveyors will also observe the quality of the environment, assistive devices, and efforts made by staff. [42 CFR 483.25 (a)(3)]

3. **Changing physicians** When a resident changes physicians, the new physician is required by standards of practice to: (a) conduct a new history and physical examination, (b) write new orders, and (c) obtain a written release from the former physician, when possible. If the former physician becomes disabled, dies, or simply neglects to provide a release as requested, this should be documented in the resident's record.

4. **Care of the deceased** When a resident dies in a facility often a sad, gloomy atmosphere descends. Residents and staff speak in subdued voices and there may be an appearance of uncertainty as to what to do next. The administrator should ensure that the facility has a step by step plan for care of the deceased. When death is imminent the plan should include discussion with the family regarding the mortuary that will be used and arrangements for the body to be transported. The plan should also include steps to take when death occurs.

Figure 12.5:

Action to Take When Death Occurs

1. Contacting family members if none are present
2. Contacting the physician to declare death
3. Completing papers for releasing the body
4. Preparation of the body for release to the mortuary
5. Conferring with the family before release

Preparation of the body for release is often an extremely upsetting experience, especially for a CNA. Some simply cannot handle their emotional reactions to this duty. Often they refuse, even if it means loss of their job. The facility should have one or more nursing-staff members trained in proper procedures, one who is able to carry out the task without being overwhelmed. Proper guidelines that direct immediate, appropriate action are helpful in lessening the impact of dealing with death. Nothing that needs to be done should be left to last minute planning.

5. **Discharge** When the facility anticipates discharge, staff must prepare a discharge summary as noted under resident rights in Chapter 11. Content of the summary is threefold: (a) it must contain a recapitulation of the entire

resident stay, (b) it is to contain a final summary of the resident's status, including all items listed in the comprehensive assessment, and (c) there must be a post-discharge plan of care, developed with the participation of the resident and his family which will assist the resident to adjust to the new living environment.

The **post-discharge plan** applies to a resident who is discharged to a private residence, another nursing facility, a residential facility, or other living arrangement. The plan describes the resident's and family's preferences for care, how the resident and family will access and pay for these services, and how care should be coordinated if continued treatment involves multiple caregivers. It identifies specific needs of the resident after discharge and describes the resident/caregiver education needs to prepare the resident for discharge.

Discharge planning should actually begin at admission, otherwise families may bring residents to the facility with the idea of **dumping** them. There may be no intention of returning the resident to his home, no matter what progress the resident may make. Essentially, the family may turn the resident's room at home over to someone else and close the door on the possibility of returning home. The social worker should be active in this area. Discussing discharge probability and plans in the event of improvement may affect the dumping syndrome. It may assist in keeping such families more involved in resident care. (See Chapter 11 for more details)

Surveyors will note whether discharge plans are properly included in the resident's record, and whether post-discharge care is addressed. They monitor whether the facility assisted the resident and family in locating post-discharge services. Also, they determine what type of predischarge preparation the facility provided. [42 CFR 483.20 (e)]

6. **Emergency care** Standard health-care practices require that a facility have plans for the care of residents in an emergency situation. This means when a resident is injured, has a heart attack, suddenly experiences acute symptoms, lapses into a coma, has seizures, or any other condition that may be life threatening. The facility should have plans posted at the nurses station to use in such emergencies. Plans should include what action to take if the physician and the backup physician are not available, instructions on transfer to a hospital emergency room, contacting the family, and so on. They should include special plans for residents with **cardiac problems**, since time is often the greatest factor. Policies and procedures should be developed and regularly reviewed by the nursing staff. Emergency care measures should never be left to memory. They should be available in written form for ready reference.

   Nursing facilities must have an **emergency drug kit** as discussed under pharmacy and medications. It must contain drugs used by a nurse during emergencies. Most SNFs have a **crash cart** which contains drugs and materials the nurse and physician may use. A common practice is to have a code that is announced when emergencies requiring use of the crash cart occur. Some facilities use **Code Blue**, followed by the room number of the emergency case. All nursing staff should be trained in exactly what to do when the emergency code is sounded.

7. **Infection control** Requirements for a facility-wide infection control program are discussed in Chapter 8. The resident-care area is a focus of the program, for its purpose is to prevent the development and transmission of disease and infection. The program is to monitor and investigate the cause of infection and the manner of spread. A **separate record** should be maintained on each infection. It should identify each resident with the infection, state the date of infection, the causative agent, the origin or site of infection, and describe what cautionary measures were taken to enable the facility to analyze clusters and/or significant increases in the rate of infection. The facility should address prevention of infection common to nursing facility residents. This includes immunization for influenza and pneumococcal pneumonia, as appropriate.

New infections, referred to as nosocomial, should be identified quickly, paying especial attention to residents at **high risk** of infection. High risk includes the immobilized who have invasive devices or procedures, pressure sores, mental disabilities or mental illness, altered immune systems, and those recently discharged from a hospital. For nonsporadic, facility-wide infections that are difficult to control, the program should have procedures for informing and enlisting the aid of local or state epidemiologists.

Reporting Most states require that an incident of a contagious disease be reported. The state designates the agency to which it must be reported, usually the state department of health.

Surveyors determine if there are unexplained and/or similar infections, and if there is a significant increase in the rate of infection. They select a sample of residents at high risk of infection, and monitor what staff has done to reduce risks. Infection control policies for residents with AIDS or hepatitis B are reviewed to determine if they meet OSHA requirements and CDC standards. Surveyors also review procedures for identifying and disposing of infectious waste. [42 CFR 483.65]

8. **New admissions** The facility should have a carefully planned program for helping new admits to become acquainted with facility practices and with other residents. Simply telling the resident when activities are planned, when meals are served, and so on is not enough.

   Example: Mr. Thomas showed shyness and uncertainty when admitted. Nursing staff spent considerable time orienting him to nursing service and told him about other facility activities. At noon mealtime he was accompanied to the dining room by an aide who told him to sit anywhere, then the aide left. He saw two men at a table, walked over and shyly sat down with them. Mr. Murphy who usually sat with these two walked over and shoved Mr. Thomas out of the chair, and he fell to the floor. The administrator handled this by counseling Mr. Murphy and staff set up a program to work with newcomers. It included staff introducing them to each activity personally. Also some of the better adjusted residents assumed the big brother role and accompanied newcomers to all activities for several days after admission.

9. **Rehabilitative nursing** Restorative nursing, as a part of the care plan, outlines the needs of the resident each day in modalities such as range of motion, ambulation, and breathing exercises. These are planned by the nursing staff, and the physician is generally not required to give specific approval. As a part of the care plan they will have general medical approval. **Range of Motion (ROM)** means the extent of movement of a joint. Even though certain joints may be immobilized due to surgery, appropriate preventive measures are to be used whenever possible. As an example, an immobilized elbow usually does not prevent range of motion exercises for wrist and fingers. As a preventive means, the resident may be taught to use active exercise himself in addition to staff measures used. Ambulation and breathing exercises are self-explanatory and may involve measures used by both the resident and the staff.

   Residents admitted with limited range of motion must receive appropriate treatment and services to increase range of motion, and/or prevent further decrease unless the resident's condition demonstrates that a reduction is unavoidable. Residents who are admitted without limited range of motion must be monitored to ensure that reduction in range of motion does not occur, unless the resident's clinical condition demonstrates that it is unavoidable.

   Clinical conditions that are considered **primary risk factors** for decreased range of motion are: (a) immobilization — bedfast, (b) strokes, multiple sclerosis, cerebral palsy, polio, (c) pain, spasms, and immobility due to arthritis or Alzheimer's Disease

Nursing and other health-care personnel should routinely perform rehabilitative measures in the daily care of residents. These measures include: (a) maintaining good body alignment and proper positioning, (b) making every effort to keep the resident active, except when contraindicated by physician's orders, and encouraging residents to achieve independence in activities of daily living by teaching self-care, and ambulation activities, (c) assisting residents to carry out prescribed therapeutic exercises between visits of the therapists, and (d) assisting residents with routine range of motion exercises.

Orthopedists often prescribe four exercises an administrator needs to be familiar with: (a) **Flexion** is bending a limb or part of the body to and fro, as moving the hand to the shoulder to exercise the elbow; (b) **Rotation** is turning a limb 180 degrees, as turning the palm of the hand over to exercise the elbow; (c) **Abduction** is moving a limb outward from the body, as raising the arm from the side to the level of the shoulder; (d) **Adduction** is moving the limb back toward the body or toward the median line of the body. Orthopedists further recommend daily movement of every body joint in every direction its structure intends it to move. Group exercise is one approach to meeting this need.

Surveyors choose a sample of residents who need routine preventive care and observe staff providing ROM exercises. They determine if there has been a decline in ROM and/or muscle atrophy that was avoidable. The facility's efforts to prevent further decline in range of motion of residents who have limited ROM is noted. Plans of care are examined to determine if objectives and progress were evaluated, and whether care planning changed as the resident's condition changed. [42 CFR 483.25 (e)]

10. **Restraints** Resident's rights regarding restraints are discussed in Chapter 11. It is important for the administrator to know when restraints may be used, and how they should be monitored. Restraints may be used only to control a resident's behavior that is harmful to the resident or to others. An appropriate safety program dictates that safety is not just a matter of environment, but also a concern for those who are in that environment. Residents exhibiting assaultive behavior toward self or others must be dealt with immediately and appropriately. Restraints may never be used for staff convenience or to discipline a resident.

Physical and chemical restraints are defined under resident rights and examples of physical restraints are given. Examples of psychoactive drugs are best discussed with the pharmacist who keeps abreast of the many changes in these drugs and their use. Physical restraints may be applied only with the doctor's orders. Previously, a facility could have a standing order that specified when physical restraints could be used and who could apply them. There is, however, the matter of a resident doing harm to himself or to another resident. It is permissible to stop this action which will probably require restraint. The minute nursing staff puts a hand on a resident to prevent his assaultive behavior that is restraint. Staff must remove the resident from an area where he can hurt someone, isolate him in a room, or physically restrain him from action. In the meantime the physician is called and asked for instructions.

If physical restraints are used, standard practice requires they be **monitored** at least every 30 minutes. They must be removed at least every two hours for ten minutes. A facility is unwise to monitor at that frequency because of inherent dangers of restraints. They should be monitored at least every 15 minutes, and in some instances more often, dependent on the resident's behavior. Chemical restraint **monitoring** schedules depend on the type of drug used. Some require monitoring as often as every 15 minutes. Standard practice specifies four hours as the maximum period, but this is a questionable procedure. It is difficult to imagine a chemically restrained resident going unobserved for that length of time.

If OBRA's goal of a **restraint free** environment is attained, monitoring procedures for physical and chemical restraints will be of no concern. OBRA recommends that staff develop **alternatives** to restraints. These could include earlier interventions when potentially harmful behavior is exhibited, temporarily isolating the resident from other residents, using diversionary activities, engaging in walking, exercising or other physical activity, conversation with a staff member, and many others.

As discussed under Legal Management, restraints represent a potentially dangerous activity. The administrator should establish carefully designed policies and procedures governing restraints. He should require that not only the physician but also the family be advised if restraints are necessary. The family should never come to the facility and find their resident in restraints without prior knowledge of why the restraint must be used.

Example: Mr. Sims, aged 89, was out of contact, confined to bed, and using an indwelling catheter. The catheter was uncomfortable and Mr. Sims, not realizing what he was doing, removed the catheter as soon as the orderly left the room. The charge nurse called his physician who ordered hand restraints. Later, his 6'4" son weighing about 250 pounds came in and saw the restraints. He went into a rage, screaming and cursing the nurses, and ordering them to remove the restraints. When the administrator arrived the son threatened to knock his teeth out. He was quieted only when the physician was called and the son talked to him.

Houdinis Every facility has one or two residents whose dexterity and ability to release themselves approaches that of the famous Houdini. No matter what restraint is used they will release themselves. This type resident must be monitored by a special plan that includes the attention of all staff and what they are to do.

The administrator would be wise to require that he be notified when any resident needs restraints, and that regular reports be made if it is necessary to continue their use for any length of time. Use of restraints should be seen as a potentially dangerous practice that is used as a last resort, and then for the shortest possible time.

11. **Routine house orders** Most health-care facilities have procedures referred to as routine house orders. These are **standing orders**, or standard operating procedure (SOP), given by the professional staff regarding procedures to follow when certain resident-care situations develop. They are rules or procedures for everyone to observe. The advantage is that routine house orders provide consistent attention to the situation, and no one depends on memory. It may differ from a PRN order which usually is ordered for a specific resident.

12. **Relationships** Staff is always concerned with relationships of residents to each other, to staff, and to their physicians. The activity director, social worker, and nurses promote resident relationships continuously. Many techniques are used, such as changing seating arrangements in group activities and at mealtime, getting small groups to socialize and become better acquainted, asking more outgoing residents to talk with the less active residents, and many more techniques. In a study by the American Health Care Association, findings indicated that a facility **newsletter** promotes more interest of residents in each other than other approaches. The newsletter of this type must be very newsy about activities of the facility and of residents including birthdays, anniversaries, accomplishments, vignettes, and news about residents that arouses interest of others. Frequently, residents say of someone who is mentioned in the newsletter, "I didn't know that about her." This is often the beginning of closer relationships. The newsletter seems quite effective in promoting personal and social relationships among residents.

Physician/resident relationships are a frequent concern to nursing staff. Many residents complain that their doctor will not listen, he will not answer their questions. Staff should coach residents on how to relate to their physician and how to obtain answers. Sometimes having them verbalize and practice what they will say to the physician helps. Writing down their questions may attract the doctors attention and a favorable response.

Example: A female resident complained that her doctor was always in too much of a hurry. He never answered her questions, or she did not even have the opportunity to ask. The nurse had her to write her questions. When the doctor visited next she handed him her questions and said, "Doctor, I have a few questions. Would you please answer them?" He took the paper, pulled up a chair and sat down, and went over each question with her for the first time.

Nurses may also coach the physician, particularly those with whom the nurse has a good relationship. Nurses often can help a physician understand his resident's need for more information and for allaying the resident's anxiety.

13. **Special needs** The facility must provide all the following services to residents who need them or assist residents in obtaining them. Nonavailability of program funding does not relieve a facility of its obligations to ensure that residents receive all needed services listed for Medicare and Medicaid. For services not listed, the facility is required to assist the resident in using any available resources to obtain these services: (a) injections, (b) parenteral and enteral fluids, (c) colostomy, ureterostomy, or ileostomy care, (d) tracheotomy care and suctioning, (e) respiratory care, (f) foot care, (g) prosthesis.

    Nurses are trained in all of these types of care. This not only includes personally providing the care, but also assisting residents to learn and carry out self-care. The facilities must have policies and procedures for each of these services readily available as guidelines. Especial attention should be given to preventing infections that result from carrying out procedures in these forms of special care. The actual procedure may be carried out by a non-staff person, but staff is responsible for careful follow-up to ensure there are no complications.

    Medical devices Sometimes devices that residents cannot pay for, and they aren't qualified for Medicare or Medicaid to pay, may be obtained from various community resources. The social worker must have a list of these, which not only includes Lions Clubs, support groups, cancer society and many others, but could also include suppliers.

    Example: The manager of a small chain of nursing homes did considerable business with a medical supply enterprise. He went to the enterprise owner and explained he occasionally needed medical devices that residents could not pay for. He asked if the supplier would consider donating a device when the resident couldn't pay. The supplier agreed and also included a significant discount for residents who could pay part of the cost of a device.

    Surveyors will select samples of residents receiving one or more of these services within *seven days* of the survey. They will monitor procedures for providing these services, observe actual providing of the services, check adequacy and use of equipment used, note results and whether any services or care affects the resident's ability to carry on usual activities, and determine whether residents who are capable are handling the service themselves. [42 CFR 483.25 (k)]

URINARY TRACT AND BOWEL PROBLEMS

Incontinence Up to 30 percent of people over age 60 have some degree of incontinence, ranging from partial to complete. Unfortunately, a recent study showed that 35 to 50 per cent of physicians did nothing when they learned a patient was incontinent. (Morris) Incontinence is not just a physical problem, it is highly emotional. Feelings range from denial, shame, and embarrassment, to humiliation and anger. Nursing home staff must recognize any problem in this area and actively deal with it as it is a part of one of the ADL's — toileting. [42CFR 483.25 (a)(iii)]

Urinary incontinence is nearly always treatable with exercise, bladder training, surgery, and other techniques. It occurs for many reasons — infections, hormones, surgery, prostate problems, dehydration, damaged muscles, diabetes, and medications. The first step is to determine the type of incontinence so the underlying problem can be treated. Virginia Morris identifies five types of incontinence.

1. **Transcient-incontinence** begins suddenly when a person who has never been incontinent can't get to the toilet quickly enough. It may be caused by medication or infection. It may disappear of its own accord, or it can nearly always be treated successfully.

2. **Stress incontinence** primarily affects women when they cough, laugh, strain, exercise, sneeze, or lift something heavy. The sphincter muscles around the urethra are loose and stretched out, usually due to bearing children or hormonal changes after menopause. The smallest amount of pressure on the bladder may cause small amounts of urine to leak.

3. **Urge or reflex incontinence** occurs when a person has a sudden urge to urinate and cannot hold it until they reach the toilet. Stroke, infections, bladder contractions and other reasons cause the bladder to release urine with little or no warning.

4. **Overflow incontinence** often occurs in men who have prostate problems. The enlarged prostate can block the urethra so urine does not drain normally. The bladder holds the urine and it eventually overflows and dribbles out. This type of incontinence also occurs in people who have other disorders or infections that block the urethra and prevent normal bladder contraction. If not treated this buildup of urine can cause kidney or bladder infections.

5. **Functional incontinence** is caused by the brain in such cases as dementia, head injury, and stroke. The brain is unable to receive the message from the bladder; therefore involuntary urination occurs. The person doesn't know what has happened. This type of incontinence is sometimes confused with inability to get to the toilet quickly enough or no bed pan is available.

Treatment or management of urinary incontinence involves correcting the underlying problem. Usually this is nonmedical — bladder training and exercises and a regular toileting schedule. Morris identifies several modalities that may be useful. See Figure 12.6.

Figure 12.6:

Methods of Handling Urinary Incontinence

1. Kegel exercises
2. Regular schedule
3. Bladder training
4. Biofeedback
5. Bedpans and commodes
6. Dietary changes
7. Medications
8. Surgery
9. Pads, diapers, catheters

Kegel exercises are designed to strengthen the sphincter muscle around the urethra where it exits the bladder. In women the exercise involves squeezing the muscles of the vagina and anus. Men tighten the muscles in the urethra and the anus. Both can benefit by stopping and starting frequently while urinating. This exercise can be done while sitting, reading, watching television, etc. It takes real commitment as it should be done one or two hundred times a day. It is particularly useful for stress incontinence, but usually requires at least a month of exercise before results are notable.

Scheduling bathroom trips and fluid intake can help both stress and urge incontinence. A resident should note about how frequently he normally urinates, then set a schedule. If frequency is about three hours, set a schedule and go to the bathroom whether there is an impulse to do so or not. This is sometimes called **prompted voiding.** Fluid intake may also be scheduled, realizing that it makes about one and one-half hours for a glass of fluid to reach the bladder and be ready for voiding.

Bladder training involves learning to extend the time between urinating periods. A resident may begin by trying to void every 30 minutes to an hour, then extend this time until they can wait two or three hours. Holding urine as long as possible helps to strengthen the sphincter muscles. (Morris)

Biofeedback in conjunction with exercise can be helpful. The biofeedback machine informs the resident on how well he relaxes the sphincter and other muscles. The resident can practice ways of manipulating muscles and gain better control.

Bedpans and commodes are useful for urge incontinence and a physical disability that makes getting to the bathroom difficult.

Dietary changes as limiting caffeine and alcohol can help some residents with incontinence. Avoiding spicy foods, tomatoes, and imitation sweeteners may also help. An overweight person is sometimes helped by losing weight. Morris warns that a resident should not drink less in order to urinate less for this can cause dehydration and make incontinence worse.

Cranberry juice is often used to lessen the odor of urine, and now scientist believe it helps prevent urinary infections thereby aiding continence. It is believed the concentrated tannins in the juice prevents the E. coli bacteria from adhering to the cells that line the urinary tract. E. coli is the principal culprit in urinary tract infections.

Medications in conjunction with exercise and training may be used to stop bladder contractions or strengthen the resistance of the urethra. This is particularly helpful with urge and stress incontinence.

On the other hand drugs such as tranquilizers, diuretics, psychotropics, sedatives, antihistamines and calcium-channel blockers can worsen incontinence. Drug lists of an incontinent resident should be checked for these medications.

Surgery is usually a last resort but sometimes it may be necessary to clear obstructions or repair the urethra. Newest studies suggest injections of collagen, silicone or other materials into the urethra can narrow the opening and help control incontinence.

Pads and diapers should be used only when all else has failed, except for trips or other occasions requiring extra care. These devices can be upsetting to residents; so much so that some refuse to use them when needed. When diapers are worn skin infections and rashes can be common. Special care of the crotch is indicated — cleaning and drying immediately after urination occurs, and using small amounts of a moisturizer rather than powder.

Catheter care [42 CFR 483.25(d)] A resident who enters a facility without an indwelling catheter is not catheterized unless the resident's clinical condition indicates it is necessary. As with pads and diapers, catheters are to be used only when other treatment modalities have proven ineffective. Examples of conditions that merit use of catheter include: (1) urinary retention that causes overflow incontinence, infections, or renal dysfunction; or cannot be corrected surgically; or cannot be managed with intermittent catheter use; (2) skin wounds, sores, or irritations that are being contaminated by urine; and (3) terminal illness.

Bowel incontinence is less prevalent, but is often more difficult to treat. Immobile, bedridden, or mentally disabled residents may require use of diapers which can be both physically and emotionally draining on staff.

Constipation is the most common cause of bowel incontinence. **Diarrhea** also causes incontinence in the elderly as they cannot hold on to soft or liquid stools. Other causes include a **cathartic colon** — overuse of laxatives — surgery, medications, dementia, and severe depression.

Treatment for bowel incontinence varies according to cause. Weak, torn sphincter muscles may be repaired surgically. Nerve damage to the sphincter may be treated by using suppositories or enemas to empty the bowel on schedule. Diet can be used to bulk up loose stools and to restore regularity, with high-fiber foods. Treatment of **constipation** should first be a high fiber diet. Laxative can cure the constipation, but with over-use can be damaging. They can interfere with vitamin absorption. (Morris)

Surveyors will monitor a sampling of residents who are incontinent. They examine the care given, whether individual goals were set and attained, whether residents are properly hydrated, and whether sampled residents have urinary tract infections. If surveyors find that incontinence is not controlled by restorative measures, they will note whether a plan has been implemented to prevent incontinent-related infections and to maintain resident dignity. Surveyors will examine a sample of residents who came to the facility without indwelling catheters and are now catheterized. They will especially note if restorative measures were attempted before catheterization, whether there are infections, and whether staff uses proper infection control measures before, during, and after providing service to the catheterized resident.

Prostate trouble Prostatitis is not common, but elderly men with enlarged prostates are more susceptible. This disorder requires medical treatment immediately or complications may occur. **Cancer** of the prostate is five times more prevalent in men in their 60's than in younger men. By age 80 nearly all men have prostate cancer. But, few men die from prostate cancer. Usually it is confined to the prostate and is slow growing. However, it should be monitored in male residents for if it metastasizes it usually spreads to the bones. (Morris)

Monitoring for prostate cancer or its spread is done by performing a prostate specific antigen (PSA) test. This is a simple blood test that should be done at least annually on all elderly male residents.

Counselling men with prostate cancer is very important. Most people equate cancer with death, so the resident with prostate cancer should be fully reassured that his "cancer" does not usually run the course of other cancers. Chances are much in his favor that he will not die from this disorder. According to the American Medical Association, less than two cases per 10,000 result in death.

AIDS CARE

When the **Acquired Immune Deficiency Syndrome** (AIDS) was first identified in America, health-care professionals frequently were seized with fear about treating it. Nursing homes refused to accept AIDS residents, and staff often resigned rather than provide care to them. In some communities that proposed to develop AIDS treatment facilities, the people rose up in protest, sometimes threatening legal or physical action.

HCFA issued directives that provided penalties to nursing homes refusing to admit AIDS residents. With infection control and blood-borne pathogens programs in place, nursing homes became more comfortable with AIDS cases. With these programs, which include CDC's **standard precautions,** it is generally accepted that there is no way nursing home staff can contract AIDS from an infected resident in the course of their regular duties. Professionals are now quite comfortable with providing service to AIDS residents.

HCFA does provide certain **precautions** as outlined in Chapter 8. AIDS residents may be isolated only when there is bleeding or a bloody discharge, except in case of communicable disease outbreak occurs in a facility. Staff may then use reverse isolation to protect the AIDS resident.

CEREBROVASCULAR ACCIDENTS (CVA)

Residents who have had a stroke are frequently admitted to SNF's and NF's after the acute phase of the CVA is past. During the post-acute phase, the CVA resident primarily needs rehabilitation and restorative nursing care. It may involve physical, occupational, and speech therapy. Based on the assessment, goals should be set, modalities selected, and treatment implemented. Since this often involves retraining in activities of daily living, all staff may be involved. Nursing staff, in particular, should understand that the CVA resident needs help in re-establishing **independence** in daily activities. They should not feel sorry for, or prematurely assist the resident in combing hair, buttoning clothes, or other activities. Encourage the resident to do it for himself, and give assistance when the resident cannot accomplish a simple task of personal care. The facility must provide an environment which helps the resident use his physical, mental, and psychosocial abilities to the fullest extent possible.

One type of CVA frequently goes unnoticed in nursing homes. The very light stroke that is often not noticed by the resident or staff is fairly common. It involves mild cortical damage characterized primarily by some loss in social judgement. Staff or family may notice a sudden change in the resident's topics of conversation and his behavior toward others.

> **Example:** Family members were very concerned about their 83-year-old mother who resided in a nursing home. They asked the social worker, "What are you people doing to mother? She's always been very prim and proper, never used curse words or told shady stories. All of a sudden she has begun to curse and talk about sex, and she plans to go to bed with one of the men residents." An examination revealed a mild CVA that explained her behavior change.

Knowledge of this type CVA and confirmation by physicians can be helpful in family counseling. However, don't be surprised if some family members refuse to believe that mother is deteriorating in this manner. They may blame the change on the type of people she associates with in the facility.

COUNSELING RESIDENTS AND FAMILY

Administrator, nurses, social worker, activity director, and other staff must do some resident/family counseling. Whatever the problem, the staff counselor must contain any feelings he has and deal with the resident/family problem. The first step in counseling is to allow the counselee to express his feelings, get it off his chest. The counselor simply listens, and asks questions that encourage the counselee to discuss his concerns further. All counselors must speak with low affect and in a nonthreatening manner. Low affect means in a soft voice, showing no irritation, impatience, or anger. If the counselor does not use this approach, the counselee may become defensive and/or angry. All energy will be directed toward defending himself, rather than discussing and solving the problem. After the resident or family member has *gotten it off his chest*, then the counselor may make necessary explanations. The next stage is to engage them in problem solving, assisting the counselee in deciding upon a solution that is best for him.

Resident Often a resident complains about almost everything, and there is no true basis for the complaints. The trained social worker should **counsel** with this type resident in an effort to explore and resolve the complaint. If the complaint is not based on fact, generally the basis of the complaint is simply that the resident wants to go home. He does not wish to be in a nursing facility, no matter how well services are rendered. Sometimes this resident can be given enough emotional support to understand what they are doing and come to accept that the facility is best for his needs.

Family member Sometimes a family member continuously complains when it is obvious the resident is doing well. In this case they often have not resolved their feelings about placing their resident in a nursing home. When this seems to be the issue and the family member ventilates his feeling, the counselor might say, "If I hear you correctly, you are saying you don't feel very good about mama being in a nursing home." If this is true and it is timed properly, the family member may say, "You are so right. I just can't stand to see her suffering so much because she's away from home." Another may look at you as if to say, or to even say, "At last someone has heard what I've been trying to say."

Often family members come to the administrator (they often want to talk to the top man) and report that, "Mama says she didn't get her bath on time today. She said her food was cold and her coffee too weak at breakfast. Also, she said nobody answers her calls to the nurses station without a long wait." If the administrator knows this is not what actually happens, he can be assured the resident just wants to go home. One effective way to handle this type problem is to go to the resident's room, have the family member stay in the hall where he is not seen but can hear what is said in the room. The administrator should go into the room, bring up a pleasant topic as discussed earlier. Then when mama is comfortable, ask about breakfast. Most likely she will say, "Oh, it was okay." Ask about her bath and bed being made up. She'll probably respond the same way. Ask about nursing staff answering her bell, and she'll probably say they respond every time.

HEARING AND BALANCE PROBLEMS [42 CFR 483.25 (b)]

Hearing loss is a common problem among the elderly. Two major types are frequently observed. **Presbycusis** is the gradual loss of acute hearing in which the resident may hear what is said but has poor word acuity. It is characterized by inability to hear certain tones such as high pitched, shrill, or low frequency sounds and to differentiate some syllables and word sounds. They often misunderstand what is said as when the nurse told a resident, "It looks like it's going to rain." The resident responded, "I don't hear any train." **Conductive** hearing loss results from impairment, damage, or malfunction of any portion of the conductive mechanisms of the ear. A resident with this type loss may not hear what is said and may not respond at all unless they are looking at the speaker.

The facility must ensure that residents receive proper treatment and assistive devices to maintain or improve hearing abilities. Staff must assist the hearing impaired to make appointments and arrange for transportation to and from professionals specializing in hearing impairment and to offices of professionals specializing in providing assistive devices. The intent is that the facility be aware of which residents need attention for their hearing, and assist each resident in obtaining the care needed.

Trauma Staff should be aware that loss of hearing is often more traumatic to residents than loss of sight. The deaf person only sees what goes on in front of him. The blind hear all that is going on around them. Staff are frequently less patient with residents who have hearing loss than with those who have visual loss. Society seems less impatient and more accepting of the blind than of the hard of hearing. As Dr. Helen Keller pointed out, "Loss of sight cuts you off from the environment; loss of hearing cuts you off from people." The facility itself is not required to conduct audiology exams or to provide hearing aids. They are to ensure availability of needed services. If a resident is financially unable to secure services and needs assistive devices, the social worker is to work with the family or legal representative in securing them.

Surveyors will select a sample of residents with hearing losses and determine whether the facility has carried out its duties. They will question certain residents about whether they asked for assistance in seeing an otologist or going to a hearing aid specialist, and how staff responded to the request. If a resident has a hearing aid and is not using it, surveyors will determine why not – is it without batteries or does it need repair?

Benign Disequilibrium of Aging (BDA) Many elderly experience a disturbance in the sense of balance. This is a serious matter as it may lead to falls and other accidents. Sometimes the inner ear that regulates balance suddenly develops a problem in the elderly. It results in what Dr. Charles Prosser, a physician writer in Louisiana, calls benign disequilibrium of aging.

Onset is anything but benign. It usually begins with vertigo — a sense of things spinning — followed by inability to stand without falling and by nausea and vomiting. Some residents compare it to severe seasickness. This phase usually passes in a day or two with treatment.

Symptoms After the initial attack, a person has poor balance. He tends to stagger, to bump into things, and sometimes to fall easily. When walking he cannot turn quickly without staggering. Some residents cannot look up while walking without falling. Usually, they are quite unsteady on their feet and find that any quick movement—standing up, turning, changing directions—causes imbalance. Occasionally, the acute onset symptoms recur, but many experience these only once.

Treatment Thus far there is no effective medication for BDA. All drugs used for dizziness and vertigo are ineffective. Dr. Prosser warns that one must learn to cope with imbalance. He should not change his gait and walk spraddle-legged as one tends to do. Staff in nursing homes need to fully evaluate this problem when it occurs.

VISUAL PROBLEMS

Visually impaired OBRA requires that a facility must provide proper services for the visually impaired. The facility must make appointments and arrange transportation for residents who need the care of a practitioner specializing in treatment of vision. When residents do not have funds to obtain needed eyeglasses, the social worker must work with the family, legal representative, and/or community resources for obtaining them. This requirement does not address acute medical problems, such as acute glaucoma or retinal detachment. Acute medical problems are handled under direct supervision of the resident's physician.

Glaucoma symptoms usually do not appear until irreversible damage is done. Fluid pressure in the eye should be 16 to 18, but when it increases dramatically sight is lost. Untreated it can cause total blindness. When discovered early, medications slow or prevent damage. When eye drops are prescribed staff should ensure they are used even though the resident experiences no symptoms. (Morris)

Recent developments provide a cure when pressure is so high that more dramatic measures are needed, especially in cases of traumatic glaucoma — due to eye injury. A filter can be implanted in the eye to control the pressure and prevent damage to sight.

Legal blindness Many facility residents are legally blind and no one is aware of it. Visual acuity of 20/200 or less, with correction, constitutes legal blindness. Facilities should arrange for periodic checkups, perhaps once each year or two, to ensure that residents are not unknowingly suffering from this degree of visual disability. Also, the legally blind are often eligible for some services offered by state programs for the blind.

AMD Age-related macular degeneration has recently attracted research interest. Elderly people with this disorder are unable to do anything that requires "straight ahead" vision, such as driving, watching TV, reading, and sewing. It steals the eyesight of one in three Americans by the age of 75. It is an intractable disease, but researchers feel they are near a breakthrough on solving the problem. Medical practitioners have given little attention to AMD, and the public knows little about it, according to Emil R. Hubka, Jr., one of the founders of the Macular Degeneration Task Force (MDTF). The MDTF is spearheading research on the disorder.

AMD is painless and can develop so slowly it is hardly noticeable, but it can also develop rapidly, resulting in impaired vision in both eyes. Common **symptoms** are blurred vision or seeing straight lines as being crooked. More than 90 percent of people with AMD have the "dry" form, and an examination reveals formation of tiny, yellow deposits known as drusen in the retina. This dry type rarely causes blindness, but the "wet" AMD can have profound effects. It is caused by leaky vessels behind the retina that can lead to blindness, although most people retain some peripheral vision. (Eastman)

The MDTF recommends that any person over 65 have at least a yearly eye examination. The Force expects drugs on the market soon that will help prevent or reverse AMD.

Staff in nursing homes should be alert to any resident complaining of not being able to see TV or read, or if they start seeing wavy lines when looking at straight lines.

Veterans have an advantage. The Veterans Administration has a new program which helps an

AMD resident adapt peripheral vision to a number of tasks — check writing, keeping records, etc. The VA program trains the veterans for four weeks with devices that greatly assist them in coping with AMD.

Surveyors will select a sample of resident's with visual disorders and question them about assistance with appointments, transportation, and obtaining eyeglasses as needed. If they observe a resident who is not wearing his eyeglasses, surveyors will determine if it is due to a problem with the eyeglasses and whether they need repair.

MENTAL AND PSYCHOSOCIAL PROBLEMS

Psychosocial problems Based on assessment, the facility must ensure that a resident who displays mental and psychosocial adjustment problems receives appropriate treatment and services to achieve as much remotivation and reorientation as possible. Psychosocial adjustment difficulty applies to problems residents have in adjusting to their life circumstances that lead to declining functional abilities. This is especially true regarding adjustment to living in the nursing facility. They may be moody and withdrawn or exhibit such behavior as anxiety, wandering, verbal or physical abuse, lack of involvement, and a sense of dissatisfaction with life. Some of the manifestations of mental social adjustment difficulties are included in Figure 12.7.

Figure 12.7:

Some Symptoms of Mental Problems

1. Impaired verbal communication
2. Depression in response to stress, characterized by a sad mood
3. Social isolation – loss of or failure to have relationships, withdrawn
4. Sense of powerlessness, apathy, or hopelessness
5. Anxiety, fear, anger, and grief
6. Sleep disturbances
8. Negative view of self
9. Sexual dysfunction
10. Alteration of thought process — confusion
11. Spiritual distress — disturbance of beliefs
12. Inability to control behavior — aggressive or potentially violent
13. Alteration of family relationships

Dependency Some residents show strong dependency needs, characterized by constantly making requests or complaints, some legitimate and some not. This person exhibits a very demanding nature that upsets staff, and often other residents. The resident cannot be ignored, for this only intensifies the dependent behavior. They may become angry and sulk, but the behavior will be resumed. Perhaps the best solution is for the social worker to counsel with the resident, identify the basis of the behavior, and help develop plans that will more effectively meet the resident's needs.

Depression Almost all long-term care residents experience some depression. This is especially true following admission. All their old familiar stimuli are removed — the sounds, smells, lighting patterns, room structure, and their personal belongings. Depression may range from the **blahs** and the **blues** to a deeper depression characterized by a mask-like expression, crying, withdrawing, and isolating themselves. A resident who is sufficiently depressed to withdraw and isolate himself needs immediate assistance. The social worker should counsel with the resident, try to determine the **depth** of the depression, and decide with the interdisciplinary team whether specialized services are needed. It is not difficult to determine the depth of a depression. When the counselor is alone with the resident, and the resident expresses sadness, cries, or shows despondency, the counselor asks, "What did you enjoy doing before you began to feel this way?" If the resident smiles, however faintly, or perks up and says, "I used to enjoy music (or reading, or television, or whatever)," the counselor responds with, "Oh, what kind of music did you like?" If the counselor can engage the resident for several minutes in discussing what the resident previously enjoyed, the depression is not too severe. The resident will likely respond to counseling and may be helped to engage in activities with others.

If the resident responds with a flattened affect and with such answers as, "Oh, I used to enjoy singing and dancing, but I just don't enjoy anything anymore." If after several efforts the counselor cannot elicit a positive response, the depression is deep enough to require specialized treatment, such as psychotherapy and/or medication.

Agitated depression Diagnosis of depression is sometimes missed because the resident shows none of the withdrawn, crying, or mask-like expressions. They are restless, pacing the floor, sometimes wringing their hands, or having sleeping problems. This type depression is often mistaken as dementia.

Medication for the depressed is now available and should be considered. One geriatric psychiatrist told a group of facility nurses and social workers that the biggest, untreated problem in the elderly is depression. Reportedly, he and his clinic have had extremely favorable results by prescribing low doses of antidepressants and carefully monitoring them for side effects.

Entertaining as an antidote to depression and loneliness has proved effective in some facilities. This activity is built on the basis that the homelike atmosphere should be extended to other than a resident's room. A facility should have several small rooms where a resident can entertain family members and friends. This gives the facility a more personalized atmosphere.

Cooperation and planning by the activity director, social worker, and nurses can make it possible for residents to have social events much as they did at home. One resident was an expert bridge player so with the help of the staff she was assigned a room an afternoon each week for her bridge club. Another was a member of a small sewing club when she came to the facility. A plan was worked out so she and the six other members of her club could use a room once each week. Dietary service brought them coffee and cookies. There was more talking than sewing, but the event boosted the resident's spirit tremendously. She changed from a rather withdrawn person to her former outgoing self as she shared her club experience with other residents.

Van Dyk Manor in Ridgewood, N.C., has these programs for residents. The facility used its formal living room instead of the dining room for a Valentine party. Staff decorated it with Valentine motif and 10 couples had a nice meal and a wonderful time. (Van Dyk)

Dementia The prevalence of dementia in nursing homes continues to rise; especially dementia of the Alzheimer's type. Although a facility may not have an Alzheimer's unit they are likely to have a number of residents with early Alzheimer's symptoms. Normally, development of a dementia-care program involves a large number of staff and increased costs. With the tightening of Medicare/Medicaid funds, many facilities feel they cannot consider a dementia-care program.

A unit can be established at nominal cost, but it will require a highly trained staff, including CNAs. A description of how this can be done appeared in the March, 1996, issue of *Nursing Homes.* The program is in operation at St. Joseph's Manor in Trumbull, CT. In addition to staff training, it involves reassignment of staff to maintain adequate coverage for other resident care. St. Joseph's believes that the responses of dementia residents, as evidenced by smiles, eye expression and other expressions, indicate they acknowledge an opportunity has been provided for them to continue to live their lives in a supportive, affirming atmosphere. (Sr. DiMaria)

St. Joseph's dementia-care program can be replicated with reasonable costs. A syllabus of the training course can be secured from St. Joseph's.

Appropriate **treatment** programs and activities to assist the resident to cope with change may include a number of specialized services: (a) crisis intervention, (b) individual, group, and family psychotherapy, (c) song therapy, (d) training in drug-therapy management, (e) structural socialization activities, (f) maintenance of daily living skills, and (g) development of appropriate personal support networks.

There are other treatment programs and services, dependent on the resident's adjustment problem. More than one therapy may be used with the same resident. For example, a confused resident who is not in good contact and shows little interest in his environment may benefit from remotivation, reality orientation, and sensory training. **Remotivation** techniques are used to encourage residents to be more interested in the immediate environment. **Reality orientation** may be used with it to assist the resident in reestablishing firmer contact with reality. Together they are often effective in assisting residents to gain a firmer hold on who they are, what is the date, the day, and the time, who are the staff people, and so on. The facility must also ensure that residents who have no psychosocial adjustment problems do not deteriorate and develop problems, unless their clinical condition demonstrates that such a pattern is unavoidable.

Surveyors will select a sample of residents who exhibit psychosocial adjustment difficulties. They will monitor the facility's efforts to accommodate the resident's usual and customary routines and the programs carried out to remotivate the resident and maintain or improve maximum psychosocial functioning. They also determine whether selected residents have shown an increase in appropriate behavior, whether they are better adjusted. Surveyors note whether treatment goals and plans have been re-evaluated as indicated. [42 CFR 483.25 (f)]

SKIN CARE

Skin changes One of the most notable degenerative processes in the elderly is changes in the skin. Older skin becomes thinner and less oily. It tends to be drier and more susceptible to bruises, tears, infections, and rashes. The slightest bump may cause a skin to tear or a bruise that results in a hematoma next day — much to the chagrin of family members who often feel the resident is being mistreated. Injuries do not heal as quickly, and minor irritations may become serious wounds. (Morris)

Shingles, cellulitis and erysipelas often occur in the elderly and staff must be attuned to the early symptoms and the need to call these conditions to the physician's attention and begin treatment at once.

Skin **reactions to medication** are common, especially swelling, burning, itching, blisters, hives and rashes.

Staff should be alert to early signs of **skin cancer.** Blemishes, warts, red dots, moles and other markings are common to old age, but staff should be alert to changes that may indicate cancer. A skin exam should be part of every physical, and staff might have to call this to the physician's attention.

Pressure sores The administrator should be especially aware of the presence and treatment of pressure sores (decubitis ulcers). It is generally considered inexcusable for residents to have pressure sores except in rare instances. Not to provide proper care when pressure sores do occur is unforgivable. The facility must ensure that a resident who is admitted without pressure sores does not develop them. In rare instances it may be unavoidable due to the resident's clinical condition.

A **pressure sore (or ulcer)** means an area where the skin and underlying tissues are eroded as a result of a lack of blood flow. It is ischemic ulceration and/or necrosis of tissues overlying a bony prominence that has been subjected to pressure, friction, or shear. Causes are pressure and friction which in turn are a result of improper turning, hard sheets, wet sheets and/or bed clothing, and lack of attention to pressure points, body casts, certain types of illness, and some types of therapy. If a resident has pressure sores the facility must provide proper treatment to promote healing and to prevent new sores and infection.

Skin care programs as a preventative measure are operated by some facilities. New admissions are evaluated for their risk level, using the Braden Scale Assessment Form. An at risk resident, mostly due to urinary incontinence, is placed on a preventative protocol which utilizes a turning and positioning schedule. Skin care products are used by CNAs who are specially trained in the proper procedure. The program should include use of special mattresses with a built-in overlay. Facilities using a skin-care program report they seldom have even a Stage I pressure sore. (Knox)

Administrators should check periodically with nursing staff on the number of pressure sores and the care that is given. The care and treatment program should include taking color pictures of pressure points and documenting skin condition at admission, and at the time of transfer to and time of return from a hospital. Frequently, residents return from the hospital with pressure sores, and the nursing facility is blamed. Proper documentation establishes where pressure sores occur and may be the beginning of resolving the problem.

Surveyors will select a sample of residents at risk of developing pressure sores and determine if routine preventive care is provided. For those who develop sores after admission, surveyors try to determine if the sores were unavoidable. They carefully monitor treatment given when pressure sores exist. [42 CFR 483.25 (c)]

Hydration The facility must provide each resident with sufficient fluid intake to maintain proper hydration. **Sufficient fluid** means the amount of fluid to prevent dehydration and to maintain health. The amount needed is specific for each resident, and it fluctuates as the resident's condition changes. Increased fluids are indicated if a resident has fever or diarrhea as output of fluids far exceeds fluid intake if proper attention is not given.

Some risk factors for a resident becoming dehydrated are: (a) coma/decreased sensorium, (b) fluid loss from fever, diarrhea, and uncontrolled diabetes, (c) difficulty with drinking, reaching and holding fluid containers, and requesting fluids, (d) dementia in which the resident forgets to drink, and (e) refusal of fluids.

A general guideline for determining baseline daily **fluid needs** is to multiply the resident's body weight in kilograms times 30cc. There are 2.2 pounds of weight to one kilogram. A 110 pound resident weighs 50 kilograms; multiplied by 30 cc, this equals 1500cc of fluids needed. Current research findings indicate a strong relationship between skin condition and water intake. Regular, adequate water intake seems to reduce skin dryness, scaling, and wrinkling. Some facilities have a hydration program that involves staff prompting water intake for all residents. Each time an employee enters a resident's room he pours part of a glass of water and hands it to the resident while talking about something else. Anecdotally, they report very satisfactory results as characterized by improved skin condition and general well-being.

Surveyors select a sample of residents who appear to have insufficient fluid intake as indicated by dry skin, cracked lips, poor skin turgor, thirst, or fever. Also, they will examine abnormal laboratory findings, such as elevated hemoglobin, potassium chloride, sodium, albumin, blood urea nitrogen, and other biochemicals which may indicate inadequate fluid intake. Surveyors will monitor the facility's hydration program to determine if adequate fluids are provided. They also determine whether alternative approaches are used when fluid intake is difficult to maintain. [42 CFR 483.25 (j)]

Nasogastric Care

Nasogastric care Based on assessment, the facility must ensure that a resident who has been able to eat alone or with assistance is not fed by nasogastric tube. An exception is the resident whose clinical condition demonstrates that use of a nasogastric tube is unavoidable. This includes residents who are unable to swallow without choking or aspirating, such as those with Parkinson's disease or esophageal diverticulum, those who are comatose, and those who are unable to maintain or improve nutritional status through oral intake. A resident fed by nasogastric or gastronomy tube must receive appropriate treatment and services to prevent complications. Complications include aspiration, pneumonia, diarrhea, vomiting, dehydration, metabolic abnormalities, and nasal-pharyngeal ulcers. Every effort must be made to restore normal feeding function if possible.

Surveyors will examine a sample of residents who are now tube fed but were not at admission. They will determine if tube feeding was unavoidable. In addition they monitor all tube feeding procedures to determine what efforts are made to prevent complications. Also, they evaluate whether the facility attempts to return the resident to eating by mouth. [42 CFR 483.25 (g)]

WANDERERS AND ELOPEMENT

Wandering means walking around aimlessly, in and out of rooms and outside the building, with little or no awareness of potential dangers. Many elderly tend to wander. Some residents insist on it and sneak outside the facility at every opportunity. This should be distinguished from pacing back and forth in the hallways or in one's room. Staff should describe behavior, not put a name on it.

> **Example:** An 80-year-old resident spent most of his time pacing up and down the hallway, sometimes wringing his hands. He never went outside unaccompanied and never threatened to leave. One morning at 3:45 he awoke, left his room, went out the door, walked onto a thoroughfare and was killed by an automobile. Both nurse and CNA were working with other residents away from the nurses station and did not hear the alarm when the resident opened the door. The family sued, and won because they had entered in his record that he was a wanderer. Had they described his behavior–pacing and wringing his hands–the outcome could have been different.

As a minimum the program should include plans shown in Figure 12.8.

Figure 12.8:

Wanderer Program

1. Find out at admission if there is tendency to wander
2. Fully assess problem
3. Develop plan of care to monitor
4. Train everyone in what to do
5. Include family in assessment and planning
6. Install automatic door locks
7. Have resident wear wrist alarm that engages door-locks when he is near
8. Develop full plan of follow-up when resident elopes — alert police, check outside, notify family, do full search

If a facility has wanderers, it is only a matter of time before one elopes. This justifies a careful plan and the wrist/door locks. The wrist alarms are not considered a restraint. A problem with this is that fire marshals will only allow the door lock to hold for 15 seconds because of danger in case of fire. Most people who push on a door that does not open turn around and walk away. However, some residents become aware that the door opens for others. They stand back until someone opens the door, then rush outside before the door closes.

Monitoring Administrators should regularly monitor, personally, their wanderer program. They should train their staff to be aware of the time of day residents usually elope. Generally it occurs in the evening or early night, hence the term "sundowners." These procedures should be a part of the facility's risk management program because an eloper who gets injured or dies will cost money. Few juries are friendly to nursing homes when they are sued in these cases.

> **Example:** In the example above, the person who ran over the resident and killed him sued the facility for negligence. Although the facility

had a wanderer program that met state standards the jury awarded the complainant $500,000 because he "suffered mental anguish" due to the nursing home's negligence.

RESTLESS LEGS SYNDROME (RLS)

Nightwalkers Every facility has residents who are victims of the restless legs syndrome. They have trouble relaxing and sleeping at night. Symptoms range from prickly, jittery, tingling, jerky sensations to actual pain in the legs. They feel compelled to stand up and walk or to stamp their feet. Some walk for an hour or more and still cannot relax and go to sleep.

> **Example:** Mrs. Smith, a 92-year-old woman, was admitted to a nursing home. The first night she jumped out of bed and started walking down the hall. A CNA told her she couldn't do that, she had to get back in bed as it was midnight. Mrs. Smith said, "You just think I can't go walking, I have restless legs, and I can't stay in bed. I have to exercise."

In a recent article in *Saturday Evening Post*, Robert H. Yoakum describes how this relatively unknown, seldom understood, disorder affects an estimated 40 million people. RLS has caused "family dysfunction, work-place accidents, automobile crashes, lost-education and income opportunities, disability, and premature death" according to a 1998 report to Congress by the National Center on Sleep Disorders Research. The report indicates that "diagnosis and treatment in primary medicine today is virtually zero..." Many victims of RLS are undiagnosed or misdiagnosed and treated as chronically ill sleep-disorder victims.

Physicians often consider RLS a mental problem needing psychiatric care. Many victims are so embarrassed by this problem they won't discuss it. There is no need to be embarrassed as it is now recognized as a disease worthy of attention and research. It is also recognized that 80 percent of RLS victims have a related disease called "periodic limb movements in sleep" (PLMS) which worsens with age. PLMS causes leg jerks and kicks during nondreaming sleep. Bed partners may complain of this even before the victim is aware that they occur.

Medical scientists now know RLS/PLMS are sensory-motor disorders of unknown origin. They respond to some medications used in Parkinson's disease and in convulsive disorders. There is great need for further research into causative factors and in treatment, but there is considerable information available. When a facility has residents with RLS/PLMS, the administrator should contact RLS Foundation, P.O. Box 7050, Department SEP, Rochester, MN 55903-7050. The Foundation provides information and publishes a newsletter called *NIGHTWALKERS.*

SEXUALITY

Increasingly, problems or potential problems arise regarding sex activity among residents. Newer residents are far more sophisticated than 20 years ago and are more likely to expect more freedom to fulfill their needs. Administrators report many more residents now engage in sex within nursing homes. As noted under resident rights this is their privilege, and the facility must plan so residents may have privacy with anyone of their choosing. Usually, facilities have a procedure by which residents are told they can have privacy when they "request it." This often poses a problem as it becomes rather obvious that the residents plan to have sex. They hesitate to make it known by requesting privacy with someone, especially if it is another resident.

In rooms with multiple beds, drawing the curtain does not provide adequate privacy.

> **Example:** A male resident and a female resident had developed a close relationship. One afternoon a CNA entered the female resident's room. Seeing the curtains drawn around her bed the aide drew it back, saw the woman and her friend having sex, hastily closed the curtain, closed the door and left. Later that afternoon the male resident came to the administrator's office and exploded with anger. He warned that if this ever happened again he would sue the facility for not following its own rules of privacy.

Administrators must take personal interest in ensuring that privacy is available. One of the best methods is providing a lock on the resident's door, as allowed by the Life Safety Code, and providing staff training on privacy. Even this plan has problems, for staff will not know how long the door has been locked. Knocking on the door and asking if one may enter can be helpful, but it is not an infallible solution.

Whatever procedures are established they should be discussed with residents shortly after admission. The procedures may require consideration of the consensual nature of the encounter, each person's competency, and whether a guardian is involved. (Gold) Residents and staff must know what is required and what is expected. It is obvious that had policies been clear and understood, the problem in the example above would not have occurred.

THE EDEN ALTERNATIVE

The medical model Dr. William H. Thomas of New Berlin, New York challenges the historical approach to nursing-home care. He contends that long-term care is based on a confusion of care, treatment, and kindness. This is due to the medical-model nursing-home's fixation on diagnosis and treatment. This guarantees that most resources will be spent on the war against diseases rather than loneliness, helplessness, and boredom that steadily decay the spirit of nursing home residents.

Dr. Thomas has started what may well be a revolution in nursing homes, a new way of thinking about nursing-home services. He has developed a program that provides, among other things, the songs of birds, the laughter of children, the companionship of pets, and the shoots of green, growing plants. He calls it the **Eden Alternative.** It uses the principles of ecology and anthropology in an effort to improve residents' quality of care. It teaches administrators to be more like naturalists in constructing "vibrant, supple habitats in which residents can live."

Overtreatment/overregulation Dr. Thomas contends the focus on treatment in nursing homes has resulted in over medication. More than half the 1.7 million nursing-home residents are on regular doses of psychotropic drugs, and many nursing homes regularly administer $200 to $300 of medicine a month per resident. Residents are regularly subjected to unnecessarily restrictive diets. Also, he believes many programs, such as activities, are more focused on complying with regulations than meeting residents' needs. He questions what would happen if surveyors began writing deficiencies on a resident's high degree of loneliness, helplessness, or boredom instead of the facility's failure to meet regulations on treatment procedures, records, the physical plant, etc.

The Eden Alternative began in 1991 at the Chase Memorial Nursing Home in New Berlin. It has spread to more than 100 other nursing homes, and information on the program and how it operates is available to all. Its focus on **care** instead of treatment utilizes, to the fullest, the "homelike" atmosphere promoted by HCFA. It tries to create a healthy, natural habitat that includes dogs, cats, birds, rabbits, plants, gardens, children, music, art, and many other resources common to a homelike atmosphere. The program emphasizes unique leadership by the administrator and the empowering of employees to provide a better, more gratifying service.

Results The Eden Alternative brought about dramatic changes for residents, staff and family. Figure 12.9 shows some of the gains the program made at Chase Memorial.

Figure 12.9:

Changes Due to Eden Alternative

1. Medication reduction — both in number and cost
2. Fewer deaths
3. Less feelings of helplessness; residents now have something that depends on them
4. Revolutionized facility management
5. Improved job satisfaction
6. CNA turnover rate decreased 26 per cent
7. Higher resident satisfaction
8. Greater family satisfaction — fewer complaints

Administrators not already involved in a program like the Eden Alternative should purchase a copy of Dr. Thomas' book *Life Worth Living.* It provides details of the program, including step by step procedures on creating a program with the use of animals, gardens, children, etc. It points out risks and how to deal with them. The book fully explains the concept of providing **care** rather than just **treatment.**

QUALITY ASSESSMENT AND ASSURANCE [42 CFR 483.75 (r)]

A facility must maintain a **quality assessment and assurance committee** consisting of: (1) the DON, (2) a physician designated by the facility, and (3) at least three other members of the facility staff. The committee is responsible for **identifying** issues that necessitate action by the committee. This includes any issue which negatively affects quality of care and services provided to residents. It develops and implements plans of action to correct quality deficiencies in such areas as pharmaceutical services and infection control. Since a safety committee is no longer required, the assessment and assurance committee might also carry out safety-program duties. Actually, OBRA appears to envision this committee supplanting pharmaceutical services, infection control, and safety committees. In smaller facilities one committee may be a real advantage, since there is limited staff to do committee work. During one meeting the committee can address all facets of quality care, safety, and more.

Meetings OBRA requires the committee to meet *at least quarterly.* In practice, some facilities convene the quality assessment and assurance committee weekly or even more frequently. One facility includes all department heads on the committee. They meet daily at 10:00 a.m. after each department head has attended to necessary departmental duties. The administrator serves as chairman, and except for the physician, they make rounds of the entire facility during each meeting. They keep the physician advised of their findings and actions taken. The physician meets monthly with the committee. These are luncheon meetings which are more appropriate to the physician's schedule.

This approach has proven very educational for department heads, and has resulted in significant changes. Department heads now identify issues in their own departments more quickly and often correct them before the next committee meeting. They simply report these issues and actions, and they are recorded by the committee. Another benefit of this approach is that after the committee has worked together for several weeks, department heads begin to identify issues in departments other than their own that the head of that department has not noticed.

A third benefit is improved interdepartmental relations. Frequency of meetings enhanced communications to the extent that issues, which previously became controversial, were resolved at their onset. A department head who noticed a potential quality assurance problem in another department, began to contact that department before the next committee meeting. Without arousing defensive feelings, as had occurred in the past, department heads now accept and act on issues identified by their cohorts.

Another benefit of this approach is better time utilization. At first, meetings required two or more hours to address all necessary issues. After three months of daily meetings, the committee seldom needs more than 45 minutes to tour the facility and act on all necessary issues. The facility is very enthusiastic about this team approach, and it is reflected in improved resident care and environmental conditions. In two surveys subsequent to instituting this program, no deficiencies were identified for the first time in the facility's existence.

Records The quality assessment and assurance committee is required to maintain records of their meetings. These are for documentation of their actions, but are for their use only. Actually, surveyors do not have access to the details of these records as they are the findings of what amounts to an internal audit and corrective actions taken voluntarily. Surveyors are required to know that the committee keeps these records, and some request the record so they can read it. In such cases it probably is best that the facility gives surveyors access to the records.

THEFT CONTROL

Many nursing facilities face the problem of theft in the resident-care areas, primarily of resident valuables and facility supplies. A number of conditions make this possible: (a) resident rooms are open to staff 24 hours per day, (b) residents may be asleep or not mentally capable of recognizing and reporting a theft, (c) most personnel are paid low wages, often the minimum required, and (d) providing security guards may not be economically feasible. A most common practice is removal of stolen items through garbage disposal practices. Items are placed in plastic bags which are periodically taken outside to a dumpster. The bags are usually white or black, rather than clear, so that objects are easily hidden from view. An employee carrying out garbage may hand it to a waiting person or hide it behind the dumpster to be picked up by a cohort later.

Prevention of the theft may be enhanced by a number of measures, some of which the administrator should discuss with his attorney before implementing. The following practices sometimes prove successful.

1. **Policies** Set up very strong policies about theft and teach them to new employees. Require applicants to take lie detector tests before employment with the emphasis on prior theft records. These tests may not always be allowed.

2. **Procedures** Set up strict procedures on taking out garbage—a regular schedule, only certain employees, at certain times. Periodically, have a supervisor check the garbage to ensure only garbage is included. Allow no one to take out garbage except at scheduled times. Check the employee out and in. Usually, it should take no more than five minutes to take garbage out and return to work.

3. **Clear plastic bags** Use only clear plastic that can be visually checked. Periodically, lift the bag to determine whether its weight is appropriate to content and/or press the side of the bag for objects that may be hidden inside.

4. **Rule** Establish a rule that an employee guilty of theft is discharged immediately. Make no exceptions.

5. **Reporting theft** Establish a procedure that every instance of theft be reported. Investigate it fully, letting all staff know the administrator is monitoring such action. Try to determine if there is a pattern to the stealing, as on the same shift, the same group of employees, and the same area.

One administrator uses a method that may be questionable legally, but it is highly effective. If he determines there is a pattern with the same employees on duty, he calls them in singly or as a group. He confronts them with the fact that the thefts occur only when they are on duty and states that they are either involved or they know who is. He tells them to speak up, put a note under his door, or use some other means of getting the word to him. He tells them if this is not done, the cost of the lost item will be taken out of their paychecks. Thus far, he has always found out who is the culprit.

GLOSSARY

The prefixes, suffixes, common medical terms, diagnoses, and health-care specialists already defined in this chapter are not repeated in this glossary. Only the other new terms used are included.

Administration of drugs The actual giving of medications to patients or residents by mouth, injections, or otherwise.

Aspirator A health care instrument used to withdraw fluids from the body.

Assessment An evaluation of a resident's physical, mental, and psychosocial functional capacity that includes deficits, strengths, and equipment and assistance needed to maintain or improve the resident's present level of functioning.

Audiologist A person duly qualified to test and work with people who have hearing problems.

Autoclave Equipment used to sterilize medical supplies, instruments, and other materials.

Automatic stop order A procedure governing administration of drugs not specifically limited as to time or number of doses when ordered by the physician.

Bathing system Generally, an automatic, whirl-type tub in which residents are placed, bathed, and/or supervised by nursing personnel.

Cathartic colon A condition in which a person has used laxatives to the extent the bowel has become inactive and will not void without a laxative.

Charge nurse A licensed nurse who supervises the total nursing activities on a given tour of duty.

Comprehensive care plan A plan that is developed from the assessment which establishes objectives for a resident's care and improvement and identifies steps to be taken in attaining these objectives.

Conductive hearing loss Impairment, damage, or malfunction of any portion of the conductive mechanism in the ear.

Crash cart A special cart containing drugs – some that can be used only by the physician – and materials needed during an emergency.

CVA Cerebrovascular accident that involves hemorrhaging in the brain – a stroke that may result in paralysis.

Dc'd drugs Drugs whose use has been discontinued by the resident's physician.

Director of nursing A registered nurse who is in charge of the nursing service in a nursing facility, unless the facility has a waiver, in which case it may be an LPN/LVN.

Discharge planning Plans for the discharge of residents when feasible.

Disposables Medical supplies that are designed to be used once then destroyed, such as underpads, dressings, needles, and syringes.

Disturbed resident An individual whose behavior is disruptive and/or a threat to himself or to others.

Drug regimen The drugs, their dosages, and directions for administration as prescribed for an individual resident.

Dumping syndrome The practice of some families to bring a resident to the facility and leave him with no thought of possible discharge.

Eden Alternative A innovative nursing-home program that focuses on care rather than treatment through use of animals, plants, gardens and other resources to create a healthy, natural habitat for residents.

Egg crate Foam rubber pad placed on top of a mattress for resident comfort.

Elopement A resident walking away from a facility without permission or knowledge of the staff, with resident usually unaware of what he is doing or the dangers.

Emergency drug kit A kit containing medications which a nurse may use during emergencies.

Emesis basin A crescent shaped basin placed under the chin of a resident when vomiting.

Health-care specialist A person qualified by training, and usually licensed, to provide specialized care for the sick and disabled.

Holistic approach A care and treatment approach that includes physical, mental, social, and spiritual needs of residents.

Invasive device Medical devices that are inserted into body cavities, as catheters and nasogastric tubes.

Isolation The reduction of a residents contact with people by confining him to an isolation room which is accessible only to authorized personnel.

Labeling The practice of labeling drugs by the pharmacist as prescribed by the physician.

Legally blind Visual acuity of no more than 20/200 with correction.

Medical director A full or part-time physician who is responsible for overall coordination of medical care in the facility.

Medical supplies Bandages, dressings, underpads, wipes, needles, syringes and other supplies required to give medical and nursing care.

Nasogastric tube A tube inserted through the nose into the stomach for feeding and for aspirating fluids from the stomach. Also called a Levin tube.

Nursing hours per resident day The number of hours of nursing care available for each patient each day.

OT A person duly qualified to practice occupational therapy.

Periodic Limb Movements in Sleep PLMS A sensory-motor disorder resulting in leg jerks and kicks during nondreaming sleep.

Pharmaceutical services committee A committee formerly required in SNF's that developed policies and procedures for effective drug therapy, distribution, control, and use.

PT a person duly qualified to practice physical therapy.

Prefix One or more letters or syllables combined or united at the beginning of a word to modify its meaning.

Presbycusis A type of impaired hearing due to old age.

Prescribe The writing of an order by a physician for medications to be administered to a patient.

Quality Assessment and Assurance Committee A committee of staff persons that meets regularly to identify issues that negatively affect care and institute corrective action.

Rehabilitation specialist A person qualified by training, license and/or registration to do physical, occupational, or speech therapy, or other specialized therapies.

Rehabilitative nursing care A required type of nursing care with the goal of assisting residents to achieve and maintain an optimal level of self-care and independence.

Remotivation therapy A therapeutic modality that seeks to stimulate a resident's interest in his environment.

Resident-care plan A written health-care plan outlining a course of action to assist a resident in obtaining desired results.

Restless Legs Syndrome RLS A condition characterized by an intolerable creeping and internal itching sensation occurring in the lower extremities.

Restraint A chemical or physical means of restricting a person's activity, as by administering a tranquilizing drug, or placing them in devices that limit movement and cannot be removed by the person.

Specialized rehabilitative service Services provided by physical, occupational, speech therapists, and other related therapists.

Speech pathologist (therapist) A person duly qualified to practice speech therapy.

Sphygmomanometer An instrument for measuring blood pressure, commonly called a cuff.

Stroke patient A resident who has suffered a cerebrovascular accident (CVA) and suffers some degree of paralysis.

Suffix An abstract element at the end of a word serving a derivative, formative, or inflectional function.

Therapeutic recreation specialist A person licensed or registered by the state and eligible for registration by the National Therapeutic Recreation Society.

Turgor Usually referring to rigidity or tightness of skin due to swelling.

Underpads An absorptive, disposable pad used under residents who have poor bladder and/or bowel control.

UR Utilization review is a formerly used method of review and assessment of a resident or resident's care and/or of the efficiency, appropriateness, and cost effectiveness of care.

Wanderer The resident who wanders about the facility and its grounds without being fully aware of the danger in what they are doing, or one who elopes.

REFERENCES

Christen, Margaret, "Adaptations of the Physical Environment to Compensate for Sensory Changes, " in G.K. Gordon and Ruth Stryker, editors, *Creative Long-Term Care Administration*, Springfield, MO: Charles C. Thomas Publisher, 1983.

DiMaria, Sister M. Peter Lillian, "Creating a Dementia Care Program – From Within," *Nursing Homes,* Vol. 45, No. 3, Cleveland: MEDQUEST Communications, 1996.

Eastman, Pegg, "When the Light Fades," *AARP Bulletin,*, Vol. 37, No. 7, Washington: AARP, 1996.

Facts and Comparisons, St. Louis, MO: J.B. Lippincott Company, 1995.

Gold, Marla Fern, "Ethics: Blending Resident Rights With Safety," *Provider,* Vol. 22, No. 6, Washington: AHCA, 1996.

Gustafsen, Judith M., "The Impact of Staff Attitudes on Resident Disability," in G.K. Gordon and Ruth Stryker, editors, *Creative Long-Term Care Administration*, Springfield, MO: Charles C. Thomas Publisher, 1983.

Hughes, Marylou, *The Nursing Home and the Resident's Relatives*, Bossier City, LA: Professional Printing & Publishing, Inc., 1987.

Knox, Leila, "Organizing for Skin Care: A Case History," *Nursing Homes,* Vol. 45, No. 3, Cleveland: MEDQUEST Communications, 1996.

Morris, Virginia, "How To Care For Aging Parents," New York: Workman Publishing Company, Inc. 1996.

Pharmacist's Manual, An Informational Outline of the Controlled Substances Act of 1970, Washington: Drug Enforcement Administration, U.S. Department of Justice, 1986.

Sander, Pamela, *Activity and Volunteer Service Policies and Procedures*, Bossier City, LA: Professional Printing and Publishing, Inc., 1989.

State Operations Manual, Provider Certification, Revisions One and Two, U.S. Department of Health and Human Resources, Springfield, VA: U.S. Department of Commerce, National Technical Information Service, 1998.

Stott, Nancy A., "Controlling Pressure Ulcer Severity," *Provider,* Vol. 22, No. 8, Washington; AHCA, 1996.

Taber's Cyclopedic Medical Dictionary, 14th Edition, Clayton L. Thomas, editor, Philadelphia: F.A. Davis Company, 1982.

Thomas, William H., MD, "Life Worth Living," Acton, MA: Vander Wyk & Burnham, 1996.

Title 42 Code of Federal Regulations, Public Health, Part 400 to 429, Washington: U.S. Government Printing Office, 1995.

Title 42 Code of Federal regulations, Public Health, Part 430 to end, Washington: U.S. Government Printing Office, 1996.

Van Dyk, Robert, "Enabling Residents to Entertain," *Provider, Vol.* 22, No. 6, Washington: AHCA, 1996.

Yoakum, Robert H., "Nightwalkers: Victims of a Hidden Epidemic," *Saturday Evening Post*, Indianapolis, IN: Benjamin Franklin Literary and Medical Society, Inc. Nov-Dec 1998.

INDEX

INDEX

A

B

C

D

E

F

G

H

I

J

K

L

M

N

O

P

Q

R

S

T

U

V

W

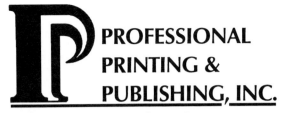